MAGRITTE:
THE TRUE ART
OF PAINTING

magritte magritte magritte

à Harry Torczyne
en toute sympathie
René Magritte
25 octobre

magritte magritte magritte magritte

MAGRITTE: THE TRUE ART OF PAINTING

HARRY TORCZYNER

With the collaboration of Bella Bessard

Translated by Richard Miller

PUBLISHED BY HARRY N. ABRAMS, INC., PUBLISHERS, NEW YORK

DISTRIBUTED BY NEW AMERICAN LIBRARY

For my friend Fritz Landshoff

Frontispiece: 1. Photograph of René Magritte

Editor: John P. O'Neill
Assistant Editor: Ellen Schwartz

Library of Congress Cataloging in Publication Data

Magritte, René, 1898-1967.
Magritte, the true art of painting.

"A concise, completely reorganized paperback version of... Magritte, ideas and images... which was itself a translation of... René Magritte, signes et images."
Bibliography: p.
1. Magritte, René, 1898-1967. I. Torczyner, Harry. II. Title.
ND673.M35A4 1978 759.9493 78-10499
ISBN 0-8109-2172-3

Library of Congress Catalogue Card Number: 78-10499

Published in 1979 by Harry N. Abrams, Incorporated, New York

Printed and bound in France

CONTENTS

PREFACE

René Magritte and I were destined to meet. Indeed, if a film projectionist were simultaneously to flash two series of images—one dealing with the first forty years of Magritte's life and the other with the first forty years of mine—onto adjoining parts of a screen, there would unroll before the viewer many of the same figures of both men and women playing various roles at different moments in both films. Some members of this cast of characters, deliberately or capriciously brought together by fate during the last decade of Magritte's life, would appear synchronously in both films.

Magritte and I were both born in Belgium, although in different centuries. Only a fortnight separated our birthdays, and we were both born under the sign of Scorpio. Magritte once pointed out to me that his birthday, November 21, meant he was born under the same sign as Edgar Allan Poe, whom he admired enormously. However, he did not enjoy it when I remarked that Charles de Gaulle, whom he disliked, was also a Scorpio. In order to tease Magritte a little about his birth date, I told him that it was on a November 21, in 1811, that the German dramatist and poet Heinrich von Kleist had taken his own kind of revenge on fate and on the victor of Wagram, Napoleon, by first killing his beloved, Henriette Vogel, and then by firing a bullet into his own head.

These remarks were exchanged during my first meeting with René Magritte and his wife Georgette, which occurred on a Saturday afternoon, October 26, 1957, at their apartment on the Boulevard Lambermont, Brussels. Their black Pomeranian Loulou was present at this meeting as a certified witness. Politely but systematically, Magritte subjected me to a close cross-examination. "Did I know his work?" "Truly?" "What was an international lawyer?" To the last question I explained that an international lawyer was one who traveled a great deal. Magritte later handed me a book. With some emotion I realized I held in my hands Magritte's copy of Lautréamont's *Les Chants de Maldoror,* a volume that in my youth had completely changed my views on life. Upon turning the pages, I discovered the images that Magritte had drawn to accompany Lautréamont's text.

"Where did my travels take me?" Magritte continued. Was I, like Maldoror, in Madrid today, in St. Petersburg tomorrow, Peking yesterday? "No, no, you'll find me in Brussels today," I explained, "Abidjan tomorrow, then Moscow, Jerusalem, even Paris!" Magritte replied, "You must travel the skies for me. It would be a pleasure to discover through you distant lands and half-barbarous tribes. Since you live in the United States, you could also give me news about my dealer, my pictures, my friends, even my critics. You could send me reports, minutes, dispatches." "So you need an ambassador to the United States?" I queried. "Exactly," he said, and then Magritte burst out laughing.

After my return to Manhattan, I received my Magrittian credentials, but they had been issued from 97 rue des Mimosas instead of the apartment on the Boulevard Lambermont, because René and Georgette had moved. They were now occupying the whole of a white house. It was in this dwelling that I visited them five or six times a year.

2. Illustration for *Les Chants de Maldoror* by Lautréamont, 1948

My conversations with René Magritte dealt principally with what he called his "labors." As I became a familiar visitor, I grew to know exactly the hiding places of his latest gouaches, or "grist," as his close friend Louis Scutenaire called them. These canvases might be casually set on the floor with their faces to the wall, like mislaid or forgotten objects. Sometimes Magritte would spontaneously show me a completed work or a sketch, observing my reaction closely out of the corner of one eye.

Oddly, despite his outward assurance and his certainty of being on the path of truth, Magritte needed reassurance. This is the reason why those friends who had formed part of his intimate circle at the outset of his career continued to be his necessary companions, despite the occasional falling-outs and misunderstandings that led frequently to touching reconciliations, and despite the dissensions that lent a perverse spice to his everyday life. I met one after the other in Magritte's home, when he still saw them, or at their own homes after they had become estranged from him, all of the members of the old-guard Surrealist group in Brussels, the true friends of Magritte. This group included Paul Nougé, biochemist, poet, and thinker; Pierre Bourgeois, the first poet to write a work inspired by one of Magritte's paintings; Camille Goemans, writer and gallery director; Marcel Lecomte, poet and essayist; André Souris, composer; E. L. T. Mesens, musician, poet, and collagist; Louis Scutenaire, Magritte's spiritual brother and the author of epigrams, poems, and stories, whose "Inscriptions" were engraved on the painter's mind; Irène Hamoir, poet; Marcel Mariën, an iconoclast by birthright, a *poète-agitateur,* a native of Antwerp, who became the devoted computer in whose memory are stored the accomplishments, deeds, and writings of this group of friends. Paul Colinet, the poet and intimate friend of the Magrittes, was also a member of this circle, but I never met him because he was dying throughout the autumn of 1957, at the time of my first visit to the Magrittes. With this group of friends, Magritte signed manifestos and took part in demonstrations, playing his intermittent role of *homo ludens;* in their company he could be solitary without being lonely. From one of their number, Paul Nougé, he had learned that "We are responsible for the universe" and that "Everything is still possible."

Much later new voices joined the chorus to which René Magritte often turned for comment. Among the new arrivals was the youthful André Bosmans, with whom Magritte shared his thoughts. When Bosmans wrote to Magritte that "Nothingness is the sole wonder of the world," it became even clearer to the artist that despair must be faced with the courage of hope.

In 1926, the members of Magritte's circle, like the artist, began to welcome the French Surrealists. From 1927 to 1930, René and Georgette, while living at Le Perreux-sur-Marne, France, often visited André Breton and his friends at Breton's house in the Rue Fontaine, Paris.

Here they met Aragon, Ernst, Éluard, Duchamp, Man Ray, and Dali. Magritte witnessed the minor and major excommunications from the Surrealist movement and participated in all its discussions. He and his work were taken seriously, but in 1928, André Breton did not mention Magritte in his volume *Le Surréalisme et la Peinture.* Magritte's relations with Breton and his circle remained courteous, but the timid artist had no intention of allowing himself to be intimidated, and he and Georgette returned to Brussels. Despite all the ensuing disagreements, Magritte and Breton retained a sincere admiration for one another. One day, when I mentioned Breton to him, Magritte said: "It was hard for me to be in tune with a man who didn't like music."

During World War II, André Breton, along with his entourage, went into exile in New York. He visited the Haitians and the Hopi Indians exactly in the manner that he had once visited the Belgians. During his New York years, I met him frequently. Early in 1945, Brentano's published a new text of Breton's essay *Le Surréalisme et la Peinture*. The cover of this edition bore a reproduction of Magritte's *Le modèle rouge (The Red Model),* a painting that Magritte had executed in 1937. In the sole paragraph of his text that Breton devoted to Magritte, the French Surrealist both judged correctly and wrote with a masterful hand:

> Magritte's nonautomatic but on the contrary fully deliberate progress is the buttress of Surrealism. Alone among us, he has approached painting in the spirit of an "object lesson," and from that angle he has presided over the systematic trial of the visual image, emphasizing its shortcomings and indicating the dependent nature of the figures of language and of thought. A unique and totally rigorous undertaking, within the confines of the physical and the mental, bringing into play all the resources of a mind demanding enough to conceive each picture as the site of the solution of a new problem.

To mark the publication of Breton's volume, my colleague Robert Tenger installed in Brentano's show window on Fifth Avenue a model of *Le modèle rouge* surrounded by copies of the book. Two large black boots ending in cleverly sculpted, flesh-colored toes were placed on the graveled floor of the window. This sight brought thousands of passersby to an abrupt halt.

The United States discovered Magritte early. In 1936, Julien Levy, a disciple of Surrealism and an art dealer, acquired Magritte's painting *La clé des songes (The Key of Dreams),* and he showed the artist's work. Shortly after its opening, the Museum of Modern Art, New York, hung on its walls in 1939 Magritte's painting *Le faux miroir (The False Mirror),* that eye with its hypnotic pupil, that black sun floating among the clouds. When the time would come for the endless hours devoted to the collective delights of shared mental sloth, millions of Americans of all ages, with eyes and ears only for their television sets, would be shaken awake and brought back to reality by this image borrowed to become the emblem of one of the largest American television networks.

In 1946, Magritte's credo, *La Ligne de Vie,* was published *in extenso* in English in an issue of the magazine *View* devoted to him. In 1947, Alexandre Iolas, a young Greek immigrant to New York, born in Egypt, exhibited paintings by Ernst and Magritte in the Galerie Hugo, which he had opened off Madison Avenue. For more than thirty years, until his retirement, Iolas was the splendid herald of these artists in the New World. That same year William Copley, who later became an imaginative painter and a unique Maecenas, began to make Magritte known in California. Copley subsequently lived for many years in Longport-sur-Orge (Seine-et-Loire), where René and Georgette often visited him.

From London, Mesens contacted the Sidney Janis Gallery, New York, to arrange the Magritte exhibition entitled *"Les Mots et les Choses,"* which opened in 1954. The young Robert Rauschenberg and Jasper Johns studied Magritte at that show. However, only one buyer materialized—Saul Steinberg, the witty virtuoso draftsman. Magritte was not yet appreciated by the art press nor by museums, except for those in New York. Modern Belgian art has not as a general rule attracted either international attention or interest. Only James Ensor was known, but who else?

The large New York exhibition of Belgian art held during the summer of 1960, a show in which I collaborated, was organized by Baron Jan Albert Goris, then minister plenipotentiary of Belgium to the United States and the most brilliant contemporary author writing in Dutch. The three paintings most often reproduced in the magazine and newspaper reports of this exhibition were by Magritte: *Le plagiat (Plagiarism), Le château des Pyrénées (The Castle of the Pyrenees),* and *Au seuil de la liberté (On the Threshold of Liberty).*

My assigned tasks as ambassador to the United States had to be carried out at Magritte's convenience. "I'm giving you a lot of difficulties," he wrote in October 1960, "but they are those given to a magnificent and outstanding ambassador." The excessive flattery of these adjectives was a diplomatic indication of the urgency of this particular dispatch.

René Magritte's letters constitute a précis of authentic Magrittism, and they reflect his spirit of precision. One word in a preface, a single turn of phrase in a text—everything in his writings was examined, reviewed, minutely gone over. His handwriting is clear, each sign giving each letter even greater impact because of his fine calligraphy.

Magritte applied his typical rigor to everything he undertook or advised someone else to undertake. When I was having difficulties in choosing the exactly right frame for *Le château des Pyrénées,* Magritte offered to make me a "Doctor of Framing." He sent me a detailed plan for the frame, while at the same time evidencing a certain amicable tolerance: "I ask you not to take my indications as ultimate dogma. If you are calling in an experienced framer (and not a mere carpenter), he may be able to suggest another shape of frame than the one I have designed."

Magritte cared little for chronology. The order in which his paintings were hung in an exhibition was unimportant to him; only the works counted, not their dates. Often, to confuse those animated by a passion for art-historical exactitude, or to confound the compilers of so-called *catalogues raisonnés,* he would inscribe a fanciful date in large numerals on the back of a picture. *Le tombeau des lutteurs (The Tomb of the Wrestlers),* painted in the peaceful summer of 1960, bears the fateful date "1944." Even the dates of his letters often mock time: for example, "Almost the end of September 1958" and "Already February 2nd, 1959." A banner bears the date "July 14," but there is no indication of the year of this particular "July 14."

The first museum exhibitions devoted solely to René Magritte's painting finally took place. They marked an end to those invitations extended to two artists at the same time because of the parsimony and narrowmindedness of curators. The Museum of Modern Art exhibition in New York in 1961, in the honorable company of Yves Tanguy, was the last show in tandem in which Magritte participated. In accord with Magritte, Douglas McAgy put together an important group of paintings, gouaches, drawings, and documents for the exhibition "René Magritte in America," which took place in 1961 at the Dallas Museum of Fine Arts, Dallas, Texas, and then moved to the Houston Museum of Fine Arts, Houston, Texas. That same year, however, the Tate Gallery in London barred its doors to the Belgian painter of mystery, despite the intervention of Mesens, Sir Roland Penrose, and other enlightened and educated spirits. Magritte's images did not illuminate this museum until after his death, when David Sylvester organized a retrospective.

As a result of continuous efforts and initiatives, a series of *vernissages* took place in the United States. Plans and projects for these exhibitions were submitted to Magritte for his approval. The artist often sent me directives, he expressed his wishes, and we collaborated on the texts and drew up meticulous memoranda for me to discuss with the authors of catalogue introductions—who often dared both to engage in explanations of his work and to indulge in comparisons that Magritte felt to be insufferable.

The triumphant and moving reception given Magritte during the opening of the Museum of Modern Art exhibition in December 1965 in New York remains unforgettable. *Le jour de gloire* had come at last. That was the day Magritte chose to pay a visit to a lifelong friend. On that rainy Sunday afternoon, I accompanied Georgette and René to Edgar Allan Poe's residence in the Bronx. What had his invisible friend said to him in that tiny bedroom? Magritte was in tears.

At the beginning of our relationship, Magritte had insisted that I create new verbal expressions, and sensitive to his taste for precise terminology, I began calling his pictures "Magrittian children," began to use the adjective "Magrittian" to describe images and ideas characteristic of him, and began to speak of "Magrittism," all with his approval.

Often, plays on words—by which I mean the spiritual exchange of serious thoughts—brought forward a problem whose solution called for Magritte's presence of mind. Thus Max Jacob's line "Seen against the light or otherwise, I do not exist, and yet I am a tree," and my lines, "Let the day sleep/Let the night wake/The living green Tree/Watches over the life/The survival of man," posed this kind of question to him. Magritte's inspired solution was that tree enhaloed with sparse leaves, that glorious image with its greens and blues that was given the only title worthy of it: *L'arc de triomphe (The Arch of Triumph).*

When Magritte painted my portrait, he executed it from a photograph, just as if he did not know me. In so doing he was following the example set by Albrecht Dürer, who made a drawing of a rhinoceros on May 20, 1515, from a friend's sketch, which had been made in Lisbon where a rhinoceros had been sent to King Manuel by an Indian grandee. Would the portrait be better if I had posed for it? One day at Le Perreux-sur-Marne, Magritte painted in one sitting the portrait of a friend of Éluard, a Madame Pomme or Apfel. When it was finished, the pretty little face resembled the sitter's face, but

3. Illustration for *Les Chants de Maldoror* by Lautréamont, 1948

the head was completely bald. Do Ionesco's *Rhinoceros* and *The Bald Soprano* speak Magritte's language?

Magritte disliked turning toward his past, but his loyalty was constant. He gratefully preserved the memory of those who had believed in him when he was the object of derision and contempt from a hostile world and those who had remained devoted to him throughout his overlong, difficult years.

Magritte introduced me to three stalwart friends who had been among the first to recognize his works—P. G. Van Hecke, M. Schwarzenberg, and Geert Van Bruaene. In 1959, when the most prestigious art dealers in the world were making proposals to him that would have quadrupled his earnings, Magritte firmly refused them and remained faithful to Alexandre Iolas, with whom, he always said, he had a contract. In fact Magritte had no contract with Iolas, but Magritte did have respect for his given word, and he never forgot that Iolas had encouraged him and continued to represent him despite the failure of the 1947 show at which not one single canvas had been sold. Magritte explained his point of view in his "pomp and circumstance" style in a letter to me, dated November 19, 1959: "Since the end of the war, Iolas has been faithfully buying from me all or almost all of my 'output.' This faithfulness (which at the outset was sometimes translated with difficulty into monetary form) is a kind of dogma.... A perfect dogma, with the minor imperfections inherent to anthropology, nevertheless, and which would be just as imperfect were that dogma adhered to by some other Iolas."

Magritte talked to me about his paintings, but he did not indulge me with talk about his family. I never met his two brothers. One day when Magritte was giving me several musical compositions of his younger brother Paul to show to New York publishers, he mentioned in passing a brother named Raymond who was comfortably off and whom he never saw.

Nonetheless, Magritte took an interest in genealogy. Were the Magrittes of the same family as General Jean-Antoine Marguerritte, the unhappy hero of the charge at Reichshoffen, of which the king of Prussia, the future Emperor William I, had remarked that it had been "as beautiful as it had been useless"? Magritte could have been related to this general's sons, Paul and Victor Marguerritte, preferably Victor (the author of the scandalous novel *La Garçonne* [the literary forerunner of today's liberated woman], who was stricken from the lists of the Legion of Honor for having "insulted French womanhood"), as his genealogy was elective. According to Georgette, three Marguerritte brothers came from France to Pont-à-Celles, in the Belgian province of Hainaut, during the French Revolution. Léopold Magritte, René's father, was supposed to have been the direct descendant of one of these brothers, Jean-Louis Magritte, known as de Roquette, the local pronunciation having altered the orthography of his name.

Magritte, however, told me many times that he had neither a predecessor nor a successor in painting. The question of influences seemed to him a superfluous one. His moving discovery of Chirico's *Le chant d'amour,* which has so often been alluded to, was a revelation to him, but not the beginning of an influence, no more so than was the discovery of certain elements or aspects of Max Ernst's work.

On the question of the quantity and the numerous variations on his images, I once asked him if he was trying to make the Magrittian children as numerous as the stars in the sky. "Yes, that is my wish," he replied. He encouraged the reproduction of his paintings in every medium, mechanical or otherwise,

4. Illustration for *Les Chants de Maldoror* by Lautréamont, 1948

as posters or as postcards. Magritte disliked the orthodox, conformist notion of the unique *exemplum.* However, while preaching the multiplication and dispersion of his images, he hated plagiarism and its ramifications. His curtain, his stone balustrade, were sincerely considered by him as trademarks that were intended to discourage or unmask counterfeiters. Unlike most artists, Magritte had no desire to retain a finished painting for study or for his personal collection. As soon as they were born, the Magrittian children were sent out into the world to make their way; however, he did not lose interest in them and he remained curious as to who took them in and how they were appreciated. For example, in regard to *L'art de la conversation (The Art of Conversation),* he was eager to know how I thought it was getting on in the New Orleans museum that had given it a home. Some of Magritte's other canvases met with a cruel fate. *Le messager (The Messenger),* now known as *Le voyageur (The Voyager),* was damaged by fragments from a V-bomb explosion in 1945 and later returned to the artist. A long time afterward, some friends saw it in his home in its sad state, and upon their urging Magritte gave it to them with permission to have it restored. In this way this astounding image was saved.

Magritte's relations with those who liked or were purported to like his painting were ambivalent. An amateur who had been interested in Magritte's work at the time when he was still comparatively unknown continued to enjoy the artist's affection because of his obvious sincerity. But after Magritte became famous, he spoke to me—not without some bitterness—about the latecomers, the *"visiteurs du soir,"* who brought him nothing and who wanted to take away everything, at any price. Just as an Englishman thinks a man should not be hanged if he is a duke, so did Magritte feel that one should not despise a man for being rich. But he also felt that there was nothing admirable about this quality. One day in New York, when a millionaire collector of Magritte's work took the artist by his arm in a familiar manner, Magritte whispered to me, "He leads me around like a racehorse wearing his colors."

Magritte fortunately had friends in the world of Belgian officialdom who formed at the same time part of his spiritual family. Émile Langui of the Ministry of Fine Arts and Robert Giron of the Brussels Palais des Beaux-Arts both served his cause. They saw to it that frescoes were commissioned from Magritte and that a large sum of money was granted to him as a "prize to crown his career"—but only after the entire world had come to know Magritte's name. Nevertheless, when the Belgian government seriously began to consider making Magritte a baron, the artist found it both ridiculous and not enough. "Tell them," he said to me, "that Maeterlinck was at least a count!"

In refusing to singularize himself, Magritte showed the world that he was not like everyone else and that he intended to protect himself from everyone else. Out of politeness, he did not interfere with the literati when they described him as they imagined him to be: as the hero of a detective story or a spy novel. To please these writers he allowed them to believe that he was a character in search of an author. Herein was born the legend that threatens to be handed down from book to book. No one was more intelligently direct than Magritte; he had no artifice. He was not a secret agent. He made known his likes and dislikes, his opinions and his prejudices. He openly confronted everyone who attempted to impose the conventional lies upon mankind, under the pretext of whatever religion or ideology.

Magritte was curious, voyeuristic, and analytical. He was often negative, like the Geist der Verneint in Goethe's *Faust,* like that Spirit of Denial who stalks the dunes, the moors, the mists in Caspar David Friedrich's landscapes, with which the artist was familiar.

Georgette was Magritte's lifelong companion. In the house that she had decorated on the rue des Mimosas, Magritte was surrounded by the *Magies noires* for which she had posed and by her portraits. For him, Georgette represented "The Likeness." For her, he had a tenderness and a concern that were evident to any visitor. He was displeased with the film Luc de Heusch had made about him because Georgette was not in it. In Nice one day in June 1964, as I was strolling with Magritte, he stopped before a shop window in which he had espied a porcelain rooster. "I must buy that for Georgette," he said to me. "She'll love it." "Are you still courting her, René?" "It's true," he replied, smiling.

I saw Magritte for the last time on the afternoon of August 8, 1967, in his room in the Clinique Edith Cavell in Brussels. Georgette, René, and I chatted as though nothing were wrong. Georgette related how Stéphane Cordier of the review L'Arc had just called to request authorization to publish Magritte's drawings for *Maldoror* in an issue of the review to be devoted to Lautréamont, and she added that René had agreed. His room gave onto the garden. That pleased him. Magritte was walking around in his dressing gown and eating some dried beef he had had smuggled in. He was completely yellow. He wasn't in great pain and he told me he was suffering from jaundice. Georgette and I looked at each other. I kissed Georgette and I kissed René and I left for New York. What could I think? What could I believe? On August 12, I telephoned the clinic and was informed that Magritte had left the hospital and gone home. I was overjoyed. I called the house on the rue des Mimosas. Georgette came to the telephone, sobbing: "It's bad, very bad," she told me.

On August 15, at 3:55 PM, I received the following telegram:

FIA 112 (27) CDV296
04918 B229221 7 PD INTL FR CD
BRUXELLES VIA WUI 15 1815
TORCZYNER
(DELR) 521 FIFTHAVE NYK
RENE DECEDE
GEORGETTE.

Magritte's Ideas and Images give evidence of a life worth living. More than fifty years ago, Magritte gave the starting signal to his Lost Jockey, that rider whose mysterious race will persist as long as men exist who know that everything is always possible. What he thought, what he believed, what he created, needs neither interpreters nor exegetes. "Women, children, men who never think about art history," Magritte said, "have personal preferences just as much as aesthetes do."

I have chosen from my book *Magritte: Ideas and Images* the necessary elements to make known and appreciated by a larger public what René Magritte considered to be the True Art of Painting.

HARRY TORCZYNER

New York, New York
October 11, 1978

THE LIVING MIRROR

THE MENTAL UNIVERSE

His gray eyes interrogated you with a curiosity mingled with a real and strange tenderness, for he knew you were the prisoner of his look, that you deserved his compassion, and yet he kept you in this uneasy state. He spoke French slowly, in an even voice, with a strong Walloon accent he made no attempt to conceal. He expressed himself in short, clear, concise sentences.

Magritte attached no importance whatsoever to his art, but the greatest importance to the problems that art posed for him. These problems obsessed him until he had solved them. He was meticulous in all things: each day had its schedule. Whatever the weather, he was on time for appointments. He liked neatness and cleanliness. He liked to receive letters, but didn't want to be burdened with them. He was a shy man, a solitary man who avoided unexpected meetings. One did not enter either his mind or his home without knocking. No physical contact. Although he liked those with whom he was on familiar terms, he detested familiarities. He expected everything from everyday life, but nothing from life itself.

Under the rain-drenched Belgian sky, the apartments and houses in which Magritte lived were all the same to him and all alike. When in 1963 he decided to build, he tried to oversee the most unimportant details and suffered the presence of an architect as had Ludwig Wittgenstein. In a short time, however, these concerns began to appear ridiculous to him and he lost interest in the project, as well as in the architect, and went back to indifference.

For Magritte, Woman was a far different thing from the synthetic, artificial, mythological creature that was the fashion with the Surrealists. She was neither destructive goddess nor guardian muse. In his work, no Pygmalion appears to bring the marble statue to life. He knew love and loved love, about which he spoke openly and without equivocation. He wished his friends a good night of love as naturally as he wished them "*bon appetit.*"

Magritte abhorred violence. He hated soldiers and detested those organized massacres, wars. Yet, under the Nazis he worked for the Resistance.

He was a hypochondriac. After he had reached sixty, however, his imaginary illnesses were succeeded by real ones: violent headaches, neuralgias, liver attacks. He injured his right wrist, which depressed him deeply, for he was afraid he had lost that absolute manual mastery that had enabled him to paint without a single smudge. He fought against and tried to master fate up until the day he succumbed to his final illness.

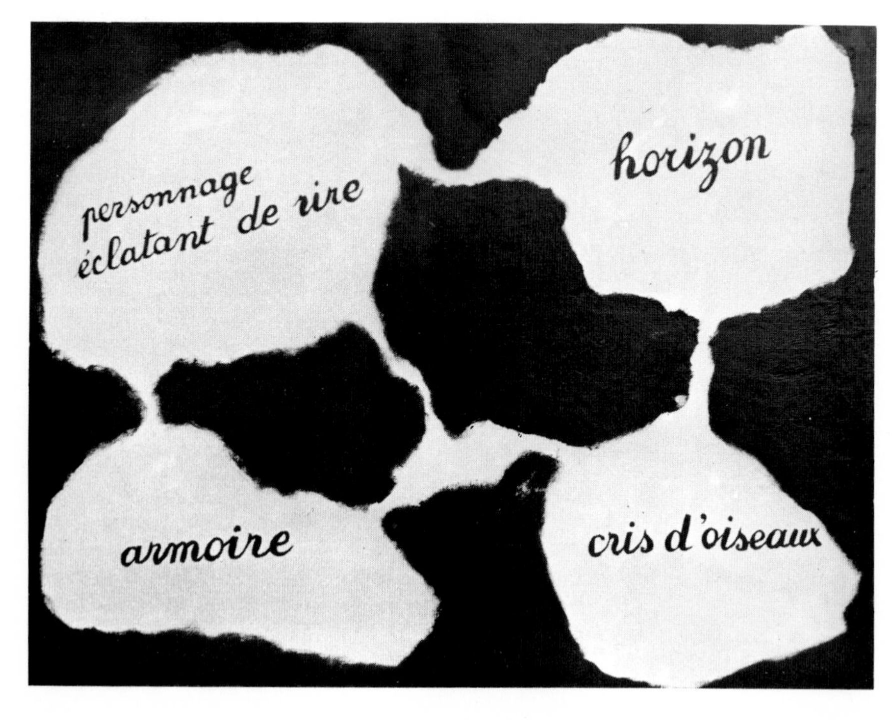

5. *Le miroir vivant (The Living Mirror)*. 1926. Oil on canvas, 21¼ x 28¾" (54 x 73 cm). Collection Mme. Sabine Sonabend, Brussels, Belgium

6. Photograph of René Magritte (holding his mother's hand) with his parents and two younger brothers, Raymond and Paul

Man

I despise my own past and that of others. I despise resignation, patience, professional heroism, and all the obligatory sentiments. I also despise the decorative arts, folklore, advertising, radio announcers' voices, aerodynamics, the Boy Scouts, the smell of naphtha, the news, and drunks.

I like subversive humor, freckles, women's knees and long hair, the laughter of playing children, and a girl running down the street.

I hope for vibrant love, the impossible, the chimerical.

I dread knowing precisely my own limitations.

—*René Magritte,* Le Savoir Vivre, *Brussels, 1946*

Painting *bores* me like everything else. Unfortunately, painting is one of the activities—it is bound up in the series of activities—that seems to change almost nothing in life, the same habits are always recurring. . . .

—*René Magritte, statement reported by A. Gomez, May-June 1948*

I hope I will never stoop to pulling strings to achieve success, which I can get along without.

—*Letter from René Magritte to André Souris, March 1953*

I dislike money, both for itself and for what it can buy, since I want nothing we know about.

—*René Magritte, statement reported by Maurice Rapin, "René Magritte,"* Aporismes, *1970, p. 23*

"According to my doctrine," it is forbidden (under pain of imbecility) to foresee anything. What I will do *in all* situations is as unpredictable as the emergence of a real poetic image. . . .

—*Letter from René Magritte to Mirabelle Dors and Maurice Rapin, December 30, 1955*

I will tell you . . . that I have some patience with the rich from whom I derive my livelihood; on occasion I may give the impression that I am their "valet": for example, I obey their idiotic caprice that I paint their portraits. I've never claimed to be a "luxury item" in the arts though, and in fact I often make gaffes *au-to-mat-i-cal-ly.* (At my Brussels retrospective in '54: the Minister of Education came to visit the exhibition and I accompanied him through the rooms "like a servant," as Breton would say. However, when looking at *Le civilisateur,* whose title surprised him, I served him with: "Indeed, we have a lot to learn from dogs," etc.)

—*Letter from René Magritte to Mirabelle Dors and Maurice Rapin, March 7, 1956*

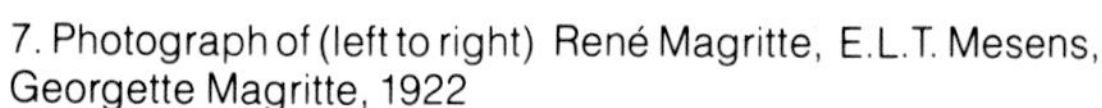

7. Photograph of (left to right) René Magritte, E.L.T. Mesens, Georgette Magritte, 1922

8. Photograph (taken by Man Ray) of René Magritte in front of his painting *Le thérapeute (The Healer)*, Brussels, Belgium, 1937

I can write texts that are interesting to people who don't play a conventional game. If one wants to reach other people, one must appear to play on their terms, while at the same time avoiding in any way being for an instant conventional. In short, I take pains never to be conventional when I am painting, and insofar as possible when I am not painting, I appear to play a conventional game: to paint, for example, or to live in a house, to eat at regular mealtimes, etc. . . . Maybe because some conventions are not stupid, but then those are not the annoying ones. Still, it's a fact that despite the conventional appearance of my paintings, they look like paintings without, I believe, fulfilling the requirements defined by the treatises on aesthetics.

—Letter from René Magritte to Mirabelle Dors and Maurice Rapin, March 15, 1956

I am *very* sensitive in some instances, I take it as a personal insult when stupidity is calmly displayed right under my eyes. On the other hand, I am delighted and my vanity is not injured when someone corrects a mistake I have made. It's not easy to correct mistakes and to say something good about something bad. It requires only a moment's discomfort.

—Letter from René Magritte to Mirabelle Dors and Maurice Rapin, March 30, 1956

I too have some horrible memories, but I'll never understand "repentance," I only feel remorse.

—Letter from René Magritte to Mirabelle Dors and Maurice Rapin, November 1956

1) My father was in the real estate business, buying and selling factories, etc. I was married when I was about 20 years of age, and I had to "earn my living," my father's support having been withdrawn (as the result of bad business deals). I don't think I know the circumstances that may have determined my character or my art. I don't believe in "determinism."

2) Married circa 1920.

3) No children.

4) Married or not, it's easy either to frequent or avoid cafés.

5) Experimentation ended in 1926, and gave way to a concept of the art of painting to which I

have remained faithful. The term "composition" supposes a possible "decomposition," for example, in the form of analysis. To the extent that my pictures have any value, they do not lend themselves to analysis.

6) The critic or the historian can do better than to put a facile label on a school or so-called school. Language and writing can bring out the unpredictable possibilities suggested by a picture. I hope so. I don't want to give a name to the images I paint.

7) My wife and I have preferred to observe Paris from a distance. This has not affected my relations with the Surrealists.

8) There is no explicable mystery in my painting. The word *Vague* (Wave) inscribed on the picture manifests inexplicable mystery.

9) The objects accompanying my wife's face are no more symbols than the face is. "Why?" is not a "serious" question; it is too easy, for example, to reply: "Familiar objects have been assembled together in the portrait to obtain a sensational result."

10) "Total portraits" are to me not worth looking at. All the information they give is meaningless.

11) Political ideas or current ideas about art cannot help me paint a picture, nor imagine one. Thus I am not *engagé,* as one generally hears. The only thing that engages me is the mystery of the world, definitively, I believe.

12) I am not trying to "provoke" anything or anyone when I paint: I have barely enough attention for the painting itself.

13) I do not feel I am "adding" something to the world: where would I get what I am adding if not from the world?

14) I have never thought such a thing. Progress is a preposterous notion.

15) André Gide's "morality" may have contributed to an increase in the criminal court clientele. But I doubt it: that clientele is not at all literary.

16) The absurd is the belief that a particular logic (called reason) can dominate the logic of mystery. A picture seems valid to me if it is not absurd and if it is capable, like the world, of dominating our ideas and our feelings, good or bad.

17) There is no choice: no art without life.

18) The basic thing, whether in art or in life, is "presence of mind." "Presence of mind" is unpredictable. Our so-called will does not control it. We are controlled by "presence of mind," which reveals reality as an absolute mystery.

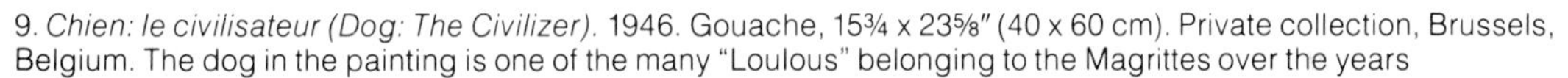

9. *Chien: le civilisateur (Dog: The Civilizer).* 1946. Gouache, 15¾ x 23⅝" (40 x 60 cm). Private collection, Brussels, Belgium. The dog in the painting is one of the many "Loulous" belonging to the Magrittes over the years

19) Without art, of course, there would be no pictures to look at. But although painters are sometimes stimulated by the strangest of motives, I recognize only one motive for the act of painting: the desire to paint an image one would like to look at.

20) Whether art is made for this or that reason makes very little difference: what counts is what it will be.

21) The language of symbols makes me miss the precision one loses in employing it. For example, a key, diamonds, insofar as they are symbols, signify confusion.

22) Great artists are against the "common meanings," but is it urgent to draw a conclusion from that (urgent for our happiness)?

23) This question seems to me to involve the isolation of the human being, whether or not he is an artist, whether or not he is "aware" of it. It is basic enough to cease being a "question" and to stand revealed as an affirmation of the mystery in which we live.

24) Like some madmen, artists have achieved similar *tours de force.* We exist within mystery, whether we know it or not.

25) The "subject," which in my opinion is the essential thing, cannot without losing this importance yield to or share its "place" with completely secondary pictorial material.

26) An object does not become more remarkable because it is represented in a picture. The error of certain painters resides in thinking the opposite.

27) In the case of great painters, "pictorial material" plays a large role on the *secondary* level. Indeed, it must be perfect and *stay in its place.*

28) In fact, looking at my pictures sometimes gives me a strange feeling. This fact is not an end I pursue, since any "end" I might imagine seems ridiculous to me.

—*Rough draft of a response to a questionnaire sent to René Magritte by M. Pierredon, pen name of Louis Thomas, journalist of* La Lanterne. *Included in a letter to Maurice Rapin, June 20, 1957*

If you look at this painting with the point of viev necessary to admit that the work is a work of ar whatever it is, you will change your opinion.* Thi point of view is not possible if outside preoccupa tions, utilitarian or rational, occupy the mind. In deed, from the point of view of immediate useful ness, what would correspond to the idea that, fo example, the sky covers the walls of a room, that a gigantic match lies on the rug, that an enormous comb is on a bed?

Such an idea would be *impotent* to resolve a utilitarian problem posed by life in society. The social individual needs a repertory of ideas ir

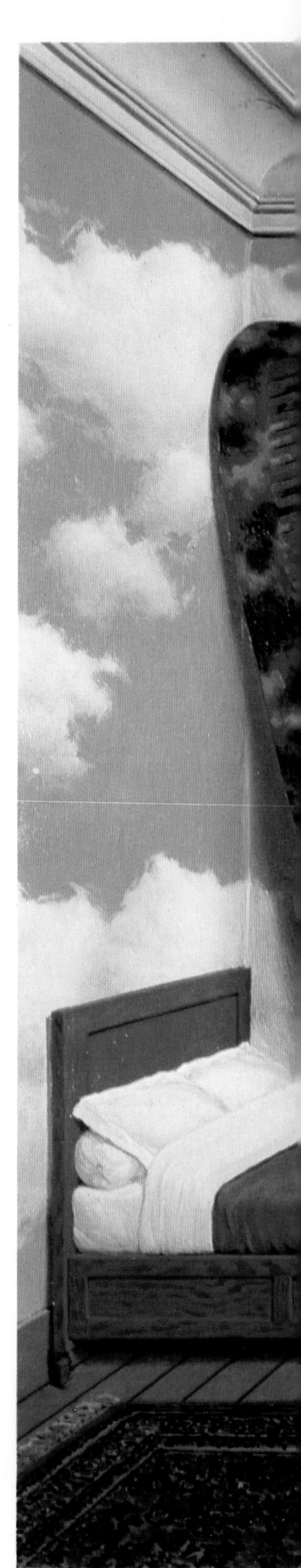

10. *Les valeurs personnelles (Personal Values).* 1952. Oil on canvas, 31⅞ x 39⅜" (81 x 100 cm). Private collection, New York, New York

which, for example, the comb becomes the *symbol* that permits him to combine certain events, permitting him, the social individual, to act in society in accordance with movements intelligible to society: the comb will part his hair, the comb will be manufactured, will be sold, etc. In my painting, the comb (and the other objects also) have lost precisely their "social character." It is only a superfluous luxury object that can, even as you put it, disarm the onlooker and even make him sick. Well, this is exactly the proof of the efficacy of this painting. A really vibrant painting has to make the onlooker sick and if the onlookers are not sick, it is because: (1) they are too gross; (2) they are used to this malaise, which they mistake for pleasure (my painting of 1931–32 (?) *Le modèle rouge* [*The Red Model*] is now accepted, but when it was new, it made quite a number of people sick). The contact with reality (and not the symbolic reality that serves social exchanges and violences) always makes people sick.

—*Letter from René Magritte to Alexandre Iolas, October 24, 1952*

*Iolas had written to Magritte on October 15, 1952, that *Les valeurs personnelles (Personal Values)* depressed him, deranged him, and made him sick.

Self-Portrait

It can happen that a portrait tries to resemble its model. However, one can hope that this model will try to resemble its portrait.
—René Magritte, *quoted by Louis Scutenaire,* Magritte, *1943*

Your idea for a "portrait of the artist" brings up a "question of conscience": I have on occasion (three times) painted myself in a picture, but at the outset there was an idea for a picture, not for a portrait. I can paint (or rather, could have) some portraits starting with the idea of a portrait, but if it concerns me, my visual appearance, that presents a problem I'm not sure I can resolve. *Of necessity* I will think about it, since the problem has come up. I cannot promise to see the end of it this year! However that may be, inspiration — which comes spontaneously — may break through in the meantime.
—*Letter from René Magritte to Harry Torczyner, July 2, 1963*

Le sorcier (The Magician) is simultaneously the *auto (mobile) portrait* (self-portrait) of its author.
—*Letter from René Magritte to G. Puel, November 4, 1953*

Maniacs of movement and maniacs of immobility will not find this image to their taste.
—*René Magritte,* Rhétorique, *no. 7, October 1962*

11. *Souvenir de voyage (Memory of a Voyage).* 1955. Oil on canvas, 63⅞ x 51¼" (162.2 x 130 cm). The Museum of Modern Art, New York, New York

12. *Le sorcier (The Magician).* Self-portrait with four arms. 1952. Oil on canvas, 13¾ x 18⅛" (35 x 46 cm). Collection Mme. J. Van Parys, Brussels, Belgium

Dernière idée = L'espoir, c'est le bien

Cher ami,

30, rue Paul Spaak - 30 - 3+0 = 3 - 3×3 = [9]

Le sort en est jetté, nous quittons Jette, le 18 crt

Vous avez déjà remarqué que le chiffre 18 - est composé de 1 et de 8, soit 1 + 8 = [9]

Il ne vous a pas échappé, je suis [illegible], que le home que nous habitons, fait 1 [illegible], celui que nous avons quittés en fait encore 1, et celui où nous allons, encore 1, ajoutés ensemble ils font 3 [illegible] et le chiffre 3 multiplié par lui même donne [9]

(Le chiffre entre pharenthèse est celui des 9 mois de la formation d'un bébé)

Bon. Le home que nous avons quitté, à Paris, avant de venir à Jette portait le no 201, soit 2 + 0 + 1 = 3 - 3 × 3 = → [9]

Le home de Jette, 135 - 1+3+5 = → [9]

Le home où nous serons bientôt a comme no, le 207, soit 2 + 0 + 7 = → [9]

Le chiffre 9, multiplié par lui même donne 81, soit 8 + 1 = → [9]

Quand pensez vous? l'endroit, c'est le Bd Lambermont, Bruxelles 3 - donc 3 × 3 = 9

Voudriez vous rédiger une formule de changement d'adresse, que je ferai imprimer, afin de distribuer votre formule - pour et [illegible] vendredi soir [illegible] t'espère [illegible] Mag

13. Letter from René Magritte to Paul Colinet, 1957. *See* Appendix *for translation*

Dwellings

Cher Bourgogne,
Vous êtes un charmant Bourgoignies,
(Et j'ai vécu jadis à Soignies)
Pour avoir apporté des plantes charmantes
à Georgette qui en était toute contente.
Je pense que vous m'écrirez: je pense
que la Pensée est ceci: elle ressemble
à la Pensée, à ce que je pense.
Et grâce à votre réponse, nous ferons ensemble
Un joli petit recueil pour l'édification
Des esprits respectueux des constitutions.
A ma future nouvelle adresse, dès le 18
de ce mois, faisant une sorte de 207
Boulevard Lambermont, je ferai de s'8
une réunion pour la mise au net
des projets relatifs à la recherche
des choses, pour les capturer avec votre perche
qui renforcera nos perches respectives
un peu démunies de forces vives.

Mag.

—*Letter from René Magritte to Paul Bourgoignie, May 8, 1954*

[Dear Bourgoignie,

You're a charming man, Bourgoignies (I once lived at Soignies), for having brought the lovely plants for Georgette, who liked them very much. I guess you're writing to me: I think the following Thought: like Thought, it resembles what I think. And thanks to your answer, we will make a nice little collection for the edification of people who like that sort of thing.

I'll be at my future new address from the 18th of this month, leaving 207 Boulevard Lambermont, and I will at once call a meeting to settle the plans with regard to the research into objects, or to catch them with your pole, all of which will reinforce our respective positions, which are somewhat drained of vital force.

Mag.]

14. Photograph of René and Georgette Magritte at 97 rue des Mimosas, Brussels, Belgium, 1965

15. Photograph of René Magritte painting at 97 rue des Mimosas, Brussels, Belgium, 1965

If all goes well, my address from the first of the year will be: 97 rue des Mimosas. In many respects, it will be better there for "living" and "working."

—*Letter from René Magritte to Maurice Rapin, December 17, 1957*

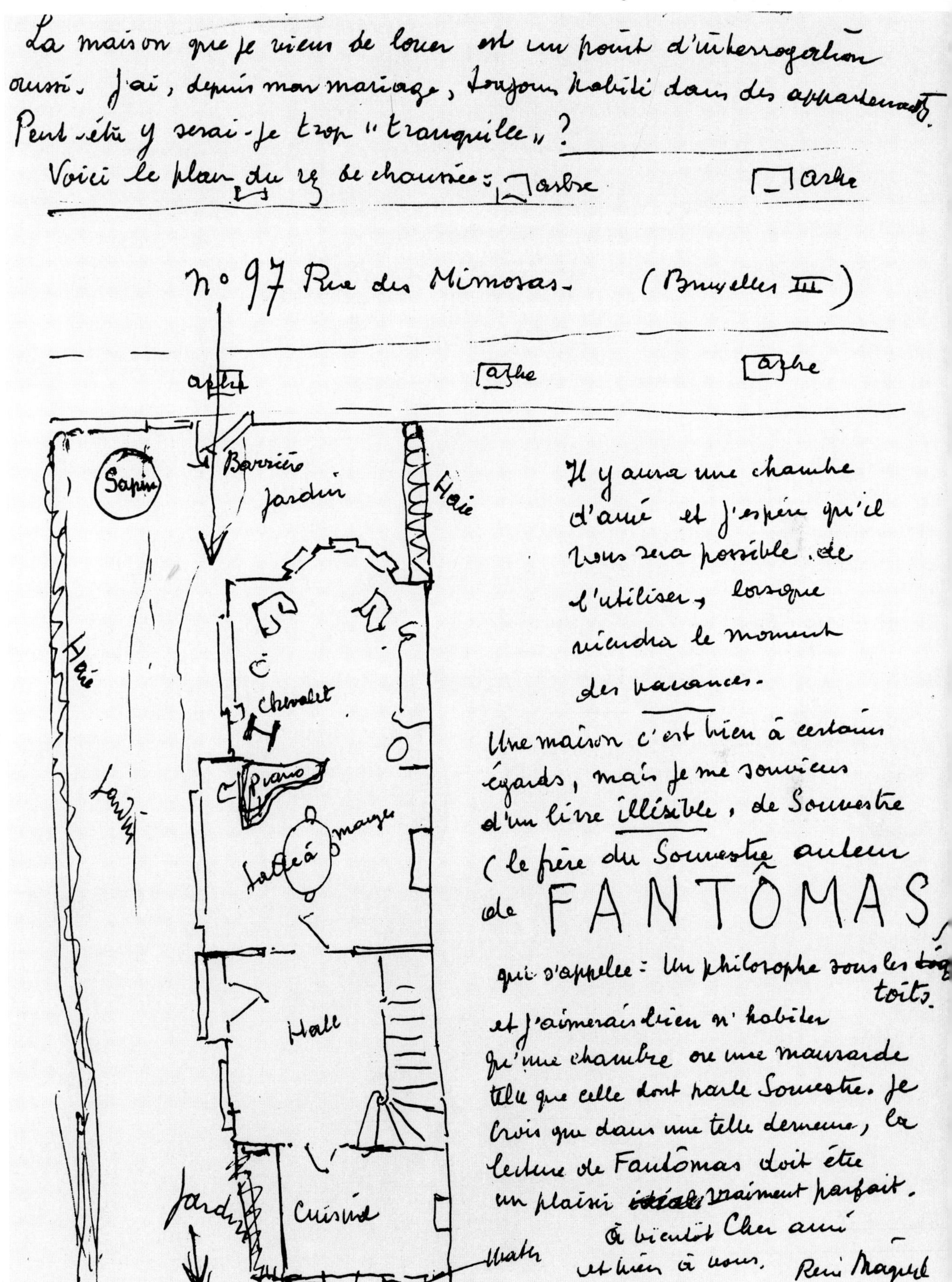

La maison que je viens de louer est un point d'interrogation aussi. J'ai, depuis mon mariage, toujours habité dans des appartements. Peut-être y serai-je trop "tranquille"?

Voici le plan du rez de chaussée: arbre arbre

N° 97 Rue des Mimosas. (Bruxelles III)

arbre arbre arbre

Barrière jardin

Sapin

Haie

Haie

Chevalet

Piano

Salle à manger

Hall

Cuisine

Jardin

Il y aura une chambre d'ami et j'espère qu'il vous sera possible de l'utiliser, lorsque viendra le moment des vacances.

Une maison c'est bien à certains égards, mais je me souviens d'un livre illisible, de Souvestre (le père du Souvestre auteur de FANTÔMAS) qui s'appelle: Un philosophe sous les toits. et j'aimerais bien n'habiter qu'une chambre ou une mansarde telle que celle dont parle Souvestre. Je crois que dans une telle demeure, la lecture de Fantômas doit être un plaisir ~~idéal~~ vraiment parfait.

À bientôt Cher ami et bien à vous.

René Magritte

16. Floor plan of the Magritte house at 97 rue des Mimosas, Brussels, Belgium, included in a letter from René Magritte to Maurice Rapin, December 20, 1957. *See* Appendix *for translation*

Woman

17. Photograph of René and Georgette Magritte, 1932

In dreams
Bordellos make
A very strong impression.
One feels one is entering
A conservatory.
—*René Magritte,* 391, *no. 19, October 1924, p. 130*

REPLIES TO THE QUESTIONNAIRE ON LOVE
I. All I know about the hope I place in love is that it only needs a woman to give it a reality.
II. The progression from the idea of love to the fact of loving is the event whereby a being appearing in reality makes his existence felt in such a way that he makes himself loved and followed into the light or shadows. I would sacrifice the freedom that is opposed to love. I rely on my instincts to make this gesture easy, as in the past.

18. *Il ne parle pas (He Doesn't Speak).* 1926. Oil on canvas, 29½ x 23⅝" (75 x 60 cm). Private collection, Belgium

I am prepared to abandon the cause I defend if it corrupts me with regard to love.

I am unable to envy anyone who will never have the certainty of loving.

A man is privileged when his passion obliges him to betray his convictions to please the woman he loves.

The woman has the right to demand such a pledge and to obtain it, if it serves the exaltation of love.

III. No, imposing limits on the powers of love must be done by experiment.

IV. Love cannot be destroyed. I believe in its victory.

—*René Magritte,* La Revolution Surréaliste, *no. 12, December 15, 1929, p. 2*

I love a woman finding herself in a man, but to my taste it becomes boring if the Holy Scriptures play the least role in this feminine inclination for X, Y, or Z. In fact, the sexual relationship should be "directed," as a doctrine of my own would prescribe, toward innocence.

—*Letter from René Magritte to Marcel Mariën, late 1937*

This afternoon, in bright sunlight, I saw a young woman waiting for the streetcar, accompanied by her body.

—*René Magritte,* Le Surractuel, *no. 1, July 1946*

19. *L'univers mental (The Mental Universe)*. 1947. Oil on canvas, 19⅝ x 28¾" (50 x 73 cm). Private collection, Brussels, Belgium

20. *L'attentat (Act of Violence)*. 1934. Oil on canvas, 27⅝ x 39⅜" (70 x 100 cm). Private collection, Belgium

19

20

21. *L'évidence éternelle (The Eternal Evidence)*. 1930. Oil on canvas, 5 panels, top to bottom: 8⅝ x 4¾" (22 x 12 cm), 7⅛ x 9" (18 x 23 cm), 10⅜ x 7¼" (26.5 x 18.5 cm), 8½ x 6⅛" (21.5 x 15.5 cm), 8½ x 4½" (21.5 x 11.5 cm). Collection William N. Copley, New York, New York

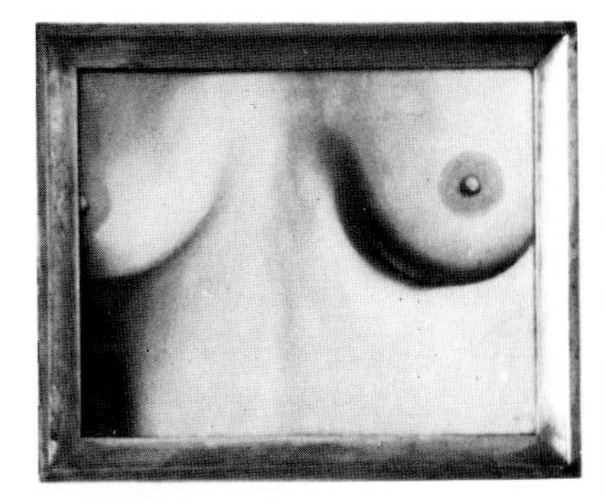

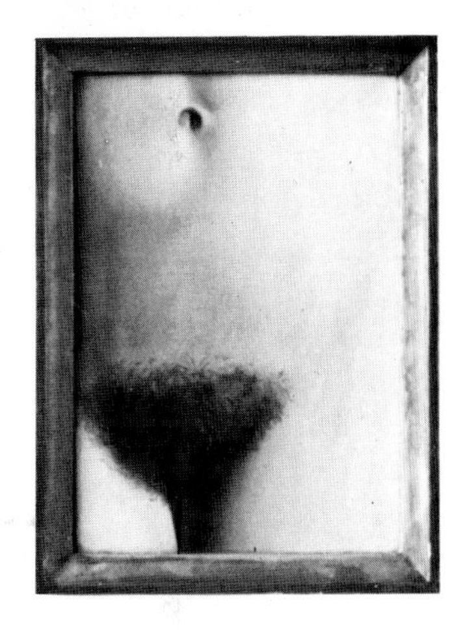

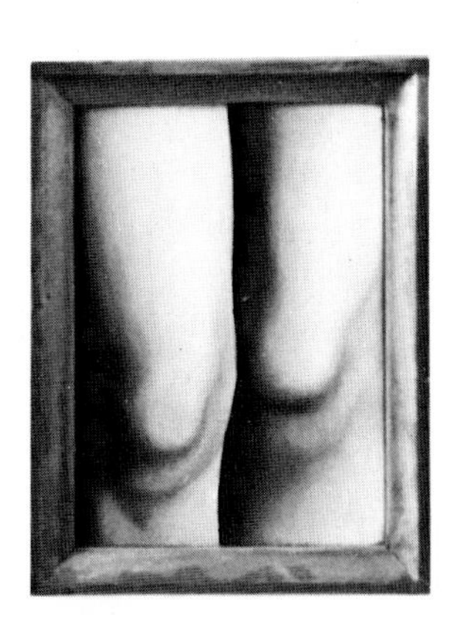

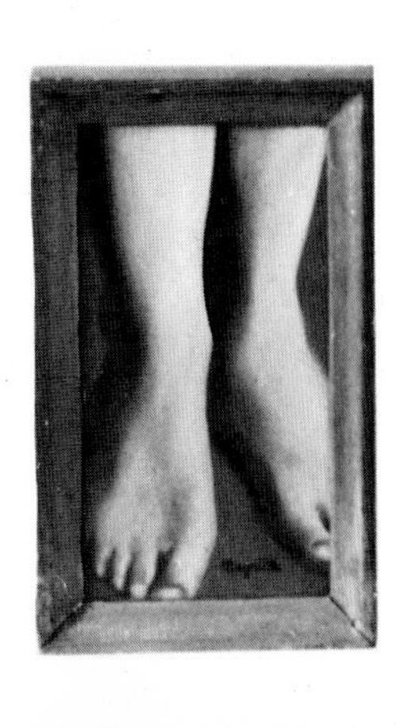

22. *La magie noire (Black Magic)*. 1935. Oil on canvas, 31½ x 23⅝" (80 x 60 cm). Collection Mme. René Magritte, Brussels, Belgium

Sexual acts amount to very little as soon as they are used to shock or to educate. There is a kind of comfortable misunderstanding that regards the understanding of sexuality as self-knowledge. Sexuality is compatible only with disinterested thought.

—*Letter from René Magritte to G. Puel, February 22, 1954*

I'm searching for a title for the picture of the nude woman (naked torso) in the room with the rock. One idea is that the stone is linked by some "affinity" to the earth, it can't raise itself, we can rely on its generic fidelity to terrestrial attraction. The woman too, if you like. From another point of view, the hard existence of the stone, well-defined, "a hard feeling," and the mental and physical system of a human being are not unconnected.

—*Letter from René Magritte to Paul Nougé, January 1948*

[Magritte] relates: The story of a short, bearded priest met at the post office, invited to the house, where he sees *La magie noire (Black Magic):* "I never knew women were made differently from men, but recently while administering Extreme Unction and annointing the feet of a dying woman, the sheet slipped off."

—*Harry Torczyner, diary entry, Nice, June 2, 1964*

25. *Les liaisons dangereuses (Dangerous Relationships)*. 1936. Oil on canvas, 28⅜ x 25¼" (72 x 64 cm). Private collection, Calvados, France

23. *La ligne de vie/La femme au fusil (The Lifeline/Woman with Shotgun)*. 1930. Oil on canvas, 28⅜ x 20⅝" (72 x 52.5 cm). Private collection, Osaka, Japan

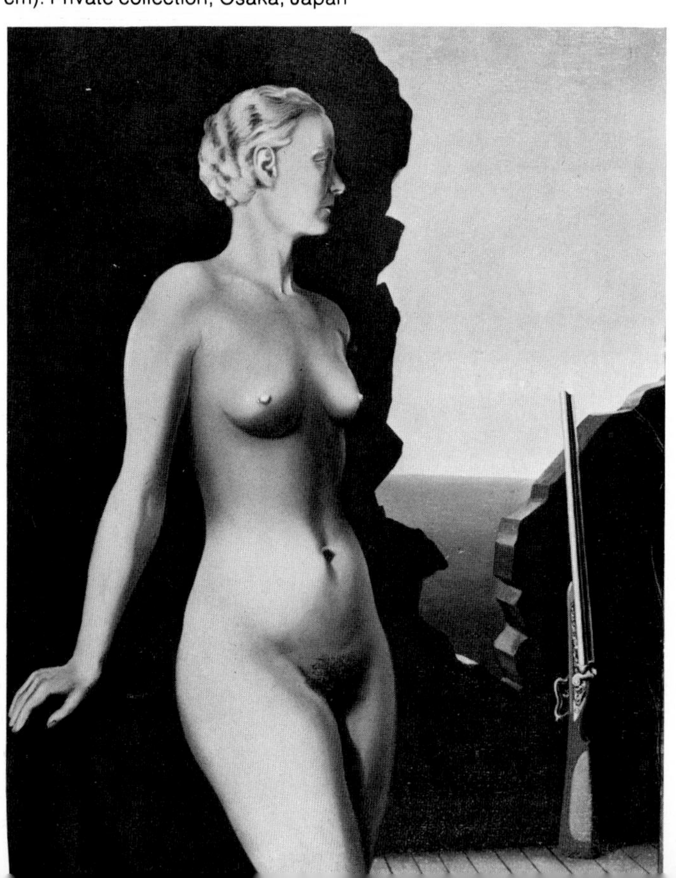

24. *La liberté de l'esprit (Freedom of Thought)*. 1948. Oil on canvas, 38⅛ x 31⅛" (97 x 79 cm). Musée Communal des Beaux-Arts, Charleroi, Belgium

Magritte

The "Surrealist" woman was as stupid an invention as the "pinup girl" who is now replacing her.
—*Letter from René Magritte to Mirabelle Dors and Maurice Rapin, August 22, 1956*

. . . for the first time I saw women in men's trousers without feeling nauseated.* What a difference there is between the apparel of this working girl, full of nobility, and that of a young girl in trousers.
—*Letter from René Magritte to Louis Scutenaire, undated*

*Magritte is referring to the film *Point du Jour.*

It seems sometimes that, as in fashion designing, it was suddenly decided that today the sack dress or sack-idea is what the world needs. And right away, if you are unable to appreciate these "fads," you are considered a backward peasant. I must have seemed one to Rachel Baes* who came to see me and, doubtless in my honor, had put on a kind of night dress of a vomitous pastel color. She also supported this sack-idea: the time had come for the authorities to recognize my "artistic worth" by making me a baron! If I should lose my powers of self-defense, I'd end up on the canvas.
—*Letter from René Magritte to Maurice Rapin, February 11, 1958*

*A Belgian painter with Surrealist leanings.

I have a great deal of admiration for admirable things, but I detest this tendency to change the forms of admirable things. If those who create fashion could change the shape of the human body (perhaps they will one day!), we would see a pretty woman with a hunchback, for example. It would be the fashion! On this question of forms, *I have nothing to say* that isn't negative: there are enough admirable forms already for the random search for new forms to be desirable. . . . I would go so far as to say that a new style is not worth knowing—no more so than an old style.
—*Letter from René Magritte to André Bosmans, August 22, 1959*

27

26. *Souvenir de voyage (Memory of a Voyage).* 1926. Oil on canvas, 29½ x 25⅝" (75 x 65 cm). Collection M. and Mme. Berger-Hoyez, Brussels, Belgium

27. Untitled. 1934–1935. Oil on canvas. Location unknown

28. *Les cornes du désir (The Horns of Desire).* 1960. Oil on canvas, 45¼ x 35" (115 x 89 cm). Collection Tazzoli, Turin, Italy

29. *La philosophie dans le boudoir (Philosophy in the Boudoir).* 1947. Oil on canvas, 31⅞ x 24" (81 x 61 cm). Private collection, Washington, D.C.

26

28

Magritte

DE GUSTIBUS ET COLORIBUS

Books were essential for Magritte's sustenance. Tempted by the role of author as a very young man, he wrote detective novels under the pseudonym Renghis, a combination of two of his given names, René and Ghislain. Later on, he was to sketch out "literary images," such as his *Théâtre en plein coeur de la vie (Theater in the Heart of Life).*

His curiosity drew him to the most diverse areas of literature. He admired Simenon as much as Conrad or Stevenson. He passed effortlessly from the world of Souvestre and Allain and their *Fantômas,* which had delighted his youth, to the philosophical garden in which he encountered Spinoza, Hegel, Nietzsche, Marx, Bergson, Heidegger, and Foucault. Foremost among his favorite poets were Edgar Allan Poe, Lautréamont, Apollinaire, and Éluard.

The brother of a composer and husband of a fine pianist, Magritte was an eclectic music lover. His tastes ranged from Bach to Schoenberg, whom he defended as early as 1929, and he was particularly fond of the music of Erik Satie.

His favorite diversions were chess and movies. He was a fervent fan of the films of Laurel and Hardy, westerns, suspense movies—the real "cinema," without pretensions or messages. An amateur filmmaker himself, he made comic or naïvely erotic films with his friends. From time to time, he made documentaries, which he showed at home, such as his last film, made in June 1967, concerning the foundry in Verona where his bronze sculptures were cast.

Chess served him as a sort of mental gymnastics. He liked to move the men around, intrigued by their shapes.

Of course, he liked to walk, or to swim during vacations, but he was not attracted to sports, and although he admired acrobats, he did not think much of athletes.

In his youth he had gone to the races, and he retained in his memory those images of jockeys and horses that we find in his pictures.

After turning sixty, he tried to become an expert driver. He bought a bright red Lancia, but after two accidents in less than one week he gave up this ambition.

Homebody though he was, he sometimes allowed himself to be enticed into traveling, without ever being at heart a tourist. What he disliked most were the preparations, vaccinations, and boring consultations of complicated timetables. In August 1929, during one of his first foreign trips with Georgette, he went to Spain with his friends Camille Goemans, and Paul and Gala Éluard. At Cadaquès, where they met Salvador Dali, they witnessed the adventure that became the soap opera of the art world: the love affair between Dali and Gala, and her leaving Éluard. In 1937, at 35 Wimpole Street, an address as literary as it is elegant, Magritte painted at the home of his host Edward James and discovered the charms of the English language. Toward the end of his life, he traveled to Texas and Israel where his fame had preceded him, and he was impressed by these new lands and customs. Still, the familiar landscapes from the Ardennes to the North Sea remained his favorites. For Magritte, the voyage he most enjoyed was the voyage around his own room.

Horses

Le jockey perdu (The Lost Jockey) is the first canvas I really painted with the feeling I had found my way, if one can use that term.
—*Remarks by René Magritte reported by E. C. Goossen, January 28, 1966*

30. *Le jockey perdu (The Lost Jockey).* 1926. Collage and gouache, 15½ x 23⅝" (39.5 x 60 cm). Collection Harry Torczyner, New York, New York

31. *Le jockey perdu (The Lost Jockey).* 1940. Oil on canvas, 23⅝ x 28½" (60 x 72.5 cm). Collection William N. Copley, New York, New York

33. *Le coeur du monde (The Heart of the World).* 1956. Oil on canvas, 26 x 20⅛" (66 x 51 cm). Museum of Art, Carnegie Institute, Pittsburgh, Pennsylvania. Gift of Mr. and Mrs. George L. Craig, Jr.

32. *L'enfance d'Icare (The Childhood of Icarus).* 1960. Oil on canvas, 38⅝ x 51⅜" (98 x 130.5 cm). Location unknown

4. *Le blanc-seing (Carte Blanche)*. 1965. Oil on canvas, 31⅞ x 25⅝″ (81 x 65 cm). Collection Paul Mellon, Washington, D.C.

35. *L'arc de triomphe (The Arch of Triumph)*. 1962. Oil on canvas, 51⅛ x 65″ (130 x 165 cm). Private collection, New York, New York

36

36. *Les grâces naturelles (The Natural Graces).* 1962. Oil on canvas, 15¾ x 11⅝" (40 x 32 cm). Collection Mme. Suzanne Ochinsky, Brussels, Belgium

37. *L'île au trésor (Treasure Island).* 1942. Oil on canvas, 27⅝ x 36⅝" (70 x 93 cm). Collection Mme. René Magritte, Brussels, Belgium

38. *La mémoire (Memory).* 1938. Oil on canvas, 28½ x 21¼" (72.5 x 54 cm). Collection Menil Foundation, Houston, Texas

37

magritte

39. *La réponse imprévue (The Unexpected Answer).* 1933. Oil on canvas, 32¼ x 21½″ (82 x 54.5 cm). Musées Royaux des Beaux-Arts de Belgique, Brussels, Belgium

40. *L'art de vivre (The Art of Living).* 1967. Oil on canvas, 25⅝ x 21¼″ (65 x 54 cm). Location unknown

Memories of Travels

Paris is a beautiful city without any raison d'être; aside from great vistas, it's a vacuum.
——Letter from René Magritte (Paris) to Paul Nougé, May 13, 1948

The few days I spent in Paris gave me the impression of a ghost town, where medieval mysticism has merely been transformed into a commercial, political, industrial, scientific mysticism . . . or artistic! (Paris is not an isolated case—it's the same everywhere.)
——Letter from René Magritte to Mirabelle Dors and Maurice Rapin, January 23, 1956

41

I saw some mountains on the way back through Switzerland (that boring country). As one nears Switzerland, France becomes Swiss and makes escape that much easier. You can't wait to get rid of the chalets and cheeses. Mountains quickly bring on indigestion (contrary to what I just read in *Le Rapport d'Uriel* by Benda,* for whom mountains command respect due to their impressive immobility). I recommend Benda to you; he's very amusing reading: he's nearly always angry and never stops attacking so-called reasonable doctors.
——Letter from René Magritte to Mirabelle Dors and Maurice Rapin, July 23, 1956

*Julien Benda (1867–1956) was a French philosopher and littérateur known for his antipathy toward Bergson and others who had turned from intellectual discipline toward a more mystical interpretation of the world

I am spending my vacation at home. During the first half of June I'll probably go to Zoute (Belgian coast resort). That will depend on the temperature, which isn't very high here: mornings and evenings one gladly wears a coat.
——Letter from René Magritte to Harry Torczyner, May 25, 1957

42

43

41. *Le temps menaçant (Threatening Weather)*. 1928. Oil on canvas, 21¼ x 28¾" (54 x 73 cm). Collection Sir Roland Penrose, London, England

42. *Le paysage isolé (The Lonely Landscape)*. c. 1928. Oil on canvas. Private collection, Belgium

43. *La seconde nature (Second Nature)*. 1965. Oil on canvas, 17¾ x 21⅝" (45 x 55 cm). Location unknown

magritte

44. *Les promenades d'Euclide (Euclidean Walks).* 1955. Oil on canvas, 64⅛ x 51⅛" (163 x 130 cm). The Minneapolis Institute of Arts, Minneapolis, Minnesota

Adresse complète :

2-75-H

La Madonnina Hôtel
Casamicciola Terme
ISCHIA (Via NAPOLI.)
ITALY

CASAMICCIOLA TERME (NAPOLI)
☎ 994062

le 22 ~~Août~~ Avril 1965

Bien cher ami,

Je reçois votre lettre du 17 Avril avec grand plaisir : c'est le premier signe pour nous de l'existence d'une autre contrée que cette île étrangère. Jusqu'à présent, il a fait un froid de canard, ici, "au pays du soleil". Je ne sais si les bienfaits de la cure ne seront pas compromis par la température peu satisfaisante qui règne ici. (L'Hôtel n'a pas de chauffage) Au point de vue gastronomique, il s'agit de "surprises étonnament "en contraire" : Poulet filandreux accompagné d'un emplâtre aux épinards. Potage "crème de légumes", difficilement à distinguer d'une papier de tapisserie. Nous sommes donc, paraît-il, le meilleur hôtel de Casamicciola. – Je pense que nous sommes venus trop tôt : la bonne saison (si elle n'est pas un mythe) se montrera après notre retour à Bruxelles.

Quant à la cure, elle dure une bonne heure : 1° bain de boue 2° bain d'eau de la montagne 3° repos 4° massage. Cela se passe vers 8 h du matin, à jeun. Pas d'amélioration déjà du statu quo sanitaire de Bruxelles. Je dois faire un effort pour écrire, pour m'asseoir, me coucher, etc.

Je ne sais que vous conseiller pour satisfaire les demandes d'expositions. Kansas City, par exemple, il faudra peut-être y renoncer si le musée de N.Y. a fixé une date qui ne permet pas d'organiser plusieurs expositions ?

Georgette et moi, nous avons été très contents d'avoir de vos nouvelles. Nos meilleures amitiés pour vous et pour Marcel.

RM.

(Je vous ai adressé le 16 une carte via air mail, ainsi qu'à Suzi).

45. Letter from René Magritte to Harry Torczyner, April 22, 1965. *See Appendix for translation*

My vacation is being spent at home—I only see the disagreeable side of travel plans. I am completely devoid of the kind of imagination one needs to "set off" on a trip.

—*Letter from René Magritte to André Bosmans, May 26, 1958*

I got back from London tired out from the opening. There are too many people to talk to. I've come away with an unpleasant feeling about airplane trips: the reduction in distance is paid for by a loss of tranquillity; I do not have total confidence in machinery. Still, London seems to have a "power" that Paris, for example, seems to lack. . . .

Finally, I had a fine idea for a painting the night I spent in London: in the middle of a large city, a candle towers very high and lights up the night. You will probably see this image when you come at the beginning of next month. I hope to be able to start painting it very soon.

—*Letter from René Magritte to André Bosmans, October 1, 1961*

We may go to America, but the decision has not been made completely. We would rather go by boat than by airplane—we don't have enough confidence where the heavier-than-air is concerned; heavier-than-water seems less dangerous.

—*Letter from René Magritte to Suzi Gablik, September 29, 1964*

Sheraton-Gladstone Hotel
114 East 52nd Street
New York, N. Y. 10022
Room 703 Phone: Plaza 3–4300
(Please write the number seven
like this: 7, because written
like this: 7, the Yankes [sic]
don't understand what number it is.

December 10, 1965.

Dear Irène and Scut, New York isn't bad. For example, a moving (to us) reminder of *Uncle Tom's Cabin*—our chambermaid is black. (Actually, this black is more brown, but you wouldn't notice that.) Upon arrival (after eight long hours on the plane and around thirty kilometers by car) we saw New York by night (at 5 p.m., or midnight Brussels time), and it was magical. By the way I am just now telling Georgette, who has just got dressed, "You're looking very pretty"—so everything is going well, and will get even better. (This "better" does not include the many invitations we are getting: various cocktail parties, etc.)

During the day we stroll around the streets, which oddly enough seem quieter than the Rue Neuve in Brussels. This seven million population seems to live slowly. The tempo of New York life is not much different from that of Braine d'Alleu or Olignie.

Harry Torczyner has a very comfortable office, two secretaries (a white woman and a black woman—another reminder of Uncle Tom), and finally a normal assistant.

Georgette fed nuts to the tame squirrels in the park. Suzi [Gablik] took us there. She is going to have a show soon and curses you because of your deliberate absence from her city. She has shown me her paintings (which are actually "photomontages" she has colored and retouched). They are nice, but, strangely enough, although she has found beautiful titles for me *(La Joconde* [*La Gioconda*], *L'arc de triomphe* [*The Arch of Triumph*]*)*, hers is, for example, *Hermaphrodite Landscape,* and she is sticking to it, despite my suggestion to change it to *The New York Poet* (or *New York 1000 Years Ago,* for example).

I will end by sending you our affectionate greetings.

Mag. Georgette

—Letter from René Magritte (New York) to Louis Scutenaire and Irène Hamoir, December 10, 1965

46. *L'étoile du matin (The Morning Star)*. 1938. Oil on canvas, 19⅝ x 24" (50 x 61 cm). Marlborough Fine Art (London) Ltd., England

We are spending two whole days in Houston, "Western" country. At St. Thomas University, I was pleasantly surprised to find a large collection of my paintings (notably *La lunette d'approche* [*The Field Glass*]). I am delighted by the Texans' interest in my painting: it appears to be considerable. We are being royally entertained by Mr. and Mrs. de Menil.

—Letter from René Magritte (Houston) to André Bosmans, December 19, 1965

47. *Le chef d'orchestre (The Orchestra Conductor)*. 1954. Oil on canvas, 23⅝ x 19⅝" (60 x 50 cm). Private collection, Belgium

48. René Magritte at a rodeo in Symington, Texas, December 1965. Photograph by Adelaide de Menil

While Georgette is praying in a *Catholic* church in Houston (Texas), I am manipulating my ballpoint to tell you that fact and to prepare you for seeing me wearing a real cowboy hat and a shirt with metal buttons when we meet again among the mimosas.
—Letter from René Magritte (Houston) to Louis Scutenaire, December 20, 1965

The trip to the "holy places" has not given me any religious feeling. But the country is very beautiful and one feels very much at home, even in the desert. Of course, we have been living here only under the best conditions.
—Letter from René Magritte (Jerusalem) to André Bosmans, April 24, 1966

Here we are, back from Israel since Friday evening. It was a fine trip: we visited the country north and south—it is very beautiful, and reminds me of a more primitive and more historic Côte d'Azur. We were given the best reception possible, like New York for that matter; despite being tired, we were enchanted, and hope to go back to Jerusalem under calmer conditions. That city's museum has some real treasures—the Dead Sea Scrolls and a beautiful Picasso exhibit. I have two pictures in the museum's (permanent) collection.

I'm starting to recover from the trip, which means that very soon I will be thinking about taking up paints and brushes again.
—Letter from René Magritte to Harry Torczyner, April 25, 1966

I don't travel in kilometers—I'm not a traveling salesman. Wherever I go, I say to myself: "It's just like I imagined it would be. I thought so."
—Remarks by René Magritte reported by Guy Mertens, Pourquoi Pas, *April 26, 1966*

It has stopped being as hot as a furnace. I wear dark glasses since the light is too brilliant and is therefore tiring. At the risk of shocking you, I will be glad to get back to the Northern mists, the Josephat Park, and the "Deux Magots" at the Porte Louise and the # 65 bus.
—Letter from René Magritte (Cannes) to Louis Scutenaire, June 27, 1966

49. Photograph of (left to right) Alexandre Iolas, Marcelle Torczyner, and René Magritte at the opening of the exhibition *René Magritte* at the Museum of Modern Art, New York, New York, 1965. On the wall hangs *Le faux miroir (The False Mirror)*

PERSONAL VALUES

René Magritte considered it almost a duty to ignore the contemporary art scene, with the exception of those painters with whom he felt natural affinities—which he hastened to elevate to the rank of elective affinities—such as De Chirico, Max Ernst, and, much later, Klapheck. Of course, he also paid homage to Picasso and Braque, but only as Cubists. He had a certain regard for such women painters as Rachel Baes, Jane Graverol, and Leonor Fini, a regard due above all to his inherent gallantry.

Criticism's evil eye watched constantly over Magritte. He was called an illustrator, postcard manufacturer, a painter of no pictorial value whatsoever; his work was said to be an insult to intelligence! The benevolent gaze of friendly criticism, even more cruel, took pains to explain Magritte. Alchemy, the cabala, tarot, the art of mime, dreams, and fantasy were all called upon. Between the enmity of one group and the incomprehension of the other, Magritte sat back and accepted the inevitable.

As one once believed in the good savage, he would believe for a long time in the "good" revolutionary, be he Surrealist, communist, or both. Life for him was a threepenny opera with a new cast of characters: Violette Nozières, who poisoned her incestuous father, earned his homage; Dominici, the peasant patriarch who murdered an English lord, his wife, and daughter, inspired him to write a ballad. Although he discoursed, wrote, published manifestos, and took part in all the ritual demonstrations, Magritte knew deep down that his sole and real calling toward changing the world was to paint his images.

Magritte did not want to listen to talk about psychoanalysis. Mad ideas are proper, madness is not. Fantasies are suitable, the fantastic reprehensible. He affirmed the presence of the spirit and denied the influence of dreams. Obstinately he shut doors and windows to the evil spirits.

This extremely inquisitive man was not curious about scientific discoveries. Paradoxically, he considered the sciences a discipline devoid of interest because they applied themselves to the world of the possible. If scientists restricted themselves to mental speculations, they earned his respect, but the concrete goals they set for themselves diminished them in his eyes. Pure research and its uncertainties escaped Magritte.

The awareness, as he told me, that he would never be able to fathom the reason for existence on this earth preoccupied him unceasingly. None of the other questions that life poses seemed to have the same importance. Death, nothingness, of which he spoke dispassionately, did not worry him. He was obsessed with the "why" of the world.

50. Photograph of (left to right) René Magritte, Marcel Duchamp, Max Ernst, and Man Ray, Amsterdam, The Netherlands, October 1966

Art

If we were to bother about an artistic hierarchy . . . André Lhote* would have little place in it, and could be left out with no great loss. On the other hand, Ingres and Picasso would have "prominent" positions. If an aesthete or art historian has any commonsense, he must agree with this. (Picasso, of course, as a Cubist, is a great figure in art history. The Picasso who followed in Lautrec's footsteps was superfluous.)
—*Letter from René Magritte to Maurice Rapin, March 15, 1958*

*André Lhote (1885–) is a French painter who has written and taught extensively about art. He was originally affiliated with the Cubists.

Unfortunately, we have to admit that many "artists" restrict their "messages" to information about the "importance" of the "material" they employ.
—*Letter from René Magritte to André Bosmans, July 10, 1963*

Abstract Art

. . . the current attempt to promote "abstract" painting on a popular level with a lot of help from artistic drill sargeants may be worthy of your assessment. In any case, one must either be for or against the stupidity that is trying to pass itself off as intelligence. Unfortunately . . . although Sacha Guitry* passes as being intelligent with those admirers who were moved by his [portrayal of] Napoleon, the Sacha Guitrys without theaters easily come to guide the consciences of "intellectuals" who think they are smarter than their grocers. In addition, the "battle" of ideas, lively though it may be, cannot at its present level excite anyone but narrow-minded people. The battle would probably be more amusing and less boring if it were not just hot air. I think that, to begin with, we must refuse to play a kind of game (the "Parisian" game, despite the "prestige" it enjoys, makes judgments on the players without the right of appeal) whose complexity is taken for profundity. The word "reaction" could signify the decision to do away with all the idiocies with which we are so busy.
—*Letter from René Magritte to N. Arnaud, May 7, 1955*

*Sacha Guitry (1885–1957) was a French writer, actor, and director active in the theater and cinema. One of his best known plays is *Castles in Spain*.

The many varieties of painting are occasionally amusing and fascinating. About 1915 I was passionately interested in Mondrian and the emergence of abstract painting. All the abstract paintings reveal only *abstract painting,* and absolutely nothing else. Painters have been making and remaking the same abstract picture since 1915 (whether red, black, or white, large or small, etc.).

The world and its mystery can never be remade; they are not a model that can just be copied. What is more, I cannot share an interest in what abstract painting is able to say, which was summed up once and for all by the first abstract painting.
—*Letter from René Magritte to André Bosmans, August 1959*

Age-old stupidity was manifested recently by a claimant that appeared when the art of painting was replaced by a so-called abstract, nonfigurative, or formless art—which consists in depositing the "material" on a surface with varying degrees of fantasy and conviction. However, the act of painting is undertaken so that poetry can emerge, not so the world is reduced to the variety of its material aspects.

Poetry is not oblivious to the world's mystery: it is neither a means of evasion nor a taste for the imaginary, but rather the presence of mind.
—*René Magritte,* Rhétorique, *no. 9, 1963*

To be curious about the reasons for or against "abstract art" is to play the "abstractionists'" game, the same game. They either have the answers to their questions or are interested in discovering further answers, but never ask themselves effective questions that are astonishing enough to stand up as questions and nothing but questions.

To say "this or that is inexplicable" is undoubtedly easy when it is easy and when one goes on to further verbal exploits with the same contempt (which one unwittingly feels) for what one says or thinks. It's no longer this easy if that which is inexplicable is forceful enough to demand our undivided attention, and thereby forbid our misplaced interest in some would-be explanation.

I hope you are going to write against "abstract art" in view of the inexplicable element that truly concerns us, sufficiently for us not to respond with curiosity or indifference.
—*Letter from René Magritte to Paul Bougoignie, undated*

Bosch

I am often asked if I feel I am the heir to the great Belgian painters. Why specifically Belgian? In my opinion, Belgian painting is only one episode among many in the overall history of art. And Bosch is singled out. . . . Hieronymus Bosch lived in a world of folklore, of hallucinations. I, by contrast, live in the real world.

—*Remarks by René Magritte reported by Claude Vial.* Femmes d'Aujourd'hui, *no. 1105, 1965*

Braque

The large Georges Braque exhibition at the Brussels Palais des Beaux-Arts deserves to be brought to our readers' attention. It is of unquestionable historical interest and illustrates an experiment that is important to grasp fully.

Braque is a "Cubist" painter.

In art history, it may be useful to make a summary distinction between two periods, that of classical art and that of modern art.

Modern art began about 1800. Such painters as Courbet, Géricault, and Delacroix created images that no longer had the conventional character of classical compositions. Millet and Manet captured life itself with such a vigor that to the eyes of their contemporaries their painting looked like a provocation, and it drove to fury both art critics and a public devoted to sterile imitations of the past.

With Corot, researches began in which specifically pictorial concerns prevailed over the subject matter, which in turn became no more than a pretext for displaying the forms created by light and shadow.

The importance bestowed upon "appearance" became even more pronounced with the Impressionist painters. They aspired to capture the real colors of the subject at the very moment it was observed; this direct observation of reality enabled them to take notice of the nuances that had either escaped classical painters or had seemed unimportant to them. The "pointillists" were to go even further in their attempt to restore the special vibrations of certain atmospheres through the breakdown of colors.

Nonetheless, these various researches were necessarily limited. At best, they enabled the sensations produced by the external world's *appearance* to be given concrete form.

Cézanne went beyond this stage. In Cézanne, we find a concept of the universe that cannot be realized through this technique. This painter attempted to penetrate the very substance of the world and the essence of space. Cézanne's pictures also departed from the relative stylization of photographic reproduction. They questioned the pictorial representation of reality.

The "Cubists," among whom Georges Braque and Pablo Picasso appear to be the most eminent, responded to this challenge in an original way.

They flatly condemned all painting that purported to be a reflection of the universe.

Cubist pictures are objects with a life of their own, not *representations*. They justify themselves by the *disparity* they bring out between the painted object and the appearance of the real object. This appearance itself is held up to question, and one discovers that the intention of the Cubists was to seek out a new means of knowledge, rather than to induce aesthetic pleasure through new means.

Has their undertaking been a success?

While some doubt may still remain, an exhibition such as the one devoted to Georges Braque deserves to be considered with the greatest attention.

51. Letter from René Magritte to Harry Torczyner, September 18, 1965. *See* Appendix *for translation*

le 18 Septembre 19[65]

Cher ami,

C'est une bonne question, dans votre lettre du 15 ct. Une bonne et une malheureuse à la fois : elle me fait mieux connaître les idées de Soby, qui ne sont pas très "catholiques": En effet, si influence il y a, on peut dire que Chirico en est responsable (dès 1925 environ, date où j'ai connu ses travaux). Par ailleurs dans un livre sur Max Ernst, Waldberg ne ca[che] pas que celui-ci, aussi, a subi l'influence de Chi[rico] Max Ernst et moi la reconnaissons volontiers, [mais] avec un peu de sens critique, il est évident que rapidement, nos "personnalités" se sont manifestées et n'avaient plus comme rapport avec Chirico — qu'un certain état esprit partagé plus ou moins avec d'autres surréalistes et de manières très différentes.

S'il s'agit de l'influence de Max Ernst, il faudrait parler de Fritz Van den Berghe, qui, lui était très éloigné de l'esprit surréaliste ; il n'a utilisé que l'aspect extérieur de la peinture de Ernst et il passe aux yeux de cata[illegible] pour un "précurseur" du Surréalisme en Belgi[que] Quant aux livres de Max Ernst, je n'en ai eu connaissance qu'en 1927, au moment où je les ai rencontrés. J'étais alors — comme maintenant — très peu "au courant" de l'actualité artistique.

Si l'on considère ce que j'ai peint depuis 1926 — "Le Jockey perdu" — 1926 — par exemple et ce qui a suivi, il ne me semble pas possible de parler "d'influence" de Chirico — J'ai été "frappé" vers 1925 en voyant un tableau de Chirico : "Le Chant d'Amour". Si influence il y a — c'est bien possible — on ne peut cependant retrouver dans "Le Jockey perdu" une ressemblance avec les tableaux de Chirico. L'influence en question se borne, en fin de compte, à une grande émotion, à une révélation merveilleuse en voyant, pour la première fois dans ma vie, une peinture vraiment poétique. Avec le temps, j'ai été amené aussi, à renoncer à des recherches de peinture où la "manière de peindre" avait la primauté. À présen[t] je sais que depuis 1926, je ne m'inquiétais plus que de "ce qu'il faut peindre". Ceci n'a été précisé que assez longtemps après avoir recherché "d'instinct" ce qu'il faut peindre.

Il y aura donc deux dessins pour Seitz et la dam[e]

À bientôt cher Harry et mes amitiés pour vou[s] et Marcelle,

René.

Finally, so as not to break with the customs of criticism, we should note that Braque uses a very limited number of colors, that he is especially devoted to contours and nuances, and that the variety of his grays, whites, and blacks frequently gives rise to surprising effects.
—*René Magritte under the pseudonym Florent Berger,* La Voix du Peuple *(Belgian Communist Party organ), December 1, 1936*

Dali

The 5000-kilo block of marble [balanced] on a bayonet is well within the style of the traditional artist who sees things "on a grand scale."* A few years ago, I dealt with a related subject without resorting to the *quantity* that impresses the empty headed. The 5000 kilos of rock will impress these idiots and, owing to the nature of their minds, they will comprehend nothing but the weight of the stone.
—*Letter from René Magritte to Mirabelle Dors and Maurice Rapin, May 9, 1956*

*During an interview, Salvador Dali had announced the construction of a sculpture made up of a five-ton block balanced on a bayonet.

Dali is superfluous: his flaming giraffe, for example, is a stupid caricature, an unintelligent bid—because it is facile and useless—to outdo the image I painted showing a piece of paper in flames and a *burning key,* an image I subsequently refined by showing only one flaming object—a trumpet (the title of it is *L'invention de feu* [*The Invention of Fire*]).

Moreover, Dali has given proof for some time that he really belongs to that vile group of individuals who drop in on the pope and value historical-religious painting without having any religious feelings whatsoever to justify this kind of behavior—which is an indication of the superficiality that is always so rampant everywhere nowadays.
—*Letter from René Magritte to André Bosmans, March 1959*

52. *Le bain de cristal (The Glass Bath).* 1946. Oil on canvas, 19⅝ x 13¾" (50 x 35 cm). Collection M. and Mme. Berger-Hoyez, Brussels, Belgium

De Chirico

He is actually the first painter to have thought of making painting speak of something other than painting.
—*Letter from René Magritte to André Bosmans, March 27, 1959*

I saw Chirico on television. He . . . made witty replies to the journalist questioning him. (He was probably trying to seem "down to earth" when he explained his paintings' Greek settings.) I noticed . . . the landscape with the men in the "foreground." All the same, I wondered whether Chirico's occasional outbursts of hilarity weren't signs that he was slightly gaga?
—*Letter from René Magritte to André Bosmans, April 8, 1964*

Delvaux

As for D[elvaux], I don't share your benevolence: he is a thousand percent *artiste-peintre* with the professional eccentricities and self-assurance that go along with it. I know him well enough to know that he's naïve, basically pretentious, respectful of and a believer in the most bourgeois "order." His success is due solely to the quantities of *naked women* he turns out continuously on immense panels. To him, they are "nudes" like those the academy professors tell us were the most sublime subjects of heroic classical painting.
—*Letter from René Magritte to Maurice Rapin, February 28, 1958*

Dubuffet

. . . it's getting easier to understand Dubuffet: one wrong note after another, his value based exclusively on imbecilic snobbery. He could go even further and exhibit used toilet paper arranged according to his "fancy" under glass; that would make some aesthetes drool.
—*Letter from René Magritte to Louis Scutenaire, 1949–1950*

Ensor

The reactions prompted by the James Ensor exhibition are extremely interesting in themselves. First, there is the critical reception, which is unanimous in declaring James Ensor to be an artist of the highest rank and of considerable influence. Yet this same body of criticism has given a cool reception to Ensor's early pictures (*Le chou* was condemned for "moral turpitude" in 1880, *L'après-midi d'Ostende* was refused by the Salon de Bruxelles in 1881, and so on). This criticism has, of course, played its habitual role, that of defending vociferously, whenever called upon, the outmoded values prevailing at the time, and the young Ensor treated [these values] with casual disrespect. Nowadays, the general consensus has changed: it seems that Ensor is some kind of summit. Ensor has had to display a certain freedom, of course, in order to seek a new pictorial climate. The French Impressionists pursued the same goals: to limit painting's professed objectives and to plumb them more deeply. Like his French friends, Ensor has achieved pictures in which color has given way to plays of subtlety or violence. The subjects are insignificant, serving as mere pretexts for unsymmetrical compositions and the decorative interplays of a colorist. It is apparent that here, by contrast to the work of Millet, Courbet, or Manet, a new way of understanding the world has not been introduced. An unenlightened euphoria and childish humor have dominated the development of James Ensor's work, and it represents fairly accurately one notion of happiness ascribed to by the bourgeoisie of 1900. A certain inconsequential nostalgia can be extrapolated from the vestiges of his disappearing world, but we must not confuse it with an exalted feeling about life.

A different kind of interest is also being shown on the occasion of this Ensor exhibit: the interest of the art dealers and speculators on the lookout for a "good deal."

The preface of the exhibition catalogue informs us that "doubtful" attributions will soon be eliminated as the result of investigations. Ensor's pictures will thus become solid investments. Poor old James Ensor! They made you a baron, and now the pictures in which you celebrated your youth have become the sorry objects of common speculation.

Finally, the interest of the visitors to the Ensor retrospective must be noted: they wander with great seriousness in front of the vegetables, the vases of flowers, the drunken Christs, and the other subjects Ensor enjoyed painting, without wondering if the seriousness they vaunt isn't somewhat out of place.

Were it possible to forget the gossip and the legend that disfigure James Ensor, a large exhibition of his works such as this one might possibly clear the artistic atmosphere that is still somewhat darkened by the Nazi occupation. However, it appears that we must go on living under this cloud.

—*René Magritte, "Homage à James Ensor,"* Le Drapeau Rouge, *no. 20–21, October 1945*

Ernst

Max Ernst's painting represents the world that exists beyond madness and reason. It has nothing to teach us, but it relates directly to us, and that is why it can surprise and enchant us.

Max Ernst clearly does not resemble the traditional artist for whom "thinking big" or "small" seems to be indispensable to his happiness or suffering. All kinds of interests are evinced for traditional painting: historical, documentary, political, etc.

If we make a distinction between Max Ernst's pictures in which virtuosity commands the professional attention of technicians, and those whose style depends on the diligent imitation of an idea, there is still only one interest that truly applies to both: an interest made up of astonishment and admiration. The odd feeling that Max Ernst's pictures are "well painted" means that we are under their spell, rather than in the presence of a manifestation of respect toward some definition of "fine painting."

Max Ernst possesses the "reality" that is able to awaken—if it be asleep—our trust in the marvelous, which cannot be isolated from the real-life situation in which it appears.

—*Letter from René Magritte to Patrick Waldberg, 1958, in Waldberg* Max Ernst, *Paris, 1958*

Imitation Art

. . . a slice of bread and jam displayed in a painting exhibition can really only fill the role of an "imitation" picture.

Bread and jam shown in an exhibition undoubtedly suggest the opposition "imitation" picture—true picture. But this relies on the usual frivolity of the viewing public, to whom it never occurs that a picture could be an imitation. I have never personally encountered this *explicit* notion of an imitation picture. One often has occasion to speak of bad painting, stupid painting, and so on, but the term "imitation" seems to be freer of ambiguity. It is worth popularizing, whereas formulas such as figurative art, nonfigurative art, etc., are not, given the confusion to which they give rise. "Imitation picture" probably has no chance of succeeding, because in order to be "fashionable" imitation is just what is called for. "Figurative art" is the equivalent of cooking with food, while nonfigurative art is nonfood cooking.

—*Letter from René Magritte to André Bosmans, July 20, 1960*

Impressionism

Unlike "Sunday painters" or Paris Salon painters, the Impressionists brought to painting a needed and intelligent new form, which was to create a contrast between living ideas and dead ideas. Today, the general public still prefers the dead idea and has not yet really absorbed the living idea of the Impressionists.

—*René Magritte,* La Lutte des Cerveaux, *1950*

Kandinsky

Le toile vide (The Empty Canvas). Kandinsky's emptiness has nothing to do with the "invisible" painting, as I once called it. To my mind, the "invisible" is the removal of the habitual meaning of the things that are visible in the picture, by means of which our mystery comes to dominate us completely.

Kandinsky's "emptiness" can easily be achieved.

Our mystery dominates us. We can do nothing to make it appear.

—*Letter from René Magritte to Maurice Rapin, March 31, 1958*

54. *Un Picasso de derrière les fagots (A Picasso from the Finest Vintage).* 1949. Painted bottle, height 12⅜" (31.5 cm). Private collection, United States

he "dominates" the situation without ever doubting that he is himself *part of the situation* without free will, whatever it may seem.
—*Letter from René Magritte to Maurice Rapin, August 6, 1956*

"Surrealism" (like "Fantastic art") has only a very vague meaning, which is false if it is given a meaning other than the very limited one it has: Surrealist is what suits Breton, what he says is valid. (This doesn't mean he really thinks it is.) So I am not very "Surrealist." For me, the word also signifies propaganda (a dirty word), with all the idiocies necessary to propaganda's success.

I may be "in practice" considered a "Surrealist," but this is part of a stupid "game." I have shows with "Surrealists," such as Labisse, Couteau, etc. . . . It goes without saying that I do not participate in, nor am I a part of, this artistic-cultural Ballets Russes movement.
—*Letter from René Magritte to Maurice Rapin, July 3, 1957*

Some Romantics are admirable, and some Surrealists are nothingness incarnate. There is a mediocre way of thinking, not necessarily Romantic, which can be classical or Surrealist. This is the one that is impossible to destroy: it has no force, it is the value that has been given it.
—*Letter from René Magritte to Harry Torczyner, 1959*

If the word *chance* exists, its meaning is in effect the same as that of the word *order.* It can be demonstrated that chance obeys a certain order, that it is the order of order, that order is due to chance, that this is so by chance, etc. . . . The Surrealists have talked a lot of nonsense, and I fear that despite their genius they are not made of the stuff to realize it. "Automatic" writing naïvely encourages this banal pretension to devise a methodical way of "forcing thought to speak"—as if thought were a machine, as if the interesting quality in writing or painting weren't *always unpredictable.*
—*Letter from René Magritte to André Bosmans, January 13, 1959*

. . . there are no Belgian Surrealists, aside from Delvaux (if even!) and myself. The Belgian artists who pass for Surrealists have only vague or false notions about it—in other words, none at all.
—*Letter from René Magritte to Harry Torczyner, January 25, 1964*

The term *Surrealism* gives rise to confusion, and the term *Realism* is not suitable for the direct apprehension of reality. Surrealism is the direct knowledge of reality: reality is absolute, and unrelated to the various ways of "interpreting" it. Breton says that Surrealism is the point at which the mind ceases to imagine nothingness, not the contrary. That's fine, but if I repeat this definition I'm no more than a parrot. One must come up with an equivalent, such as: Surrealism is the knowledge of absolute thought.
—*Notes written by René Magritte at the Gladstone Hotel, New York, New York, December 16, 1965*

Tachisme/Action Painting*

Nothing very exciting is achieved by "action painting" [*tachisme*] or "automatic writing." "Detachment" is also easy to understand. These methods of painting or writing make short work of all the problems that arise when one is looking for something truly different. We are talking about "technique," a word that in itself suggests a way of "cutting" a Gordian knot, because technique, conscious thought, and unconscious thought are all ways of thinking that are mistaken for thought itself.

Of immediate concern to us is a painted or written language that does not leave us indifferent, not the knowledge that it is conscious or unconscious, spontaneous or deliberate. The level on which such opposites become meaningful may be as scientific as you like, but I can't accept that. To follow Boileau or the *Surrealist Manifesto* is to affirm that hope may be ridiculous and easily satisfied. There are things done spontaneously that have no grace, and carefully thought out things that do. This doesn't depend on the chance that always seems to come along when one believes in it.
—*Letter from René Magritte to Maurice Rapin, March 7, 1958*

*Action painting, the more gestural manifestation of Abstract Expressionism, was known in France and Belgium as "art tachiste." This name was derived from the "taches"—paint stains, spots, or splashes—that were characteristic of such paintings. Magritte here plays on the double meaning of the term "art tachiste," which is largely lost in translation.

Tanguy

The idea of showing Tanguy's paintings along with mine isn't bad . . . it's fine of itself, but it takes a museum curator's mentality to have thought it up, since such an exhibition would point up the clash (almost total) between Tanguy's ideas and my own. It is apparent to everyone (except a curator) that Tanguy always stuck to redoing the same painting. The modifications [apparent in] the countless versions are negligible. The curator's idea is good because it will demonstrate the opposite of what he believes. As far as he is concerned, there can be no question in his mind of either nuances or incompatible differences.
—*Letter from René Magritte to Harry Torczyner, September 30, 1961*

As for painters like Tanguy [or] Miró, I think they behave like priests: they always use the same recipe for invoking the God of the Catholics. Both of them have renounced (or are unaware of) the distinction between imaginary and imagined, and have settled on the imaginary, which never varies.
—*Letter from René Magritte to André Bosmans, November 13, 1965*

Van Gogh

I don't really respond to Van Gogh's paintings. I mention this because I've been asked to write something about this painter; I don't know if I'll manage to do it [since] I'm not very "enthused." There is, of course, the story of the ear, cut off and cleaned up, put in an envelope, and given as a gift to prostitutes. If I do write something, I'll try to convey what happened as being more important than the actual pictures that elicit the obligatory admiration of intellectuals.
—*Letter from René Magritte to G. Puel, March 8, 1955*

Philosophy

If society weren't ignorant of what we are like, don't you think it would find us suspicious? Society plays its role. We're surrounded by jokers who have forgotten what they're about. Yet we have to take society into account. It uses poor judgment, but it is isolated. Otherwise. . . .
—*Letter from René Magritte to Marcel Lecomte, September 1928*

There is an established "beauty" that is like a self-satisfied person with a solid income; there's another kind of beauty that sears our souls. I love this beauty that has no protection or strength except its own force and charm. For me, thought and language cannot be reduced to their function (as alleged by sociologists), which would involve the social structure and bring about changes in it. Thought and language clearly possess this function as far as orthodox sociologists and philologists are concerned. I don't feel obliged to think as they do, nor have I any desire to do so!
—*Remarks by René Magritte quoted by Maurice Rapin,* Aporismes, *1970*

It's as though we were in a cave without ventilation.
—*Remark by René Magritte reported by Louis Scutenaire,* René Magritte, *1942, p. 36*

Life is supposed to be better appreciated through displeasure, uncertainty, pain, terror. We find "completely natural" the unceasing efforts that continue to be made to turn the world into a torture chamber. We don't protest because the mind has been twisted into thinking as follows: we believe that tragic lighting is better suited to reveal life, and that this is how we come into contact with the mystery of existence. Sometimes we even believe that we are successful, thanks to this illumination, this objectivity. This objectivity becomes greater as the terror becomes more vivid.
—*René Magritte, notes written to Marcel Mariën regarding the* Manifeste de L'extramentalisme, *1946*

We mustn't fear daylight just because it almost always illuminates a miserable world.
—*René Magritte,* Le Surréalisme en Plein Soleil, *October 1946*

When we consider philosophy, it's like considering painting or writing. We aren't thinking of what the professional philosophers, painters, or writers mean. Whence the danger of using the words *philosophy, painting,* etc.

Beauty is a promise of happiness (happiness for twentieth-century Westerners).
—*Letter from René Magritte to Paul Nougé, October-November 1946*

I consider valid the linguistic attempt to say that my pictures were conceived as material signs of freedom of thought.
—*René Magritte,* La Pensée et les Images, *catalogue of the Magritte exhibition, Brussels, May 1954*

A pictorial (or other) language impresses the yokels insofar as it is *dull.* Let me explain: the artist paints dull pictures so that they seem to mean something important. If the picture were to state clearly what the artist thought, we would recognize it as an open secret, as a banal idea or feeling. Thanks to obscurity, however, the untutored believes the picture to have some wonderful meaning.

What I paint is addressed to those who *"live" in the present,* or rather, *for* it. . . . An artist who paints for posterity has an intention that I do not have. In my opinion, he is doing something idiots understand very well—those who do not concern "living" men. The man who seems to be alive, whom one refers to as "alive," is an enigmatic reality that need not be lent a meaning that would *interpret* that reality as one that is concerned with posterity. We *see* that after a time reality abandons what we perceive in it, that it abandons its form and means of communication (death no longer speaks our language, since if it speaks we cannot hear it). I think of my pictures as being truly in touch with the living, but there is no reason for expecting these pictures to outlive the living, when the latter do not have a parallel ambition or [entertain] such facile notions.
—*Letter from René Magritte to Louis Scutenaire, February 24, 1955*

This business of the [art] public might also be clarified. (Van Gogh showed his pictures without saying anything to the "respectable" people who barely glanced at them. Now, everyone is more "sensitive" than those "respectable" folk, and everyone recognizes Van Gogh's greatness now that he is dead.) In this regard, I think that my painting has real interest only for those who are alive now. In the future, it will have nothing but some historical value (if it still has any value at all). Why do we care about creating works that will last, when man doesn't have similar ambitions for himself? This surrogate survival through one's work is nonsense.
—*Letter from René Magritte to G. Puel, March 8, 1955*

55. *Les vacances de Hegel (Hegel's Holiday).* 1958. Oil on canvas, 23⅝ x 19⅝" (60 x 50 cm). Galerie Isy Brachot, Brussels, Belgium

56. Letter from René Magritte to Maurice Rapin, May 22, 1958. *See* Appendix *for translation*

Mon dernier tableau a commencé par la question : Comment peindre un tableau dont le verre d'eau est le sujet ? J'ai dessiné de nombreux verres d'eau :

etc. —.

une ligne se trouvait toujours dans ces dessins.

Ensuite cette ligne s'est évasée et a pris la forme d'un parapluie,

Puis ce parapluie a été mis dans le verre : et pour finir le parapluie s'est ouvert et a été placé en dessous du verre d'eau :

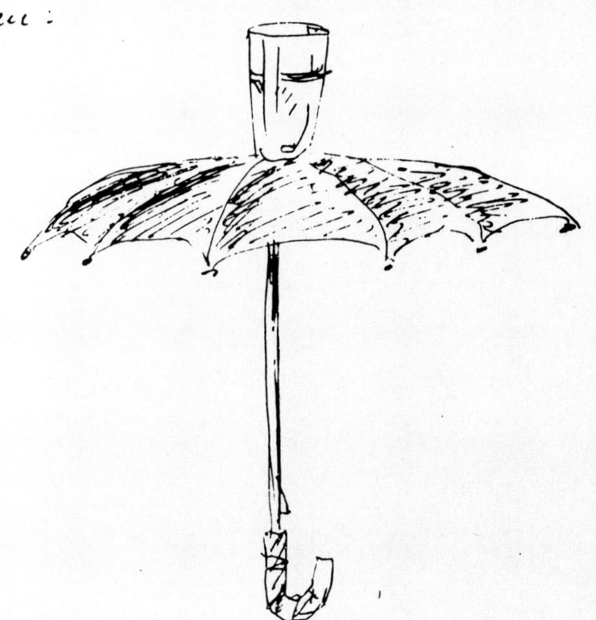

Ce qui me semble répondre à la question initiale.

Le tableau ainsi conçu s'appelle :

« Les Vacances de Hegel »

Je crois que Hegel aurait aimé cet objet qui a deux fonctions contraires : repousser et contenir de l'eau. Cela l'aurait sans doute amusé comme on le peut en vacances ?

Bien amicalement à vous

René Magritte

The criterion that Valéry condemns doesn't yet exist, as far as I know. There is this need I mentioned to you in which an interest in the most difficult things and the passion for research are replaced by an interest or desire for the result.

—*Letter from René Magritte to G. Puel, May 22, 1955*

VARIETIES OF SADNESS*

Dinos: But doesn't the All High know all things?
Agathos: And it is the *only thing* (since he is the All Highest) that should remain unknown to Himself.
—*Edgard* [*sic*] *Poe*

Freedom is the possibility to be, and not the obligation to be.

The sad heart can beat, it can cease to beat; it makes acquaintance with freedom. Sadness knows freedom; it imposes nothing.

Freedom is an "old acquaintance" that we bear as badly as sadness and being. The will intervenes to control or stop palpitations. All the feelings that judge, serve, represent, deny, or utilize freedom *are not distracted by sadness,* are not led astray as to the extent of their ignorance of freedom.

Ignorance is surely not total save in [a state of] absolute nothingness.

In a world that puts a price tag on usefulness, we tolerate freedom, sadness, and being, which are duly motivated by their obedience to the laws of chance, necessity, or experience. We respect sadness, but want to alleviate it: "Travel is an effective diversion for moral afflictions," said Larousse, whose gargantuan labors were indicative of a normal insanity, a tenacious will to "banish dark thoughts." There are many ways to "alleviate sadness": learned discoveries teach us, among other things, that love is hate, that sadness stems from a childhood complex, etc. However energetic the search for error or truth, the entertaining outcome outweighs all other aspects.

Caricatures of sadness command respect. . . . The knowledge of freedom prescribes nothing useful. Rather, it distinguishes with some difficulty between the useful and the useless.

Respect turns into suffering when certain faces express arrogance, brutality, cruelty, or the other emotions that would impose their wills, no matter the abjectness that may result. This spontaneous or methodical will is stupid insofar as it is unfamiliar with freedom and lacks sadness.

Like love, honest emotions can be distracted by sadness. They counter the knowledge of freedom with no disinterested or passionate motives. They are happy, they can suffer the most acute unhappiness.

"Unmotivated and inconsequential" emotions such as nostalgia, congeniality, pity, boredom, charm, and humor are variations of unedifying sadness.

Edgard [sic] Poe wrote "The Genesis of a Poem." He tells us that one kind of logical method decides on the treatment to be inflicted on a "theme" chosen for its *utility:* NEVERMORE! Obviously, *no one* believes the utility of NEVERMORE! to be more than marginal, more than a negligible quantity. NEVERMORE! is only suitable for assisting in something such as, for example, the conception of a poem. Poe humorously brings his discourse into line with the truth in popular opinion, which attributes to sadness the power of leading the will down solemn or merry paths. Truth does not contradict the truth of the heart or mind.

"The Raven" and "The Genesis of a Poem" express the sadness that has never abandoned poets of freedom.
—*René Magritte, 1955*

*An earlier, shorter version, *Two Variations of Sadness*, was contained in a letter to Louis Scutenaire. 1955

Being the "master of one's fate" can't be accomplished without automatic recourse to the faculty of comparing oneself to a master of fate or maintaining a privileged relationship with fate. To believe in fate, one has to compare future time with past time, and believe in both past and future.
—*Letter from René Magritte to Mirabelle Dors and Maurice Rapin, March 13, 1956*

I think a lot about . . . the impossibility of perceiving anything other than ideas, feelings, or sensations. What we imagine to be *links* between these things are in turn only an idea or feeling, and to my knowledge nothing can be seriously considered a *link, relationship, cause* or *effect.*

In rereading Nietzsche, I find exactly the same idea, but expressed with a word that revolts me—*atomism:* "Our conscience (as we call it) is composed of atomic phenomena," meaning separate, autonomous, isolated, indivisible things. He also stresses what I already thought: we can predict nothing; everything that happens is an "effect" whose "cause" is beyond what happens to us, beyond our horizon. He goes on at great length about our civilization, its decadence. He isn't very attractive here. But his disciples seem to have misunderstood him precisely to the extent they were "concerned" with social questions. The Nazis "were fond of" Nietzsche, Beethoven, Wagner, as though, had they been alive, they wouldn't have gone straight to the gas chamber.
—*Letter from René Magritte to Mirabelle Dors and Maurice Rapin, June 19, 1956*

The fact of living is of great importance for everyone, but the life of someone else doesn't have the same importance. . . .

Since death is absolute nothingness, it will be an absolute comfort to us mortals. The moral question will not come up in the absolute absence of "point of view" (lack of "conscience"). Since it is absolute nothingness, then, death would be a program of absolute comfort that is attained no matter what means are employed to achieve it. The idea that death is absolute nothingness is not contradicted by the idea that we live in mystery. Mystery is not penetrated by this supposition. On the contrary, it appears to respect the idea of mystery, and thus should be respectfully considered.
—*Letter from René Magritte to Paul Colinet, 1957*

It's "normal" to think sometimes of putting an end to what we call life. It would be possible, like other possibilities we occasionally think about without "following through."

All the same, there is something so uninteresting about blowing one's brains out that such a project couldn't hold our interest for long, and once you've given it up you're impervious (as I am, I think) to things that may appear sensational but that are in the end more or less nothing.
—*Letter from René Magritte to Maurice Rapin, February 18, 1958*

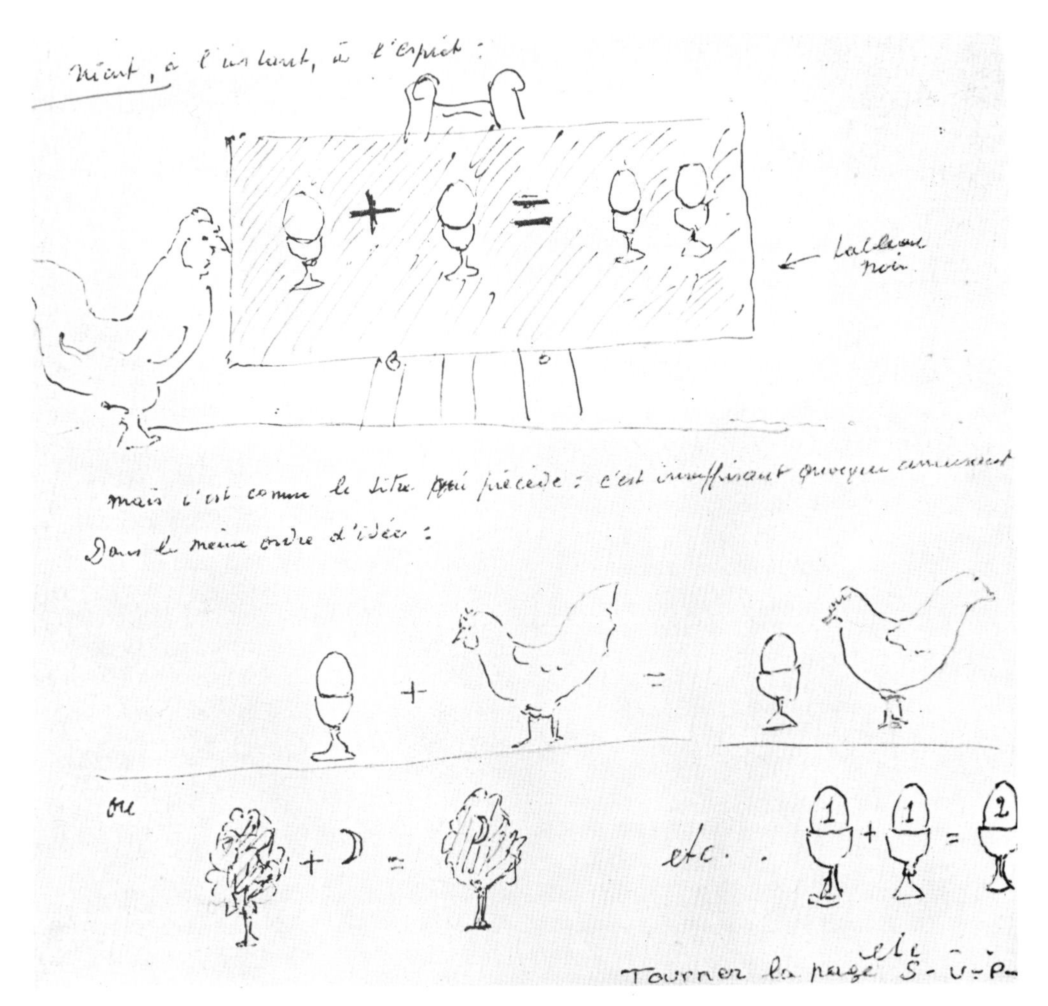
vient, à l'instant, à l'esprit :

tableau noir.

mais c'est comme le titre qui précède : c'est insuffisant quoique amusant

Dans le même ordre d'idée :

ou

etc.

Tourner la page S.V.P.

57. Letter from René Magritte to Paul Colinet, 1957.
See Appendix *for translation*

58. *Variante de la tristesse (Variation of Sadness)*. 1955. Oil on canvas, 19⅞ x 23⅜" (50.5 x 59.5 cm). Private collection, Chicago, Illinois

I am planning to paint a picture on the idea of the chicken with a boiled egg. (I'm wondering if the egg should be decapitated or intact?) Nocturnal and sunlit variations are a possibility.
——*Letter from René Magritte to Paul Colinet, 1957*

59. *La statue volante (The Flying Statue)*. 1927. Oil on canvas, 23⅝ x 19⅝" (60 x 50 cm). Private collection, Belgium

Words have all kinds of meanings. Take the word *serious,* for example: "serious" people such as scientists, businessmen, strategists, etc. A French biologist (Rostand) states with the scientist's solemnity: "Once past childhood, we should know that nothing is serious." This superiority, which does not lack serious irony, illustrates the seriousness of "serious" people, and is a prime example of the stupidity of specialists who try to "deal with everything." Poets can reclaim this word *serious* by giving it a *truly* serious meaning. Poetry is a more serious "business" than science, strategy, finance, or another supposedly serious thing.

The poet can seriously judge what is not poetic. The scholar, the man of war, the empire builder, cannot seriously judge poetry.

The meaning of the word *logic* has never to my mind followed the scholastic rules of reasoning when it designates that which should join images together so that a poem can be what we have the right to expect of it. I don't put any more stock in the word *logic* than in any other. Poetic "meaning," "rigor," "enlightenment," or "logic" are all the same. The important thing is the poem, in which nothing is unimportant, and which is able to give the feeling of something truly "serious."

—*Letter from René Magritte to André Bosmans, May 1959*

. . . I *jokingly* said that clever people would reproach the "heaviness" of what I might write to elucidate an idea. . . . It's what one says that counts above all; the way one says it is important only if it is suited to saying exactly what must be said.

—*Letter from René Magritte to André Bosmans, July 20, 1960*

After a discussion about my text *La Voix du Mystère (The Voice of Mystery),* I'm afraid that the mystery I'm talking about may be confused with the one priests propagandize. Someone told me that they would be able to convince me that I'm a "believer" as they understood the term. . . .

Is it perhaps a question of distinguishing between Nothingness and the Nirvana touted by Eastern priests? But this is a difficult matter. In "distinguishing" Nothingness, we already define it and give it a form it couldn't possibly, as Nothingness, have.

I believe that what we don't yet know about Nothingness is necessary.

—*Letter from René Magritte to André Bosmans, September 25, 1961*

If someone likes you for your good qualities, it's only your good qualities they like.

—*Letter from René Magritte to André Bosmans, March 1962*

I chose "idea" to differentiate between thought composed of words (speech) and thought composed of another language (music, painting, mathematics, etc.).

What is appealing about ideas is that they are so often questionable. It seems that the sum is not greater than the part ad infinitum, which accounts for that immediate effectiveness [of ideas] that suffices for our happiness.

—*Letter from René Magritte to André Souris, December 7, 1963*

The first feeling I remember is when I was in a cradle, and the first thing I saw was a chest next to my cradle. . . . The world presented itself to me in the guise of a chest.

—*Remarks by René Magritte, reported by Jean Neyens, January 1965*

I don't know the reason (if there is one) for living or dying.

—*Letter from René Magritte to Chaim Perelman, March 22, 1967*

"We never see but one side of things," Victor Hugo said, I believe. . . . It's precisely this "other side" that I'm trying to express. . . .

—*René Magritte, 1967, quoted in* Lectures pour Tous, *Pierre Cabane, Paris, no. 167, November 1967*

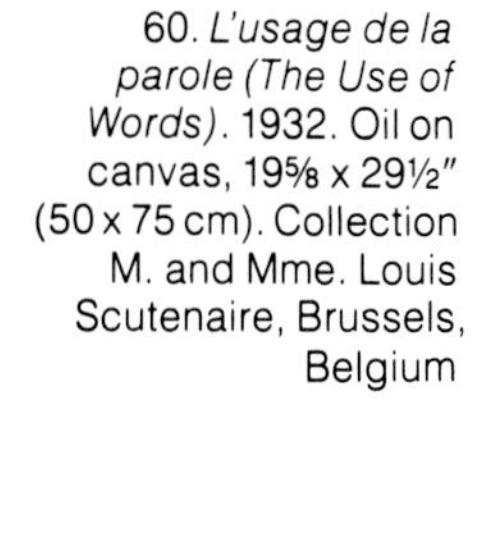

60. *L'usage de la parole (The Use of Words)*. 1932. Oil on canvas, 19⅝ x 29½" (50 x 75 cm). Collection M. and Mme. Louis Scutenaire, Brussels, Belgium

Politics

Man's will is being enlisted to engage in the accomplishment of a utopian task.

The consent of the workers is obtained by employing threats and words that seem to point out indispensable realities.

The world is blinded by this blackmail, and yet it manifests a legitimate concern—quickly allayed, to be sure, by the vague hope that its desires will somehow be fulfilled.

As long as we have the means to do so, we Surrealists cannot discontinue the activity that puts us in direct opposition to the myths, ideas, feelings, and behavior of this ambiguous world.

—*Letter from René Magritte to Louis Scutenaire, December 12, 1932*

The Communist point of view is my own. My art is valid only insofar as it opposed the bourgeois ideal in whose name life is being extinguished.

—*René Magritte,* Les Beaux Arts *(Brussels), no. 164, May 17, 1935, p. 15*

I distrust this folk art the Fascists have chosen to promote. Art-for-the-people is spurious because it is based on a superficial point of view. I too am part of the people. What a painter must do is to see mankind in workman's overalls. This is what Courbet did when he painted *Les Casseurs de Pierre (The Stone Breakers),* which caused a scandal among gallery-goers because its subject was new. For that matter, I have often met with greater understanding from the working class than from the most refined aesthetes. As for the snobs, they have wildly applauded Surrealist projects because they have to be "with it." Today, they are being lulled by the deplorable singsong of Existentialism, and tomorrow. . . .

—*René Magritte,* Clarté, *December 16, 1945*

At present artists cannot survive unless they allow their works to be exploited. A painter who turns down a contract with a dealer or who refuses to sell his pictures to collectors on the pretext that he

61. *L'intelligence (Intelligence).* 1946. Oil on canvas, 21¼ x 25⅝" (54 x 65 cm). Collection M. and Mme. Louis Scutenaire, Brussels, Belgium

has the right to greater returns has no way of acquiring those greater returns; he lacks that effective means available to other professions—the strike. A strike by professional painters or poets would create hardship for no one.

The only way poets and painters have of struggling against the bourgeois economic system is to give their works a content that rejects the bourgeois ideological values that underlie the bourgeois economic system.

In actuality, the only writers and painters working toward this goal in Belgium (along with scientists in their respective field) are the signatories of this letter, and their public adherence to the Communist cause is being met with real hostility and mistrust on the part of the Communist Party. Indeed, their efforts are never discussed when the Communist press takes up cultural problems (not a word in *Le Drapeau Rouge* about the works that have been submitted to it by Nougé, Scutenaire, Mariën, and Magritte; on the other hand, the bourgeois press exhibits its perspicacity in doing them the honor of considering them enemies), but rather it seems to be the rule that only representatives of bourgeois thought are given much consideration.

The articles in *Le Drapeau Rouge* devoted to contemporary art exhibits mention:

1) Ensor (who showed in Germany during the Occupation) and other "stars" established by the bourgeoisie.

2) Dead artists, the fact of their death having aroused some "rather belated" interest, and apparently being sufficient to confer exceptional value on their works.

3) An anarchical group of experiments by "young" [painters], from which nothing can be extrapolated at this juncture.

* * * *

The Party refused, it says, to take a stand on these questions: in fact, if the Party has no confidence in the content of these works, it is because that content is nonexistent as a force of opposition to bourgeois thought. Nevertheless, the Party wants to get some use out of artists who are *incapable of inventing new emotions,* and requires them to engage in political agitation. Yet since artists cannot go on strike, the absurdity of artists' political agitation is only too obvious.

The only *correct* attitude the Party can take with regard to the aesthetic question, *and which it is refusing to take,* is that of requiring an artist to give his works a revolutionary content. This is our conviction, and it prevents us from attending the meetings at Antwerp, which will be held with the absurd notion of seeking ways for artists to engage in political agitation.

—*René Magritte* et al., Lettre au Parti Communiste de Belgique, *1946*

Have I discovered something? I thought that the idea *progress doesn't exist* was dangerous to our health, since it prevents a greater contact with reality: good and bad things (for us as well as others, for the dead and the yet unborn) that continually happen, struggle, are replaced, and so on.

The notion of progress facilitates cerebral suppurations such as: "The dunce cap is an advance over the tricorn," "The revolver is an advance in the art of killing," "Death and suffering in an ultramodern hospital is an advance," etc.

The idea of progress is linked to the belief that we are coming closer to absolute good, which permits a lot of today's evil to emerge.

—*Letter from René Magritte to Paul Nougé, August 14, 1946*

All my latest pictures are leading me to the simplified painting I have sought for so long. In short, it is the increasingly rigorous research into what is, to me, the essential in art: a purity, a precise image of mystery that, having abandoned all extraneous conjecture, is decisive. . . . It seems that in this way I express what was overwhelming about *Le viol (The Rape)* with forms identical to those in nature. The reading of it becomes internalized.

—*Letter from René Magritte to Claude Spaak, undated*

On the other hand, in order to attract the interest of the artistic, political, and literary population, this title was chosen because of the "sensitivity" to current events that makes these cultivated individuals so impressionable. Having thus gained the attention of this group for the few moments it is capable of maintaining a semblance of thought, one notices that on their level—the level of unskilled art—folk objects are the equivalent of the so-called secrets of alchemy in another area.

Just as propaganda for alchemy could only be made with an ignorance of today's scientific knowledge, so the arguments for folk art can only be explained by the reprehensible ignorance of spiritual things shared by the cultural specialists who are responsible for or support this shameful enterprise.

Whereas the least objective of minds would readily judge the call for a return to alchemy to be an attempt to destroy scientific progress and a desire to return to the adoration of icons or to the fear of forbidden fetishes in the hope of rediscovering a so-called age of gold, a parallel and large-scale endeavor in favor of folk art is now underway and is being supported by both those who are for reaction and those who seek change in the world economic system.

The agreement these opponents have reached on the benefits of folklore is unusual and significant enough to merit examination.

The fact that the Catholic and revolutionary newspapers are united in this affair leads one to believe that what divides them exists on another level than that of cultural matters, and that there is nothing to keep them from agreeing on "minor questions."

In short, these political foes give little importance to the feelings a man has about life and the enhancement of those feelings by artistic means. What divides them makes them alike. These foes are made of the same stuff: second-rate stuff that has nothing to do with either the noble spirit of the alchemists or with the enthusiasm of unknown folk artists. Alas! This stuff is the stuff of inertia, an inertia made monstrous by its permanence and its extent!

There are some men here on earth who know what true intellectual honesty is and who want no part of this inertia nor expect any help from it. The countless others are indifferent, passive, clumsy calculators, or dishonest. Their number is not enough to make them right.

In the artistic sphere in 1949, we are called upon to dismiss the case involving the fraudulent attempts to revive feudal obscurantism based on folk material. Also, to refuse to respect the myriad selfish hopes one could place on this kind of undertaking.

Simple honesty demands that such attempts—doomed, in any case, to failure—be called by their rightful name: the sign of contemptibility.

—*René Magritte,* Nous N'Avons Pas Choisi Le Folklore, *1949*

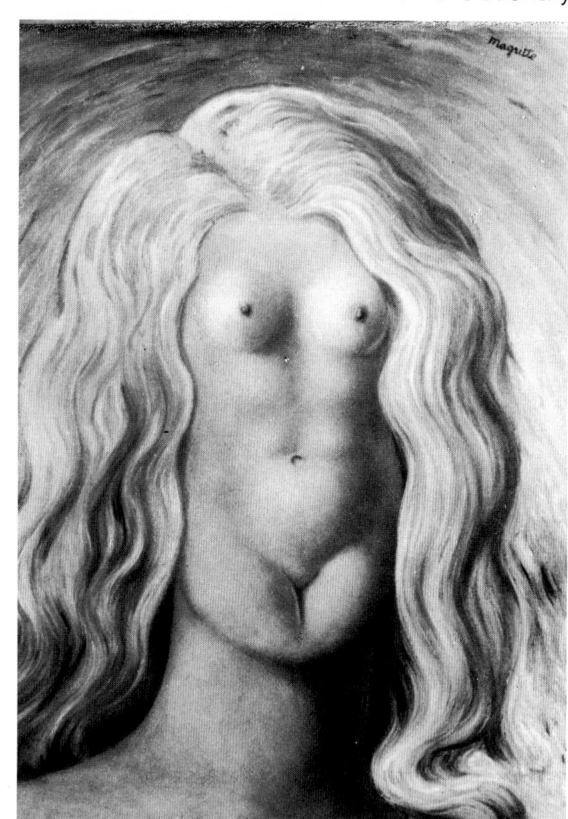

62. *Le viol (The Rape).* 1945. Oil on canvas, 25⅝ x 19⅝" (65 x 50 cm). Collection Mme. René Magritte, Brussels, Belgium

Le viol (The Rape). This painting was part of a 1947 show organized by Communist intellectuals and sympathizers at *Le Drapeau Rouge* offices, rue des Casernes, Brussels, and was lost subsequent to the exhibition. It was found by Pierre Alechinsky, who returned it to Madame Magritte after Magritte's death.

NOTE FOR THE COMMUNIST PARTY

The workers have been exposed to paintings under poor conditions as a result of initial confusion in regard to artistic activity and political action. While the political struggle must, under present circumstances, concentrate on the demand for our rights to, for example, adequate nourishment and minimum comforts, the battle being waged by revolutionary artists can now be understood as a response to a maximum need: the conquest of the mind's wealth, a conquest that must never be abandoned.

In their encounter with artists, the workers were only permitted to contemplate those pictures strictly limited to the plastic expression of political ideas or sentiments; and the architects of the Party's cultural policy are making the error of leading the workers to believe that this is the only kind of painting for which they are suited.

Although the pictorial translation of political ideas is useful for illustrating Party posters, it does not automatically follow that the artist's only valid role is to paint pictures that in more or less lyric terms express the social struggle, and that the workers must forgo the pleasure of looking at pictures that can enrich their minds without teaching them class consciousness.

Class consciousness is as necessary as bread; but that does not mean that workers must be condemned to bread and water and that wanting chicken and champagne would be harmful. If they are Communists, it is precisely because they hope to attain a better life, worthy of man.

For the Communist painter, the justification of artistic activity is to create pictures that can represent mental luxury, a luxury for Communist society quite different from the useless, ostentatious, tasteless luxury of the existing exploiting classes.

To want systematically to exclude this luxury from the socialist world is to condone a sordid and culpable establishment of mediocrity, at least insofar as the mind is concerned.

A better life cannot be conceived without some real luxury. It cannot be achieved without political struggle and the difficult struggle waged by revolutionary artists, those who do not limit their efforts solely to the expression of political ideas or to the representation of familiar scenes in the life of the working class for the purpose of edification.

—*René Magritte,* Note Pour Le Parti Communiste, *April 24, 1950*

Revolt is a response of active man that need not be legitimized by more or less comprehensible motives.

Revolt against the world of today signifies the refusal to participate willingly in activities dominated by hoodlums and imbeciles. It likewise signifies the will to act against this world and to seek ways of changing it.

—*René Magritte, "La Révolte en Question,"* Le Soleil Noir *(Paris), no. 1, February-March 1952, p. 68*

PEACEFUL EVENING*

As a patriarch and small landowner
I don't like strangers
who shamelessly and without permission trample
the arable soil which I work with my hands.
One fine evening after the family meal,
I was told that an Englishman, his wife, and
daughter
were camping on my property
without having advised or consulted me.
At first it was the vision of a slip-clad woman,
allowing a glimpse of soft curly hair,
that arose in my imagination,
and then the idea of spying on her from behind a
bush.

You already know what happened next:
my rough laborer's hand
took my carbine, fired, and hit her
with great accuracy on her exposed parts.
I left my empty shells lying in the dew;
my educated son says he collected them
and changed the position of the bodies
while I slept peacefully in my bed.
Thanks to my cleverness and experience,
I had a good laugh on the police
until the moment during the reenactment [of the
crime],
when I was no longer able to maintain my
cover-up.

—*René Magritte, 1952*

*Written at the time of the Dominici affair, to be sung to the tune of "Le Chant du Départ"

Progressive atheists and Fascist Catholics are not very interesting. While on the way to Antwerp yesterday, I passed near the camp at Breendonc [sic] (the Belgian Buchenwald), and the memories this camp brought back are far from being able to provide any rationale for the universe. As for the progressive atheists you mention, who dream of horsewhipping the whole world, they are obviously incapable of making anything but trouble. We don't have to do anything about such "engagés" so long as they leave us more or less in peace. However, when "culture" is at stake, their titles—Catholics, Fascists, atheists, progressives, etc.—are reason enough for one to be disgusted at the prospect of collaborating with them. For them, it's not enough to take a "quick turn round the floor with a modicum of elegance." They wouldn't hesitate to stop you if it were necessary.

—*Letter from René Magritte to G. Puel, May 22, 1955*

One idea that's occurred to me—I don't know what it's "worth." What we call a "work of art" is usually "defended" with the same tenacity with which one would defend—to cite the same example—the subway if it came under attack. Painters are born, live, and die "for painting" (preferably abstract) as they would "for France." The idea occurred to me that what is to be defended cannot be defined as easily as can old or fashionable "pictorial values." It seems to me that it is the vision of the world that must be defended, *because it cannot be separated from the viewer.*

—*Letter from René Magritte to Mirabelle Dors and Maurice Rapin, January 23, 1956*

L'impromptu de Versailles (Versailles Impromptu): Homage to Violette Nozières, who poisoned her incestuous father

—*René Magritte, in* Violette Nozières, *Brussels: Éditions Nicolas Flamel, 1933*

63. *L'impromptu de Versailles (Versailles Impromptu).* Illustration for *Violette Nozières,* Brussels: Édition Nicolas Flamel, 1933

Psychoanalysis

64. Letter from René Magritte (written in London) to Louis Scutenaire and Irène Hamoir, March 12, 1937

12th March, 1937.

Dear Friends,

I am, at the moment, seated before my coffee, and Mrs. Paige is in front of me, and in front of Mrs. Paige is a type-writer. Before commencing the letter, we have verified the date on the calendar. At last, speaking of serious things, yesterday the young Matta brought me to the home of two psychoanalysts but let us not speak too quickly, it is necessary to put things clearly.

First, Matta is a young man who comes from South America. I think he has a little Indian blood in his veins. He does paintings which are a thousand times better than those of Miro. He has many ideas. He received a religious education and he lives in a flat in a white house. That for Matta!

Second, Dr. Matté is also a young South American. At first he was a surgeon, but then he became interested in the work of our friend, Freud. He also lives in a flat, only it is in a street where all the doctors live. At the moment he treats young boys of five years and his treatment consists in painting with these young boys. It seems that the brushes represent the sexes (masculine) for the boys. This young doctor is very much interested evidently (that goes without saying) by sur-realism.

Third, Dr. Vits is a man of about 50 years of age, andhe has no hair. He finds Brussels very erotic but London not the least so (according to Mrs. Paige New York is in this respect like London). He left Germany for the reason that Hitler is making thought impossible in Germany. Obviously, he is a doctor who treats fatal diseases. On the whole, he is sympathetic.

Now you know with whom I passed yesterday evening. They questioned me on the subject of my painting and they now understand the interpretations of my paintings. Thus, they think my picture, "The Red Model" is a case of castration. You will see from this how it is all becoming very simple. Also, after several interpretations of thiskind, I made them a real psychoanalytical drawing (you know what I mean):'canon bibital' etc. Of course, they analyzed these pictures with the same coldness. Just between ourselves, its terrifying to see what one is exposed to in making an innocent picture.

I received the account of your journey . It seemed to me a little complicated, but as I am a good boy, I do not mind.

I want you to do whatever you can to make my absence less distressing to my wife, I thank you in advance and I send you my regards 'bibitals'.

Magritte

65. *Le modèle rouge (The Red Model).* c. 1935. Pencil drawing, 12⅜ x 9" (31.5 x 23 cm). Collection Melvin Jacobs, New York, New York

66. *Le modèle rouge (The Red Model).* 1935. Oil on canvas, 22 x 18" (55.9 x 45.8 cm). Musée National d'Art Moderne, Centre National d'Art et Culture Georges Pompidou, Paris, France

The problem of shoes demonstrates how the most frightening things can, through inattention, become completely innocuous. Thanks to *Le modèle rouge (The Red Model),* we realize that the union of a human foot and a shoe is actually a monstrous custom.

——*René Magritte,* La Ligne de Vie, *lecture, November 20, 1938*

67. *Les belles relations (The Beautiful Relations).* 1967. Oil on canvas, 15¾ x 12⅝"
(40 x 32 cm). Collection M. and Mme. Pierre Scheidweiler, Brussels, Belgium

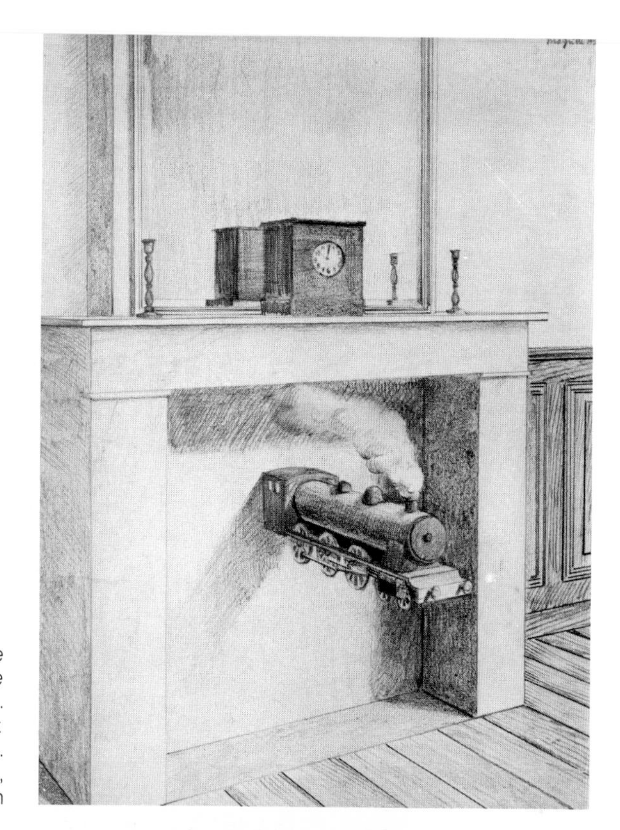

68. Study for *La durée poignardée (Time Transfixed).* 1935. Pencil drawing, 11¾ x 9⅞" (30 x 25 cm). Private collection, Brussels, Belgium

69. *La durée poignardée (Time Transfixed).* 1939. Oil on canvas, 57½ x 38¾" (146 x 98.5 cm). The Art Institute of Chicago, Chicago, Illinois

I apologize for the delay in answering your letter of April 25th, although it wasn't my fault. I had to wait for a translation of what you wrote in English.

The question you ask concerning the conception of the painting *La durée poignardée (Time Transfixed* doesn't seem to be a very accurate translation) can be given an exact answer insofar as *what I was thinking of.* As for trying to explain *why* I thought of painting the image of a locomotive and *why* I was convinced this painting should be executed, I cannot know nor do I wish to know. Even the most ingenious psychological explanations would have validity only with regard to "possible" interest in an understanding of an intellectual activity that posits relationships between what is thought and what has nothing to do with thought. Thus, I decided to paint the image of a locomotive. Starting from that possibility, the problem presented itself as follows: how to paint this image so that it would evoke mystery—that is the mystery to which we are forbidden to give a meaning, lest we utter naïve or scientific absurdities; mystery *that has no meaning* but that must not be confused with the "non-sense" that mad men who are trying hard to be funny find so gratifying.

The image of a locomotive is *immediately* familiar; its mystery is not perceived.

In order for its mystery to be evoked, another *immediately* familiar image without mystery—the image of a dining room fireplace—was joined with the image of the locomotive (thus I did not join a familiar image with a so-called mysterious image such as a Martian, an angel, a dragon, or some other creature erroneously thought of as "mysterious." In fact, there are neither *mysterious* nor unmysterious creatures. The power of thought is demonstrated by unveiling or evoking the mystery in creatures that seem familiar to us [out of error or habit]).

I thought of joining the locomotive image with the image of a dining room fireplace in a moment of "presence of mind." By that I mean the moment of lucidity *that no method can bring forth.* Only the power of thought manifests itself at this time. We can be proud of this power, feel proud or excited that it exists. Nonetheless, we do not count for anything, but are limited to witnessing the manifestation of thought. When I say "I thought of joining, etc., . . ." exactitude demands that I say "presence of mind exerted itself and showed me how the image of a locomotive should be shown so that this presence of mind would be apparent." Archimedes' "Eureka!" is an example of the mind's unpredictable presence.

The word *idea* is not the most *precise* designation for what I thought when I united a locomotive and a fireplace. *I didn't have an idea;* I only thought of an *image.*

The power of thought or "presence of mind" manifests itself in different ways:

—For the painter, thought becomes manifest in *images* (for the exacting painter, and not the painter who has "ideas" or who "expresses" his "sublime" emotions).

—For Bergson, thought manifests itself in *ideas.*

—For Proust, it manifests itself in *words.*

I am very exacting, and in conceiving a painting I avoid "ideas" or "expressing emotions." Only an image can satisfy these demands.

La durée poignardée is only an image. Because of that it testifies to the power of thought—to a certain extent. While looking at this painting, you think of Bergson and Proust. That does me honor and demonstrates that an image *limited strictly to its character as an image* proves the power of thought just as much as Bergson's *ideas* or Proust's *words. After* the image has been painted, we can think of the relation it may bear to ideas or words. This is not improper, since images, ideas, and words are *different* interpretations of the *same* thing: thought.

However, in order to state what is *truly necessary* about an image, one must refer exclusively to that image.

This is what I have tried to write to you—clumsily, and in French, which I fear will be much less clear than if I had been able to put it into English for you.

In any case, I hope you will not doubt my goodwill to answer you as well as possible.

Very cordially,
René Magritte

P.S.—The title *La durée poignardée* is itself an image (in words) joined to a painted image.

The word *durée* was chosen for its poetic truth—a truth gained from the union of this word with the painted image—and not for a generalized philosophical sense or a Bergsonian sense in particular.

NOTE:

I think the following points should be clear:

1. Psychological theories "explain" nothing. They are possible *thanks to thought*. They give expression to thought—*but they do not make thought possible*. Thought exists without psychology. It is thought that illuminates what it sees: ideas, images, emotions, sensations, and psychology!—not vice versa.

2. "Presence of mind" (or the power of manifest thought) can be found in Bergson, in Proust, in other men.

Hegel, for one, experienced this presence of mind. But, in his old age, when he found the sight of the starry sky banal, *which is true* (along with the sight of a locomotive), he overlooked as a philosopher the fact that the starry sky imitated in an image would no longer be banal if this image were to evoke mystery, thanks to the lucidity of a painter who could paint the banal image of the starry sky in such a way that it appeared in all its evocative force.

Hegel saw only a "given" image, without the intervention of thought. I believe Hegel only gave validity to the manifestation of thought *through ideas*. He might perhaps have allowed himself to be distracted while looking at images; it might have been a kind of vacation for him. Would my picture entitled *Les vacances de Hegel (Hegel's Holiday)* have amused Hegel? Would another, older picture, *Le travail caché (The Hidden Work)*, perhaps have "taught" him that images are as valid as ideas? This painting actually shows the trite spectacle of a starry sky . . . (The stars spell out the word *DESIRE.)*

Philosophers attempt to concern themselves with art. But so far as I know, none of them tell us about what is *inside* art.

When will the philosopher construct a system that powerfully conveys mystery? (Although philosophers make brilliant *attempts* at theories about mystery.)

—Letter from René Magritte to Hornik, May 8, 1959, in André Bosmans archive

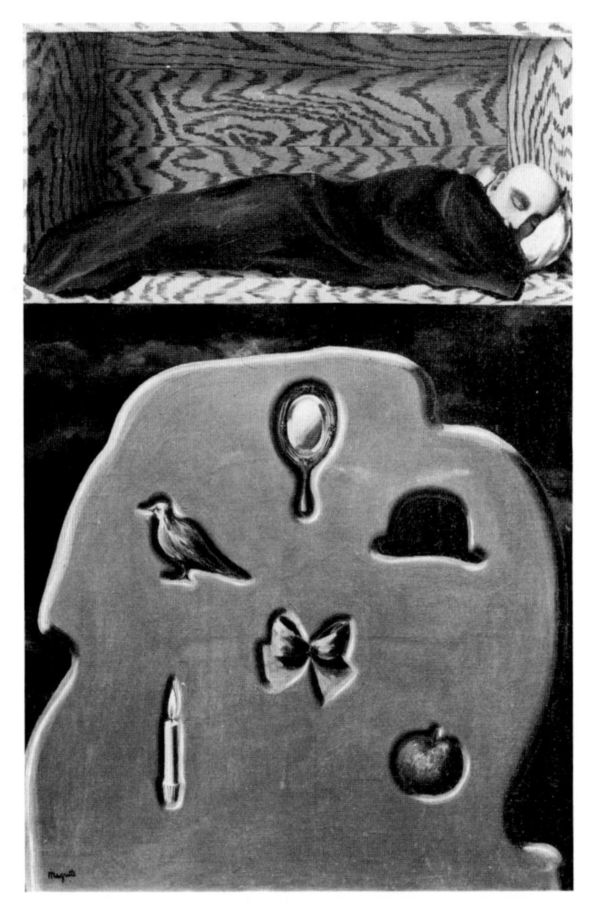

70. *Le dormeur téméraire (The Reckless Sleeper).* 1927. Oil on canvas, 43¼ x 33½" (110 x 85 cm). The Tate Gallery, London, England

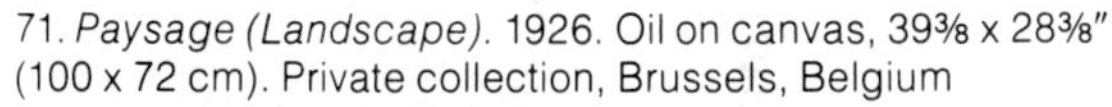

71. *Paysage (Landscape).* 1926. Oil on canvas, 39⅜ x 28⅜" (100 x 72 cm). Private collection, Brussels, Belgium

[Here's] something pretty amusing: On a television program, a doctor was telling how the art of lunatics differed from that of the Surrealists. He commented on a patient's drawing and later regretted his words. He was interpreting it (according to the sacrosanct habit of seeing everything as a symbol), and in his scientific ardor he forgot scientific discretion to such an extent that he said, "And this is a symbol of the female sex organ, *with all its disgusting attributes.*" He realized after it was too late that he had expressed his own opinion rather than that of the author of the drawing, and that maybe he would be mistaken for a homosexual. Even if one could have corrected the tape, the imprudent psychiatrist must have been made keenly aware of the dangers inherent in interpretation.
—*Letter from René Magritte to Harry Torczyner, August 18, 1961*

Psychoanalysis only allows interpretation of that which lends itself to interpretation. Fantastic Art and Symbolic Art present it with numerous occasions for intervention. With respect to these Arts, there is often the question of more or less apparent delirium.

Art, as I conceive it, is resistant to psychoanalysis. It evokes the mystery without which the world would not exist, that is, the mystery one should not mistake for some sort of a problem, however difficult.

I see to it that I paint only images that evoke the world's mystery. To make this possible, I have to be wide-awake, which means I have to cease to identify myself completely with ideas, sentiments, and sensations. (Dreams and madness, on the contrary, are propitious to absolute identification.)

Nobody in his right mind believes that psycho analysis could elucidate the mystery of the uni verse. The very nature of the mystery annihilates curiosity. Nor has psychoanalysis anything to say about works of art that evoke the mystery of the universe. Perhaps psychoanalysis is the best sub ject to be treated by psychoanalysis.
—*Statement by René Magritte (Brussels), May 21, 1962, in* The Vision of René Magritte, *exhibition catalogue, Walker Art Center, Minneapolis, Minnesota, September 16–October 14, 1962.*

. . . the Surrealists' taste for dream narratives is o no interest to me. Maybe the judgment that "my paintings are dreams" contributes to my indiffer ence. I never put any stock in this judgment. don't mean to say that dreams aren't interesting to doctors; that is their business (like penicillin).
—*Letter from René Magritte to André Bosmans, May 8, 1962*

The title is *Gradiva* (even if I mistakenly pu *Gravida,* as you spell it). *Gradiva* is a novel by . . . forget the name, with an analysis by Freud. I'c also forgotten I had given the drawing a title Maybe that would be significant to a Freudiar specialist.*
—*Letter from René Magritte to Harry Torczyner, October 29, 1965*

*Magritte is referring to *Gravida* (a pregnant woman), as distinguished from *Gradiva* the title of a story by Wilhelm Jensen, which was the subject of Freud's first psychoanalytic study of a literary work, *Illusions and Dreams in Jensen's "Gradiva."*

72. *Personnage méditant sur la folie (Person Meditating on Madness).* 1928. Oil on canvas, 21¼ x 28¾" (54 x 73 cm). Collection M. and Mme. Louis Scutenaire, Brussels, Belgium

73. *La présence d'esprit (Presence of Mind).* 1960. Oil on canvas, 45⅝ x 35" (116 x 89 cm). Collection Pirlet, Cologne, Germany

74. Study for *La présence d'esprit (Presence of Mind).* 1960. Drawing, 5⅞ x 4½" (15 x 11.5 cm). Private collection, New York, New York

Sciences

Poets were able to enjoy Jules Verne's *Journey to the Moon,* and they will pay no attention to such a voyage as is presently being planned by serious people, generals, journalists, financiers, etc. . . .
—Letter from René Magritte to André Bosmans, January 10, 1958

I am, of course, unable to appreciate science, not being a scientist. That doesn't imply contempt for it, merely lack of interest. It seems to me that skepticism consists not only in withholding judgments, but above all in avoiding error and consequently in thinking of truth as something inaccessible (which is already an infidelity to skepticism, since truth is what is being judged).

It happens that scientific conquests and the more or less precise goals of scientific endeavor don't interest me at all. As for the value of science and its capabilities, I am maintaining a spontaneous "scientific" discretion, which may be uninformed, but which is nevertheless final.

I believe everything is always possible, but there is only mediocrity in anything one might desire of the possible. For example, it's possible that one day we may see a squared circle or live centaurs. In what way can hope for a particular possibility force us to esteem some science that may enable us to realize those possibilities?
—Letter from René Magritte to Maurice Rapin, May 7, 1958

The "illustration" of the themes of science, scientific research, mankind can to my mind be nothing more than a joke (albeit an innocent one). I painted an image entitled *La présence d'esprit (Presence of Mind),* which exactly *fit* (without "illustrating") the ideas and emotions relevant to the varied possibilities of the theme. Thus, the painting *La présence d'esprit* shows the sky, earth, a bird, a man, and a fish—in other words, all aspects of the world with which science is concerned (it researches what they are, at least for the science-minded). This image, *La présence d'esprit,* does not prejudge what they represent for the scientifically inclined, nor for those subject to any discipline whatsoever: commercial, political, military, or anything else. It shows aspects of the world with which all kinds of people are concerned, including scientists, in their own way. If we accept this [proposition], I believe we can hold that these aspects of the world interest mankind in general. . . .

The "idea" of mankind . . . can in turn be "presented" in the painting due to the fact that a man depicted in it "symbolizes" the "unity of man." Furthermore, the picture is called *La présence d'esprit*—that which is absolutely indispensable to any program that is to encompass "science, scientific research, and mankind."
—Letter from René Magritte to Harry Torczyner, July 1960

75. *Un peu de l'âme des bandits (A Little of the Bandits' Soul).*
1960. Oil on canvas, 25½ x 19¾" (65 x 50 cm). Location unknown

BY MYSTERY POSSESSED

"The visible presented by the world is rich enough to constitute a language evocative of mystery," Magritte told us. The division of the painting; the painting within the painting; the dismemberment of the image; the use of words; the juxtaposition of unrelated objects set in the sky, on the ocean, or on earth—all these inventions of his mind had no purpose other than to mark out and to make remarked this empire, possessed by mystery. It is this ultimate confrontation with mystery that Magritte's work forces upon us, whence its power and its spell.

He was concerned with the problems of similarity and of resemblance; finding for them a simple and perfect solution gave him intellectual pleasure. "Peas share a relationship of similarity. . .only thought has resemblance," he wrote to Michel Foucault. In fact, analogy and *rapprochement* are mental operations. In his variations on one of his best-known themes, *L'empire des lumières (The Empire of Lights),* Magritte gives us a precious example of these inspired games. From the time he discovered his path and adopted his particular gait, he never again deviated from his pictorial style. One can say that his other modes of expression—Cubist, Impressionist, and Fauvist (which lasted only for a moment, the moment of the exhibition "The Black Period")—are merely interludes in his life as a deliberate magician.

Magritte never hesitated to represent the human figure as an object, but he was not attracted by the self-portrait or portrait. He did not like using a mirror to reflect either his person or his personality. Nevertheless, out of friendship he consented to paint a few portraits of friends, thereby giving them the satisfaction of observing themselves in a false mirror.

Mystery—without which no world, no thought, would be possible—corresponds to no doctrine, and does not deal with possibilities. Thus, a question such as "How is mystery possible?" is meaningless because mystery can be evoked only if we know that any possible question is relative only to what is possible.

Some mediocre or absurd things do not really cast doubt on the concept of mystery; nothing beautiful or grandiose can affect it. Judgment as to what is, was, or will be possible does not enter into the concept of mystery. Whatever its manifest nature may be, every object is mysterious: the apparent and the hidden, knowledge and ignorance, life and death, day and night. The attention we give to the mystery in everything is deemed sterile only if we overlook the higher sensibility that accompanies that attention, and if we grant a supreme value to what is possible. This higher sensibility is not possible without freedom from what we call "the laws of the possible."

Freedom of thought alert to mystery is always possible if not actually present, whatever the nature of the possible: atrocious or attractive, mean or marvelous. It has power to evoke mystery with effective force.

—*René Magritte, "La Voix du Mystère,"* Rhétorique, *no. 4, January 1962, p. 1*

Resemblance—which can be made visible through painting—only deals with figures as they appear in the world: people, curtains, weapons, stars, solids, inscriptions, etc. . . . spontaneously united in the order wherein the familiar and the strange are restored to mystery.

What one must paint is the image of resemblance—if thought is to become visible in the world.

—*René Magritte, catalogue of the Magritte exhibition, Paris, Galerie Rive Droite, 1960*

MAGIC CATALOGUE

Naming Things

76. Notes for an illustrated lecture given by René Magritte at Marlborough Fine Art (London) Ltd., February 1937; published in facsimile in the catalogue of the exhibition *Magritte* held at Marlborough Fine Art (London), October–November 1973, pp. 21–23. *See* Appendix *for translation*

Mesdames et Messieurs,

La démonstration que nous allons faire ensemble tendra à montrer quelques caractères propres aux mots, aux images et aux objets réels.

(1) Un mot peut remplacer une image:

Chapeau HAT.

(2) Une image peut remplacer un mot. Je vais le démontrer en me servant d'un texte d'André Breton où je remplace un mot par une image:

Si seulement IF ONLY THE SUN WOULD SHINE TONIGHT.

[de Jean Scutenaire] On ne peut pas ONE CANNOT GIVE BIRTH TO A FOAL WITHOUT BEING ONE ONESELF.

de Paul Eluard:
Dans les plus sombres yeux se ferment les plus clairs.
THE DARKEST EYES ENCLOSE THE LIGHTEST.

[de Paul Colinet] Il y a THERE IS A SPHERE PLACED ON YOUR SHOULDERS.

de David Gascoigne

[de Mesens] Masque de veuve WIDOW'S MASK FOR THE WALTZ.

de Humfrey Jennings

THE FLYING ~~la~~ the OF EDUCATION

- 2 -

(3) Un objet réel peut remplacer un mot:

Le pain du crime. THE BREAD OF CRIME.

(4) Une forme quelconque peut remplacer ~~l'image d'un objet:~~ un mot

Les naissent THE ARE BORN IN WINTER.

(5) Un mot peut faire l'office d'un objet:

Ce bouquet THIS BOUQUET IS TRANSPARENT

(6) On peut désigner une image ou un objet par un autre nom ~~mot~~ que le sien:

L'oiseau THE BIRD

La montagne THE MOUNTAIN

Voici le ciel BEHOLD THE SKY (skaie)
~~Bihôlde ti skaie~~
Bis is de skaje

(7) Il existe une affinité secrète entre certaines images. Elle veut également pour les objets représentés par ces images. Recherchons ensemble ce qui doit être dit. Nous connaissons l'oiseau dans une cage. L'intérêt est éveillé davantage si l'oiseau est remplacé par un poisson, ou un soulier.

Ces images sont curieuses. Malheureusement elles sont arbitraires et accidentelles.

- 3 -

Il est possible pourtant d'obtenir une image nouvelle qui résistera mieux à l'examen du spectateur. Un grand oeuf dans la cage parait être la solution requise.

Occupons nous maintenant de la porte. La porte peut s'ouvrir sur un paysage vu à l'envers.

Le paysage peut être représenté sur la porte.

Essayons quelque chose de moins arbitraire: à côté de la porte faisons un trou dans le mur qui est un autre porte aussi.

Cette rencontre sera perfectionnée si nous réduisons ces deux objets à un seul. Le trou se place donc tout naturellement dans la porte et par ce trou l'on voit l'obscurité.

Cette image pourrait de nouveau s'enrichir si l'on éclaire la chose invisible cachée par l'obscurité ~~que l'obscurité nous cache~~. Notre regard veut toujours aller plus loin, veut voir enfin l'objet, la raison de notre existence.

Texte de la Démonstration faite par René Magritte, à Londres, à la London Gallery, le février 1937.

Un objet ne tient pas tellement à son nom qu'on ne puisse lui en trouver un autre qui lui convienne mieux :

Il y a des objets qui se passent de nom :

Un mot ne sert parfois qu'à se désigner soi-même :

Un objet rencontre son image, un objet rencontre son nom. Il arrive que l'image et le nom de cet objet se rencontrent :

Parfois le nom d'un objet tient lieu d'une image :

Un mot peut prendre la place d'un objet dans la réalité :

Une image peut prendre la place d'un mot dans une proposition :

Un objet fait supposer qu'il y en a d'autres derrière lui :

Tout tend à faire penser qu'il y a peu de relation entre un objet et ce qui le représente :

Les mots qui servent à désigner deux objets différents ne montrent pas ce qui peut séparer ces objets l'un de l'autre :

Dans un tableau, les mots sont de la même substance que les images :

On voit autrement les images et les mots dans un tableau :

Une forme quelconque peut remplacer l'image d'un objet :

Un objet ne fait jamais le même office que son nom ou que son image :

Or, les contours visibles des objets, dans la réalité, se touchent comme s'ils formaient une mosaïque :

Les figures vagues ont une signification aussi nécessaire, aussi parfaite que les précises :

Parfois, les noms écrits dans un tableau désignent des choses précises, et les images des choses vagues :

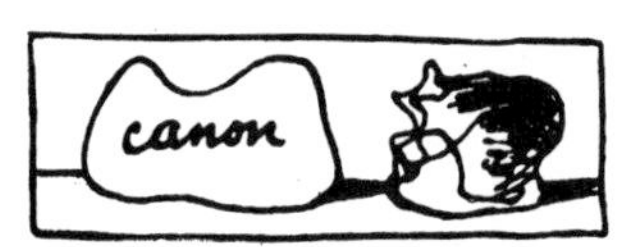

Ou bien le contraire :

René Magritte

77. *Les mots et les images (Words and Images).* Illustration in *La Révolution Surréaliste* (Paris), vol. 5, no. 12 (December 15, 1929), pp. 32–33. *See* Appendix *for translation*

Man/Object

78. *Golconde (Golconda)*. 1953. Oil on canvas, 31⅞ x 39⅜" (81 x 100 cm). Private collection, United States

79. *Le fils de l'homme (The Son of Man)*. 1964. Oil on canvas, 45⅝ x 35" (116 x 89 cm). Collection Harry Torczyner, New York, New York

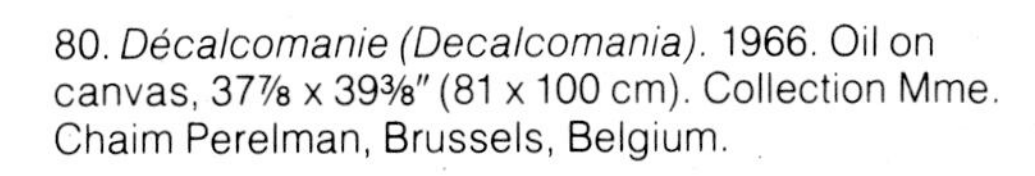

80. *Décalcomanie (Decalcomania)*. 1966. Oil on canvas, 37⅞ x 39⅜" (81 x 100 cm). Collection Mme. Chaim Perelman, Brussels, Belgium.

81. Photograph of René Magritte as *The Healer,* rue Essegham, Brussels, Belgium, 1937

82. *Le thérapeute (The Healer).* 1937. Oil on canvas, 36¼ x 25⅝" (92 x 65 cm). Collection Baron Joseph-Berthold Urvater, Paris, France

83. *Le thérapeute (The Healer).* n.d. Gouache, 18⅞ x 13⅝" (48 x 34.5 cm). Private collection, New York, New York

84. *Le libérateur (The Liberator).* 1947. Oil on canvas, 39 x 31⅛" (99 x 79 cm). Los Angeles County Museum of Art, Los Angeles, California. Gift of William N. Copley

Pipe

"The famous pipe. How people reproached me for it! And yet, could you stuff my pipe? No, it's just a representation, is it not? So if I had written on my picture 'This is a pipe,' I'd have been lying!"
—*René Magritte, remarks reported by Claude Vial, "Ceci n'est pas René Magritte,"* Femmes d'Aujourd'hui, *July 6, 1966, pp. 22–24*

85

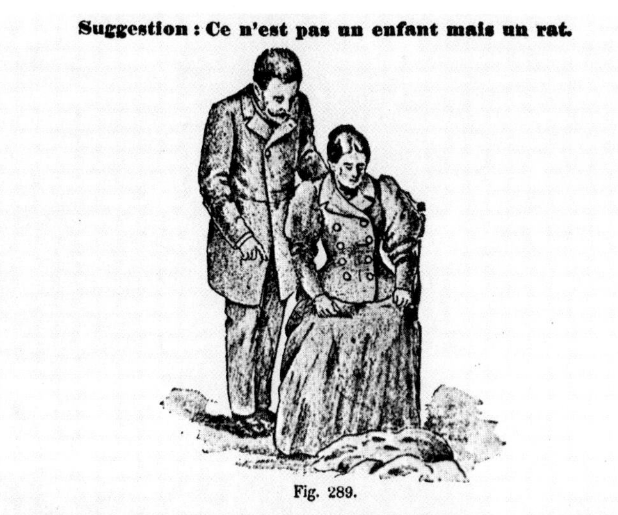

86

85. *Suggestion: Ce n'est pas un enfant mais un rat (Suggestion: This is Not a Child, But a Rat).* Illustration in *La Nouvelle Médication Naturelle* by F. E. Bilz (edition translated from German), 1899, fig. 289

86. *La lampe philosophique (The Philosopher's Lamp).* 1935. Oil on canvas, 23⅝ x 19⅝" (60 x 50 cm). Private collection, Brussels, Belgium

87. *Ceci n'est pas une pipe (This is Not a Pipe).* 1928–1929. Oil on canvas, 23¼ x 31½" (59 x 80 cm). Collection William N. Copley, New York, New York

87

Rose

According to the method that I think is exclusively my own, I have been looking for about two months for the solution to what I call "the problem of the rose." At the end of my search, I realize that I have probably known the answer to my question for a long time, but dimly, in the same way as everyone else. This knowledge, which is apparently organic and not conscious, has been there at the beginning of every search I've undertaken. The first sign I instinctively dashed off on paper when I decided to resolve the rose problems is this one:

and that oblique line diverging from the stem of the flower has required long, hard research for me to unravel its meaning. Of the many objects I imagined, I recall these:
the line is the pole of a green flag

the line is a tower of a feudal castle

or an arrow:

finally, I hit on it: it was a dagger, and the rose problem was pictorially solved as follows:

Finally, after the search is concluded, it's easy to "explain" that the rose is perfumed air, but it is also cruelty, and reminds me of your "patricidal rose." I also recall this passage of forbidden images by Nougé: "We perceive the rose's faint perfume by means of a heartrending memory."

And a curious fact—in 1942 or 1943 I made a picture with the cover of the first volume of *Fantômas,* but replacing the murderer's bloody knife with a rose.

—*Letter from René Magritte to Paul Colinet, November 27, 1957*

88. *La boîte de Pandore (Pandora's Box).* 1951. Oil on canvas, 18¼ x 21⅝" (46.5 x 55 cm). Yale University Art Gallery, New Haven, Connecticut

The presence of the rose next to the stroller signifies that wherever man's destiny leads him he is always protected by an element of beauty. The painter hopes that this man is heading for the most sublime place in his life. The rose's vividness corresponds to its important role (element of beauty). The approach of nightfall suits withdrawal, and the bridge makes us think something will be overcome.

—*Letter from René Magritte to Mr. and Mrs. Barnet Hodes, undated, 1957*

89. *La voix des vents (The Voice of the Winds).* 1928.
Oil on canvas, 25⅝ x 19⅝" (65 x 50 cm). Private collection, United States

I'd prefer to believe that the iron bells hanging from our fine horses' necks grew there like poisonous plants on the edge of precipices.
—*René Magritte, "La Ligne de Vie,"* Combat, *vol. 3, no. 105, December 10, 1938*

90. *Les fleurs de l'abîme I (Flowers of the Abyss I).* 1928. Oil on canvas, 21⅝ x 28¾" (55 x 73 cm). Private collection, New York, New York

91. *Grelots roses, ciels en lambeaux (Pink Bells, Tattered Skies).* 1930. Oil on canvas, 28¾ x 39⅜" (72 x100 cm). Collection Baron Joseph-Berthold Urvater, Paris, France

le 19 Août 1960

Bien Cher ami,

Je reçois votre lettre du 16 août et les documents "spéciaux". Je vous en remercie et vais me mettre en rapport avec la direction du Mayfair, dont le nom me semble avoir quelque chose de Hollandais.

J'apprends avec plaisir quel accueil "Le Tombeau des lutteurs" a reçu chez vous. La date 1944 confirme qu'à cette époque, la peinture que je concevais — en essayant de l'accorder à l'esprit de l'impressionnisme — n'était pas toujours (en 1954) accordée à cet esprit. "Ma manière habituelle" était, loin, au contraire, toujours là pour témoigner que j'y reviendrais définitivement — Des tableaux de 1944 ont en effet, tels que "Le Tombeau des lutteurs", été peints dans "ma manière habituelle", redevenue depuis exclusivement la seule qui me semble vraiment nécessaire pour peindre sans fantaisie ni originalité des idées suffisamment "sublimes" pour qu'elles ~~puissent~~ doivent se passer d'autre chose que d'une description précise. Je crois fermement qu'une belle idée est desservie par une expression "intéressante": l'intérêt y étant pour l'idée. Celles qui ont besoin ou "passes", d'éloquence par exemple, sont incapables à valoir par elles-mêmes — Ceci fait partie de mes convictions qui sont la plupart du temps fort mises à l'épreuve, par les interprètes de tout poil qui veulent y mettre "du leur" en récitant des poèmes, en peignant des tableaux, etc —

J'attendrai, à présent, que vous soyez délivré des chaînes qui vous attachent à votre bureau et que vous puissiez envisager un petit tour en Belgique —

Bien à vous et à votre famille à qui ma sympathie est acquise spontanément.

René Magritte

Room

Late-nineteenth-century authors are not devoid of charm: Lorrain's *Mr. de Baugrelon,* for example, is highly to be recommended. Once I called a picture *Le tombeau des lutteurs (The Tomb of the Wrestlers)* in memory of a book by Cladel* I read in my youth and that I've completely forgotten. I felt the title fit the idea of a huge red rose filling the space of a room.

——*Letter from René Magritte to André Bosmans, July 23, 1960*

92. Letter from René Magritte to Harry Torczyner, August 19, 1960. *See* Appendix *for translation*

94

93. *Le tombeau des lutteurs (The Tomb of the Wrestlers)*. 1960. Oil on canvas, 35 x 46⅛" (89 x 117 cm). Collection Harry Torczyner, New York, New York

94. *Le tombeau des lutteurs (The Tomb of the Wrestlers)*. n.d. Drawing, 3⅞ x 5½" (10 x 14 cm). Private collection, New York, New York

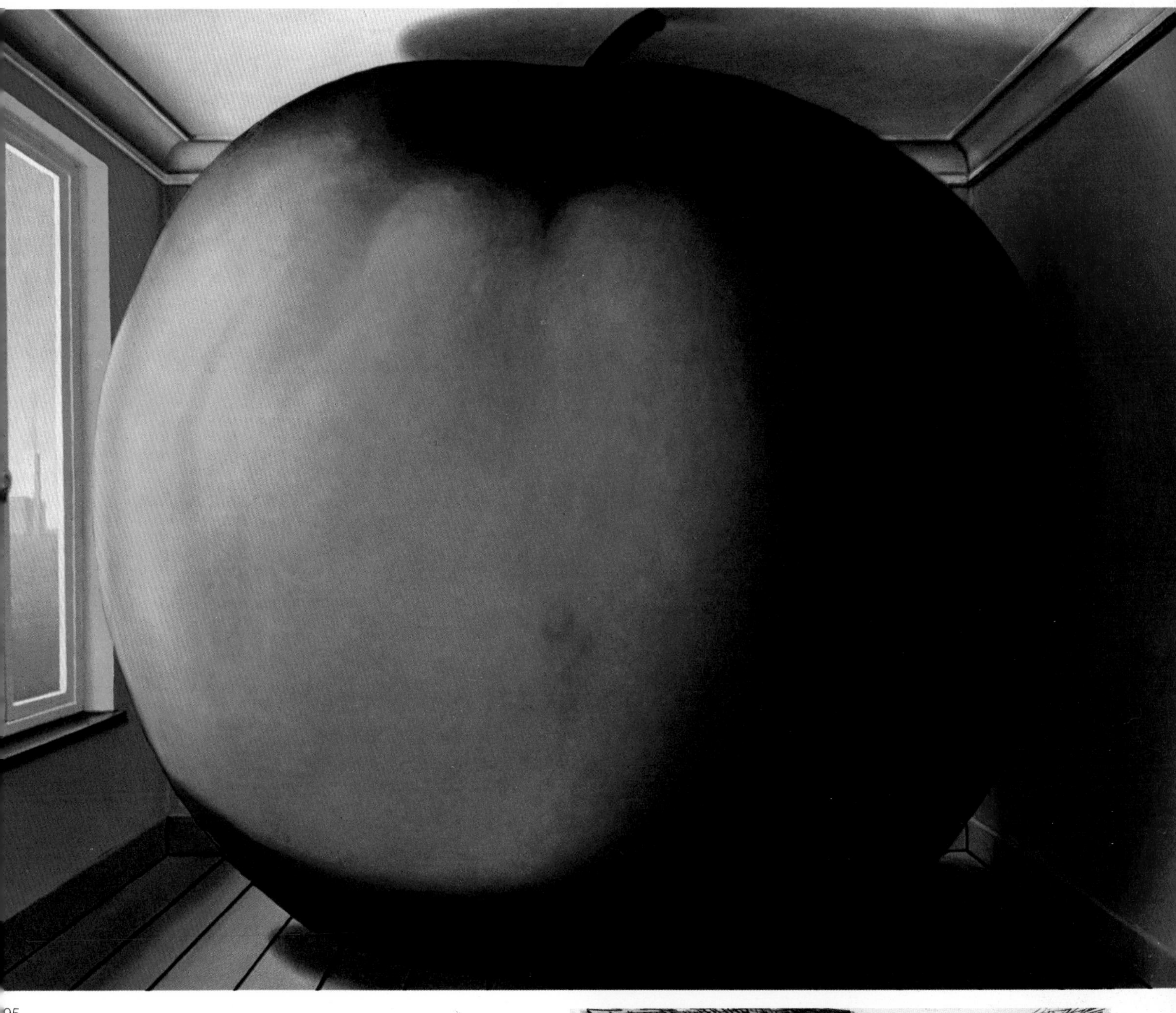

95

95. *La chambre d'écoute I (The Listening Room I).* 1953. Oil on canvas, 31½ x 39⅜" (80 x 100 cm). Collection William N. Copley, New York, New York

96. *La chambre d'écoute (The Listening Room).* n.d. Drawing. Private collection, United States

96

97. *L'anniversaire (The Anniversary)*. 1959. Oil on canvas, 35¼ x 45⅞" (89.5 x 116.5 cm). Art Gallery of Ontario, Toronto, Canada

Chair

My current "problem" consists in wondering how to show a chair (as subject) in a painting, and in speaking to you specifically about chairs and mimosas. My question must be answered by discovering the thing, the object destined to be joined with a chair. (For the cage, it's an egg; for an umbrella, a glass of water; for a door, an opening one can pass through, etc.)

—*Letter from René Magritte to André Bosmans, July 23, 1958*

I'm happy with my chair, and with the title, which I feel fits it; it's called *Une simple histoire d'amour (A Simple Love Story)* (just to make it worse in the eyes of the comfortably "installed").

—*Letter from René Magritte to Harry Torczyner, September 20, 1958*

My chair with the tail appears in the film.* Some people comfortably "installed" (in chairs) have understood *Une simple histoire d'amour* in various ways, but they have all burst out laughing (astonishing to think that a chair could get such a rise out of people).

—*Letter from René Magritte to Harry Torczyner, September 1958*

*A motion picture made by Dr. Eugene Lepesckin, Burlington, Vermont.

98. *Une simple histoire d'amour (A Simple Love Story)*. 1958. Oil on canvas, 15¾ x 11¾" (40 x 30 cm). Galleria La Medusa, Rome, Italy

99. *Une simple histoire d'amour (A Simple Love Story)*. n.d. Gouache. Private collection, United States

J'attends de vos nouvelles, comme nouvelles je ne vois rien de mieux que de vous faire connaître la solution trouvée à ce problème de peindre un tableau avec une chaise comme sujet. J'ai cherché longtemps avant de savoir que la chaise devait avoir une queue (qui est plus "parlante" que les timides pattes d'animaux qui servent parfois de pieds aux chaises) Je suis très satisfait de cette solution. Qu'en pensez-vous?

100. Letter from René Magritte to Harr Torczyner, July 1958. *See* Appendix fo *translation*

101. *L'automate (The Automaton).* 1928. Oil on canvas, 39⅜ x 31½" (100 x 80 cm). Moderna Museet, Stockholm, Sweden

ree

2. *Campagne III* *(ountryside III)*. 1927. on canvas, 28⅞ x ¼" (73.5 x 54 cm). alerie Isy Brachot, ussels, Belgium

3. *Le dernier cri (The* *st Scream)*. 1967. on canvas, 31½ x ⅝" (80 x 65 cm). Col- ction Dr. Jean Robert, ussels, Belgium

4. *Passiflore (Pas-* *nflower)*. 1936. on canvas, 17¾ x ⅝" (45 x 55 cm). Col- ction M. and Mme. uis Scutenaire, ussels, Belgium

102

103

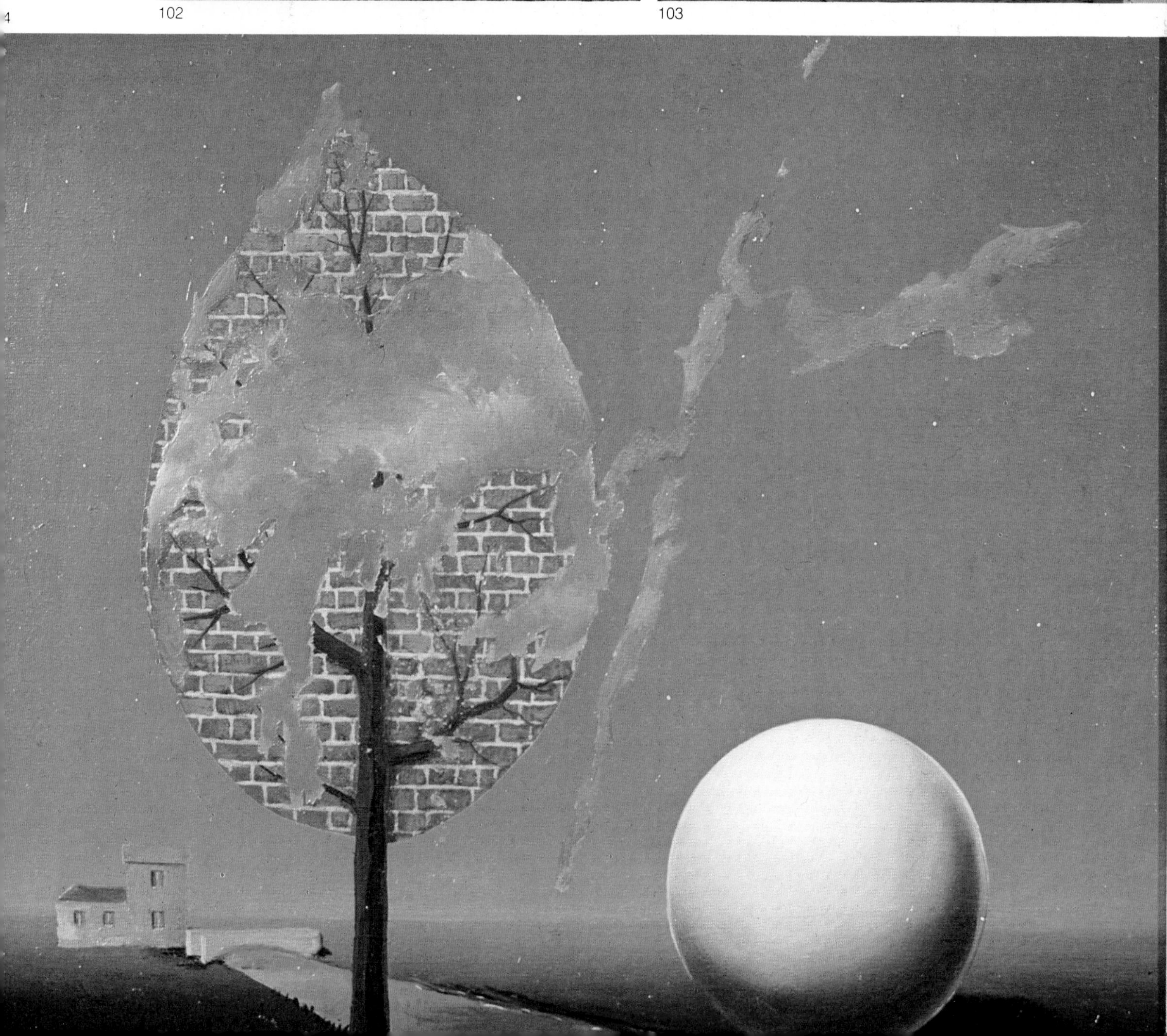

The sphere and the house suggest enigmatic measurements to the tree. The curtain conceals the usele

—René Magritte, 1950, Le Fait Accompli, no. 76, December 1972

105

106

105. *Le plagiat (Plagiarism).* 1960. Gouache, 12⅝ x 9⅞" (32 x 25 cm). Private collection, New York, New York

106. *Le pays des miracles (The Country of Marvels).* c. 1960. Oil on canvas, 21⅝ x 18⅛" (55 x 46 cm). Private collection, Brussels, Belgium

107. *La voix du sang (The Call of Blood).* 1961. Oil on canvas, 35⅜ x 39⅜" (90 x 110 cm). Private collection, Brussels, Belgium

Cloud

108. *Le souvenir déterminant (The Deciding Memory).* 1942. Oil on canvas, 25⅜ x 19⅞" (64.5 x 50.5 cm). Private collection, New York, New York

109. Untitled. 1964–1965. Engraving for *Aube à l'Antipode* by Alain Jouffroy, Édition Soleil Noir, 1966

110. *Les marches de l'été (The Progress of Summer).* 1938. Oil on canvas, 23⅝ x 28¾" (60 x 73 cm). Private collection, Paris, France

108

109

110

111. *La grande famille (The Large Family).* 1947. Oil on canvas, 39⅜ x 31⅞" (100 x 81 cm). Collection Nellens, Knokke-Le Zoute, Belgium

Bottle

112

113

114 115 116

Curtain

The work that I am thinking about painting . . . will be a combination of curtains, of which one will be painted as a sky, another as a fire, another as a forest, and another as a house. They will be placed against a dark background. *Les goûts et les couleurs (Tastes and Colors)* seems a good title for this painting, and in any case it's as good as the title for the painting of the tree and the leaves, which is now called—as you know—*L'arc de triomphe (The Arch of Triumph).*

—Letter from René Magritte to André Bosmans, April 24, 1962

117. *L'ovation (The Ovation).* 1962. Oil on canvas, 34⅝ x 45¼" (88 x 115 cm). Private collection, New York, New York

112. Painted bottle. n.d. Height 11⅜" (29 cm). Collection M. and Mme. Marcel Mabille, Rhode-St.-Genèse, Belgium

113. *L'explication (The Explanation).* 1954. Oil on canvas, 31½ x 23⅝" (80 x 60 cm). Private collection, New York, New York

114. *La dame (The Lady).* 1943. Painted bottle, height 12" (30.5 cm). Collection Hoursi Siva, New York, New York

115. *La dame (The Lady).* n.d. Painted bottle, height 12⅝" (32 cm). Collection Mme. René Magritte, Brussels, Belgium

116. *Ciel (Sky).* n.d. Painted bottle, height 11¾" (30 cm). Collection Mme. René Magritte, Brussels, Belgium

118. *Le beau monde (The Beautiful World).* c. 1960. Oil on canvas, 39⅜ x 31⅞" (100 x 81 cm). Private collection, Brussels, Belgium

119

120

121

119. *Les mémoires d'un saint (The Memoirs of a Saint).* 1960. Oil on canvas, 31½ x 39⅜" (80 x 100 cm). Collection Menil Foundation, Houston, Texas

120. *Les goûts et les couleurs (Tastes and Colors).* 1962. Oil on canvas, 51⅛ x 38⅛" (130 x 97 cm). Private collection, Milan, Italy

121. *La peine perdue (Wasted Effort).* 1962. Oil on canvas, 39 x 31¼" (99 x 79.5 cm). Private collection, New York, New York

Sun/Moon

Je viens de peindre la lune sur un arbre dans les couleurs gris-bleu du soir. Scutenaire a trouvé un très beau titre: "Le seize septembre". Je crois que "c'est bien", donc qu'à partir du "16 Septembre" il n'y a rien à fonder -

122. Letter from René Magritte to Mirabelle Dors and Maurice Rapin, August 6, 1956. *See* Appendix *for translation*

123. *Le seize septembre (September Sixteenth).* 1957. Oil on canvas, 63⅝ x 51⅛" (161.5 x 130 cm). Collection Menil Foundation, Houston, Texas

24. *Le banquet (The Banquet).* 1957. Oil on canvas, 19⅝ x 23⅝" 50 x 60 cm). Collection William Alexander, New York, New York

125

12

126

125. *L'au-delà (The Beyond)*. 1938. Oil on canvas, 28⅜ x 19⅝" (72 x 50 cm). Private collection, Brussels, Belgium

126. *La voie royale (The Royal Road)*. 1944. Oil on canvas, 29½ x 18⅛" (75 x 46 cm). Private collection, Zurich, Switzerland

127. Study for *Le banquet (The Banquet)*. 7⅞ x 10¼" (20 x 26 cm). Collection Harry Torczyner, New York, New York

In answer to the sun, I have come up with: a tomb There's a gravestone on the ground, and the sur lights the sky, earth, and tomb. This is today's answer and will perhaps be inadequate in the future. Actually, by taking the sun as the point o departure for the voyage we are making, by taking the sun as our origin, it isn't yet possible for us to envisage any ending for this voyage beyond death. This is a present certainty, and the picture's title, *L'au-delà (The Beyond)*, recreates an affective content for the term.
—*From a lecture by René Magritte, 1939*

After *La fée ignorante (The Ignorant Fairy)*, I'vе painted a picture in which one sees the moor hidden by a tree at night. Here in Brussels, they are felling trees on the boulevards and avenues (not forgetting to fell a lot of old houses that are now being replaced by horrid constructions). "Progress" has not yet "improved" Wilfingen, I believe; you're lucky!
—*Letter from René Magritte to E. Junger, June 5, 1956*

The subject that you asked about on Sunday, as to whether or not it had already attracted my attention, has become uppermost in researching the problem of the sun. It was death, indeed, so that it is not possible for fruitless doubts to arise. In passing, I point out to you that the truism "The sun shines for all" is coincidentally illustrated here.
—*Letter from René Magritte to Paul Colinet, Friday the 13th, 1957*

128. *Le banquet (The Banquet).* 1956. Gouache, 14⅛ x 18½" (36 x 47 cm). Private collection, United States

129. *Le chef d'oeuvre ou les mystères de l'horizon (The Masterpiece or The Mysteries of the Horizon).* 1955. Oil on canvas, 19½ x 25⅝" (49.5 x 65 cm). Collection Arnold Weissberger, New York, New York

130 Fig. 523.

Flaming Object

La découverte du feu (The Discovery of Fire) allowed me the privilege of experiencing the same feeling that was felt by the first men who created flame by striking together two pieces of stone.

In turn, I imagined setting fire to a piece of paper, an egg, and a key.

—*René Magritte,* La Ligne de Vie, *lecture, November 20, 1938*

131

30. *Bain de vapeur en chaise nattée ouché (Steam Bath Using Caned Chairs).* lustration in *La Nouvelle Médication Jaturelle* by F. E. Bilz (edition translated rom German), 1899, vol. 2, p. 1777, fig. 523. Archives Pierre Alechinsky, Bougival, France

31. *Les fanatiques (The Fanatics).* 1945. Dil on canvas, 23⅝ x 19⅝" (60 x 50 cm). Collection Nellens, Knokke-Le Zoute, Belgium

32. *L'échelle de feu (The Ladder of Fire).* 933. Oil on canvas, 21¼ x 28⅞" (54 x 73.5 cm). Private collection, England

33. *L'échelle de feu (The Ladder of Fire).* 939. Gouache, 10⅝ x 13⅜" (27 x 34 cm). Collection Edward James Foundation, Chichester, England

132

33

Word

134. *Les six éléments (The Six Elements).* 1928. Oil on canvas, 28⅜ x 39⅜" (72 x 100 cm). Philadelphia Museum of Art, Philadelphia, Pennsylvania. Louise and Walter Arensberg Collection

135. *Le palais des rideaux (The Palace of Curtains).* 1934. Oil on canvas, 11 x 16½" (28 x 42 cm). Collection Pierre Alechinsky, Bougival, France

136. *Les reflets du temps (The Reflections of Time).* 1928. Oil on canvas remounted on cardboard, 22½ x 30¼" (57 x 76.5 cm). Collection Dr. Robert Mathijs, Brussels, Belgium

134

136

137. *Le sens propre (The Proper Meaning).* 1928–1929. Oil on canvas, 28¾ x 21¼" (73 x 54 cm). Collection Robert Rauschenberg, New York, New York

135

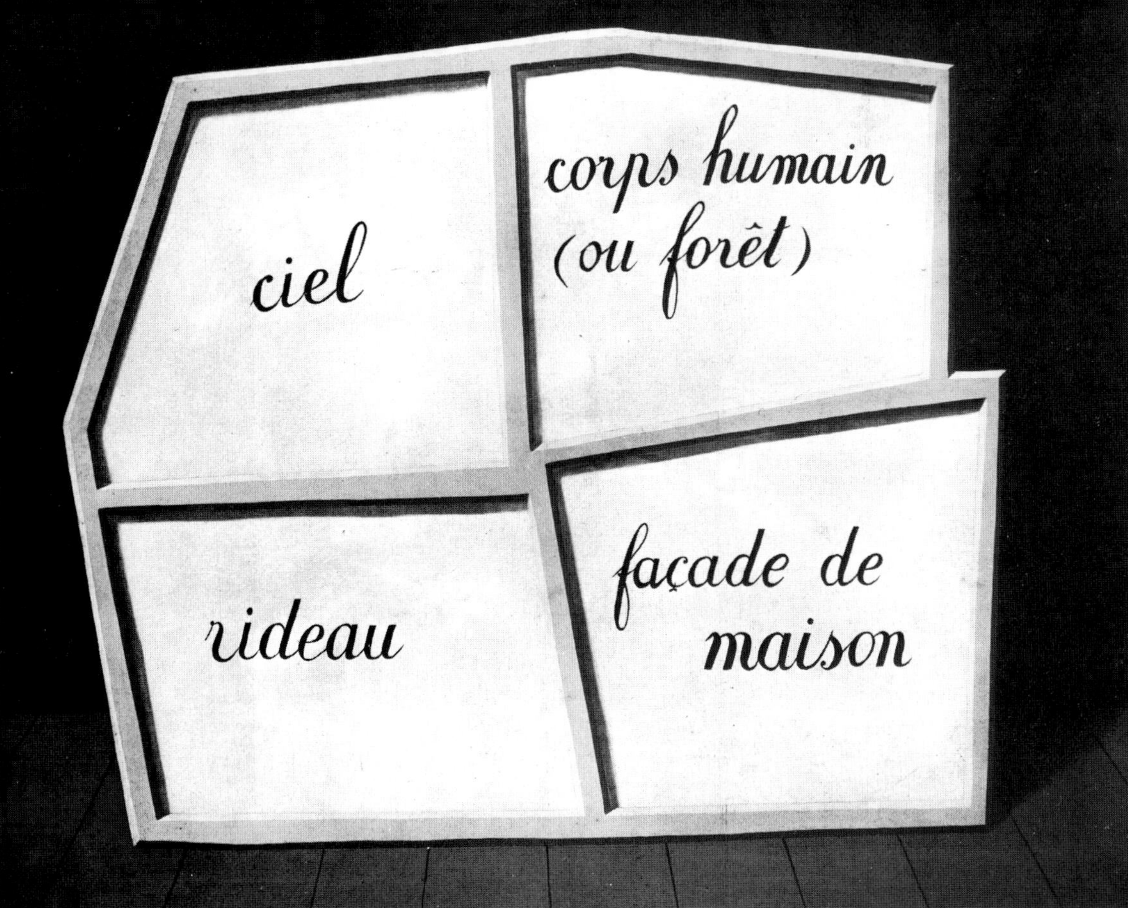

138. *Le masque vide (The Empty Mask).* 1928. Oil on canvas, 28¾ x 36¼″ (73 x 92 cm). Garrick Fine Arts Inc., Philadelphia, Pennsylvania

138

7

Apple

139

140

139. Untitled drawing. n.d. 6¾ x 7¼" (17 x 18.5 cm). Collection Joshua Nahum Musher, New York, New York

140. *La grande table (The Large Table).* 1959. Oil on canvas, 21⅝ x 25⅝" (55 x 65 cm). Collection Mme. Sabine Sonabend, Brussels, Belgium

141. *L'idée (The Idea).* 1966. Oil on canvas, 16⅛ x 13" (41 x 33 cm). Location unknown

Bilboquet

142. *Le joueur secret (The Secret Player).* 1926. Oil on canvas, 59⅞ x 76¾" (152 x 195 cm). Collection Nellens, Knokke-Le Zoute, Belgium

43. *Le beau ténébreux Dark and Handsome).* 1950. Oil on canvas, 2⅞ x 18⅞" (58 x 48 cm). The Israel Museum, Jerusalem, Israel

Anthropoid Bilboquet

144. *Les rencontres naturelles (Natural Encounters).* 1945. Oil on canvas, 31½ x 25⅝"
(80 x 65 cm). Collection M. and Mme. Louis Scutenaire, Brussels, Belgium

Stone and Rock

Now if, for example, weight can play a part in poetry, it is evoked by a stone (as in *La bataille de l'Argonne* [*The Battle of the Argonne*]). What is evoked is weight, *not its laws;* it is evoked *without physics*. The sensation, feeling, or idea of weight is enough for poetry; *laws would be too much,* and there would be too much as soon as physics intervened. The appearance of the word "physics" asserts a belief in the interest physics has for poetry. Now, interest in physics, while valid for an engineer or a physicist, means that there's no longer any question of poetry. If the physicist grants a greater spiritual importance to physics than to poetry, then the question of truth arises.

—*Letter from René Magritte to André Bosmans, July 24, 1961*

By confronting us with a massive rock in midair*—something we know cannot happen—we are somehow forced to wonder *why* doesn't the rock come plunging down into the sea? We know, of course, that it should. But *why* should it? . . . What fails to happen in the painting reminds us of the mystery of what actually does happen in the real world.

Space, time, and matter are dramatized here in suspended animation. The force of gravity, which we dismiss as commonplace in our daily lives, becomes powerful and awesome here. We can step on an ordinary stone any day without giving it a second thought, but the stone in the painting is compelling. The artist has made it extraordinary. It reminds us that all stones are extraordinary. . . . It is a wonderful picture to remind us that the world of our senses, the world of stones and castles, of oceans, clouds and waves, is the world that we must study before we can comprehend the more subtle world of atoms and molecules, of which the world of our senses is composed. Even more important, perhaps, it has the power to evoke a feeling of wonder. This is the ingredient that can make both a painting and physics exciting.

—*Letter from Albert V. Baez, physicist, to Harry Torczyner, September 8, 1963*

*The author is referring to *Le château des Pyrénées*.

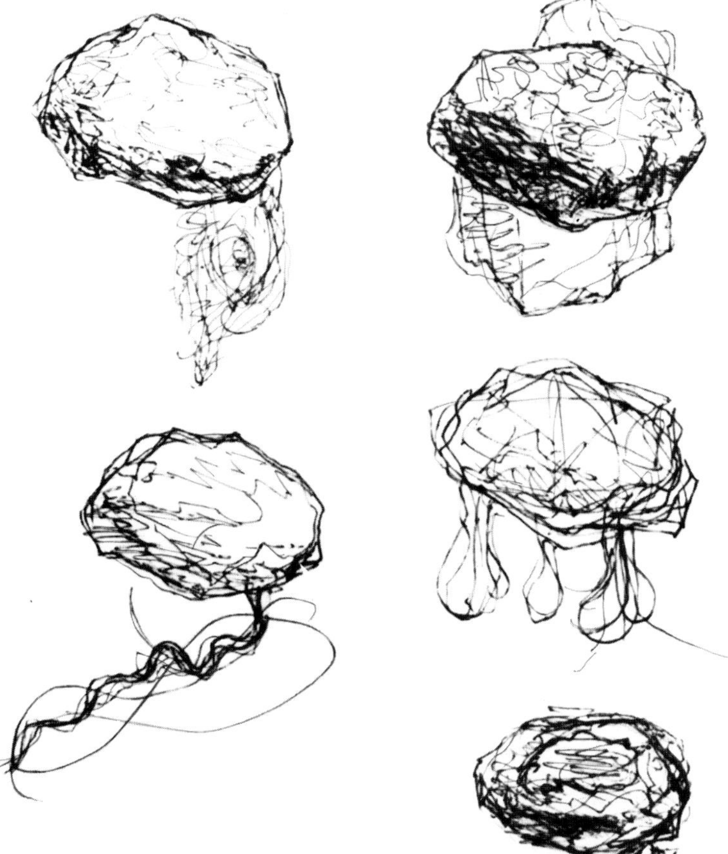

146

145. *Les origines du langage (The Origins of Language)*. 1955. Oil on canvas, 45⅞ x 35⅜" (116.5 x 90 cm). Collection University of St. Thomas, Houston, Texas

146. Untitled drawings. c. 1959. Private collection, New York, New York

149. *Le château des Pyrénées (The Castle of the Pyrenees)* 1959. Oil on canvas, 78¾ x 57⅛" (200 x 140.5 cm). Collection Harry Torczyner, New York, New York

147. *Le trou dans le mur (The Hole in the Wall).* 1956. Oil on canvas, 39⅜ x 31½" (100 x 80 cm). Collection Hans Neumann, Caracas, Venezuela

148. *La bataille d'Argonne (The Battle of the Argonne).* 1959. Oil on canvas, 19½ x 24" (49.5 x 61 cm). Collection Tazzoli, Turin, Italy

Easel

The problem of the window gave rise to *La condition humaine (The Human Condition).* In front of a window seen from inside a room, I placed a painting representing exactly that portion of the landscape covered by the painting. Thus, the tree in the picture hid the tree behind it, outside the room. For the spectator, it was both inside the room within the painting and outside in the real landscape. This is how we see the world. We see it outside ourselves, and at the same time we only have a representation of it in ourselves. In the same way, we sometimes situate in the past that which is happening in the present. Time and space thus lose the vulgar meaning that only daily experience takes into account.

—*René Magritte,* La Ligne de Vie II, *February 1940*

150. *La condition humaine (The Human Condition).* 1934. Oil on canvas, 39⅜ x 31⅞" (100 x 81 cm). Private collection, Paris, France

Object

151. *Fromage sous cloche (Cheese under Bell Glass).* n.d. Collection M. and Mme. Marcel Mabille, Rhode-St.-Genèse, Belgium

152. *La métamorphose de l'objet (Metamorphosis of the Object).* 1933. Study for an ashtray. Gouache, 3⅞ x 3⅞" (10 x 10 cm). Private collection, Brussels, Belgium. *See* Appendix *for translation*

153

154

153. *L'empire des lumières (The Empire of Lights)*. 1953. Oil on canvas, 14⅝ x 17¾" (37 x 45 cm). Collection Arnold Weissberger, New York, New York

154. *L'empire des lumières II (The Empire of Lights II)*. 1950. Oil on canvas, 31⅛ x 39" (79 x 99 cm). The Museum of Modern Art, New York, New York. Gift of Dominique and John de Menil, 1951

155. *L'empire des lumières (The Empire of Lights)*. 1948. Oil on canvas, 39⅜ x 31½" (100 x 80 cm). Private collection, Brussels, Belgium

156. *Le salon de Dieu (God's Drawing Room)*. 1958. Oil on canvas, 16⅞ x 23¼" (43 x 59 cm). Collection Arnold Weissberger, New York, New York

Sky/Landscape

For me, the conception of a picture is an idea of one thing or of several things that can become visible through my painting.

It is understood that all ideas are not conceptions for pictures. Obviously, an idea must be sufficiently stimulating for me to undertake to paint faithfully the thing or things I have ideated.

The conception of a picture, that is, the idea, is not visible in the picture: an idea cannot be seen with the eyes.

What is represented in a picture is what is visible to the eyes, it is the thing or things that must have been ideated.

Thus, what is represented in the picture *L'empire des lumières (The Empire of Lights)* are the things I ideated, i.e., a nighttime landscape and a sky such as we see during the day. The landscape evokes night and the sky evokes day.

I find this evocation of night and day is endowed with the power to surprise and enchant us. I call this power: poetry.

If I believe this evocation has such poetic power, it is because, among other reasons, I have always felt the greatest interest in night and in day, yet without ever having preferred one or the other.

This great personal interest in night and day is a feeling of admiration and astonishment.

——*René Magritte, late April 1956*

INTERMISSION

Cubist Period

I'm neither a "Surrealist" nor a "Cubist" nor a "'Patawhatever,'"* even though I have a fairly strong weakness for the so-called Cubist and Futurist "schools." Were I really an *artiste-peintre*, I would waver between these two disciplines. Were I an innocent intellectual, I would be content with what Surrealism entails in a large, very large part of unimportant matters.
—*Letter from René Magritte to André Bosmans, April 1959*

* Pataphysics ("Patawhatever") is a philosophy invented by Alfred Jarry, which was taken up by the Surrealists and Dadaists.

157. *Jeune fille (Young Woman)*. 1924. Oil on canvas, 21⅝ x 15¾" (55 x 40 cm). Collection Mme. René Magritte, Brussels, Belgium

158. *La baigneuse (The Bather)*. 1923. Oil on canvas, 19⅝ x 39⅜" (50 x 100 cm). Collection M. and Mme. Berger-Hoyez, Brussels, Belgium

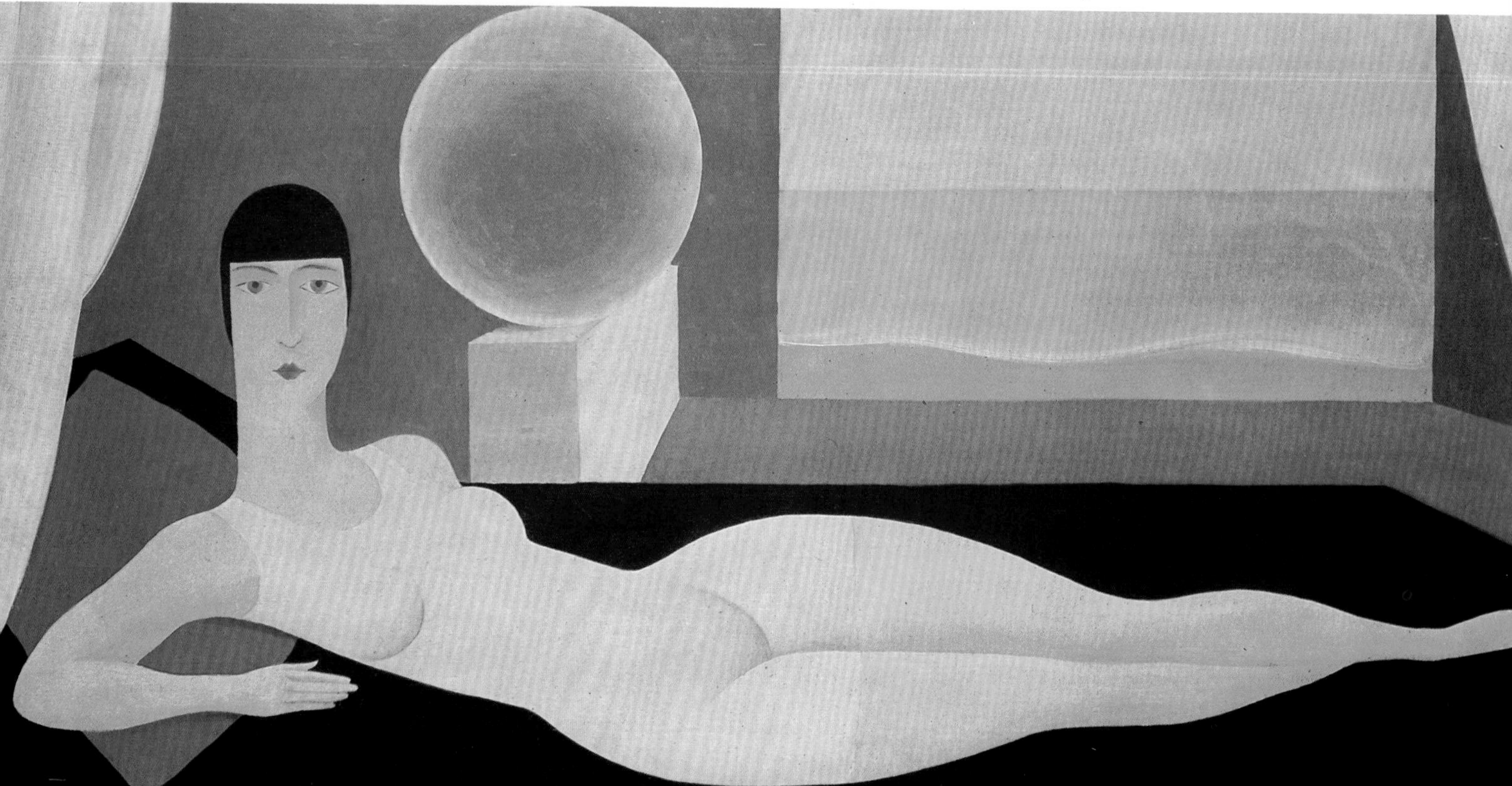

Renoir Period

For the period I call "Surrealism in full sunlight," I am trying to join together two mutually exclusive things:

1) a feeling of levity, intoxication, happiness, which depends on a certain mood and on an atmosphere that certain Impressionists—or rather, Impressionism in general—have managed to render in painting. Without Impressionism, I do not believe we would know this feeling of real objects perceived through colors and nuances, and free of all classical reminiscences. The public has never liked the Impressionists, although it may seem to; it always sees these pictures with an eye dominated by mental analysis—otherwise, we must agree that freedom runs riot.

and, 2) a feeling of the mysterious existence of objects (which should not depend upon classical or literary reminiscences), which is experienced only by means of a certain clairvoyance.

Some of the paintings of this period have succeeded in uniting these two mutually exclusive things. I gave up—why? It's not too clear—perhaps out of a need for unity?

—Letter from René Magritte to G. Puel, March 8, 1955

. . . pictures of "Surrealism in full sunlight." Pictures we say—to laugh and to stop laughing—are from my "Black Period," given the futility of having shown them to the public up to now.

—Letter from René Magritte to Mirabelle Dors and Maurice Rapin, March 30, 1956

59. *Les heureux présages (The Good Omens).* 1944. Oil on canvas, 15¾ x 23⅝" 40 x 60 cm). Collection M. and Mme. Berger-Hoyez, Brussels, Belgium

160. *La moisson (The Harvest).* 1944. Oil on canvas, 23⅝ x 31½" (60 x 80 cm). Collection M. and Mme. Louis Scutenaire, Brussels, Belgium

Fauvist Period

This is probably my last holographic ejaculation for you from Paris. Taking stock, we come to the result zero, as our friends warned us. (Zero if the results are indeed measurable.) Spiritually, however, I have made a few acquisitions: for example I think (provisionally) that what distinguishes us from the genial way of thinking (in spite of ourselves, since it would be out of the question to want to distinguish oneself at any price) is for example our total lack of belief in substance and in form. Those who are very active here seem to cling to form, the only bone they have left to gnaw on. Thus this shit Baron Mollet, who honeyed up to me and now tells everyone that *Les pieds dans le plat (The Faux Pas)* wasn't suitable for Paris (true, it doesn't suit, but not in the way this cretin thinks). The basics: feelings are "basically" totally boring, except when they are experienced in daily life (outside literature).

The whole thing makes me think that my "business" of making pictures boils down to mere fabrication, like making old furniture, for example. Surrounding this enterprise are other forms of craftsmanship, such as writing, theater, etc. . . . that is what makes up the art world—but its substance and form don't interest me.

There are some visitors to the exhibition (the young girls have a tendency to laugh, but they restrain themselves since it's unbecoming in art galleries), visitors who make the usual asshole remarks: "It's less profound than it was," it's "Belgian wit," you can feel it's not "Parisian," "What brush work!", "What a lovely torso" (for the "psychologist"), etc. . . . There's a review in *Arts*, which you can buy for yourselves in Brussels. I'm incapable of buying the issue and sending it to you. I feel nauseated just thinking of it. As for sales, that too is Zero up until now; perhaps it will change, nothing is permanently decided. Also, for pleasure, we go for walks in the Bois de Vincennes, which is near to our quarters so we can avoid trips and noises. Another source of pleasure is that there are some good charcuteries here. I'm expecting a visit from Iolas in a day or two. Even if he doesn't come or is late, I'm taking off on Thursday. If you'd like, we could see each other Friday at my place, as usual.

—*Letter from René Magritte to Irène Hamoir and Louis Scutenaire, May 17, 1948*

161

162

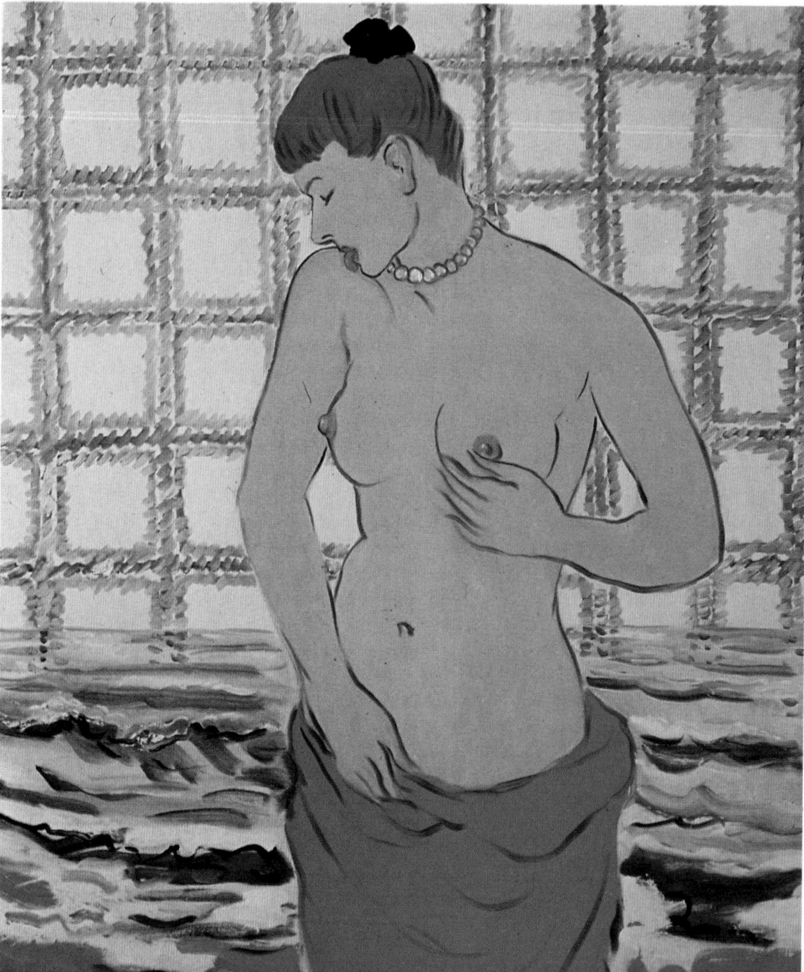

161. *Le prince charmant (Prince Charming).* 1948. Gouache, 17¾ x 12⅝" (45 x 32 cm). Collection M. and Mme. Louis Scutenaire, Brussels, Belgium

162. *Le galet (The Pebble).* 1948. Oil on canvas, 39⅜ x 31½" (100 x 80 cm). Collection Mme. René Magritte, Brussels, Belgium

TOWARD PLEASURE

For Magritte, inspiration was very simply the recognition of a subject worthy of being represented in painting. He did not begin with an idea, but, on the contrary, he arrived at an idea that had to be able to stand up to his criticism and to impose itself upon him. Sometimes, this inspiration was slow to come. Bad luck. He refused to provoke or to hasten its arrival through imagination. Inspiration permitted him to evoke mystery by uniting in one image the visible offered by the world.

Once painted, this image had to be given a name, like a newborn child that must be baptized. A strange and indissoluble bond exists between each newborn and its name. A name is annunciatory, revelatory, serving neither to define nor to interpret its bearer. So it is with the titles given Magritte's pictures. Sometimes he asked advice by letter, or he would convoke an actual family council. His circle of close friends would then gather under his presidency to decide on a name. Sometimes Magritte would decree that a work was to bear the title of one of his favorite books.

What mattered to him was discovering what must be painted, not the way to paint. In order to discover an answer to his research, Magritte had to solve a series of problems and relentlessly to pursue his mental calculations.

He followed his pictorial "Lifeline" obstinately, faithfully, and not without a certain austerity; and with characteristic lucidity and sense of moderation, he has explained to us why his images demand no explanation.

163. *Le chant de la violette (The Song of the Violet).* 1951. Oil on canvas, 39⅜ x 31⅞" (100 x 81 cm). Private collection, Brussels, Belgium

164. Photograph of René Magritte, Brussels, Belgium, 1934

65. *A la rencontre du plaisir (Toward Pleasure)*. 1950. Oil on anvas, 19¼ x 23" (49 x 58.5 cm). Collection Harry Torczyner, New York, New York

POETIC ATTRIBUTIONS

The flesh statue of a young woman holding a rose made of flesh in her hand. Her other hand is leaning against a rock. The curtains open onto the sea and a summer sky.
—*René Magritte, June 22, 1946, in* Fait Accompli, *nos. 111–113, April 1974*

166. *Les fleurs du mal (The Flowers of Evil).* 1946. Oil on canvas, 31½ x 23⅝" (80 x 60 cm). Collection M. and Mme. Berger-Hoyez, Brussels, Belgium

Les Fleurs du Mal

Unexpected images sometimes appear to m when my eyes are open or closed, and they be come the models of pictures I like to paint.

In depicting the image that appeared to me on day, I painted *Les fleurs du mal (The Flowers c Evil).* It was the unexpected image of a statu made of flesh, a woman made completely of flesh holding in her hand a rose made of flesh, in front c the sea I had seen between two red curtains.

The title *Les fleurs du mal* goes with the pictur just as a noun corresponds to an object withou either illustrating or explaining it.

It would be useless to posit some mental prc cess of which I am ignorant and to charge it wit having determined the content of what I call a "unexpected image." It would be just as easy t assert that latent memories of Baudelaire' poems were, unbeknownst to me, the origin fc the painting *Les fleurs du mal.*
—*René Magritte, address given upon being made a member of th Académie Picard, April 5, 1957*

A title "justifies" the image by completing i Nietzsche also said "there is no thought withou language." Could the painting that affects us be language without thought? Because it is evider that pictures representing ideas—justice, fc example—fail to affect us.
—*René Magritte,* Paroles Datées, *June 19, 1956, in* Les Brouillor Sacrés, *I, Paris, November 1956*

The titles of my paintings accompany them lik the names attached to objects without illustratin or explaining them.
—*Letter from René Magritte to Barnet Hodes, 1957*

Titles . . . become "eloquent" as names for paint ings on condition that they fit exactly. Their mean ing has strength and charm thanks to the paint ings, and paintings acquire greater precision b being well named.
—*Letter from René Magritte to André Bosmans, March 7, 1959*

Titles should be images that are precisely joinec with the pictures. In fact, the titles I might ca purely "intellectual" are not satisfactory at all. Ti tles that can suit any picture are hardly any better such as *The Image Itself, Resemblance,* anc others that are intelligent, but perhaps too much so.
—*Letter from René Magritte to Marcel Lecomte, June 13, 1960*

The titles go with my paintings as well as they can They are not keys. There are only false keys.
—*From an interview with René Magritte by Guy Mertens,* Pourquc Pas, *1966*

The Domain of Arnheim

For the development of *La fontaine de jouvence (The Fountain of Youth),* I can say that it began about 1933–1934; I was trying to paint a mountain and thought of giving it a bird's shape and calling this image *Le domaine d'Arnheim,* the title of one of Poe's stories. Poe would have liked seeing this mountain (he shows us landscapes and mountains in his story).

Fortune faite (The Fortune Made) and *La fontaine de jouvence* are stones bearing such inscriptions as "Coblenz," "Roseau" (or the date in *Les verres fumés [The Dark Glasses]*) "à boire," "à manger" *(to drink, to eat)* as in *Fortune faite.* These stones can be seen as a little piece of *Le domaine d'Arnheim.*

To be more thorough, I mustn't forget to say that between *Le domaine d'Arnheim* and *La fontaine de jouvence* came *Le sourire (The Smile),* which was a very old stone—without the bird's head—bearing a date of five figures.

—Letter from René Magritte to André Bosmans, April 6, 1959

Literary Sources

Many of Magritte's images are known to have derived their titles from happy memories of reading:

L'Au-Delà (F. Grégoire)
"The Domain of Arnheim" (Edgar Allan Poe)
Les Fleurs du Mal (Charles Baudelaire)
Gaspard de la Nuit (Bertrand)
"La Géante" (Charles Baudelaire)
Treasure Island (L'Ile du Trésor) (Robert Louis Stevenson)
Les Liaisons Dangereuses (Choderlos de Laclos)
Souvenirs du Voyage (J. A. Gobineau)
Visions of a Castle of the Pyrenees (Ann Radcliffe)

167. *Les épaves de l'ombre (The Shadow's Wreckage).* n.d. Oil on canvas, 47¼ x 31½" (120 x 80 cm). Musée de Grenoble, Grenoble, France

The first concept of a mountaintop shaped like a bird, which led to *Le domaine d'Arnheim* some thirty years later.

168. Untitled drawing. n.d. 4⅜ x 5⅞" (11 x 15 cm). Collection M. and Mme. Marcel Mabille, Rhode-St.-Genèse, Belgium

169. *Le domaine d'Arnheim (The Domain of Arnheim)*. 1962. Oil on canvas, 57½ x 44⅞" (146 x 114 cm). Collection Mme. René Magritte, Brussels, Belgium

170. *Fortune faite (The Fortune Made)*. 1957. Oil on canvas, 23⅝ x 19⅝" (60 x 50 cm). Location unknown

The Well of Truth

171

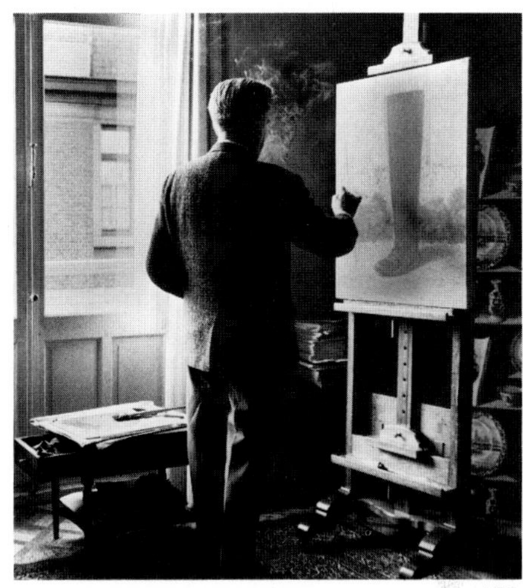

172

171. *Le puits de vérité (The Well of Truth).* c. 1962–1963. Pen and ink drawing, 11⅜ x 8¼" (30 x 21 cm). Collection Mme. Sabine Sonabend-Binder, Brussels, Belgium

172. Photograph of René Magritte painting *Le puits de vérité (The Well of Truth)*, 1963

173. Pen sketch of *Le puits de vérité (The Well of Truth)* in a letter from René Magritte to Harry Torczyner, January 13,1962. *See* Appendix *for translation*

173

J'ai envoyé il y a quelque temps à Suzi
le dessin d'un nouveau tableau (une
jambe de pantalon et un soulier) en
lui demandant comment
elle l'appelerait. Le
titre est trouvé enfin :
"L'Etalon"
(dans le sens de l'unité
immuable – ou presque –
de mesure).

The Voyager

174. *Le voyageur (The Traveler)*. 1935. Oil on canvas, 21⅝ x 26" (55 x 66 cm). Private collection, Brussels, Belgium

175. Ink drawing in a letter from René Magritte to Mirabelle Dors and Maurice Rapin, August 22, 1956

THE TRUE ART OF PAINTING

176. *Découverte (Discovery)*. 1927. Oil on canvas, 25⅝ x 19⅝" (65 x 50 cm). Collection M. and Mme. Louis Scutenaire, Brussels, Belgium

I believe I've made an altogether startling discovery in painting: up until now I used combined objects, or perhaps the position of an object was enough to render it mysterious. But as a result of the research I have pursued here, I have found a new possibility things may have: that of *gradually* becoming something else—an object *melts* into an object other than itself. For instance, at certain spots the sky allows wood to appear. This is something completely different from a compound object, since there is no break between the two materials, no boundary. Using this means, I get pictures in which the eye "must think" in a way entirely different from the usual; the things are tangible, yet a few planks of ordinary wood grow imperceptibly transparent in certain areas, or a nude woman has parts that also become a different material.

—*Letter from René Magritte (Le Perreux-sur-Marne) to Paul Nougé, November 1927*

The Lifeline

Comrades, Ladies and Gentlemen.

That old question "Who are we?" receives a disappointing answer in the world in which we must live. Actually, we are merely the subjects of this so-called civilized world, in which intelligence, baseness, heroism, and stupidity get on very well together and are alternately being pushed to the fore. We are the subjects of this incoherent, absurd world in which weapons are manufactured to prevent war, in which science is used to destroy, to construct, to kill, to prolong the life of the dying, in which the most insane undertaking works against itself; we are living in a world in which one marries for money, in which one constructs palaces that rot, abandoned, by the sea. This world is still holding up, more or less, but we can already see the signs of its approaching ruin glimmering in the darkness.

It would be naïve and useless to restate these facts for those who are not bothered by them, and who are peaceably taking advantage of this state of affairs. Those who thrive on this disorder hope to consolidate it, and, the only means available to them being further disorders, they are contributing to its imminent collapse, albeit unwittingly, by replastering the crumbling structure in their so-called realistic way.

Other men, among whom I am proud to count myself, despite the utopianism they are accused of, consciously desire the proletarian revolution that will transform the world; and we are acting toward this end, each according to the means available to him.

Nevertheless, we must protect ourselves against this second-rate reality that has been fashioned by centuries of worshipping money, races, fatherlands, gods, and, I might add, art.

Nature, which bourgeois society has not completely succeeded in extinguishing, provides us with the dream state, which endows our bodies and our minds with the freedom they need so imperatively.

Nature seems to have been overly generous in creating for those who are too impatient or too weak the refuge of insanity, which protects them from the stifling atmosphere of the real world.

The great strength for defense is the love that binds lovers together in an enchanted world made precisely to their order, and which is admirably protected by isolation.

Finally, Surrealism provides mankind with a methodology and a mental orientation appropriate to the pursuit of investigations in areas that have been ignored or underrated but that, nonetheless, directly concern man. Surrealism demands for our waking lives a liberty comparable to that that we possess in dreams.

The mind possesses this freedom to a high degree, and as a practical matter new technicians must devote themselves to the task of destroying some complexes—such as ridicule, perhaps—and of looking for those slight modifications that must be made in our habits so that this faculty that we possess of seeing only what we choose to see might become the faculty of discovering at once the object of our desires. Daily experience, even hobbled as it is by religious, civil, or military moralities, is already achieving these possibilities to some degree.

In any case, the Surrealists know how to be free. As André Breton cries: "Liberty is the color of man."

In 1910, Chirico played with beauty; he imagined and achieved what he wanted: he painted *Le chant d'amour (The Song of Love),* in which we see boxing gloves together with the face of an antique statue. He painted *Melancholia* in a land of high factory chimneys and infinite walls. This triumphant poetry replaced the stereotyped effects of traditional painting. It was a total break with the mental habits characteristic of artists who were prisoners of talent, virtuosity, and all the minor aesthetic specialities. It meant a new vision in which the spectator rediscovered his isolation and listened to the world's silence.

In his illustrations to Paul Éluard's *Répétitions,* Max Ernst superbly demonstrated, through the shattering effect of collages made from old magazine illustrations, that one could easily dispense with everything that had given traditional painting its prestige. Scissors, paste, images, and some genius effectively replaced the brushes, colors, model, style, sensibility, and the divine afflatus of artists.

The labors of Chirico, of Max Ernst, certain works by Derain, *L'homme au journal (Man with Newspaper)* among others, in which a real newspaper is pasted into a figure's hands, Picasso's experiments, Duchamp's anti-artistic activity, which casually proposed using a Rembrandt as an ironing board: these are the beginnings of what is now called Surrealist painting.

In my childhood, I liked playing with a little girl in the old, abandoned cemetery of a small country town. We visited those underground vaults whose heavy iron doors we could lift and we reascended into the light, where an artist from the capital was painting in one of the cemetery's paths, picturesque with its broken stone columns amid piles of dead leaves. At that moment, the art of painting seemed somehow magical, and the painter endowed with superior powers. Alas! I later learned that painting had little to do with real life, and that each attempt at freedom had always been foiled by the public: Millet's *Angelus* created a scandal when it appeared; the painter was accused of having insulted the peasants by representing them as he had. People wanted to destroy Manet's *Olympia,* and the critics reproached the painter for showing women cut into pieces because he had only shown the top half of a girl standing behind a bar counter, the bottom half being hidden by it. During Courbet's life, it was agreed that he showed very poor taste in vociferously showing off his spurious talent. I also saw that examples of this kind were infinite, and that they extended into every realm of thought. As for the artists themselves, most readily renounced their freedom and placed their art at the service of anyone or anything. Their concerns and ambitions were usually the same as those of any opportunist. In this way I acquired complete mistrust of art and artists, whether they were officially blessed or only aspired to be, and I felt I had nothing in common with such company. I possessed a point of reference that placed me elsewhere—it was that magic of art that I had known in my childhood.

In 1915, I tried to rediscover the stance that would enable me to see the world other than as others wanted to impose it upon me. I had mastered certain techniques of the art of painting, and, in isolation, I made attempts that were deliberately different from anything I knew in painting. I tasted the pleasures of freedom in painting the least conformist images. Then, by a singular chance, I was handed—with a pitying smile and probably the idiotic idea of having a good joke on me—the illustrated catalogue of an exhibition of Futurist paintings. I had before my eyes a powerful challenge to the good sense with which I was so bored. For me, it was like the light I had found again upon emerging from the underground vaults of the old cemetery where I had spent my childhood vacations.

In a state of real intoxication, I painted a whole series of Futurist pictures.

Yet, I don't believe I was a truly orthodox Futurist because the lyricism I wanted to capture had an unchanging center unrelated to aesthetic Futurism.

It was a pure and powerful feeling: eroticism. The little girl I had known in the old cemetery was the object of my reveries, and she became involved in the animated ambiences of stations, fairs, or towns that I created for her. Thanks to this magical painting I recaptured the same sensations I had had in my childhood.

The elements that entered into the compositions of my paintings were represented by means of flexible shapes and colors, so that those shapes and colors could be modified and shaped to the demands imposed by a rhythm of movement.

For example, the elongated rectangle representing the trunk of a tree was sometimes sectioned, sometimes bent, sometimes barely visible, according to the role it played. These completely free forms were not in disagreement with nature, which does not insist (in the case of the tree in question) on producing trees of a rigorously invariable color, dimension, and form.

These kinds of concerns gradually raised the question of the relationship between an object and its form, and between its apparent form and the essential thing it must possess in order for it to exist. I tried to find the plastic equivalents of this essential thing, and my attention turned away from the movement of objects. Then I painted pictures representing immobile objects shorn of their details and their secondary characteristics. These objects revealed to the eye only their essentials, and, in contrast to the image we have of them in real life, where they are concrete, the painted image signified a very lively perception of abstract existence.

This contrast was reduced; I ended up by finding in the appearance of the real world itself the same abstraction as in my paintings; for despite the complex combinations of details and nuances in a real landscape, I managed to see it as though it were only a curtain hanging in front of me. I became uncertain of the depth of the countryside, unconvinced of the remoteness of the light blue of the horizon; direct experience simply placed it at eye level.

I was in the same innocent state as the child in his cradle who believes he can catch the bird flying in the sky. Paul Valéry, it seems, experienced this same state by the sea, which, he says, rises up before the eyes of the spectator. The French Impressionist painters, Seurat among others, saw the world in exactly this way when they broke down the colors of objects.

Now I had to animate this world that, even when in motion, had no depth and had lost all consistency. I then thought that the objects themselves should eloquently reveal their existence, and I looked for the means to achieve this end.

The novelty of this undertaking made me lose sight of the fact that my earlier experiments, which had led to an abstract representation of the world, had become useless when this very abstraction became characteristic of the real world. In addition, it was still with my old manner of painting that I began to execute paintings with a new point of departure; this discord kept me from thoroughly exploiting the researches I was undertaking; my attempts up to this point to show the evidence, the existence of an object, had been hampered by the abstract image I was giving of that object. The rose I put on the bosom of a nude girl did not create the overwhelming effect I had anticipated.

I subsequently introduced into my paintings elements complete with all the details they show us in reality, and I soon realized, that when represented in this fashion, they immediately brought into question their corresponding elements in the real world.

Thus I decided about 1925 to paint only the superficial characteristics of objects because my researches could be developed under no other condition. I was actually renouncing only a certain manner of painting that had brought me to a point I had to go beyond. This decision, which caused me to break with a comfortable habit, was the outcome of a lengthy meditation I had in a working-class restaurant in Brussels. My state of mind made the moldings of a door seem endowed with a mysterious existence, and for a long time I remained in contact with their reality.

That was when I used to meet my friends Paul Nougé, E. L. T. Mesens, and Jean [sic] Scutenaire. We were united by shared concerns. We met the Surrealists, who were violently demonstrating their disgust for bourgeois society. Since their revolutionary demands were the same as ours, we joined with them in the service of the proletarian revolution.

This was a setback. The politicians leading the workers' parties were in fact too vain and too lacking in perspicacity to appreciate the Surrealists' contribution. These people in high places were allowed to compromise seriously the proletarian cause in 1914. They also indulged in every cowardice, every baseness. In Germany, at a time when they still represented a perfectly disciplined worker population and when this power could have been exploited to crush easily that asshole Hitler, they gave in to him and his handful of fanatics. Recently, in France, Monsieur Blum helped the Germans and Italians murder the young Spanish Republic and, purportedly fearing a revolutionary situation, he seems to be ignoring the people's rights and prerogatives by giving way in his turn to a threatening reactionary minority. It should be noted in passing that a political leader of the proletariat has to be very courageous to dare declare his faith in the cause he defends. Such men are assassinated.

The subversive aspect of Surrealism has clearly worried the traditional labor politicians, who at times are indistinguishable from the most fanatic defenders of the bourgeois world. Surrealist thought is revolutionary on all levels and is necessarily opposed to the bourgeois conception of art. As it turns out, the leftist politicians ascribe to this bourgeois conception, and they want nothing to do with painting if it does not conform.

However, the bourgeois conception of art should be inimical to the politician who calls himself revolutionary and who should thus be looking toward the future, since [this conception's] characteristics are a cult dedicated exclusively to past achievements and a desire to halt artistic development. Further, the value of a work of art is gauged in the bourgeois world by its rarity, by its value in gold; its intrinsic value interests only a few old-fashioned innocents who are as satisfied by the sight of a wildflower as by the possession of a real or paste diamond. A conscientious revolutionary like Lenin judges gold at its true value. He wrote: "When we have achieved victory on a world scale, I think we will build public latrines in gold on the streets of some of the world's largest cities." A feeble-minded reactionary such as Clemenceau, the zealous lackey of every bourgeois myth, made this outrageous statement about art: "Yes, I won the World War, but if I am to be honored in future history, I owe it to my incursions into the realms of art."

Surrealism is revolutionary because it is the indomitable foe of all the bourgeois ideological values that are keeping the world in its present appalling condition.

From 1925 to 1926, I painted some sixty pictures, which were shown at the Centaur Gallery in Brussels. The proof of freedom they revealed naturally outraged the critics, from whom I had expected nothing interesting anyway. I was accused of everything. I was faulted for the absence of certain things and for the presence of others.

The lack of plastic qualities noted by the critics had actually been filled by an objective representation of things, which was clearly understood and comprehended by those whose taste had not been ruined by the literature that had been created around painting. I believed this detached way of representing objects corresponded to a universal style, in which one person's manias and petty preferences no longer played a part. For example, I used light blue to represent the sky, unlike the bourgeois artists who paint sky as an excuse to show their favorite blue next to their favorite gray. I consider such petty little preferences to be irrelevant, and these artists to be lending themselves to a most ridiculous spectacle, albeit with great seriousness.

Traditional picturesqueness, the only one granted critical approval, had good reasons for not appearing in my paintings: by itself, the picturesque is inoperable and negates itself each time it reappears in the same guise. Before it became traditional, its charm was derived from unexpectedness, the novelty of a mood, and unfamiliarity. But by repeating a few such effects, picturesqueness has become disgustingly monotonous. How can the public at each spring salon continue to look without nausea at the same sunny or moonlit old church wall? Those onions and eggs either to the right or to the left of the inevitable copper pot with its predictable highlights? Or the swan that since antiquity has been about to penetrate those thousands of Ledas?

I think the picturesque can be employed like any other element, provided it is placed in a new order or particular circumstances, for example: a legless veteran will create a sensation at a court ball. The traditional picturesqueness of that ruined cemetery path seemed magical to me in my childhood because I came upon it after the darkness of the underground vaults.

I was criticized for the ambiguity of my paintings. That was quite an admission for the ones who were complaining: they unwittingly reveal their timidity when, left to themselves, they no longer have the guarantees of some expert, the sanction of time, or any other guideline to reassure them.

I was criticized for the rarefied nature of my interests—a singular reproach, coming from people for whom rarity indicates great value.

I was also criticized for many other things, and finally for having shown objects situated in places where we never really find them. Yet this is the fulfillment of a real, if unconscious, desire common to most men. In fact, ordinary painting is already attempting, within the limits set for it, to upset in some small way the order in which it generally views objects. It has allowed itself some timid bravado, a few vague allusions. Given my desire to make the most ordinary objects shock if at all possible, I obviously had to upset the order in which one generally places them. I found the cracks we see in our houses and on our faces to be more eloquent in the sky; turned wooden table legs lost their innocent existence if they suddenly appeared towering over a forest; a woman's body floating above a city advantageously replaced the angels that never appeared to me; I found it useful to envisage the Virgin Mary's underwear, and showed her in this new light; I preferred to believe that the iron bells hanging from our fine horses' necks grew there like dangerous plants on the edge of precipices. . . .

As for the mystery, the enigma my paintings embodied, I will say that this was the best proof of my break with all the absurd mental habits that commonly replace any authentic feeling of existence.

The pictures painted in the following years, from 1925 to 1936, were also the result of a systematic search for an overwhelming poetic effect through the arrangement of objects borrowed from reality, which would give the real world from which those objects had been borrowed an overwhelming poetic meaning by a natural process of exchange.

The means I used were analyzed in a work by Paul Nougé entitled *Les images défendues (Forbidden Images).* Those means were, first, the displacement of objects, for example: a Louis-Philippe table on an ice floe, the flag on a dung heap. The choice of things to be displaced was made from among very ordinary objects in order to give the displacement maximum effectiveness. A burning child affects us much more than the self-destruction of a distant planet. Paul Nougé rightly noted that certain objects, devoid of any special affective content in themselves, retained this precise meaning when removed to unfamiliar surroundings. Thus, women's undergarments were particularly resistant to any sudden change.

The creation of new objects; the transformation of known objects; the alteration of certain objects' substance—a wooden sky, for example; the use of words associated with images; the false labeling of an image; the realization of ideas suggested by friends; the representation of certain day-dreaming visions—all these, in sum, were ways of forcing objects finally to become sensational.

In *Les images défendues,* Paul Nougé also remarks that the titles of my paintings are conversational commodities rather than explications. The titles are chosen in such a way that they also impede their being situated in some reassuring realm that automatic thought processes might otherwise find for them in order to underestimate their significance. The titles should provide additional protection in discouraging any attempt to reduce real poetry to an inconsequential game.

One night in 1936 I awoke in a room in which someone had put a cage with a sleeping bird. A wonderful aberration made me see the cage with the bird gone and replaced by an egg. There and then, I grasped a new and astonishing poetic secret, for the shock I felt had been caused precisely by the affinity of two objects, the cage and the egg, whereas previously this shock had been caused by the encounter between two completely unrelated objects.

From that moment, I sought to find out whether objects besides the cage could also disclose—by bringing to light an element characteristic of them and absolutely predestined for them—the same unmistakable poetry the union of the egg and cage had managed to produce. In the course of my experiments I came to the conviction that I always knew beforehand that element to be discovered, that certain thing above all the others attached obscurely to each object; but this knowledge had lain as if lost in the depths of my thoughts.

Since this research could only yield one right answer for each object, my investigations were like problem solving in which I had three givens: the object, the entity linked with it in the recesses of my mind, and the light under which that entity would emerge.

The problem of the door called for an opening one could pass through. In *La réponse imprévue (The Unexpected Answer),* I showed a closed door in a room; in the door an irregular-shaped opening revealed the night.

Painting *La découverte du feu (The Discovery of Fire)* granted me the privilege of sharing early man's feeling when he gave birth to fire by striking together two pieces of stone. In my turn, I imagined setting fire to a piece of paper, an egg, and a key.

The problem of the window gave rise to *La condition humaine (The Human Condition).* In front of a window seen from inside a room, I placed a painting representing exactly that portion of the landscape covered by the painting. Thus, the tree in the picture hid the tree behind it, outside the room. For the spectator, it was both inside the room within the painting and outside in the real landscape. This simultaneous existence in two different spaces is like living simultaneously in the past and in the present, as in cases of déjà vu.

The tree as subject of a problem became a large leaf whose stem was a trunk with its roots stuck straight into the ground. In remembrance of a poem by Baudelaire, I called it *La géante (The Giantess).*

For the house, I showed, through an open window in the façade of a house, a room containing a house. This became *L'éloge de la dialectique (In Praise of Dialectic).*

L'invention collective (The Collective Invention) was the answer to the problem of the sea. On the beach I laid a new species of siren, whose head and upper body were those of a fish and whose lower parts, from stomach to legs, were those of a woman.

I came to an understanding of the problem of light by illuminating both the bust of a woman painted in a picture and the painting itself with the same candle. This solution was called *La lumière des coïncidences (The Light of Coincidences).*

La domaine d'Arnheim (The Domain of Arnheim) is the realization of a vision Edgard [sic] Poe would have liked: it shows a vast mountain shaped exactly like a bird with spread wings. It is seen through an open bay window on whose ledge sit two eggs.

Woman gave me *Le viol (The Rape)*. It is a woman's face comprised of parts of her body: the breasts are eyes, the navel the nose, and the sexual organs replace the mouth.

The problem of shoes demonstrates how the most frightening things can, through inattention, become completely innocuous. Thanks to *Le modèle rouge (The Red Model)*, we realize that the union of a human foot and a shoe is actually a monstrous custom.

In *Le printemps éternel (The Eternal Spring)*, a dancer has replaced the genitals of a Hercules lying by the sea.

The problem of rain led to huge clouds hovering on the ground within the panorama of a rainy countryside. *La sélection naturelle (Natural Selection)*, *Union libre (Free Union)*, and *Le chant de l'orage (The Song of the Storm)* are three versions of this solution.

The last problem I addressed myself to was that of the horse. During my researches, I was again shown that I had known unconsciously long beforehand the thing that had to be brought to light. Indeed, my first idea was a vaguely perceived notion of the final solution: it was the idea of a horse carrying three shapeless masses whose significance I did not understand until after a series of trials and errors. I made an object consisting of a jar and a label bearing the image of a horse and the inscription in printed letters *Confiture de cheval (Horse Preserves)*. Next I imagined a horse whose head was replaced by a hand with the little finger pointing forward, but I realized that this was merely the equivalent of a unicorn. I dwelt for some time on one intriguing combination: in a dark room I placed a horsewoman sitting by a table, her head resting on her hand while she gazed dreamily at a landscape shaped like a horse. The horse's lower body and legs were the colors of the sky and clouds. What put me at last on the right track was a rider in the position one takes when riding a galloping horse; from the sleeve of the arm thrust forward emerged the head of a race horse, and the other arm, thrown back, held a whip. Next to this horseman, I placed an American Indian in the same posture, and suddenly I sensed the meaning of the three shapeless masses I had set upon the horse at the beginning of my experiments. I knew they were riders, and I finished off *La Chaine sans fin (The Endless Chain)* as follows: in a deserted landscape, under a dark sky, a rearing horse carries a modern horseman, a knight of the Late Middle Ages, and a horseman from antiquity.

Nietzsche believed that without an overheated sexual makeup Raphael would never have painted his hordes of Madonnas. . . . This is at

177. *L'annonciation (The Annunciation)*. 1930. Oil on canvas, 44⅞ x 57½" (114 x 146 cm). Private collection, Brussels, Belgium

178. *Le mois des vendanges (The Time of the Harvest).* 1959. Ink drawing, 7 x 10½" (17.8 x 26.7 cm). Private collection, New York, New York

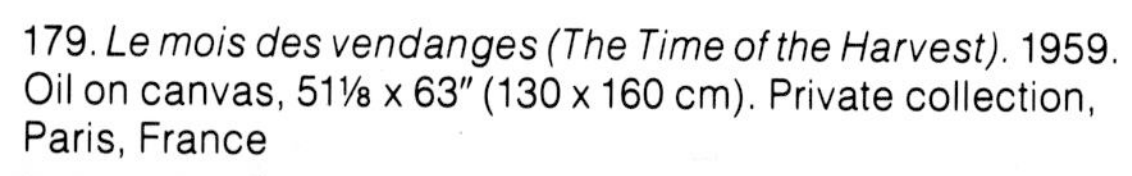

179. *Le mois des vendanges (The Time of the Harvest).* 1959. Oil on canvas, 51⅛ x 63" (130 x 160 cm). Private collection, Paris, France

striking variance with the motives usually attributed to this Old Master; according to priests, it was the ardor of his Christian faith; aesthetes contend it was the desire for pure beauty, etc. . . . But [Nietzsche's] opinion brings us back to a healthier interpretation of pictorial phenomena. This disorderly world of ours, full of contradictions, keeps going more or less because of explanations, by turns complex and ingenious, that seem to justify it and render it acceptable to the majority of mankind. Such explanations account for one kind of experiment. It must be remarked, however, that what is involved is a "ready-made" experiment and that while it may give rise to brilliant analyses, this experiment is not itself based on an analysis of its own real circumstances.

Future society will develop an experiment that will be the fruit of a profound analysis, whose perspectives are being outlined under our very eyes.

It is thanks to a rigorous preliminary analysis that pictorial experiment as I understand it can now be set up. This pictorial experiment confirms my faith in life's unexpected possibilities.

All these overlooked things that are coming to light lead me to believe that our happiness, as well, depends on an enigma concerning man, and that our only duty is to attempt to understand it.

—René Magritte, lecture given November 20, 1938, at the Musée Royal des Beaux-Arts, Antwerp. A later abridged version, La Ligne de Vie II, *dates from February 1940*

The True Art of Painting

The effects of the art of painting are as numerous as the possible ways of understanding and practicing it.

The earliest drawings of prehistoric times required an immense mental effort from the caveman, not only to conceive them, but also to *dare* to conceive them despite the prejudices that held sway.

It is extremely likely that the first draftsman was killed for practicing black magic, and afterwards, when people had grown used to it, other draftsmen probably came to be regarded as gods, and finally, in the dawning age of heraldry, as mere disseminators of information.

In the twentieth century, these different prehistoric ways of understanding the art of painting persist. The painter who desires spiritual freedom still encounters widespread hostility, the official painter is an honored figure, the commercial painter is a salaried employee commissioned to decorate bordellos, churches, department store windows, advertising posters, and other means of modern propaganda.

Archaeology, both past and present, made note of all the methods of painting. But this reckoning is not very useful to someone who is looking for a manner of painting that would be useful to mankind.

The art of painting is an art of thinking, and its existence emphasizes the importance to life of the human body's eyes; the sense of sight is actually the only one concerned in painting.

The goal of the art of painting is to perfect sight through a pure visual perception of the exterior world by means of sight alone. A picture conceived with this goal in mind is a means of replacing nature's awesome spectacles, which generally require only a mechanical functioning of the eye because of the familiarity that obscures such repetitious or predictable natural phenomena. On the other hand, should nature suddenly take on a threatening aspect, it is not only sight but also the other senses—hearing, smell, touch, taste—that help throw us into a state of panic hardly conducive to our making fruitful contact with the exterior world.

Thus we see that a painter is mediocre if he doesn't give special consideration to the importance of his spectators' eyes. One example of a mediocre painting would be one executed to flatter a rich banker's patriotic sentiments and libidinous proclivities. It might show the banker before an unfurled flag, one arm brandishing an unsheathed sword and the other holding a lovely, swooning woman, her flesh revealed by a dress that has been torn by some routed barbarian. Clearly sight plays no especial role in such a painting: it presents the same painful spectacle as the sight of the door to a safe. The painting may be useful to the banker as an erotic or heroic stimulant, but these utterly banal excitements do not allow for a pure visual perception of the exterior world.

A less mediocre painter, one who recognized that the sole aim of painting is to involve the sense of sight, would still misunderstand this aim if he executed a painting like the following: a blindfolded man walking through a forest is being approached by a murderer armed with a knife. This would be a mistake, because although the man's sight would be necessary for his survival, it only becomes important at this moment of danger due to a temporary feeling of anxiety. This picture would mean that if it weren't for the murderer the man's sight would be less important.

Modified, the same subject could give way to the following: a blindfolded man walking through a forest (without a murderer). In this case the importance of the man's sense of sight would undoubtedly be called into question, but not as effectively as it would if the spectator's own eyes were given the opportunity to realize their full potential.

To achieve this result, the painter must invent his pictures and bring them to completion under very difficult circumstances. He must start off with a contempt for fame and thus forgo the material comforts that might enable him to work in peace. He must have contempt for fame, since in order to win that fame he would have to paint mediocre pictures like those described earlier. Fame will come on its own, or it won't. (The fame of Da Vinci, Galileo, [or] Mozart adds nothing to their achievements.)

In addition to a life subject to ridicule, insult, or worse (since he will be considered a humbug or degenerate), the painter is constantly faced with professional problems because his way of understanding and practicing the art of true painting obeys an implacable law: the perfect picture does not allow for meditation, which is a feeling as banal and uninteresting as patriotism, eroticism, etc. The perfect picture produces an intense effect only for a brief moment, and the feelings that recall the initial response are to a greater or lesser degree mitigated by habit. This inexorable law forces the painter to outdo himself with each new picture, not in the sense of some futile elaboration but rather as a productive renewal. In accordance with this law, the spectator must be disposed to experience a moment of unique awareness and to admit his powerlessness to prolong it. This unique contact for the spectator takes place in front of the picture (the first spectator is the painter himself), and it is vital at the moment this contact is made that the picture not be divorced from the wall on which it is hung, the floor, the ceiling, the spectator, or from anything else that exists.

The special problems the painter must resolve are psychological in nature. The painter must not allow himself to be led astray by the technique of the art of painting, which has been further complicated by the succession of different manners of painting that have emerged over the past century. The caveman's simple linear representation was replaced by the same representation increasingly perfected so as to fill in the body's outline with its apparent volume. The science of perspective and the study of anatomy placed at the painter's dis-

180. *La place au soleil (The Place in the Sun)*. 1956. Gouache, 6¼ x 8⅛" (16 x 20.5 cm). Galerie Isy Brachot, Brussels, Belgium

posal infallible means for achieving trompe l'oeil effects to the point where easy experiments can leave no room for doubt of this fact.

About 1900, at the moment when this technique had reached perfection, it became clear that it was operating in a vacuum: the countless landscapes and portraits were unable, despite their numbers, to inspire anything but boredom.

The century began with discoveries that replaced old techniques with new ones in every field of endeavor. Painters, tired of lifeless painting, joined in the general infatuation with technique and attempted to give painting renewed youth. The cinema showed them images in motion on a screen, and this astonishing novelty incited them to compete with it. Unfortunately, the problem was badly posed. The technique of the art of painting having been perfected, it was useless to seek painting's rejuvenation in still another technique. In fact, a perfect technique of the art of painting was available, but it was being used without intelligence or effectiveness while the clumsy technique of the newborn art of cinema still derived its effects from its novelty.

So painters, misunderstanding the problem of painting, cast about for new techniques, and through them managed to restore to painting a few fleeting moments of superficial vitality. The Impressionists, Cubists, Futurists, all experienced moments of agitation and excitement due to original techniques, but they were futile, since these same moments of agitation and excitement could be achieved, and better, through other means than those related to painting.

Now that these technical experiments have come to an end (along with their successors such as abstract or nonfigurative art, Constructivism, Orphism, etc.), the technical problem can be posed to the painter correctly as a function of the desired result; and the great importance of technique, assuming one has mastered it, can be restored to its proper proportions as a *means*.

Since the true goal of the art of painting is to conceive and execute paintings that are able to give the viewer a pure visual perception of the exterior world, the painter must not contravene the natural workings of the eye, which sees objects according to a universal visual code: for example, the eye perceives the object "sky" as a blue surface. If the painter wishes to give a pure visual perception of the sky, he must employ a blue surface, adopting all the visual characteristics of that surface (nuances, perspective, luminosity, etc.). This presents no technical problem to the painter who has mastered the technique necessary to represent this blue surface, which, for the sense of sight, is all that is needed to depict the sky. However, it does present a psychological problem: how can the sky be represented according to the desired result? What should be done with the sky? There are some fine possibilities open to us; we have only to know how to use them. Some solutions will be found in the painter's technique, while others are better suited to the cinematographic technique, which is also capable of creating pure visual perception. Thus, the idea of an immobile flash of lightning can be of little help to a painter, since this image in a painting would be associated with the idea of its flashing movement; whereas on a screen, by means of simple trick photography, the spectator could see a stroke of lightning immobilized in a tumultuous sky. In this regard, the cinema ideally should, like painting, obey the psychological law mentioned earlier and only show a stroke of lightning long enough for the eyes to register its immobility, because once this moment has passed the lightning's immobility will become devoid of any interest.

For the painter, the search for ways to convey the sky, a pipe, a woman, a tree, or any other object, is his principal labor. This work is carried out in total obscurity, even though [the painter] must protect his sense of freedom within his obscurity if he wants to keep from being carrie off course by the magnetic pull of chance.

——*René Magritte,* Le Véritable Art de Peindre, *1949*

I am thinking of further researches, because the idea I had about what could make certa pictures valid. Their realization depended on th exactness of the solutions found for the problem that had been posed, in the following manne once an object or any subject had been chose as a question, another object had to be found answer, one secretly linked to the first by comple bonds so as to verify the answer. If the answe asserted itself, self-evident, the union of the tw objects was striking. . . .

The researches that led up to these revelatior were undertaken, I realize now, to find a unilatera irreversible meaning in some objects. Althoug the answers clarify the questions, the questior do not clarify the answers. If the dagger is th answer to the rose, the rose is not the answer t the dagger; neither is water to the boat, nor th piano to the ring. This verification allows us to g on to investigate the answers that are also ques tions, resolved by the objects that originall played the role of questions. Is this possible? seems to demand that the human will attain tha quality Edgard [sic] Poe attributes to divin works, "where cause and effect are reversible." we can conceive this quality, it is perhaps nc impossible for us to attain it through a process c enlightenment.

——*René Magritte,* La Carte d'Après Nature, *no. 1, October 1952*

I had a little idea: instead of writing a strange wor under an object, I thought of trying to paint a plur on a pear, or something else, such as a locc motive on a recumbent lion, etc.

——*Letter from René Magritte to Mirabelle Dors and Maurice Rapin February 14, 1956*

I'm also sending you a sketch of a variant of *La place au soleil (The Place in the Sun).* It occurs to me that this image could be joined successfull with a volume of *La Femme Assise (The Seated Woman)**. Be joined with, not illustrate.

——*Letter from René Magritte to Mirabelle Dors and Maurice Rapin February 24, 1956*

*By Guillaume Apollinaire

I'm continuing *La place au soleil.* The latest thing I've done is the delineation of the Egyptian scribe on a lovely apple.

——*Letter from René Magritte to Mirabelle Dors and Maurice Rapin March 13, 1956*

I would reproduce six different paintings* of *La place au soleil,* including:

The scribe "on" the apple

Botticelli's *Primavera* "on" a bowler-hatted individual seen from behind

Gérard's *Madame Recamier* "on" her chair

A bird "on" a leaf, and two other pictures whose objects remain to be found. . . .

The *origin* that I *know* for *La place au soleil* was an often overlooked "chance." On sketches we often see indications that remind the painter of what he has seen: one painter, for example, *writes* "pale green, red," etc., on his sketches. On a map

181. Pen sketch in a letter from René Magritte to Mirabelle Dors and Maurice Rapin, February 24, 1956

183. Drawing for *Le bouquet tout fait (Ready-Made Bouquet)*. n.d. Collection Robert Rauschenberg, New York, New York

182. *La place au soleil (The Place in the Sun)*. 1956. Oil on canvas, 19⅝ x 25⅝" (50 x 65 cm). Private collection, Brussels, Belgium

made to give directions, we write: "road to . . . square, theater, etc. . . ." On an architect's plan: "room, corridor, garden, etc. . . ."

The words written on drawings are not put there without some mental process. "Chance" intervenes when one realizes one can write words on a drawing not to "inform," but just to write them, to describe a drawing on which words are written. And these words are not meant to be decorative motifs, but rather to be joined with images—to the extent of words that mean what they designate; to the extent of images that represent objects. . . .

La place au soleil is an "objective stimulation," if you like, with the difference that the image placed "on" another takes on an even stranger character: instead of an apple "on" the same apple, we have a scribe.

—*Letter from René Magritte to Mirabelle Dors and Maurice Rapin, March 21, 1956*

*For a book whose title, *La Place au Soleil*, would relate to these new images.

I have continued my *Places au soleil* [sic], but see how the title is no longer good for a big tree in the evening on which one sees a crescent moon! In this case, we are given a better, or in any event another, description of *La place au soleil:* what we see on one object is another object hidden by the one that comes between us and the hidden object.

—*Letter from René Magritte to Mirabelle Dors and Maurice Rapin, April 20, 1956*

I have just painted the moon on a tree in the blue-gray colors of evening. Scutenaire has come up with a very beautiful title: *Le seize septembre (September Sixteenth)*. I think it "fits," so from September 16th on, we'll call it done.

—*Letter from René Magritte to Mirabelle Dors and Maurice Rapin, August 6, 1956*

One can question the obligation to experience a feeling "determined" by what we look at. Something familiar is sometimes seen with a feeling of strangeness, and we can have a familiar feeling with regard to so-called mysterious things. In both possibilities, one finds the union either of a feeling of strangeness, the familiar object, and ourselves, or of a familiar feeling, the mysterious object, and ourselves. This does not imply that our feelings are "determined," nor that the painter can decide which feeling a painting ought to inspire. It should be noted in this regard that everything that is "determined" (or rather is considered to be) conspicuously lacks charm and interest: we don't really like a picture upon learning what it has allegedly "determined." It is immediately "lost sight of" in favor of a tedious and irrelevant commentary.

The feeling we experience while looking at a picture cannot be separated from either the picture or ourselves. The feeling, the picture, we, are joined in our mystery.

—Letter from René Magritte to Paul Colinet, 1957

If painting were obliged to express emotions or set forth ideas, I would express neither optimism nor its opposite.

We cannot be too unsure of the effectiveness of our so-called power of expression. What we feel when looking at a painting, or when looking into a blue distance, for example, does not imply that we are "determined" by what appears to us. Yet painting—like the blue distance and everything else—reveals images of the world, and it can happen that in looking at them, painting them, thinking about them, we have this unfamiliar feeling of our mystery—one we also have sometimes with our eyes closed.

—Letter from René Magritte to Paul Colinet, 1957

Things are neither as simple nor as complicated; in my opinion, the *theme* consists of the following: *a picture inside out*—whatever the subject it represents in this way—within something (like a landscape) right side out. One version of the picture *Le réveille-matin (The Alarm Clock)* would be possible by representing a face (or a landscape) on the inside-out picture. But if I paint on an easel representing, for example, an afternoon sky (right side out) against a nocturnal sky (right side out), it's another "theme," although there's still a picture and an easel.

I'm called a "Surrealist," but I don't worry about it. I sometimes care about stating clearly certain ideas that are completely useless. I consider "wasting one's time" in this way is as good as another. Like everyone, I believed in the existence of the "unconscious" as though I really needed to believe in it. I've given that and other things up without feeling diminished or extended and without becoming simpler or more complicated.

—Letter from René Magritte to Defosse, February 3, 1958

"Large formats." Their dimensions alone produce an "effect." Any idiot's picture enlarged on a 50-yard-high surface set up in a field would create a sensational "effect." I am wary of such an effect, and that of miniatures. . . .

The question of "going beyond" art seems to exist on a level that means nothing to me. I "paint pictures," officially I am an *artiste-peintre*. I'm neither this side nor the other of artistic thought: I think I'm somewhere else.

—Letter from René Magritte to Maurice Rapin, March 31, 1958

Attached are the replies I made during an interview that's supposed to be broadcast. I hope they amuse you. Yours, René Magritte.

1. René Magritte, at this moment an exhibition of your paintings is being held at the Museum of Ixelles. I believe it's a retrospective, isn't it?

Yes, it is. The Museum of Ixelles has hung almost a hundred pictures chosen from among those painted from 1926 to fairly recently.

2. How do you feel when you see your works again some time after having painted them?

My feeling is that I didn't do too badly in painting pictures that can surprise me as though I hadn't actually created them.

3. Don't you feel somewhat paternal when you see such a large exhibition of your work?

Of course, but with the perplexity of a father who doesn't really know why his children turned out so beautiful or ugly.

4. If you, the painter, are perplexed when you look at your paintings, it's understandable that people visiting your exhibition are confused, especially if they have some aesthetic preference for painters they feel they can more easily understand.

It's not only understandable, but I think it demonstrates that if certain things seem familiar or "nonperplexing" to us, it's because of notions that make them pass as such. I've taken care to paint precisely those pictures that don't have a familiar look and have nothing to do with naïve or sophisticated notions.

5. One could say, then, that you avoid like the plague expressing ideas in your painting?

I avoid it as much as possible. I feel that words express enough ideas, sometimes very beautiful ones but all too frequently tedious, without painting having to add its own. As I see it, painting is not meant to express ideas, even ideas of genius. If the painter has genius, he has a genius for images, not for ideas.

6. But don't the titles of your paintings evoke ideas?

Perhaps, since even a misunderstood word can evoke the idea that there is meaning. But the words we do understand do not always necessarily evoke ideas. The title of a picture is an image made up of words. It joins up with a painted image without trying to satisfy a need to understand ideas. The title and the picture enrich and refine thought, which enjoys images whose meaning is unknown.

7. I'm tempted to ask you why thought enjoys images with unknown meanings?

It seems obvious that enigmas and puzzles are appealing to thought. The game consists in finding what is hidden. But the game has nothing to do with images whose meanings remain unknown. I believe that thought enjoys the unknown, that is to say, what is unknowable, since the meaning of thought itself is unknown.

—Letter from René Magritte to André Bosmans, April 16, 1959

The pictorial language, like other languages, evokes mystery de facto if not de jure.

I try—insofar as possible—to paint pictures that evoke mystery with the precision and charm necessary to the realm of thought. It's obvious that

184. *Le réveil-matin (The Alarm Clock).* 1953. Oil on canvas, 20½ x 24⅝" (52 x 62.5 cm). Private collection, Rome, Italy

this precise and charming evocation of mystery is composed of images of familiar objects, brought together or transformed in such a way that they no longer satisfy our naïve or sophisticated notions.

In coming to know these images, we discover the precision and charm that are lacking in the "real" world in which they appear.

—*René Magritte, Preface to exhibition catalogue,* René Magritte, *Musée d'Ixelles, April 19, 1959*

An image (after having been conceived with the sole intention of creating a beautiful image) can be successfully joined with a text. . . . The word "illustration" should be eliminated. It is the "joining" of an existing text with an image chosen from among preexisting images that establishes the felicitous encounter between images and words. . . .

—*Letter from René Magritte to André Bosmans, May 11, 1959*

This manner [of representing the image] is indispensable, otherwise there is no visible representation of the image. What is superfluous and best avoided are the originality, fantasy, and awkwardness that can become part of the manner.

—*Letter from René Magritte to André Bosmans, October 1960*

Have thought some more about the "art of mime." It must be avoided as far as possible. Mime "expresses" emotions (if one indeed recognizes a certain facial expression as expressing a specific emotion, as taught us by convention).

If you could tell Dallas that my painting is wholly alien to anything conventional, it would be wonderful, but would it be difficult to say? Especially since in Dallas they seem so taken with the notion of mimicry!

I'm giving you a lot of problems, but fortunately they are only those befitting a magnificent and outstanding ambassador.

—*Letter from René Magritte to Harry Torczyner, October 21, 1960*

I'm happy to learn that you put "squarely" to Dallas what I thought about comparing mime and my painting. I particularly maintain that my painting *expresses nothing* (nor do other paintings, for that matter). Just because painting corresponds to (or engenders) some of our feelings doesn't mean it expresses them. To believe it expresses feeling would be to admit, for example, that an onion expresses the tears we shed when peeling it. The tear-onion peeling relationship is an obvious and inevitable one (except for those with blocked tear ducts). The painting-emotion relationship is just as clear (except for the blind or the wooden). But the conclusion—onion expressing tears or painting-onion the emotions we feel upon looking at it—is one of those mistaken notions whose elimination is a utopian dream. (A brave man asked me only yesterday, "What painting 'expresses' joy?"! With all the goodwill in the world, I was unable to make him understand that it was the painting he took joy in looking at.)

—*Letter from René Magritte to Harry Torczyner, October 24, 1960*

As for the onion story—written in a letter—if it is to be printed. I think it should be "cleaned up" as follows:

There is a mistaken idea about painting that is very widespread—namely, that painting has the power to express emotion, something of which it is certainly incapable. It is possible that one may be moved while looking at a painting, but to deduce by this that the picture expresses an emotion is like saying, for example, that a cake "expresses" the baker's feelings and expresses the pleasure we derive from tasting it. . . . (I've replaced onion with cake, thereby avoiding the objection that the onion is not [like the picture] a manmade object.)

—*Letter from René Magritte to Harry Torczyner, November 1960*

Mr. McAgy has unintentionally given me the opportunity to clear up this question of "expression": a mime doubtless "expresses" emotions, if one agrees that this or that grimace is the expression of this or that feeling. Without forgetting that the mime is not expressing his own feelings—in fact, he can express goodness and yet be wicked and thoroughly incapable of a good action—without forgetting this, can we still believe that what he is expressing deserves to be called an expression of goodness? And what interest does this kind of caricature of expression have?

—*Letter from René Magritte to Harry Torczyner, November 14, 1960*

Resemblance—as the word is used in everyday language—is attributed to things that have or do not have qualities in common. People say "they resemble each other like two drops of water," and they say just as easily that the imitation resembles the original. This so-called resemblance consists of relationships of similarity and is distinguished by the mind, which examines, evaluates, and compares. Such mental processes are carried out without being aware of anything other than possible similarities. To this awareness things reveal only their similar qualities.

Resemblance is part of the essential mental process: that of resembling. Thought "resembles" by becoming what the world presents to it, and by restoring what it has been offered to the mystery without which there would be no possibility of either world or thought. Inspiration is the result of the emergence of resemblance.

The art of painting—when not construed as a relatively harmless hoax—can neither expound ideas nor express emotions. The image of a weeping face does not express sorrow, nor does it articulate the idea of sorrow: ideas and emotions have no visible form.

I particularly like this idea that my paintings *say nothing.* (Neither, by the way, do other paintings.)

There is a mistaken idea about painting that is very widespread—namely, that painting has the power to express emotion, something of which is certainly incapable. Emotions do not have an concrete form that could be reproduced in pain

It is possible that one may be moved whil looking at a painting, but to deduce by this that th picture "expresses" that emotion is like sayin that, for example, a cake "expresses" the idea and emotions of those of us who see it or eat it, c again, that the cake "expresses" the thought of the chef while baking a good cake. (To th man who asked me, "Which is the picture that 'ex presses' joy?" I could only answer "The one tha gives you joy to see.")

The art of painting—which actually should b called the art of resemblance—enables us to de scribe in painting a thought that has the potentia of becoming visible. This thought includes onl those images the world offers: people, curtains weapons, stars, solids, inscriptions, etc. Re semblance spontaneously unites these figures i an order that immediately evokes mystery.

The description of such a thought need not b original. Originality or fantasy would only add weakness and poverty. The precision and charm of an image of resemblance depend on the re semblance, and not on some imaginative manne of describing it.

"How to paint" the description of the resem blance must be strictly confined to spreading col ors on a surface in such a way that their effective aspect recedes and allows the image of re semblance to emerge.

An image of resemblance shows all that there is, *namely, a group of figures that implies nothing* To try to interpret—in order to exercise some sup posed freedom—is to misunderstand an inspired image and to substitute for it a gratuitous interpre tation, which, in turn, can become the subject c an endless series of superfluous interpretations.

An image is not to be confused with any aspec of the world or with anything tangible. The image of bread and jam is obviously not edible, and b the same token taking a piece of bread and jan and showing it in an exhibition of paintings in nc way alters its effective aspect. It would be absurc to believe [this appearance] capable of giving rise to the description of any thought whatsoever The same may be said in passing to be true o paint spread about or thrown on a canvas whether for pleasure or for some private purpose

An image of resemblance never results from the illustration of a "subject," whether banal or extraordinary, nor from the expression of an idea or an emotion. *Inspiration gives the painter what must be painted:* that resemblance that is a thought capable of becoming visible through painting—for example, an idea the component terms of which are a piece of bread and jam and the inscription, "This is not bread and jam"; or further, an idea composed of a nocturnal landscape beneath a sunlit sky. De jure such images suggest mystery, whereas de facto the mystery would be suggested only by the slice of bread and jam or the nocturnal scene under a starry sky.

However, all images that contradict "commonsense" do not necessarily evoke mystery de jure. Contradiction can only arise from a manner of thought whose vitality depends on the possibility

RENÉ MAGRITTE

97, RUE DES MIMOSAS, BRUXELLES 3

TÉL. 15.97.30

Après avoir suivi les cours de l'Académie des Beaux Arts, en 1916 et 1917, j'ai cherché avec les moyens dont je disposais comment peindre des tableaux qui ne me soient pas indifférents (la peinture dite "d'expression de sentiments" me laissant indifférent, et, d'autre part, la peinture bornée aux effets picturaux purement formels ne me paraissant pas valoir la peine d'être regardée) j'ai essayé avec l'aide des théories futuristes, cubistes et dadaïstes — de peindre d'une manière satisfaisante — Ce fut une période de recherches qui a duré près de dix années, sans être convaincantes.

C'est vers 1926 que ces diverses recherches ont été abandonnées grâce à ce que je considère comme étant la révélation de ce qu'il fallait peindre : ce qu'il fallait peindre était ce qu'il faut peindre à présent, en 1962. Ce qu'il faut peindre se borne à une pensée qui peut être décrite par la peinture. Étant donné que les sentiments et les idées n'ont aucune apparence visuelle, cette pensée (qui peut être décrite par la peinture et devenir visible) ne comprend aucune idée ni aucun sentiment. Elle s'identifie à ce que le monde apparent offre à notre conscience. Cependant, cette pensée n'a pas la passivité d'un miroir : elle est éminemment active, elle unit dans l'ordre qui évoque le mystère du monde et de la pensée — les figures du monde apparent : ciels, personnes, rideaux, inscriptions, solides, etc. Il est à remarquer que cette pensée (qui vaut la peine d'être décrite par la peinture) n'"assemble" pas n'importe quoi, ne "compose" pas : elle unit les choses de telle sorte que ces choses visibles évoquent le mystère sans lequel il n'y aurait rien. Comme exemples, un paysage nocturne sous un ciel ensoleillé et une montagne en forme d'oiseau, (d'autre part) démontrent que la peinture — telle que je la conçois — n'est pas orientée par des recherches formelles, mais concerne la pensée, exclusivement par son manque de solution de continuité avec le monde et son mystère.

René Magritte

le 20 Mars — 1962

of contradiction. Inspiration has nothing to do with either bad or good will. Resemblance is an inspired thought that cares neither about naïveté nor sophistication. Reason and absurdity are necessarily its opposites.

It is with words that titles are given to images. But these words cease being familiar or strange once they have aptly named the images of resemblance. Inspiration is necessary to say them or hear them.

—*René Magritte, statement in exhibition catalogue* René Magritte in America, *the Dallas Museum for Contemporary Arts and The Museum of Fine Arts of Houston, 1960*

. . . the word *illustrator* (here in its true sense: one who renders illustrious) also means in other cases something we should be wary of. An image that accompanies a text—if it is valid—is never an "illustration," and it never results from an illustrator's procedure. Yes, there are sometimes pleasant illustrations, but they add nothing to the text illustrated. However, an image conceived with no thought other than its conception can felicitously *join* a text and enrich it by accompanying it. Then it's not a question of illustration, nor of pleasant art.

—*Letter from René Magritte to Pierre Demarne, July 22, 1961*

185. Autobiographical statement by René Magritte, March 20, 1962. *See* Appendix *for translation*

186. *L'idole (The Idol).* 1965. Oil on canvas, 21¼ x 25⅝" (54 x 65 cm). Private collection, Washington, D.C.

APPENDIX/TRANSLATIONS

This appendix contains English translations of the fifty-one letters and documents printed in facsimile in the text either in whole or in part. The figure number of each facsimile illustration, together with the number of the page on which it appears, has been provided for each item in this appendix.

1 Fig. 13 (page 20)
Letter from René Magritte to Paul Colinet, 1957

Latest idea; *Hope is well-being*
Dear Friend,
30 rue Paul Spaak. 30—3+0 = 3—3×3 = 9
The die is cast, we are leaving *Jette* on the 18th.
You will have already noticed that 18 consists of 1 and 8, thus 1+8=9.
You will also, I'm sure, have noticed that the *home* we are living in is 1 *home,* the one we left makes another 1, and the one we are moving to another 1. Together, they make 3 *homes,* and the number 3 multiplied by itself gives 9.
(The number in brackets is the same as the 9-month formation of a baby.)
Fine. The *home* we left in Paris before we moved to Jette was number 201, or 2+0+1=3, 3x3=9
Our *home* in Jette was 135—1+3+5=9
The *home* we will soon be in bears the number 207—2+0+7=9
The number 9, multiplied by itself, gives 81, and 8+1=9
What do you think?
It's on the Boulevard Lambermont, Brussels, 3, thus 3x3=9
Would you work out a formula for changing addresses that I could have printed up for distribution? For and until Friday evening, or 11 o'clock with the [?]?
I hope,

Mag.

2 Fig. 16 (page 21)
Letter (excerpt) from René Magritte to Maurice Rapin, December 20, 1957, showing floor plan of the Magritte house at 97 rue des Mimosas, Brussels, Belgium

The house I've just rented is also a question mark. Since my wedding, I've always lived in apartments. Will I be too "calm" there?
Here's the plan for the ground floor:

tree tree

No. 97, rue des Mimosas (Brussels III)

tree tree tree

There will be a guest room and I hope you'll use it when vacation time comes.

A house is fine in some ways, but I recall an *unreadable* book by Souvestre (the brother of the author of FANTÔMAS), called *A Garret Philosopher,* and I'd like just to live in a room or a garret like the one Souvestre describes. I think it must be a really perfect pleasure to read FANTÔMAS in such a dwelling.

Until soon dear friend,
yours,
René Magritte

[*The words in the floor plan are*]
pine tree, gate to the garden, easel, piano, dining room, hall, kitchen, toilet, and fence.

3 Fig. 45 (page 39)
Letter from René Magritte to Harry Torczyner, April 22, 1965

22 ~~August~~ April 1965

Dear Friend,
I got your letter of April 17 with great pleasure: it's the first sign we've had of the existence of a land other than this Italian isle. Until now, it's been awfully cold here in the "land of sun." I don't know whether the benefits of the treatment aren't being compromised by the unsatisfactory temperature that prevails here. (The hotel doesn't have heat.) From a gastronomical point of view, there are astonishing "surprises" *ex contrario:* stringy chicken comes covered with a mound of raw spinach. "Cream of vegetable" soup is hard to tell from wallpaper paste. We are said to be in the best hotel in Casamicciola. I think we got here too early: the good season (if it's not a myth) will appear after our return to Brussels.
As for the cure, it lasts for a good hour: 1st, a mudbath; 2nd, a bath in mountain water; 3rd, rest; 4th, massage. This takes place at around 8 AM on an empty stomach. There hasn't been any improvement as yet in the health *status quo* that prevailed in Brussels. It's an effort for me to write, to sit, to lie down, etc.
I don't know what to tell you about filling requests for exhibitions. Kansas City, for example, ought perhaps to be canceled if the N.Y. museum has set a date that doesn't allow for organizing several exhibitions?
Georgette and I were very happy to hear your news. Our best wishes to you and Marcel [sic].

R.M.

(On the 16th I sent you an airmail card, and one to Suzi.)

4 Fig. 51 (page 44)
Letter from René Magritte to Harry Torczyner, September 18, 1965

18 September 1965

Dear Friend,
Your letter of the 15th contains a good question. Both good, and unfortunate: it makes me understand better Soby's ideas, which aren't very "catholic." In-

deed, if there is any influence, it can be said that Chirico is responsible for it (since about 1925, the date when I first knew his work). For that matter, in a book on Max Ernst, Waldberg does not hide the fact that Ernst also underwent Chirico's influence. Max Ernst and I admit to it readily, but with a little bit of critical sense it is soon obvious that our "personalities" rapidly came to the fore and that our relationship to Chirico was no more than the one the other Surrealists shared to a greater or lesser degree, and in very different ways.

If it's a question of Max Ernst's influence, one has to talk about Frits van den Berghe, who was far from the Surrealist spirit; he only used the exterior aspect of Ernst's painting and in some people's eyes he passes for a "precursor of Surrealism in Belgium."

As for the books of Éluard and Ernst, I didn't know them until I met them in 1927. Then—as now—I was very little "in the know" about artistic goings on.

If one takes into consideration what I've painted since 1926 (*Le jockey perdu*—1926—for example, and what followed), I don't think one can talk about "Chirico's influence"—I was "struck" about 1925 when I saw a picture by Chirico: *Le chant d'amour*. If there is any influence—it's quite possible—there's no resemblance to Chirico's pictures in *Le jockey perdu*. In sum, the influence in question is limited to a great emotion, to a marvelous revelation when for the first time in my life I saw truly poetic painting. With time, I began to renounce researches into pictures in which the *manner of painting* was uppermost. Now, I know that since 1926 I've only worried about *what should be painted*. This became clear only some time after having "instinctively" sought what should be painted.

So there will be two drawings for Seitz and Lady X.

Until soon, dear Harry, and friendly greetings to you and Marcelle.

R.M.

5 Fig. 53 (page 46)
Letter (excerpt) from René Magritte (written in London) to Louis Scutenaire and Irène Hamoir, February 18, 1937

I'm writing to you since I suppose that since you're crippled up—as Scut tells me among his usual jokes—you won't be coming to London this weekend.

London is a revelation. Of course, I'm only just beginning to discover it. But until now, everything is perfect (of course I don't speak English, but "there's something"). Yesterday evening we went to visit Henry Moore, a charming sculptor, sort of Arp-Picasso, the son of a miner, with a young Russian wife ADMIRABLY stacked (a sort of robust wasp). I'm expecting Georgette this coming Friday. Maybe Colinet will come with her? The joker hasn't written me yet. What does this mean?

Until soon, my friends, with my best wishes—

Magritte

6 Fig. 56 (page 51)
Letter (excerpt) from René Magritte to Maurice Rapin, May 22, 1958

My latest picture began with the question: how to paint a picture with a glass of water as the subject? I drew a number of glasses of water:

[illustrations]

a line [illustration] always appeared in these drawings.

Then this line [illustration] became deformed [illustration] and took the form of an umbrella [illustration]. Then this umbrella was put into the glass [illustration], and finally the umbrella opened up and was placed under the glass of water [illustration]. Which I feel answers the initial question.

The picture so conceived is called:

Les vacances de Hegel

I think Hegel would have liked this object that has two contrary functions: to repel and contain water. Wouldn't that have amused him as we are amused when on vacation?

Your friend,
René Magritte

7 Fig. 57 (page 53)
Letter (excerpt) from René Magritte to Paul Colinet, 1957

... springs immediately to mind:

[illustration] blackboard

however, it's like the preceding title: however amusing, it's insufficient. Along the same lines:

[illustrations]

PTO

8 Fig. 76 (page 67)
Notes (complete) for an illustrated lecture given by René Magritte at the Marlborough Fine Art Gallery, London, February 1937

THE NAMING OF THINGS

Ladies and Gentlemen,

The demonstration we are about to embark upon will attempt to show some of the characteristics proper to words, to images, and to real objects.

(1) A word can replace an image:

Chapeau HAT.

(2) An image can replace a word. I will demonstrate this by using a text of André Breton, in which I will replace a word with an image:

	[illustration]
Si seulement	IF ONLY THE *SUN* WOULD SHINE TONIGHT.
(Jean Scutenaire)	*On ne peut pas* ONE CANNOT GIVE BIRTH TO A *FOAL* WITHOUT BEING ONE ONESELF [illustration]
Paul Éluard:	*Dans les plus sombres* yeux *se ferment les plus clairs*. THE DARKEST *EYES* ENCLOSE THE LIGHTEST. [illustration]
	[illustration]
(Paul Colinet)	*Il y a* THERE IS A *SPHERE* PLACED ON YOUR SHOULDERS.
David Gascoigne (Mesens)	*Masque de veuve* WIDOW'S *MASK* FOR THE WALTZ.
Humfrey [sic] Jennings	THE FLYING BREATH OF EDUCATION [illustration]

(3) A real object can replace a word:

Le pain du crime. THE *BREAD* OF CRIME.

(4) An undifferentiated form can replace a word:

Les naissent THE [illustration] ARE BORN IN WINTER.

(5) A word can act as an object:

Ce bouquet	THIS BOUQUET IS TRANSPARENT

(6) An image or an object can be designated by another name:

L'oiseau	[illustration]	THE BIRD
La montagne	[illustration]	THE MOUNTAIN
Voici le ciel	[illustration]	BEHOLD THE SKY (skaie) (dis is de skaye)

(7) Certain images have a secret affinity. This also holds true for the objects these images represent. Let us search for what should be said. We know the bird in a cage. Our interest is increased if we replace the bird with a fish, or with a slipper.

These images are strange. Unfortunately, they are arbitrary and fortuitous.

[illustrations]

However, it is possible to arrive at a new image that will stand up better beneath the spectator's gaze. A large egg in the cage seems to offer the required solution.

[illustration]

Now let us turn to the door. The door can open onto a landscape seen backwards.

The landscape can be represented on the door.

Let us try something less arbitrary: next to the door, let us make a hole in the wall that will be another door.

This juxtaposition will be improved if we reduce these two objects to one. Thus, the hole comes naturally to be in the door, and through this hole we see darkness.

This image can be further enhanced if we illuminate the invisible object hidden by darkness. Our gaze always tries to go further, to see the object, the reason for our existence.

Notes for an illustrated lecture given by René Magritte at the London Gallery, London, February 1937.

9 Fig. 77 (page 68)
***Les mots et les images (Words and Images).* Illustration in *La Révolution Surréaliste* (Paris), vol. 5, no. 12 (December 15, 1929), pp. 32–33**

WORDS AND IMAGES

[*first column*]

An object is not so linked to its name that we cannot find a more suitable one for it

[illustration]

Some objects can do without a name:

[illustration]

Often a word is only self-descriptive:

[illustration]

An object encounters its image, an object encounters its name. It can happen that the object's name and its image encounter each other:

[illustration]

Sometimes an object's name can replace an image:

[illustration]

A word can replace an object in reality:

[illustration]

[*second column*]

An image can replace a word in a statement:

[illustration]

An object makes one suppose there are other objects behind it:

[illustration]

Everything leads us to think that there is little relation between an object and what it represents:

[illustration]

Words that serve to designate two different objects do not reveal what can separate these objects from each other:

[illustration]

In a picture, words have the same substance as images:

[illustration]

In a picture, we see images and words differently:

[illustration]

[*third column*]

An undifferentiated form can replace the image of an object:

[illustration]

An object never performs the same function as its name or its image:

[illustration]

Now, in reality the visible outlines of objects touch each other, as if they formed a mosaic:

[illustration]

Vague figures have a necessary meaning that is as perfect as precise figures:

[illustration]

Written words in a picture often designate precise objects, and images vague objects:

[illustration]

Or the opposite:

[illustration]

René Magritte

10 Fig. 92 (page 75)
Letter from René Magritte to Harry Torczyner, August 19, 1960

August 19, 1960

Dear Friend,

I have received your letter of August 16th and the "special" documents. Thank you. I'll get in touch with the manager of the Mayfair, whose name has something Dutch about it.

I am happy to hear about the welcome you've given *Le tombeau des lutteurs*. The date 1944 shows that during that period the painting I envisaged—attempting to bring it into harmony with the Impressionist spirit—wasn't *always* (in 1954) in accord with that spirit. "My usual manner" was sometimes, rather always, there to testify that I would recover once and for all. The 1944 pictures, such as *Le tombeau des lutteurs,** were, in fact, painted in "my usual manner," which has since come to be the only one that I feel is truly necessary for painting, without fantasy or eccentricity, ideas already "sublime" enough that they do not need to be anything but a precise description. I firmly believe that a beautiful idea is ill served by being "interestingly" expressed: the interest being in the idea. Those ideas that need eloquence to "get across," for example, are incapable of making an effect on their own.

This is one of my convictions—which are often solely tested by all kinds of interpreters, who try to add something "of themselves" when they recite poems, paint pictures, etc.

At the moment, I'm waiting for you to be freed from the chains fastening you to your desk so that you can think about making a little trip to Belgium.

Best wishes to you and your family, who have my heartfelt feelings,

René Magritte

**Le tombeau des lutteurs* was, of course, painted in 1960

11 Fig. 100 (page 80)
Letter (excerpt) from René Magritte to Harry Torczyner, July 1958

I await your news. As for mine, the best I can do is tell you the solution to the problem of painting a picture with a chair as subject. I looked for a long time before realizing that the chair had to have a tail (which is more "striking" than the timid animal feet that chairs sometimes have). I'm very satisfied with this solution. What do you think?

Yours,
René Magritte

12 Fig. 122 (page 89)
Letter (excerpt) from René Magritte to Mirabelle Dors and Maurice Rapin, August 6, 1956

I have just painted the moon on a tree in the blue-gray colors of evening. Scutenaire has come up with a very beautiful title: *Le Seize Septembre*. I think it "fits," so from September 16th on, we'll call it done.

13 Fig. 152 (page 103)
Gouache study for an ashtray, *La métamorphose de l'objet (Metamorphosis of the Object),* 1933

[illustration]

Dear Lady Admirer,
Here's the bottom. If the person with ashtrays wants to put a border on it, he should simply put equal concentric circles on a white border: [illustration] the same white as in the drawing. I hope it will please you as much as Cleopatra pleased Bonaparte. Until one of these days soon. Yours, M

14 Fig. 173 (page 115)
Letter (excerpt) from René Magritte to Harry Torczyner, with pen sketch of *Le puits de vérité (The Well of Truth),* January 13, 1962

A while ago I sent Suzi the design of a new picture (a pant leg and a shoe), asking her what she would call it.

[illustration]

The title has finally been found: *L'étalon* [*The Standard*] (in the sense of the immutable—almost—unity of measurement.

15 Fig. 185 (page 133)
Autobiographical statement by René Magritte, March 20,1962

After having taken courses at the Académie des Beaux-Arts in 1916 and 1917, I tried with the means I possessed to find a way to paint pictures that would interest me (I was indifferent to the paintings said to "express feelings," and, on the other hand, painting restricted to purely formal pictorial effects didn't seem to me worth looking at), and I tried—with the help of Futurist, Cubist, and Dadaist theories—to paint in a way that would satisfy. That was a research period that lasted for nearly ten years, without reaching any conclusion. About 1926, these various investigations were abandoned because of what I deem to have been the revelation of *what was to be painted: what was to be painted was what must be painted now, in 1962*. What must be painted is limited to a thought that can be described in painting. Given the fact that feelings and ideas have no visible appearance, this thought (which can be described by painting and therefore becomes visible) includes no idea and no feeling. It is like what the apparent world offers to our awareness—Yet this thought is not passive, like a mirror: it is highly ordered, it unites—in the order evocative of the world's mystery and of thought—figures from the apparent world: skies, characters, curtains, inscriptions, solids, etc.—It should be noted that this thought (which is worth describing in painting) does not "assemble" just anything, it doesn't "compose": it unites objects in such a way that visible objects evoke the mystery without which there would be nothing. As examples, a nocturnal landscape beneath a sunny sky and, on the other hand, a mountain shaped like a bird, both demonstrate that painting—as I conceive it—is not guided by formal researches, but involves thought, exclusively because of its lack of solution of the world's continuity and mystery.

René Magritte
March 20, 1962

MAGRITTE/CHRONOLOGY

1898 René-François-Ghislain Magritte born November 21 in Lessines, in the Belgian province of Hainaut, the son of Léopold and Régina Magritte (née Bertinchamp)

1910 the Magrittes move to Châtelet (Hainaut), where René studies drawing

1912 Magritte's mother commits suicide by drowning in the River Sambre. René studies at the Lycée Athénée

1913 Magritte, his father, and his brothers Raymond and Paul settle in Charleroi. Magritte meets the thirteen-year-old Georgette Berger at a fair

1916-18 Magritte studies, intermittently, at the Académie Royale des Beaux-Arts in Brussels

1918 The Magritte family moves to Brussels. René works in Pierre Flouquet's studio and discovers Futurism

1920 First exhibition in Brussels at the Galerie Le Centre d'Art

1921 Military service

1922 Magritte marries Georgette Berger. Works as a designer in a wallpaper factory with the painter Victor Servranckx. Together they write *L'art pur: Défense de l'esthétique* (unpublished). Magritte discovers De Chirico's painting *Le chant d'amour (The Song of Love,* 1914). Magritte's paintings are influenced by Cubism, Futurism, and abstract art. He makes poster designs and advertising sketches

1926 Paints *Le jockey perdu (The Lost Jockey)* and receives a contract from the Galerie le Centaure in Brussels. In one year, he paints sixty canvases

1927 First one-man exhibition at the Galerie Le Centaure is unfavorably received. Moves to Le Perreux-sur-Marne, near Paris. Plays an active role in the Parisian Surrealist circle and shows his work at Camille Goemans' gallery the following year

1929 Publishes "Les mots et les images" ("Words and Images") in *La Révolution Surréaliste*. Visits Dali in Cadaqués, Spain

1930 Magritte returns to Belgium and resides at 135 rue Esseghem in Jette-Brussels

1936 First one-man exhibition in the United States at the Julien Levy Gallery, New York

1937 Stays for three weeks in London at the home of Edward James

1938 First one-man show in London at the London Gallery. On December 10 Magritte delivers a lecture entitled "La Ligne de Vie" ("The Lifeline") in Antwerp

1940 Joins the exodus of Belgians following the German invasion of May 19. Spends three months in Carcassonne, France, before returning to Georgette in Brussels

1943-45 Attempts Surrealist paintings "in full sunlight," employing the technique of the Impressionists

1945 Joins and abandons the Communist Party

1948 Fauvist period Magritte calls "l'époque vache"

1952-53 Paints *Le domaine enchanté (The Enchanted Domain),* a series of eight panels later enlarged under his supervision for murals at the Casino Communal Knokke-Le Zoute, Belgium

1954 Retrospective at the Palais des Beaux-Arts, Brussels. Writes "La pensée et les images" ("Thought and Images") for the catalogue

1956 Awarded the Guggenheim Prize for Belgium

1957 Moves to 97 rue des Mimosas, Brussels-Schaerbeek. Paints *La fée ignorante (The Ignorant Fairy),* the design for a mural in the Palais des Beaux-Arts at Charleroi, later executed under his supervision

1960 Retrospective exhibitions at the Dallas Museum for Contemporary Arts and The Museum of Fine Arts, Houston. Luc de Heusch makes a film with and about Magritte entitled *La leĉon des choses, ou Magritte* premiered April 7, 1960

1961 Designs and supervises a mural for the Palais des Congrès, Brussels, entitled *Les barricades mystérieuses (The Mysterious Barricades).* Writes "Le rappel à l'ordre ("The Call to Order"), *Rhétorique* no. 1, May 1961

1962 Writes "La leçon des choses" ("The Object Lesson") *Rhétorique,* no. 4, January 1962. Exhibition at the Walker Art Center, Minneapolis

1964 Writes "Ma conception de l'art de peindre" ("My Conception of the Art of Painting"), *Rhétorique,* no. 11 May 1964. Exhibition at the Arkansas Art Center, Little Rock

1965 Retrospective at The Museum of Modern Art, New York. Georgette and René Magritte visit the United States for the first time

1966 René and Georgette Magritte visit Israel

1967 Exhibition at the Museum Boymans-van Beuningen in Rotterdam. Magritte dies on August 15. Exhibition at the Moderna Museet, Stockholm

1969 Retrospective exhibitions at The Tate Gallery, London; Kestner-Gesellschaft, Hanover; and Kunsthaus, Zurich

1971 Exhibition at the National Museum of Modern Art, Tokyo, which travels to the National Museum of Modern Art, Kyoto

1973 Retrospective loan exhibition at Marlborough Fine Art, London

1976 Exhibition at the Institute for the Arts, Rice University, Houston

1977 Exhibition, "René Magritte: Ideas and Images," Sidney Janis Gallery, New York. The eight panels constituting *Le domaine enchanté* (from the Casino Communal, Knokke-Le Zoute, Belgium) exhibited at Metropolitan Museum of Art, New York

1978 Retrospective exhibitions at the Palais des Beaux-Arts, Brussels, and at the Centre National d'Art et Culture Georges Pompidou, Paris

SELECTED BIBLIOGRAPHY

WRITINGS BY MAGRITTE

René Magritte was a prolific writer of manifestos, statements, articles, and personal letters, which dealt with his own artistic activities and also constituted a running account of his views on the general artistic, political, and social issues of his time. The following material has been consulted in the formulation of this volume.

Dors, Mirabelle, and Rapin, Maurice. *Quatre-vingts Lettres de René Magritte à Mirabelle Dors et Maurice Rapin*. Paris: CBE Presses, 1976

Magritte, René. Unpublished letters and statements from the personal archives of Georgette Magritte, Pierre Alechinsky, André Blavier, André Bosmans, Dominique de Menil and the Menil Foundation, Pierre Demarne, Mirabelle Dors and Maurice Rapin, Marcel Mariën, Irène Hamoir and Louis Scutenaire, André Souris, and Harry Torczyner

Mariën, Marcel (ed). *René Magritte: Manifestes et autres écrits*. Brussels: Les Lèvres Nues, 1972

Rapin, Maurice. "René Magritte," in *Aporismes*. Viry-Chatillon, France: S.E.D.I.E.P., 1970, pp. 20–36

BOOKS ABOUT MAGRITTE

Blavier, André. General bibliography up to 1965 in Waldberg, Patrick, *René Magritte*. Brussels: André de Rache, 1965, pp. 285–336

———. *Ceci n'est pas une pipe. Contribution furtive à l'étude d'un tableau de René Magritte*. Verviers, Belgium: Temps Mêlés (publication of the Fondation René Magritte), 1973

Bussy, Christian. *Anthologie du Surréalisme en Belgique*. France: Éditions Gallimard, 1972

Demarne, Pierre. "René Magritte," *Rhétorique*, no. 3, September 1961

Foucault, Michel. *Ceci n'est pas une pipe*. Montpellier, France: Fata Morgana, 1973

Gablik, Suzi. *Magritte*. Greenwich, Connecticut: New York Graphic Society, 1973

Hammacher, A. M. *Magritte*. New York: Harry N. Abrams, 1974

Larkin, David. *Magritte*. New York: Ballantine Books, 1972

Lebel, Robert. *Magritte, peintures*. Paris: Fernand Hazan, 1969

Mariën, Marcel. *René Magritte*. Brussels: Les Auteurs Associés, 1943

Michaux, Henri. *En rêvant à partir des peintures énigmatiques*. Montpellier, France: Fata Morgana, 1972

Noël, Bernard. *Magritte*. Paris: Flammarion, 1976

Nougé, Paul. *Renè Magritte, ou les images défendues*. Brussels: Les Auteurs Associés, 1943

Passeron, René. *René Magritte*. Paris: Filipacchi-Odégé, 1970

Robbe-Grillet, Alain. *René Magritte: La belle captive*. Brussels: Cosmos Textes, 1975

Robert-Jones, Philippe. *Magritte: Poète visible*. Brussels: Laconti, 1972

Schneede, Uwe M. *René Magritte: Leben und Werk*. Cologne: M. DuMont Schauberg,1973

Scutenaire, Louis. *René Magritte*. Brussels: Éditions Librairie Sélection, 1947

———. *René Magritte* (Monographies de l'Art Belge). Brussels: Ministère de l'Éducation nationale et de la Culture, 1964. First edition published by De Sikkel, Antwerp, 1948

———. *La Fidélité des images—René Magritte: Le cinèmatographe et la photographie*. Brussels: Service de la Propagande Artistique du Ministère de la Culture Française, 1976

———. *Avec Magritte*. Brussels: Lebeer-Hossman, 1977

Vovelle,José. *Le Surréalisme en Belgique*. Brussels: André de Rache, 1972, pp. 63–164

Waldberg, Patrick. *René Magritte*. Brussels: André de Rache, 1965

MAJOR EXHIBITION CATALOGUES (arranged chronologically)

Sidney Janis Gallery, New York. *Magritte: Words vs. Image*. March 1–20, 1954. 21 works

Palais des Beaux-Arts, Brussels. *René Magritte*. Brussels: Éditions de la Connaissance, 1954. May 7–June 1, 1954. 93 works

Dallas Museum for Contemporary Arts. *René Magritte in America*. December 8, 1960–January 8, 1961. In collaboration with The Museum of Fine Arts, Houston. 82 works

Obelisk Gallery, London. *Magritte: Paintings, Drawings, Gouaches*. September 28–October 27, 1961. 28 works

Alexandre Iolas Gallery, New York. *René Magritte: Paintings, Gouaches, Collages, 1960–1961–1962*. May 3–26, 1962. 23 works

Casino Communal, Knokke-Le Zoute, Belgium. *L'Oeuvre de René Magritte*. Brussels: Éditions de la Connaissance, 1962. July–August, 1962. 104 works

Walker Art Center, Minneapolis. *The Vision of René Magritte*. September 16–October 14, 1962. 92 works

Arkansas Art Center, Little Rock. *Magritte*. May 15–June 30, 1964. 97 works

The Museum of Modern Art, New York. *Magritte*. Introduction by James Thrall Soby. 1965. In collaboration with the Rose Art Museum (Brandeis University, Waltham, Massachusetts), The Art Institute of Chicago, the University Art Museum (University of California, Berkeley), and the Pasadena Art Museum. 82 works

Museum Boymans-van Beuningen, Rotterdam. *René Magritte*. August 4–September 24, 1967

Moderna Museet, Stockholm. *René Magritte: Le mystère de la vérité*. October 7–November 12, 1967

Byron Gallery, New York. *René Magritte*. November 19–December 21, 1968. 55 works

The Tate Gallery, London. *Magritte*. London: Arts Council of Great Britain. Introduction by David Sylvester. February 14–March 30, 1969. 101 works

Kestner-Gesellschaft, Hanover. *René Magritte*. 1969. 107 works

National Museum of Modern Art, Tokyo. *Rétrospective René Magritte*. Traveled to National Museum of Modern Art, Kyoto. 1971

Grand Palais, Paris. *Peintres de l'imaginaire: Symbolistes et surréalistes belges*. 1972. Included 46 works by Magritte

Marlborough Fine Art, London. *Magritte*. October–November, 1973. 87 works

Institute for the Arts, Rice University, Houston. *Secret Affinities: Words and Images by René Magritte*. October 1, 1976–January 2, 1977. 48 works

LIST OF ILLUSTRATIONS

Each of the 55 colorplates is indicated by an asterisk (*)

82 *Le thérapeute (The Healer)*. 1937
83 *Le thérapeute (The Healer)*. n.d.
84 *Le libérateur (The Liberator)*. 1947
85 *Suggestion: Ce n'est pas un enfant mais un rat (Suggestion: This is Not a Child, But a Rat)*. Illustration in *La Nouvelle Médication Naturelle* by F.E. Bilz, 1899
86 *La lampe philosophique (The Philosopher's Lamp)*. 1935
87 *Ceci n'est pas une pipe (This is Not a Pipe)*. 1928–1929
88 *La boîte de Pandore (Pandora's Box)*. 1951
*89 *La voix des vents (The Voice of the Winds)*. 1928
90 *Les fleurs de l'abîme I (Flowers of the Abyss I)*. 1928
91 *Grelots roses, ciels en lambeaux (Pink Bells, Tattered Skies)*. 1930
92 Letter from René Magritte to Harry Torczyner, August 19, 1960
*93 *Le tombeau des lutteurs (The Tomb of the Wrestlers)*. 1960
94 *Le tombeau des lutteurs (The Tomb of the Wrestlers)*. n.d.
*95 *La chambre d'écoute I (The Listening Room I)*. 1953
96 *La chambre d'écoute (The Listening Room)*. n.d.
*97 *L'anniversaire (The Anniversary)*. 1959
98 *Une simple histoire d'amour (A Simple Love Story)*. 1958
99 *Une simple histoire d'amour (A Simple Love Story)*. n.d.
100 Letter from René Magritte to Harry Torczyner, July 1958
101 *L'automate (The Automaton)*. 1928
*102 *Campagne III (Countryside III)*. 1927
*103 *Le dernier cri (The Last Scream)*. 1967
*104 *Passiflore (Passionflower)*. 1936
*105 *Le plagiat (Plagiarism)*. 1960
*106 *Le pays des miracles (The Country of Marvels)*. c. 1960
*107 *La voix du sang (The Call of Blood)*. 1961
108 *Le souvenir déterminant (The Deciding Memory)*. 1942
109 Untitled. 1964–1965. Engraving for *Aube à l'Antipode* by Alain Jouffroy, Édition Soleil Noir, 1966
*110 *Les marches de l'été (The Progress of Summer)*. 1938
*111 *La grande famille (The Large Family)*. 1947
*112 Painted bottle. n.d.
113 *L'explication (The Explanation)*. 1954
114 *La dame (The Lady)*. 1943.
*115 *La dame (The Lady)*. n.d.
*116 *Ciel (Sky)*. n.d.
117 *L'ovation (The Ovation)*. 1962
*118 *Le beau monde (The Beautiful World)*. c. 1960
*119 *Les mémoires d'un saint (The Memoirs of a Saint)*. 1960
120 *Les goûts et les couleurs (Tastes and Colors)*. 1962
121 *La peine perdue (Wasted Effort)*. 1962
122 Letter from René Magritte to Mirabelle Dors and Maurice Rapin, August 6, 1956
*123 *Le seize septembre (September Sixteenth)*. 1957
*124 *Le banquet (The Banquet)*. 1957
125 *L'au-delà (The Beyond)*. 1938
126 *La voie royale (The Royal Road)*. 1944
127 Study for *Le Banquet (The Banquet)*
128 *Le Banquet (The Banquet)*. 1956
129 *Le chef d'oeuvre ou les mystères de l'horizon (The Masterpiece or The Mysteries of the Horizon)*. 1955
130 *Bain de vapeur en chaise nattée couché (Steam Bath Using Caned Chairs)*. Illustration in *La Nouvelle Médication Naturelle* by F. E. Bilz, 1899
131 *Les fanatiques (The Fanatics)*. 1945
132 *L'échelle de feu (The Ladder of Fire)*. 1933
*133 *L'échelle de feu (The Ladder of Fire)*. 1939
134 *Les six éléments (The Six Elements)*. 1928
135 *Le palais des rideaux (The Palace of Curtains)*. 1934
136 *Les reflets du temps (The Reflections of Time)*. 1928
137 *Le sens propre (The Proper Meaning)*. 1928–1929.
138 *Le masque vide (The Empty Mask)*. 1928
139 Untitled drawing. n.d.
140 *La grande table (The Large Table)*. 1959
*141 *L'idée (The Idea)*. 1966
142 *Le joueur secret (The Secret Player)*. 1926
143 *Le beau ténébreux (Dark and Handsome)*. 1950
*144 *Les rencontres naturelles (Natural Encounters)*. 1945
145 *Les origines du langage (The Origins of Language)*. 1955
146 Untitled drawings. c. 1959
147 *Le trou dans le mur (The Hole in the Wall)*. 1956
148 *La bataille d'Argonne (The Battle of the Argonne)*. 1959
*149 *Le château des Pyrénées (The Castle of the Pyrenees)*. 1959
*150 *La condition humaine (The Human Condition)*. 1934
151 *Fromage sous cloche (Cheese under Bell Glass)*. n.d.
*152 *La métamorphose de l'objet (Metamorphosis of the Object)*. 1933
*153 *L'empire des lumières (The Empire of Lights)*. 1953
*154 *L'empire des lumières II (The Empire of Lights II)*. 1950
*155 *L'empire des lumières (The Empire of Lights)*. 1948
*156 *Le salon de Dieu (God's Drawing Room)*. 1958
*157 *Jeune Fille (Young Woman)*. 1924
*158 *La baigneuse (The Bather)*. 1923
*159 *Les heureux présages (The Good Omens)*. 1944
*160 *La moisson (The Harvest)*. 1944
*161 *Le prince charmant (Prince Charming)*. 1948
*162 *Le galet (The Pebble)*. 1948
163 *Le chant de la violette (The Song of the Violet)*. 1951
164 Photograph of René Magritte, Brussels, 1934
165 *A la rencontre du plaisir (Toward Pleasure)*. 1950
166 *Les fleurs du mal (The Flowers of Evil)*. 1946
167 *Les épaves de l'ombre (The Shadow's Wreckage)*. n.d.
168 Untitled drawing. n.d.
*169 *Le domaine d'Arnheim (The Domain of Arnheim)*. 1962
170 *Fortune faite (The Fortune Made)*. 1957
171 *Le puits de vérité (The Well of Truth)*. c. 1962–1963
172 Photograph of René Magritte painting *Le puits de vérité (The Well of Truth)*. 1963
173 Pen sketch of *Le puits de vérité (The Well of Truth)* in a letter from René Magritte to Harry Torczyner, January 13, 1962
*174 *Le voyageur (The Traveler)*. 1935
175 Ink drawing in a letter from René Magritte to Mirabelle Dors and Maurice Rapin, August 22, 1956
176 *Découverte (Discovery)*. 1927
*177 *L'annonciation (The Annunciation)*. 1930
178 *Le mois des vendanges (The Time of the Harvest)*. 1959
*179 *Le mois des vendanges (The Time of the Harvest)*. 1959
180 *La place au soleil (The Place in the Sun)*. 1956

181 Pen sketch in a letter from René Magritte to Mirabelle Dors and Maurice Rapin, February 24, 1956

182 *La place au soleil (The Place in the Sun)*. 1956

183 Drawing for *Le bouquet tout fait (Ready-Made Bouquet)*. n.d.

184 *Le réveil-matin (The Alarm Clock)*. 1953

185 Autobiographical statement by René Magritte, March 20, 1962

*186 *L'idole (The Idol)*. 1965

PHOTOGRAPH CREDITS

Archives Pierre Alechinsky, Bougival, France: 130; Archives de l'Art Contemporain, Brussels, Belgium: 185; Archives Iolas: 32, 43, 75, 117, 120, 148; Archives Mme. René Magritte, Brussels, Belgium: 27; Jacqueline Hyde, Paris, France: 46.

The World Beneath Our Feet

A Guide to Life in the Soil

The World Beneath Our Feet

A Guide to Life in the Soil

James B. Nardi

OXFORD
UNIVERSITY PRESS

This book is dedicated to my mother and Mother Earth,
who have each nurtured me in their own ways.

OXFORD
UNIVERSITY PRESS

Oxford New York
Auckland Bangkok Buenos Aires Cape Town Chennai
Dar es Salaam Delhi Hong Kong Istanbul Karachi Kolkata
Kuala Lumpur Madrid Melbourne Mexico City Mumbai Nairobi
São Paulo Shanghai Singapore Taipei Tokyo Toronto

Published by Oxford University Press, Inc.
198 Madison Avenue, New York, New York, 10016
www.oup.com

Library of Congress Cataloging-in-Publication Data

Nardi, Jim.
The world beneath our feet / Jim Nardi.
cm.
Summary: A close look at what soil is, how it evolved, how it supports life, and why it wears out, plus profiles of the plants and animals that form the ecosystem of healthy soil and how we can help to nurture them.
Includes bibliographical references (p. 215).
ISBN 0-19-513990-9 (alk. paper)
1. Soil animals—Juvenile literature. 2. Soil ecology—Juvenile literature. [1. Soil animals. 2. Soil ecology. 3. Ecology.] I. Title.
QL110 .N37 2002
577.5'7—dc21

2002001202

Printing number: 9 8 7 6 5 4 3 2 1

Printed in Hong Kong on acid-free paper

Photo on page 159 is courtesy of Walter Tschinkel, photographed by Charles F. Badland.

CONTENTS

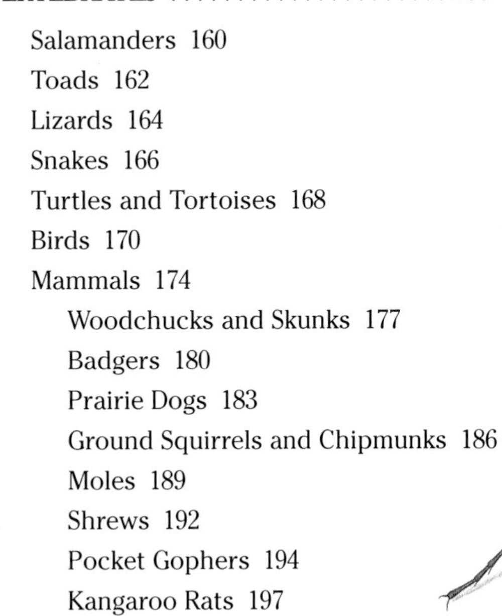

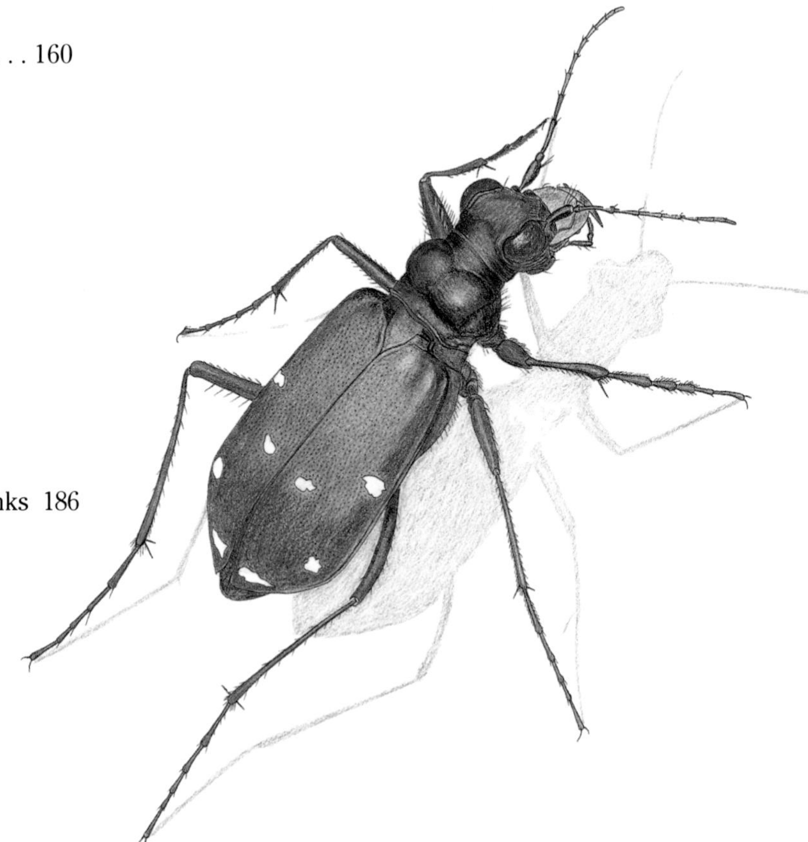

PREFACE

All creatures are nourished by minerals from the soil during their lives, and they ultimately return to minerals of the soil at their deaths. There are many kinds of soils and, like living creatures, soils are far more than the sum of their many chemicals and minerals. Soils represent the marriage of the mineral world and the organic world. Until recently the organic partner had not received its share of credit for the success of the marriage. Biologists had often focused on particular groups of soil organisms and often overlooked general relationships among organisms, soil fertility, and plant growth. We are now beginning to realize that a soil is not fertile and complete until creatures occupy it and contribute their organic portion to the mineral portion of the soil. "A dynamic natural medium in which plants grow made up of both mineral and organic materials as well as living forms" is a definition of soil that covers its attributes very well.

If biologists overlooked relationships among soils, plants, and soil creatures, it was probably because they were too busy examining and cataloging all the new creatures that kept showing up in soils wherever they looked. There is a staggering amount of life in the soil—plants, animals, fungi, bacteria, protozoa—representing all the kingdoms of life and many species within these kingdoms. Many groups of organisms never leave the soil; others live only part of their lives or part of each day in the soil. Some may be extremely abundant in some places but absent in others. Many live in dung, decaying plants, or dead animals that will eventually return to soil.

The variety of soil types and the health of soils are reflected in the diversity of their living inhabitants that either directly or indirectly contribute to a soil's fertility. Countless small, retiring inhabitants carry out their indispensable business in the soil. Although we tend to underestimate the abilities and the significance of such diminutive organisms, they happen to be the recyclers that can produce that key organic ingredient of healthy soil known as "humus."

Humus is the substance that gives soil its rich, dark color and its crumbly structure. After these creatures of the soil have thoroughly digested plant and animal debris that falls to the ground, humus is the substance that remains in their droppings. Humus is the substance that has the ability to latch onto minerals and keep them within easy reach of plant roots.

There is a very good reason why organic farmers add manure and compost to soil rather than commercial fertilizers. Compost and manure come with a good supply of minerals and with their own populations of soil creatures that convert the manure and compost to humus. Humus holds soil nutrients and water within reach of plant roots and gives soil a structure that plants promptly sink their roots into.

In the rich, productive soil of this American farm, billions of organisms are busy converting dead plant and animal matter to humus.

A backyard compost heap is a good place to see humus formation in action. Compost represents a microcosm of the soil surface and offers an alluring view of what transpires in the leaf litter of a forest or the plant debris of a prairie. The speed and thoroughness with which plant debris breaks down in a compost heap is testimony to the efficiency of the creatures who convert plant matter to humus. Stirring up a compost heap turns up a great number and variety of decomposers, or creatures that obtain nutrients from the plant litter, and are responsible for recycling and humus formation.

These decomposers and scavengers are all recyclers of dead plant as well as animal matter. They are the abundant creatures in many soils and compost heaps. It is too bad that another group of soil animals, ranging in size from tiny arthropods to fat rodents, are considered pests just because they dig holes and pile up mounds of soil; even they have redeeming virtues that are all too often overlooked. Diggers keep soil in circulation, mixing lower mineral layers with the upper organic layers and enriching the soil in ways that fertilizers never manage to do.

A variety of creatures—fungi, protozoa, mites, centipedes, beetles, birds, and snakes—act as predators, feeding on other animals and constantly keeping the populations of the more abundant decomposers and diggers in check. Bacteria are the only soil organisms that not only recycle the remains of plants and animals but also liberate all the essential elements from soil particles in forms that living plants need for their survival. All life in the soil, as well as all other forms of life on earth, ultimately depend on these bacteria and the plants that they support. In a healthy soil with its mix of decomposers, diggers, and predators, a harmony pervades both the mineral world and the organic world.

Healthy soil, good nutrition, and good health go hand in hand; and those creatures that contribute to the health of soils are of the utmost importance for the well-being of the planet. They are the ones that steadfastly keep the world running and include creatures as strange and as bizarre as any that a science fiction movie can offer. Yet, we really know very little about so many of them.

Tree roots, rain, and ice slowly break down rock, like the boulder above, into mineral particles of soil. Decomposers on the forest floor recycle the organic matter of logs and fallen leaves. Burrowing animals of the forest thoroughly mix these organic and mineral portions of the soil.

Leonardo da Vinci's observation that "we know more about the movement of celestial bodies than about the soil underfoot" is sadly as true today as it was in the 15th century. The intent of this book is to assure the reader that new discoveries and new surprises await those who stop to look a little closer at these creatures in "the soil underfoot," the unsung heroes that give the gift of good earth.

How to Use This Book

This book is divided into three parts. Part 1: Working Partnerships explains how the organisms in the soil interact with their mineral and organic neighbors. Part 2: Members of the Soil Community highlights individual inhabitants of the soil and shows how particular groups of creatures contribute to the soil environment. This second part is organized in three sections: Microbes, Invertebrates, and Vertebrates. If you are not sure what group the organism you are looking for belongs to, you can also find it listed alphabetically in the index. Part 3: The Gift of Good Earth discusses ways to enrich the soil of our farms as well as our gardens, including how to start a backyard compost pile.

At the back of the book, a glossary defines scientific terms that are frequently used. The back of the book also lists resources for additional study including further reading and Web sites. The last section of this book is an index, which will direct you to information you may not find in the table of contents.

FACT BOXES

A fact box accompanies each entry in Part 2. Each fact box is a quick reference that contains information about the common name for the group of organisms, its classification, place in the food web, size, and number of species. Fact boxes in the Vertebrates section also contain information on lifespans and gestation periods.

Common Name

The title of the fact box gives the common name for the group of organisms.

Classification

In order to keep track of relationships among organisms, creatures are grouped and named according to their similarities and the features they share. Naming or classification of each organism proceeds in a definite sequence. Groups of organisms are arranged in a definite order or hierarchy from the smallest number of groups (kingdoms) to the largest number of groups (species), from the most general at the topmost level to the most specific at the bottom of the hierarchy. The most general groups are the kingdoms, and there are six kingdoms that include all organisms: Archaebacteria (also known as Archaea), Eubacteria (also known as Bacteria), Protista, Fungal, Plant, and Animal. Microbes are found in the first four kingdoms and a few belong to the Plant kingdom; invertebrates and vertebrates belong to the Animal kingdom. The most specific groups in the classification of organisms are species, and the number of known species on earth is currently well over a million. The other levels in the hierarchy of classification are listed below between kingdom and species.

Kingdom
 Phylum
  Class
   Subclass
    Order
     Suborder
      Superfamily
       Family
        Subfamily
         Genus
          Species

Each group is given a name often derived from Latin or Greek that tells something about the group. For example, slow-moving organisms known as tardigrades are classified in the phylum Tardigrada, which is Latin for "slow stepper". Biologists may name an organism according to one or more of these levels of classification; they do not have to use them all.

Place in the Food Web
The food web is a network of organisms within which nutrients—the substances that plants, animals, fungi, and microbes need for survival—are circulated. The organisms in this book all belong to such a network. Each organism may play one or more of the following roles in the food web:

Algal eaters—organisms that eat those creatures known as algae that are capable of producing their own nutrients.

Bacterial partners of plants—bacteria that live within plant roots and form a mutually beneficial relationship with plants.

Coprophages—organisms that feed on dung.

Decomposers—organisms that break down the remains or waste products of other organisms.

Detritivores—organisms that feed on dead plant and animal matter.

Diggers—organisms that facilitate the circulation of nutrients between layers of soil and help stimulate the growth of plants.

Fungivores—organisms that feed on fungi.

Herbivores—organisms that feed on plants.

Fungal partners of plants—fungi that form mutually beneficial relationships with plant roots.

Parasites—organisms that live in or on other living organisms (hosts) and obtain nutrients from their hosts, often without killing them.

Predators—organisms that obtain nutrients from other living organisms (prey) but do not live in or on their prey.

Producers—organisms that produce their own nutrients from only air, water, minerals and energy.

Scavengers—organisms that feed on dead plant or animal matter.

The interactions among members of the soil community are shown in the food web diagram on page 30.

Size
Sizes are given in metric units—micrometers (µm), millimeters (mm), and centimeters (cm). There are a thousand micrometers in each millimeter and ten millimeters in each centimeter. Microbes, measured mostly in micrometers (µm), are so small that they will go unnoticed unless viewed under a magnifying lens. Although the sizes of most soil creatures are specified in length, the size of an organism that has the form of a filament, such as a fungus or an alga, is given as the diameter of the filament. The size of a bird or a mammal includes the length of its head and body without its tail.

5 mm

Number of Species
The number of species found worldwide is an estimate because new species continue to be discovered, especially in groups of organisms representing many of the smaller creatures. For these groups, the number of species described in scientific literature often represents only a small fraction of the species that actually exist. For the larger vertebrates, almost all species have been discovered. The number of vertebrate species, however, may change slightly from year to year. This fluctuation arises because biologists often debate whether populations that are considered one species should really be considered more than one species or whether populations that are placed in more than one species should be grouped as a single species.

PART 1

WORKING PARTNERSHIPS

The Marriage of the Mineral World and the Organic World

Every rock has what it takes to be part of a soil someday. Even the hardest of rocks will eventually succumb to the unremitting action of weather and plants. In the early days of the earth there was neither soil nor living creatures—only rocks, water, wind, and the sun. But these were ingredients enough for the making of earth's first mineral soils. Soil began to form slowly, imperceptibly, as large rocks transformed into small rocks, and small rocks into even smaller rocks.

The ultimate result of the weathering of most rocks is the formation of the three main mineral particles that make up all soils: sand, silt, and clay. These are the particles that give each soil its distinctive texture. With the appearance of these three different mineral particles, soils begin to take on particular characteristics.

The particular combination of mineral particles found in a soil determine that soil's texture. Sand particles that range in diameter from 1/500 inch (0.05 millimeter) to 1/12 inch (2.1 millimeters) impart a coarse texture to sandy soil. Minuscule particles of clay, on the other hand, that are smaller than 1/12,500 inch (0.002 millimeter) in diameter impart a sticky texture to clay soil. Silt particles, whose diameters are smaller than those of sand particles but larger than those of clay particles give silt a silky or powdery texture.

A soil in which the stickiness of clay particles, the silkiness of silt particles, and the coarseness of sand particles contribute almost equally to the soil's texture is known as "loam soil," or simply "loam." All other soil textures with names like clay loam, sandy loam, silty clay, or sandy clay represent combinations of soil particles with textures lying somewhere between any two of the four major types of soil texture: sand, silt, clay, and loam.

These sandstone rocks in the hills of southern Illinois have been weathered and sculpted by thousands of years of rain, wind, and snow.

The soil-forming forces are as effective now as they were when the earth was much younger. Soil is being born today just as it has since the early years of the earth. But the birth of soil is a slow and labored process. Building a soil takes time. By one liberal estimate, just an inch (25.4 millimeters) of soil takes on the order of 500 years to form; by a more conservative estimate one inch of soil forms only about every 1,000 years.

A complete soil represents the marriage of the mineral or inorganic world with the organic world. Each partner's attributes are often enhanced in the other's company. Minerals come from the breakdown of rocks; organic matter arises from the decay of animals and plants. Minerals provide many essential elements for plant life, but so does organic matter. The marriage of the mineral world and the organic world is a combination that improves the longer the two partners work together.

Mineral soils form from rocks, air, and water without any contributions from living creatures. These soils, however, are missing one final element that is essential for the survival of all creatures. This element is nitrogen.

Even though roughly 3/4 of the air we breath is nitrogen in the form of dinitrogen (N_2) gas and 34,500 tons (31,050 metric tons) of the gas lie over every acre of land, very few of our fellow creatures can use nitrogen as it exists in the air. Animals depend on plants and other animals as sources for their nitrogen, but green plants can use only two forms of nitrogen. One is ammonia, formed by combining nitrogen with hydrogen; the other is nitrates, which is formed by combining nitrogen with oxygen. Billions of years before life appeared on earth, lightning was the only agent that could transform nitrogen of the air into nitrogen of ammonia.

As life began to appear on earth, a few specialized bacteria, some algae, and certain filamentous bacteria called actinomycetes that live in the soil began to take on the task of converting dinitrogen gas to ammonia, a process known simply as nitrogen fixation.

Rain, wind, sun, and ice all help convert rock to soil, but it is the living creatures that clearly make the soil hospitable for other

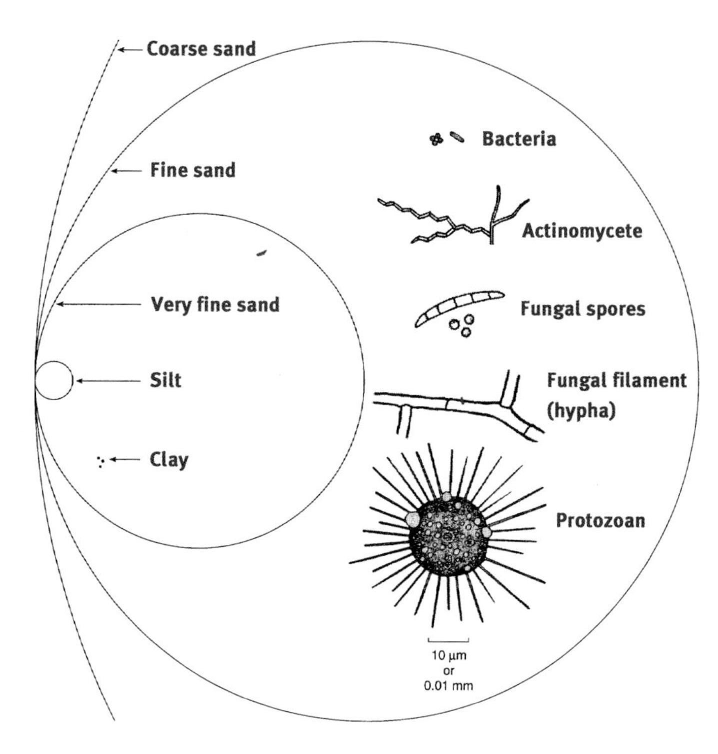

A world of soil creatures can live on a grain of sand. Here, the sizes of soil particles are compared with the sizes of soil microbes.

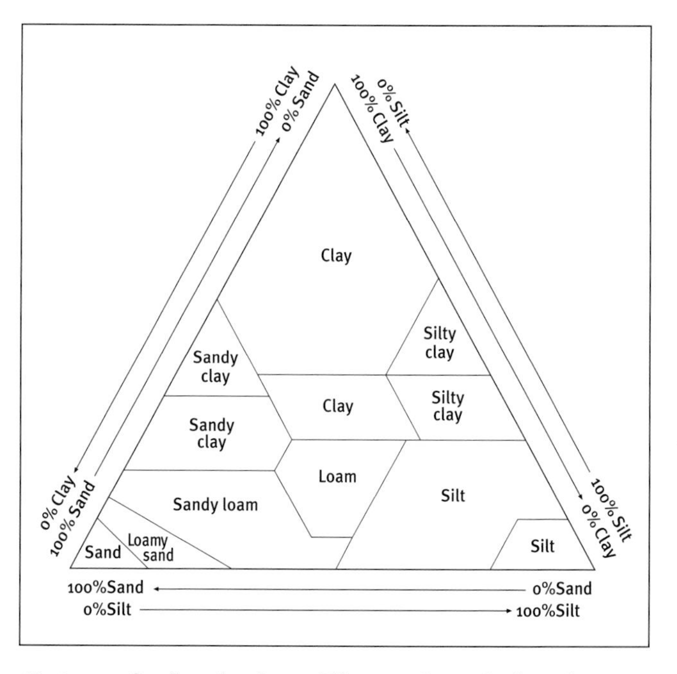

Textures of soils arise from different mixes of mineral particles. At a particular corner of the triangle 100 percent of the particles are either sand, clay, or silt. The percentage of this particle then diminishes gradually to 0 percent at each of the other two corners.

living forms. Only hardy and intrepid pioneers can move in and eke out a meager existence on the barren and nutrient-poor stretches of uninhabited soil and rock. New pioneers appear and new nutrients are added as other creatures pass away. As early generations of microbes, plants, and animals die and decay, later generations of creatures take up residence among their remains. Once pioneers are established on a rocky and barren soil, they begin to create soil particles from rock and the remains of the creatures that preceded them. The slow and often imperceptible breakdown of rocks and the build-up of soil by the weather proceeds a little faster with help from plants, their roots, and their various partners.

Alliances between organisms have been very important, if not essential, in colonizing soils for the first time. By sharing their talents and working together, the partners survive where either one alone would have perished. Four very successful partnerships are those of the algae and fungi that form lichens, the plants and bacteria that form nitrogen-fixing knots or nodules on roots, the fungi and plant roots that form mutually beneficial associations, and the diggers and decomposers that circulate and recycle the soil nutrients that plants need for survival.

The lowly lichens and algae are usually the first signs of life on barren, uninhabited surfaces of the earth. The rugged, tenacious lichen is half alga, half fungus and combines the best attributes of each partner. The algal partner not only captures the energy of sunlight to produce sugars and oxygen but often also fixes nitrogen from the air by converting dinitrogen gas to ammonia. The fungal partner provides water and essential elements for survival and growth. Lichens are especially gifted at breaking down rocks.

First of all, lichens are extremely abundant and occupy 8 percent of the earth's land surface. Second, a lichen can live a very long time in one place on a rock—a few hundred, even a few thousand years. Therefore, a lichen can afford to be unhurried and persistent in its affairs. Third, lichens are among the very few organisms of the earth that can penetrate and, over a span of many generations, ultimately eat their way into their rocky homes.

Lichens and mosses are some of the first plants to colonize barren rocks. Once these tiny plants have settled down on a rock, such as the one above, they can remain for hundreds, sometimes thousands, of years.

What lichens have that other organisms do not is the ability to produce a variety of acids, many of which are found nowhere else in the kingdoms of life. The names of some of the acids are taken from the scientific names given to the lichens that produce them: usnic acid of *Usnea* lichens, lobaric acid of *Lobaria* lichens, gyrophoric acid of *Gyrophora* lichens, and evernic acid from *Evernia* lichens.

Mosses, too, can gain footholds on bare rock. They grip the surfaces of rocks with tiny rootlets, or rhizoids. These green pioneers obtain enough water and elements from the surfaces of rocks to sustain them as generations of mosses claim the bare rock for their home. Mosses, unlike lichens, are not known to produce special acids that can digest rocks, but this matter has not been studied closely. Even if mosses only occupy

Continued on page 16

How Soil Is Formed

Sun, ice, water, and wind are all constantly changing the face of the earth. Where once a field of boulders covered the landscape, grasses and other plants may spread their roots into a rich, dark soil. Where once its granite roots anchored a mountain to the earth, massive trees may now spread their gnarled branches and twisted roots.

As the sun beats down on a rock, its surface heats up, while just beneath the surface, where the heat does not penetrate, the temperature is many degrees cooler. The rock's surface expands during the heat of the day and contracts during the cool of the night, but the well-insulated core of the rock remains unperturbed by the rising and falling temperatures. After many cycles of expansion and contraction, the outer layers of the rock begin to flake off, and a first step in the conversion of rock to soil has begun. The deserts of the world are the best places to observe this gradual wearing down of rocks by the intense heat of the midday sun and the cold of the desert night.

As water freezes in cracks of rocks, it expands and widens the cracks as well as making more, smaller cracks. Every time water freezes, it expands almost 10 percent in size. Freezing water can expand enough to completely split a rock. By acting as a wedge in crevices and cracks, ice is a large contributor to rock breaking and the early stages of soil formation.

Wind works best as a former of soil when it works together with dust and sand, blowing, blasting, and scraping whatever rocks lie along its path. The rocks are eventually worn smooth and smaller as a few more mineral particles are removed by each gust of wind.

Over millennia, rain, snow, and flowing water wear away at rocks by the force and friction of their movements. Look at any rock canyon or rocky shoreline to see how water has sculpted its surface, carrying off tiny particles of rock that may some day form part of a rich soil, far from the rocks of its origin.

Rain helps convert rock to soil by two different means. The force of raindrops falling from the sky physically wears away at rock surfaces to form particles of sand and silt. Raindrops also mix with the carbon dioxide in the air to form a weak acid called carbonic acid—the acid that produces the fizz of carbonated beverages. Carbonic acid is very effective at corroding surfaces of rocks such as limestone.

Acid corrosion is a process of interaction and exchange of chemical elements that can be expressed in the simple, straightforward shorthand of a chemical equation. The *elements* in the equation are substances that cannot be broken down into other substances with different properties, but these elements can join to form *compounds* that are made up of more than one element. For example, hydrogen and oxygen combine to form water. Carbon, in turn, can combine with hydrogen and oxygen to form simple sugar compounds as well as long chains of sugars like cellulose.

Each element in a chemical reaction is represented by a capital letter or a capital letter and a small letter (for example, C = carbon; Ca = calcium). Some elements and some compounds have either a negative charge or a positive charge. Those with a positive charge are referred to as cations, while those with a negative charge are referred to as anions. When nitrogen (N) and oxygen (O) join, they often form negatively charged nitrate (NO_3^-), but when nitrogen and hydrogen join they form positively charged ammonium (NH_4^+). In every chemical equation, the number and the types of elements as well as the number and types of charges on the left side of the equation (the reacting chemicals) must equal the number as well as the types of elements and charges on the right side of the equation (the chemical products). Therefore another, quicker way to say that rain reacts with carbon dioxide to form carbonic acid is to write:

$$\underset{\text{rain}}{H_2O} + \underset{\text{carbon dioxide}}{CO_2} \rightarrow \underset{\text{carbonic acid}}{H_2CO_3}$$

The carbonic acid of rain drops is corrosive and chemically transforms rocks by removing certain elements from them. This transformation occurs when the positively charged hydrogen in carbonic acid replaces other positively charged elements in rocks like limestone and granite and over time dissolves them. Caves are formed and calcium ions are liberated by the corrosive action of carbonic acid on limestone. Limestone is also known as the compound calcium carbonate ($CaCO_3$).

$$H_2CO_3 + CaCO_3 \rightarrow Ca^{+2} + 2OH^- + 2CO_2$$

A variety of clays are also formed as rocks like granite and schist encounter carbonic acid.

Like all acids, carbonic acid releases positively charged hydrogen ions that continually exchange places with other positively charged elements like aluminum, magnesium, iron, sodium, and potassium. These elements are found in many of the compounds found in rocks and soils. The more rain that falls, the more carbonic acid forms, and the more hydrogen ions are added to the soil. These hydrogen ions by their sheer numbers continually displace other positive ions from rocks and contribute to the slow and steady conversion of rocks to particles of clay, sand, and silt.

The most abundant mineral of granite, and just about all other rocks, is a mineral known as feldspar. Feldspars come in a variety of forms. What they all have in common is that they share the elements of aluminum (Al), oxygen (O), and silicon (Si). All

Water and lichens work together to transform rock to soil.

feldspars contain either one or two other elements. These can be potassium (K), calcium (Ca), sodium (Na), or barium (Ba), with potassium usually being the most common.

When a feldspar encounters carbonic acid, they react and leave behind several compounds.

$$\underset{\text{feldspar}}{2K(AlSi_3O_8)} + \underset{\text{water}}{H_2O} + \underset{\text{carbonic acid}}{H_2CO_3} \rightarrow$$

$$\underset{\text{potassium carbonate}}{K_2CO_3} + \underset{\text{clay}}{Al_2Si_2O_5(OH)_4} + \underset{\text{sand/silt}}{SiO_2}$$

One of the compounds of the reaction, potassium carbonate, is formed when carbonate anions join with potassium cations. Large particles of silicon dioxide, better known as sand, as well as smaller particles of silicon dioxide, better known as silt, result as different elements change partners during the reaction. The particles of clay are a mixture of aluminum, silicon, oxygen, and hydrogen.

Continued from page 13

space on rocks and do not send their rootlets into the rock, they still shelter bacteria, fungi, and other tiny organisms among their rootlets that may help transform rock to soil.

Even some fungi can chew away at rocks. Only in the last few years have researchers shown that fungi have some ability to convert rocks to soil. The acids secreted by the thin, delicate filaments, or hyphae, allow them to perforate even the most substantial rocks.

Atop barren rocks and the sands of deserts, one of the first signs of life is the formation of a thin, fragile crust, known among ecologists as a cryptobiotic (*crypto* = hidden; *bios* = life) soil, that harbors bacteria, lichens, algae, protozoa, some fungi, and some mosses. These pioneers settle down in sterile environments, adding nitrogen, storing water, stopping erosion, and generally enriching the soil by intertwining their living filaments with the lifeless grains of sand and the solid crystals of rocks. But none of these pioneers have roots that can delve deep beneath the surface of the new soil.

Hardy plants that do extend roots are drawn to these fragile sites and soon transform them into green oases where other creatures can gain a foothold in the young soil. These plants with roots get a great deal of help along the way from bacteria, from fungi, and from animals of the soil that form some remarkable partnerships with their green allies.

Plants and Their Bacterial Partners

As soil begins to appear on the surface of sand or rock, every now and then a seed lands, germinates, and extends its newly formed roots into the young soil. Few seedlings, however, can survive in the newly-wrought soil prepared by bacteria, algae, lichens, and mosses. Even though these soils have most of the mineral nutrients that a plant needs to get a start, they are still deficient in that one essential nutrient: nitrogen.

Because practically all of a soil's nitrogen is stored in organic rather than mineral matter, rocks and soils that contain no living things also have no organic matter and nitrogen. However, some of the plants that pioneer these new soils have the ability to establish themselves—root, stem, and shoot-on nitrogen—poor soil where no plants other than lichens, algae, and mosses have managed to gain a foothold.

These early roots have established special partnerships with certain rod-shaped bacteria called rhizobia (*rhizo* = root; *bio* = life) and other filamentous bacteria called actinomycetes. The roots accommodate these bacteria in special knots or nodules. Each root nodule shelters millions of bacteria and provides a perfect environment for them to convert dinitrogen gas of the air to the compound of nitrogen and hydrogen called ammonia. Although neither bacteria nor plants can use nitrogen in the form of dinitrogen gas, they both can use nitrogen in the form of ammonia.

Each root is covered with very fine hairs that project at right angles to the surface of the root, giving it a distinctly fuzzy appearance. All these root hairs, even though each is only a fraction of a millimeter in diameter, vastly expand the area of a root that comes in contact with soil and the minerals and creatures inhabiting it. The root hairs of each nodule-bearing plant secrete substances that attract particular bacteria.

However, not just any root hair and any bacteria can get together. Each plant requires a special type of rhizobium or actinomycete, and only when substances on the root hairs match substances on the bacteria do the plant and the bacteria strike up an intimate relationship. Those soil bacteria that are compatible with root hairs they encounter latch on to the hairs and spread into the root; there they stimulate root cells to divide and

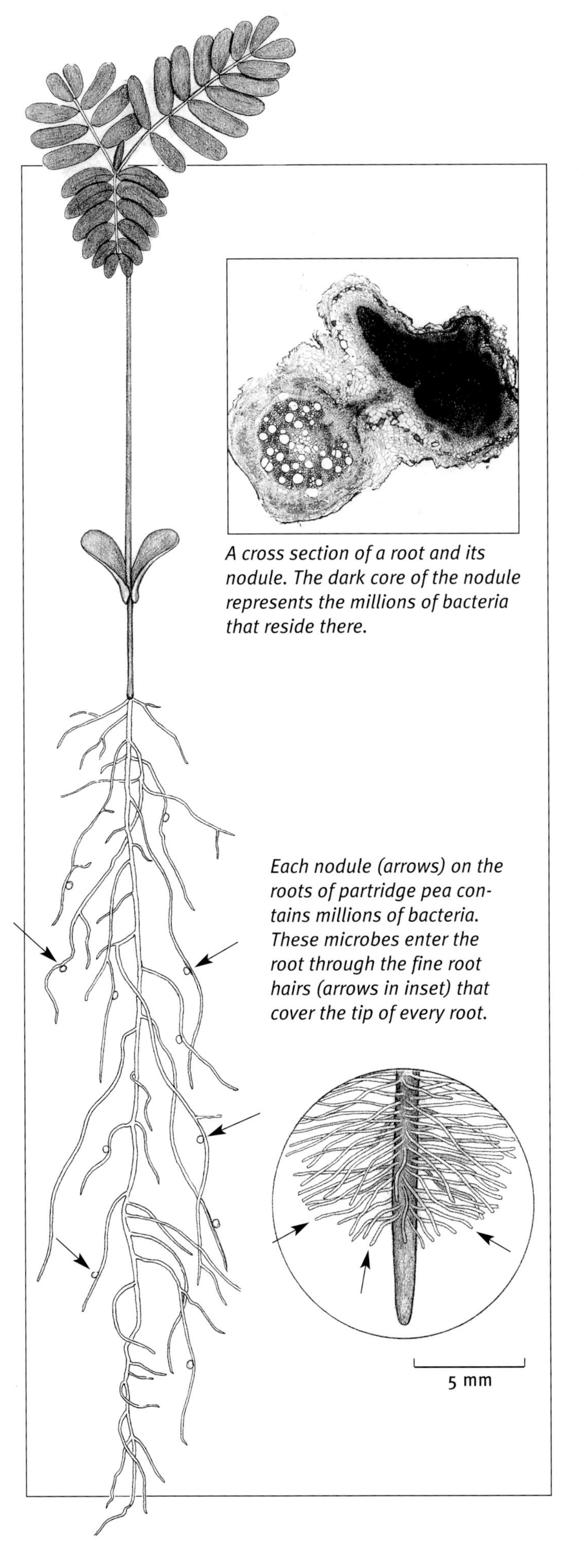

A cross section of a root and its nodule. The dark core of the nodule represents the millions of bacteria that reside there.

Each nodule (arrows) on the roots of partridge pea contains millions of bacteria. These microbes enter the root through the fine root hairs (arrows in inset) that cover the tip of every root.

to form a knot or nodule of cells. The bacteria have an enzyme that converts dinitrogen from the air to ammonia. The plant roots in turn supply the energy that the enzyme needs to carry out nitrogen fixation. The ammonia produced in the root nodules nourishes both plant and bacteria.

Their teamwork allows them to settle in soils that other plants without nodules would never consider proper environments to sink their roots into. But after they have been settled on an inhospitable soil for a while, plants with root nodules leave enough nitrogen compounds in the soil to support a new wave of plant settlers that have neither root nodules nor the ability to supply their own nitrogen compounds.

Plants and Their Fungal Partners

Although only the roots of a relatively few plant species and even fewer plant families team up with rhizobial bacteria and actinomycetes to produce root nodules and nitrogen compounds, the roots of all types of plants, from mosses to trees, have teamed up with long filaments of fungi in special partnerships that benefit them both. Together the two partners retrieve elements from deep in the soil and eventually return the elements to the topsoil, where they once again begin their journey downward. The filaments of fungi surround plant roots and usually extend well beyond the reach of the longest plant roots. Since the thin fungal filaments can grow into tinier spaces of the soil than can plant roots, the fungi tap resources that are otherwise inaccessible to roots, sending back water and a variety of minerals to the plant.

The plant reciprocates by sharing with fungi the energy of sunlight as well as the sugars that it makes with this energy. At certain seasons fungi use some of this energy from their green partner when they send forth their fruiting bodies, or mushrooms. Thousands of fungal filaments from the soil come together to form these colorful mushrooms. The thousands of spores that each mushroom produces are carried off by wind and animals of the forest floor to new sites where they settle in the leaf litter, sprout their filaments, and start new partnerships.

It is easy to imagine how plants and fungi first became steadfast partners. Early, barren soils were most likely without organic matter as well as many elements like nitrogen, phosphorus, and sulfur found in organic matter. In extracting elements from those soils, green plants probably needed all the help they could get, and fungi turned out to be committed allies. Fungi have been found in association with the first green plants that colonized the land about 400 million years ago. The development of partnerships between green plants and fungi might just have been a critical step in the early colonization of soils by green plants.

There was a time when soil fungi and moldy soil were considered harmful to plants. Since the few soil fungi that had been studied at the time did cause diseases of plants, people had the naive view that all fungi were harmful to plants and impeded their growth. How a few careful observations can change our views of the world! Not only do many soil fungi improve the health of plants that grow with them, but some of these fungi are actually essential for survival of the plants they associate with. This idea was first proposed in an article published in 1885 by a professor of biology in Berlin.

Professor A. B. Frank had originally been commissioned in 1881 by the German government to find a way to increase the supply of delicious and highly prized fungi called truffles, which grow among the roots of beech and oak trees. For centuries pigs and dogs have been trained to locate these woodland fungi, which fetch a high price at market, and German politicians naturally wished to encourage this lucrative harvest in their country.

When weather conditions are just right, mushrooms arise from the miles of fungal filaments that live in the soil and leaf litter of the forest.

Although Frank never did find out how to improve Germany's truffle harvest, he found something very unexpected and even more important. Almost all the trees that Professor Frank examined did not show any evidence of damage even though molds and fungi encircled their roots. The fungi formed regular networks around the healthy roots. The intimate association of soil fungi with roots represents neither an ordinary root nor an ordinary fungus but a structure with properties of both. Since those early investigations, these special structures of the soil have been referred to as mycorrhizae (*myco* = fungus; *rhizae* = roots).

Professor Frank had enough confidence in his observations to claim that the fungi of the mycorrhizae pass on water and nutrients to the roots. For years other scientists challenged his view that the association of fungi and roots was a healthy association and not a harmful one. Investigators have now traced the flow of nutrients between roots and fungi. They have also shown that pine seedlings with mycorrhizae absorb more nitrogen, more potassium, and more than twice the amount of phosphorus from the soil than pine seedlings planted in the same soil that do not have fungal partners. Fungi and plants grow up together, sharing nutrients, but always respecting each other's integrity.

Ironically, although thousands of papers and books have been published about mycorrhizae since Professor Frank's pioneering work, no one yet knows how to increase the truffle population in an oak or beech forest.

The Virtues of Roots

Once established in the soil with help from their pioneering partners—algae, lichens, mosses, bacteria, and fungi—plants with roots can manage very well at living off the land and at the same time enriching the earth. Green plants contribute to the process of soil formation in two ways: by breaking down rocks and adding mineral matter to a soil, and by adding their organic matter to the soil whenever they return to it, in part or entirely. The plant roots not only exert forces strong enough to crack rocks, they also release compounds potent enough to gradually and inexorably transform some of the largest and hardest rocks to the finest of mineral particles.

In its early days a plant puts most of its energy into growing down into the soil. Enough nutrients are stored in its seed to tide the seedling over for a few days until its leaves start to form and expand. Roots, however, are the first part of a new seedling not only to form but also to function in carrying water and nutrients from the soil to parts above ground. Small roots branch from large roots, and tiny root hairs branch from small roots. A typical Midwestern prairie produces three tons of roots for every ton of shoots. Through the months of the winter, roots are often the only parts of plants that live on.

Plant roots contribute to soil formation by physically cracking rocks. Roots also chemically alter rocks as the carbon dioxide they produce combines with water in the soil and forms corrosive carbonated water.

Even after plants are well established above and below ground, the roots of most plants actually outweigh and outgrow all the leaves, stems, flowers, and fruits that the plants produce above ground.

As roots navigate through the soil, they force their way into whatever passageways they encounter between particles of soil, often pushing soil to one side as they forge ahead. Look at a sidewalk that has been built over roots of trees to see just how forceful a growing root can be. An introductory botany text written in 1925 cites an example of the roots of a birch tree entering a crevice and lifting a 20-ton (18-metric-ton) boulder. By exerting a force of up to 150 pounds per square inch (11 kilograms per square centimeter), a root can lift and even crack a slab of concrete weighing hundreds of pounds. Or to put it another way, a root measuring four inches (100 millimeters) in diameter and three feet (1 meter) in length can lift 50 tons (45 metric tons).

High above the ground and roots, leaves capture the sun's energy to produce sugars and, like all other living tissues, to release carbon dioxide gas. Roots—whether large, small, or tiny—may not directly capture the sun's energy, but they still need some of this energy for their survival. As roots break down sugars and release energy for their own use, they also release carbon dioxide into the surrounding soil in the same way that the leaves at the other end of the plant release carbon dioxide into the surrounding air. Each root is surrounded by a halo of carbonic acid that forms as carbon dioxide leaves the root and reacts with water in the nearby soil. The carbonic acid reacts with rocks such as granite to release nutrients for plant growth and to form the mineral particles of soil known as clay, sand, and silt. This simple acid has far-reaching effects on the future of the soil and the mineral nutrients that the soil can furnish to the roots of plants.

In a prairie, forest, or desert, the roots of different plants partition the soil space so that competition for nutrients and water is minimized. Some plants have shallow roots that rarely extend more than a few inches or a couple of feet below the surface of the soil. In deserts where only about 3 percent of the rainfall penetrates more than a few inches below ground, cacti of all sizes—from giant saguaros to small, round cacti not much bigger than a nickel—have shallow, sprawling root systems that catch and absorb whatever rain happens to fall.

The roots of other plants extend down well beyond two feet (60 centimeters), some as far as five feet (1.5 meters), but even more roots, as in the case of desert mesquite trees, venture well beyond that to depths of as much as 100 feet (30.5 meters). Roots of some prairie plants, as well as trees like mesquite that live in some of the driest sections of a desert, extend below ground more than ten times as far as their leaves and stalks reach above ground.

Fungal filaments wrap around roots of trees and exchange water and minerals for the sugars produced by the tree. The fungus uses the nutrients it obtains from the tree to produce its fruiting bodies, the mushrooms.

As young seedlings they devote practically all their energy to growing underground. They expend relatively little energy growing toward the light until they have finally discovered a reliable source of water. Water and mineral elements beyond the reach of shallow roots may still be within reach of roots that extend deep into the soil. By having roots that extend to different layers of the soil, plants in a community reduce their competition for resources like water and minerals that may be scarce in certain soils.

Roots grow and travel through soils of many textures, wending their way among soil particles and along earthworm tunnels, always in search of the water and oxygen that every root must have. Roots are capable of growing to phenomenal lengths. After only four months of growth, one rye plant had extended 15 million roots, and the total length of these roots was about 380 miles (610 kilometers). In terms of surface area, these roots came in contact with 2,554 square feet (284 square yards; 238 square meters) of soil. And if the lengths and surface areas of all the minuscule but innumerable root hairs covering each root are taken into consideration, the figures for root length and surface area soar to 7,000 miles (11, 260 kilometers) and 7,000 square feet (778 square yards; 651 square meters).

Having roots with such incredibly large surface areas assures that a plant gathers enough of the mineral nutrients that are present in low concentrations in the surrounding soil. By establishing mycorrhizal associations, roots increase even more the surface area available for uptake of water and nutrients. While roots are alive, they help hold soil particles together. Even after they die, roots leave a legacy to the soil that nurtured them. New spaces are continually being created in soil whenever roots rot and leave their vacant passageways in the soil.

Alive or dead, roots actually improve the movements of water, air, and other roots through the soil by helping to form clumps and aggregates in the soil. However, because roots are so hard to observe deep underground, very few people have studied them. When they do, scientists will probably discover that roots of many plants grow much longer and much deeper than they originally suspected.

Roots can be very choosy about the soils they associate with; they grow well only in soils that have a suitable assortment of nutrients. And often the nutrients can be used only if suitable mycorrhizal fungi are present in the soil to help the roots tap these resources. The essential nutrients in soils that all plants demand for their growth and survival come in the form of elements and compounds. The 18 essential elements that plants need for growth and survival come from the air and from water, but mostly from the soil. The three elements from water and air—carbon, hydrogen, and oxygen—make up 95 percent of a plant's weight. The other 15 essential elements derived from the soil represent a mere 5 percent of a plant's weight.

Roots mine the mineral resources of the soil, and roots can make these 18 essential minerals available to animals of the land. In going from soil to plant, calcium, for example, is first concentrated eightfold; and in going from plant to animal, this element is then concentrated fivefold more, for a total of 40 times the concentration found in soil. Not only are

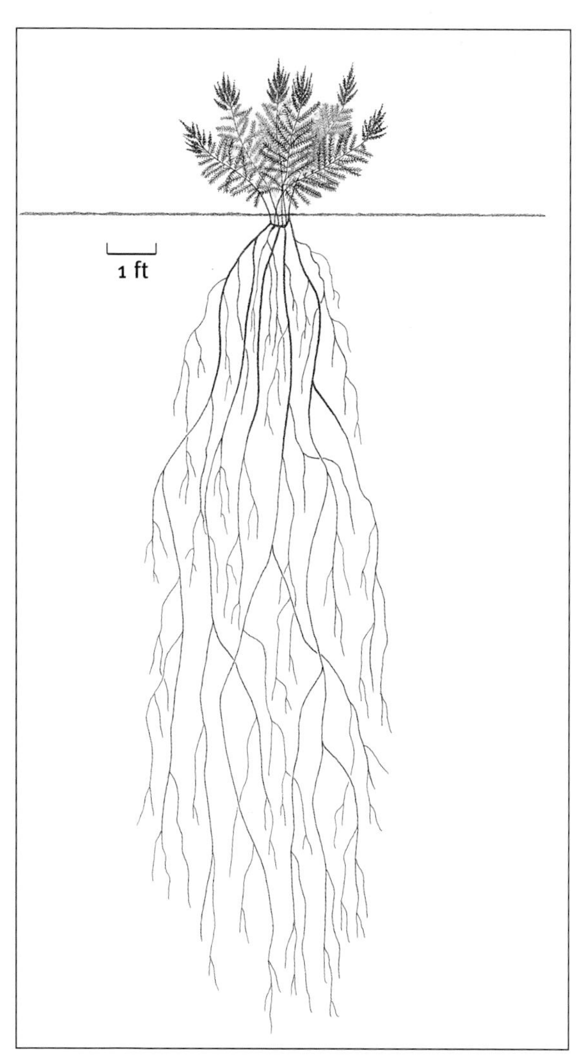

The deep roots of leadplant improve the structure of soil as they grow and enrich soil when they die. Each year prairie plants add to each acre of soil about three tons of roots for every ton of shoots.

Tall saguaro cacti and short mesquite shrubs share the Arizona desert. The shallow roots of saguaro and the deep roots of mesquite do not compete for the sparse water of desert soil.

we human animals entirely dependent on energy that is ultimately derived from sugars that plants produce during photosynthesis, we are also almost entirely dependent on plant roots for concentrating from the soil the many mineral nutrients that sustain our lives.

To establish how much nutrition a plant gets from the soil, a Belgian scientist by the name of van Helmont performed a long but simple experiment more than 350 years ago that we still cite today as a particularly informative experiment on plant nutrition. First, van Helmont filled a large pot with exactly 200 pounds (90.8 kilograms) of soil that he had thoroughly dried in an oven. Next he watered the soil and planted a shoot that he had cut from a willow tree. He weighed the willow shoot at the time he planted it and then again five years later.

The shoot that initially weighed 5 pounds (2.3 kilograms) grew into a small tree weighing 169 pounds 3 ounces (76.7 kilograms). Throughout the experiment, he added only water to the soil to keep it moist, and he carefully covered the surface of the pot with a sheet of metal perforated with tiny holes to keep dust from accumulating on the surface of the soil. In addition to weighing the tree after five years' growth, van Helmont also dried the soil from the pot and found that the soil had lost only 2 ounces (0.057 kilogram) of its initial starting weight of 200 pounds (90.8 kilograms). Most of the 164 pounds (74.5 kilograms) that the willow shoot had gained in the five years must have come from the water and air, but only a tiny fraction of the plant's increase in weight could have come from the soil.

In the engaging little book *Lessons on Soil* that he prepared for students at the village school of Wye in Kent, England, Sir John Russell went on to demonstrate even more illuminating features about the nutrition that plants derive from the soil. Van Helmont had shown how very little plant food is actually found in soil and how little food a plant receives from the soil during its growth. Yet without these small, practically undetectable amounts of food from the soil, plants barely survive and grow poorly.

Russell asked the students to plant mustard seeds in a pot of topsoil where rye plants had previously grown (pot 1). The mustard plants that subsequently grew only weighed 0.63 ounces (17.8 grams), while mustard plants that grew in topsoil where no other plants had grown (pot 2) weighed 2.2 ounces (62.3 grams), or almost three and a half times as much as the mustard plants that shared their soil with rye plants. Van Helmont could have predicted exactly what the students found when they dried and weighed the soil of pot 1 both before planting the rye and after harvesting it. Even though the rye plants had used most of the nutrients in the soil of pot 1, the dried soil neither gained nor lost weight while the rye plants grew on it.

When the students repeated the experiment using subsoil rather than topsoil, mustard plants that had grown in subsoil where rye had previously grown (pot 3) weighed

Mustard plants grow better in soil to which dead plant matter has been added (pots 5 and 6, topsoil and subsoil, respectively) than they do in soil to which no plant matter has been added (pots 2 and 4, topsoil and subsoil, respectively). However, they do not grow as large in soil where rye plants had previously grown (pots 1 and 3, topsoil and subsoil, respectively). They grow best in soil that contains both dead plant matter and a greater number of living soil creatures (pot 5, topsoil).

slightly less than mustard plants grown in soil that had not been previously planted with rye (pot 4). Although the topsoil provides nutrients for the growth of mustard plants, the subsoil offers less in the way of nutrients to either rye plants or mustard plants.

To help pinpoint the origin of these nutrients in the soil, the students at Wye School were then asked to compare the growth of mustard plants in specially prepared pots of topsoil (pot 5) and subsoil (pot 6). To both of these pots, the same weight of such plant remains as stems, leaves, and grass were added before the mustard seeds were planted. The mustard plants always grew larger in both topsoil and subsoil to which plant pieces had been added (pots 5 and 6) than they did in soil to which no plant remains had been added (pots 2 and 4). Once again the mustard seedlings grew better in the pots with topsoil (pots 2 and 5) than in the pots with subsoil (pots 4 and 6). Adding pieces of plants to the subsoil (pot 6) increased the growth of mustard plants, but not as much as adding the same weight of plant pieces to topsoil increased their growth (pot 5).

The plant pieces that the students had added to the soil provided nutrients to the growing mustard seedlings, but the plants were not able to take nutrients directly from the pieces of plants. If the mustard seedlings had been able to obtain nutrients this way, they would have grown as well in subsoil containing plant remains (pot 6) as they grew in topsoil containing the same amount of plant pieces (pot 5). When the pots were emptied after the mustard plants had completed their growth, more original plant pieces remained in the subsoil than in the topsoil. Some change occurs in pieces of plants when they are exposed to the soil that makes them more nutritious to growing plants. Whatever this change is, it is more evident in topsoil than it is in subsoil, and the agents that bring about this change are clearly more effective in the topsoil than they are in the subsoil.

The experiments that the students at Wye School carried out call our attention to the special attributes of topsoil. One obvious difference between topsoil and subsoil is that topsoil is inhabited by creatures whose chief occupation is decomposing and recycling plant and animal remains that fall to the surface of the soil. These creatures are busiest and most abundant in the topsoil, because it is here that their food and nutrients are most plentiful. The fertility of a soil comes from the life that it supports.

The Elements of Plant Growth

Elements and compounds in the soil come as either positively charged ions (cations), negatively charged ions (anions), or uncharged ions. Like charges repel and opposite charges attract. When negative charges combine with an equivalent number of positive charges, the resulting compound is uncharged or neutral. That is what happens, for example, when a calcium cation meets a carbonate anion:

Ca^{+2}		CO_3^{-2}		$CaCO_3$
calcium cation	+	carbonate anion	→	calcium carbonate-or lime

Plant roots cannot use a number of elements, such as phosphorus, unless they occur as compounds with another element. Nitrogen, phosphorus, sulfur, and boron can be used by plants only when they form compounds with hydrogen such as ammonium cations (NH_4^+) or when they form compounds with oxygen such as nitrate (NO_3^-), phosphate (PO_4^{---}), sulfate (SO_4^{--}), or borate (BO_4^{--}).

Even though positive cations and negative anions attract and bind one another, under certain circumstances they can separate, exchange, and form new combinations. Exactly which exchange of cations and anions will occur in the soil depends first on how strongly the anions and cations bind to each other, and second on how many there are of each. Compounds and elements interact in the soil to either enhance or suppress each other's uptake by plant roots or movement in the soil. If one compound or element in a soil increases or decreases, other compounds or elements, as well as the plants and animals that live in that soil, are often affected.

The chart below lists the elements that are essential for plant growth along with the ionic forms that they assume in soils.

The first nine elements are those that are required in relatively large amounts (more than 0.1 percent of a plant's dry weight); the remaining elements in the list are those that are used in relatively small quantities (less than 0.1 percent of a plant's dry weight).

Names and symbols for elements	Symbols (and names) for ionic forms of elements	
Elements derived mostly from water and air		
Carbon, C		
Hydrogen, H	H^+	
Oxygen, O		
Elements derived from soil		
Nitrogen, N	NO_3^-, NH_4^+ (nitrate, ammonium)	
Phosphorus, P	HPO_4^{--} $H_2PO_4^-$ (orthophosphates)	
Potassium, K	K^+	
Calcium, Ca	Ca^{++}	
Magnesium, Mg	Mg^{++}	
Sulfur, S	SO_4^{--}	(sulfate)
Boron, B	BO_4^{--}	(borate)
Copper, Cu	Cu^{++}	
Chlorine, Cl	Cl^-	(chloride)
Iron, Fe	Fe^{++}, Fe^{+++} (ferrous, ferric)	
Manganese, Mn	Mn^{++}	(manganous)
Molybdenum, Mo	MoO_4^{--}	(molybdate)
Zinc, Zn	Zn^{++}	
Nickel, Ni	Ni^{++}	
Cobalt, Co	Co^{++}	

Plants and their Animal Partners

Decomposers And Recyclers

Many of the animals of the soil look like creatures from another world, and they really are creatures from a world that is totally alien to most of us. Few people ever see these creatures, not because they are rare but because they lead retiring lives in the leaf litter and soil. Try looking for them, however, and you are very likely to succeed in your search. Despite their uniqueness, these small animals without backbones share a number of features with other animals of the soil, both large and small.

A great many of the soil creatures are pale and white. In the dark recesses of the soil, pigments that give color to skin and other natural body coverings are embellishments that none of their blind fellow creatures would appreciate anyway. Pigments often protect from sunlight; but in the soil, pigments are usually superfluous since rays of sunlight almost never reach these recesses. There is no point in wasting energy on producing pigments that serve no useful function.

In totally dark surroundings there is not much point in having eyes, either. Since eyes

Getting Closer: A Berlese Funnel

A good way to make the acquaintance of the creatures that live in the soil beneath our feet is to set up a Berlese funnel. This useful device is named after the Italian scientist Antonio Berlese, from whose writings and beautiful, detailed drawings came some of our first close-up views of the subterranean world. The heat and brightness of an electric light placed above a Berlese funnel drives creatures that are accustomed to dark, moist habitats down into the dark chamber below the funnel. Here they can be collected and observed at close range. It is hard to believe that a device so simple to make can be so effective at revealing who lives in the leaf litter and soil.

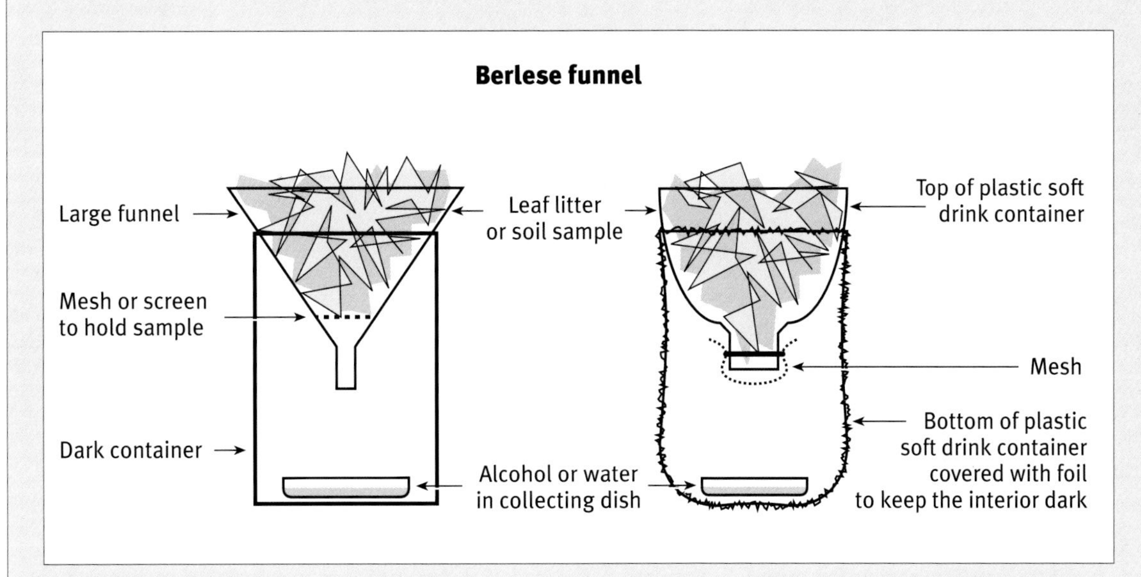

Berlese funnels are easy to make and easy to use. Sooner or later all the arthropods of a soil or leaf litter sample leave the funnel to escape the bright light overhead and look for a darker home.

are often absent or very small in soil creatures, senses other than sight have been enhanced to compensate for visual deficiencies. Touch and smell seem to be particularly acute. One feature of most creatures from the underground is their abundance of touch-sensitive hairs, bristles, and whiskers. These sensory structures can be quite large and can come in any number of shapes: some long, fine, and tapered; some like fine feathers; some paddle-shaped, and a few club-shaped.

Predators are usually endowed with well-developed sense organs since their livelihood depends on finding particular prey. A good sense of touch and smell go well with speed and agility in tracking down prey. In the labyrinthine passageways of the soil, long, sinuous bodies are often a definite advantage for a predator. Nonpredators often just move along until they stumble upon their dinner—sometimes living, sometimes dead.

Rather than trying to outrun or outmaneuver agile predators, certain prey have adopted a different strategy for escaping harm. They often use energy to form hard, protective shells that are part of their bodies. If these shells are not sufficient protection, the prey often curl or roll into a ball with all their soft, vulnerable parts tucked away beneath the ball's hard surfaces.

Mites, millipedes, woodlice, and armadillos have all independently discovered this strategy for protection. When curled into a ball, one genus of woodlouse looks so similar to a curled armadillo, the Spanish name for "little armored one," that the person who initially named the woodlouse decided, most appropriately, to name it *Armadillidium*.

Beetle or oribatid mites of soils also have hard, slick shells covering most of their spherical bodies. A hungry predator finds it difficult to sink its jaws, or mandibles, into the protective shell, but the mite's eight legs are still vulnerable bite-size morsels. These legs can, however, be drawn beneath the protective shell at the rear end of the mite while the hard shell at the head end that is hinged

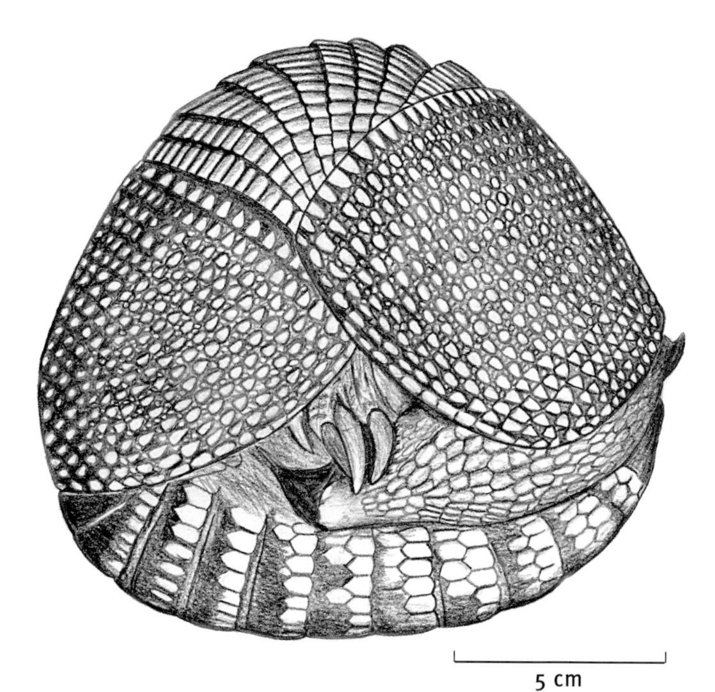

The armadillo belongs to a group of armored mammals that dig burrows and feed on soil insects. These slow-moving creatures escape the teeth of their predators by rolling up so that only their hard armor is exposed.

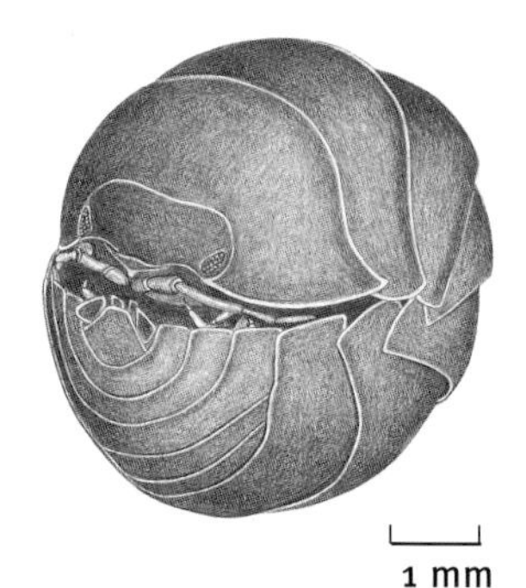

The Armadillidium is a slow-moving woodlouse that avoids the jaws of its predators by tucking all its appendages beneath its hard plates of cuticle.

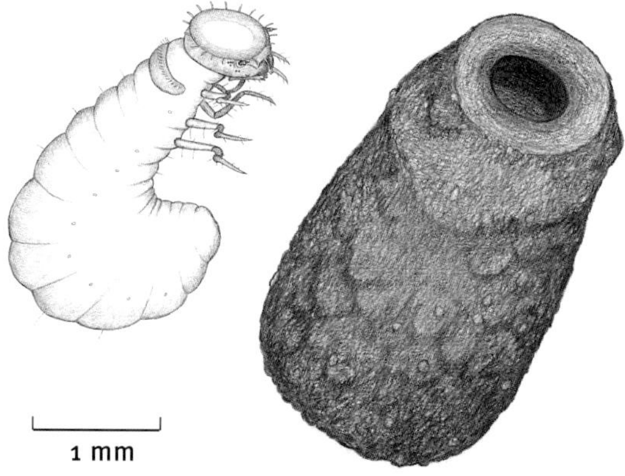

The head of this beetle larva forms a snug-fitting plug for its case, fashioned from its droppings and shed skins.

to the rear end swings backward. The two shells clamp down like those of a clam, with barely a space between them. By thus rolling into a ball, the oribatid leaves no vulnerable parts of its body exposed. Predators are foiled by this maneuver, and the mites are also protected from drying out if the soil ever becomes too dry.

Other animals of the soil protect themselves by building cases in which to retreat or in which they lay their eggs. A few beetle larvae and a few moth caterpillars use a combination of silk, saliva, and soil particles to fashion the cozy cases in which they live and travel. The rear end of a case is usually open to expel the droppings of the larva, and the larva can quickly seal the front end by plugging the entrance to the case with its very hard, snug-fitting head.

Although millipedes and pseudoscorpions do not carry cases wherever they go, they do build shelters for themselves at each molt, a time in their lives when they are most vulnerable. As they grow, their old, hard shells are shed, exposing new, soft shells underneath. During this molting period several days may pass before the new shell expands and hardens. A mother millipede also builds a case for each of her eggs and then stands guard over her nest as the young millipedes develop inside. Cases made from particles of soil defy the jaws of predators and blend in so well with surrounding soil that they easily go unnoticed.

Another feature shared by many of these soil animals is the sheer abundance with which they occur. Some of the most abundant soil animals are represented by the arthropods (*arthro* = jointed; *pod* = feet). These are animals that do not have backbones but do have jointed legs. Well over a billion arthropods may live on an acre (4,840 square yards; 4,050 square meters) of pasture soil. In a hardwood forest, the layers of leaf litter and the tiny passageways that permeate the rich soil provide even more habitats and niches for animals of the soil.

The figures that have been calculated for the number of individuals of a particular group of soil creatures may vary depending on the time of year the population was examined, the particular habitat occupied by the population, and the method used to count portions of the total population. Since figures calculated for human populations can also vary with season and place, taking a census of a country like the United States with a population of well over 200 million people is a monumental task. The final count of people represents not an exact total but nevertheless a good estimate of the actual size of the population.

Making a census of an entire acre of soil with animal populations many times the size of the human population of the United States also demands great effort. Different census takers have arrived at different figures for the numbers of different animals per acre of soil. The figures, however, always give the same impression about creatures of the soil. They are extremely abundant, and certain groups are always more abundant than others. The number of creatures on a single acre of land far exceeds the entire human population of the world.

Think of organizing all the creatures in a 3-foot by 3-foot area (one square yard, or almost one square meter) of soil into categories according to their abundance. We can do this by arranging the categories as a series of stacked layers with the dimensions of each layer reflecting the number of creatures in a particular category. When the layers are stacked in order of their sizes, they form a pyramid of numbers. The most abundant creatures will be represented by the very bottom layer, and the least abundant animals will be represented by the layer at the very top of the pyramid.

Even though they are the smallest of the soil creatures, bacteria can easily claim to be the most abundant—on the order of thousands of billions in each square yard or meter of soil. There are so many bacteria that despite their individual tiny sizes, as a group

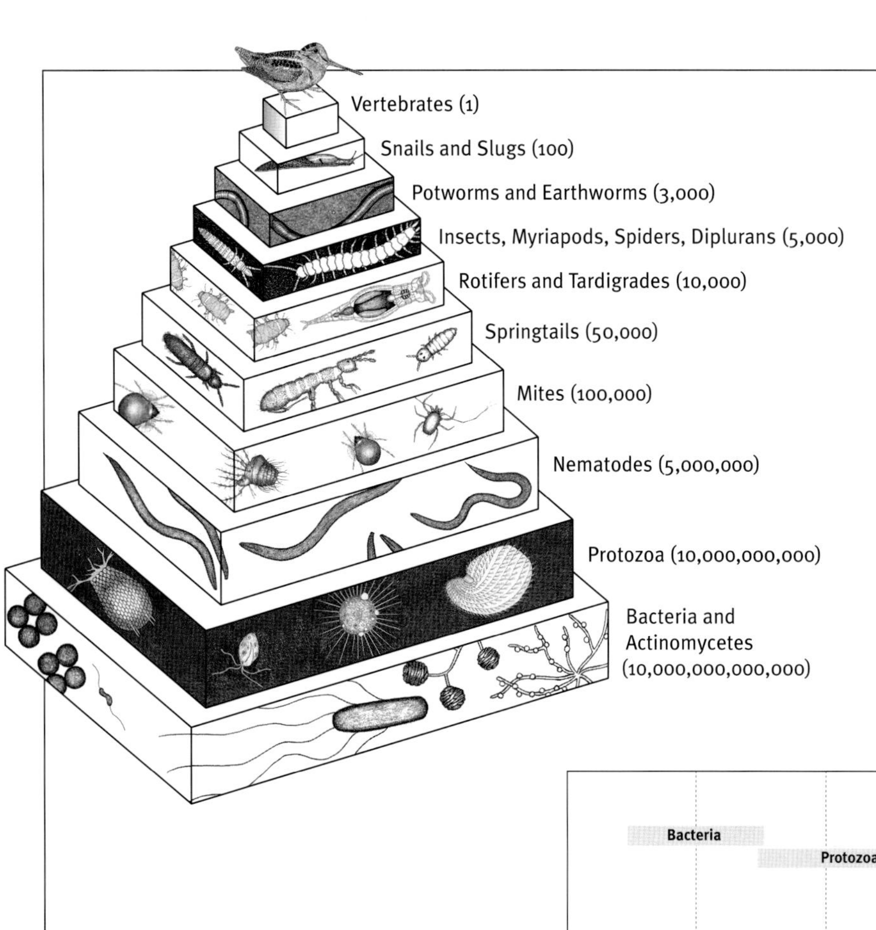

The number of creatures that live on a square meter of ground can be arranged in a pyramid of layers according to their sizes. There are millions of creatures at the bottom layer of the pyramid, a few in the top layer, and thousands of other invertebrate creatures in layers in between. If the dimensions of each layer in the pyramid were drawn proportionally to the number of animals that they represent, then the bacteria and actinomycetes layer would be 100 million times the volume of the mite layer and the mite layer, in turn, would be 100,000 times the volume of the vertebrate layer.

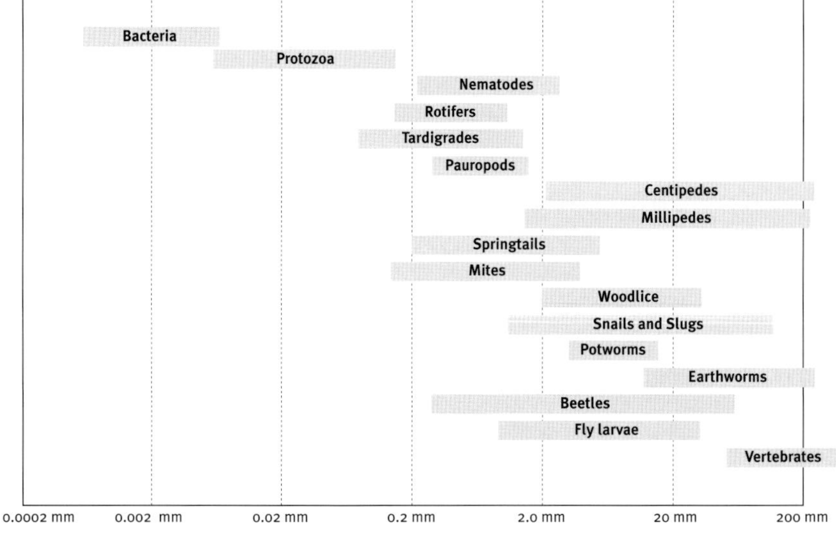

Creatures in the soil vary vastly in length, from 1/1,000 mm for bacteria to about 1,000 mm for badgers, some burrowing snakes, and a few earthworms.

they easily outnumber, and often outweigh, all other categories of soil creatures.

As soil creatures increase in size, fewer of them are found in a square meter (or yard) of soil. So by ranking the categories of creatures according to their size, we can predict the arrangement of layers in the pyramid. One-celled organisms, known as protozoa, would be represented by a layer above the smaller, more numerous bacteria but below the layer for the larger, less numerous eelworms or nematodes. Then, seven more layers—representing (1) mites, (2) relatives of insects known as springtails, (3) tiny invertebrates known as rotifers and tardigrades, (4) all arthropods other than mites and springtails and including, including insects, (5) potworms and earthworms, and finally (6) snails and slugs—would be stacked one on top of the other in roughly the order of their increasing sizes.

The topmost and smallest layer of the pyramid would represent the vertebrates—toads, frogs, salamanders, turtles, snakes, mammals, and birds. Soil is sparsely populated by these creatures whose survival depends in one way or another on creatures that are smaller but more abundant than they—those creatures represented by all the lower layers of the pyramid.

These larger animals may dispatch large numbers of earthworms, insect larvae, and slugs; but the pyramid of which they represent the topmost layer neither wobbles nor tips. The vast mosaic of soil life needs its predators and producers as well as its decomposers, its minuscule creatures as well as its hefty creatures, all subsisting in an exquisite state of balance and mutually sustaining one another. The interactions of all these members of the soil community take the form of an intricate web, showing how the various members depend on one another for their nutrition and survival.

How Creatures Give Soil Its Fertility

As he watched leaves fall gently to the earth one autumn day, the naturalist Henry David Thoreau realized that even death and decay have a grander and brighter side than most of us appreciate. He wrote in his journal:

> How pleasant to walk over beds of these fresh, crisp, and rustling fallen leaves. . . . How beautiful they go to their graves! They that waved so loftily, how contentedly they return to dust again and are laid low, resigned to lie and decay at the foot of the tree and afford nourishment to new generations of their kind. . . . They are about to add a leaf's breadth to the depth of the soil. We are all richer for their decay.

The people of the Aran Islands, off the west coast of Ireland, have known for centuries that to grow vegetables on their rocky islands they must pulverize their rocks and mix them with decaying seaweed. Not much but algae and lichens and mosses can grow on rocks and minerals alone. The organic matter contributed by plants and animals enriches a soil's physical as well as chemical properties, providing the essential conditions for survival of practically all of the soil's plant and animal life.

All living plants and animals take elements and compounds from the soil. In death they all actually return more to the soil than they ever took during their lifetimes. Not only do they return elements and compounds that they obtained from the soil, they also add organic matter made up almost entirely of elements that initially came from water and air. Much of the energy that plants capture from the sun during photosynthesis is passed on to the soil and to the animals that feed on the plants.

Plants are nourished by resources of the soil, and they eventually return all elements to the soil, but not without a great deal of help from the decomposers. In addition to returning to the soil all the elements that plants once borrowed from it, decomposers inherit the energy that plants once captured from the sun as they grew and flourished. The decomposers pass on their inheritance to the soil as they actively decompose the remains of plants and as they in turn are eventually decomposed by other decomposers. The energy from the faraway sun is put to use by the decomposers of the soil as they break down dead plant and animal matter into compounds that dissolve in soil and water.

Traces of plant and animal matter often stubbornly resist decay. The tough and fibrous traces of plant remains, such as leaf veins and heartwood, are made up of sugars strung together to form chains of cellulose as well as compounds known as lignins that hold the chains of cellulose together. A few creatures of the soil, such as snails, termites, and fungi can digest some of these tough plant remains; however, most decomposers simply pass them through their guts undigested, but at least chewed down in size.

Even though they decompose at a very slow rate, the tough plant remains become smaller and smaller as they pass through one soil animal after another. Organisms in the

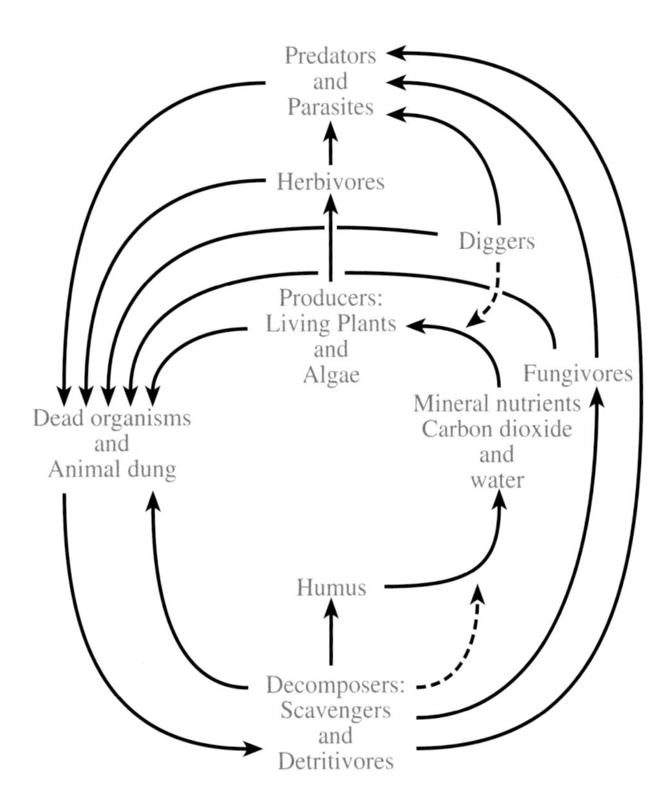

This food web shows how both living and dead creatures interact with each other as well as with minerals, water, and carbon dioxide of the soil. Solid arrows show the flow of nutrients between the living world and the mineral world of the soil; and dashed arrows indicate how the flow of nutrients from debris and soil is affected by the activities of decomposers, scavengers, detritivores, and diggers.

soil eventually pulverize these persistent plant fragments, although the compounds of cellulose and lignin making up the fragments remain mostly intact. By the time bacteria have traveled through the guts of the decomposers, they have often multiplied many times over, and they continue breaking down whatever organic matter remains in the droppings of the larger decomposers.

After organic matter passes through an earthworm, for example, its bacterial population can increase fivefold. Droppings made up of these pulverized fragments of leaf litter are even more inviting to bacteria and fungi since there are now many more pores and niches for them to occupy. The fungi that dwell in the forest litter are continually consumed in vast numbers and their spores are continually carried to new homes by decomposers.

As microbes and animals of the soil break down the remains of various creatures into simpler compounds, they add organic matter to the soil. Such organic matter also happens to be the main source of certain essential elements of the soil such as nitrogen, phosphorus, and sulfur. Eventually, the organic matter transforms into tiny particles of a dark organic matter known as "humus." Humus consists of the hard-to-digest plant materials that remain in organic matter after the easily digested portions have been consumed at least once by decomposers. It is made up of persistent organic molecules from plant cells such as oils, resins, lignins, and waxes, as well as remains of bacteria and fungi that pass through the digestive tracts of larger decomposers and end up in their droppings.

Organic matter can actually be consumed a number of times, since there are some decomposers that prefer feeding on organic matter that has already been digested by some other decomposers. Other soil arthropods and worms also find nutrition in these droppings. One creature's meal today can be another creature's meal tomorrow. These decomposers of dung, called coprophages, redigest the droppings of other soil animals. Among the better known decomposers of dung are certain potworms, springtails, and woodlice. With time even the well-digested humus formed by the coprophages slowly and gradually decays. But while it lingers in the soil it has some remarkable effects on soil properties.

Because humus particles are acidic and contain high concentrations of positively charged hydrogen ions, for each hydrogen ion lost the humus particle gains a negative charge. The negative charges that accumulate on humus particles act as magnets for any positively charged elements (cations) or compounds that pass their way. Humus binds many of these cations that are essential for plant growth, like calcium and potassium, and

Death and decay, life and rebirth flow together among the decaying leaves and logs of this forest floor in the Adirondack Mountains of New York.

prevents their being leached from the soil. Humus serves as an important intermediary between fresh organic matter, from which it is derived, and the carbon dioxide, minerals, and water to which it eventually returns, often years later.

Under certain weather and soil conditions, humus never manages to accumulate and contribute to the structure of a soil. Where soils are sandy, rocky, and porous, as they are in deserts, organic matter decays more rapidly than it does in soil that is dense, compact, and poorly aerated.

Organic matter also decays more rapidly in warmer climates. When temperatures rise above 80°F (27°C), organic matter actually decays faster than it is generated. That is why practically all organic matter in the tropics is found aboveground in the living forest. Any organic matter that falls to the ground is quickly reduced to carbon dioxide, minerals, and water. There are practically no earthworms and few insects in tropical soils. The bacteria and fungi quickly go to work on any organic matter that falls to the ground and reduce it to simple compounds of water, carbon dioxide, and minerals, leaving no debris or humus for larger creatures of the soil such as earthworms and insects.

Even the phenomenon of global warming is linked to the well-being of the obscure microbes and tiny fauna of the forest floor. Living plants take carbon dioxide from the air to produce oxygen and carbon-containing compounds that are stored in plant tissues and in tissues of animals that feed on plants. Eventually the decomposers break down these carbon stores from dead plant and animal matter. New humus is constantly being formed from dead plant matter and constantly replacing the old humus that is being reduced to carbon dioxide, water, and minerals.

The rate at which new humus replaces old humus determines just how thick the layer of humus on the forest floor will be. In tropical forests where bacteria and fungi convert the litter directly to water, carbon dioxide, and minerals, little humus manages to accumulate. Only in the cooler forests at higher latitudes does humus have a chance to build up and slow the production of carbon dioxide. If global warming increases, not only will the humus content and the richness of soils imparted by humus diminish, but the generation of carbon dioxide in the soil and air will also undoubtedly rise.

The Importance of Nitrogen

Bacteria and fungi are the microbes of soil that initiate recycling of dead plant and animal matter. Microbes have been around longer than any of the other creatures of the soil, and as we are continually discovering, they have adapted to just about every environment and every diet. They can ingest, digest, and process just about any compound known to humans. That virtue has made microbes extremely useful in cleaning up many of our human-made messes as well as processing compounds in the soil that no other creatures can deal with. Without this processing, nature's chemical cycles would screech to a halt. Microbes get involved in the rather unsavory task of feeding on rotting plants and animals in order to tap the reserves of energy that remain in them after death. Energy is a resource of unparalleled importance. All creatures need energy for survival. Whenever the supply of dead matter that falls to the ground increases, microbes of the soil quickly multiply to use every bit of this new energy source.

Just as all creatures need energy for survival, they also need large amounts of certain elements—in particular, carbon and nitrogen—to grow and multiply. Microbes can usually get all the carbon and other elements they need from dead plant matter, but nitrogen is often in short supply. The proportion of carbon to nitrogen in many fallen leaves and logs is greater than 100 to 1, but in bacteria this proportion is around 5 to 1. For these bacteria to survive and multiply, they need to find a source of food that can provide carbon and nitrogen in proportions ranging between 5 to 1 and 30 to 1.

As microbes undertake the job of decomposing fallen leaves or rotting logs, they obviously need more nitrogen than the leaves or the logs can supply. For microbes to continue multiplying and decomposing, they must get nitrogen from whatever source is nearby. Microbes that feed on organic matter in its early stages of decay multiply and act most efficiently as decomposers if they can take nitrogen from the neighboring soil. This usually means competing with plant roots for nitrogen. The growth of plants in the area of decaying organic matter slows down as microbes compete with roots for the nitrogen that they need. The addition of nitrogen-rich manure or fertilizer to soil with decaying organic matter gives both roots and microbes enough nitrogen to satisfy their needs. Likewise, adding nitrogen to compost in the form of manure or fertilizer provides the missing element for microbial growth and speeds up the decay of compost heaps.

Fresh, green plant matter is higher in nitrogen than dry, dead plant matter such as straw, sawdust, or dry leaves and is always a good addition to a compost pile. Once the decay of organic matter in soil or in compost is complete, and the energy source for bacteria is used up, most of the bacteria will die and return the nitrogen they used to grow and multiply so rapidly. Soil and compost are now the richer for the demise of the decomposers, and enough nitrogen is now available to meet the needs of plants and microbes alike.

Different plants and different parts of plants have different proportions of carbon and nitrogen, so naturally they differ in their ability to supply the nitrogen that microbes need to continue growing. Not surprisingly, those plants or plant parts that can offer decomposing microbes ample quantities of nitrogen rot faster than those with meager quantities of nitrogen.

Some leaves are thin and delicate, like those of elms and alders; these leaves contain more nitrogen than leaves like those of oaks and beeches that are thick and tough. Elm and alder leaves, for which the ratio of carbon to nitrogen is about 20 to 1, rot faster than oak, pine, and beech leaves that have a carbon to nitrogen ratio of about 50 to 1; they decay in one year as opposed to three years for the tougher leaves.

Leaves like those of maple and basswood trees with carbon to nitrogen ratios of about 40 to 1 are not quite as tender as elm leaves, or as tough as oak and beech leaves, and completely decay in two years. Sawdust, wood chips, logs, and branches contain an even

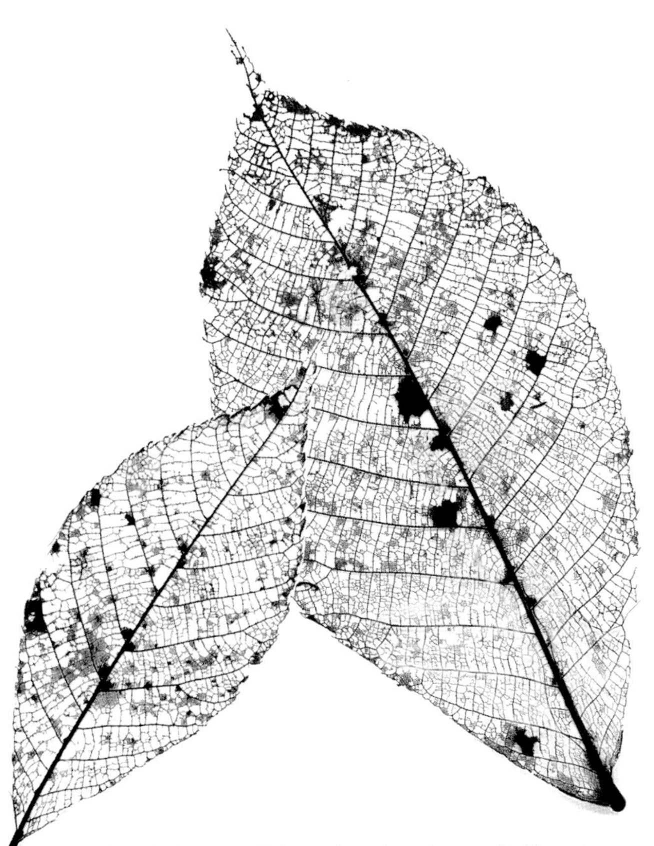

The skeletons of these hop hornbeam (left) and hickory (right) leaves are rich in lignin, a principal ingredient of woody fibers that is always the last portion of leaves and logs to decay.

smaller proportion of nitrogen than beech leaves and oak leaves. Woody materials that contain far more carbon-containing compounds than nitrogen-containing compounds, with a carbon to nitrogen ratio as high as 400 to 1, rot the slowest of all the organic matter.

An oak leaf experiences many changes from the time it falls from a tree until the time it is transformed to particles of humus by the many decomposers of the forest floor. There are always plenty of springtails on the forest floor waiting to chew holes in this freshly fallen leaf, and they are often joined by woodlice and millipedes that usually live in the leaf litter. Fungal filaments and bacteria invade the leaf tissue through the holes and improve the flavor of the decaying leaf for larvae of crane flies and midges. These fly larvae begin widening the holes chewed by springtails, woodlice, and millipedes, and add some of their own holes to the fallen leaf.

At this stage, when the leaf is pulverized and perforated with holes, even more soil arthropods join in the feast on the fallen leaf. Snails, oribatid mites, earwigs, a few crickets, other fly larvae, and maybe a few bristletails now widen the holes in the leaf until only its skeleton remains. Most of the soft, nitrogen-rich tissue of the leaf has been eaten, and only the tough, nitrogen-poor leaf skeleton or veins still persist. The many jaws that have chewed on the leaf have left many little pockets and irregularities in the leaf.

Bacteria move into these many microhabitats and now colonize more of the leaf than was ever exposed or colonized before. Bacterial decomposition progresses rapidly. Minuscule relatives of earthworms, called enchytraeid worms or potworms, along with the ubiquitous oribatid mites and springtails continue chewing what remains of the leaf's skeleton. Earthworms soon pull the remains of the fallen leaf into their extensive burrows where they mix this organic matter with mineral matter from below.

Earthworms can be particularly abundant and are especially good processors of organic matter, but the smaller enchytraeid worms and other burrowing animals also contribute to the mixing and churning of particles from the decomposed leaf. By this stage the leaf has been so thoroughly chewed and fragmented that only indigestible, dark, and enriching particles of humus remain. The decomposers have thus transformed a relatively nitrogen-poor oak leaf to relatively nitrogen-rich humus, and the soil is all the richer for the transformation.

Soil Structure

During a good portion of the 19th century, most chemists were convinced that understanding the soil's contribution to plant nutrition was simply a matter of understanding which chemicals, such as nitrates or phosphates, should be provided to a plant and in what proportions. In the 20th century it became increasingly clear that the growth of plants is influenced not only by the chemicals

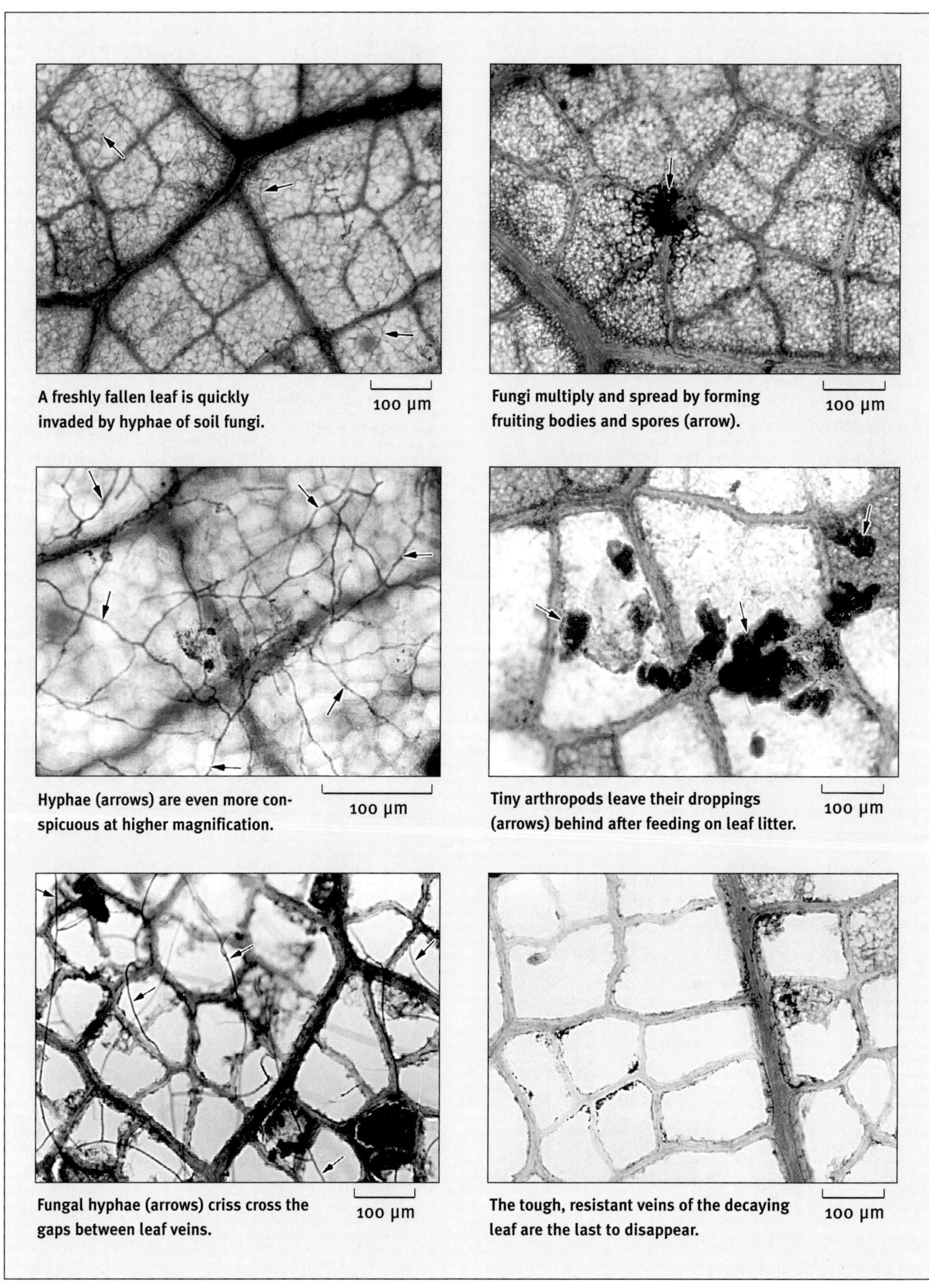
A freshly fallen leaf is quickly invaded by hyphae of soil fungi.
100 µm
Fungi multiply and spread by forming fruiting bodies and spores (arrow).
100 µm
Hyphae (arrows) are even more conspicuous at higher magnification.
100 µm
Tiny arthropods leave their droppings (arrows) behind after feeding on leaf litter.
100 µm
Fungal hyphae (arrows) criss cross the gaps between leaf veins.
100 µm
The tough, resistant veins of the decaying leaf are the last to disappear.
100 µm

As oak leaves return to the earth, they pass through various stages of decay. They are skeletonized, shredded, and digested by arthropods as well as colonized by fungi (indicated by arrows) and microbes. The droppings that the arthropods leave behind (also shown with arrows) contribute to formation of humus.

that make up the soil's solid ingredients, but also by the structure of the soil—the way in which these solid ingredients aggregate in the soil. By adding and mixing humus with soil particles, decomposers and recyclers encourage the aggregation of soil particles as well as improve the structure and, consequently, the fertility of soil.

Humus can affect the structure of soil in at least two ways. It can hold soil particles together in clumps or aggregates and thus reduce erosion of what otherwise would be soil that is too loose. On the other hand, the presence of humus can loosen the structure of a soil that is too tight and compact by facilitating movement of air and water into the soil as well as by encouraging the growth of roots and the movement of animals through the soil. The structure of a soil is often described as the size and shape of the small pieces into which a soil breaks up when crumbled in the hand. A crumbly structure has spaces and pores among the solid ingredients of a soil through which air, water, roots, and soil creatures can freely move.

Although the solid ingredients appear to fill practically all the space occupied by a crumbly structured soil, they actually share about half of their space with air and water. Tiny mineral particles of the soil, like clay, are separated by tiny pore spaces. Large mineral particles like sand are separated by large pore spaces. Even though larger sand particles may have larger pores between them, smaller clay particles have more of their surface area exposed to surrounding pores. Clearly, a mineral particle will increase its total area of exposed surface if it breaks into smaller particles.

Incalculable numbers of tiny creatures live in the spaces between the solid matter of crumbly soil and on the vast area of solid surfaces lining the spaces. The smaller spaces are occupied by water, while the larger spaces are filled with air. A researcher at Rothamsted, Britain's premier agricultural experiment station, once calculated that the surfaces lining all the tiny pores and passageways in a couple of tablespoons of soil add up to 250,000 square feet (27,800 square yards; 23,250 square meters)—the area occupied by a city block. No wonder there is room for so many creatures to live on the surfaces of soil crumbs.

If the mineral particles of sand, silt, and clay were packed tightly together in the absence of organic matter, pore spaces would remain among the particles, but the soil in these cases would be referred to as structureless. The smaller the mineral particles, the stickier the soil would be when wet and the harder it would be when dry. In such a tight, dense material, even the stronger roots of a plant could not penetrate, while air and water could barely circulate. Sticky clay soils that lack structure are almost impermeable to water, while sandy soils without structure can lose water rapidly.

It is amazing how a little organic matter added to the soil by living creatures or once living creatures can aggregate mineral particles and greatly improve the structure of a soil—and therefore the movement of water, air, and roots through it. But to maintain crumbs in the soil requires constant addition of organic material and the constant activity of microbes. Fresh supplies of plant and animal material are needed to keep up with their constant decomposition by microbes. When organic material is partially decomposed and exists as long sinuous fibers that stretch from mineral particle to mineral particle, it is most effective at binding particles in crumbs. But eventually even these organic molecules are broken down by soil bacteria to the simple compounds of CO_2 and water. Soil that loses more plant and animal material than it gains over time eventually loses its crumbs, its structure, its pores, and its air spaces. Creatures that stir up the soil, that mix mineral matter with fresh supplies of organic matter, help keep the structure, the crumbs, and the pores in a soil.

Diggers and Tillers

This morning the ground beneath the oaks and maples of the neighborhood park is covered with many tiny piles of soil. Yesterday the same soil surface had been perfectly smooth, but during last night's rain, the neighborhood earthworms were busy. As they fed and burrowed, they were constantly swallowing soil, essentially eating their way through the soil and then piling their droppings as casts on the surface. Charles Darwin calculated that these casts can soon add up to 10 tons (9 metric tons) of soil brought to the surface in just one year on only an acre of land. Now that is a substantial amount of earth moving!

Creatures that tunnel and burrow and dig participate in mixing the lower mineral-rich layers of the soil with the upper organic-rich layers. Their tunnels carry air and water to the deeper layers of the soil and provide channels along which roots often grow as they follow routes of least resistance. Many of the burrowing mammals can move massive amounts of soil—hundreds of pounds—when excavating a single den.

Spiders and insects, earthworms and crayfish may be much smaller than moles, gophers, and groundhogs, but they are certainly more abundant. When the earth-moving abilities of just one of these small creatures is multiplied by the number of creatures that work the soil over time and over area, one realizes that collectively these creatures are capable of moving a phenomenal amount of soil.

Who are some of these diggers of the earth? Where do they dig, how much soil do they move, and how does their earth moving affect nearby plants and animals? To answer these questions, we should first examine the layers of soil through which these various diggers travel, the properties of the layers, and how mixing and redistributing these layers is important for the continual circulation of mineral nutrients in a soil. Without creatures living among its layers, a soil becomes static and its nutrients halt their circulation from one layer to another. Without the circulation of minerals, only a few rugged pioneers can establish a foothold on what has become a lifeless soil.

How Plants and Animals Affect the Layers of Soil

The mineral particles in a soil come from rocks that have worn down over the ages; the organic particles come from the decay of plants and animals that once lived in, on, or over the soil. The elements and compounds of a soil come from air, water, and rocks, as well as from plants and

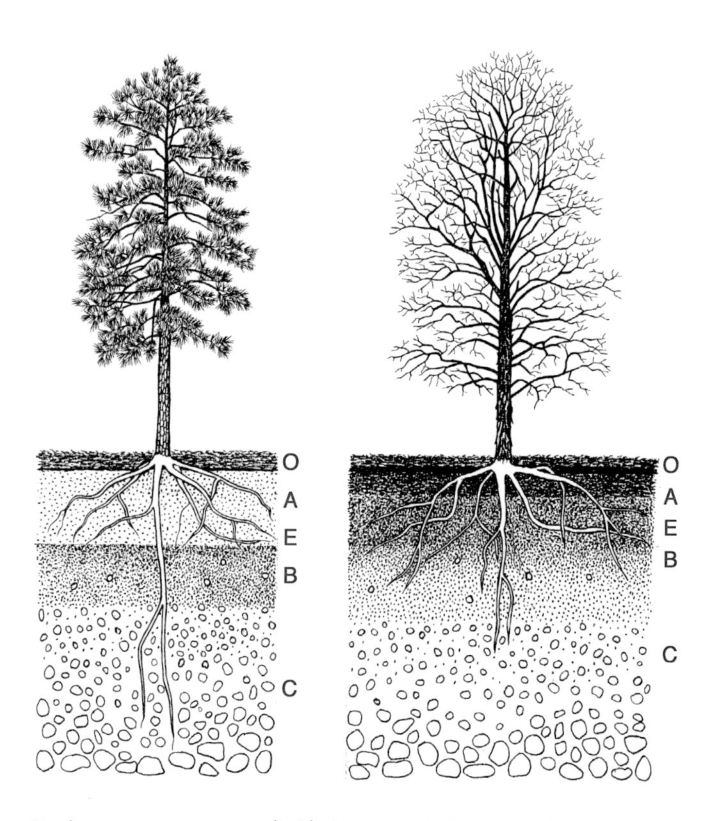

Under evergreen trees (left) the organic horizon of the soil is clearly a separate layer from the underlying mineral horizons, but in a deciduous forest (right), animals of the soil constantly mix the organic and mineral horizons.

Soil Horizons

Road cuts, trenches, and stream banks often expose the colorful and distinctive horizontal layers or *horizons* of a soil. These horizons tell about the elements and compounds that can be found in the soil. Over time, variations in the slope of the land as well as different climates, different plants, and different materials from which soils originate combine to give each soil a unique layering, from its surface down to its bedrock. Water that percolates down through a soil carries along with it elements and compounds from the soil's surface that settle at particular levels along the way. Often certain elements or compounds react with other elements and compounds that have already settled at another level in the soil. Wherever elements and compounds settle, combine, or react in the soil, they often leave colorful evidence of their whereabouts and give each soil its distinctively colored and textured layers.

Soil layers were first named after the first three letters in the alphabet: A, B, C. As studies of soils continued, other horizons were identified and their new names were added: O, E, R. Transitional horizons, such as AE, EB, BC, are found between these six so-called master horizons. Each of these main horizons of the soil are often even further subdivided into thinner horizons according to their special properties of color or chemistry.

At the surface of the soil, the *O* (organic) horizon consists entirely of organic matter, both recently added and decayed. Beneath the *O* horizon lies the *A* horizon, often known as topsoil, where organic matter and mineral particles intermingle. Roots seem to grow best in the *A* horizon. In soils of grasslands, surface debris as well as the thick mat of decaying roots assure that the *A* horizon is thick and deep. In woodland soils, however, the *A* horizon is thinner than in grassland soils and is built up almost entirely by the decay of surface debris such as logs and fallen leaves. Relatively few tree roots decay each year to add their organic matter to the woodland soil.

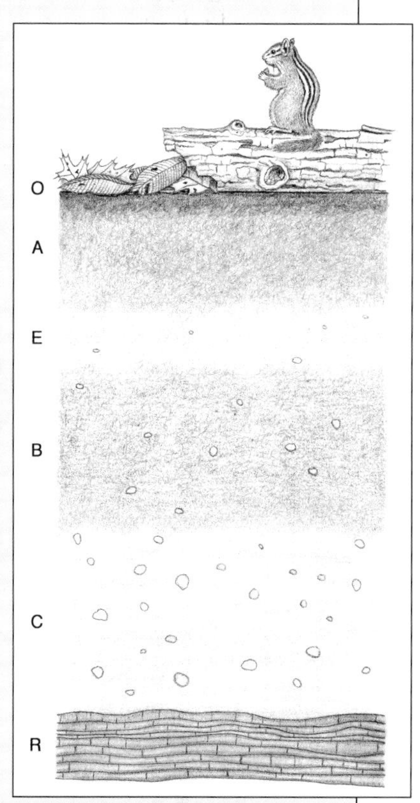

In grasslands, with their deep *A* horizons, most of the organic matter lies underground, whereas in a forest most of the organic matter is found above ground in the living trees rather than in its shallow *A* horizon.

The *E* horizon was once considered part of the *A* horizon. This layer loses most of its organic matter, clay, and nutrients from the leaching action of rain and melting snow as they percolate down through the horizons. The loss of matter and chemicals that give color to soil leaves little but pale sand in the *E* horizon.

The *B* horizon, or subsoil, is where many elements, clay particles, and some organic matter accumulate as they are leached out of the overlying *E* horizon by rainfall or snow. Beyond the *B* horizon and beyond the reach of most plant roots lies the *C* horizon, which is neither perturbed by the activities of soil creatures nor any longer involved in the process of soil formation. This quiet horizon of the soil represents materials such as gravel and sand from which the soil above initially began to form.

Beneath all the other soil horizons, usually anywhere from 20 to 60 inches (50 to 150 centimeters) below ground, lies the *R* horizon, the layer of underlying bedrock. Rocks like limestone, sandstone, granite, schist, or slate may occupy this horizon. As long as the other horizons from *O* to *C* remain in place and uneroded, the *R* horizon remains solid and unaffected by any weathering and soil formation that takes place in the horizons above.

animals. The various elements in a soil not only affect a variety of physical and chemical attributes of the soil, they also influence which plants will send down roots in the soil and which animals will take up residence in it. Plants and animals that live in a particular soil are not only a consequence of that soil's properties—its texture, its water, its nutrient elements and compounds—but they are also frequently responsible for them as well. From observations made over many years in many places, we know that certain plants and animals are associated with certain soils. We can tell a lot about the layers of a soil from the plants and animals that live in it, and we can also tell a lot about who lives in a soil by examining its various layers.

Because there are few diggers and burrow makers, little of the plant litter in a pine, hemlock, or other evergreen coniferous forest gets mixed with the deeper mineral soil. The soil shows a distinct layering, with the dark layer of plant litter clearly distinct from the pale, underlying mineral soil. In a forest of broadleaf deciduous trees, there are many soil dwellers. Their tillage and mixing of soil produce well-mixed layers of soil that look very different from the distinct layers in a coniferous forest. The striking difference between the way organic layers of soils blend with mineral layers in different types of forests was first noted more than a century ago by the Danish forester P. E. Müller. In deciduous forests the dark surface layer of plant debris or *mull* layer blends imperceptibly with the brown mineral layer of the deep soil, and no obvious soil horizons can be seen. In a pine forest, the organic layer of plant debris or *mor* layer remains separate and unmixed with the underlying mineral layers.

The surface layer of dark plant litter in a pine forest abruptly switches after a few inches to a white or gray mineral soil. These soils of coniferous forests are known as *podzols,* a Russian name meaning "ashes underneath" and referring to the bleached appearance of the mineral soil that was once

On the floor of a pine forest, mosses and pine needles contribute to the formation of a distinct organic or mor layer.

believed to represent the ashes left by forest fires. What has happened in the bleached, or *E,* layer of the podzol is that nutrients have been washed out of the layer by rain and melting snow. Almost the only materials left behind are the insoluble grains of sand. The light-colored sand gives the mineral soil its bleached appearance, and the nutrients that trickle downward come to lie in a red, brown, or black layer. Since the dark color of this soil layer comes from the toxic iron and aluminum ions that have settled in this horizon, tree roots in an evergreen forest tend to avoid these elements and grow best at the boundary between the sandy, bleached layer and the toxic, dark layer.

Obviously, it takes living organisms to keep various layers of soil in constant circulation, to keep essential nutrients from settling too deep in the soil, and to keep other toxic elements from concentrating and forming inhospitable layers in a soil. It also takes the decomposers to free these essential nutrients from dead plant and animal matter. Looking in on some of the many creatures that contribute their share to the circulation of nutrients in the soil, we can see how they impart to soil its amazing complexity, its fertility, and its health.

PART 2

MEMBERS OF THE SOIL COMMUNITY

MICROBES • INVERTEBRATES • VERTEBRATES

MICROBES

BACTERIA

CLASSIFICATION
Kingdom Archaebacteria (also known as Kingdom Archaea)
Kingdom Eubacteria (also known as Kingdom Bacteria)

PLACE IN FOOD WEB
Decomposers, Bacterial partners of plants, Producers

SIZE
1–10 µm in diameter

NUMBER OF SPECIES
4,888

Bacteria

For years, scientists considered the decay and recycling of plant and animal debris in the soil to be a purely chemical reaction that did not involve any living creatures. But then the clever experiments of the French biologist Louis Pasteur in the latter half of the 19th century established beyond question the importance of bacteria in decomposing organic matter and liberating its nutrient elements in forms that plants could use. Every naturally occurring organic compound, derived from living or once living organisms, and even many humanmade compounds like pesticides, are decomposed by bacteria. After all, there are plenty of bacteria to handle decomposition—33 billion of them in each ounce of fertile soil. If all of the bacteria on a single acre of soil were weighed, they would tip the balance at one and a half tons (1.2 metric tons).

The number of different bacteria in a given area of soil has not been easy to estimate, for few bacteria have distinguishing physical characteristics. They have more or less the same size, shape, and overall appearance. Although they look the same on the outside, their genetic makeup can be very different. By analyzing genes and the deoxyribonucleic acid (DNA) that makes up these genes, two biologists from Norway set out to estimate the number of bacterial DNAs from a sample of forest soil that were at least 30 percent different from one another.

For some larger animals, such as birds and mammals, the genetic differences separating species are often far less than 30 percent. The genetic difference between humans and chimpanzees, for example, is only 2 or 3 percent. From their analysis of all the DNA extracted from all the bacteria in just 3/100 ounce (1 gram) of woodland soil, the Norwegian biologists concluded that anywhere from 4,000 to 5,000 species of bacteria live in that one little parcel of the earth's surface. Bacteria seem to inhabit more areas of the soil than any other creatures; scientists have found bacteria dwelling more than two miles below the surface of the soil. Imagine how many different species of bacteria—with many different talents—inhabit

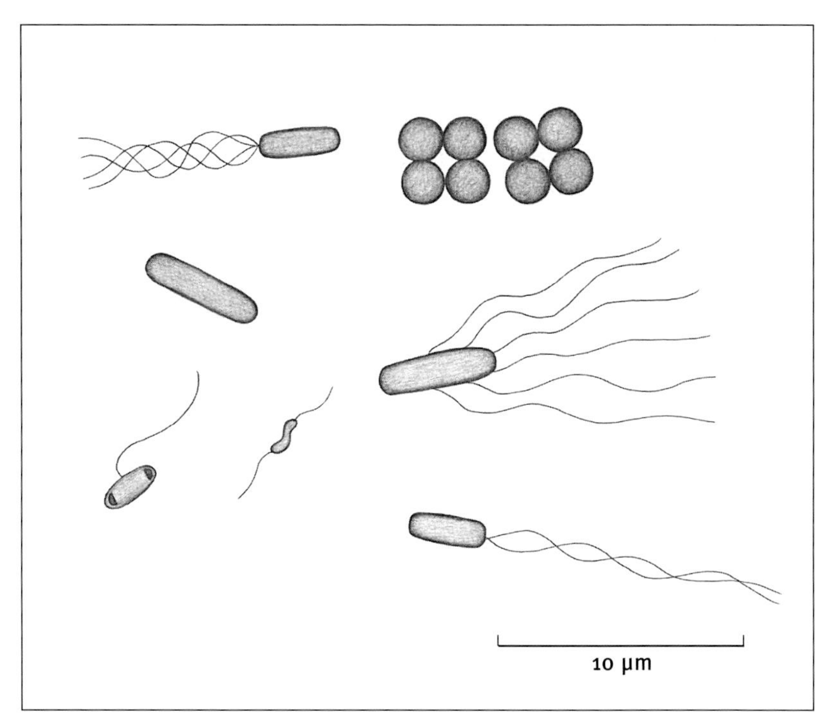

Bacteria of the soil come in a variety of sizes and shapes. Bacteria carry out jobs involving chemical transformations that are essential for the survival of all life on earth. The bacteria seen here are (clockwise from upper left): Pseudomonas, Sarcina, Azotobacter, Rhizobium, Thiomicrospira, Desulfuromonas, and Clostridium.

the soil of our planet if thousands of species occur in less than a teaspoonful of it.

Bacteria of the soil are more abundant around roots, in a zone known as the rhizosphere, than they are anywhere else in the soil. The number of bacteria that inhabit the rhizosphere are 10, 20, or even several hundred times more common than the number of bacteria in areas of the soil that are rootless. Roots are constantly releasing organic substances, including dead cells, that can be broken down and used as a source of energy by certain bacteria. The plant benefits from the proximity of these numerous bacteria and their talents for enriching the soil.

Plants are dependent on bacteria to ensure that the essential elements of soil are available to their roots. Two types of bacteria provide nutrients to the roots from different sources: heterotrophic ("other nourishing") and autotrophic ("self nourishing"). Heterotrophic bacteria depend on other organic substances in the soil for their nourishment and transform this organic matter into plant nutrients. Autotrophic bacteria generate their own organic matter from CO_2 and in addition transform inorganic matter and minerals into nutrients that bacteria and plants can use. Whichever route bacteria follow, they all ultimately provide elements in forms that plant roots can readily absorb and use for their growth. Bacteria oversee a vast range of chemical transformations in the soil. All of the 18 essential elements used first by plants and then by animals are continually recycled, thanks to the bacteria of soil.

The billions upon billions of soil bacteria exert an extraordinary influence on the health of the earth. Acting as crucial recyclers and decomposers of plant and animal remains, heterotrophic bacteria control the amount of organic matter remaining in the soil as well as the levels of carbon dioxide released from soil into our atmosphere. Ninety percent of the carbon dioxide produced by life on earth arises from the activities of bacteria and their fellow microbes, the fungi. The metabolic activity of the microbes in the top six inches (15 centimeters) of a single acre of rich soil easily surpasses the metabolic activity of 50,000 human beings.

In the final stage of decomposition of organic matter in soils, heterotrophic bacteria liberate minerals essential for survival of all plant and animal life on earth. Autotrophic bacteria convert many inorganic compounds that contain essential but inaccessible elements for plant growth to compounds that plants can avidly consume. Like green plants, they consume carbon dioxide, thus diminishing the levels of this gas that has been implicated in global warming. Pesticides and other pollutants are metabolized and detoxified by many heterotrophs.

These simple creatures, the bacteria, have managed to carry out certain transformations of elements from one inorganic form to another inorganic form, from organic to inorganic, from living organisms to minerals—transformations that no plants or animals have managed to achieve during their history on earth. It is to the bacteria of the soil, with a little help from the larger soil inhabitants, that the credit for the constant renewal of our earth is due.

Actinomycetes

The hearty smell of good earth that rises from a newly plowed field or from digging in the rich, dark soil of a hardwood forest is the odor given off by the millions of actinomycetes that live in the soil. This earthy odor comes from a compound appropriately known as geosmin (*geo* = earth; *osmi* = odor) that arises as actinomycetes break down organic matter. Actinomycetes resemble both fungi and bacteria. They form fungal-like colonies in the soil with their filaments radiating outward; the forms of these colonies have earned them a scientific name that translates to ray (*actino*) fungi (*mycos*). Like fungi, actinomycetes form networks of filaments in the soil. However, the spores from which these filaments sprout look more like bacterial spores than fungal spores. Even after being studied for many decades, actinomycetes still puzzled those who tried to pigeonhole them. Did they represent a common ancestor of fungi and bacteria, or were they somewhere in between? Although on the outside actinomycetes can take on forms that resemble both bacteria and fungi, on the inside their molecules clearly look more like molecules of bacteria.

Actinomycetes help in the decomposition of soil's organic matter, but they are better known as sources of antibiotics for medicine. In the soil, antibiotics like actinomycin, tetracycline, neomycin, and candicidin help maintain checks and balances on burgeoning bacterial and fungal populations. One of the better known antibiotics, streptomycin, is produced by a common actinomycete named *Streptomyces.* The antibiotics of actinomycetes had been controlling soil bacteria for millions of years before we discovered their usefulness in controlling our own disease-causing bacteria.

ACTINOMYCETES

CLASSIFICATION
Kingdom Eubacteria (also known as Kingdom Bacteria)

PLACE IN FOOD WEB
Decomposers, Bacterial partners of plants

SIZE
0.05–2 µm in filament diameter

NUMBER OF SPECIES
1,460

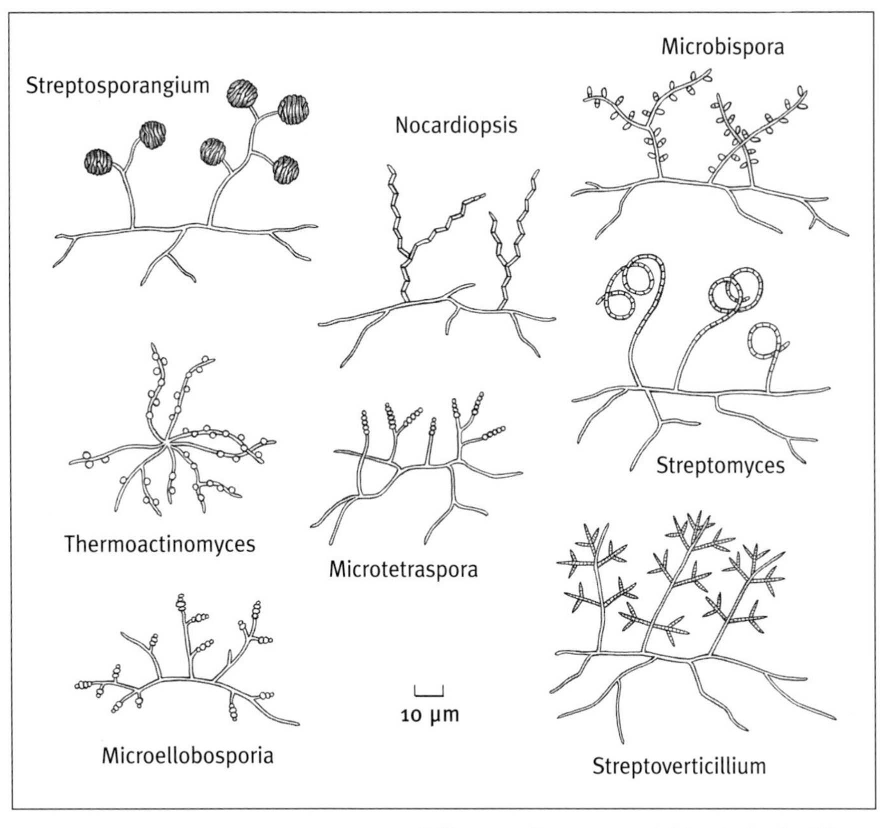

Actinomycetes are special bacteria that form networks of filaments and produce spores.

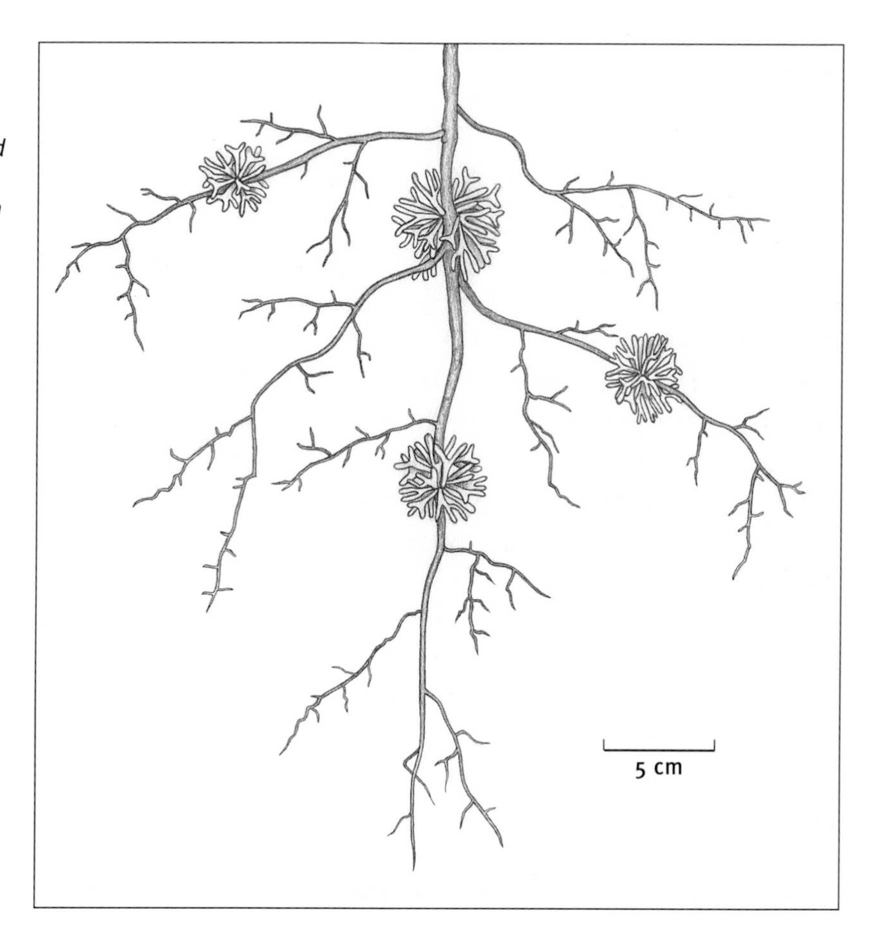

Some actinomycetes associate with roots of woody shrubs and form nitrogen-fixing nodules where dinitrogen gas in the air is converted into usable nitrogen compounds. These nodules, each about an inch in diameter, form on roots of the prairie plant, New Jersey tea.

Actinomycetes are among the few soil organisms that are nitrogen fixers, taking dinitrogen gas (N_2) from the air and converting it to ammonia (NH_3) in the soil. Unlike the rhizobial bacteria that associate only with the roots of legumes like peas, beans, and clovers, actinomycetes only associate with plants that are woody and are not legumes. The actinomycetes invade root hairs of these plants just as rhizobia invade root hairs of legumes. Also like rhizobia, actinomycete filaments penetrate through the root cells and induce special growths, or root nodules; but unlike the small, round nodules formed by rhizobia, nodules formed by actinomycetes are knobby and branched and sometimes up to an inch in diameter.

New plants that bear root nodules with actinomycetes are continually being found, and their contribution to worldwide nitrogen fixation only became appreciated in the latter half of the 20th century. Certain free-living bacteria of the world, with the help of rhizobia, actinomycetes, and a few algae, add about 140 million tons (126 million metric tons) of nitrogen to the soil each year.

Algae

Algae are usually associated with ponds, streams, marshes, and mud puddles, but closer looks at the algae that live in soil have changed this narrow view of them a great deal. Algae are even common in the soils of deserts around the world and have been revived from soils that have been stored dry for as long as 83 years. While they are in a dry, dormant state, algae can endure temperatures exceeding the boiling point of water at 212°F (100°C) as well as low temperatures down to -320°F (-195°C). In the soil is where algae and fungi probably first discovered that they could establish compatible and fruitful partnerships in the form of lichens.

Like the lichens that arose from them, algae can be hardy pioneers and builders of soil. They were the first colonists on the Indonesian island of Krakatau after its volcano violently erupted in 1883. Like other green plants, algae have the ability to capture the sun's energy and produce their own sugars and organic matter. As they use the energy they produce from

BLUE-GREEN ALGAE

CLASSIFICATION
Kingdom Eubacteria

PLACE IN FOOD WEB
Producers

SIZE
2–25 µm in filament or cell diameter

NUMBER OF SPECIES
1,500

GREEN ALGAE AND RED ALGAE

CLASSIFICATION
Kingdom Plant

PLACE IN FOOD WEB
Producers

SIZE
2–25 µm in filament or cell diameter

NUMBER OF SPECIES
7,000 green algae
4,000 red algae

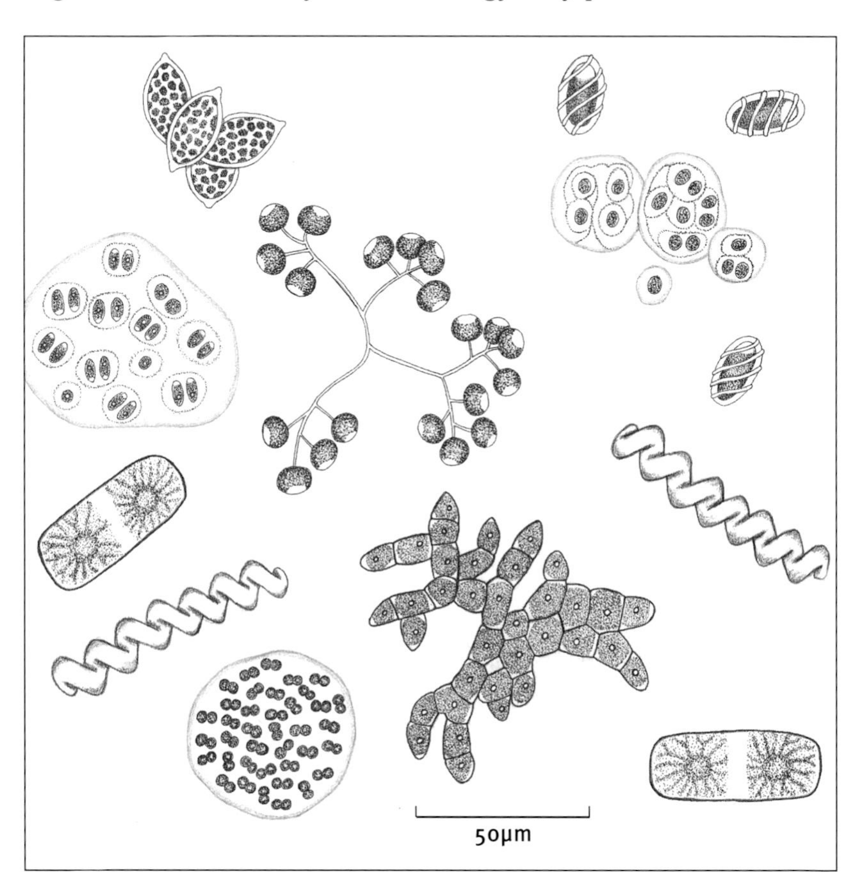

Some algae are plants, some are bacteria, and some are related to one-celled animals. They all use the energy of sunlight to produce their own nutrients. Pictured here are a variety of algae (clockwise from center): Dictyosphaerium, Gleocapsa, Scotiella (3 cells), Spirulina, Cylindrocystis, Protoderma, Aphanocapsa, Spirulina, Cylindrocystis, Palmella, Oocystis.

ALGAE WITH FLAGELLA, YELLOW-GREEN ALGAE, AND DIATOMS

CLASSIFICATION
Kingdom Protistan

PLACE IN FOOD WEB
Producers

SIZE
2–25 µm in in filament or cell diameter

NUMBER OF SPECIES
800 algae with flagella
5,900 yellow-green algae and diatoms

photosynthesis, they give off carbon dioxide like all other living creatures. The corrosive carbonic acid that forms when carbon dioxide combines with water contributes to soil formation by helping to digest any rocks that might be in the immediate vicinity. As many as 3 billion algae have been counted per ounce (30 grams) of soil. All these algae add a phenomenal amount of organic matter to the soil. In some Arizona soils the amount of organic matter added annually to the top three inches (7.6 centimeters) of an acre comes out to be about six tons (5.4 metric tons). Many algae, like certain bacteria and actinomycetes, can fix nitrogen from the atmosphere and add this essential nutrient to impoverished soil, once again pioneering the way for the plants that will follow.

The organic matter that algae add to the soil is often sticky and helps improve the structure of soil by holding particles together in loose clumps. When soil structure is improved, the soil is able to hold more water in its pore spaces and erosion is markedly reduced. The soil of bare, eroded fields that has been colonized by soil algae contains about 10 percent more water than comparable soil without algae.

As producers of organic matter from the energy of sunlight, algae give more to the soil community than they take. Algae nurture the soil with organic matter and nitrogen that they leave behind; they also provide nutritious feasts for the many small arthropods that feed on them.

Fungi

Along with bacteria, fungi are the main recyclers of nutrients and a major source of nutrition for many soil animals. But fungi are versatile and play many other roles in the soil community. In addition to forming their remarkable partnerships with green plants, soil fungi also protect plants by eating nematodes and insects before these animals have a chance to feed on plant roots. Many fungi have established a number of mutually beneficial relationships with green plants, with only a minority of fungi damaging the plants by infecting their roots. Because only about 5 percent of the estimated 1.5 million species of fungi have been described, we can anticipate discovering new species of molds and mushrooms for years to come.

Plant debris that falls to the ground is colonized by a succession of fungi. As fresh plant matter gradually decomposes, the simplest compounds of the dead plant matter are broken down first by a group of fungi that have been named sugar fungi. These molds of the soil, the first colonizers of leaf litter, are only able to obtain their energy for survival from simple sugars. They can digest simple sugars but not the tough fibers made up of chains of sugars known as cellulose and the even tougher compounds,

FUNGI

CLASSIFICATION
Kingdom Fungi
Phylum Zygomycota (molds)
Phylum Ascomycota (yeast and sac fungi)
Phylum Basidiomycota (mushrooms)

PLACE IN FOOD WEB
Decomposers, Bacterial and fungal partners of plants

SIZE
3–10 µm in filament diameter

NUMBER OF SPECIES
75,000

Fungi can extend miles of filaments, or hyphae, through a square meter of soil and litter. Without having a sexual encounter with a different hypha, a single hypha can divide to form asexual spores of all imaginable shapes at the ends of these filaments.

Mushrooms arise when two different fungal hyphae have a sexual encounter, shuffle their different genetic information, and produce sexual spores containing new arrangements of genes from both hyphae.

called "lignins," that hold cellulose chains together. To deal with possible competition for the sugars in the leaf litter, these pioneer decomposers of newly fallen plant debris grow very quickly and are very abundant in the soil; in addition, they secrete antibiotics that discourage growth of nearby bacteria and fungi.

They are also among the few fungi that can survive the high temperatures that they often generate as they extract the first nutrients from fresh plant debris. In a compost pile these sugar fungi begin the decomposition by releasing a burst of energy that can raise the temperatures in the center of the compost pile to 150°–165° F (65°–75° C). After the sugar fungi have exhausted their food resources of simple sugars and begin to die, the next stage of colonization begins as other fungi move in to begin devouring the tough fibers that remain in the partially decomposed plant litter. The filaments of the sac fungi and mushrooms that take the place of the sugar fungi set about digesting the cellulose of the plant litter with great efficiency. These fungi are fewer in number and work at a slower pace, but they do their work thoroughly. Even fewer in number, but no less thorough, are the fungi that can decompose lignin, one of the most resistant of plant compounds to decomposition. The filaments that tackle the decomposition of lignin are produced by the fungi that are most familiar and most attractive, the mushrooms.

Fungi are specialized not only for decomposing plant remains but also for decomposing animal remains and animal dung. Hair and hooves, claws and feathers are food for certain sac fungi, and many molds grow on the droppings of animals.

Whether several fungal filaments, or hyphae, that are recovered from the soil are part of just one fungus or are part of different fungi is by no means easy to determine without laboratory testing. Estimates of the abundance of fungi in the soil are usually made in terms of lengths of fungal filaments rather than in terms of numbers of individuals that are each descended from a different spore. So when scientists actually started looking carefully at the total length of hyphae in a single soil fungus, they were rather astounded by the lengths to which fungal hyphae can grow and the acreage over which a single fungus can roam. First, a 38-acre (183,920-square-yard; 154,000-square-meter) fungus was reported from the woods of Iron County, Michigan, in 1992; soon thereafter a fungus occupying 1,500 acres (7.26 million square yards; 6.1 million square meters) was reported in a forest of the Pacific Northwest. By some measures, these fungi are the largest living creatures on earth. Fungi this large are at least 1,000 and maybe even 10,000 years old. For fungi to reach this size takes many years. A fungus can cover quite a bit of ground when it is growing at the rate of about eight inches (20 centimeters) a year.

Soil fungi are easy to observe in the field and in the laboratory. Damp, rainy weather encourages their growth, so not surprisingly mushrooms are most common after rainy weather in spring, late summer, and fall. Many of these have mutually beneficial associations with roots of nearby trees. Mushroom filaments sometimes aggregate into strands made up of several thousand individual filaments. These strands look and act like growing plant roots, forcing their way into hard, dead wood and accelerating its decomposition. These rhizomorphs (*rhizo* = root; *morph* = form) look like roots, but they look even more like boot laces; in fact, the dark rhizomorph of one tasty autumn mushroom is known as bootlace fungus.

The morel is a sac fungus of spring, whose spores form within tiny sacs that line the pits on its surface.

Rhizomorphs and hyphae can be found on fallen logs, under their bark or throughout the rotting wood, at almost any time of year, even on hot, dry days. Leaves of the forest floor are coated with hyphae that form a variety of delicate, intertwined patterns. Many fungi that happen to be present on a small fragment of wood, fallen leaf, animal dropping, or soil can be enticed to grow by placing the fragment on a moist piece of sterile filter paper in a clean, covered dish. By examining them under a microscope, you can gain a firsthand and close-up appreciation of how fungi and their soil companions are able to recycle the ton and a half of leaves that fall to the ground each autumn on every acre of deciduous forest.

The dark rhizomorphs of bootlace fungus form intertwining strands on the surface of this decaying maple log.

ACELLULAR SLIME MOLDS

CLASSIFICATION
Kingdom Protista
Phylum Gymnomycota
Class Myxomycota

PLACE IN FOOD WEB
Predators of bacteria and protozoa, Decomposers

SIZE
5 µm in cell diameter
Up to 5 mm in height of fruiting body

NUMBER OF SPECIES
700

CELLULAR SLIME MOLDS

CLASSIFICATION
Kingdom Protista
Phylum Gymnomycota
Class Acrasiomycota
Class Dictyosteliomycota

PLACE IN FOOD WEB
Predators of bacteria and protozoa, Decomposers

SIZE
5 µm in cell diameter
Up to 5 mm in height of fruiting body

NUMBER OF SPECIES
65

Slime Molds

The creatures known as slime molds that creep through decaying wood and between rotting leaves seem to be part fungus, part animal. They have fruiting bodies like fungi at certain times in their life cycles, but they move and act like protozoa at other times. Like amoebae, they creep and spread over logs, twigs, and fallen leaves, leaving a trail of slime in their wake. As they glide along they engulf bacteria, some protozoa, and small pieces of decaying plant remains. In one of nature's tricks of magic, these blobs of undifferentiated tissue can transform within only a few hours into fungal-like masses of often richly colored and elaborately sculptured fruiting bodies.

Not surprisingly, biologists have never been too sure where to place these creatures in the tree of life. Some have considered slime molds to be fungi, while others have placed them among the protozoa. Actually, they are neither fungus nor animal. Slime molds are now considered to be members of the same kingdom to which the protozoa belong, the kingdom Protista; but within this kingdom, they are still considered unique enough to be given a phylum of their very own.

Even among the slime molds, two clearly distinct groups—the acellular slime molds and the cellular slime molds—are found in the soil and on decaying leaves and wood. The acellular slime molds grow and move as a single immense amoeba known as a plasmodium, often many inches across and usually

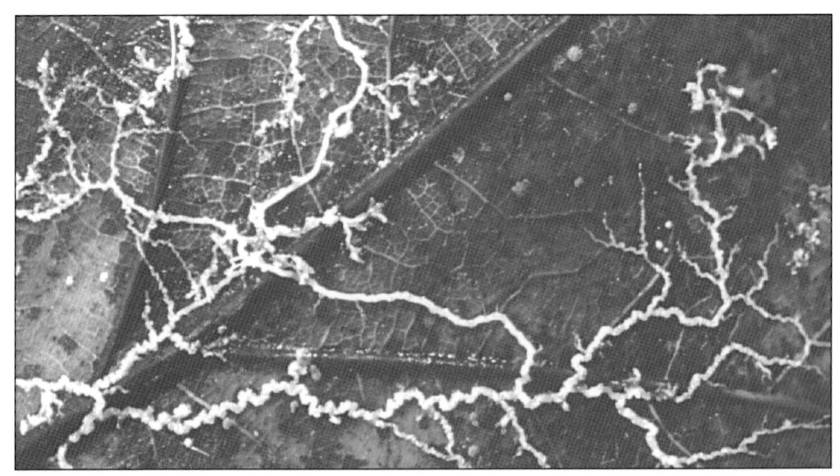

The bright yellow plasmodium of slime molds changes its shape within minutes as it oozes over leaves and logs. The slime mold engulfs most of the microbes that lie in its path.

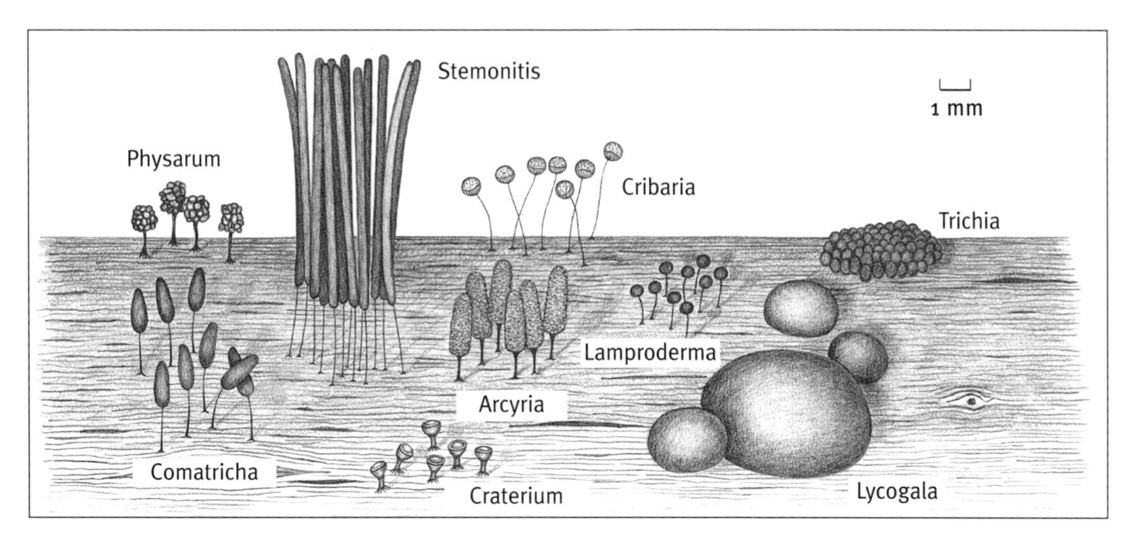

The fruiting bodies or sporangia of slime molds often have unusual and colorful forms.

bright yellow. The cellular slime molds, on the other hand, grow by dividing into many little independent amoebae.

Eventually this multitude of amoebae gather together to form a slug-shaped blob in which the individual amoebae interact in unison and harmony as the tiny slug imperceptibly creeps over the forest floor. When the surroundings of a slime mold become drier and brighter, and food becomes scarcer, it settles down to the sedate life of a fruiting body. The single, large plasmodium of each acellular slime mold turns into a cluster of fruiting bodies, whereas the cluster of many small amoebae that make up each slug of a cellular slime mold turns into a single fruiting body.

Slime molds are everywhere, but unless you set out to find them you will probably never see them. On a walk through the woods in summer or fall when logs and leaf litter are moist from earlier rains, you are very likely to spot small patches of what can best be described as bright yellow, lacy jelly spread thinly over the surfaces of rotting logs, twigs, or leaves. At drier times during the year, you are more likely to spot clusters of the colorful fruiting bodies of the slime molds on the same surfaces. If you spot a slime mold, for instance a yellow plasmodium on a well-decayed log, you can try raising it. Take a fragment about the size of a dime and place it on a piece of absorbent paper, such as a paper towel, at the bottom of a glass jar. Keep the jar out of the direct sun, in a somewhat dark place, like a basement. Keep the paper moist but not wet and feed the plasmodium some uncooked rolled oats every few days. Like a giant amoeba, the organism will take solid food into its jellylike body and creep from place to place. In a week or so, you may have more plasmodium than you know what to do with.

Lichens: A Mix of Several Kingdoms

> **LICHENS**
>
> **CLASSIFICATION**
> Mixture of Kingdom Eubacteria, Kingdom Plant, and Kingdom Fungi
>
> **PLACE IN FOOD WEB**
> Decomposers, Producers
>
> **SIZE**
> Algae, 2–25 µm in filament or cell diameter
> Fungi, 3–10 µm in filament diameter
>
> **NUMBER OF SPECIES**
> 14,000

Many of the soil algae and soil fungi gave up their free-living existences to become members of a very successful alliance that draws on the strengths of each partner. Fungi are heterotrophs that survive on organic molecules and absorb inorganic nutrients, while algae are autotrophs that can capture the energy of sunlight and manufacture their own organic nutrients. The algal member of the partnership provides organic nutrients, and the fungal filaments that embrace the algae absorb essential inorganic nutrients from rock or soil.

Usually one, but sometimes two species of algae join with a specific fungus to form a lichen that can survive harsher conditions than can either the algal or the fungal partner on its own. Lichens have an uncanny ability to extract minuscule quantities of nutrients from the poorest of soils and the hardest of rocks. Even subfreezing temperatures, scorching sunlight, and long droughts do not trouble the steadfast alliance of algae and fungi; the lichen partnership endures the most adverse conditions. Only in the presence of unlimited nutrients and plenty of moisture, when the living is easy, may algal cells of a lichen grow as a free-living algae, abandoning their fungal partners.

Another attribute arising from this partnership or symbiosis (*sym* = together; *bio* = life; *sis* = the act of) of algae and fungi is the production of the unusual acids of lichens. Alone, neither algae nor fungi normally produce the 100 or so organic acids that are unique to lichens. In addition to corroding rocks, the acids of lichens readily combine with elements from rocks and enhance the solubility of these elements in the soil. These acids also inhibit the growth of other microbes and show antibiotic activity. Since lichens grow extremely slowly, expanding at the rate of 1/25 inch (1 millimeter) or less each year, a little antibiotic activity can protect them from encroachment by more rapidly growing microbes that share their rock or patch of soil.

Lichens can also warn of pollutants in the environment. Their ability to scavenge and concentrate trace amounts of elements from the environment—even toxic ones—has had disastrous consequences for lichen populations in polluted places. Their disappearance from a landscape is a warning to the rest of us.

Lichens are among those very few creatures that can colonize bare rocks.

Protozoa

Over 300 species of one-celled animals, or protozoa, live in the very thin film of water that usually lines the innumerable pores of the soil. If the water film that lines the pores in a couple of tablespoons of soil were spread out flat, it would cover an area of about 250,000 square feet (27,800 square yards; 23,250 square meters). Quite a few protozoa, measuring anywhere from 0.0002 to 0.0064 inch (0.005 to 0.16 millimeter), can squeeze into a city block, so estimates of 10 billion protozoa living in the top 6 inches (12 centimeters) of a square yard of meadow should not seem outlandish.

Soil protozoa occur in four main forms: those that have flagella (*flagellum* = whip); those that are covered with cilia (*cilium* = small hair); and two that are amoeboid (*amoeba* = change) and constantly change their shapes—one form with a protective shell called a test (*testa* = shell), the other with no shell at all. Protozoa have definite preferences for certain soils. Shell-bearing amoebae, or testacea, are more common in forests than they are in plowed fields. Whereas about 100 testacea may live in a teaspoon of plowed soil or desert soil, about 1,000 times the number can be found in the litter and soil of forests. Amoebae without shells but with fine, radiating rodlike pseudopods (*pseudo* =false; *pod* =feet) are more common in wet soils. Their graceful, starlike forms have suggested the name of heliozoa (*helio* = sun; *zoa* = animals). The smaller amoeboid protozoa and protozoa with flagella seem to be the more common forms in most soils; members of the genus *Colpoda* seem to be the most common protozoa with cilia.

Soils often dry out, and water films can evaporate from pores of the soil. When this happens, soil protozoa lose their normal shapes and enter an immobile, inactive state called a cyst. There they wait until damper days arrive. In some soils and at particular times of year, most of the protozoa may exist in this state of suspended animation.

Although larger protozoa, such as testacea that travel with their shells, sometimes feed on algae, fungi, and even plant debris, protozoa feed mostly on bacteria. So their major influence on the cycling of organic matter and on humus formation is through their control of bacterial populations. Protozoa seem to be the principal predators of soil bacteria.

PROTOZOA

CLASSIFICATION

Kingdom Protista
- Phylum Protozoa
  - Class Rhizopodea (amoebae)
  - Class Ciliatea (ciliated protozoa)
  - Class Actinopodea (heliozoa)
  - Class Zoomastigophorea (flagellates)

PLACE IN FOOD WEB

Predators of bacteria, Detritivores, Fungivores

SIZE

5–160 μm in diameter

NUMBER OF SPECIES

65,000

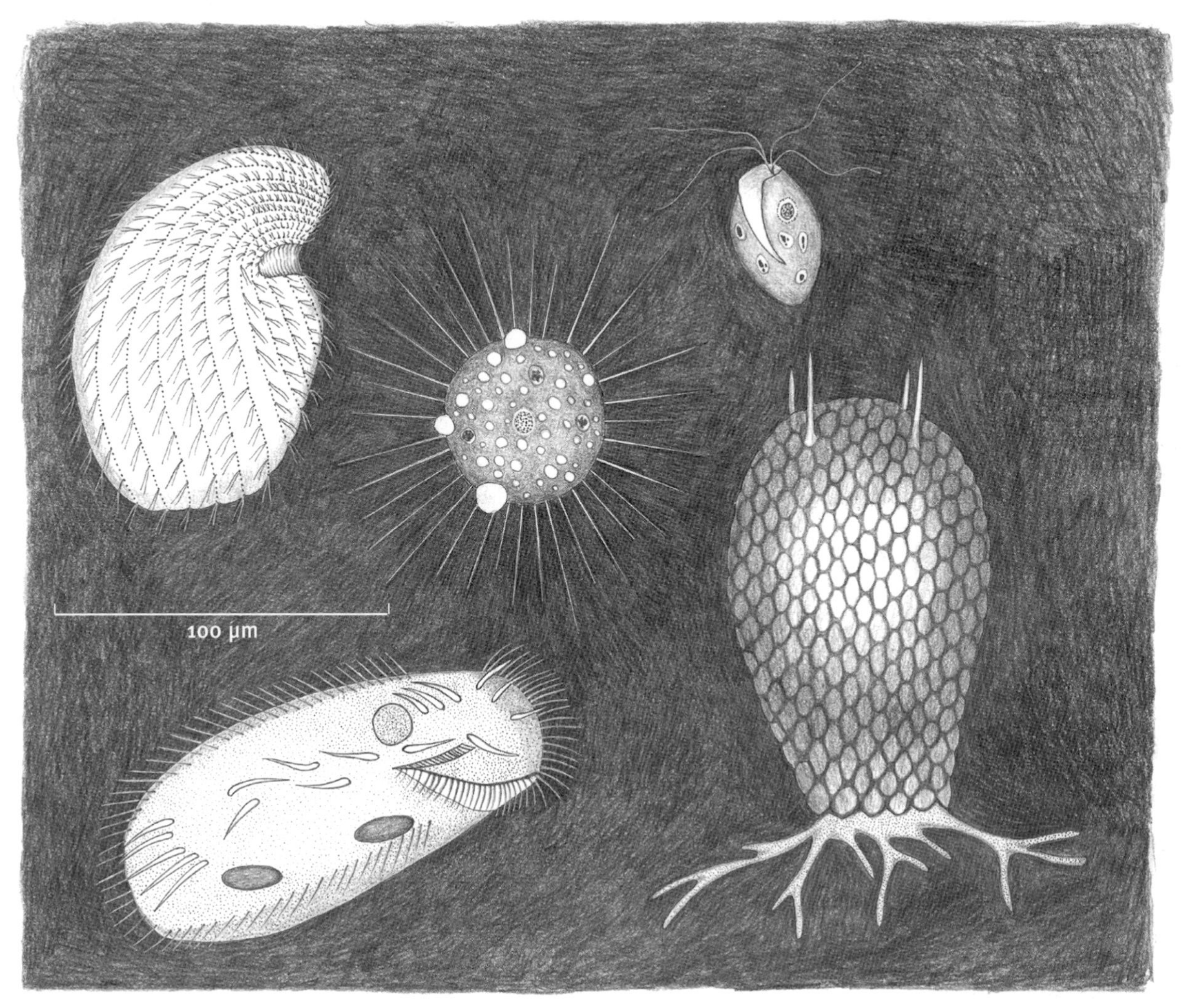

Different shapes and sizes of protozoa swim in the film of water that covers soil particles. The protozoa here are (clockwise from center): heliozoa, Actinophrys*; flagellate,* Tetramitus*; testacea,* Euglypha*; ciliate,* Oxytricha*; ciliate,* Colpoda.

By one estimate, 90 percent of the bacteria consumed in the soil are eaten by protozoa, and the other 10 percent are eaten by small worms called nematodes, most of which are no more than a 1/25 inch (1 millimeter) long. Larger nematodes, in turn, eat many of the protozoa that have fattened on bacteria.

INVERTEBRATES

FLATWORMS: Soil Planarians

Flatworms are creatures of the night, the time when they can glide from beneath rocks, logs, and leaf litter with little danger of drying up during their rovings. In addition to having nocturnal habits, our native American flatworms are cryptically colored to match their surroundings and are tiny, ranging in size from 1/12 to 2 3/4 inches (0.2–70 millimeters). They have a well-deserved reputation for being difficult to find. Even though some tropical flatworms can grow to 24 inches (600 millimeters) in length and often have stripes and bright colors, they have very simple body plans.

FLATWORMS

CLASSIFICATION
Phylum Platyhelminthes
Class Turbellaria

PLACE IN FOOD WEB
Predators

SIZE
200 µm–60 cm in length

NUMBER OF SPECIES
3,000

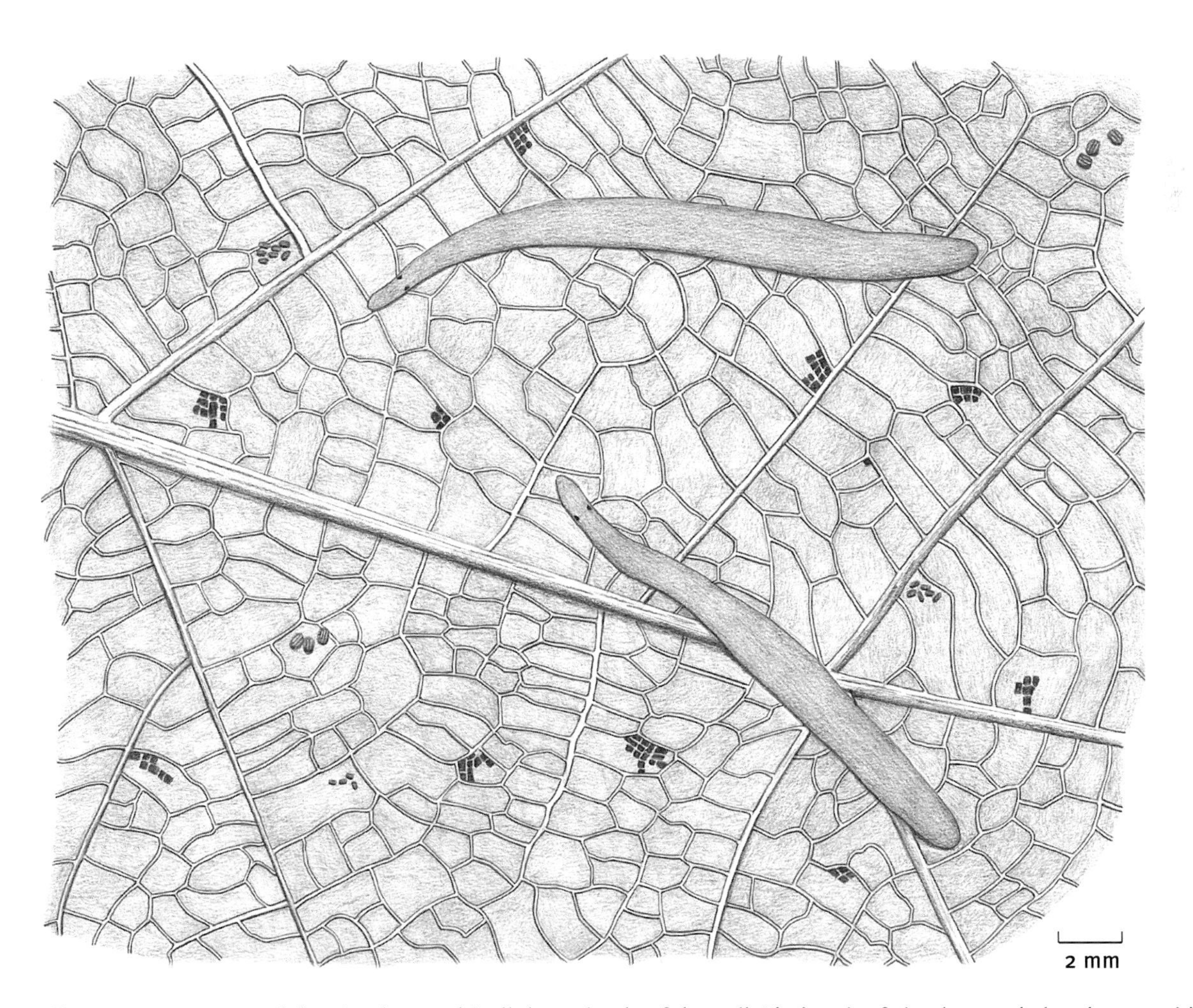

Flatworms are some of the simplest multicellular animals of the soil. Their pair of simple eyes helps them avoid light.

Not only do all flatworms survive without a circulatory system or a respiratory system, but they also have a gut with only one opening that serves as both mouth and anus. The flatworm's two-way gut has so many branches and subbranches throughout its body that whatever nutrients it obtains from digestion are quickly passed to every tissue of the body. By being so flat, a flatworm has a large surface area for inhaling oxygen and exhaling carbon dioxide. It manages quite well without the special respiratory organs such as lungs, gills, and tracheae that many other animals have. Even though soil planarians, like potworms and earthworms, each have both male and female reproductive organs, they still get together every so often to exchange sperm and to fertilize each other's eggs. As two flatworms go their own ways after mating, their eggs are left behind in a round, leathery cocoon. When the newly hatched flatworms leave the cocoon after about a month, they look like miniature versions of their parents and begin feeding on the many protozoa that share the water film with them. After a few weeks, young flatworms are ready for heftier prey such as slugs, potworms, earthworms, springtails, larvae of insects, and even other planarians.

Since flatworms cannot burrow, they glide through the soil. Squeezing through narrow passageways and sliding over leaf litter on their flat bellies, flatworms have been clocked moving along at speeds of 3/4 to 2 inches (20–50 millimeters) per minute.

The graceful movement of flatworms results from a combination of waving cilia, similar to those that propel smaller protozoa, and slimy mucus, similar to that used by the larger snails and slugs of the soil. For life in the dark and damp environments of the water films that cover soil and leaf litter, the simple body plan of flatworms has served them very well. It has enabled them to colonize soils around the world, wherever they have been inadvertently transported in the soil of potted plants.

EELWORMS and POTWORMS: Nematodes and Enchytraeids

Everyone knows earthworms, but the other true worms of soils—potworms and eelworms—are far less familiar and one and two orders of magnitude smaller than earthworms, as wells as many orders of magnitude more abundant. An earthworm measures 4 inches (100 mm); a potworm or enchytraeid worm measures at most 9/16 inch (15 mm) and an eelworm or nematode averages only 1/25 inch (1 millimeter) in length. Grasslands, pastures, and prairies always support the greatest numbers of worms, with plowed fields supporting only about a tenth of that number. Whereas only 50,000 to 8 million earthworms can live on an acre (4,840 square yards; 4,050 square meters) of grassland soil, some 80 billion eelworms and 400 million potworms can live in the same area. The total number of individuals representing each type of worm may be very different, but the total weight per acre of each type is comparable, ranging from 100 to several hundred pounds.

Earthworms prefer alkaline soils rich in calcium and low in hydrogen ions. Their smaller relatives, the potworms, however, are found primarily in soils with lots of decaying matter, and they actually prefer acid soils with high concentrations of hydrogen ions, like the soil of pine forests. Nematodes are the

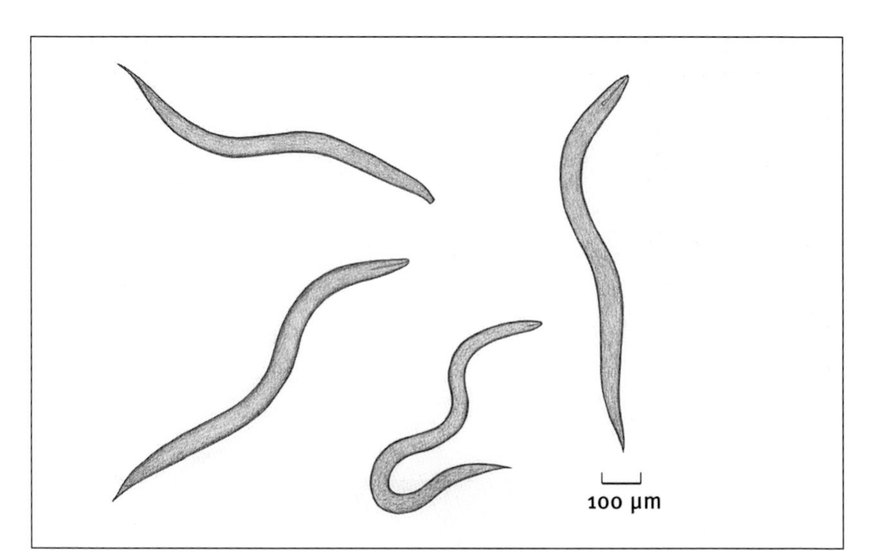

Nematodes twist and turn through the innumerable microscopic spaces between soil particles.

EELWORMS

CLASSIFICATION
Phylum Nematoda

PLACE IN FOOD WEB
Predators, Herbivores, Fungivores, Parasites

SIZE
300 µm–1 cm in length

NUMBER OF SPECIES
15,000

POTWORMS

CLASSIFICATION
Phylum Annelida
Family Enchytraeidae

PLACE IN FOOD WEB
Decomposers, Detritivores

SIZE
5 mm–15 mm in length

NUMBER OF SPECIES
600

least finicky and seem at home in just about every type of soil. In trying to convey an impression of their abundance and their omnipresence, one authority on nematodes, Dr. N. A. Cobb, wrote in the *Yearbook of the United States Department of Agriculture* for 1914 that "if all matter in the universe except the nematodes were swept away, our world would still be dimly recognizable . . . we should find its mountains, hills, vales, rivers, lakes, and oceans represented by a film of nematodes." However, our ignorance of the estimated half a million different species of nematodes that share this earth with us is as vast as the habitat they occupy. Only about 15,000 or 3 percent of those half-million species have been described, so many new discoveries and surprises await those who study nematodes.

Earthworms and potworms feast on the plant debris that ends up on the ground, quickly transforming it to humus. The smaller animals that contribute their share to humus formation, however, often end up as dinner for the smallest of the worms, the nematodes. Nematodes that feed on bacteria and

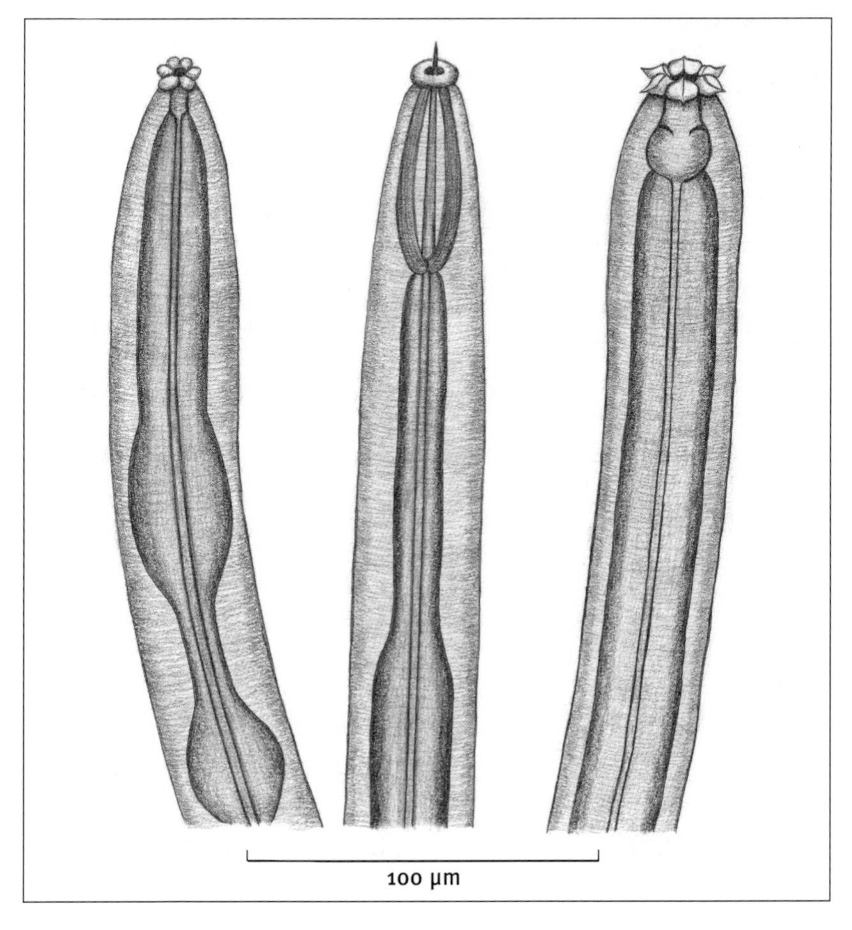

A closer look at the heads of nematodes reveals mouths that are specialized for different eating habits. Nematodes that feed on roots and fungi (center) have piercing mouthparts that drain sap. Nematodes that feed on protozoa, rotifers, and other nematodes (right) have large teeth lining their mouths, but nematodes that feed on tiny bacteria (left) do not have these imposing teeth.

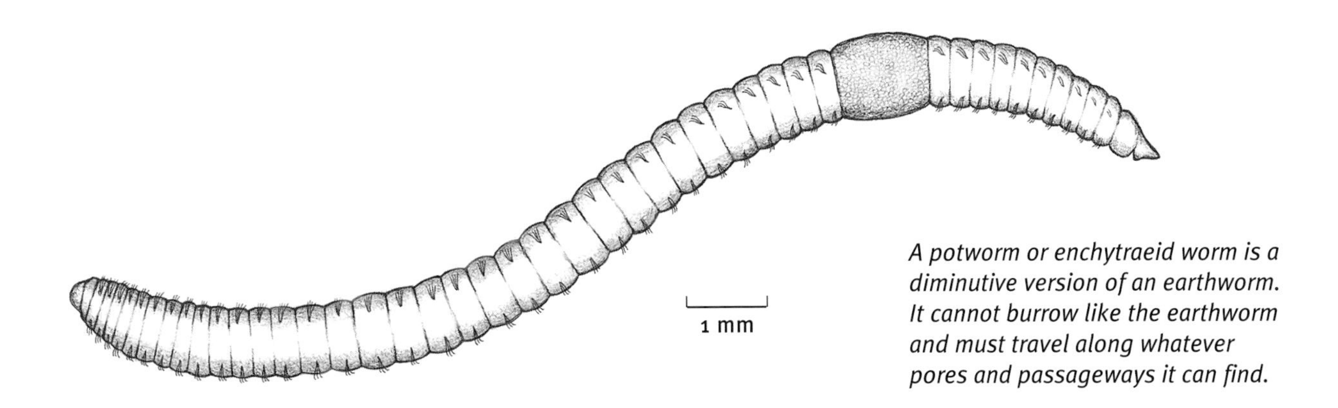

A potworm or enchytraeid worm is a diminutive version of an earthworm. It cannot burrow like the earthworm and must travel along whatever pores and passageways it can find.

actinomycetes often have several lips surrounding a narrow mouth that vacuums up food from pores in the soil. Nematodes that are root feeders have mouths with hollow, piercing spears that they ram into roots to tap juices of the plant. The larger nematodes are predators of protozoans, rotifers, and tardigrades, as well as smaller nematodes, They are often well-endowed with as many as six lips at the entrance to their mouths, and grinding plates or a few teeth just inside. They must look ferocious and formidable to the humus builders who share their topsoil. Behind each nematode's mouth lies a proportionately large and muscular esophagus; with this feeding pump, the nematode gulps down its meal, whether it be root juices or rotifer meat.

There are even some nematodes that attack insects of the soil. A special pouch in such a nematode's intestine carries symbiotic bacteria that act as accomplices in dispatching insects. When the nematode penetrates the body cavity of an insect host, it releases thousands of these bacteria into the insect's blood. There the bacteria quickly multiply, soon killing the insect but providing a rich source of nutrition for the nematode. Some farmers are using these nematodes as a natural, nontoxic form of control for such insect pests of soil as weevil larvae and fly larvae known as leatherjackets.

Nature is always enterprising and opportunistic. As long as nematodes have dwelled in the soil, there have been creatures whose survival has depended on exploiting the vast, protein-rich resource the nematodes represent. Creatures called springtails have been observed grasping nematodes at one end and then sucking them up in a few seconds like long strands of spaghetti. Tardigrades and certain mites probably also eat their share of nematodes, but one of the greatest threats to the well-being of nematodes are certain fungi that have developed not only an appetite for nematodes but also a way to detect their odors and ingenious ways to trap them. There are at least 150 species of fungi that feed entirely on nematodes or that supplement their diets of rotting leaves and wood with nematode tidbits. A meal of a nematode or two improves the nutrition of a fungus by adding a good dose of nitrogen to a bland diet of plant debris that is notably high in carbon and low in nitrogen.

Most soil fungi seem deceptively placid as their hyphae meander through the pores of soil, but they can be deadly to nematodes that meander through the same pores. Some of these fungi have sticky spores that latch on to the skin of nematodes. There they germinate and hyphae begin growing into the nematode. Once the hyphae have filled the nematode and digested its contents, they grow out of the mummified worm and produce more sticky spores that wait for a new nematode to pass by. Another group of fungi produce sticky hyphae rather than sticky spores and catch passing nematodes just as fly paper catches flies. Many of these same fungi produce an alluring odor that attracts nematodes and rotifers, adding to their success as hunters and carnivores.

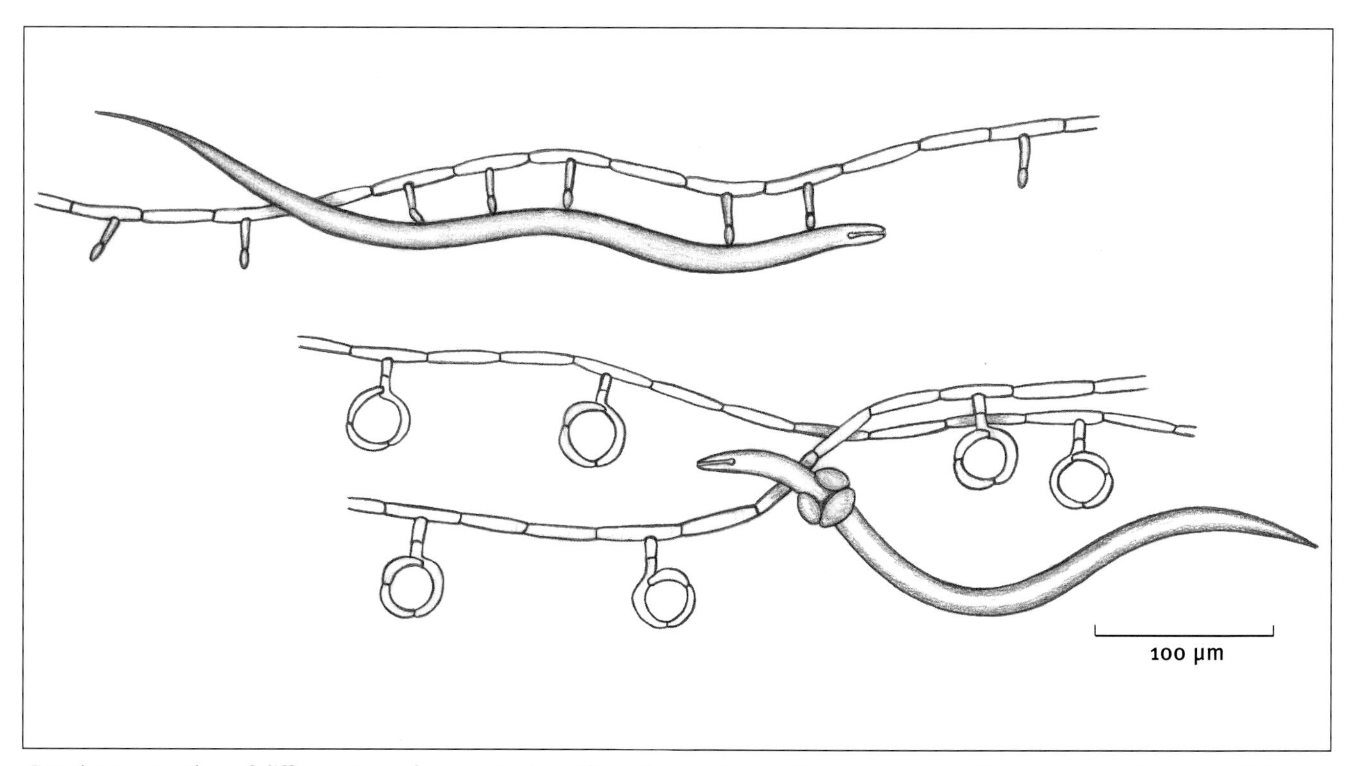

Fungi set a number of different traps for nematodes. After a fungus immobilizes a nematode in a noose or sticky trap, it then sends its hypha into the nematode's body to digest all of the nematode except its hard, outer cuticle.

Baermann Funnel

The variety of nematodes in a handful of soil can be easily sorted from the humus and mineral particles. To do so, wrap the soil in cheesecloth or muslin and place it in a small funnel that is filled with water after its stem has been corked or clamped at the bottom. In a short time most of the nematodes wriggle out of the inundated soil, through the pores of the cloth, and into the water. They soon gravitate to the stem of the funnel. When the cork or clamp is removed, many nematodes can be collected for closer inspection under a microscope.

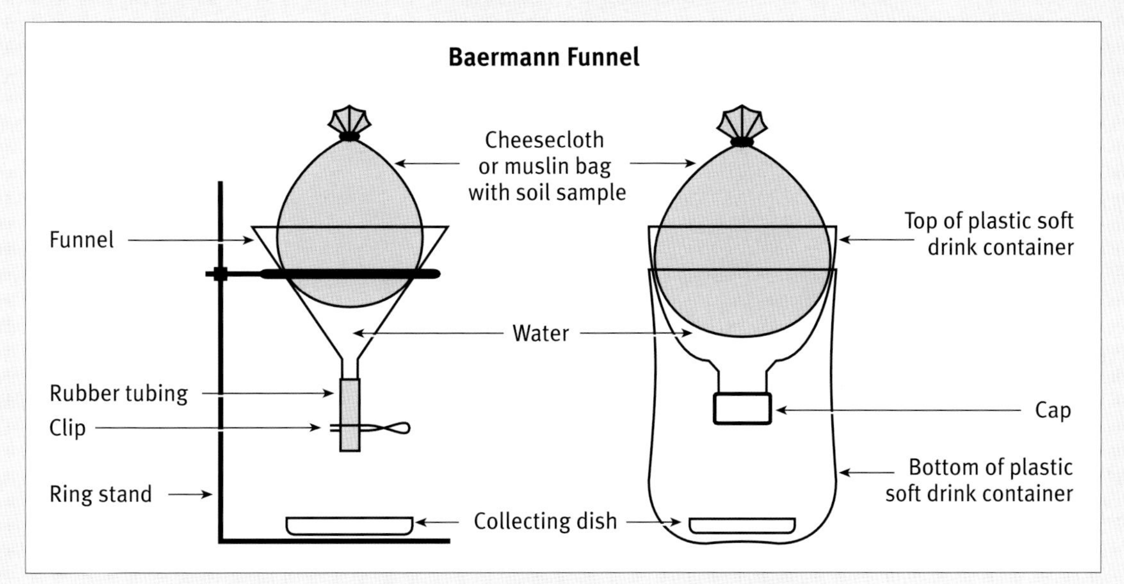

Baermann funnels extract nematodes and potworms from a handful of soil.

The most remarkable of the nematode-eating fungi, and also the most common, are snare-forming fungi which have developed the most elaborate traps of all. These traps only form if the fungi are informed in some way that nematodes are in the vicinity. Just the nearby presence of nematodes and the chemicals they exude is sufficient stimulus for the fungi to form the loops, and even water that once contained nematodes will trigger trap formation. In some species the inside of each loop is just wide enough for a nematode to slip through part way and then get stuck long enough for the fungus to finish it off by piercing it with its hyphae. Some species of loop-bearing fungi have developed loops that can constrict and strangle a victim. If a nematode should chance to poke its head into one of these loops and touch one or more of the loop cells, the cells will swell with water in a flash of a second and grip until the struggling worm wriggles no more.

EARTHWORMS

CLASSIFICATION
Phylum Annelida
Class Oligochaeta
Order Opisthopora

PLACE IN FOOD WEB
Decomposers, Detritivores

SIZE
1–40 cm in length

NUMBER OF SPECIES
7,260

Earthworms

Every farmer tries to make his land more productive by using fertilizers and tilling the soil. Although the earthworm works at a much slower pace and on a much smaller scale, it achieves the same effect. As it plows through the soil, often as deep as 7 or 8 feet (2 to 2.5 meters) and occasionally as deep as 10 feet (3 meters), an earthworm swallows mineral particles and plant matter, partially pushing its way through the soil and partially eating its way through. Inside the earthworm, mineral particles and plant debris are mixed together and pass out as "castings," or "casts." Most casts are left on the surface of the soil and are especially obvious at entrances to earthworm burrows after a spring rain.

Earthworm manure is always finer, richer, and less acidic than the soil and litter the earthworm initially swallowed. By the time the bits of soil, plant material, and bacteria have passed through the earthworm's gut, many minerals that were previously unavailable to plant roots can now be found in the casts. In passing through earthworms, soil takes on new properties. Along its long gut each earthworm has three pairs of glands that secrete calcium carbonate ($CaCO_3$), the same compound that farmers add to soil to lower its acidity. Earthworm casts contain around 50 percent more calcium, nitrogen, phosphorus, potassium, and bacteria than the surrounding soil. In this way earthworms contribute to the formation of rich, productive soils that are not too acidic, and they prefer these soils above all others. Considering this distinct preference, it is not surprising that not many earthworms are found in the generally acidic soils of the tropics and evergreen forests.

In his book *Soil,* G. V. Jacks tells a revealing anecdote about earthworms, moles, and the chalk lines of a tennis court. Dr. Jacks, a soil scientist at Rothamsted Experimental Station in Britain, lived near a tennis court that had been built on acidic soil. The calcium of the chalk ($CaCO_3$) that had been used to mark the lines on the court had locally neutralized the acid and created a soil environment that attracted earthworms. Long after the surface chalk had been washed away by rains, runways of moles still faithfully followed the former chalk lines. The moles had clearly discovered that their favorite food, earthworms, preferred to live along these long,

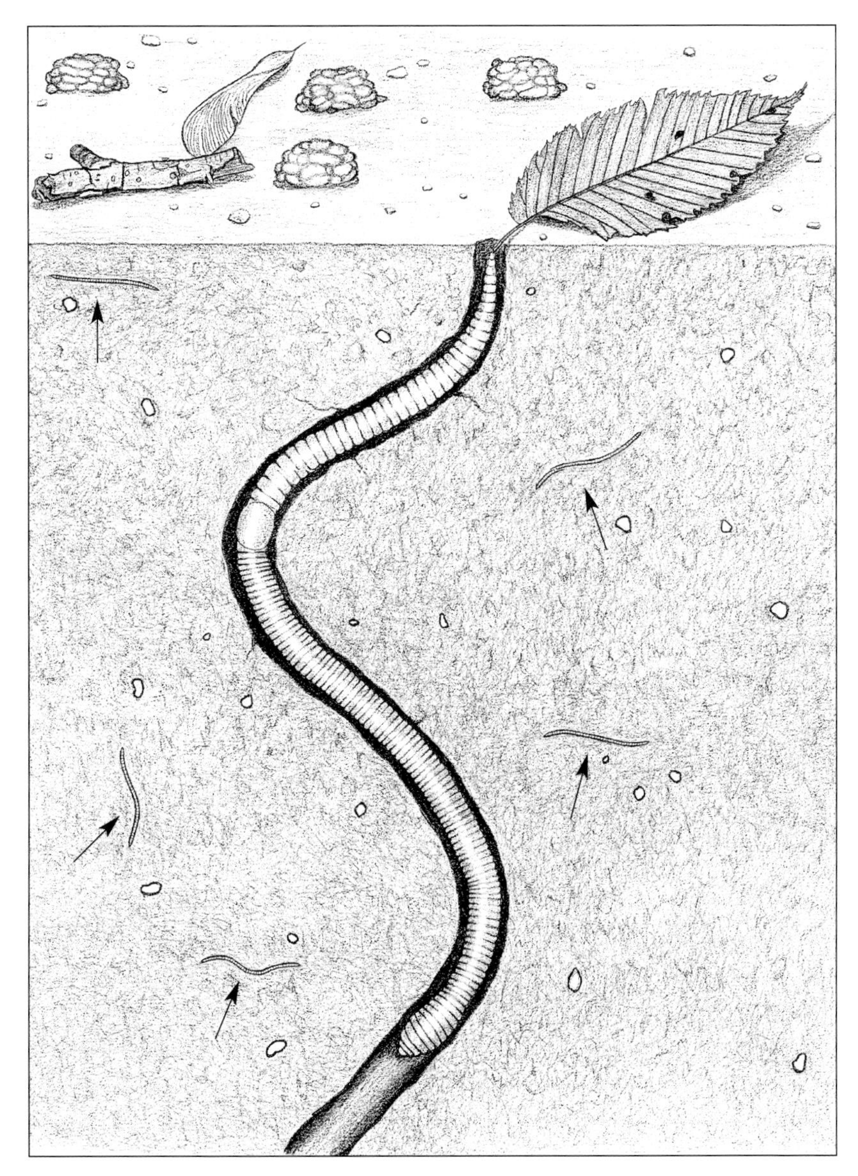

Earthworms pull fallen leaves into their burrows and leave their droppings or casts on the soil's surface. Five potworms (three to the left of the earthworm and two to its right) move through the spaces in the soil.

narrow stretches of soil where they were able to avoid the surrounding acidic soil.

Years before earthworms were appreciated as beneficent tillers of the soil, a clergyman named Gilbert White, who lived in the small English village of Selborne, came to their defense in his book, *The Natural History of Selborne.* When White wrote down his observations in 1777, most people had poor opinions of "this small and despicable link in the chain of nature." Gardeners considered them a nuisance for leaving their

The Earthworm's Dilemma

In the dark of night earthworms issue forth from their burrows to harvest fallen leaves and plant debris aboveground. They avoid the bright light of day and the invisible ultraviolet rays of the sun, to which they are especially sensitive. Even on an overcast day, enough ultraviolet penetrates the cloud layers to harm a sensitive earthworm after a few hours' exposure. On rainy days when water floods their burrows, earthworms are faced with drowning if they stay underground or being burned by the short wavelengths of ultraviolet light if they surface for oxygen. Next time you see earthworms that have emerged from the soil after a rainy night and have perished on sidewalks and in puddles, you will have a better appreciation for the challenges they face from living in poorly drained burrows.

unsightly casts along garden walks, and farmers believed that earthworms ate seedlings of wheat and corn. How ironic that men who tilled the soil had failed to appreciate what an English clergyman observed so clearly: "Worms seem to be the great promoters of vegetation by boring, perforating, and loosening the soil, and rendering it pervious to rains and the fibres of plants; by drawing straws and stalks of leaves and twigs into it; and most of all, by throwing up such infinite numbers of lumps of earth called worm-casts, which, being their excrement, is a fine manure for grain and grass."

In 1881, Charles Darwin devoted his last book to earthworms and the many observations of them that he had recorded over his lifetime. What he had observed over a long period was that these lowly, legless creatures showed a surprising amount of intelligence—earthworms can actually arrive at conclusions based on their experiences. Earthworms drag fallen leaves into the entrances of their burrows to serve as protection from predators or as part of an evening meal. Earthworms, however, do not just pull any part of a leaf into their burrows. Darwin found that they systematically feel around the edge of a leaf until they find the leaf's tip or its stalk. Some leaves fold and curl more readily at one end or the other, while others can be pulled down a worm's burrow equally well from either end. After examining a particular type of leaf, an earthworm can assess which end it should drag into its burrow.

Later in the book Darwin also documented the earth-moving prowess of earthworms by presenting specific examples of Roman ruins and ruins of prehistoric Britons being buried by many centuries' worth of earthworm casts. Darwin estimated that in places these objects get buried at the rate of a tenth of an inch each year, with up to 40 tons (36 metric tons) of casts per acre being added each year to the surface of the soil. As a conclusion for his tribute to earthworms, Darwin wrote, "The plough is one of the most ancient and most valuable of man's inventions; but long before he existed the land was in fact regularly ploughed by earthworms. It may be doubted whether there are many other animals which have played so important a part in the history of the world, as have these lowly organised creatures."

Few people realize that the familiar earthworms of our gardens, yards, and fields are actually immigrants like most

Americans, having accompanied humans in their travels from the Old World to the New World. Most undoubtedly arrived as stowaways in potted plants and root stocks. The smaller, native earthworms have been largely displaced by these larger immigrants, but they still hang on in those remote, uninhabited, and increasingly rare spots where native vegetation still endures and the soil lies undisturbed by cultivation. These native species of earthworms work at a measured pace that always maintains an abundant supply of leaf litter and humus on the soil's surface.

In contrast, species of earthworms introduced from other parts of the world are now depleting the leaf litter of many forests and eliminating the rich fauna and flora associated with the litter. Within a few weeks they can recycle and completely remove the layer of leaf litter on the floor of a deciduous forest that normally takes three to five years to decompose. Only recently have we discovered that, depending on particular circumstances, earthworms can contribute either positively or negatively to the fertility of soils as well as to the native plants and animals associated with those soils.

Down in the leaf litter and soil live other relatives of the beneficent earthworms. These other segmented worms have developed reputations as infamous bloodsuckers. In southeast Asia and the surrounding islands, horror stories are told of leeches that stealthily emerge from the forest litter to suck the blood of people and other mammals. Most people know about the leeches that live in ponds and streams, but not about these leeches of the land.

In Mexico, Guatemala, and southern Europe, the bloodsucking land leeches have not established the sordid reputation of their Asian relatives. These leeches feed on the cold blood of salamanders rather than the warm blood of animals like ourselves. While bloodsucking leeches do not live in the soils of the United States, these soils, as well as soils in Latin America, Asia, and Hawaii, are host to large land leeches that prey on earthworms and snails. Leeches are always associated with swamps and ponds, but some of these segmented worms left their aquatic habitats long ago to explore opportunities in the soil. There, they discovered a limitless supply of earthworms on which to feast, and have stayed ever since.

ROTIFERS

CLASSIFICATION
Phylum Rotifera

PLACE IN FOOD WEB
Predators of bacteria and protozoa, Scavengers, Algal eaters, Fungivores

SIZE
100–500 µm in length

NUMBER OF SPECIES
100 in soil

Rotifers

After observing these creatures with crowns of cilia waving in circular patterns like the motion of a wheel, the early scientists chose the Greek name of "wheel bearers" for them. These animals may be as small as 1/250 inch (0.1 millimeter) or as large as 1/50 inch (0.5 millimeter). Most rotifers live in ponds, lakes, and streams, but about 5 percent of the estimated 2,000 species have found a home in the soil or on nearby mosses and lichens.

Rotifers usually navigate in the water films that cover the leaf litter, mosses, and soil particles by swimming with their crowns of cilia. As the water films shrink on hot, dry days, a rotifer resorts to creeping across surfaces in inchworm fashion: using its head and two toes to contact particles of soil and alternately stretching and buckling the portion of its body between its head and toes. If the water films completely disappear, as a last resort rotifers form dehydrated cysts like those of protozoa, tardigrades, and nematodes that enable them to enter a state of suspended animation until wetter and better times return. During hard times, one particularly common rotifer of the soil called *Philodina* (*philo* = love; *dina* = whirling) transforms to a colorful pink cyst.

For millions of years rotifers have given birth to daughters in a totally female-dominated world. These animals have multiplied and spread without the distractions of courtship and mating. Their principal concerns seem to be surviving droughts, avoiding predators, and finding enough bacteria, algae, protozoa, and plant debris to satisfy their hungers. For most rotifers sex is as superfluous as males, and abstinence is a way of life.

Philodina *(above) is a common rotifer of ponds as well as soils. Rotifers (below) travel through the soil using the same locomotion as inchworms.*

50 µm

Snails and Slugs

Like woodlice, which have the distinction of being the only crustaceans that ventured from the sea onto the dry land, slugs and snails left their ancestral homes in the sea long before the ancestors of whales left the land to dwell in the sea, even long before dinosaurs appeared. Snails and slugs are the only mollusks to leave not only their saltwater homes in the oceans but also their freshwater homes in lakes and streams. About 1,000 species are at home in the forests and fields of America north of Mexico. Their needs are simple—a little moisture, some calcium in the soil for producing shells, and a good supply of rotting vegetation. Only a few snails and slugs are predators and feed on earthworms, potworms, or others

SNAILS AND SLUGS

CLASSIFICATION
Phylum Mollusca
Class Gastropoda

PLACE IN FOOD WEB
Decomposers, Detritivores, Scavengers, Predators

SIZE
1.5 mm–12 cm in length

NUMBER OF SPECIES
30,000 land snails
500 land slugs

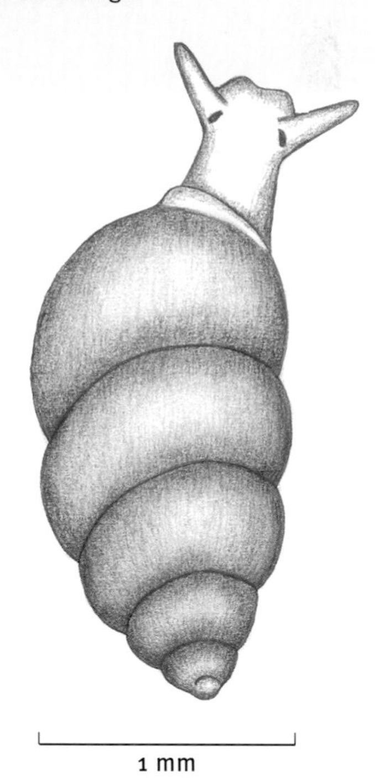

Tiny, cone-shaped snails are common scavengers on the forest floor that usually go unnoticed.

These snails have gathered on a moist log in the southern Appalachians.

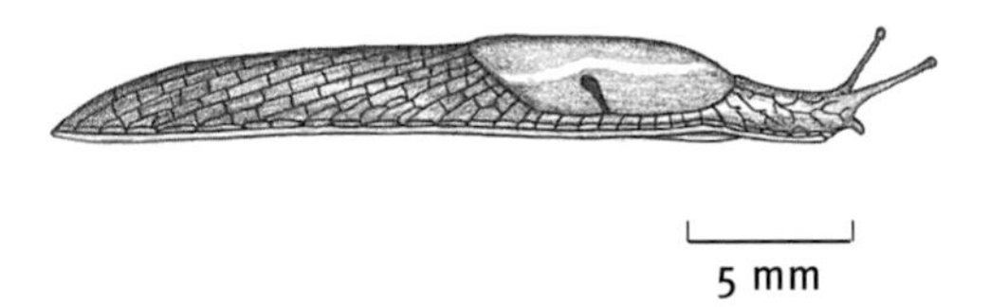

Beneath their soft exteriors, slugs carry small, hidden shells.

of their kind. Each of these soil mollusks is bathed in a slimy, protective mucus layer that avidly holds water and allows each animal to venture across dry stretches of the forest floor without inevitably shriveling and dehydrating.

Collectively, snails and slugs are known as gastropods or "belly feet," creatures whose feet spread out beneath them as they crawl along. Each slug and each snail has one large muscular foot on which it gracefully glides over the swells and swales of the forest floor. As successive waves of contraction pass along the muscles of the foot, the gastropod inches along. Watching the "belly" of a gastropod from below, as the animal moves across the clear surface of a jar or terrarium, is the best way to appreciate the nimble-footed movements of these animals.

As it consumes plant litter, each animal extends a structure in its mouth that looks and works like a tongue but is covered with many hard, sharp teeth; it is called a "radula." So many teeth are found in the mouth of one common snail that they are arranged in 120 rows of 91 teeth each. The teeth of the radula rasp away at decaying leaves, making distinctive imprints on a leaf's smooth surface. The material that the radula scrapes from a leaf passes into a digestive tract where the variety of enzymes involved in breaking down the tougher fibers of leaves and wood is probably greater than that found in the gut of any other animal of the soil.

Gastropods are considered delicacies in many countries, appearing on restaurant menus under their French name, "escargot." Other creatures share our fondness for escargot and have special adaptations for hunting and eating their catch. Certain ground beetles and a couple of families of daddy longlegs have long, powerful mouth parts that enable them to reach deep within the openings of snail shells. The snail-eating ground beetles have narrow, scissorlike mandibles; the jaws of the daddy longlegs are often longer than their bodies. Glowworms, the larvae of many species of fireflies, can track down snails by following their slime trails. After overtaking a snail, a firefly larva paralyzes it with toxin from its sharp, hollow jaws. Next the needlelike jaws inject enzymes that begin digesting the snail and enable the larva to suck in juicy gastropod. There is even one family of flies whose larvae specialize in being predators of gastropods.

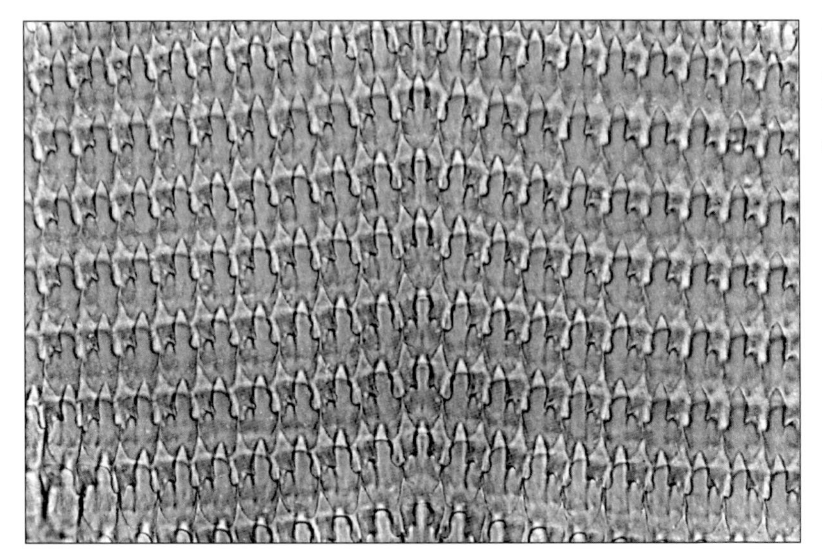

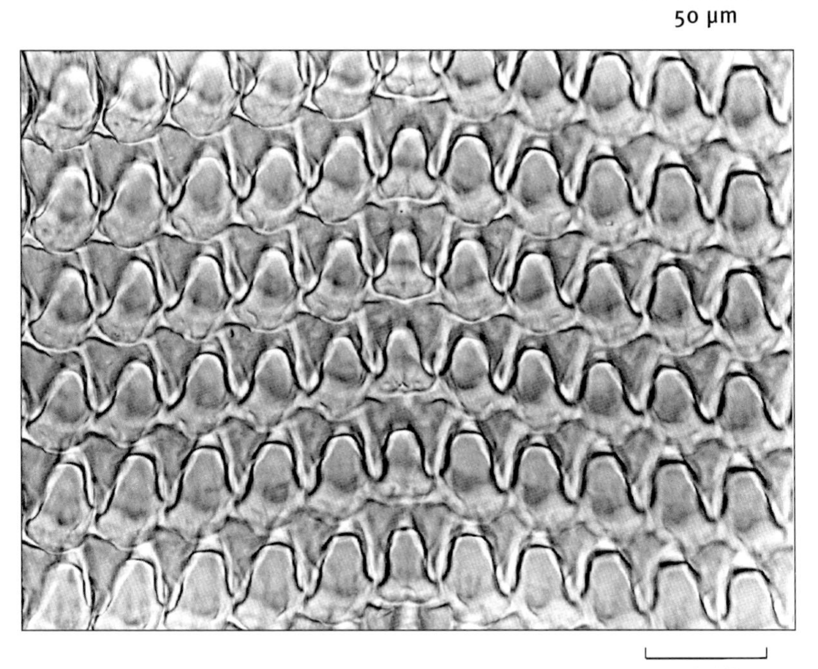

The teeth of a slug (top) and a snail (bottom) are precisely arranged and very effective at rasping and tearing mushrooms and dead leaves.

In the woodlands of Britain and Europe, birds regularly smash the shells of snails on rocks in order to get at the meal within. To avoid hungry thrushes, snails have shells with many different color patterns—bands or no bands, yellow or brown—that camouflage them and vary with the snail's habitat. A great range of forms and colors have evolved and are still evolving among the gastropods as snails and slugs continually find new ways to avoid becoming someone's "escargot."

TARDIGRADES

CLASSIFICATION
Phylum Tardigrada
Class Eutardigrada (naked tardigrades)
Class Heterotardigrada (armored tardigrades)

PLACE IN FOOD WEB
Predators, Fungivores, Algal eaters

SIZE
50 µm–1.2 mm in length

NUMBER OF SPECIES
400

Tardigrades

Only in the last 200 years have we humans even known that such creatures as tardigrades exist. A German naturalist and priest named Johann Goeze published the first account of a tardigrade in 1773 referring to the tiny rotund animal as a *Kleiner Wasser Bär,* or "little water bear." Only a few years later, Bonaventura Corti and Lazzaro Spallanzani, Italian abbots and professors of natural science, contributed their accounts and impressions of tardigrades. Corti referred to them as *brucolini,* or "little caterpillars," and what caught Spallanzani's attention was the slow, resolute movement of these little animals that walked like turtles. He chose the name *Il Tardigrado,* or "slow stepper." To this day both Goeze's and Spallanzani's names for these animals have stuck.

Water bears are considered to be related to arthropods, such as insects and millipedes; but they are also unique enough to be placed in their own phylum—Tardigrada. Like arthropods, tardigrades shed an exoskeleton as they grow, and the structure of this cuticle distinguishes the two different types of tardigrades: Heterotardigrades, or armored tardigrades, have thick cuticles that are divided into plates; eutardigrades, or naked tardigrades, have thinner cuticles that may be sculptured but are without any plates. The charm of these little water bears is often enhanced by their appealing colors. Although many tardigrades are colorless, white, or brown, some are red, green, orange, yellow, and even pink.

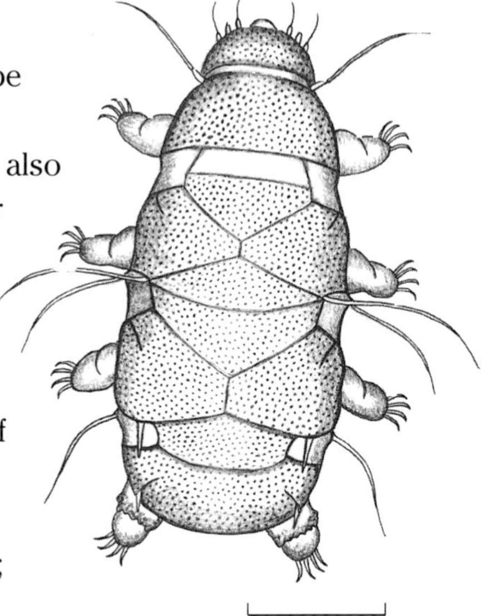

Some tardigrades have cuticles with plates and four claws on each leg (bottom). Other tardigrades have thinner cuticles with a few bumps and two double claws on each leg (top).

Most tardigrades are about $1/50$ inch (0.5 millimeter) long and dine on just about all the creatures in the soil that are their size or smaller, including protozoa, algae, fungi, rotifers, nematodes, and other tardigrades. There are plenty of larger creatures in the soil that in turn feed on tardigrades—large protozoa, nematodes, carnivorous fungi, mites, spiders, and insect larvae.

The ornate eggs of tardigrades

At certain times and in certain places, tardigrades can be as abundant as the mites and springtails that are about everywhere in the soil and leaf litter. However, tardigrades prefer certain microenvironments with just the right food, humidity, ventilation, temperature, and other conditions that adequately satisfy their needs. When these conditions are met, as many as 400,000 tardigrades and 1.2 million tardigrade eggs can be found in a square yard (9 square feet; 0.84 square meter) of soil. Few eggs are as lovely as tardigrade eggs. They are spherical globes almost one-tenth as large as a full-grown tardigrade and are ornamented with pores, spines, knobs, ridges, and assorted processes arranged in attractive geometric patterns.

Even in their favorite habitats, environmental conditions can often go awry. The temperature can drop too low or rise too high. Drought can lower the humidity to zero. When faced with these dire circumstances, tardigrades have a talent for slowly losing all but about 3 percent of their water and shriveling into unrecognizable forms, yet remarkably remaining alive. This state of suspended animation has been given the impressive-sounding name of cryptobiosis, or "hidden life," and is being actively studied by those who would like to find out if humans also can enter a cryptobiotic state. In their almost completely dehydrated forms, tardigrades can survive high temperatures well above that of boiling water and low temperatures well below -200°F (-130°C). Even after being left on a dried museum specimen of moss for 120 years, a slumbering tardigrade can be awakened from its long sleep.

ONYCHOPHORANS

CLASSIFICATION
Phylum Onychophora
Class Onychophora
Order Onychophora

PLACE IN FOOD WEB
Predators

SIZE
1.5–15 cm in length

NUMBER OF SPECIES
80

Onychophorans

The onychophorans are an ancient group, and their distribution in such widely scattered lands as New Zealand and the islands of the Caribbean suggest that they appeared on earth at a time when the far-flung continents were all part of a single large land mass known as Pangaea. Around 180 million years ago this land mass began to fragment into the continents and islands that we know today, and the onychophorans went along for the ride.

Today onychophorans are barely hanging on in the hot, humid forests of the West Indies, South America, Africa, Australia, New Zealand, and the Malay Archipelago. They hunt for arthropods under rotten logs and in the leaf litter. Just anterior to its mouth, each onychophoran has a pair of glands that explosively expel a sticky material as far as half a meter, entangling and entrapping its arthropod prey. This life style, however, is probably no longer optimal in today's world, as populations of onychophorans steadily continue to dwindle.

Although the first biologist to encounter an onychophoran in 1826 described it as a mollusk, some biologists have since then considered them members of the earthworm phylum Annelida, while others have placed them among the spiders, mites, myriapods, insects, and crustaceans of the phylum Arthropoda. Now most biologists consider them such an exceptional and distinctive group of soil organisms that they have placed them in their own phylum, the Onychophora ("claw bearers"), a name that refers to the curved claws on the ends of their unsegmented legs.

Onychophorans are the best candidates for organisms that represent a "missing link" between the annelids and the arthropods. On one hand, they have the arthropod attributes of having dorsal hearts extending from head to tail as well as air tubes known as tracheae that repeatedly branch throughout their bodies. On the other hand, beneath their thin, velvety cuticles are layers of muscles like those of earthworms. Cilia, such as those found on the surfaces of certain protozoa,

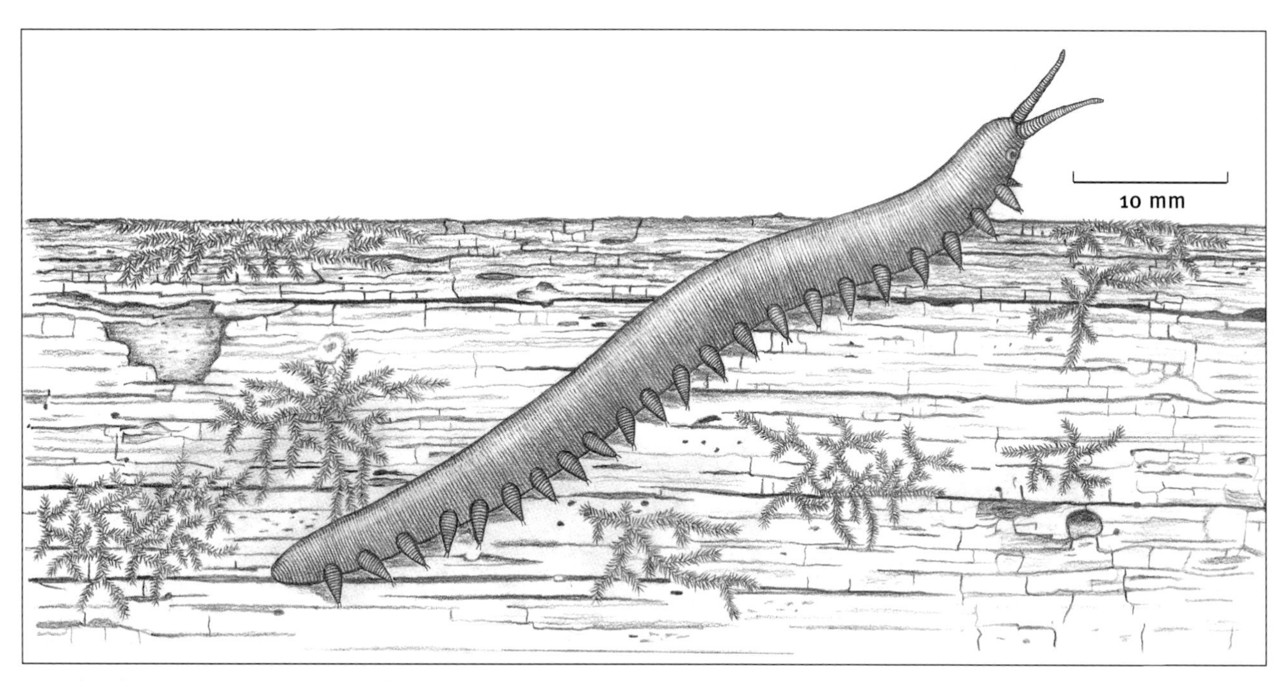

Onychophorans are rare animals of tropical forests that share attributes with both earthworms and arthropods.

line the reproductive and excretory organs of onychophorans. These tiny hairs that sweep fluids through their reproductive and excretory ducts are found in earthworms and other annelids but never in arthropods. For good reasons, onychophorans are considered survivors of an ancient lineage that probably eventually gave rise to both the annelids and the arthropods.

MITES

CLASSIFICATION
Phylum Arthropoda
Class Arachnida
Subclass Acarina

PLACE IN FOOD WEB
Decomposers, Detritivores, Predators, Fungivores

SIZE
100 µm–4 mm in length

NUMBER OF SPECIES
30,000

Mites and Springtails

Arthropods all have exoskeletons and jointed legs, and are by far the most abundant and most diverse animals of the soil. They can be as small as a fraction of a millimeter or as large as four inches (100 millimeters). They can be found in every imaginable habitat the soil has to offer and just about every habitat found on our planet. In soils of pastures, forests, and plowed fields, mites and springtails represent the undisputed majority of these arthropods.

To the unaided eye, a mite or a springtail is neither imposing nor prepossessing, but it is amazing how a little magnification can change our views of these creatures. They may be small, but they come in an enchanting diversity of forms, colors, and textures. In most moist soils they are the most important producers of humus. Although few mites and springtails survive in arid and semiarid soils, ants seem to do quite well. Ants are probably the most abundant arthropods in many desert soils, but in other soils mites and springtails outnumber them by at least 100 to 1.

Wherever mites and springtails are found, mites are usually more abundant than springtails, often several times more so. Half of the 30,000 species of mites that have been described are dwellers in the soil. Anywhere from 100,000 to 400,000 mites live in a square yard (9 square feet; 0.84 square meter) of moist forest soil. Up to 10,000 individuals per square yard are predatory mites, but most mites of the topsoil and litter are the shiny, scavenging beetle, or oribatid, mites. The larger, predatory gamasid mites have long protruding

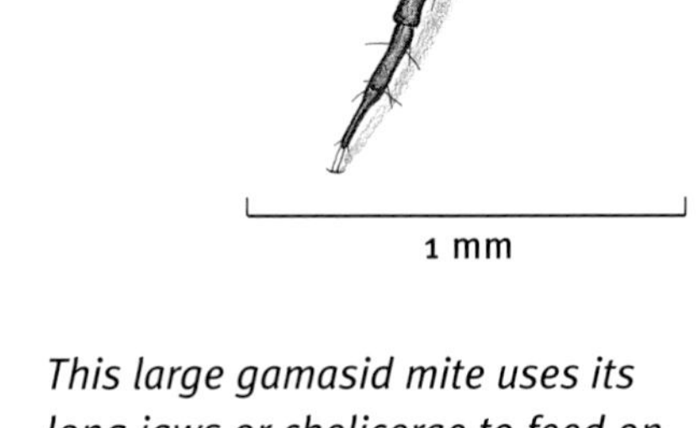

This large gamasid mite uses its long jaws or chelicerae to feed on smaller arthropods and their eggs.

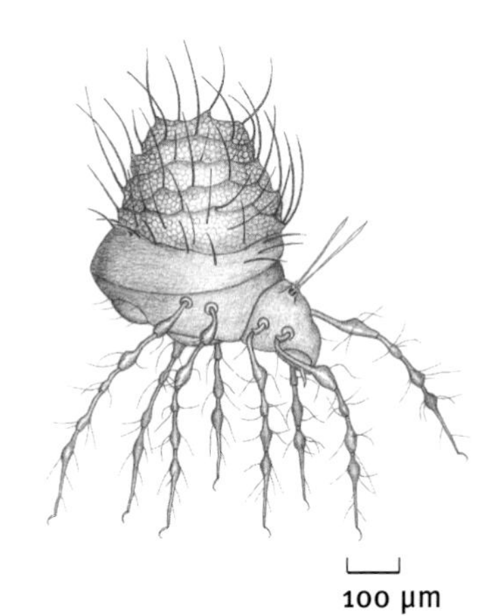

This long-legged oribatid mite carries a pile of its shed skins on its back.

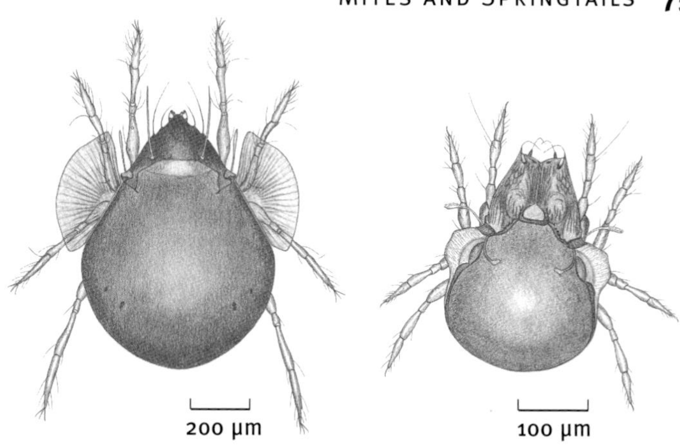

Many oribatid mites look as though they have tiny wings. Mites cannot fly, but they can tuck their legs under their "wings" and protect them from the jaws of predators.

mouth parts, or chelicerae, with which they stalk nematodes, potworms, springtails, and other tiny arthropods. The smaller oribatid mites eat fungi and leaf litter with their less conspicuous chelicerae.

The oribatid mites that feed on decaying leaves set the stage for smaller decomposers like bacteria and fungi to free most of the energy and nutrients stored in those leaves. Oribatid mites and fungi, however, do not seem to tolerate each other's company very well. They compete for the same supply of decaying plant litter. Eventually either oribatids or fungi predominate, and bacteria are left to finish the job of decomposing. The mites seem to work best at chewing the fallen leaves and other plant debris into small pieces, making the leaf litter more accessible to smaller decomposers and providing a larger surface area over which microbes can act. Their healthy appetites ensure that each oribatid mite consumes roughly 20 percent of its weight in leaf litter every day. The tiny droppings that they leave behind add to the soil's stockpile of humus.

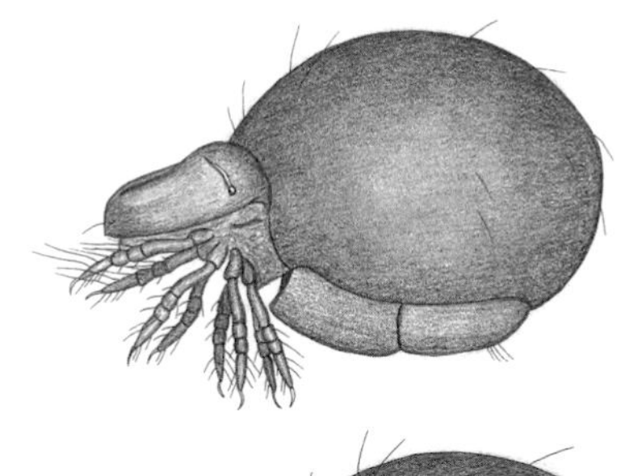

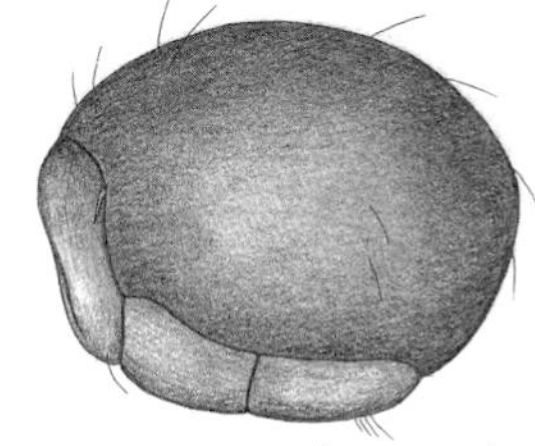

No trace of an oribatid mite's legs or mouthparts remain exposed after an oribatid closes its shell.

These darkly pigmented soil mites are an exception to the rule that soil-inhabiting arthropods are usually soft, pale, and white. Their hard, dark shells serve them well as safeguards from predators and drought. Oribatid mites go by a variety of common names. They are often referred to as beetle mites because they look like small, dark, and round beetles. Since many other oribatid mites live among mosses, they have earned the name moss mites. The third common name for oribatids is seed mites and refers to a group of mites that can mimic seeds.

The seed mites are one of two main groups of oribatid mites: those that close up their shells like clams, and those that do not. With a hinge between the shell at the front end of the body and the shell at the rear of the body, seed mites can tuck in their legs and clamp their front and rear shells shut so that all their appendages are safely covered by their hard shells. The folded mite looks just like a small, round seed. Those species that lack this hinge cannot fold their bodies like the seed mites. Instead, they resort to other strategies for defense.

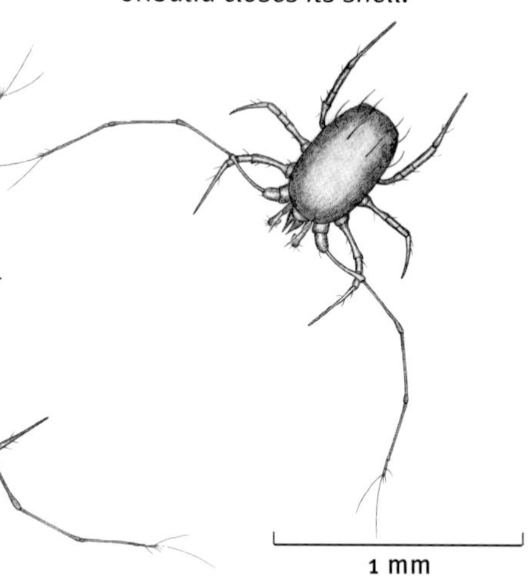

Rather than using their first pair of legs for walking, these small gamasid mites use their exceptionally long legs to explore their environment.

SPRINGTAILS

CLASSIFICATION
Phylum Arthropoda
Class Collembola
Order Collembola

PLACE IN FOOD WEB
Decomposers, Detritivores, Fungivores, Herbivores, Algal eaters

SIZE
100 µm–8 mm in length

NUMBER OF SPECIES
7,500

Some of the mites that cannot fold their bodies like jackknives have a feature that no other mites have. They have winglike projections on their sides called pteromorphs (*ptero* = wing; *morph* = form). These lateral projections are the closest things to actual wings that any mite has developed. Insects are the only flying invertebrates, but with their pteromorphs, mites come very close to having real wings. Pteromorphs have never gotten mites off the ground and into the air, but they have probably saved the lives of a number of mites. Legs tuck neatly beneath the pteromorphs if the mite feels threatened, and there they remain until all seems well again.

Although oribatid mites only lay one or a few eggs at a time, they somehow have succeeded remarkably well in populating the upper layers of the soil as judged from censuses of soil animals in a variety of forests, fields, and pastures. One such census that was taken of the upper 12 inches (30 centimeters) of soil in an English pasture arrived at a figure of 137,000 per square yard (164,000 per square meter) for the density of all mites. In the month of May, oribatid mites made up about 60 percent of the pasture's total mite population, while in the month of November oribatid mites represented 45 percent of all mites in the soil samples from the pasture.

Some of the most extraordinary mites can be found far below the soil's surface, where the passageways of the soil are too narrow and too torturous for most mites. Some of these deep dwellers are so long and thin and their legs are so short that they look more like nematodes than mites.

Very little is known about the mites in this out-of-the-way, inaccessible habitat. They surely do not encounter many other creatures in the deep soil layers where they roam, so most likely they survive on what little organic debris, such as that left behind by plant roots, finds its way to these depths.

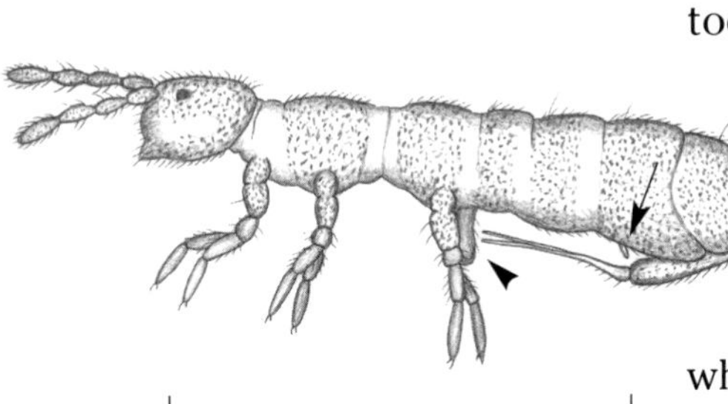

In this side view of a springtail, the fork of its tail as well as the catch (retinaculum, arrow) that holds the tail in place are clearly visible. Its "glue peg" is located behind and between its third pair of legs (arrowhead). A springtail might have six legs like other insects, but it has half the number of segments in its abdomen that insects have.

Even with all the mites inhabiting the leaf litter and soil, there still seems to be space for the next most populous group of arthropods, the springtails or Collembola. Although springtails have diverse shapes, habits, and diets, their tastes in food are not as wide-ranging as those of the mites; and they are far more prolific egg layers than the mites. Encountering springtails frolicking on the snow is probably the best way to get some idea of how extremely abundant these arthropods can be. On winter days when thick blankets of snow begin melting in the warm sunshine, the water descends into the leaf litter, inundating the countless pores, spaces, and passageways inhabited by springtails. This is when the springtails climb to the top of the snow, and millions of them pepper its surface. Springtails hop about wherever they are, and their antics on the snow have earned them the name snow fleas (even though they are only distantly related to fleas). On top of the snow, the winter springtails number around 500 per square foot (900 square centimeters); but around tree trunks and in depressions into which they fall, they accumulate by the thousands.

Springtails and mites are both successful animals, but they are successful for very different reasons. Each group has developed its own strategy for success. Most springtails are prey and very few are predators. Most make a livelihood as scavengers of decaying plant and animal litter, as well as grazers of living mosses, lichens, algae, and fungi. Springtails have learned to cope with predators in ways that are different from the ways used by mites. The most obvious difference between the two is the presence of a springing organ that lies tucked beneath the abdomen of the springtail and can instantaneously launch or "spring" a springtail to safety. With their springs, some animals can jump as much as 20 times their own length to avoid the jaws of a predator. Such jumping feats are impossible, however, down in the narrow, tortuous passageways of the soil. Only the springtails that live on the surface have the space in which to leap to safety.

Springtails that live just below the surface do not have quite as much room in which to leap and maneuver. As a result, springtails found in the upper layers of soil usually have shorter legs, shorter antennae, and shorter springing organs than those that live overhead in the leaf litter. Even further down in the soil, the pore spaces become smaller, and springtails appear that have completely lost their springing organs and whose legs and antennae are even shorter. The widths of their bodies are not much smaller than the widths of the pores through which they crawl. The springtails that inhabit deeper layers have lost their eyes as well as their pigment, but their sense of touch is enhanced by well-developed tactile sensors located near the base of each antenna, called "postantennal organs."

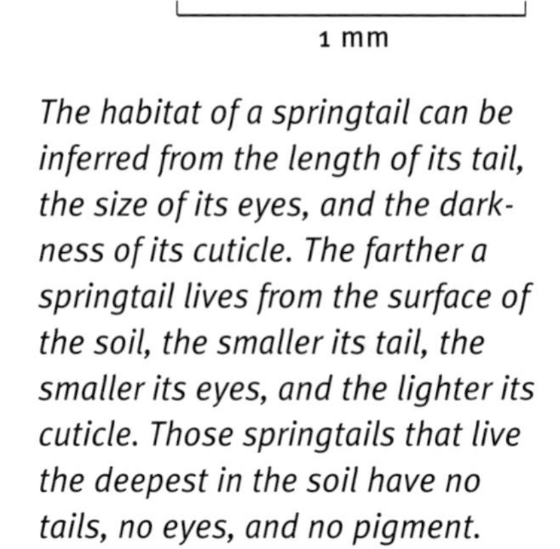

The habitat of a springtail can be inferred from the length of its tail, the size of its eyes, and the darkness of its cuticle. The farther a springtail lives from the surface of the soil, the smaller its tail, the smaller its eyes, and the lighter its cuticle. Those springtails that live the deepest in the soil have no tails, no eyes, and no pigment.

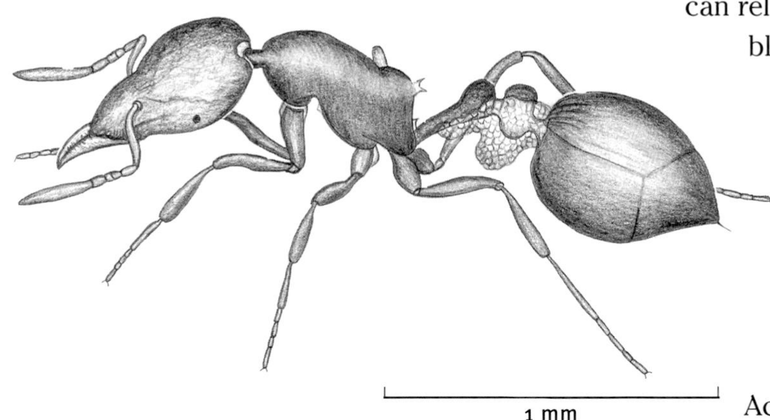

This tiny ant of forest soils is a predator of springtails. It lies in wait for a springtail to come within striking range of its large jaws and quickly paralyzes its prey with its stinger. The spongy structure between its thorax and abdomen is believed to produce an odor that springtails find enticing.

These tiny, blind springtails navigate through the small pore spaces assisted by their keen sense of touch. They cannot outrun or outleap predators that they encounter, but they can release small droplets of their toxic blood from pores called pseudocelli (*pseudo* = false; *ocelli* = little eyes) that are scattered over their bodies. One taste of this blood soon destroys the appetite of a prospective predator. Ants that attempt to eat one of these pale, helpless-looking springtails are in for an unpleasant surprise. According to one observer of an ant-springtail encounter, the unsuspecting ants "clean their mouth parts very quickly and most suffer from temporary paralysis in their feelers, mouth parts, and even legs."

Springtails lack the hard, protective armor that covers the bodies of the oribatid mites and that keeps them from drying out during a drought. Many springtails have thin cuticles that are covered with scales like those on moths and butterflies; these waterproof structures help the animals retain moisture. The distinctive water-conserving device shared by all springtails, however, is a tube found on each animal's ventral surface that can extend or retract as humidity rises and falls. A springtail walking on the side of a glass container will often check out the moisture in its strange environment by extending its ventral tube. The tube appears to stick to the surface of the glass and explains why the scientific name chosen for the springtails, Collembola, translates to glue peg (*coll* = glue; *embol* = peg). Even as leaf litter dries out, springtails are still able to soak up enough vestiges of moisture with their ventral tubes to survive throughout the drought.

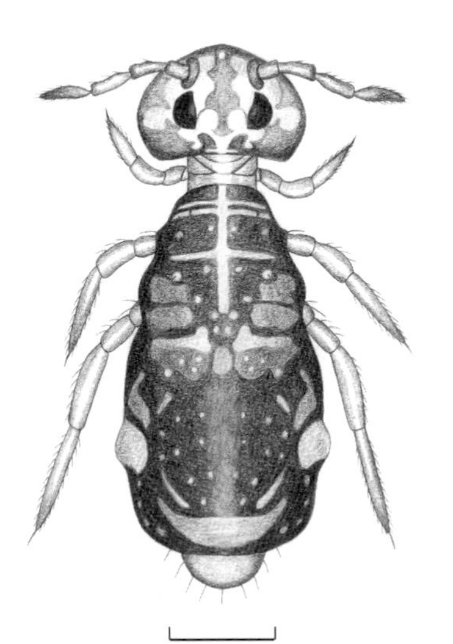

This springtail lives in the leaf litter on the forest floor.

The various adaptations of springtails to life in the soil are remarkable examples of how animal forms have been molded by their immediate surroundings. Springtails that live only a thin soil layer from each other look and behave very differently. In the soil, microenvironments separated by only a few inches or centimeters can be as different as the Arctic and the Amazon.

Proturans and Diplurans

Some soil-dwelling arthropods, such as insects and mites, have close relatives that are found in ponds, on trees and flowers, and even as parasites on larger animals. Other groups, such as the diplurans and proturans, have been very conservative about adapting to different habitats. They are pale, eyeless animals that may venture no further from the soil than a rotten log.

Proturans have a distinctive yellow-brown color that makes them easy to spot in a soil sample; they are by far the smaller of the two groups and rarely grow to more than 1/12 inch (2 millimeters) in length, whereas diplurans are about

PROTURANS

CLASSIFICATION
Phylum Arthropoda
Class Protura
Order Protura

PLACE IN FOOD WEB
Fungivores, Algal eaters

SIZE
600 µm–1.5 mm in length

NUMBER OF SPECIES
400

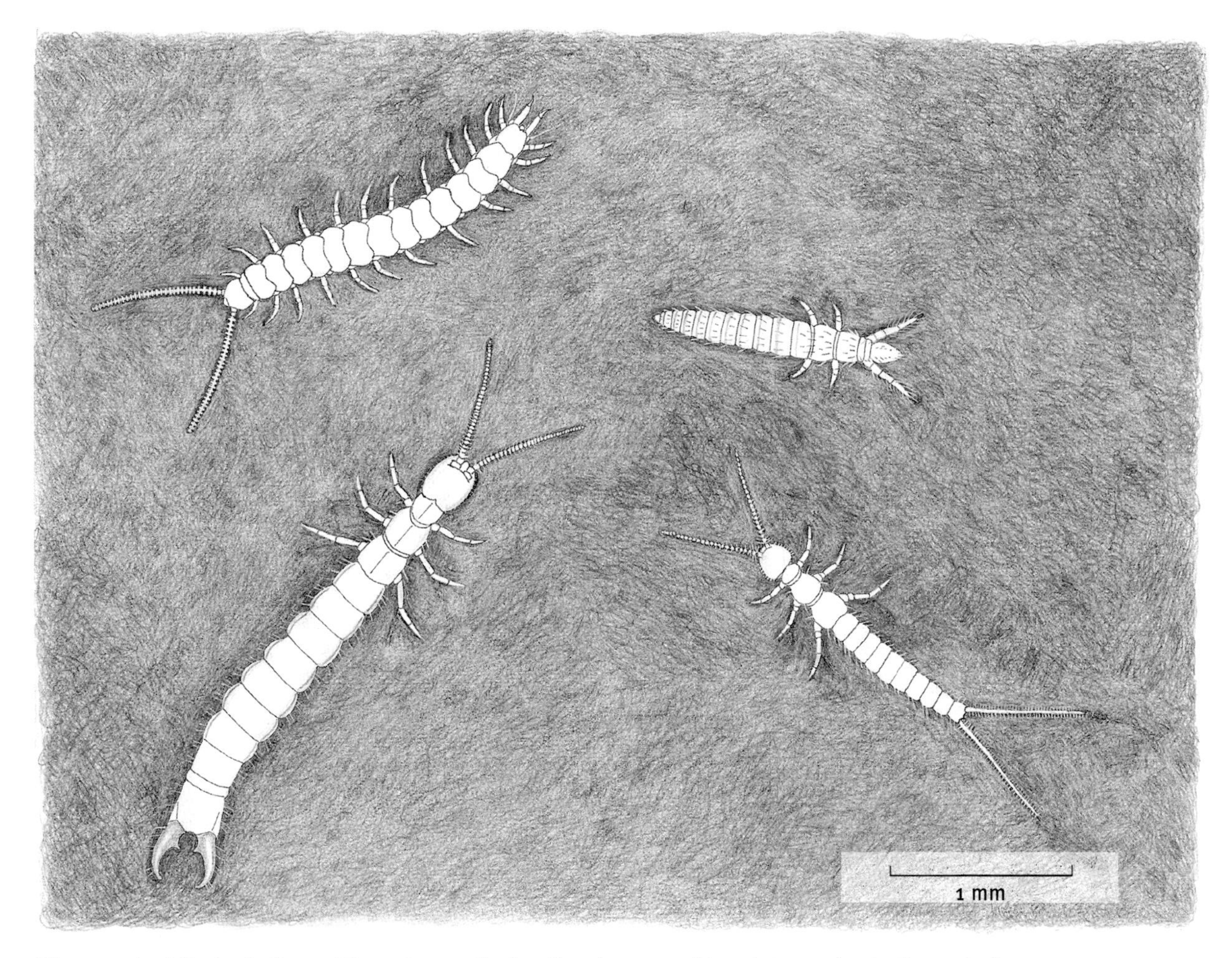

These pale, blind relatives of insects use their refined sense of touch to navigate through the passageways of the soil. To the right of the 24-legged symphylan is a proturan; below the symphylan is a japygid. To the right of the japygid is a campodeid.

DIPLURANS

CLASSIFICATION
Phylum Arthropoda
Class Diplura
Order Diplura
Family Campodeidae
Family Japygidae

PLACE IN FOOD WEB
Predators, Detritivores

SIZE
2 mm–5 cm in length

NUMBER OF SPECIES
400

4 to 40 times larger. Proturans and diplurans resemble insects in that they have six legs, but there most of the resemblance ends. Soil creatures like diplurans and proturans that are without eyes compensate for their lack of sight with enhanced senses of touch and smell. Diplurans have long antennae at one end, and equally long sensory appendages called "cerci" that project from the other end of their bodies. A variety of sensory bristles are scattered elsewhere over their bodies. What one soon notices about the smaller proturans is that they are missing both the antennae and the cerci. Proturans usually walk on only two pairs of legs and use their first pair of legs as antennae. They wave their front legs about just like an insect trying to locate a particular scent in its environment would do.

As predators, diplurans need a sophisticated sense of touch to enable them to snatch prey in half a shake of an antenna. The smaller and more delicate diplurans called "campodeids" are known to prey on wriggling midge larvae. The larger and more robust diplurans are called "japygids." Their cerci look like those of earwigs and have taken on the form and function of pincers. Japygids use their pincers to seize smaller campodeids and springtails. The long, sinuous bodies of these diplurans give them the ability to whip through the narrow pore spaces of the soil.

For proturans which feed on algae and other soil fungi, split-second responses to the world around them are probably unnecessary and excessive. Neither do proturans need to make quick escapes from predators—a pair of defensive glands at the end of each animal's abdomen produces a repellent that discourages attacks from the rear. For a small group of arthropods with only a few species, the proturans have thrived in their dark world, and as many as 5 million can live on a single acre.

Myriapods

Nature has been uninhibited about designing legs of soil arthropods. All insects, diplurans, proturans, and springtails each have three pairs of legs. All spiders, daddy longlegs, mites, and pseudoscorpions each have four pair of legs. Woodlice manage nicely with seven pairs of legs. All those arthropods with more than seven pairs of legs are considered myriapods (*myria* = very numerous; *poda* = legs), having anywhere from nine pairs of legs in pauropods (*pauro* = little; *poda* = legs) to 177 pairs of legs in soil centipedes and 375 pairs of legs on a tropical species of millipede. Many arthropods with more than three pairs of legs as adults start out in their youth with only three pairs, adding legs and body segments as they grow and molt. Young larvae of mites, millipedes, and pauropods hatch from their eggs with three pairs of legs and are often mistaken for insect larvae until they molt and develop some more legs. Surprisingly, the soil centipedes hatch from their eggs with all their legs already formed. With their additional joints and additional legs, the myriapods excel, not necessarily in speed but in their agility and ability to maneuver in tight and twisting passageways.

The smallest, least studied, and most recently discovered myriapods with the fewest legs are the symphylans and the pauropods. These two groups are often the most common myriapods in some soils, yet despite their relative abundance, symphylans were not described until the second half of the 18th century, and pauropods were not discovered until the second half of the 19th century. Both groups feed on decaying vegetation, fungi, and dead animals, but in other ways, they are very different arthropods. Pauropods are only a few

PAUROPODS

CLASSIFICATION
Phylum Arthropoda
Class Pauropoda

PLACE IN FOOD WEB
Decomposers, Detritivores, Scavengers, Fungivores

SIZE
500 µm–1.5 mm in length

NUMBER OF SPECIES
500

SYMPHYLANS

CLASSIFICATION
Phylum Arthropoda
Class Symphyla

PLACE IN FOOD WEB
Decomposers, Detritivores, Scavengers, Fungivores

SIZE
1–8 mm in length

NUMBER OF SPECIES
120

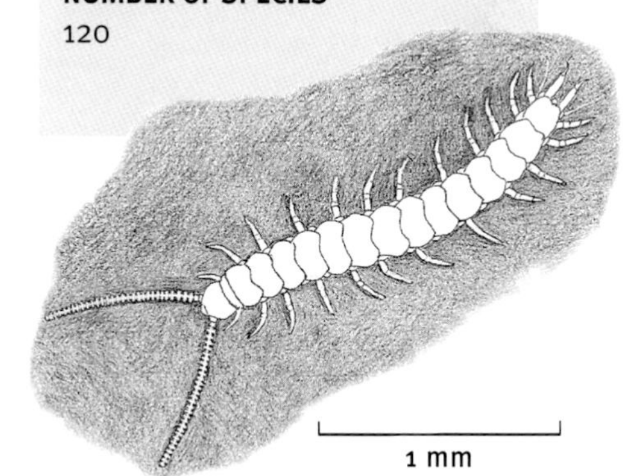

A 24-legged symphylan

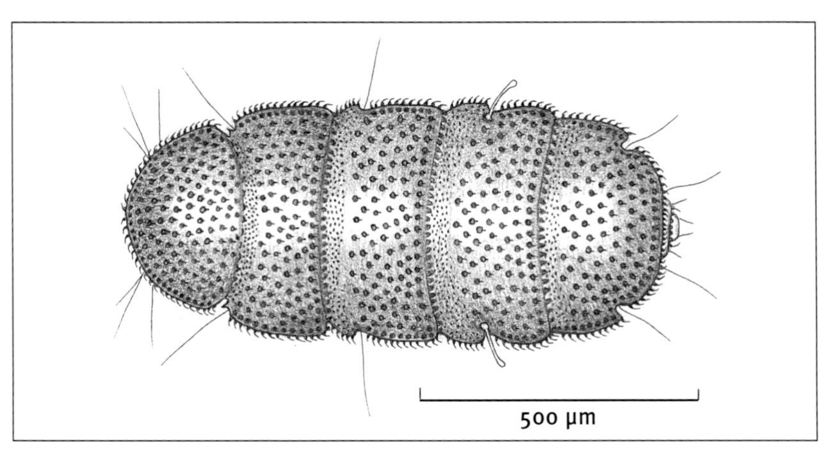

Pauropods have been known to science for slightly over a hundred years. Sir John Lubbock, a friend and neighbor of Charles Darwin, first discovered pauropods in his garden south of London.

CENTIPEDES

CLASSIFICATION
Phylum Arthropoda
Class Chilopoda
Order Geophilomorpha (soil centipedes)
Order Lithobiomorpha (stone centipedes)

PLACE IN FOOD WEB
Predators

SIZE
3 mm–30 cm in length

NUMBER OF SPECIES
3,000

LIFESPAN
5–6 years

MILLIPEDES

CLASSIFICATION
Phylum Arthropoda
Class Diplopoda

PLACE IN FOOD WEB
Decomposers, Detritivores, Scavengers

SIZE
2 mm–28 cm in length

NUMBER OF SPECIES
10,000

LIFESPAN
11 years

millimeters long, have nine pairs of legs, unusual forked antennae, and many, long paddle-shaped sensory bristles that warn of approaching trouble. Symphylans are about 10 millimeters long, have 12 pairs of legs, long, beaded antennae, and a pair of spinnerets on their last segment that spews out silk to foil any predators such as ants that approach from the rear.

Biologists have long pondered how the different groups of myriapods are related to one another. Since millipedes are built in many ways like pauropods and centipedes are built a lot like symphylans, biologists have been tempted to think that sometime many millions of years ago millipedes descended from ancestors resembling pauropods and centipedes descended from ancestors resembling symphylans. If this is actually the way the myriapod family tree grew, then centipedes and millipedes have gained legs, eyes, and many new colors in the intervening years.

Millipedes feed on plant debris, leaving behind their numerous droppings that contribute to humus and soil formation. Droppings are good for the soil, and they are good for constructing the nests that most millipedes build for their eggs. Each millipede egg is quite large as eggs go and can be more than a 1/25 or 2/25 inch (1–2 millimeters) in diameter. The mother millipede often envelops each of her eggs in a hollow ball made of soil particles and droppings and then places each of these nests in a pile that she guards very attentively. As newly hatched millipedes leave their nurseries and wander off into the soil, they build similar nests of their own for shelter when they feel a molt coming on and they are about to shed their thick, protective shells. In addition to their nests and thick shells, millipedes protect themselves with repellent or toxic substances

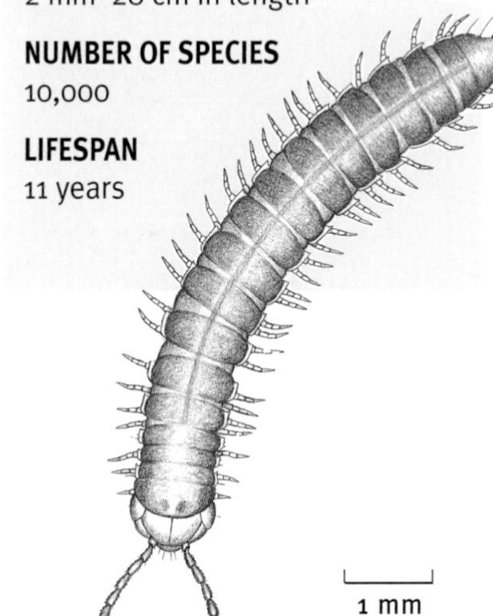

Some millipedes are cylindrical (right), some are cylindrical with a pair of projections on each body segment (above), and some are flat. All these millipedes have two pairs of legs on most of their body rings.

that they release from pairs of defensive glands found on the lateral surfaces of most body segments. Millipedes save a great deal of energy by always having an abundance of food within easy reach. All the energy saved can be used for the more pressing concern of protecting themselves from predators.

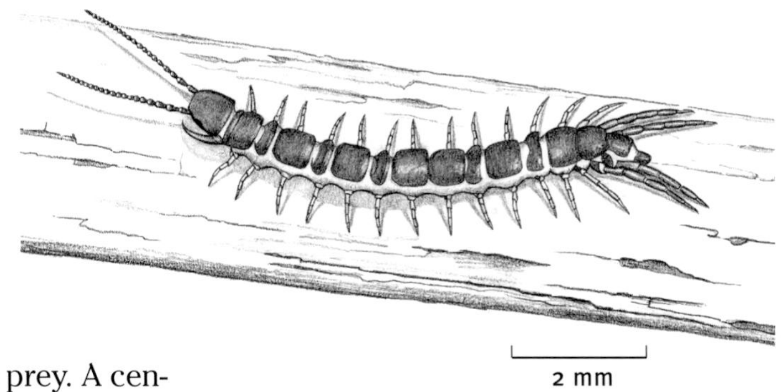

Stone centipedes prowl the forest floor, searching for prey on logs, between fallen leaves and under stones.

Centipedes, on the other hand, must expend considerable energy to stalk and capture prey. A centipede's diet of meat, however, does provide more energy than a millipede's diet of rotten leaves. For subduing its prey, a centipede's first pair of legs has been specially recruited and remodeled as a pair of poison fangs.

Even though they are predators, centipedes still have to worry about being eaten. Like the symphylans, stone centipedes are prepared for possible attacks from the rear. Symphylans eject silk from spinnerets on their last segment, and stone centipedes have glands on their last pair of legs that expel a similar sticky, stringy substance that quickly gums up the mandibles, antennae, and legs of attackers like ants. Since stone centipedes live on the surface of the soil, beneath rocks, under the bark of fallen trees, and in the leaf litter, they are bound to encounter different enemies from those of soil centipedes that live as deep as two feet (60 centimeters) below the surface. When a soil centipede is assaulted, it quickly draws its long body into a coil and secretes a repulsive fluid from glands on its underside. Soil centipedes are master contortionists that can maneuver their long bodies through the tiny spaces of the soil. They have muscles and flexible joints in places where few other animals do and are able to ferret out potworms and small earthworms from their deep burrows.

Mother centipedes guard their eggs and have been observed to lick them. The eggs are susceptible to attack by fungi, and the licking coats the eggs with salivary secretions containing natural fungicides. Whatever the ingredients may be in these secretions, they are probably more effective and more environmentally friendly than our commercially available fungicides. Soil fungi seem to be a constant threat to eggs in the humid environment of the soil, and maternal care of eggs is fairly common among soil arthropods. As centipedes do, diplurans, symphylans, millipedes, and many soil insects remain with their eggs until they have hatched, ensuring that fungi are kept at bay.

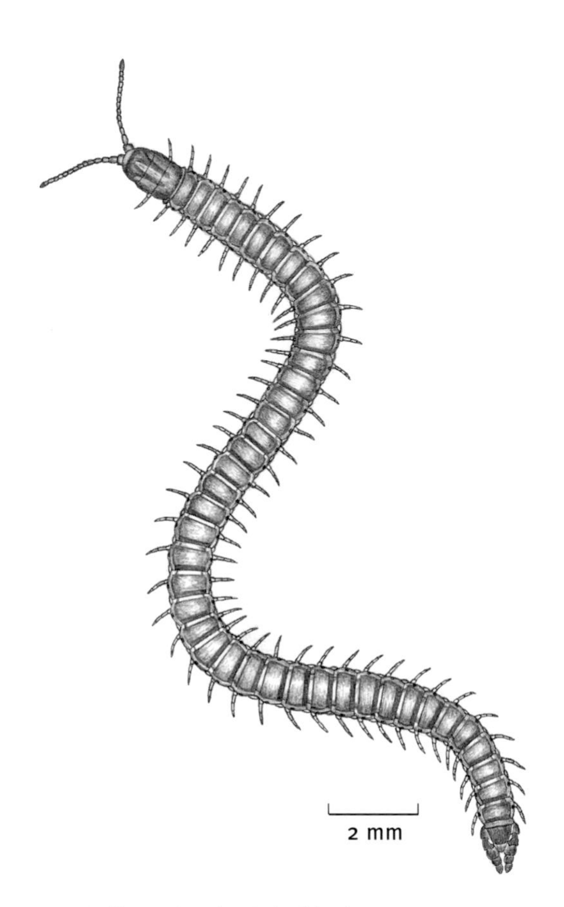

Soil centipedes inhabit deeper recesses of the soil and rotten logs.

SPIDERS

CLASSIFICATION
Phylum Arthropoda
Class Arachnida
Order Araneae

PLACE IN FOOD WEB
Predators, Diggers

SIZE
3 mm–5 cm in length

NUMBER OF SPECIES
34,000

Spiders

Spiders are without exception predators, and they have developed a variety of hunting skills. Some, like the swift wolf spiders, simply run down their prey, while others spin elaborate webs in the shape of funnels, tubes, or domes that trap their prey. Some of the smallest spiders of the family Hahniidae spin simple sheet webs over tiny depressions in the soil. Most spiders, regardless of their hunting or spinning skills, have a retreat in the soil in addition to their web aboveground.

Various estimates of spider densities in forests and fields are in amazingly close agreement. In the leaf litter of a German forest, the number of spiders on an area of soil 10.8 square feet (1 square meter) in size ranges from 50 to 150. On the same area of English pasture, the number of spiders was calculated to be 142. With populations like this, spiders readily keep in check populations of arthropods that grow too large for the available resources.

Spiders are known to shower their young with maternal care. The mother wolf spider carries her egg sac in tow while she hunts, and even helps her newly hatched spiderlings escape from the egg sac by tearing it with her chelicerae, or jaws, when she senses their impending birth. The baby spiders quickly clamber up their mother's legs and ride about on her back until they have exhausted the yolk reserves of their eggs and must hunt for themselves. Baby funnel-web spiders stay in their mother's web for several weeks and coax regurgitated prey from their mother's chelicerae.

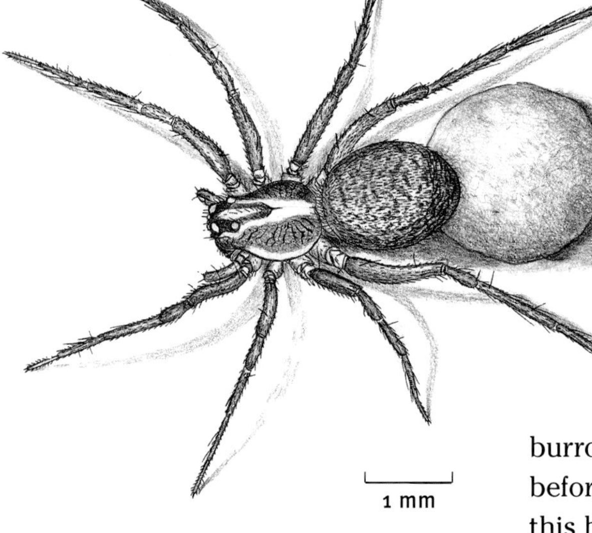

A mother wolf spider travels with her egg case over terrain covered with dead leaves, sticks, and stones. Even after her eggs hatch, she carries her spiderlings on her back until they molt for the second time.

Young trapdoor spiders stay in their mother's burrow and share her meals for several months after hatching before they venture out to dig their own burrows. Only during this brief debut aboveground does a trapdoor spider leave its burrow. During the rest of its days, it lurks beneath the trapdoor of its burrow. There the spider waits to snatch unwary prey that it can reach with its forelegs without losing a safe grip on the burrow with its hindlegs.

In digging their burrows, trapdoor spiders use their chelicerae for loosening the soil; then they spin silk around the loose soil to hoist it from the burrow. Once the burrow of a

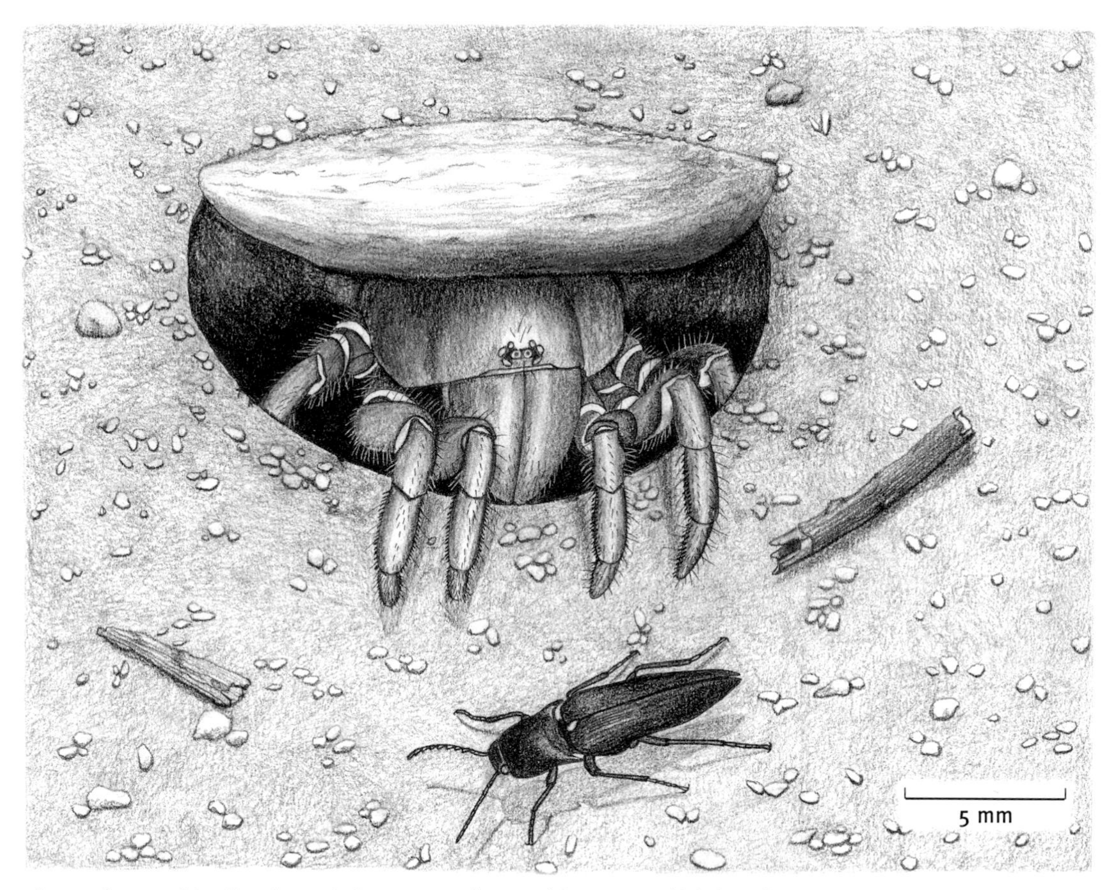

A trapdoor spider lies in wait for passersby. In this case a click beetle is about to become a meal for the spider.

trapdoor spider is about 6 inches (15 centimeters) deep and 3/4 inch (2 centimeters) wide, the spider lines all the walls with a smooth layer of silk, fashions a trap door with silk that fits snugly at the top, and finally covers it with particles of surrounding soil. The fit of the door and its camouflage are so good that the door is practically invisible when it is closed.

At night wolf spiders can often be spotted on the ground by looking for the red glow of their eight eyes in the beam of a flashlight. This works especially well if you wear the light on a hat. These wolf spiders run down their prey on the surface of the soil; but another group of wolf spiders known as Geolycosa (*geo* = earth; *lyco* = wolf) dig shafts as deep as about 39 inches (1 meter) in sandy soils. Geolycosa, like trapdoor spiders, hunt from the safety of their burrows. Glowing eyes peering up from tiny holes in the ground probably belong to these burrowing wolf spiders.

DADDY LONGLEGS

CLASSIFICATION
Phylum Arthropoda
Class Arachnida
Order Opiliones

PLACE IN FOOD WEB
Decomposers, Detritivores, Scavengers, Herbivores, Predators

SIZE
2 mm–1.2 cm in length

NUMBER OF SPECIES
2,950

Daddy Longlegs

Both spiders and daddy longlegs have eight legs, but while practically every spider has the same number of eyes as legs, a daddy longlegs has only two eyes, perched almost in the middle of its back. If daddy longlegs were true inhabitants of the underground, they would have a difficult time navigating in the narrow passageways with their eight gangly legs. Instead, they travel on the ground where they survive on plants, animals, and fungi—either dead or alive. You can often see daddy longlegs waving their legs about, as though testing the air and the objects along their paths. They give the appearance of reaping as they walk, waving their legs to and fro, and this motion long ago earned them the additional name of harvestmen.

Even though a daddy longlegs that is missing several legs may manage quite well, one that has lost its second pair of legs will gingerly pick its way across the ground like a blind person, seemingly unsure of what lies ahead. Unlike insects, whose antennae pick up enticing odors of foods and prospective mates, daddy longlegs use their exceptionally long second pair of legs in place of antennae. They are constantly grooming and preening these long, sensitive legs by pulling them between their jaws to remove any debris that could possibly diminish their sensitivity.

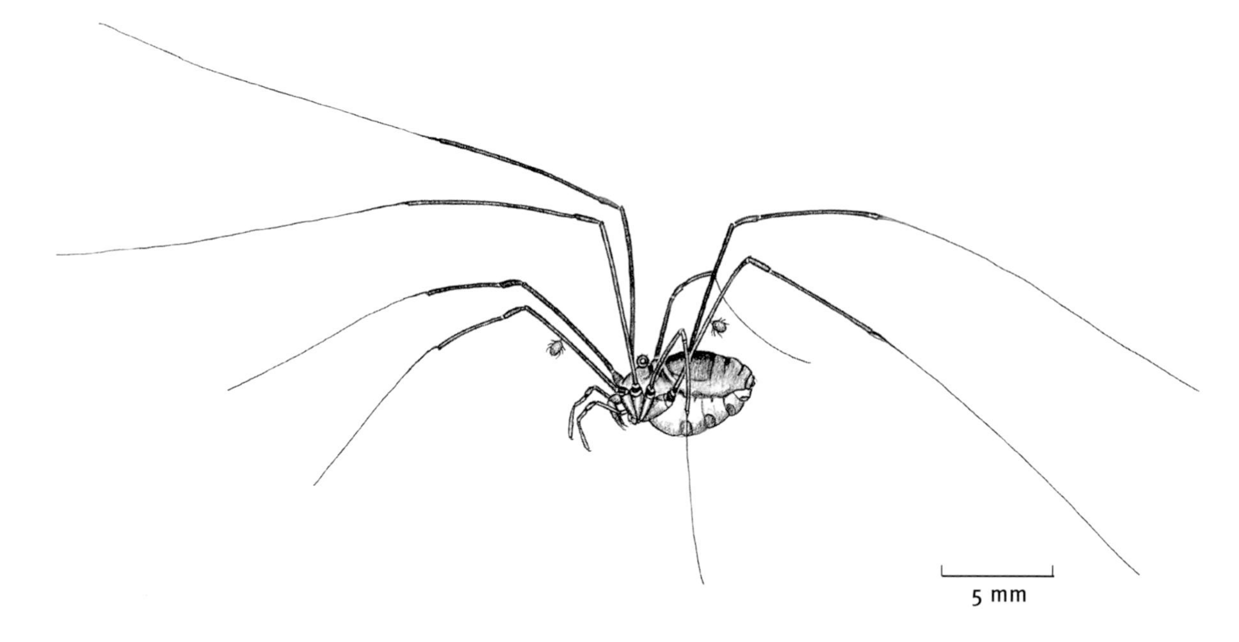

A daddy longlegs often carries hitchhiking mites.

Daddy longlegs often venture into the vegetation that covers the forest floor.

Although daddy longlegs are meticulous about leg grooming, they somehow often end up with small hitchhikers that latch on to their legs. By climbing aboard a passing leg, mites and pseudoscorpions set off for new territories and colonize new habitats. Their own short little legs could never carry them as far as those of a passing daddy longlegs, and daddy longlegs do not seem to mind accommodating their small passengers.

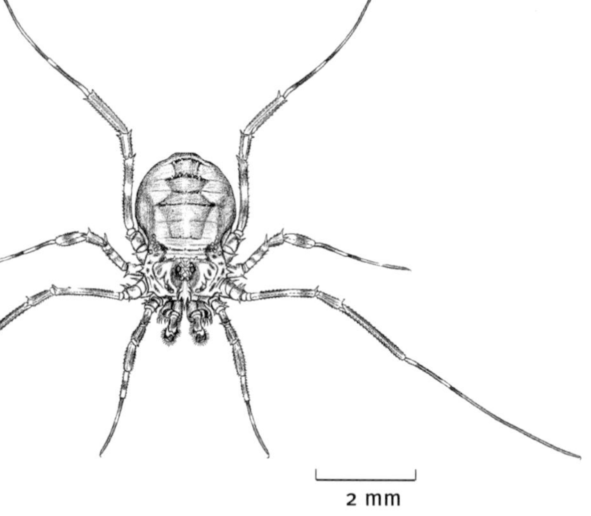

The two eyes of a daddy longlegs are perched high on its back. The body as well as the legs of the one above is covered with many spines.

The trip of such a hitchhiker is almost assured of being a safe one, for each daddy longlegs is well protected from larger animals that are always looking for a tasty meal. A daddy longlegs can certainly not be a tasty morsel, since it secretes a foul-smelling fluid from two glands, one located below its only pair of eyes and the other behind its first pair of legs. Spiders have been observed attacking daddy longlegs but then quickly backing off to wipe the disgusting taste from their jaws.

Several daddy longlegs that are confined to the same chamber must share their potent odor, and even they are not insensitive to its influence. The substance secreted by the two glands of each daddy longlegs has an anaesthetizing effect on the confined animals. They all remain in a stupor until their odors are diluted by some fresh air, and the daddy longlegs can eventually amble off.

PSEUDOSCORPIONS

CLASSIFICATION
Phylum Arthropoda
Class Arachnida
Order Pseudoscorpiones

PLACE IN FOOD WEB
Predators

SIZE
2–7 mm in length

NUMBER OF SPECIES
2,000

Pseudoscorpions

The best way to become acquainted with pseudoscorpions is to look for them as they fall from leaf litter or seasoned manure that has been placed in a Berlese funnel. As they drop into a container below the funnel, they will draw in their eight legs and remain motionless after the shock of being suddenly transported to this new, strange environment. Within a few seconds, however, they muster the courage to begin exploring the alien world about them. They stretch their legs and hold their large pincers in front of them like the antennae of an insect as they begin to walk slowly across the bottom of the container with the manner of creatures on some very important mission.

There are at least 2,000 species of these stingless little scorpions that most people never see or even know exist. Pseudoscorpions are attracted to habitats where springtails, their favorite prey, are most abundant. Pseudoscorpions usually ignore the more numerous but better armored oribatid mites of the soil. In the dark passageways of leaf litter and compost, a pseudoscorpion stretches forth its pincers like a person groping about in the dark. Long, touch-sensitive hairs on the pincers signal the presence of a springtail. Instantly it is recognized as a meal and seized with pincers and mouth parts known as chelicerae.

A pseudoscorpion waves its pincers as it ventures across a log.

These elaborate mouth parts of this simple creature are not only involved in eating. The chelicerae also function as the source of silk with which pseudoscorpions mix small pieces of sand and plant debris to build igloo-shaped cocoons. In these silken chambers they spend the unpleasant days of winter and their vulnerable days of molting. By spinning a silklike strand from its mouth parts, a pseudoscorpion's artistry resembles that of its distant relative, the caterpillars, more than it its close relative, the spiders. A caterpillar spins silk from its mouth parts, while a spider spins silk from the tip of its abdomen.

Some silk-spinning creatures can use their silk as a means of transportation. An inchworm caterpillar can drop from one branch to another as it feeds out a silk strand from the end of its spinneret, and a spiderling can sail off into the air when a

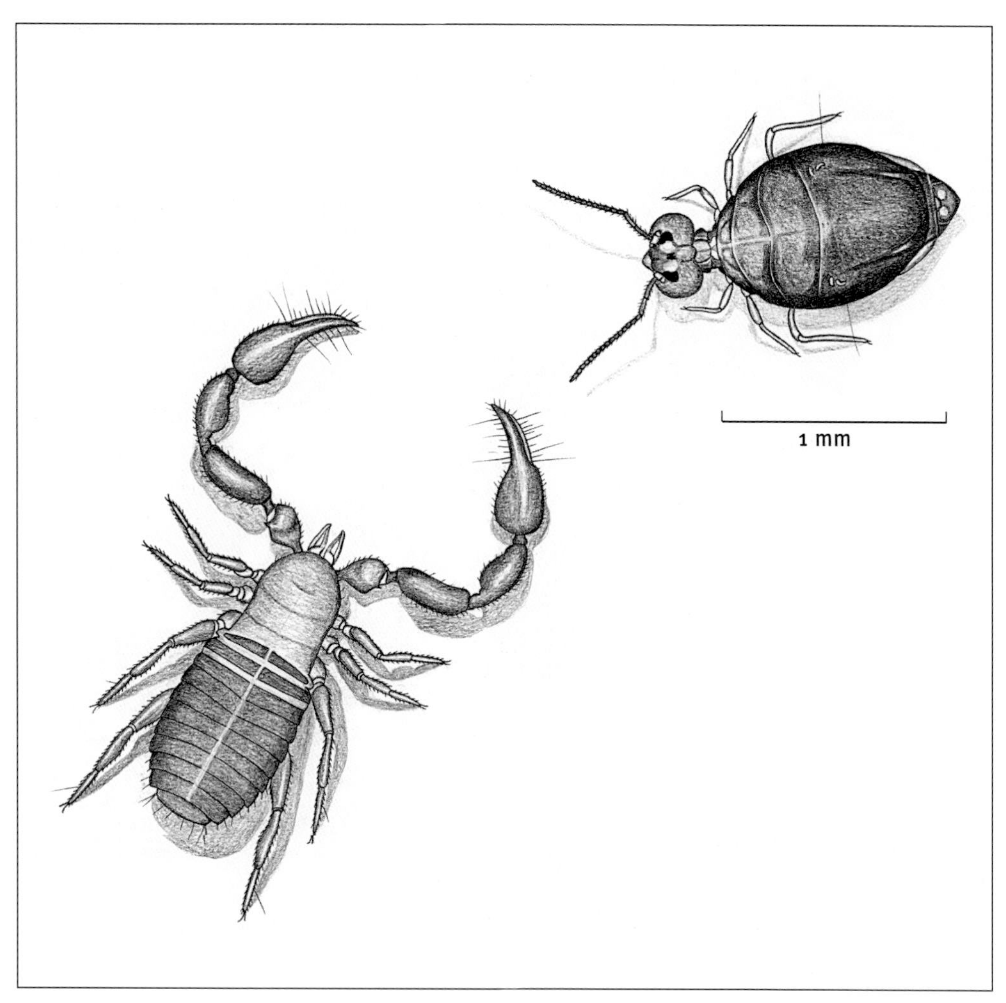

A pseudoscorpion eyes a rotund springtail as a possible meal.

gust of wind catches the strands of the diminutive silk balloon that fans out from its spinnerets. Pseudoscorpions, however, have not discovered a way to use their silk for transportation. They use little or no energy for transportation; instead they rely on others to supply the energy for them. What they do is hop aboard the long legs of some large passing insect or daddy longlegs and rely on those arthropods with much longer strides to carry them to destinations they could never reach on their own short, tiny legs. Thanks to this form of public transportation provided by larger arthropods, hardly a patch of leaf litter in the forest is without a population of pseudoscorpions.

TRUE SCORPIONS

CLASSIFICATION
Phylum Arthropoda
Class Arachnida
Order Scorpiones

PLACE IN FOOD WEB
Predators

SIZE
4–17 cm in length

NUMBER OF SPECIES
700

WINDSCORPIONS

CLASSIFICATION
Phylum Arthropoda
Class Arachnida
Order Solifugae

PLACE IN FOOD WEB
Predators

SIZE
1–5 cm in length

NUMBER OF SPECIES
800

WHIPSCORPIONS

CLASSIFICATION
Phylum Arthropoda
Class Arachnida
Order Uropygi

PLACE IN FOOD WEB
Predators

SIZE
2.5–8 cm in length

NUMBER OF SPECIES
70

True Scorpions, Windscorpions, Whipscorpions, and Schizomids

Of all the animals of the soil, only the scorpion has the distinction of having a constellation of the zodiac named for it. Scorpius, on the southern horizon, also happens to be one of the few constellations that is really shaped like the creature it is supposed to depict. The path that our sun appears to follow through the stars passes through a series of 12 constellations that together are known as the zodiac. This set of constellations has figured prominently in the history of mythology as a way to foretell the fate of an individual according to the sign of the zodiac under which he or she is born. Woe to those born under the sign of the scorpion, because this inauspicious sign is associated with war, plagues, and storms. Woe, too, to the reputation of the poor scorpion, which really prefers to hide rather than fight and only stings in self-defense.

Several arachnids go by the name of scorpion, but they are considered different enough to be placed in orders of their own. There are whipscorpions and windscorpions, true scorpions and pseudoscorpions, and there are tiny relatives of scorpions called schizomids whose place in the family tree of arachnids is far from certain. Unlike pseudoscorpions—which live in all climates where they can find shelter under bark and stones, in the soil, and in leaf litter—other scorpions are found in warm, often hot, climates. Whipscorpions and schizomids prefer warm and humid habitats. Some true scorpions also live in warm, humid places, but others, such as windscorpions, find a home in hot, dry deserts.

Most scorpions can burrow, and they sometimes dig burrows several feet beneath the soil's surface to escape the heat and light of the sun. Many also dwell under stones or logs, in crevices of the earth, or even in burrows of larger animals.

With their poor vision, scorpions depend largely on their sense of touch to maneuver in their dark surroundings. Arachnids might not have antennae, but they have resorted to using a number of different appendages in lieu of antennae.

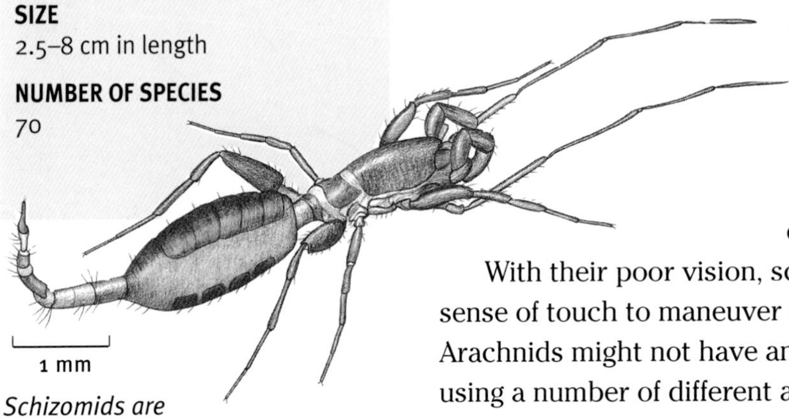

1 mm

Schizomids are tiny, blind arachnids that live under rocks, logs, and in leaf litter.

Arachnids have pedipalps (*pedi* = foot; *palp* = feel) at their head end that are just one of several pairs of appendages they can use as feelers. True scorpions, pseudoscorpions, and whipscorpions use these pedipalps as strong pincers as well as sensitive feelers; they rely on the long, sensitive hairs of their pedipalps as their main sense of touch. The pedipalps of schizomids are covered with spines and look more like the prey-grabbing legs of a praying mantis than the pincers of other scorpions. Windscorpions, however, use their enormous jaws or chelicerae as pincers and their pedipalps strictly as feelers. Many arachnids also use some of their legs as feelers. True scorpions and pseudoscorpions use all eight of their legs for walking, but whipscorpions, windscorpions, and schizomids wave their first pair of legs about—just as daddy longlegs wave their second pair—investigating their environments as they move through the leaf litter. Arachnids have perfected their skills of navigation without any antennae and often without any eyes.

All scorpions watch over their young until the little scorpions reach their first molt. Many dig deep burrows for egg laying. Whipscorpions and windscorpions have nurseries that can be 16 inches (40 centimeters) underground. True scorpions give birth to live young that soon find their way to their mother's back, where they ride about during the next two weeks of their lives. Each mother pseudoscorpion or whipscorpion carries about two dozen eggs in a sac under her abdomen. The young hop aboard the backs of their mothers as soon as the eggs hatch. Although mother windscorpions carry neither an egg sac on their bellies nor newly hatched young on their backs, many of them lay as many 100 to 200 eggs in a deep burrow and closely guard the young windscorpions until they shed their first exoskeletons. A mother schizomid builds a small chamber in the earth where she lies with her few eggs until they hatch. The time invested by these arachnids in maternal responsibilities probably saves many young from the jaws of predators and the filaments of fungi.

TAILLESS WHIPSCORPIONS

CLASSIFICATION
Phylum Arthropoda
Class Arachnida
Order Amblypygi

PLACE IN FOOD WEB
Predators

SIZE
8 mm–4.5 cm in length

NUMBER OF SPECIES
50

SCHIZOMIDS

CLASSIFICATION
Phylum Arthropoda
Class Arachnida
Order Schizomida

PLACE IN FOOD WEB
Predators

SIZE
5–7 mm in length

NUMBER OF SPECIES
35

Both true scorpions and windscorpions live in desert soils. Windscorpions (left) can bite with their huge jaws, and true scorpions (right) can sting with their long tails.

WOODLICE

CLASSIFICATION
Phylum Arthropoda
Class Crustacea
Order Isopoda
Suborder Oniscoidea

PLACE IN FOOD WEB
Decomposers, Detritivores, Scavengers, Coprophages

SIZE
1 mm–3 cm in length

NUMBER OF SPECIES
1,000

LIFESPAN
2–3 years

Woodlice

Crustaceans are the dominant arthropods of the oceans, while insects are the undisputed arthropod masters of the land. Once upon a time all crustaceans lived in the sea, but a few managed to colonize freshwater habitats and eventually the land. Although these pioneers have forsaken their homes in the water, they have found ways to conserve and carry water with them.

Water-conducting channels run around the body of each woodlouse and beneath the surface of each body segment. Urine from the woodlouse's equivalent of kidneys is recycled through these channels and additional water from the environment is taken up as needed by capillary action, just as water is automatically drawn up the channel formed by a straw that is placed in a glass of water. Ammonia from the urine quickly evaporates, and oxygen is readily absorbed at the posterior end of each animal by its pleopods (*pleo* = full; *pod* = leg), remnants of its aquatic heritage. Beneath the outer surface of their pleopods, woodlice have retained gills that are bathed by the recycled water that constantly circulates around their bodies.

As an additional adaptation to life in dry soils, some woodlice also have oxygen-absorbing sur faces on their pleopods that look and act like tiny lungs. These "lungs" are not bathed with oxygen-enriched water but take oxygen directly from the air, as our own lungs do.

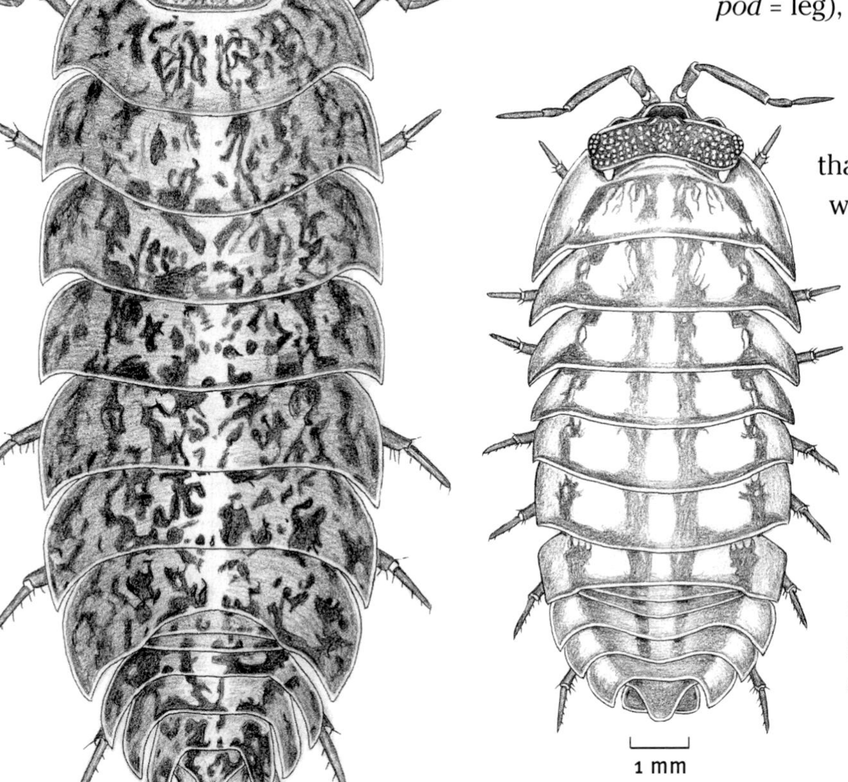

Woodlice have been named after both armadillos and pigs. Woodlice that can roll into balls belong to the family Armadillididae. Woodlice, known as sow bugs, probably because they root around in the soil like pigs, belong to the family Porcellionidae (porcelli = *a little pig).*

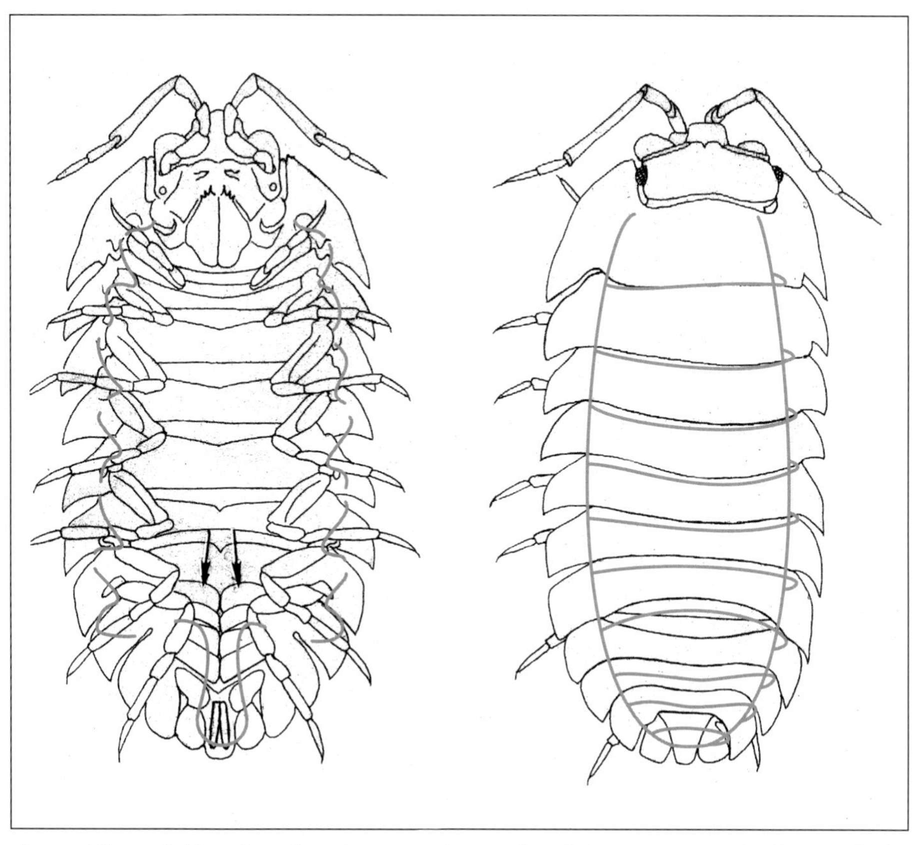

Around the outside edge of each segment as well as between segments the recycled urine of a woodlouse continually flows; the four pairs of pleopods are indicated with arrows.

In the soil community, woodlice begin the process of converting freshly fallen leaves to humus. They quickly skeletonize and fragment the leaves, setting the stage for beetle mites, certain springtails, potworms, and bacteria to continue the process of humus formation. Woodlice clearly prefer the taste of maple and beech leaves to oak leaves, and prefer the flavor of newfallen leaves to the leaves that have spent the winter on the ground. Not only are woodlice primary decomposers of the leaf litter, they are also secondary decomposers of each other's dung. An interesting physiological phenomenon underlies this behavior. The oxygen-absorbing pigment in the blood of woodlice contains copper, an element reasonably common in their ancestral seas but relatively uncommon in most land environments, and one that is lost from a woodlouse's body every time it defecates. Just as they recycle urine in their water-conducting channels, woodlice recycle their droppings and the precious copper that they contain.

CRAYFISH

CLASSIFICATION
Phylum Arthropoda
Class Crustacea
Order Decapoda

PLACE IN FOOD WEB
Diggers, Scavengers, Decomposers, Detritivores, Predators

SIZE
8–10 cm in length

NUMBER OF SPECIES
600

Crayfish

Crayfish may be abundant in low-lying forests and fields where they dig deep holes in the moist soil. Although crayfish are rarely as numerous as earthworms, one crayfish can make a significant contribution to the turnover of soil. Crayfish can never stray too far from water, and their vertical tunnels always descend as deep as the underlying layer of soil that is saturated with water. Since this layer, known as the water table, may lie as deep as 15 feet (4–5 meters) below the surface, excavating a shaft to it can bring many other soil layers to the surface, each with a different texture and with different minerals. During the digging of its tunnel, a crayfish pushes soil to the surface and piles it in an orderly fashion around the hole. Eventually the pile can grow to a tube that is eight inches (20 centimeters) tall and that may weigh 3 to 4 pounds (1.4–1.8 kilograms). On an acre of ground, several hundred such chimneys may dot the landscape at one time. The weight of all those chimneys can add up to over a ton of soil that is carried to the surface of a single acre of soil by crayfish alone.

Beneath crayfish chimneys lie tunnel systems that are often a meter deep.

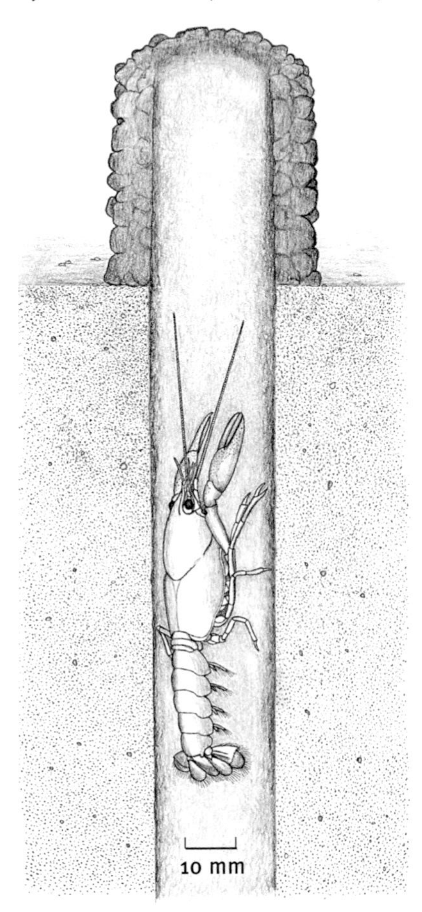

The mound of soil excavated by a crayfish adds new nutrients to the topsoil of a field.

Jumping Bristletails

Insects have colonized the earth, the air, and the waters. They feed above ground as well as below and are the only invertebrates that can fly above the earth. Sometimes drawing the line between those members of the class Insecta that live in soil and those that live in decaying plants or dead animals that will eventually return to soil can be tricky and arbitrary.

The jumping bristletails are clearly insects of the soil surface. One of the first features a person notices about the bristletails is their large, bulging eyes. A bristletail can also jump several times its length by quickly and firmly shoving the end of its abdomen against the ground. This ability makes them very effective at evading predators. As grazers in the leaf litter, they feed on algae, fungi, and lichens found among the decomposing leaves.

Like many other soil arthropods, jumping bristletails are very sensitive to the moisture in their microenvironments and do not survive long if the humidity drops too low. Bristletails, springtails, and other arthropods such as myriapods, diplurans, and proturans have developed special water-absorbing vesicles and special moisture-sensitive receptors that trigger the activity of these vesicles.

The vesicles are located on the underside of the animal and are inflated by an increase in blood pressure whenever the humidity drops too low; they are retracted by muscles once the animal's delicate water balance is restored. Each vesicle is lined by cells that secrete a thin cuticle and that are specialized for rapid uptake of water from the environment. The vesicles pop in and out of these moisture-sensitive arthropods as the humidity rises and falls, guaranteeing that the bristletail neither shrivels from lack of water nor swells from imbibing too much.

JUMPING BRISTLETAILS

CLASSIFICATION
Phylum Arthropoda
Class Insecta
Order Microcoryphia

PLACE IN FOOD WEB
Decomposers, Detritivores, Scavengers, Fungivores, Algal eaters

SIZE
1–1.2 cm in length

NUMBER OF SPECIES
350

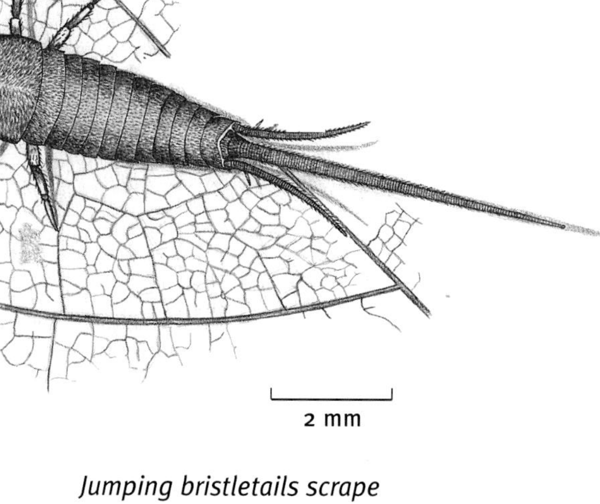

Jumping bristletails scrape fungi and algae from surfaces of decaying leaves.

EARWIGS

CLASSIFICATION
Phylum Arthropoda
Class Insecta
Order Dermaptera

PLACE IN FOOD WEB
Decomposers, Detritivores, Scavengers, Herbivores, Fungivores, Algal eaters, Predators

SIZE
4 mm–2 cm in length

NUMBER OF SPECIES
1,500

Earwigs

Earwigs are creatures of the night that spend their evenings abroad and their days sheltered in the soil or leaf litter. Most earwigs feed on plant debris, algae, and fungi, but a few hunt small insects and spiders. During the day they feel most at home in tight crevices and close quarters where as much of their body surface as possible can contact its surroundings. This typical earwig behavior assures that they are often inaccessible to the beetles, spiders, centipedes, and birds that might appreciate dining on earwig meat. Their strong pincers, or cerci, offer extra protection by delivering a good pinch to any predator that ventures too close. And if a pinch is not sufficient to deter a predator, some species of earwigs, such as the one illustrated here, emit a foul-looking, foul-smelling brown fluid. On the dorsal surface of the third and fourth segments of their abdomens they have pairs of glands from which they can squirt this repellent as far as four inches (10 centimeters).

In late winter or early spring, an earwig mother retires to a snug chamber in the soil to lay about 50 eggs. There she stays and guards the eggs until they hatch several days later. Down in the soil the young earwigs stay close together through their first four to six molts before appearing aboveground for the summer.

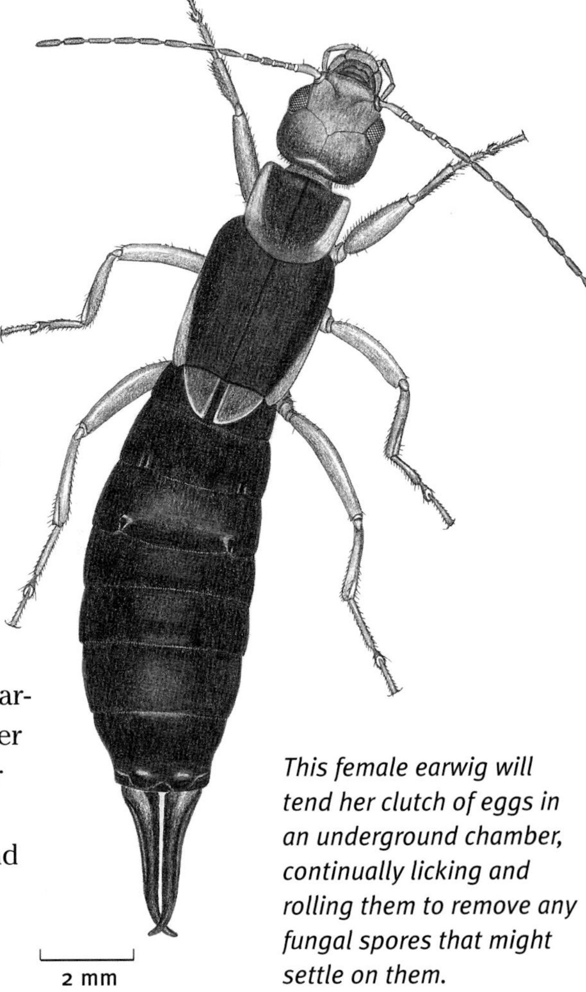

This female earwig will tend her clutch of eggs in an underground chamber, continually licking and rolling them to remove any fungal spores that might settle on them.

Cockroaches

People rarely appreciate how beautifully adapted cockroaches are to life in leaf litter and rotten logs, probably because people have never considered appreciating cockroaches even when they are found far from the kitchen or bathroom. The country relatives of our much maligned household cockroaches lead respectable lives as recyclers of the forest floor. By having long legs designed to fold closely against their bodies, cockroaches can readily slip their oval, flattened bodies under logs and between layers of leaves on the forest floor. The long antennae of a cockroach swing freely in broad arcs and explore a wide area around each insect, while bristles on appendages known as cerci at the tip of its abdomen detect the slightest movements of air that might portend the approach of danger. Not all cockroaches live in perpetual fear of predators such as ground beetles, centipedes, and shrews; one of the smallest cockroaches, named Attaphila (*atta* = generic name for leaf-cutting ants; *phila* = love), lives in the relative security of nests built by leaf-cutting ants and survives on leftovers and handouts from the worker ants. But for many cockroaches, feeding on decaying vegetation of the forest floor can often be as dangerous as feeding on leftovers in the kitchen.

Some cockroaches not only live with social insects such as ants but also have social lives of their own. These are a special family of wood-feeding cockroaches called cryptocercids that are found in only three places on earth: the Pacific Coastal foothills of the western United States, the Appalachian Mountains of the eastern United States, and China. One big difference between cryptocercids and other cockroaches is conveyed by the family name, which translates to "hidden cerci." The cerci of cryptocercid cockroaches are hidden under the abdomen rather than extending from the tip of the abdomen. The animals live in small colonies made up of two parents that often live for several years along with their 15 to 20 immature offspring, called nymphs. Like termites, these cockroaches can survive on rotten wood that is very nutrient-poor because in their hindguts they harbor protozoa and bacteria that enhance their digestion and nutrition. Social life in the log involves nymphs feeding on the cast-off skins of their parents as well as on fluids from their parents' hindguts, both of which contain the indispensable microbes that are unfailingly passed from one generation of cockroaches to the next.

COCKROACHES

CLASSIFICATION
Phylum Arthropoda
Class Insecta
Order Blattodea

PLACE IN FOOD WEB
Decomposers, Detritivores, Scavengers

SIZE
3 mm–5 cm in length

NUMBER OF SPECIES
3,680

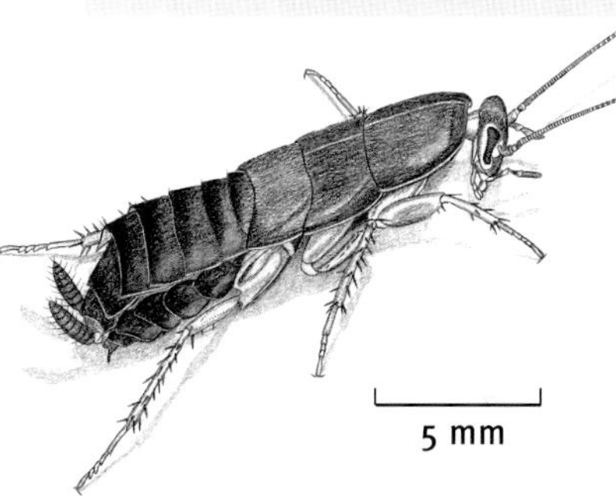

Cockroaches have a pair of long, slender antennae at their head end and another pair of short, stout, bristled appendages at their tail end that can detect the slightest disturbances in the leaf litter.

CAMEL CRICKETS

CLASSIFICATION
Phylum Arthropoda
Class Insecta
Order Orthoptera
Family Rhaphidophoridae

PLACE IN FOOD WEB
Decomposers, Detritivores, Scavengers, Predators

SIZE
5 mm–4 cm in length

NUMBER OF SPECIES
1,000

MOLE CRICKETS

CLASSIFICATION
Phylum Arthropoda
Class Insecta
Order Orthoptera
Family Gryllotalpidae

PLACE IN FOOD WEB
Diggers, Predators, Herbivores

SIZE
2.5–5 cm in length

NUMBER OF SPECIES
50

Camel Crickets and Mole Crickets

A dark and damp cellar with a dirt floor is a popular habitat for camel crickets. In fact, such a bleak place, with its molds and mold-eating animals, is probably the closest place to heaven for them. With their hunched backs, these crickets may look incapable of swift escapes, but they can easily evade curious humans who want to get a closer look at them.

The crickets that most of us are familiar with chirp away their evenings in treetops or among grasses. However, camel and cave crickets, the wingless members of cricket families, lead chirpless lives under stones, logs, piles of leaves, or even in the burrows of larger animals like gophers and kangaroo rats. Since they like dark, moist environments where long, sensitive antennae are more useful than eyes, some of these crickets have lost their eyes all together. Down in the dark passageways of their homes, they may feed on plant debris but probably they also eat smaller arthropods that come their way.

10 mm

*Most camel crickets belong to the genus Ceuthophilus (*ceutho *= concealment;* philus *= lover of), a name that conveys their love of dark hiding places.*

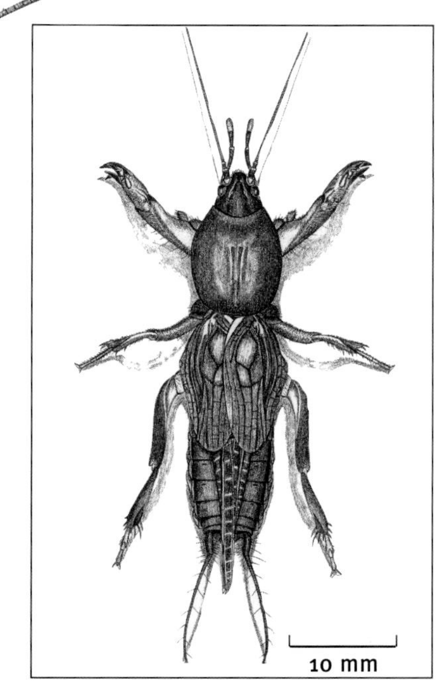

*Mole crickets belong to the family Gryllotalpidae (*gryllus *= cricket;* talpa *= mole), a scientific name that exactly matches their common name.*

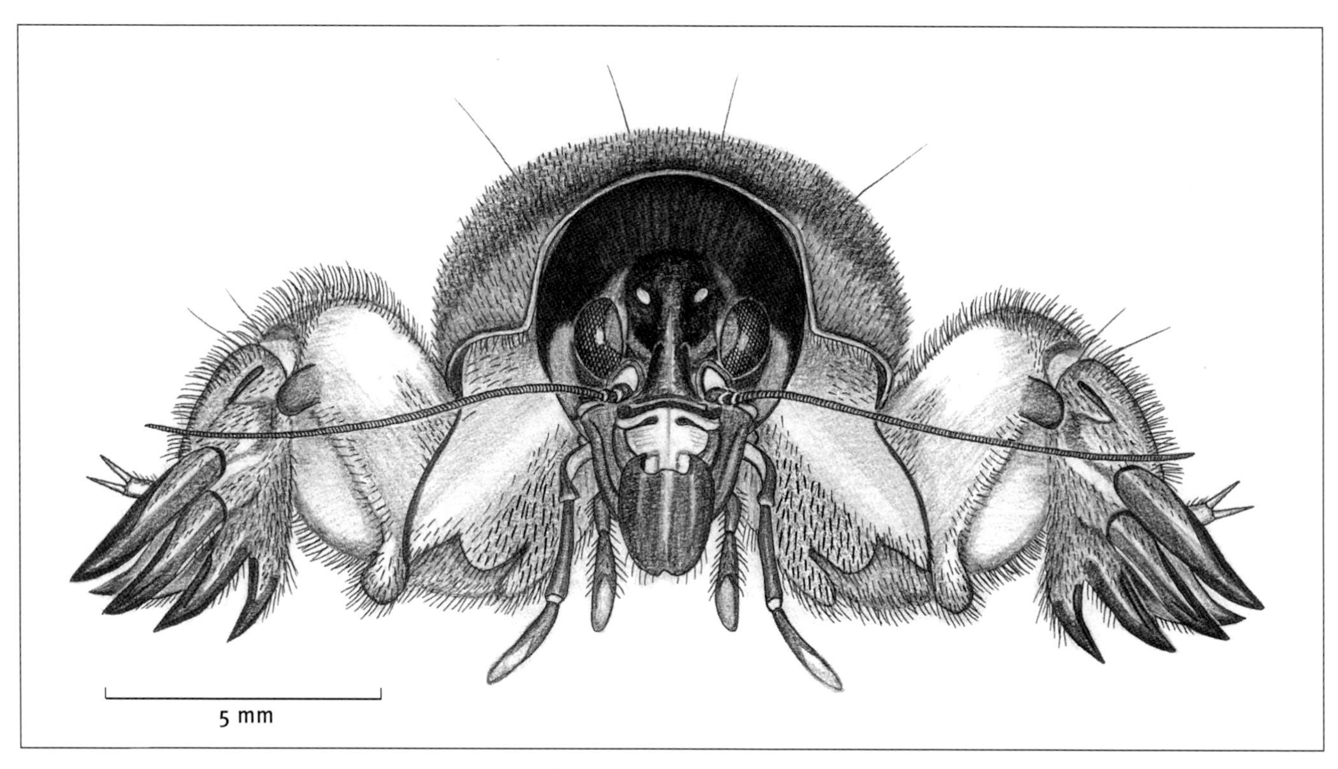

*Mole crickets have classic fossorial (*fossor *= digger) front legs. Their bodies are covered with a velvety layer of dense hairs that repel water and mud.*

Mole crickets have not given up chirping and have even gone to great lengths to dig and mold underground tunnels of exceptional acoustical design. Mole crickets are clearly designed for digging. Their front legs are broad, flat, and very muscular, and look remarkably like the front legs of that master burrower, the mole. As mole crickets look for earthworms, small insects, or plant roots, they burrow 6 to 8 inches (15–20 centimeters) belowground. But during courtship, the male uses much of his precious energy to dig a shallow burrow designed to enhance the sound of his courting chirps.

The burrow looks and sounds like a subterranean megaphone. At the bottom the male chirps away with his head facing the narrow, dead end of the burrow and his tail facing the wider entrance to the burrow. The chirps are generated as the mole cricket raises its wings and rubs them together. His chirps are amplified and carried afield by his carefully constructed megaphone, advertising his whereabouts and romantic intentions. He vigorously fiddles away with one wing scraping against the other, trusting that some female will eventually hear his earnest calls.

TERMITES

CLASSIFICATION
Phylum Arthropoda
Class Insecta
Order Isoptera

PLACE IN FOOD WEB
Diggers, Decomposers, Detritivores

SIZE
6–7 mm in length

NUMBER OF SPECIES
2,300

Termites

While the earthworm is the chief tiller of soils at temperate latitudes, in warmer and more tropical climes the termite is undoubtedly the principal purveyor of leaves, twigs, and wood to the underworld. So efficient are these tropical insects at clearing plant litter from the soil surface and so efficient are the soil bacteria and fungi of the tropics at further degrading the plant matter that humus never really has a chance to accumulate, much to the detriment of tropical agriculture.

Tropical soils are notoriously poor for agriculture even though they can nurture lush vegetation and magnificent trees. The tropical forest quickly recycles—from plants back to soil—whatever nutrients are produced by termites, fungi, and bacteria. Practically all the organic matter of a tropical forest is tied up in the living plants of the forest; organic matter quickly disappears from the soil once the forest is gone. In a patch where all the trees have been cleared for crops, rains quickly leach the few remaining nutrients of the soil beyond the reach of the crops' roots. After only three or four years the nutrients of the tropical soil have been exhausted, leaving the land practically useless for agriculture.

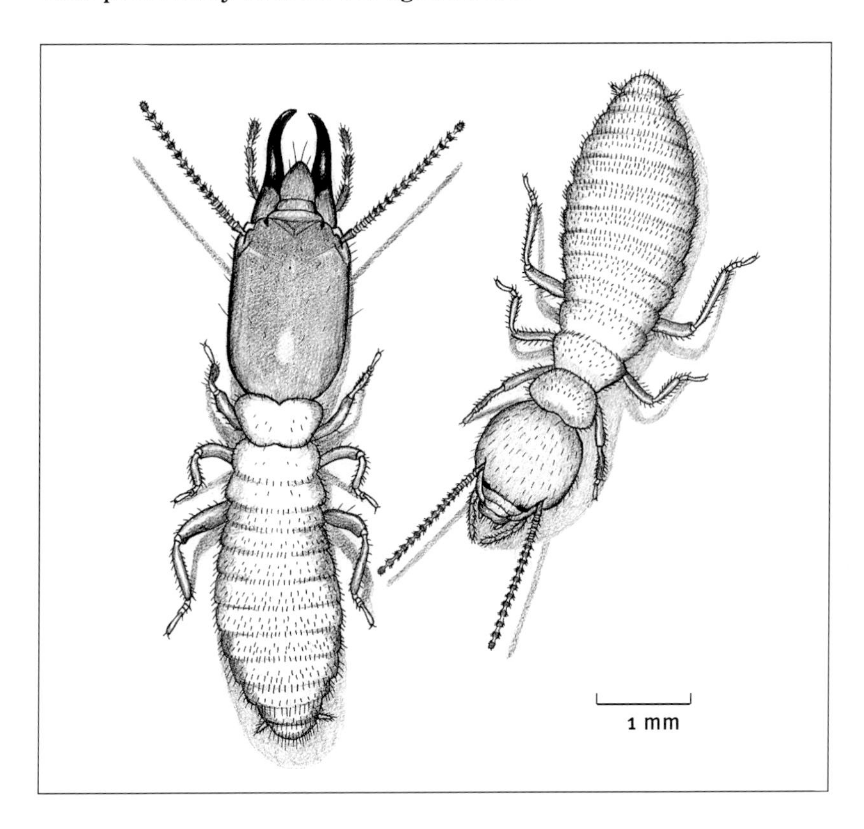

A soldier (left) and a worker (right) share the work in a termite colony. Soldiers protect the colony from intruders, and workers see to the foraging and housekeeping.

Termites that feed on dead wood and grass, some of the most indigestible and nonnutritious foods on earth, must consume vast quantities of this carbon-rich, nitrogen-poor food in order to survive and grow. In fact, termites of the African savannahs eat more grass than all the grazing mammals, such as wildebeests, zebras, and gazelles, put together.

However, tucked away at the rear end of a termite's gut are colonies of microbes that share every meal with their host. The microbes provide enzymes that supplement those produced by cells of the termite gut. They also use up some of the excess carbon and help concentrate the nitrogen that the termites need to grow. You might ask where the microbes get the supply of nitrogen that they need for their own growth among all this nitrogen-poor cellulose. In return for their contributions to the good digestion of the termite, the termite provides the microbes with chewed wood, a home, a share of the digested wood, and a rich source of nitrogen in the form of its recycled urine.

Termite mounds dominate many savannahs of Africa, Australia, and South America.

The insect equivalent of kidneys are structures called "Malpighian tubules" that excrete urine. In termites these tubules lie against the outer surface of a termite's gut; and rather than excreting nitrogen with the termite's urine, the tubules recycle nitrogen back into the termite gut. There, certain bacteria convert nitrogen in the form of uric acid to nitrogen in forms nutritious to both bacteria and termites. So many bacteria and protozoa may dwell in a termite's gut that they often make up one-third of the termite's weight.

Termites of a colony are constantly grooming one another and sharing these microbes. Any termite that fails to get its share of these creatures or in some way loses them from its gut quickly starves to death, even when surrounded by vast supplies of plant materials. The microbes of termite guts can take some of the credit for the annual ability of termites in the dry grasslands of Arizona to clear up to 92 percent of the approximately 400 pounds (182 kilograms) of plant litter found on an acre (4,840 square yards; 4,050 square meters) of ground.

In the tropics, termites have even gone a step further in recruiting help from others in improving the nutrient content of their diet. They have actually become farmers of fungi. In large chambers of their colonies, termites cultivate fungi on the droppings that accumulate after pieces of wood and grass have passed through the termites' guts the first time around. The wood and grass that pass through the guts the second time around have been predigested not only by microbes of the gut but also by the fungi in the termites' garden. Most of the carbon has been reduced to methane gas by microbes, and nitrogen from the original plant litter is now highly concentrated in the nutritious fungi. The termites feast from the gardens of fungi that they raise on their droppings, eventually extracting a phenomenal amount of nutrition from what starts out as a poor diet for any creature.

Whenever or wherever termites colonize aboveground, they carry soil with them. Whether to establish an outpost in a nearby tree or to invade the upper floors of a wooden house, termites are able to advance into the alien environment aboveground and in the daylight by building tunnels of soil wherever they go. These foraging tunnels are constantly being remodeled, abandoned, and extended as new plant litter is discovered on the surface of the ground. In these tunnels the termites bring with them the darkness and dampness of the underground that they need.

The familiar termites of temperate latitudes lead rather retiring lives underground. Only when they construct earthen tunnels and venture aboveground into our homes and buildings do we take notice of them. Their relatives in the tropics, however, build imposing edifices of soil that dot the landscape like gnarled and ghostly figures. To raise these mounds of soil, and to construct their labyrinthine galleries underground, the termites are constantly moving soil about.

Over centuries, thousands of tons of soil are mixed by termites, especially the large colonies of mound-building termites that are found in Africa, Australia, and South America. Their mounds can take on familiar or outlandish forms. Turrets, spires, obelisks, pyramids, or mesas may rise 10 feet (3 meters) above the ground and extend 50 feet (15 meters) in diameter. A network of tunnels radiates from each mound for about 160 feet (50 meters) in every direction. Frequently as many as 30 such mounds may occupy an acre (4,840 square yards; 4,050 square meters) and more than 5,000 tons or 10 million pounds (4.5 million kilograms) of soil may be moved aboveground during the construction of 30 mounds. These monumental mounds are a testament to the prowess of tropical termites as earth movers and architects.

Thrips

Thrips do not seem to do things the way other insects do. A thrips' mouth parts look like a cone-shaped beak and are positioned at the base of the head rather than at the front. While other insects have two symmetric jaws or mandibles, thrips have only one mandible (and for some unexplained reason it is always a left mandible). The mandible works along with a second, symmetrical pair of mouth parts or maxillae to rasp and punch food while the cone of tissue that surrounds the mandible and two maxillae is used to suck the fluids from the food.

The legs of thrips can have one or two claws; but at the very tips of the legs are rounded bladders on which thrips actually walk. These bladders do not look like they provide a very substantial grip on surfaces over which thrips tread, but these insects have apparently not fared any the worse for having such strange feet. As they walk across a fallen leaf, they give the impression of ballerinas gliding past on tiptoe.

Thrips of different sizes, shapes, and families live in the leaf litter and soil. Many are spore feeders or fungus feeders; others survive as predators of eggs, mites, springtails, and insects that are smaller than they are. Before young larval thrips grow their wings, they settle down, stop eating, and stop walking. So many tissues are undergoing remodeling at this time that the young thrips remain immobile as old tissues break down and new tissues take their places. This stage in the life of a thrips is often called the "pupa," but it is not like the pupae of other insects. In young thrips, wing buds form on the outside at the very beginning of development. In other insects, wing buds first form inside the bodies of larvae, and only later do the future wings move from inside to out as the insect transforms into a pupa.

No other insects feed quite like thrips, walk like thrips, or develop like thrips. Thrips clearly constitute a unique order of insects.

THRIPS

CLASSIFICATION
Phylum Arthropoda
Class Insecta
Order Thysanoptera

PLACE IN FOOD WEB
Fungivores, Algal eaters, Predators

SIZE
500 µm–2 mm in length

NUMBER OF SPECIES
4,700

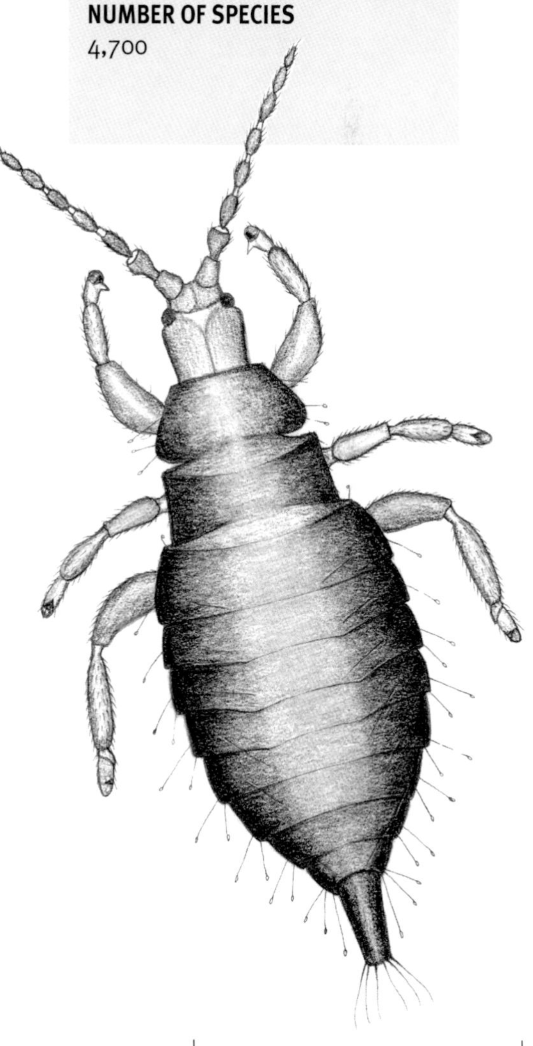

The group to which thrips belong is the order Thysanoptera (thysano = *fringe;* ptera = *wings). Most thrips have fringed wings and live above ground on plants; but all immature thrips and some of the soil thrips are completely wingless, as is the one above.*

BIG-EYED BUGS

CLASSIFICATION
Phylum Arthropoda
Class Insecta
Order Hemiptera
Family Lygaeidae
Subfamily Geocorinae

PLACE IN FOOD WEB
Predators

SIZE
3–5 mm in length

NUMBER OF SPECIES
200

BURROWER BUGS

CLASSIFICATION
Phylum Arthropoda
Class Insecta
Order Hemiptera
Family Cydnidae

PLACE IN FOOD WEB
Herbivores

SIZE
5–7 mm in length

NUMBER OF SPECIES
300

Big-Eyed Bugs and Burrower Bugs

As ground-dwelling predators of a mainly seed-eating, plant-dwelling family of insects, these geocorine bugs (*geo* = earth; *coris* = bug) have adapted to a lifestyle very different from that of most other family members.

With broad heads and large eyes, these bugs look well-suited for surveying their hunting territories among the grass roots and grass litter of meadows. Big-eyed bugs typically scurry over the ground beneath tall stalks of grasses until they spot prey that they can easily outrun. The prey often happen to be lethargic thrips or juicy springtails. With mouth parts molded into a long, pointed beak that is used for sucking rather than for chewing, a bug's feeding is a very different enterprise than it is for creatures with jaws.

There are two channels in the beak of the big-eyed bug just as there are in the beaks of all true bugs; one channel carries saliva and enzymes into the body of its prey and the other carries partially digested body fluids of the prey back to the bug's gut. Massive muscles that fill the bug's broad head pump the fluids into the esophagus and gut for final digestion of the prey. As it roams over the top of the soil, the big-eyed bug crosses paths with decomposers, diggers, and a wide variety of prey; but even this swift and sharp-eyed bug has to watch out for predators like ground beetles and rove beetles that can outweigh, outrun, and outmaneuver it.

Burrower bugs are clearly designed for digging among plant roots. The segments of its front legs are broad, and fringed with strong spines for scooping. Some bugs dig as deep as a foot and a half (45 centimeters) into the ground looking for roots. There, in a chamber among the roots, a female burrower bug lays 30 to 150 eggs and steadfastly stays with them until they hatch. Like the spiderlings of a mother wolf spider, the young burrower bugs crawl onto their mother as soon as they hatch. They stay with her for several days as she nurses them with drops of fluid from her anus that they avidly gobble up.

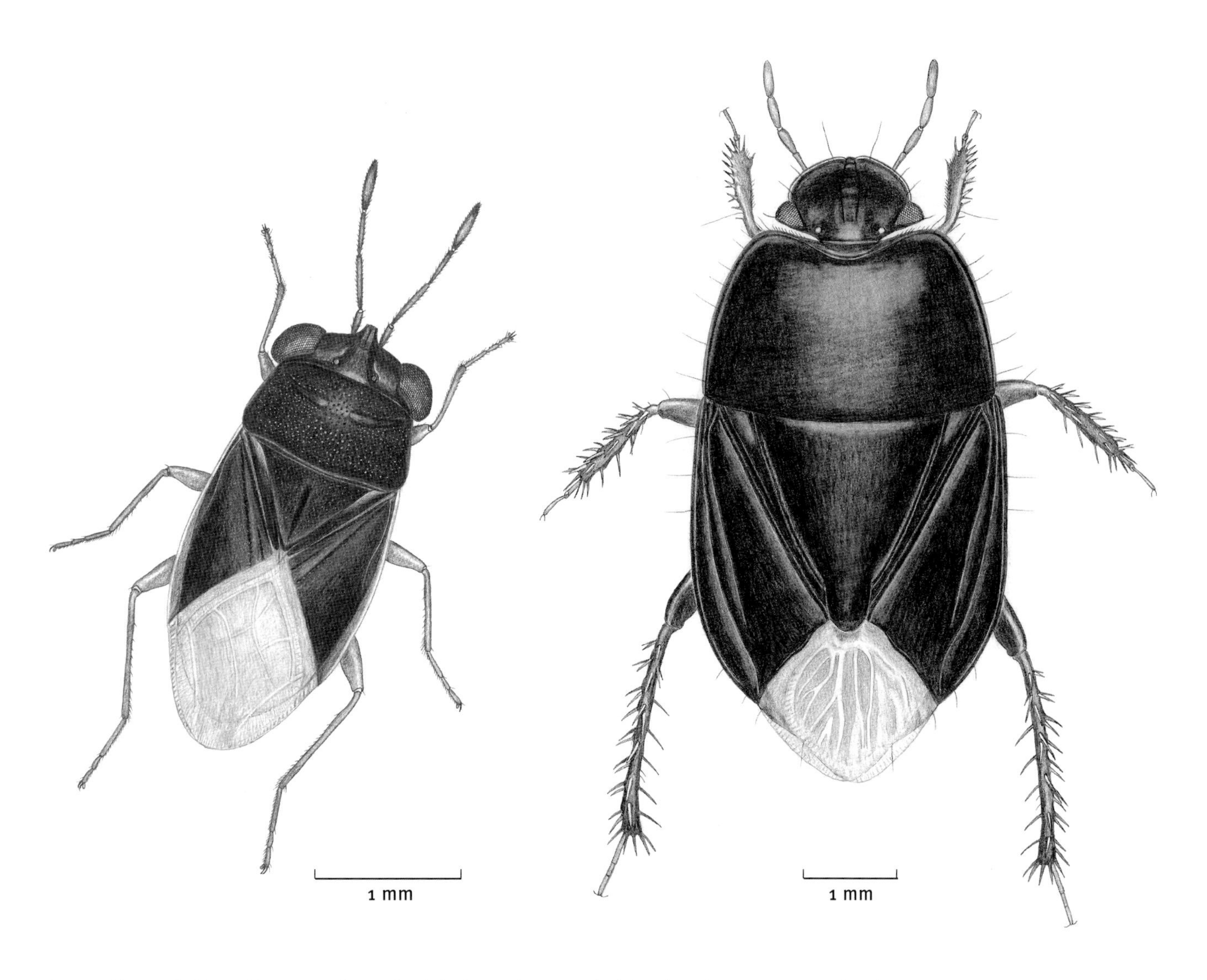

Big-eyed bugs (left) and burrower bugs (right) share the same habitat but do not compete for the same resources. The big-eyed bug is a swift hunter, and the burrower bugs dig for roots.

For the first few days of their lives, their mother's fluid is their only nourishment. Only young bugs nursed by their mothers survive to feed on plant roots. What the mother bug passes on to her children are bacteria that live in the gut of every healthy burrower bug. These bacteria produce vitamins and other nutrients that supplement the bugs' unvaried diet of root juice.

APHIDS

CLASSIFICATION
Phylum Arthropoda
Class Insecta
Order Homoptera
Family Aphididae

PLACE IN FOOD WEB
Herbivores, Fungivores

SIZE
1–8 mm in length

NUMBER OF SPECIES
3,500

Aphids and Coccoids

Scale insects (coccoids) and aphids are closely related insects. They both have beaks for sucking plant juices, some have glands on the surfaces of their bodies that secrete waxy fibers, many females give birth to living young, and some females give birth without even mating.

Most aphids live aboveground on leaves and stems, but there are a few that pass their days underground. Those that reside in leaf litter sometimes poke their beaks in the abundant filaments of fungi found on decaying leaves and feed on fungal juices. Aphids are not equipped for digging, but they can sometimes be found deep below the layer of fallen leaves, where they feed on root sap.

Ants and aphids have established mutually beneficial partnerships in which ants take responsibility for the welfare of the aphids, and the aphids reward their masters with their sugary droppings, commonly known as honeydew. There are ants that dutifully carry eggs of root aphids into their nests every autumn, and in the spring they dutifully carry the newly hatched aphids to newly sprouted roots. Throughout the growing season the ants carry the aphids from root to root to assure a steady supply of sweet honeydew.

Scale insects, also known as coccoids, are a very diverse group of plant feeders, so diverse in their forms that they represent a superfamily, Coccoidea, that has been separated into 16 different families. Some scale insects are represented only by females, and in those species the mother scales give birth without ever mating. In those species that do have males, the males have wings and legs but no mouth parts with which to feed; their lives as adults are very ephemeral. They quickly mate and live only one or two days. The females are the ones with mouth parts, even though they are wingless and usually legless as well.

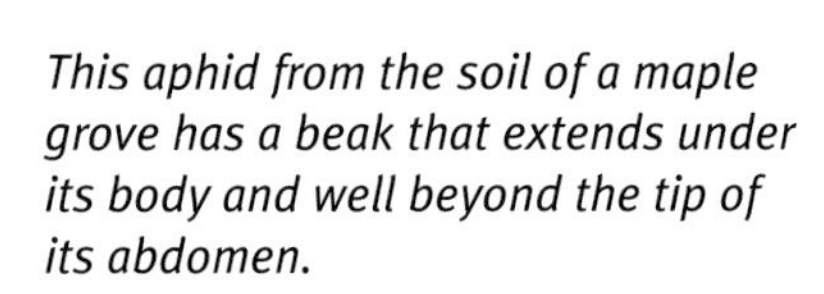

This aphid from the soil of a maple grove has a beak that extends under its body and well beyond the tip of its abdomen.

As newly hatched nymphs, scale insects have legs and are nomadic; but at their next molt the legs are lost and the nymph settles down to feed in one spot. If the nymph is a female, it usually stays there for the rest of its life. A male nymph will usually fly off once it becomes an adult. Many members of the coccoid families feed on the parts of plants found aboveground. On twigs and leaves, armored scales, wax scales, tortoise scales, pit scales, and soft scales are totally sedentary as females and reside under a scalelike covering that the coccoid secretes from glands on its body surface. A good number of coccoids, however, have settled down to life in the underground, feeding on the sap of roots and of fungi.

Female members of one coccoid family have smooth metallic gold or pearly shells, feed on rootlets, and are so round that they are referred to as ground pearls. In parts of Africa and on St. Vincent in the Lesser Antilles, these hard, rotund insects are strung as beads on necklaces. Members of another family, the ensign scales, are covered with white, waxy plates and lumber around rootlets and filaments of fungi in their white armor. Some subterranean coccoids can be so flat that it is a wonder there is space enough for heart, nerve cord, and other essential organs between their backs and their bellies. A variety of shapes and forms serve quite well for the coccoids that live in the soil.

COCCOIDS

CLASSIFICATION
Phylum Arthropoda
Class Insecta
Order Homoptera
Superfamily Coccoidea

PLACE IN FOOD WEB
Herbivores, Fungivores

SIZE
1–4 mm in length

NUMBER OF SPECIES
6,000

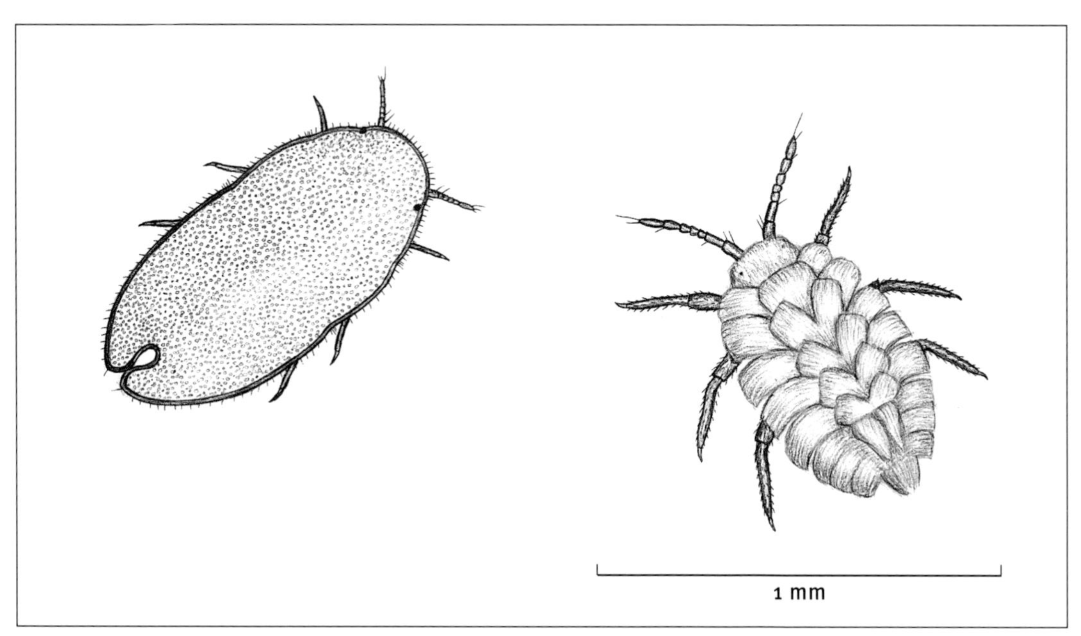

These two coccoids from the soil of an American forest are representative of the great diversity of forms among the coccoids. An ensign scale insect (right) that secretes waxy plates from its skin and a very flat scale insect (left) can each have 1,000 to 2,000 siblings.

CICADAS

CLASSIFICATION
Phylum Arthropoda
Class Insecta
Order Homoptera
Family Cicadidae

PLACE IN FOOD WEB
Herbivores

SIZE
2.5–5 cm in length

NUMBER OF SPECIES
1,500

RHIPICERID BEETLES

CLASSIFICATION
Phylum Arthropoda
Class Insecta
Order Coleoptera
Family Rhipiceridae

PLACE IN FOOD WEB
Parasites

SIZE
2.1–2.4 cm in length

NUMBER OF SPECIES
52

Cicadas and Rhipicerid Beetles

Witnessing an emergence of red-eyed cicadas in late May and early June is an experience never to be forgotten and one that occurs only once every 13 or 17 years in any one location. As the nymphs of these periodical cicadas emerge en masse after spending years belowground, they leave the soil surface perforated with their emergence holes. Twenty thousand of these holes just 1/4 inch (6 millimeters) wide were counted under a single apple tree in Indiana. This one example provides an idea of how abundant the nymphs must be in the soil. The millions of male cicadas that soon fill the trees raise a deafening racket as they vie for the attentions of the noiseless females. After mating in the treetops, the females insert their eggs in twigs by slicing through the bark with their sharp ovipositors (*ovum* = egg; *positum* = deposited).

Within a few days, tiny cicada nymphs emerge from the eggs, falling many feet to the ground and beginning their long

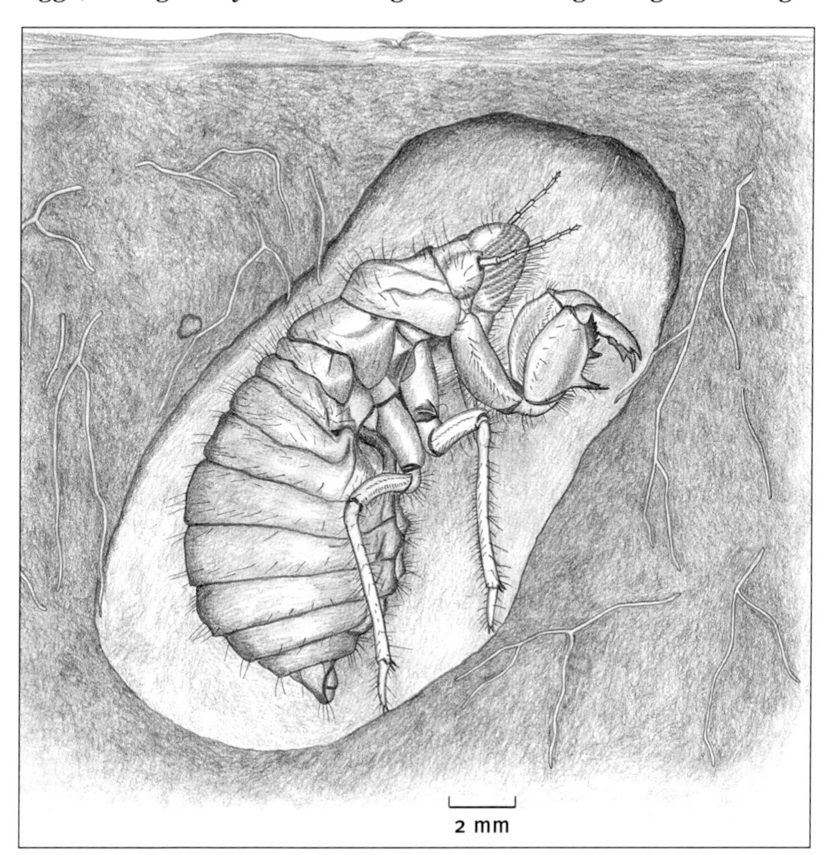

After spending most of its life in the soil, a cicada sheds the skin of its youth, unveiling its glistening wings and lovely colors.

A periodical cicada spends only a few days of its 17-year life aboveground.

journeys among the roots. The nymphs immediately tap the roots with their sharp beaks and feed on sugary sap until one day, many years later, some unknown cues tell the nymphs that the time has come to leave the soil, mate, and die.

The larger cicadas that emerge during the hot "dog days" of July and August have brown eyes and shorter life cycles than the periodical cicadas. They are known to have life cycles that last as long as seven years, and the shortest time that they spend underground is four years.

We know that the larvae of one family of beetles, the Rhipiceridae, are parasites of cicada nymphs. The name for the family (*rhip* = fan; *ceri* = horn) comes from the beautiful fan-shaped antennae of the adult beetles. They use their antennae to find trees where cicadas have recently laid their eggs and then lay large numbers of their own eggs on the trunks of these trees. The tiny, but very active, beetle larvae that hatch from the eggs are able to wend their way down through the pores and cracks of the soil until they find cicada nymphs. Even deep beneath the soil surface these nymphs must contend with parasitic insects. Once the fast and agile rhipicerid larva finds a cicada nymph, it becomes sedentary and obese, leading the decadent life of a typical parasite.

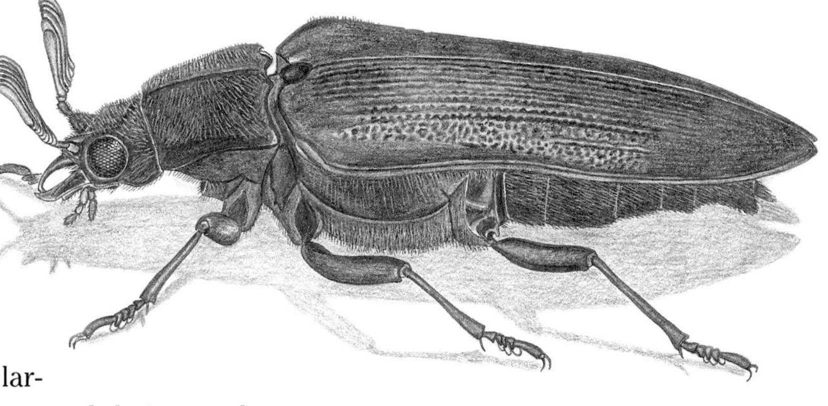

Larvae of parasitic rhipicerid beetles use the nymphs of cicadas as hosts. These beetles do not compete with many predators and other parasites for this well-hidden resource.

ROVE BEETLES

CLASSIFICATION
Phylum Arthropoda
Class Insecta
Order Coleoptera
Family Staphylinidae

PLACE IN FOOD WEB
Predators, Scavengers, Fungivores

SIZE
700 µm–2.5 cm in length

NUMBER OF SPECIES
31,200

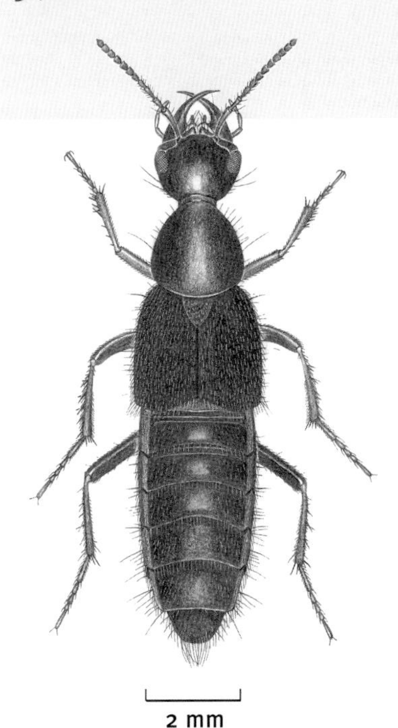

Even after metamorphosis, the fierce demeanor of larval rove beetles (below) is maintained by the adult beetles (above).

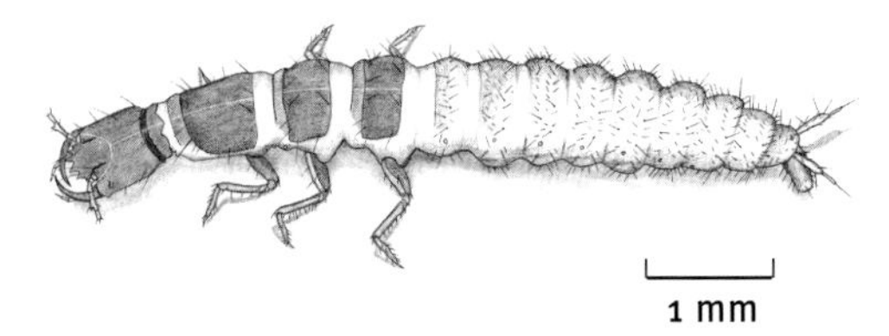

Rove Beetles and Ground Beetles

In North America, rove beetles are the largest family of beetles. Most match the soil in color, but some of the rove beetles found on fungi can be attractively iridescent.

Rove beetles can be intimidating beetles, especially the larger ones that are about an inch (25 millimeters) long. One particularly fierce-looking British rove beetle goes by the name of Devil's Coach Horse. Like the wing covers, or elytra, of the short-winged mold beetle, those of a rove beetle give its long abdomen a great deal of freedom to maneuver in the tight spaces of the soil. Rove beetles are swift and often dash about with their abdomens threateningly raised and poised like a scorpion's tail. The raised abdomen is an empty threat, but the long, sickle-shaped jaws at the other end of the beetle can deliver a good bite.

Rove beetle larvae, like their parents, have powerful jaws, speed, and agility. They also live in the same habitats and prey on some of the same animals as their parents. They are often confused with the larvae of ground beetles. However, while each leg of a rove beetle larvae ends in a single claw, ground beetle larvae have a pair of claws on each of their six legs, and a pair of what look like tails at the tip of their abdomens. These structures are known as urogomphi (*uro* = tail; *gomphi* = tooth) and can either be jointed where they meet the abdomen, as they are in rove beetle larvae, or nonjointed, as they are in ground beetle larvae.

Each ground beetle usually consumes well over its own weight in food—sometimes even two and a half times its own weight each day. Like rove beetles, ground beetles are the predominant beetle predators of the soil and leaf litter. Once prey is crushed by the mandibles of either kind of beetle, the beetle regurgitates its digestive juices so that digestion of its prey is well along by the time it finally swallows the now tenderized and liquefied meal.

A series of field experiments in Britain offers a good example of how effective ground beetles and rove beetles are as predators, as well as a good example of how pesticide application can often be counterproductive. These experiments involved application of insecticides to cabbage fields to control damage from maggots of the cabbage root fly. Ironically,

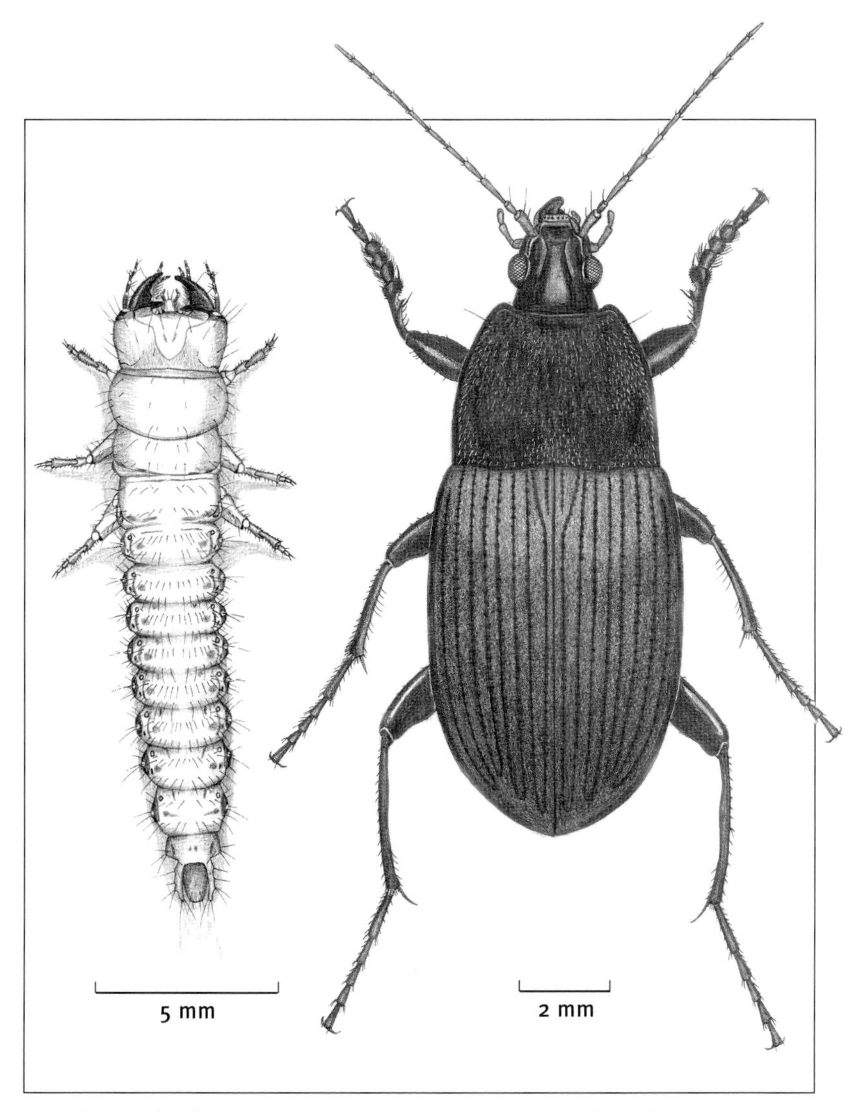

The larvae (left) blend with the soil, but the adults (right) can be colorful, iridescent, and flashy.

GROUND BEETLES

CLASSIFICATION
Phylum Arthropoda
Class Insecta
Order Coleoptera
Family Carabidae

PLACE IN FOOD WEB
Predators, Scavengers

SIZE
1.5 mm–3.5 cm in length

NUMBER OF SPECIES
30,000

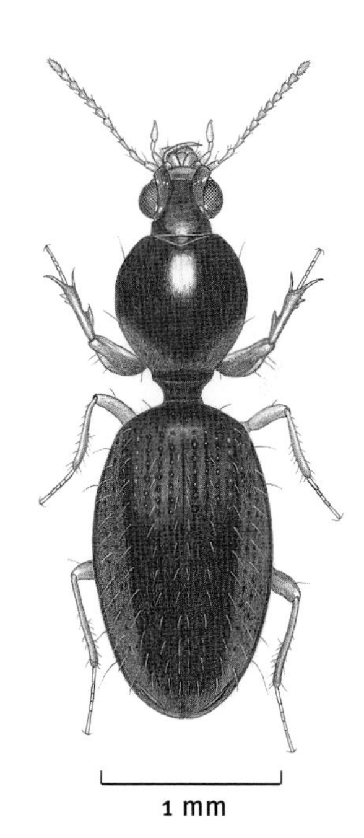

The burrowing ground beetle is a tiny predator of rove beetles.

fields treated with pesticides suffered more damage than fields that were left untreated. A closer look at the situation revealed that over 30 species of beetles were eating the eggs, larvae, and pupae of the cabbage root fly, but the pesticides were killing the beetles. If left to their own devices, the beetles were far more effective than pesticides in keeping the root flies under control.

While most ground beetles run down their prey and hunt on the soil's surface and in the leaf litter, some of the smaller ground beetles, known as burrowing ground beetles, actually live in burrows rather than under stones or logs. These sleek and compact little beetles have large front legs clearly designed for digging after the small rove beetles and mud-loving beetles that make up a good portion of their diet.

TIGER BEETLES

CLASSIFICATION
Phylum Arthropoda
Class Insecta
Order Coleoptera
Family Carabidae
Subfamily Cicindelinae

PLACE IN FOOD WEB
Diggers, Predators

SIZE
6 mm–4 cm in length (mature larvae)

NUMBER OF SPECIES
1,300

5 mm

Tiger beetles show off their colorful iridescence on sunny paths and sandbars.

Tiger Beetles

Tiger beetle larvae start out living in burrows that are about six inches (15 centimeters) deep, but by the time they are full grown, the larvae have excavated vertical burrows down into the subsoil as deep as a foot and a half (45 centimeters). The burrows are often close together in places where the soil is exposed and vegetation is sparse, not because the larvae are the least bit social, but because their mother generally left several eggs in one spot.

Rather than searching for its food, the larva lies in its burrow waiting for prey to pass by. By placing its jaws right at the entrance to the burrow, it seals the opening with its broad head and part of its thorax. Since each larva covers the exposed portions of its head and thorax with soil particles from the edge of the burrow, the tiger beetle larva becomes almost invisible. By maintaining a firm grip on the vertical wall of its burrow with the sharp dorsal hooks on its abdomen, it is ready to tackle most insect passersby and to subdue even insects larger than itself. The tiger beetle larva eventually drags its prey deep into the burrow and devours it at the bottom of the pit.

While tiger beetle larvae use subterfuge and stealth to ambush their prey, adult tiger beetles use speed in the air and on the ground to chase down other insects. The glistening colors of these flashy beetles make them easy to spot, but their long legs, sharp eyes, and strong flight muscles make them hard to catch. They are constantly wary and rarely turn their backs on pursuers. The life of a tiger beetle is in many ways like the tale of the ugly duckling: from a grotesque larva that lives in a dark burrow comes a lovely and graceful beetle found in sunny clearings.

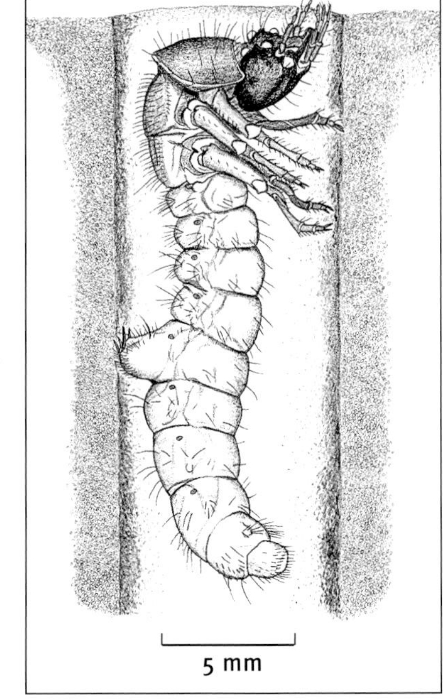

At the entrance to its vertical burrow, a tiger beetle larva waits to ambush a passing insect.

Short-Winged Mold Beetles

Short-winged mold beetles, or pselaphine (*pselaph* = grope around) beetles, may be found among the molds of the soil, but they are also on the prowl for meatier fare: springtails, mites, symphylans, diplurans, and even small worms. These tiny beetles have beautiful beady antennae that expand at their tips and give them a very appealing and distinct character. The pselaphines, as their name implies, use these sensitive antennae to full advantage as they grope and wend their way through the labyrinthine passageways of the soil.

Like other members of the rove beetle family, the pselaphine beetles have short wing covers, or elytra, that only cover a portion of their abdominal segments. Normally elytra restrain the movement of a beetle's abdomen, so with such short elytra these beetles are exceptionally limber and are free to move their long abdomens in just about any direction as the need arises. The pselaphine beetles that live the deepest in the soil are those with the shortest legs, the shortest elytra, and the fewest segments of their abdomens covered by the elytra.

SHORT-WINGED MOLD BEETLES

CLASSIFICATION
Phylum Arthropoda
Class Insecta
Order Coleoptera
Family Staphylinidae
Subfamily Pselaphinae

PLACE IN FOOD WEB
Predators, Fungivores

SIZE
0.5–5.5 mm in length

NUMBER OF SPECIES
8,300

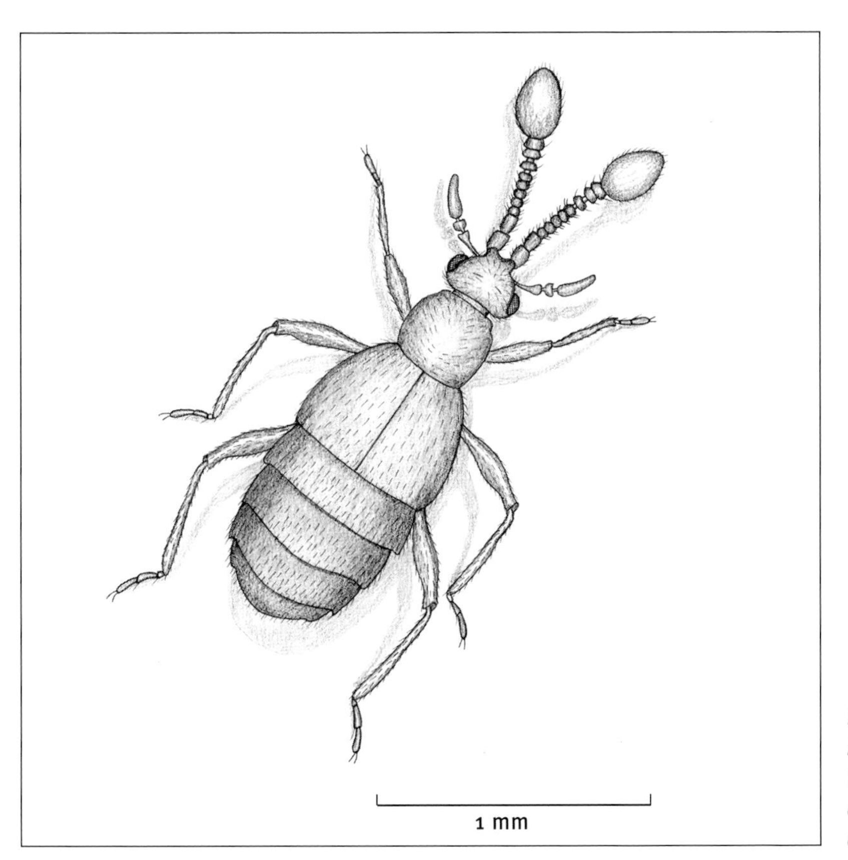

In addition to living under logs, rocks, and decaying leaves, short-winged mold beetles dwell in caves, burrows of mammals, and ant or termite colonies.

FEATHERWING BEETLES

CLASSIFICATION
Phylum Arthropoda
Class Insecta
Order Coleoptera
Family Ptiliidae

PLACE IN FOOD WEB
Fungivores

SIZE
0.4–1.5 mm in length

NUMBER OF SPECIES
400

This featherwing beetle is caught in the act of folding its feathery hind wings under its hard fore wings.

Featherwing Beetles

The featherwing or ptiliid (*ptilon* = feather) beetles include the smallest known beetles. Most members of the family measure less than 1/25 inch (1 millimeter) long. Their wings, however, are usually more than twice this length and look more like tiny bird feathers or the fine tufts on dandelion seeds than insect wings. A few fungal spores are just about a mouthful for one of these beetles.

Even though a mother beetle lays only a single large egg at a time, she puts a great deal of energy into it because the egg can be as large as half her own length. What emerges from this egg is a miniature, scaled-down version of a rove beetle larva but without pigment, eyes, and sickle-shaped jaws. Some species of featherwing beetles lay normal, fertilized eggs, but many mother featherwings are virgins and lay only unfertilized eggs that produce only daughters. The progression from egg to adult for these little beetles takes only about a month, so even though these beetles are rarely noticed, they are still very abundant on the forest floor.

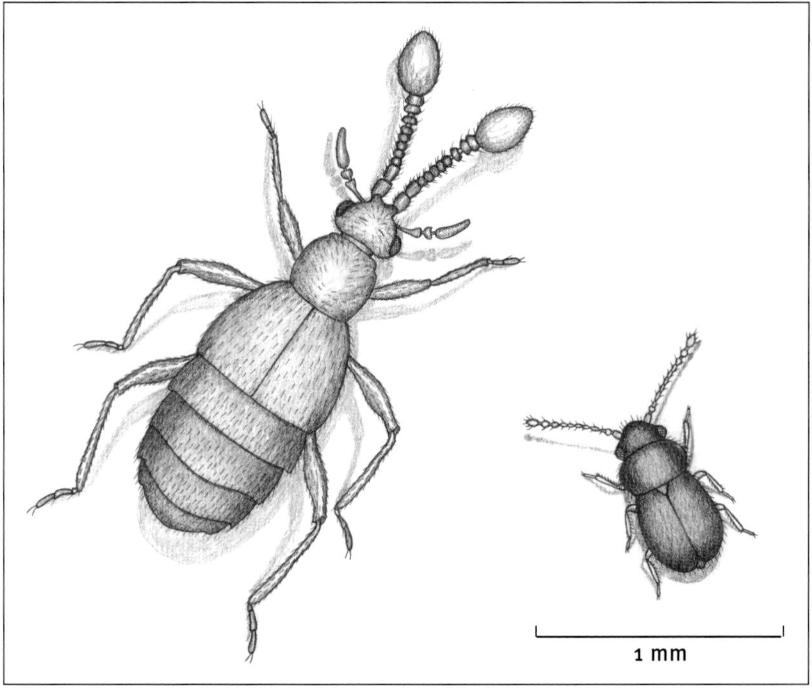

Tiny featherwing beetles (right) often fall prey to larger pselaphine beetles.

Sap Beetles

The sap beetles, or nitidulids (*nitid* = shining; *-uli* = small), love saps from all sources, at all stages of fermentation and decay: sap from rotting fruit, sap flowing from trees, sap from fungi above or belowground. The smell of decay attracts nitidulids, and they join in to promote the whole process of decay and recycling. In the soil, fermentation and decay are so pervasive that adult and larval sap beetles can feed on a variety of saps with little possibility of ever depleting their abundant food source.

Not all nitidulids lead such placid lives. Along the foraging trails of certain ants live some notorious nitidulid beetles that act like highwaymen. During the hours of daylight these beetles lie in the leaf litter, but at nightfall they patrol the ant trails looking for some unsuspecting ant that might part with food it is carrying back to the nest. By tapping their antennae on the ant's mouth parts, these highwaymen induce the ant to regurgitate the food it is carrying. Often the ant realizes she has been duped by the beetle. In retaliation she attempts to lay her mandibles on the beetle; but by the time she acts, the beetle has flattened itself on the ground, pulling all its legs and an–tennae under its body. It grips the ground with strong bristles on its legs so the ant is neither able to attack it from above nor to flip the beetle over and attack it from below. As soon as the outwitted ant moves on, the beetle waits for the next ant it will deceive and pillage.

SAP BEETLES

CLASSIFICATION
Phylum Arthropoda
Class Insecta
Order Coleoptera
Family Nitidulidae

PLACE IN FOOD WEB
Decomposers, Detritivores, Scavengers

SIZE
1 mm–1.5 cm in length (mature larvae)

NUMBER OF SPECIES
3,000

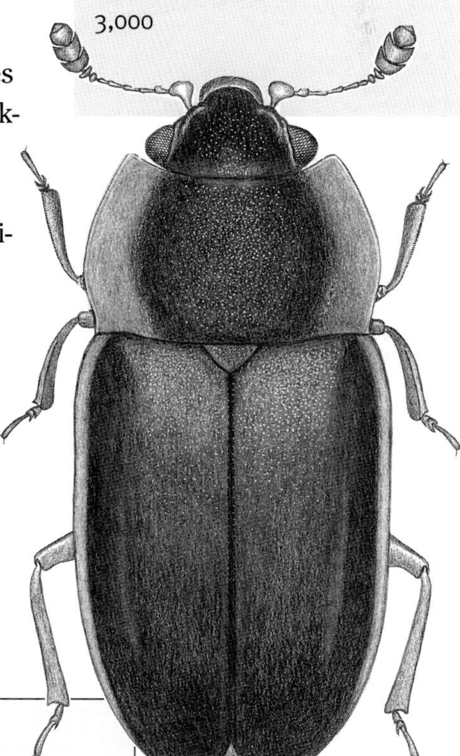

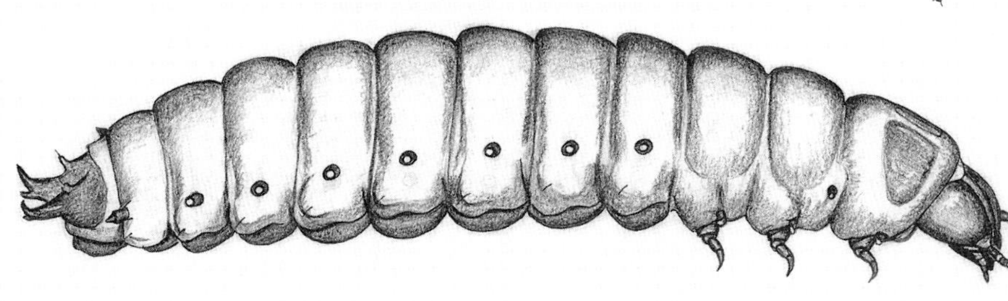

Most species of sap beetles live aboveground on green plants, but a few species of sap beetles (above) and their larvae (left) dwell in the soil among fungi and rotting plants.

ANTLIKE STONE BEETLES

CLASSIFICATION
Phylum Arthropoda
Class Insecta
Order Coleoptera
Family Scydmaenidae

PLACE IN FOOD WEB
Scavengers, Predators

SIZE
0.6–2.5 mm in length

NUMBER OF SPECIES
3,570

Antlike Stone Beetles

Although antlike stone beetles can easily be mistaken for ants at first glance, a closer look shows that their antennae are too straight to be ant antennae and their bodies are too hairy to be ant bodies. Like nitidulid beetles, many of these scydmaenid (*scydmaen* = angry) beetles have found ways to deceive and exploit other soil insects, living as scavengers in ant or termite colonies. Although the ants and termites probably can tell the difference between these beetles and the members of their own colony, they somehow tolerate the intruders and treat them with indifference. Antlike stone beetles that roam the leaf litter and hollow trees beyond the confines of ant and termite colonies survive both as adults and larvae on a diet rich in oribatid mites. Breaking through the hard shells of oribatid mites undoubtedly demands some sharp and hard mandibles for the job.

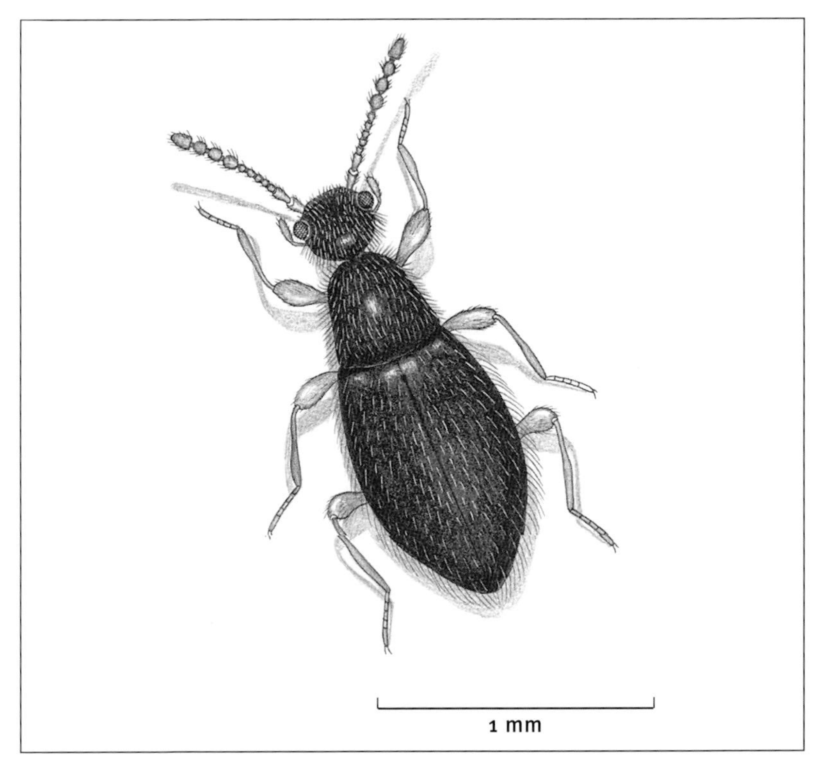

Antlike stone beetles live in the leaf litter, under bark, or as scavengers in ant and termite colonies.

Minute Fungus Beetles

The larvae of minute fungus beetles, or corylophids (*cory* = helmet; *lophi* = crown), are probably the most unforgettable beetle larvae of the leaf litter. They are flat, broad, and shaped like a turtle. The scientific term for this body shape is cheloniform (*chelona* = turtle; *form* = shape). A series of flat, ornate scales are arranged around the edge of the larva's body, similar to the colorful scales that cover butterfly and moth wings. On the back of the larva are openings of glands which probably function for protection from predators that prowl between the fallen leaves. It is easy to imagine one of these tiny pancake-shaped larvae roaming the narrow spaces between layers of fallen leaves on the forest floor. Soil fungi wend their way between the fallen leaves, where their spores and hyphae offer a feast for these little larvae.

In the adult beetles, the first segment of the thorax, known as the "pronotum," extends forward over the head, hiding the eyes, the mouth parts, and the bases of the antennae. This protruding portion of the thorax was apparently construed as a crown or helmet by the person who chose the family name Corylophidae for these beetles. This "helmet" for the beetle's head probably helps the beetle plow its way through layers of leaves on the forest floor. These rotund beetles, along with the featherwing beetles, have long hairs adorning the margins of their hindwings and are some of the smallest of all beetles. They are among the many beetles that, like their larvae, are also found in the company of molds and fungi.

MINUTE FUNGUS BEETLES

CLASSIFICATION
Phylum Arthropoda
Class Insecta
Order Coleoptera
Family Corylophidae

PLACE IN FOOD WEB
Fungivores

SIZE
1–3 mm in length (mature larvae)

NUMBER OF SPECIES
400

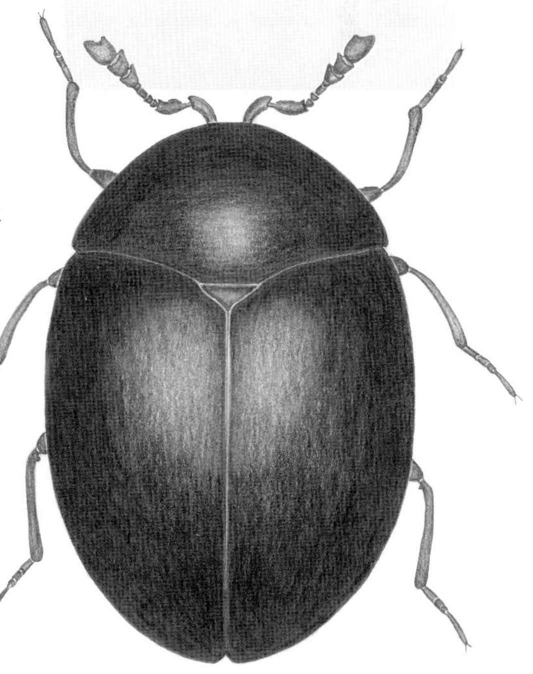

Populations of minute fungus beetles (above) and their larva (left) live in the flat world between layers of decaying leaves. There, they graze on fungi and spores that coat the leaf surfaces.

PTILODACTYLID OR WINGED-TOE BEETLES

CLASSIFICATION
Phylum Arthropoda
Class Insecta
Order Coleoptera
Family Ptilodactylidae

PLACE IN FOOD WEB
Decomposers, Detritivores, Scavengers

SIZE
3 mm–2.5 cm in length (mature larvae)
4 mm–1 cm in length (adults)

NUMBER OF SPECIES
450

Ptilodactylid or Winged-Toe Beetles

Beginning in early spring, you can find the bristly larvae of ptilodactylid beetles in forest soil and leaf litter, under the wildflowers that cover the forest floor. These larvae are occupied in converting the abundant leaf litter into the humus that nourishes the rich flora of the forest. Judging from the frequency with which they are encountered during the spring, the larvae must contribute a good share to the enrichment of the forest soil. But the distinctive adult beetles are rarely seen until later, at evening lights in late June. At that time of year, they turn out to be frequent visitors. The beetles move about quickly, waving their long, comblike antennae if they are males; or they wave equally long, but less handsome, sawtoothed antennae if they are females.

If one looks closely at the feet of these beetles, the origin of their strange family name soon becomes apparent. Like most scientific names, the long, five-syllable name for this family of beetles points out a distinguishing feature of these beetles. Near the very end of each foot of a ptilodactylid (*ptilo* = wing; *dactyl* = toe), a large, winglike lobe extends down and back, almost to the tip of the claws. Many small beetles, like other small creatures, look nondescript and featureless until one is treated to close-up views of them. Through the lenses of microscopes features appear that surprise even the most seasoned observer of the living world.

2 mm

Ptilodactylid beetles (above) are rarely seen, but down in the soil their larvae (below) are busy making important contributions to the recycling of leaves, roots, and wood.

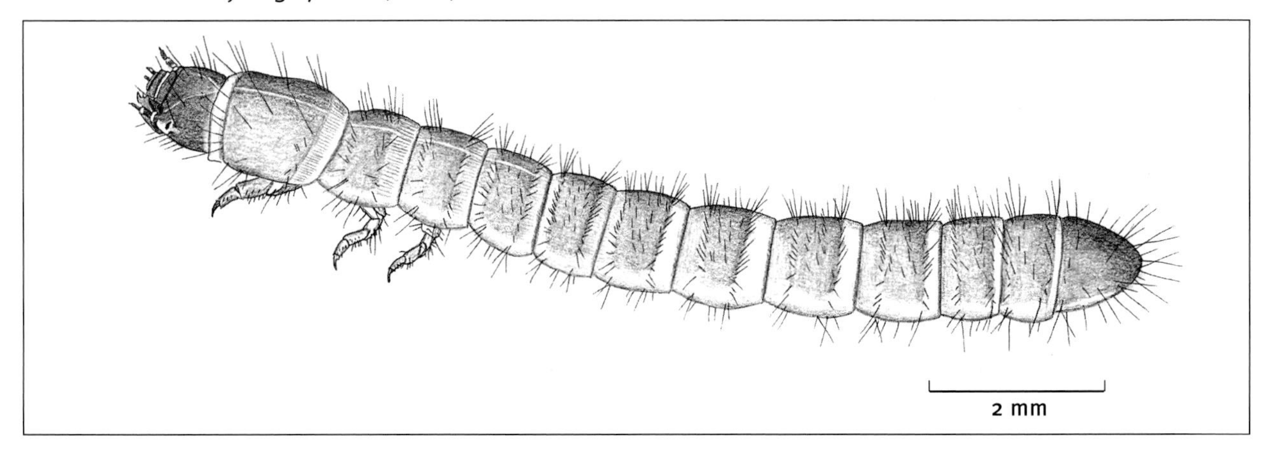

Glowworms and Fireflies

In June and July, those who live in the eastern half of North America are treated to the sight of thousands of flashing fireflies lighting the evening skies. Between the Great Plains and the Atlantic Coast about 150 species of fireflies, or lampyrids (*lampyri* = glowworm), can be found. In the rest of the world more than 10 times this number are found, most in the tropics. In North America, the biggest contributors to the midsummer displays of lights as well as the most familiar of the fireflies are the 28 species of *Photinus* and the 20 species of *Photuris*.

Even though not all adult fireflies flash, all glowworms—as firefly larvae are usually known—turn out to be flashers. Many fireflies even start out in the soil as glowing, luminescent eggs. If we looked at the soil more often and more carefully during the summer and autumn, we might see that the ground at times can be thickly covered with their lamps; several hundred glowworms can often occupy a square foot (900 square centimeters) of soil. As fast-moving predators, these larvae seize their prey with sickle-shaped jaws and inject both a neurotoxin that paralyzes their victims as well as digestive juices that help liquify muscles, nerves, and other tissues that can then be sucked back along a groove in each jaw. Larvae of the genus *Photuris*

GLOWWORMS AND FIREFLIES

CLASSIFICATION
Phylum Arthropoda
Class Insecta
Order Coleoptera
Family Lampyridae

PLACE IN FOOD WEB
Predators

SIZE
1.7–5 cm in length (mature larvae)
4.5 mm–2 cm in length (adults)

NUMBER OF SPECIES
1,900

Larvae of the firefly genus Photuris *are predators of snails and slugs.*

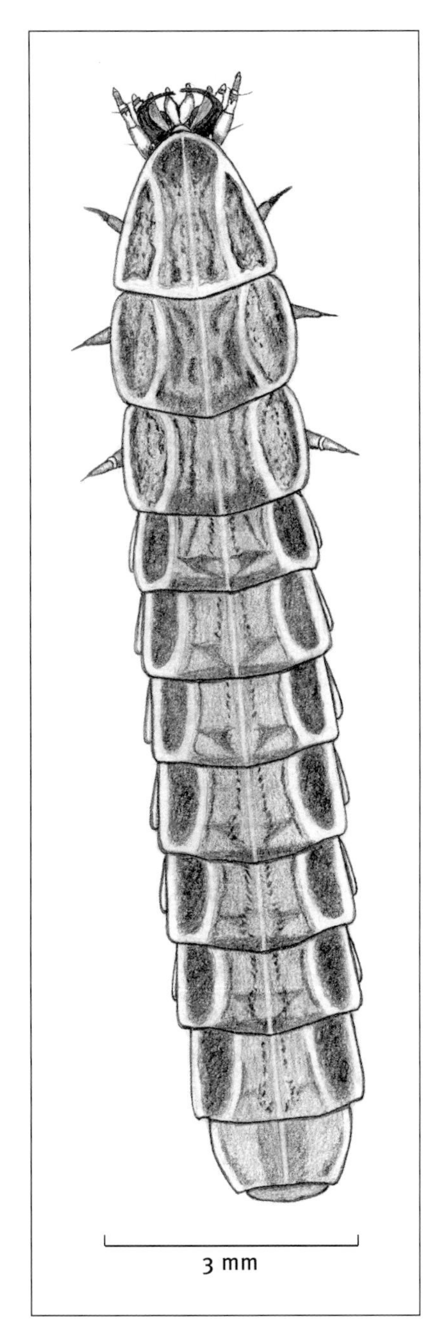

Larvae of the firefly genus Photinus *attack earthworms with their sickle-shaped jaws.*

A male firefly glides a short distance aboveground and flashes to female fireflies down below.

apparently prefer feeding on snails and slugs, while the more slender larvae of the genus *Photinus* search the narrow underground passageways frequented by earthworms. The European glowworm *Lampyris* has been observed tracking down snails and slugs by following their slime trails through the leaf litter. At the approach of winter, the larvae burrow into the the soil; in the spring they transform to pupae and adults.

The adults soon spread their wings and set about the business of courting. The males cruise over fields and clearings, each species flashing its own distinctive code that is translated by the females as "Here I am, and I'm available"; and the females fly off to a plant or spot on the ground where they can pick and choose their favorite flashers. The flashing patterns for the different species are so distinctive that most of these beetles can be recognized from the number, duration, and intervals between their flashes. Although the adults flash as part of their courtship ritual, eggs and larvae light up to warn toads and other possible predators of the soil surface that glowworms not only do not taste very good but they are also downright toxic.

Sadly, many areas are losing the magic that fills the air on summer evenings when hundreds, often thousands, of fireflies perform. Fireflies are becoming rarer wherever soil habitats that support firefly larvae and the earthworms, snails, and slugs on which they feed are paved over, plowed under, and eliminated by human encroachment on the few remaining wild places.

Soldier Beetles

SOLDIER BEETLES

CLASSIFICATION
Phylum Arthropoda
Class Insecta
Order Coleoptera
Family Cantharidae

PLACE IN FOOD WEB
Predators

SIZE
5 mm–2 cm in length (mature larvae)
1 mm–1.5 cm in length (adults)

NUMBER OF SPECIES
5,100

Although these beetles neither flash nor glow, they still share a number of other attributes with their close relatives the fireflies and glowworms. Most soldier beetle larvae run about in the soil and leaf litter, dispatching other soil creatures with large, sickle-shaped jaws. Like the larvae of fireflies, these larvae have grooves on the surfaces of their mandibles that drain the body juices of their victims. Their life cycle also closely parallels that of fireflies. After a summer of prowling and hunting, the mature larvae retire to sheltered spots in the soil and leaf litter, where they stay through the winter. Lengthening days and rising temperatures of spring signal that the time has come to pupate and leave the soil. While fireflies court in the evening skies of early summer, soldier beetle romances begin on sunny days among the flowers.

A number of features set soldier beetle larvae apart from other beetle larvae. Larval soldier beetles are covered with a dense coat of short, fine hairs that makes them look and feel as though they are attired in velvet. Deep colors of brown, purple, burgundy, or black are the most common colors for the coats of larvae, but those larvae destined to become aphid eaters as adult beetles have pink velvety covers. Soldier beetle larvae have few predators because chemicals from the many stink glands found on their backs soon obliterate any appetite that a predator might have for a meal of larval soldier beetles. Their chemical repellents as well as their velvet coats give each larva a distinctive smell and an unmistakable look.

Adult soldier beetles have soft, leathery bodies and are almost always decked out with a combination of orange or yellow and black or brown pigments. They often congregate on flowers in large numbers where they share nectar and pollen with bees, flies, and butterflies. Some of the darker soldier beetles gather on plants where aphids or scale insects (coccoids) are feeding and share their meals of aphids with ladybugs and lacewings. Once you start looking for these beetles, you will discover that they are quite common and colorful; they just are not as flashy as their relatives the fireflies.

5 mm

Soldier beetles can be very common visitors to flowers such as goldenrod and milkweed. Some flowers can have several beetles visiting at the same time.

5 mm

The dark, velvety larvae of soldier beetles are fast-moving predators

DUNG BEETLES

CLASSIFICATION
Phylum Arthropoda
Class Insecta
Order Coleoptera
Family Scarabaeidae

PLACE IN FOOD WEB
Decomposers, Detritivores, Scavengers, Coprophages

SIZE
2 mm–3 cm in length

NUMBER OF SPECIES
25,000

HISTER BEETLES

CLASSIFICATION
Phylum Arthropoda
Class Insecta
Order Coleoptera
Family Histeridae

PLACE IN FOOD WEB
Predators

SIZE
500 μm–2 cm in length

NUMBER OF SPECIES
3,700

All animals contribute dung to the soil, but some dung enriches the soil more than others.

Dung Beetles and Hister Beetles

Certain beetles dine solely on dung and share their stinky meals with fungi, nematodes, and flies. Transforming dung to humus is a faster process than converting dead grass, sawdust, or an oak leaf to humus. Organic matter in dung is not only more finely divided than an oak leaf but it is also much richer in nitrogen. There is no shortage of insects that compete with one another for coveted dung piles and are instrumental in converting them to humus. But they can be very particular about whose dung they recycle.

All the continents of the world but Australia originally had native populations of large grazing animals like cattle, horses, elephants, and buffalo; each of these animals consumes large quantities of vegetation and can drop enough dung pads in one year to cover a tenth of an acre (4,840 square yards; 4,050 square meters) of soil. Fortunately, these grazing animals share their habitats with beetles that have found a use for the dung pads and ensure that the soil surface does not become smothered beneath a layer of dung. No one really thought too much about the usefulness of these dung beetles, and their achievements were mostly taken for granted until cattle, horses, and sheep were introduced to Australia and dung pads quickly began to overrun pastures. The native Australian dung beetles had not evolved to handle the dung pads of the large livestock imported from Europe and showed no inclination to do so. Only after dung beetles were imported from Africa and southern Europe was the Australian dung dilemma solved.

Kangaroos had been the largest mammals to graze the pastures of Australia, and they left dry dung pellets no larger than golf balls. Even though some dung beetles have relatively undiscriminating tastes, many of them are very finicky about their choice of dung pads. Only those pads with particular textures, vegetable composition, water content, or specific dimensions are acceptable. For the Australian dung beetles, kangaroo dung was an acceptable meal but cow dung was not.

The dung beetles of Africa are accustomed to dung pads of every imaginable size, texture, and composition, from the large imposing pads of elephants and rhinos to the small pellets of antelopes and gazelles. Even before dung hits the ground, some dung beetles have picked up its scent and rush to claim these highly prized resources. Elephant dung alone is the preferred

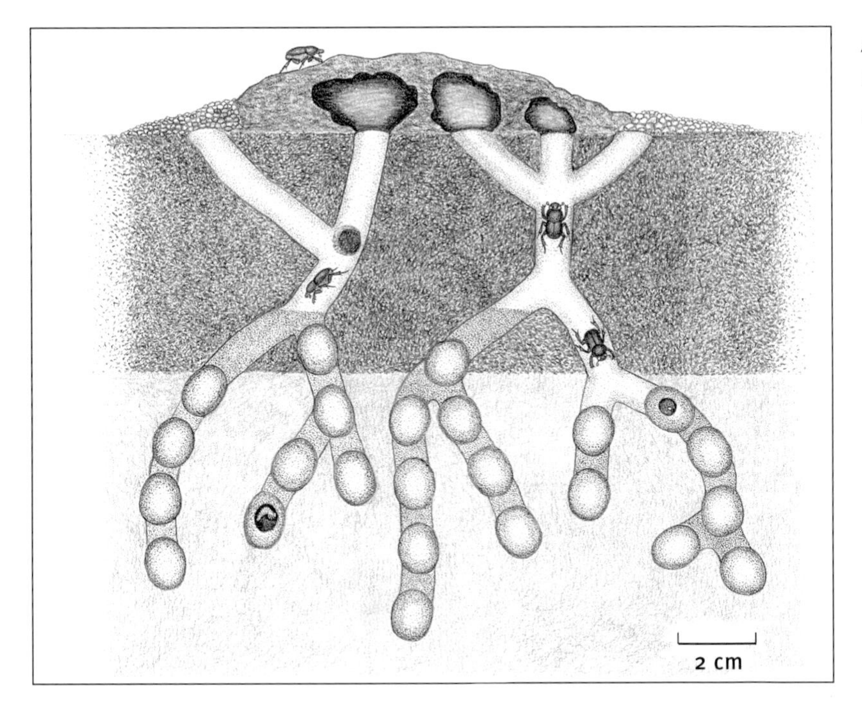

As scarab beetles position their dung balls beneath a dung pad, dung goes down and subsoil goes up.

habitat for 150 species of dung beetles. A count of more than 7,000 of these beetles on a pad of fresh elephant dung hints at just how popular dung pads can be. Adult beetles feed on the more nutritious juices of the dung, and they move solid dung to underground chambers for their larvae. With help from the bacteria in their guts, the larvae are able to digest even the cellulose fibers that make up so much of a herbivore's dung. Also, by eating their own droppings, these larvae enrich their diet with all the bacteria that go along with the droppings.

Some of the chambers that adults provide for their larvae are elaborate and extensive; one species of beetle may leave up to 40 dung balls in its underground chambers. Others excavate only shallow pits in the soil and dexterously maneuver dung balls into these pits that often are larger than themselves. Dung beetles clearly take great care in providing a dung ball for each of their larvae. By constructing their nests underground, they protect the larvae from many predators, parasites, competitors, and often from bad weather.

As part of their ancient routine of excavating chambers to accommodate their dung balls and their larvae, all dung beetles participate in mixing nutrients from dung with minerals of the soil. This activity increases the permeability of soil to air and water, increases its organic content, and improves the soil structure. In the process of doing all this, each year dung beetles can bury up to a ton of dung on two and a half acres (10,000 square meters, or 1 hectare) of soil.

Many dung beetles are dark and earth-colored, but a few are known for their brilliant colors.

An elephant or a cow may be efficient in obtaining energy from the food it eats, but it does not quite extract all the energy. All animal droppings retain some food and energy value. Someone once calculated that in the course of a year, one cow leaves enough food and energy in its droppings to support an insect population equivalent to at least 20 percent of the cow's weight as well as millions of bacteria and thousands of nematodes, protozoa, and fungi. The Plains Indians of North America were well aware that buffalo dung was a rich source of energy. They cooked and warmed themselves by fires fueled with dried buffalo dung.

The dung from herbivores—plant-eating animals—is high in energy value. The food consumed by meat-eaters,or carnivores, however, contains little energy value after it is converted to droppings. Carnivore dung neither makes a good fuel for a fire nor does its poor energy value attract many hungry insects.

Other insects are also fond of dung, and struggles often arise over who lays claim to this coveted resource. Fly maggots and dung beetles are the two main contenders for every new pile of dung. Dung beetles happen to have a number of allies in their clashes with flies and their maggots. Among their larger allies are shiny black hister beetles and sleek, sinuous rove beetles that spend most or all of their lives in dung pads where they prey on fly maggots and fly pupae. Like dung beetles, hister beetles and rove beetles usually carry mites as tiny allies on their bellies and under their wing covers, or elytra. When the beetles land on the dung pads, the mites leap off and scurry about in search of fly eggs or newly hatched maggots. Each beetle can carry up to 30 mites; and if a beetle somehow loses its mites, it simply cannot compete as well with the maggots for its fair share of the dung pad. These mites can significantly reduce the population of maggots before maggots take over the dung pad. After beetles and mites satisfy their appetites in the dung and before the last beetles leave the dung pad, mites hop aboard the beetles and set off for a new destination.

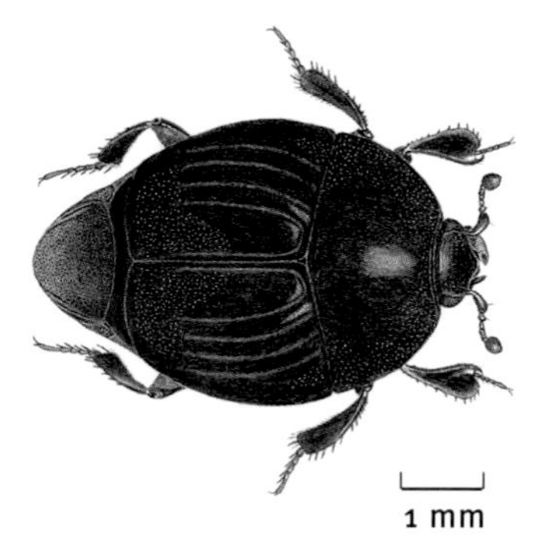

Many hister beetles have the luster of burnished ebony.

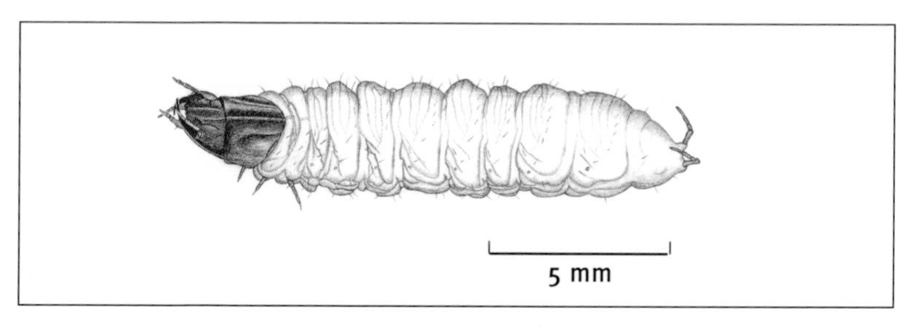

The larva of a hister beetle has imposing jaws but legs that are disproportionately small and skinny for its size.

Carrion Beetles and Burying Beetles

The only dining experience that sounds even more unappetizing than dining on dung is dining on the dead. Carrion beetles are the vultures of the insect world and see to it that the corpses of dead animals are returned to the soil that nourished them during their lifetimes. Their clubbed antennae are finely tuned to the potent odors of dead animals—always animals with backbones. Fierce competition often develops among beetles for the limited number of dead animals that happen to be on the ground at any given time or in any given place. Battles between beetles are often waged for possession of these valuable resources.

One type of carrion beetle, the colorful sexton or burying beetle, is named after the church official in charge of grave digging. These beetles are appropriately decked out mostly in black, but they also have splashes of red or orange to relieve their somber

CARRION BEETLES AND BURYING BEETLES

CLASSIFICATION
Phylum Arthropoda
Class Insecta
Order Coleoptera
Family Silphidae

PLACE IN FOOD WEB
Scavengers, Decomposers, Detritivores, Predators

SIZE
1.2–4 cm in length

NUMBER OF SPECIES
215

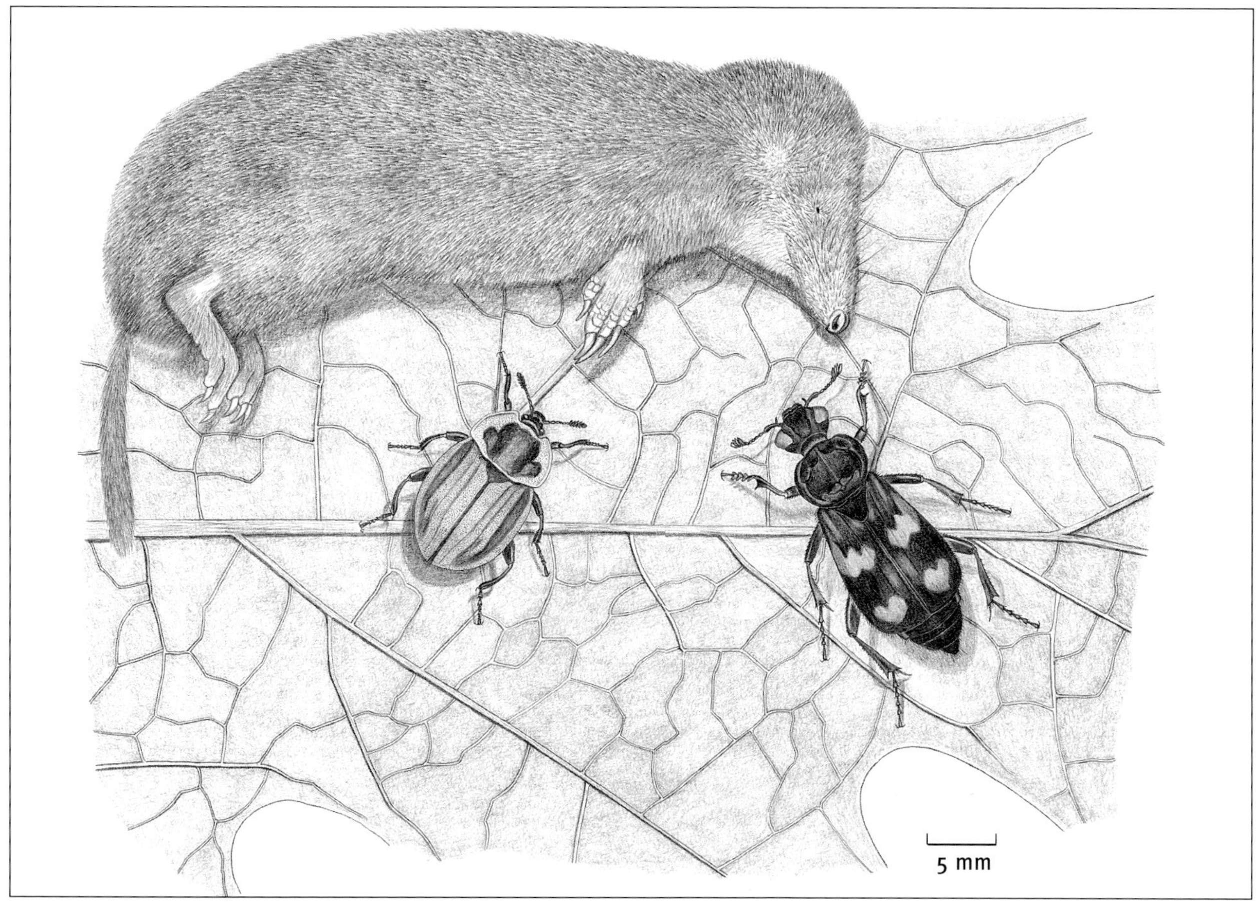

A dead shrew is a resource that is much coveted by carrion beetles. Silpha *approaches from the left and a sexton beetle approaches from the right.*

The larva of the carrion beetle is sleek and shiny.

attire. Male and female beetles work as a team to bury their find as quickly as possible before fly maggots or other beetles can establish a foothold on the dead body. Small birds and mammals are obviously preferred for logistical reasons; it is far easier for these inch-long (25-millimeter) beetles to maneuver a mouse than a cow. The generic name of the sexton or burying beetles, *Nicrophorus,* aptly translates to "carrier of the dead." Those fly eggs and fly maggots that hatch are soon dispatched by the beetles themselves or by the mites that travel with the beetles.

After a few hours of digging, shifting, and molding, the dead body is reduced to a round, unrecognizable ball buried several inches belowground. The mother beetle moves about this underground chamber, laying about 20 eggs along its walls. Next she begins chewing a little hole at the top of the ball of flesh that will serve as a nest for her larvae when they hatch in a few days. For the first few hours after the larvae have moved into the nest, the mother beetle feeds her brood just as a mother bird would feed her nestlings. After their second molt, however, the larvae are on their own and eat their way deeper into the ball of flesh until they are ready for metamorphosis.

The other carrion beetle, known as *Silpha,* is nowhere near as sophisticated about its larval rearing. Silpha does not bury the corpses that its antennae lead it to nor is it particularly concerned about the size of the corpse. A dead horse or even a large, well-rotted mushroom will suffice as well as a dead shrew. Silpha and its larvae are not adverse to sharing their rotten find with maggots and other beetles, for they add these creatures to their meal.

Jet-black, oval, and shiny, many hister beetles keep company with the carrion beetles. Hister beetles survive primarily on a diet of maggots and any other smaller insects they come across. The lower segments of their legs are broad and spiny, clearly built for digging in dung, carrion, or fungi that are past their prime. A few hister beetles and their larvae are very flattened and live under bark of decaying trees; some are long and cylindrical, and live in the tunnels of wood-boring insects; still other members of this beetle family move into nests of ants or rodents. By reducing the populations of voracious maggots in carrion and dung, hister beetles are welcome allies for the dung beetles and carrion beetles with whom these maggots compete for very popular, but limited, resources. Most hister beetles also carry a crew of predatory mites wherever they go, and these mites begin devouring fly eggs and tiny maggots as soon as they alight on dung or a dead animal.

Wireworms and Click Beetles

Anyone who has worked the soil or looked inside a rotting log has most likely come across wireworms—long, sleek, and hard like an electrical wire. There may be many other insect larvae that dwell in the soil, but wireworms are among the most conspicuous. Each wireworm probably spends more of its life in the soil than any other insect, with the exception of cicadas. Except for some of the smallest of the wireworms, most will spend at least three years and perhaps as many as seven years underground.

Wireworms are not only active but also dominant in a variety of subterranean roles: recycling plant debris, preying on other arthropods, and chewing on roots. Their sleek bodies slide easily through the soil, and although the larvae do not have eyes, the multitude of sensory bristles that cover their bodies from head to tail keep them well informed about what is happening around them.

Wireworms eventually become the click beetles (p.85), or elaterids (*elater* = hurler), of acrobatic fame that are known for their ability to hurl themselves into upright positions if they ever land or are placed on their backs. An upside-down beetle cocks its head and part of its thorax back, forming an arch between them and the rest of its body. When the tension is suddenly released, the beetle's arched back strikes the ground with such force that it springs into the air, most of the time landing upright on all six legs.

Wireworms can be a blessing as well as a curse in fields where crops are grown. Predatory wireworms prefer fields that are rich in plant debris, and they eliminate respectable numbers of insects, including other species of wireworms, that may be detrimental to the crops. Root-feeding wireworms, on the other hand, can inflict a significant amount of damage on crops once their population grows to more than a few hundred thousand larvae per acre. Root crops like potatoes and carrots seem to be especially sensitive to the ravages of these wireworms. By considering how the soil is prepared for planting each spring and prepared for winter each fall, soil conditions may be found that favor the populations of predatory wireworms. By encouraging these predators to eliminate enough of the root-feeding wireworms, pouring pesticides on the soil will become an unnecessary effort and expense.

WIREWORMS AND CLICK BEETLES

CLASSIFICATION
Phylum Arthropoda
Class Insecta
Order Coleoptera
Family Elateridae

PLACE IN FOOD WEB
Decomposers, Detritivores, Herbivores, Predators

SIZE
1–6 cm in length (mature larvae)
1.5 mm–4.5 cm (adults)

NUMBER OF SPECIES
9,000

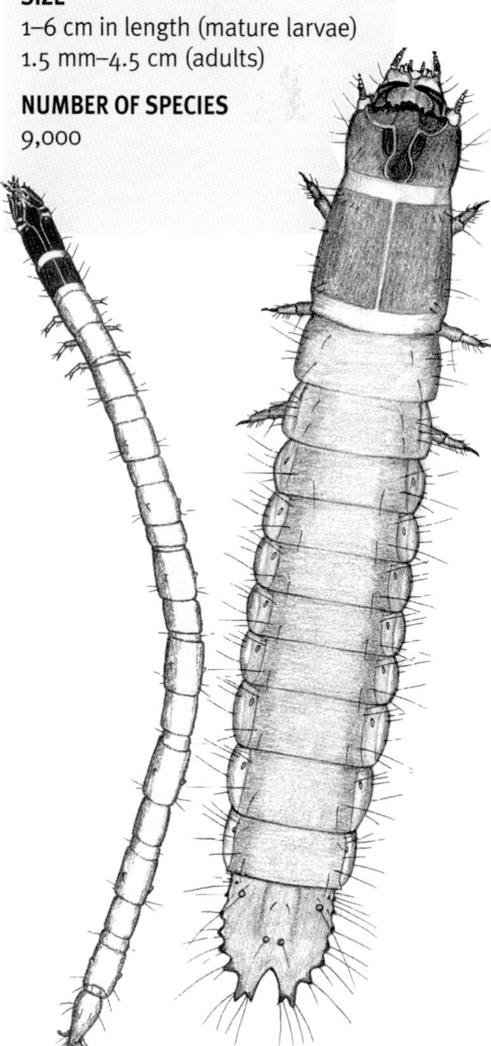

Wireworms live in soil, litter, or rotten wood. Some are long, thin, and sinuous and others are shorter, stouter, and armed with spiny tails, or urogomphi.

RETICULATED BEETLES

CLASSIFICATION
Phylum Arthropoda
Class Insecta
Order Coleoptera
Family Cupedidae

PLACE IN FOOD WEB
Decomposers, Detritivores, Fungivores

SIZE
7 mm–2 cm in length

NUMBER OF SPECIES
26

TELEPHONE-POLE BEETLES

CLASSIFICATION
Phylum Arthropoda
Class Insecta
Order Coleoptera
Family Micromalthidae

PLACE IN FOOD WEB
Decomposers, Detritivores, Fungivores

SIZE
1–2.5 mm in length

NUMBER OF SPECIES
1

Beetles of Rotten Logs

Dining on logs takes not only a good deal of chewing, but also some help with the digestion of the tough wood fibers. Years before a dead tree falls to the ground, legions of bark beetles, wood-boring beetles, and wood wasps settle under the bark and in the heartwood as they begin preparing the tree for its eventual resting place in the soil. Microbes that live in the digestive tracts of wood-feeding insects have been recruited as the insects' best antidotes for indigestion. Larvae and adult insects depend on the bacteria, protozoa, and fungi of a rotting log and will slowly starve if they are fed logs in which these microbes have been killed. Larvae of many beetles and flies that feed on rotting wood also have specialized pouches in their intestines, where the bacteria or fungi reside, that help digest some of the tough wood fibers of cellulose the larvae swallow.

In this respect these insects resemble large herbivores like cows and goats that have special chambers in their digestive tracts (rumens) teeming with bacteria and protozoa. The bacteria and protozoa help digest the large amounts of cellulose that those animals swallow with each bite of grass or hay. The nitrogen content of the wood fibers eaten by insects is probably often so low that some of these microbes of beetle and fly guts must convert (fix) dinitrogen from air to a form of nitrogen that insects can use. At metamorphosis the microbes pass from the intestine to the reproductive ducts that are forming in the females, and there they coat the surface of each egg as it is laid. When the larvae hatch, they devour pieces of their eggshells and thereby populate their intestines with the same microbes that lived in the intestines of their mothers.

Based on what we know about beetle genealogy, the first beetles that walked the earth about 240 million years ago were most similar in appearance and habits to the telephone-pole beetles and reticulated beetles that today live in moist and well-rotted logs. These are not only the most primitive living beetles, they are also some of the most unusual. By chance someone once discovered that male reticulated beetles find the odor of laundry bleach irresistible. The odor is so similar to the attractant emitted by the female beetles that a few teaspoons of bleach are sufficiently alluring to entice these rarely seen beetles from their retreats in the deep woods.

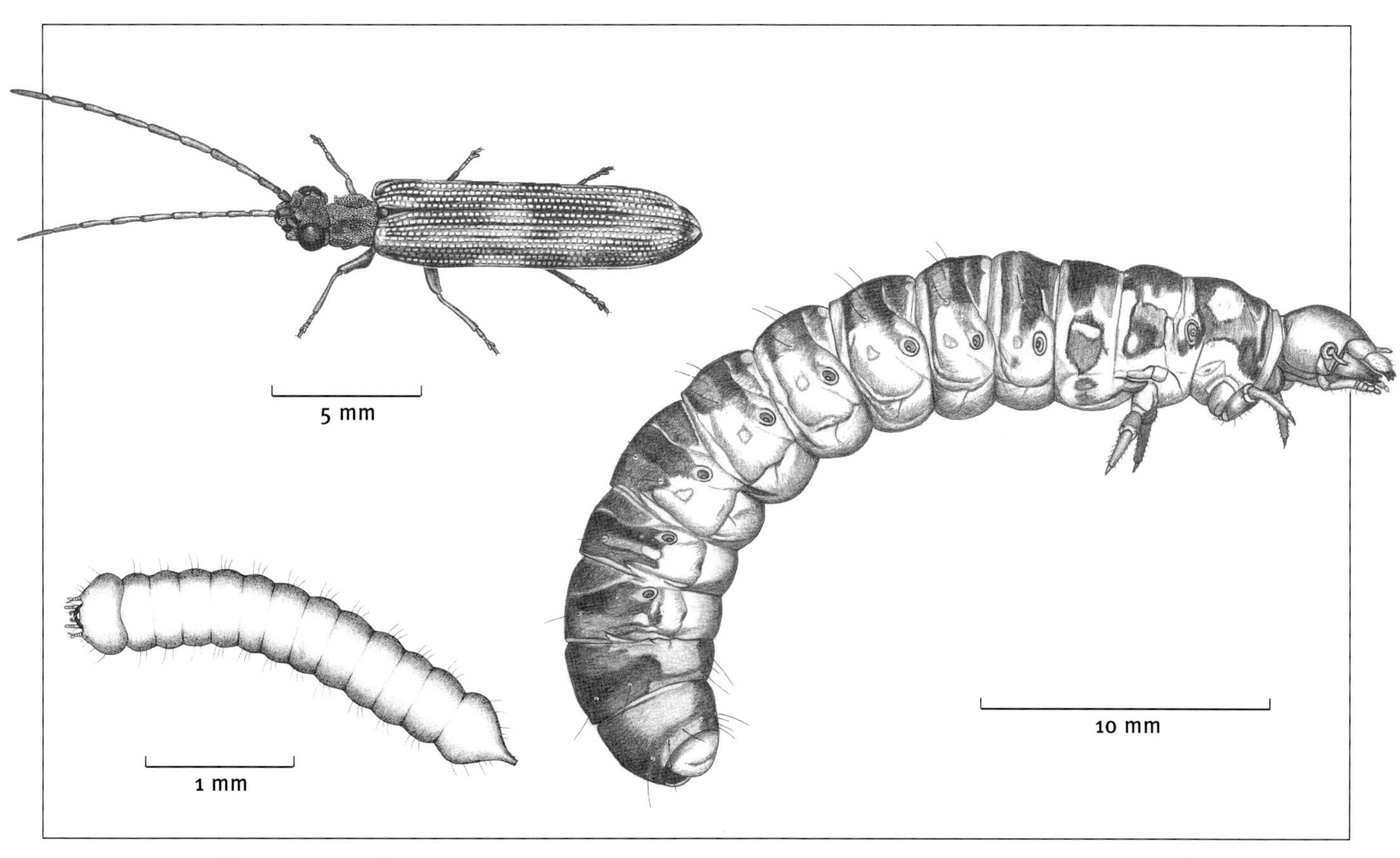

Many species of beetles contribute to the recycling of logs, branches, and stumps. Some are primitive beetles such as reticulated beetles (top) and larvae of micromalthid beetles (bottom); others are large larvae, such as those of patent-leather beetles (right).

Even fewer people have seen the tiny telephone-pole beetles. Their unusual common name was chosen because these beetles have been found in old, rotting telephone poles; however, they are most often referred to as micromalthid beetles, since they belong to the family Micromalthidae that contains only one genus, *Micromalthus*. The largest specimens of this beetle measure only 1/10 inch (2.54 millimeters) in length. Although they have the reputation of being quite rare, the larvae can be found in large numbers in certain logs. They have a definite preference for logs in the oak family that are at just the right stage of decay. Once they have found the right log, the larvae of micromalthid beetles begin multiplying as rapidly as possible to take full advantage of this ideal habitat before it disappears. To use the ephemeral resources of their log most efficiently, the larvae begin reproducing before they undergo metamorphosis and even before they mate.

These larvae are both paedogenic and parthenogenic; that is, they give birth while they are still larvae (*paedo* = child;

FALSE CLICK BEETLES

CLASSIFICATION
Phylum Arthropoda
Class Insecta
Order Coleoptera
Family Eucnemidae

PLACE IN FOOD WEB
Decomposers, Detritivores, Fungivores

SIZE
3 mm–3.5 cm in length

NUMBER OF SPECIES
1,300

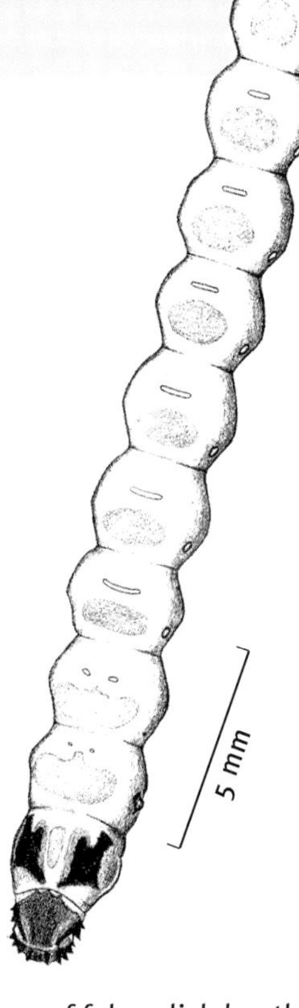

The larvae of false click beetles are strange in many ways. They are legless and eyeless, their antennae are absent or reduced to tiny stubs, and they have jaws that move out instead of in.

genesis = birth) and without mating (*parthenos* = virgin; *genesis* = birth). This policy clearly enables the beetles to share their resource with as many relatives as possible in as short a time as possible. No other beetle is known to use such a strategy. Within the beetle order Coleoptera, micromalthid beetles and reticulated beetles are considered unique enough to be placed in their very own suborder appropriately named Archostemata (*arch* = ancient; *stema* = line).

The larvae of the various wood-boring beetles that are found in rotting logs often look very much alike. As their name implies, false darkling beetles of the family Melandryidae (*melan* = black; *dry* = tree) resemble darkling beetles of the family Tenebrionidae (*tenebrio* = lover of darkness). The adult beetles look alike, and the larvae do also. Larvae of darkling beetles are also known as false wireworms because they happen to look like the wireworms that are larvae of click beetles (p.127). Wireworms that live in the soil generally chew on roots, but the wireworms of rotting logs chew mostly on the other beetle larvae that live there. As adults, another family of beetles look so similar to click beetles that they are referred to as false click beetles. Most wood-boring insects bore with the grain of the wood, but larvae of false click beetles bore across the grain; and they bore with jaws that curve out instead of in. Their eating habits must be quite unusual. Despite all the similarities among darkling beetles, false darkling beetles, click beetles, and false click beetles, the larvae of false click beetles are clearly different from all other beetle larvae.

The jaws of stag beetles can be deceiving; beetles with small jaws usually deliver harder pinches than beetles with the largest jaws.

This patent-leather beetle inspects the surface of a rotting log as it transports a group of soil mites on the top of its head.

The patent-leather, or bess, beetles like rotting logs that are well on their way to becoming humus. Adult beetles hang around the log in which their larvae are growing and even present finely chewed wood pulp to their hungry, rapidly growing larvae. The squeaky noises that both larvae and adults produce represent a language that these beetles use among themselves. The noises or stridulations arise whenever a young or old beetle rubs together two different parts of its body. A larva uses its short, stubby, and twisted third pair of legs to strum rough patches of cuticle just above its second pair of legs. The adult beetle rubs a rough patch on the underside of its wings against another rough patch on the dorsal surface of its body.

In the same well-decayed log inhabited by bess beetles, there may be larvae of the stag beetle, a rather formidable-looking relative of the patent-leather beetle. Stag beetle larvae look a great deal like their placid relatives, but the adult beetles can be as threatening as they look. Their large and pointed jaws can deliver a good pinch. Just as certain flashy beetles have been given the name lightningbugs, these beetles with king-size jaws are often called pinchingbugs. The large, lumbering larvae of pinchingbugs and patent-leather beetles devote many hours to wood chewing as they go about converting old, rotting logs to humus and extracting enough nourishment from these old logs to support their large bodies.

STAG BEETLES

CLASSIFICATION

Phylum Arthropoda
Class Insecta
Order Coleoptera
Family Lucanidae

PLACE IN FOOD WEB

Decomposers, Detritivores, Fungivores

SIZE

1.5–4 cm in length

NUMBER OF SPECIES

1,200

PATENT-LEATHER BEETLES

Phylum Arthropoda
Class Insecta
Order Coleoptera
Family Passalidae

PLACE IN FOOD WEB

Decomposers, Detritivores, Fungivores

SIZE

3–4 cm in length

NUMBER OF SPECIES

500

SCARABS AND WHITE GRUBS

CLASSIFICATION
Phylum Arthropoda
Class Insecta
Order Coleoptera
Family Scarabaeidae

PLACE IN FOOD WEB
Herbivores, Diggers

SIZE
1–12.5 cm in length

NUMBER OF SPECIES
25,000

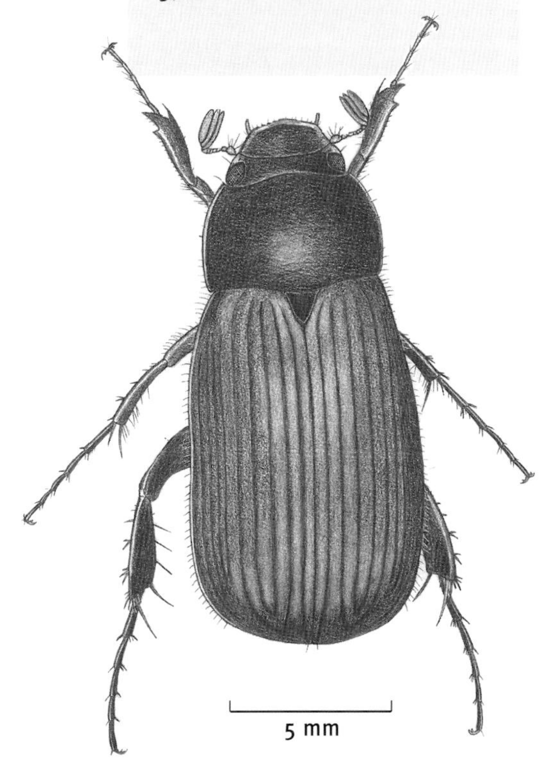

After feeding on roots as larvae, the adult beetle feeds aboveground on leaves, flowers, and fruit.

Scarabs, Weevils, and Grubs

White grubs are sluggish, C-shaped larvae of beetles known as scarabs. These include the well-known May beetles, June beetles, and Japanese beetles. Their appetites for roots of grasses, grains, legumes, trees, and shrubs combined with their abundance in the soil have earned these larvae reputations as devastating pests. To give you some idea just how abundant these white grubs can be, consider the following numbers. Larvae of Japanese beetles average about 175 per square yard or square meter in areas infested by the beetle, but one heavily infested golf course had a population of 1,500 larvae per square yard. For another species of white grub, the density of larvae for the same area was 4,500. One poor, unfortunate corn plant was found to have 200 white grubs between half an inch and 1 inch (12 to 25 millimeters) in length feeding on its roots.

These larvae move up and down in the soil according to the season and the amount of precipitation. Some can descend as deep as 5 feet (1.5 meters) in cold or dry weather, yet at other times they feed only an inch below the soil surface. During their migrations through the soil, white grubs stir up the soil quite a bit. They might wreak havoc with the roots in the neighborhood, but they do improve soil structure and fertility for the roots that will take their place. Some white grubs, like those of Japanese beetles, mature in a single year; others feed on roots for two or three years. In colder climates some may feed underground for four or five years.

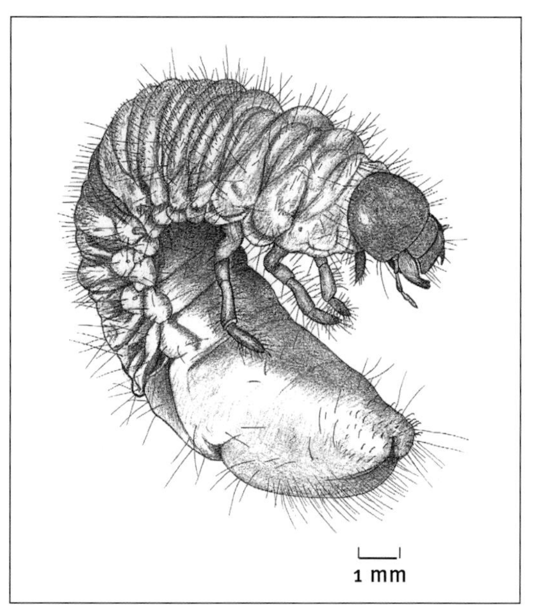

White grubs often spend several years underground.

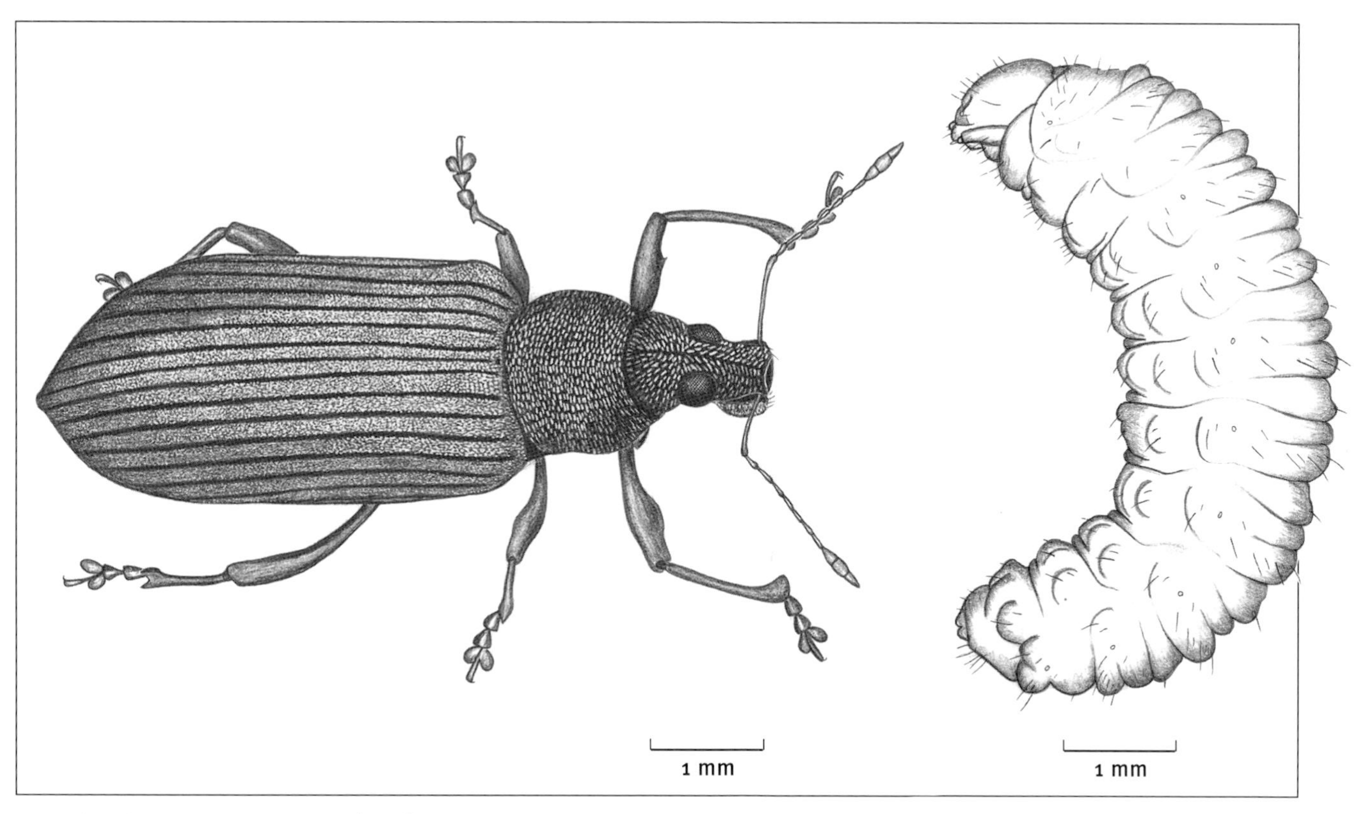

Weevil grubs that feed on roots (right) may be sluggish and sedentary, but they can inflict phenomenal damage on plants. As adult broad-nosed weavils, these beetles can strip many leaves from the same plants.

All weevils are plant feeders and are members of the largest family of beetles on the planet. Because beetles are the largest group of animals, weevils can probably claim to be the largest family in the whole Animal kingdom. All weevils have their jaws located at the end of their prominent snouts that are often referred to as "noses." Different weevils feed on different plant parts, and every plant part is eaten by some weevil somewhere. Some weevils use their snouts for drilling into nuts and have snouts that are longer than their bodies, but the broad-nosed weevils have shorter and broader snouts.

While the adult broad-nosed weevils chew on plants aboveground, the legless larvae or grubs of these weevils nestle underground in cozy chambers within roots. Roots are eaten and occupied by grubs throughout the summer, fall, and winter. As the ground warms in spring, the full-grown larvae pupate and adults emerge in late spring. Adults and grubs usually share the same host plant, and together they can devastate entire fields of vegetables and clover.

WEEVILS AND WEEVIL GRUBS

CLASSIFICATION
Phylum Arthropoda
Class Insecta
Order Coleoptera
Family Curculionidae

PLACE IN FOOD WEB
Herbivores, Diggers

SIZE
2 mm–3 cm in length

NUMBER OF SPECIES
50,000

VARIEGATED MUD-LOVING BEETLES

CLASSIFICATION
Phylum Arthropoda
Class Insecta
Order Coleoptera
Family Heteroceridae

PLACE IN FOOD WEB
Diggers, Dentritivores, Decomposers, Scavengers

SIZE
1–8 mm in length

NUMBER OF SPECIES
300

Variegated Mud-Loving Beetles

Mud-loving beetles hang out in the muddy soil around the edges of ponds and streams. There are actually two families of closely related mud-loving beetles. The minute mud-loving beetles are small and rarely seen. The variegated mud-loving beetles, or heterocerids (*hetero* = different; *ceri* = horn), are larger, more common, and, as their name implies, have a varied coloring: splotches of dull yellow on a background of brown or black. Both the adult beetles and the larvae dig long, winding burrows in the soil. Like moles they often burrow just beneath the surface, heaving the soil as they go and leaving tiny ridges to mark their travels. Sometimes the beetles also erect tiny mud chimneys along their ridges.

Not only are their front pair of legs broad and flat and bordered by spines, but their other two pairs of legs are also beautifully designed for digging. The broad, flat, and powerful mandibles of the mud-loving beetle share in the digging and quicken the pace of excavation. As they dig, the beetles scavenge on the remains of plants and animals that have washed ashore or ended their days on the water's edge. Considering their mucky environments, it is surprising that mud-loving beetles always remain clean and dry. Each beetle is covered with dense silky hair that repels both water and mud. Getting soaked by water or mired in the mud is physically impossible for these beetles.

These beetles are clearly perfectly adapted to life in the mud and can be extremely abundant on the banks of streams and the shores of ponds. One way to find out if there are any mud-loving beetles about is to splash water over the mud by the water's edge. When their burrows are flooded, they quickly head for higher ground and often take to the air.

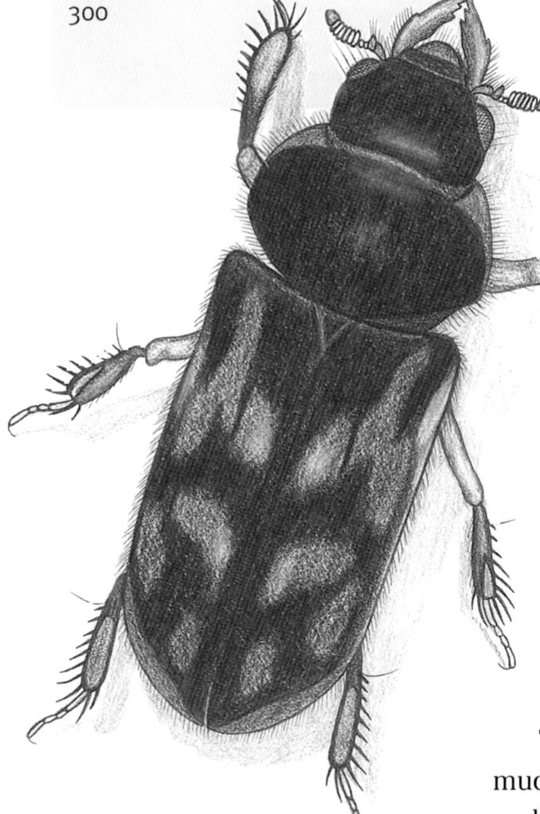

The mud around ponds and streams can be thickly populated and thoroughly excavated by mud-loving beetles.

Fungus Beetles

More species of beetles inhabit our planet than any other order of animals. Many, such as ground beetles and rove beetles, are fast predators both as larvae and adults. Others, such as fireflies, soldier beetles, and click beetles, are predators only as larvae. The sluggish larvae of certain beetles known as grubs lie in underground chambers where they chew on plant roots. Others are attracted by the smell of decay—rotting plants, dead animals, or dung.

Among the most diverse of the beetles are those that live on fungi. Many fungus beetles are unique enough to merit families of their own. There are minute fungus beetles, handsome fungus beetles, hairy fungus beetles, pleasing fungus beetles, dry fungus beetles, shining fungus beetles, round fungus beetles, tooth-necked fungus beetles, silken fungus beetles, and minute tree-fungus beetles. These families of very different fungus beetles contain just some of the beetles that dwell on or feed on fungi of the soil.

Other families of beetles whose contribution to fungal ecology should be acknowledged include the featherwing beetles, sap beetles, hister beetles, short-winged mold beetles, rove beetles, and members of a few other families of the more than 150 families of beetles that are found worldwide. Beetles transport spores of fungi while butterflies and bees transport the pollen of flowering plants. These ancient partnerships have molded the lives and forms of insects, flowers, and fungi.

FUNGUS BEETLES

CLASSIFICATION
Phylum Arthropoda
Class Insecta
Order Coleoptera

PLACE IN FOOD WEB
Fungivores

SIZE
1 mm–2.2 cm in length

NUMBER OF SPECIES
79,000

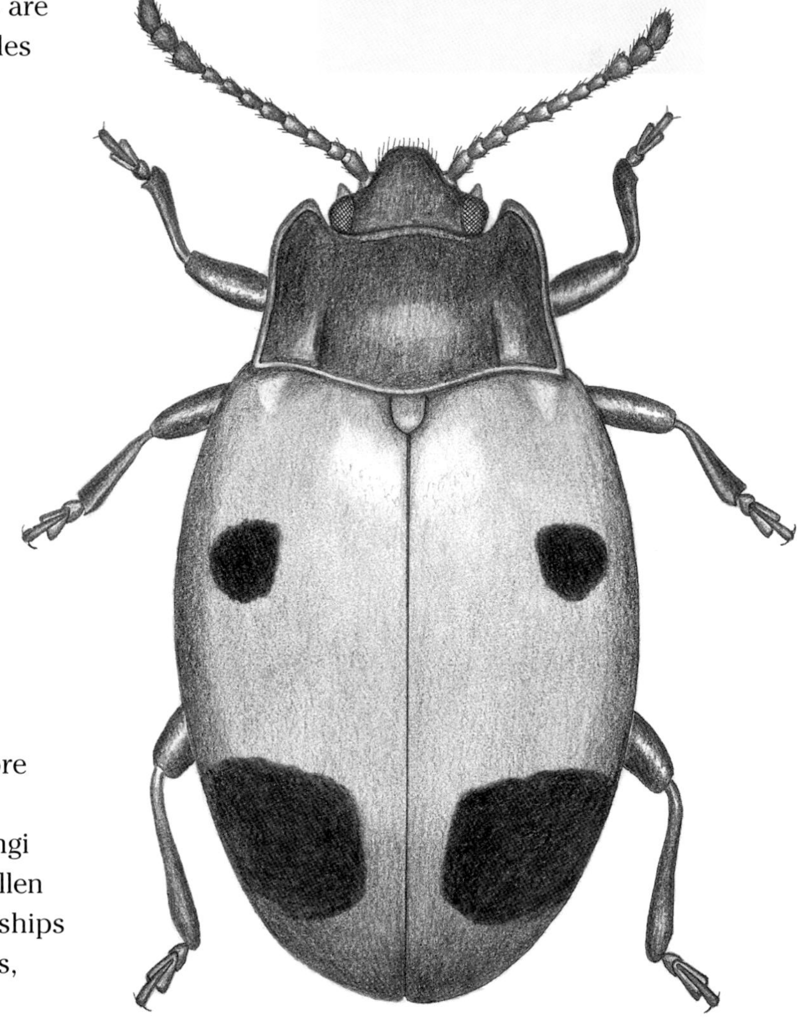

A handsome fungus beetle is only one of many beetles that spend their entire lives in the company of mushrooms and a few other fungi.

SCORPIONFLIES

CLASSIFICATION
Phylum Arthropoda
Class Insecta
Order Mecoptera
Family Bittacidae
(hangingflies)
Family Panorpidae
(common scorpionflies)

PLACE IN FOOD WEB
Decomposers, Detritivores,
Predators

SIZE
1–1.5 cm in length

NUMBER OF SPECIES
400

Scorpionflies

Scorpionflies spend their days and nights in the shadows and thickets of woodland ravines. They begin life in the soil as eggs, larvae, and pupae; only as adults do they leave the soil behind. To anyone who has seen how the males of the scorpionfly family Panorpidae go around with the tips of their abdomens in the air like the tails of scorpions, the choice of name for this group of insects is obvious. The males cannot sting with their tails, but they do use them to maintain a firm grip on the females during mating. Hangingflies, the other common family of scorpionflies, are often mistaken for the more common crane flies. Only crane flies, however, are true flies. Hangingflies and crane flies both have long, spindly legs; hangingfly has four wings, while crane fly has two wings. Only the hangingfly has jaws at the end of its snout. The crane flies, like other true flies, have just two wings and no jaws for chewing, only piercing stylets for retrieving nectar. The hangingfly drapes itself across an insect flyway waiting for whatever insects fly by. The two front legs of the hangingfly firmly grip an overhanging leaf or twig while its other four legs remain poised to snap shut on whatever insect victim happens by. The long legs close like a clamp and then bring the struggling prey to its jaws.

Covered with bumps, spines, and pieces of dirt, scorpionfly larvae scour the litter and surface of the soil for dead worms and insects. In the leaf litter of the forest, one animal's corpse quickly becomes another animal's meal. Here recycling is not optional, but a matter of survival.

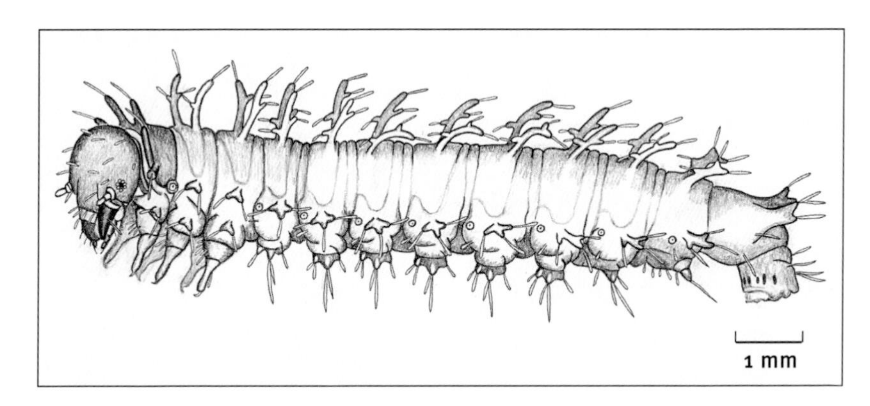

This scorpionfly (left) that hangs from vegetation spreads its legs and awaits the passage of a flying insect. Their characteristic pose has earned these gangly insects the name hangingflies. While the larva of the scorpionfly (above) could be easily mistaken for a caterpillar, the cuticle covering the front of its head is smooth and does not have the lines that divide a caterpillar's head into distinct regions.

Ant Lions

As an ant lion flutters by on a hot summer evening, there is little to hint that this delicate, airborne creature was only a few days earlier a ferocious-looking, earthbound larva. Its family name, Myrmeleontidae, reflects the fierce nature of its larval stage (*myrmex* = ant; *leo* =lion). The best known ant lion larvae are the pit diggers. Since digging a pit takes a good investment of the larva's energy, the mother ant lion has enough forethought to place her eggs in soft soil or sand. The soft, dry soil beneath overhanging cliffs or under the eaves of roofs are often favored spots for egg laying. The newly hatched larva immediately begins construction of the pit that it continually expands and remodels as it molts. For the rest of its larval life, each larva lies buried in the soil at the bottom of its pit, where it grows and molts with only its jaws protruding.

Insects that chance upon the edge of the pit all too often slip inexorably down the slope into the jaws of the ant lion larva. If for any reason an insect's descent into the pit is interrupted, the ant lion will facilitate its fall by flicking sand or soil at the prey. Escape is very unlikely. Once the prey is in the grip of its sickle-shaped jaws, the ant lion secretes digestive juices that pass through its hollow jaws and begin digesting the prey. The two parts of each jaw, the smaller maxilla and the larger mandible, nestle together, with the maxilla overlaying a groove in the mandible. The snug interlocking of maxilla and mandible forms the hollow jaw. A few minutes after the digestive juices have been at work on the prey, the ant lion larva can begin sucking nutrients from its victim.

The body of an ant lion larva is covered from head to tarsal claws with thousands of sensory bristles that are sensitive to even the slightest vibrations of the soil. An ant lion larva is aware that some creature is approaching well before the prey reaches the rim of its pit. By capitalizing on their uncanny abilities to detect nearby movements, larvae of most species of ant lions do not even bother to excavate pits. Instead they can be found patrolling runways on the surface or just beneath the surface of a sandy soil, waiting for some insects or spiders to cross their paths.

ANT LIONS

CLASSIFICATION
Phylum Arthropoda
Class Insecta
Order Neuroptera
Family Mymeleontidae

PLACE IN FOOD WEB
Predators

SIZE
1–2.2 cm in length

NUMBER OF SPECIES
2,000

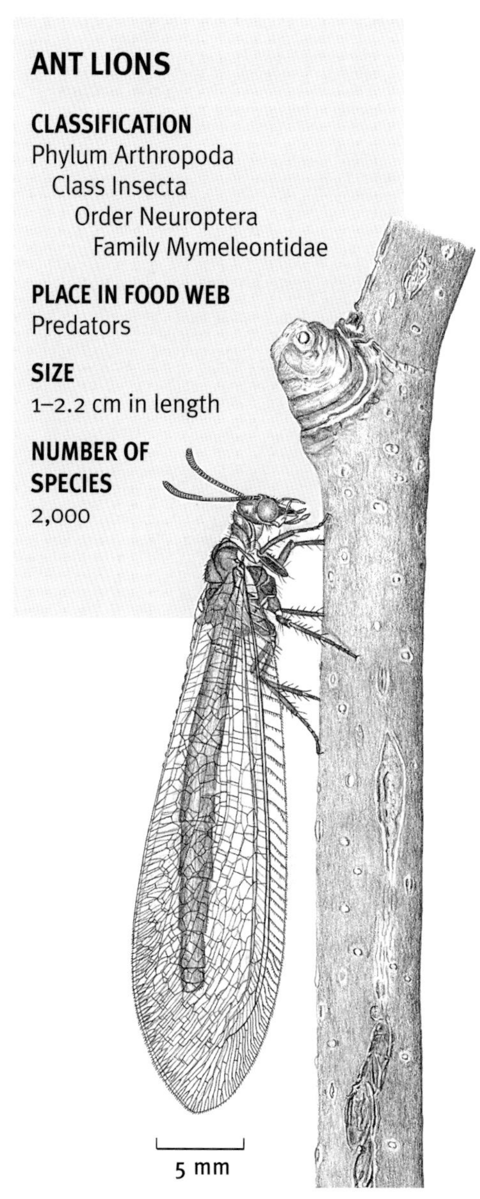

An adult ant lion perches on a sycamore branch.

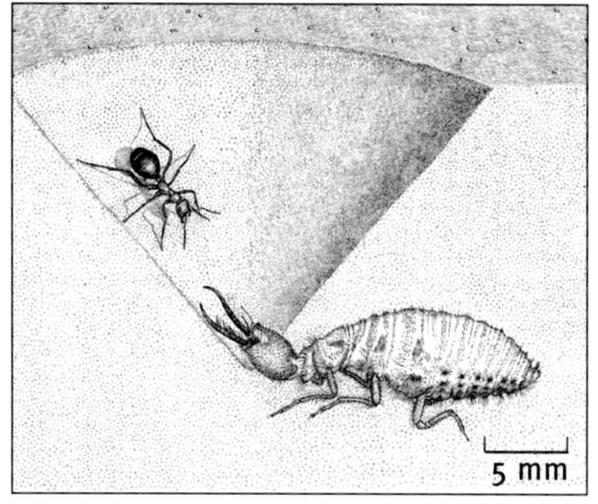

An ant lion larva waits for an ant to slide to the bottom of its pit.

CATERPILLARS AND MOTHS

CLASSIFICATION
Phylum Arthropoda
Class Insecta
Order Lepidoptera
Family Tineidae (clothes moths and relatives)
Family Noctuidae (cutworms)
Family Psychidae (bagworms)

PLACE IN FOOD WEB
Decomposers, Detritivores, Herbivores, Predators

SIZE
6 mm–5 cm in length (mature larvae)

NUMBER OF SPECIES
3,000 clothes moths and relatives
20,000 cutworms
600 bagworms

Caterpillars and Moths

Most of us do not think of those insects with scale-covered wings, the butterflies and moths, as living in the soil, but a few of them actually do live there as caterpillars. Very few of these caterpillars ever turn into butterflies; the majority turn into a number of different moths. Although most caterpillars eat the leaves of green plants, the few that are soil-dwellers survive on roots, decaying plants, and even ants. Some bore into roots where they live and eat until it is time for them to change into moths. Some live in tunnels in the soil into which they retreat when they are not feeding on roots. Wherever logs and leaf litter are decomposing, caterpillars can be found eating the fungi and plant debris. A few butterfly caterpillars even live with ants and feed on ant larvae.

Considering that all together there are about 70 families of moths and eight families of butterflies, it is obvious that not many caterpillars are cut out for life in the soil. Most of the soil-dwelling moths belong to one of three families. The same family to which the infamous clothes-eating moth belongs contains many ground-dwelling caterpillars that spin cases of silk and debris, and then, carry these cases wherever they go. The equally infamous larvae of the bagworm moth family that can strip entire shrubs of leaves have many members of their family begin life in the soil. Each species of bagworm has its own distinctive case made from sand or pieces of plants held together with silk.

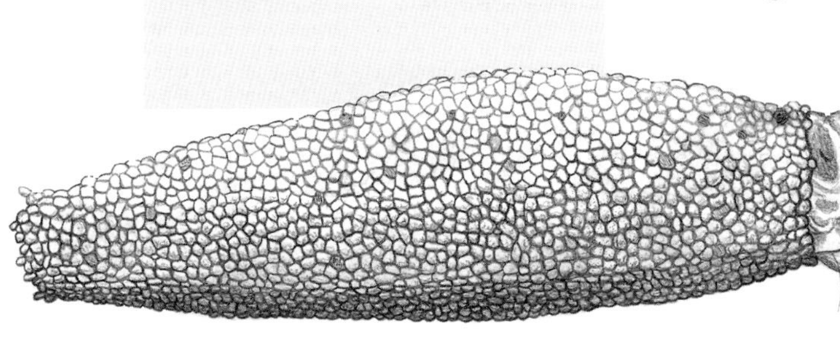

This bagworm caterpillar fashions its portable home from particles of the soil as well as with silk from glands near its jaws.

A few other ground-dwelling caterpillars belong to the family that includes the armyworms and cutworms—caterpillars that are considered serious pests of gardens and crops. Certainly some of the more eccentric caterpillars live in the soil. They have forsaken eating fresh, green leaves for brown, decaying leaves; a few of these ground-dwelling caterpillars have even developed a taste for dung. One desert caterpillar is known to have a preference for the dung of gopher tortoises, and a tropical species feeds exclusively on sloth dung.

March Flies, Crane Flies, and Soldier Flies

In most soils and leaf litter, fly larvae can often outnumber any other group of insects, even the very abundant beetles. Like beetle larvae, the larvae of flies have adapted to a wide range of diets—decaying leaves, fungi, algae, and other insects. Some fly larvae can be very abundant in particular soils. Flies, like the March flies, are not only most abundant in March and other months of spring, but they also have a tendency to place all of their 200 to 300 eggs in a single batch rather than scattering them over the ground. March fly larvae may number 3,000 to 12,000 per square yard or square meter, yet be nonexistent only a few feet or meters away. A few March fly larvae may chew on roots of living plants and are considered pests, but most species chew on dead parts of plants and are considered important recyclers.

Most people have the impression that all fly larvae look more or less the same, but a quick comparison of March fly larvae, crane fly, or tipulid larvae, and soldier fly, or stratiomyid (*stratio* = soldier; *myia* = fly) larvae, from leaf litter points out some obvious differences. Tipulid larvae usually have fleshy lobes on only their rear segment while larvae of March flies often have fleshy lobes on all body segments behind their heads. The flat larvae of soldier flies have none of these lobes, but they do have a very tough skin covered with calcium deposits. Tipulid larvae and stratiomyid larvae have two conspicuous spiracles, or breathing holes, on their rear segment, but larvae of March flies have spiracles on all but one segment of the thorax and all but one segment of the abdomen. After seeing them a few times, these larvae are easily distinguished from each other.

Judging from the large numbers of tipulid larvae, as well as the numerous stratiomyid larvae that are usually found in samples of leaf litter, these fly larvae are important recyclers of decaying leaves. Crane flies make up the largest family of flies with 14,000 species worldwide, about a tenth of them are

MARCH FLIES

CLASSIFICATION
Phylum Arthropoda
Class Insecta
Order Diptera
Family Bibionidae

PLACE IN FOOD WEB
Decomposers, Detritivores, Fungivores, Algal eaters, Herbivores

SIZE
6 mm–2.5 cm in length (mature larvae)

NUMBER OF SPECIES
700

CRANE FLIES

CLASSIFICATION
Phylum Arthropoda
Class Insecta
Order Diptera
Family Tipulidae

PLACE IN FOOD WEB
Decomposers, Detritivores, Fungivores, Algal eaters, Herbivores

SIZE
3 mm–6 cm in length (mature larvae)

NUMBER OF SPECIES
14,000

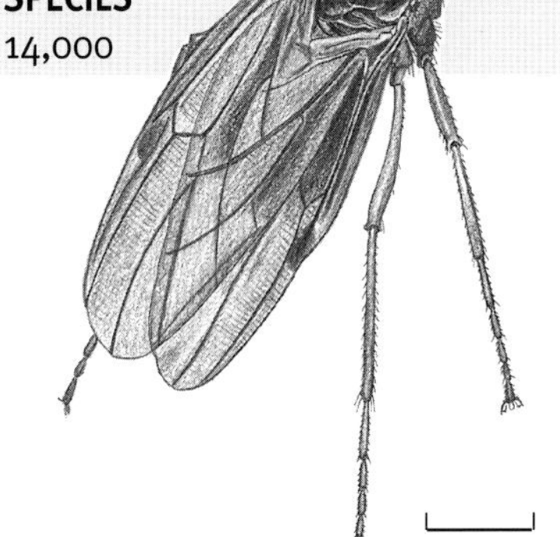

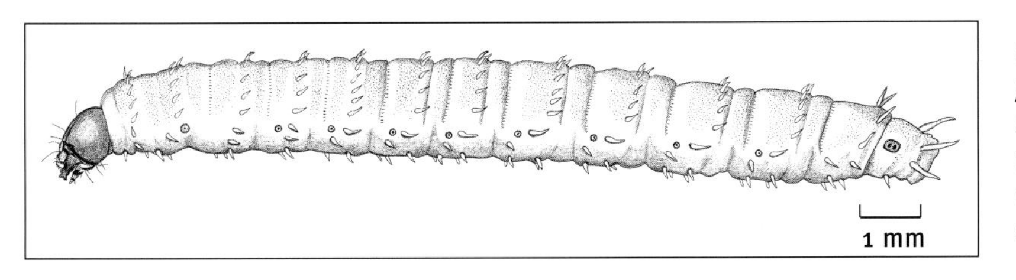

In the American Midwest this March fly is more common in April than it is in March. In April, vast numbers of these flies can emerge from the soil where they have spent the last year as larvae (left).

SOLDIER FLIES

CLASSIFICATION
Phylum Arthropoda
Class Insecta
Order Diptera
Family Stratiomyidae

PLACE IN FOOD WEB
Decomposers, Detritivores, Fungivores, Algal eaters, Herbivores

SIZE
5 mm–3.5 cm in length (mature larvae)

NUMBER OF SPECIES
2,000

found in the United States. Soldier flies, with 2,000 species around the world and about 300 in North America, are still considered a large family. A tipulid larva has rasping jaws and a head that can be retracted into its thorax.

Most larvae use their jaws to chew on moldy leaves; but a few tipulid larvae known as leatherjackets have acquired a taste for roots of crop plants and, at least in Europe, have been a considerable annoyance to farmers. The tough skins of soldier fly larvae are covered with a few long bristles and are reinforced with thousands of grains of calcium carbonate. Under the microscope these circular grains that measure about 1/5,000 inch (5 µm) across are arranged in highly ordered geometric arrays over the entire surface of the larva. With this impervious armor, the larvae can survive the summer droughts that often strike even moist pockets of leaf litter. Although the soil algae and fungi that the larvae often swallow along with decaying leaves may wither and perish, the stratiomyid larvae endure until the rains come again.

After metamorphosis, life changes drastically for fly larvae. Tipulids transform into thin flies with long, spindly legs and are often mistaken for overgrown mosquitoes or certain scorpionflies. The family name of Tipulidae is derived from a Latin name for spider (*tipula*) and no doubt refers to those long, ungainly legs. It is hard to imagine that some of these delicate flies in their younger days were tough, voracious larvae known as leatherjackets. These flies have exchanged the hard chewing mandibles of their larval days for delicate stylets that sip nectar and feed at sap flows.

Adult soldier flies give up life in the leaf litter to spread their wings and fly among the flowers. They are nectar feeders, many of them being colorful and uncanny impersonators of wasps. Those of one species, with their metallic blue color and white-stockinged feet, look just like mud dauber wasps. After being stung once, most birds know enough to stay clear of wasps and their stingers; any insect that looks like a wasp is given the same respect.

2 mm

Crane flies gracefully maneuver their long, lanky legs as they fly through the forest undergrowth. Their larvae (below), however, are completely legless and only have appendages at their tail ends.

2 mm

2 mm

This soldier fly (above) is a common visitor to compost piles, where its larva (below) is a common resident.

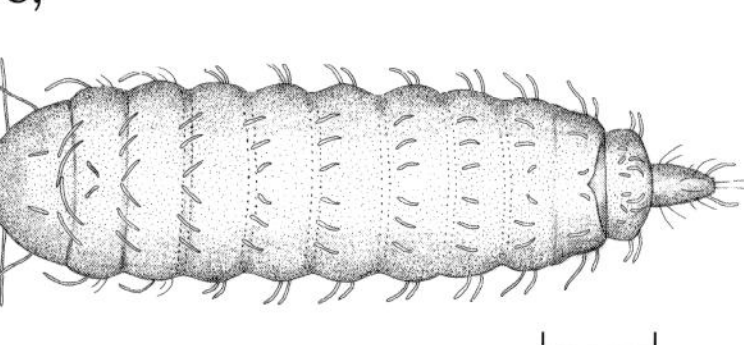

1 mm

Midges and Biting Midges

Larvae of midges are considered useful indicators of water quality in flowing waters. Some species can tolerate polluted streams, while other species are only found in unpolluted waters. The presence of certain midge larvae in a soil is probably also a good indication of soil quality. Species of soil-dwelling midges are not as numerous as those of ponds and streams nor are they as well studied as the aquatic members of their family. Like their aquatic relatives, however, soil midges recycle plant debris and feed on the tiny algae that are scattered throughout the debris.

Midge larvae, like all fly larvae, do not have true jointed legs, but they do have two pairs of fleshy prolegs without any joints whatsoever. One of these pairs projects beneath and behind the head of the larvae, the other pair is found on the very last segment. The tip of each proleg is crowned by a circle of curved spines. These spines and prolegs probably provide enough traction for the larvae to wriggle their way through the leaf litter.

Small clouds of adult midges often hover just above the ground where they once wriggled as larvae. An insect net swept through one of these swarms almost always catches only male midges. A female periodically flies into the swarm, and one of the males immediately claims her as a mating partner. There is little time and little place for courtship in midge society.

Midges of the family Chironomidae have some infamous relatives in the smaller family Ceratopogonidae, known as biting midges, no-see-ums, or punkies. These minuscule flies not only annoy us humans with their blood-sucking habits, they also take blood from the wing veins of larger insects like moths, dragonflies, and beetles. Biting midges may not feast as well on insect blood as they do on human blood, but at least they do not have to worry about being swatted; they may be smaller than 1/25 inch (1 millimeter), but their bites are mighty and out of proportion to their diminutive sizes.

MIDGES

CLASSIFICATION
Phylum Arthropoda
Class Insecta
Order Diptera
Family Chironomidae

PLACE IN FOOD WEB
Decomposers, Detritivores, Fungivores, Algal eaters

SIZE
1.5 mm–3 cm in length (mature larvae)

NUMBER OF SPECIES
5,000

BITING MIDGES

CLASSIFICATION
Phylum Arthropoda
Class Insecta
Order Diptera
Family Ceratopogonidae

PLACE IN FOOD WEB
Decomposers, Detritivores, Fungivores, Algal eaters

SIZE
2 mm–1 cm in length (mature larvae)

NUMBER OF SPECIES
1,200

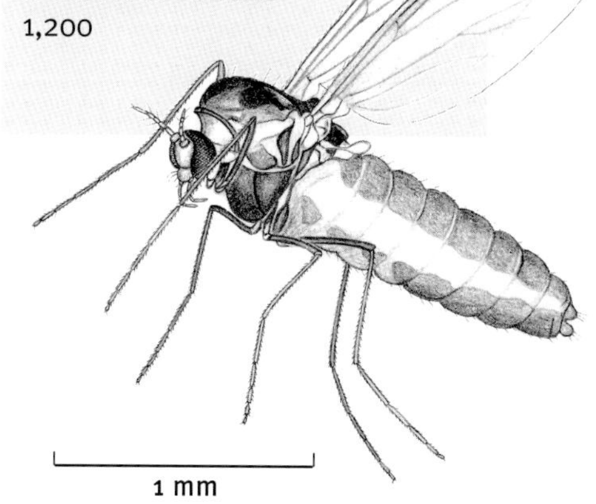

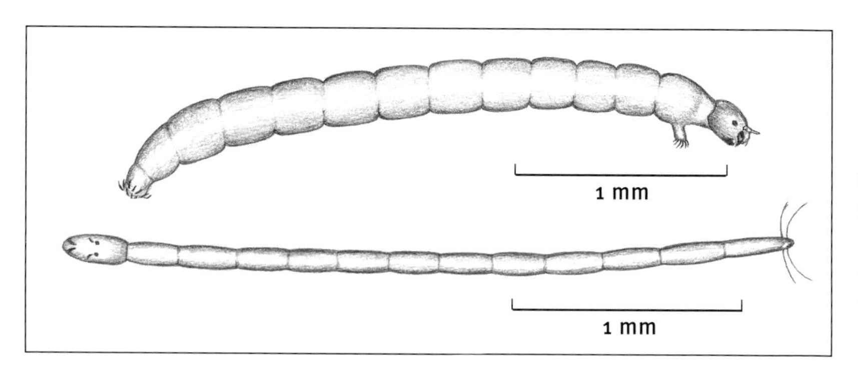

The clouds of midges that hover a few inches or a few feet above the soil are often made up of hundreds, sometimes thousands, of males. In a small scoop of forest soil, midge larvae (upper left) as well as biting midge larvae (lower left) can be unbelievably abundant.

MOTH FLIES

CLASSIFICATION
Phylum Arthropoda
Class Insecta
Order Diptera
Family Psychodidae

PLACE IN FOOD WEB
Decomposers, Detritivores, Fungivores, Algal eaters

SIZE
3–6 mm in length (mature larvae)

NUMBER OF SPECIES
450

Moth Flies

Most of us are acquainted with the fuzzy moth flies that parade at times on the edges of our bathroom sinks and the walls of our showers. They actually look like tiny moths with exceptionally long antennae and fidgety movements. The country relatives of our household moth flies live in the leaf litter and are far less conspicuous, but nevertheless they are down there at all seasons, scavenging decaying plant matter along with algae and fungi.

Some moth fly larvae, like the one pictured below, don chunks of soil upon the long bristles that cover their backs. Their earthy attire probably serves as an effective camouflage and protection, at least from us humans, for the only time you are likely to spot any of these earth-colored larvae from soil and leaf litter is when they happen to fall into a white-bottomed collecting jar.

1 mm

This moth fly grew up in the moist soil of an oak forest, but a few desert species live in animal burrows. Most adult moth flies survive on sugary or decaying plant material; but in the tropics and around the Mediterranean, some flies are blood suckers and carriers of human disease.

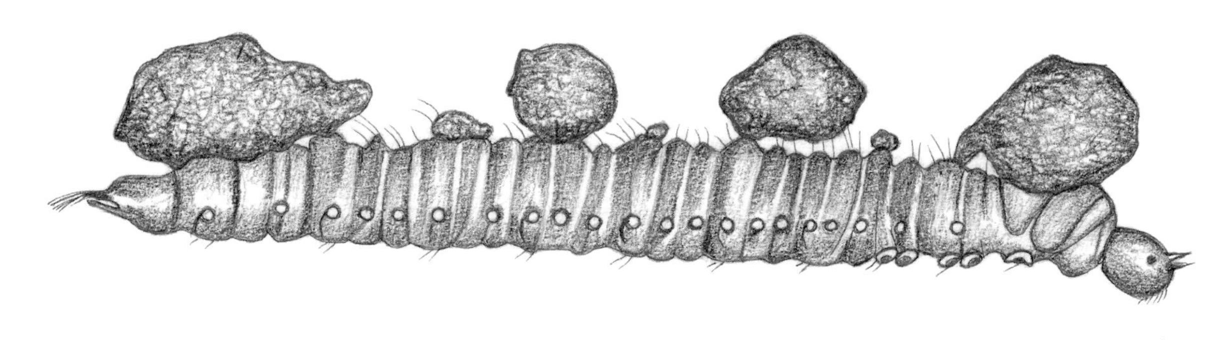

Snipe Flies

SNIPE FLIES

CLASSIFICATION
Phylum Arthropoda
Class Insecta
Order Diptera
Family Rhagionidae

PLACE IN FOOD WEB
Predators

SIZE
6 mm–1.5 cm in length (mature larvae)

NUMBER OF SPECIES
400

In late spring and early summer, snipe flies leave the forest litter where they have lived for most of the past year. They search for perches on plants of the forest understory and there await the arrival of passersby that are slow enough for them to catch and eat. A common and lovely snipe fly by the name of *Chrysopilus* (*chryso* = gold; *pilus* = cap) stands out among the flies. The iridescent disc of gold scales on its thorax and the patches of white scales on its black abdomen impart a singular beauty to this fly with dappled wings. But its stay aboveground is an ephemeral one. By the end of June few snipe flies remain to cruise the understory of the forest. They have laid their eggs in the soil litter, and their larvae will prey on other insects of the leaf litter until the following spring when they grow their first legs, spread their wings, and take to the air.

Some close relatives of snipe flies live in sandy or dusty habitats where the larvae lie at the bottom of pits, waiting until some insect or spider chances by and slips into their jaws. This lifestyle may sound very familiar. Because larvae of ant lions use a very similar strategy to capture prey, the fly larvae are by analogy called worm lions. Their scientific names were also chosen to reflect their parallel lives. Ant lions belong to the family Myrmeleontidae (*myrmex* = ant; *leo* = lion), and worm lions belong to the family Vermileonidae (*vermi* = worm; *leo* =lion). Until recently worm lions were considered eccentric members of the snipe fly family, but now they have been assigned to this small family of their own with about 27 species of flies found in dusty places around the world.

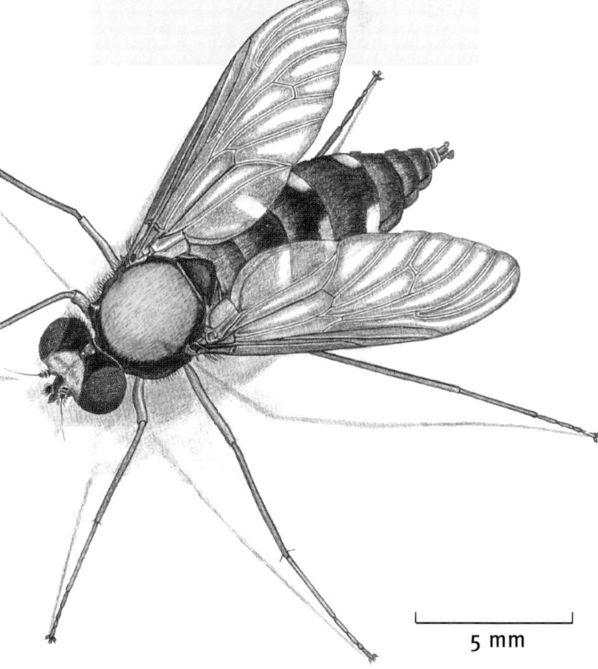

From the leaf litter, these larvae of rhagionid flies (below) snipe at other soil arthropods; and from the dense undergrowth of the forest, the adult flies (above) later snipe at passing insects.

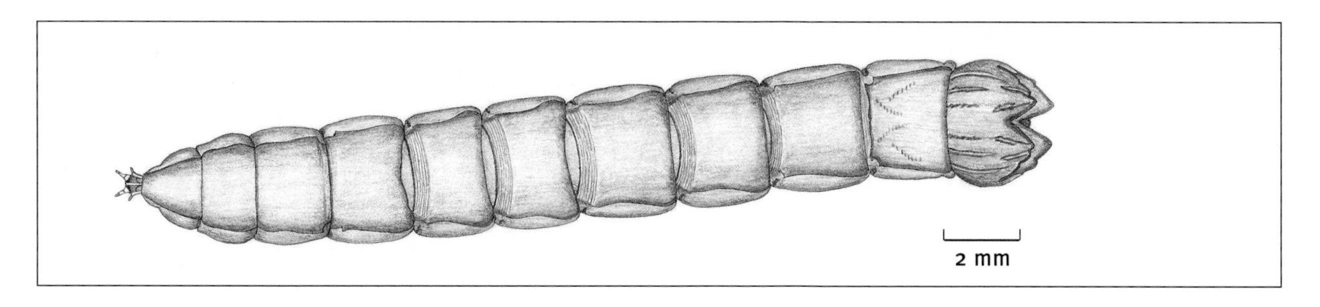

ROBBER FLIES

CLASSIFICATION
Phylum Arthropoda
Class Insecta
Order Diptera
Family Asilidae

PLACE IN FOOD WEB
Predators

SIZE
8 mm–3.5 cm in length (mature larvae)

NUMBER OF SPECIES
5,000

Robber flies can be considered the thugs of the flies, pouncing on prey as large as grasshoppers and dragonflies or as threatening as stinging bees and wasps. The larvae (below) will attack beetle grubs that are twice their size.

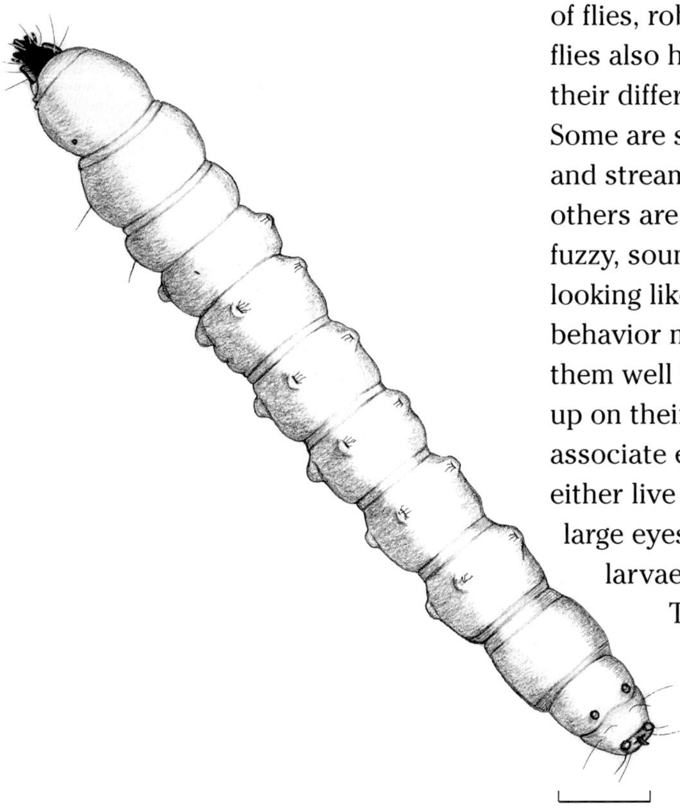

1 mm

Robber Flies

Slightly later in the summer, robber flies take up some of the same posts that were occupied by snipe flies. Robber flies constantly dash off in pursuit of passing insects but return again and again to their favorite posts. These flies have all the features an effective predator should have. With their long, sturdy legs and big claws, they do not hesitate to pounce on insects just as large or even larger than they are. Their bite is quick and potent, as anyone who has tangled with one knows. Their large, bulging eyes endow them with keen vision for discerning shapes and movements.

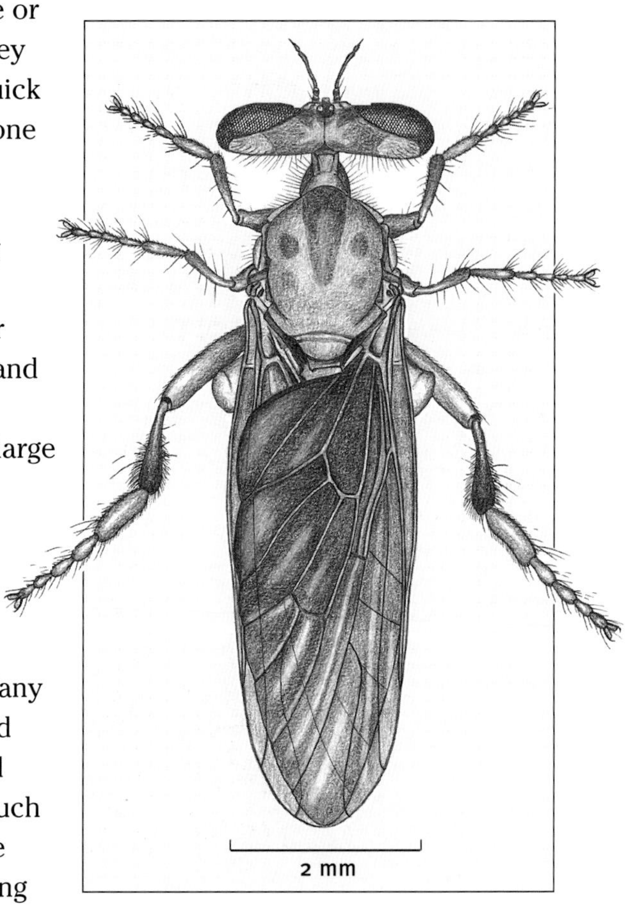

Coming from a large and diverse family of flies, robber flies also have their differences. Some are slender and streamlined. Many others are stout and fuzzy, sounding and looking like bees. Such behavior may serve them well in sneaking up on their prey as well as protecting them from birds that associate eating a bee with being stung. Larvae of robber flies either live in the soil or in well-decayed logs. Even without the large eyes, sturdy legs, and strong wings of their parents, the larvae manage quite well as predators of other larvae. Their bodies are long, smooth, and tapered at both ends. They can probably move faster than most soil larvae, and they feed on enough of these larvae to grow as long as an inch (25 millimeters) or more.

2 mm

Bee Flies

The parasitic larvae of an unusual family of flies have an uncanny ability to find hosts that live underground. These are the bee flies. The adults are fuzzy like bees; they buzz like bees; and they are shaped like bees. They even hover and visit flowers like bees. They are among the few insects that visit the very first flowers of spring. The mother bee fly simply drops an egg near the burrow of a likely host, and the lively larva that hatches from the egg goes off on its own in pursuit of a host. Several hundred different species of bee flies live in the United States, and they choose their hosts from among the beetles, flies, moths, ant lions, digger bees, and grasshopper eggs that are found in the soil. Some bee fly larvae specialize in finding ant lion larvae, others feed only on grasshopper eggs, and one common species is a parasite of the ferocious-looking larvae of tiger beetles. Having expended a great deal of energy finding its host, the bee fly larva finally settles down and molts into a lethargic larva that grows at its host's expense.

BEE FLIES

CLASSIFICATION
Phylum Arthropoda
Class Insecta
Order Diptera
Family Bombyliidae

PLACE IN FOOD WEB
Parasites

SIZE
9 mm–2.2 cm in length (mature larvae)

NUMBER OF SPECIES
3,000

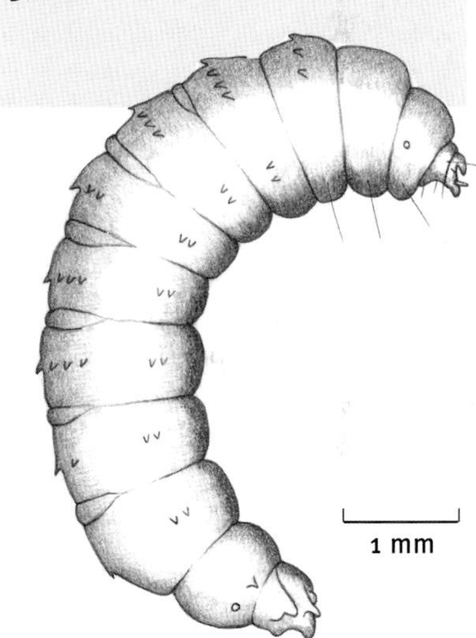

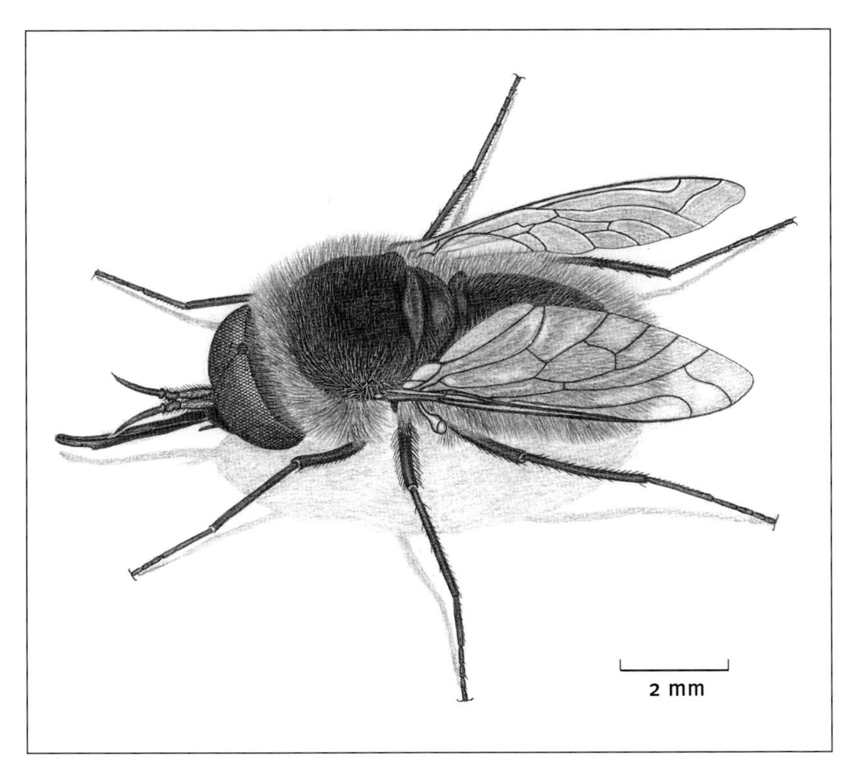

The bee fly may look like a bee and buzz like a bee, but it neither stings nor bites. Its menacing-looking proboscis is used only for sipping nectar. Its larva (above right) is a sluggish parasite of other insects that live underground.

LONG-LEGGED FLIES

CLASSIFICATION
Phylum Arthropoda
Class Insecta
Order Diptera
Family Dolichopodidae

PLACE IN FOOD WEB
Decomposers, Predators, Detritivores

SIZE
6 mm–2.2 cm in length (mature larvae)

NUMBER OF SPECIES
6,000

Long-Legged Flies

These sprightly flies prance about on vegetation with their long, spindly legs. Their family name, Dolichopodidae (*dolicho* = long; *podi* = foot, leg), conveys just one of the many striking features of these handsome little flies. They have long legs as well as long feet, or tarsi. Both males and females are iridescent green and blue. As if their lustrous colors were not sufficient embellishment, male flies have a variety of other adornments that impress female flies looking for just the right mates. During courtship the males show off the ornaments on their legs or antennae as well as their large, conspicuous genitalia. Some insects may lead retiring lives and are rarely observed, but dolichopodid flies are commonly seen and are rarely forgotten.

As predators of smaller flies, the adults move in quickly to attack and feed. Like the larvae of all flies, those of long-legged flies are legless, but they have streamlined forms and wriggle gracefully through the humus and rotting leaves that they call home. Far more is known about the colorful adults than the larvae that travel the passageways of the leaf litter. Like the adult flies, some larvae may be hunters of other insects, but probably most dolichopodid larvae graze on decaying plant matter, breaking it down in order to build the rich reserves of humus that characterize healthy soils.

1 mm

Long-legged flies often perch on the vegetation bordering ponds or small streams, not far from the moist soil where they spent their days as larvae (below).

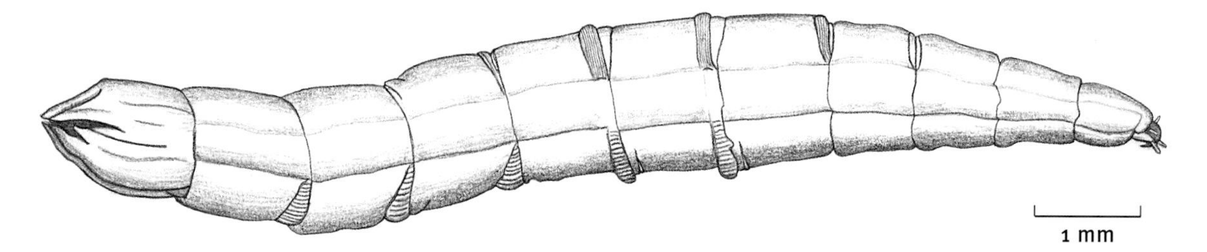

Picture-Winged Flies

Root nodules are remarkable resources that nourish plants, bacteria, and certain animals of the soil that have discovered the nodules to be some of the most nutritious portions of plants. Even though plant tissues are always rich in sugars and carbohydrates, root nodules of plants contain all these nutrients as well as millions of bacteria. Certain enterprising maggots of one fly family have developed a special relationship with rhizobia and root nodules. Maggots of platystomatid (*platy* = flat; *stomato* = mouth), or picture-winged flies, may look like ordinary maggots, but they certainly do not behave like ordinary maggots. Unsavory environments like decaying flesh or rotting leaves are the usual haunts of most maggots; but rather than scavenge in such places, platystomatid maggots have acquired distinctive and refined tastes. Newly hatched maggots navigate through the soil beneath plants with root nodules and survive by eating these nodules. Since a single plant can have hundreds of nodules on its roots, these maggots always have an abundant source of nutrient-packed food. What is surprising is that more creatures have not discovered this resource of the soil.

PICTURE-WINGED FLIES

CLASSIFICATION
Phylum Arthropoda
Class Insecta
Order Diptera
Family Platystomatidae

PLACE IN FOOD WEB
Herbivores

SIZE
4–9 mm in length (mature larvae)

NUMBER OF SPECIES
1,000

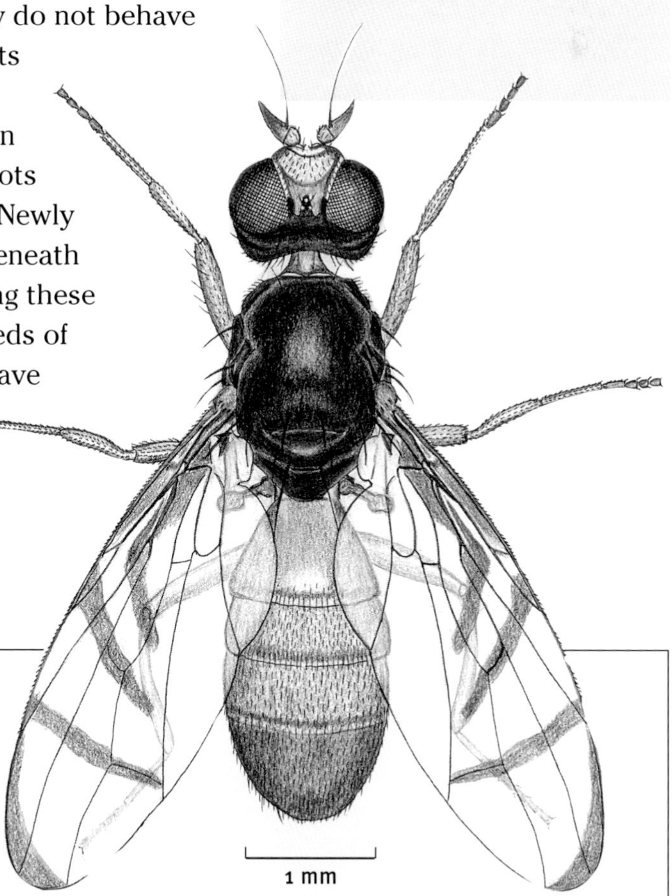

1 mm

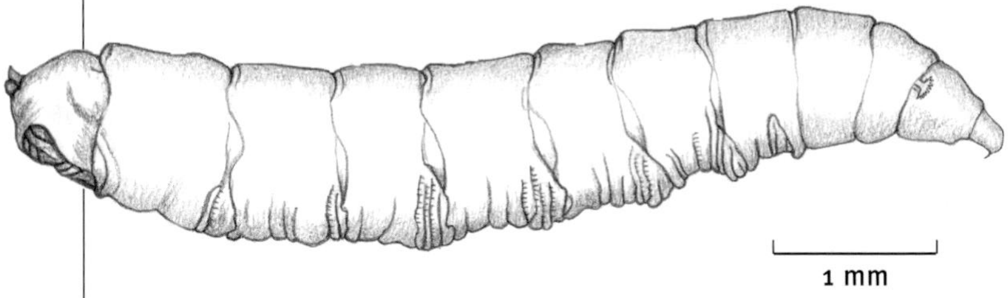

1 mm

Picture-winged flies have developed a special relationship with root nodules. Rhizobial bacteria of root nodules not only enrich the soil by converting dinitrogen gas from the air to ammonia, but they also nourish the larvae of this picture-winged fly (left).

GALL WASPS

CLASSIFICATION
Phylum Arthropoda
Class Insecta
Order Hymenoptera
Family Cynipidae

PLACE IN FOOD WEB
Herbivores

SIZE
1–8 mm in length

NUMBER OF SPECIES
1,200

Gall Wasps

On February days, often on snow-covered ground, tiny, stingless wasps crawl out of the leaf litter and begin their long trek from the soil to the treetops. These obscure little wasps have one of the strangest genealogies you can imagine. Not many people witness the migration of these wingless insects that look more like fleas than wasps. They have just emerged from chambers in the leaf litter, called galls, where they have passed the autumn and the earlier days of winter. Their lives began the summer before when their mothers laid eggs on leaves or buds of an oak tree. Either the act of the mother wasp's egg laying or some stimulus from the newly hatched wasp larva resulted in the part of the leaf or bud around the egg growing into a gall that sheltered and nourished the young gall wasp until the lengthening days of February told it that the time had come to begin its pilgrimage back to the branches where it had spent its youth.

Some galls are plain and simple growths, others are elaborate and ornate. All the wasps that emerge from the galls in the leaf litter are virgin females, and they are on their way to lay eggs on the new buds of the oak trees, where new and different galls will form around the eggs that they lay. Wasps that issue from these galls look very different from their mothers. In the insect world, virgin births are commonplace events. Even though a wingless female has no males to court her and does not expend any precious energy on mating during the chilly days of February, her children will include both males and females.

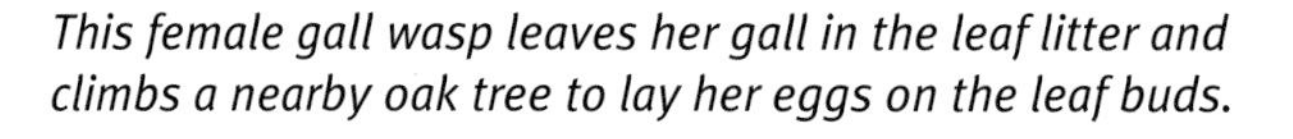

This female gall wasp leaves her gall in the leaf litter and climbs a nearby oak tree to lay her eggs on the leaf buds.

1 mm

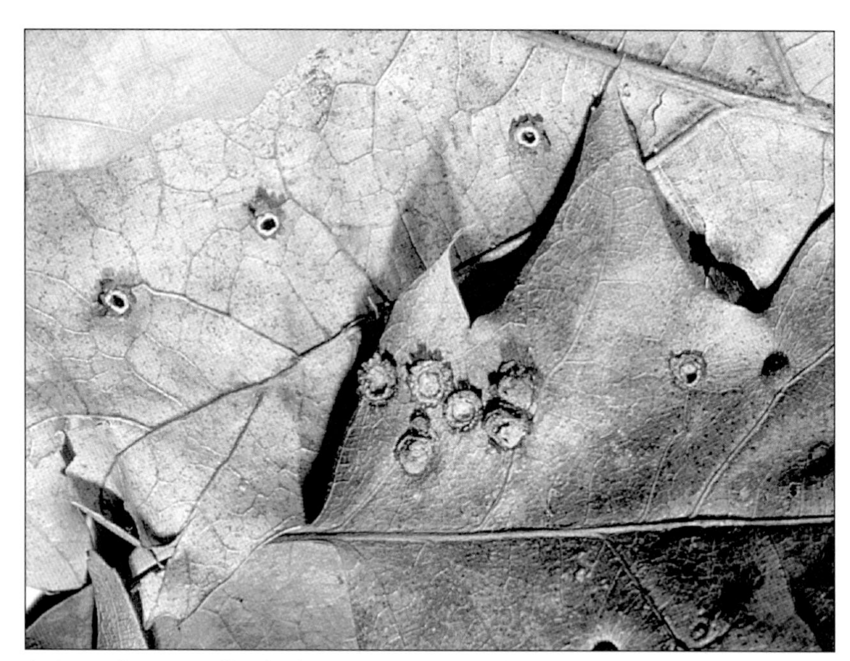

In late winter, small, stingless wasps emerge from these galls that have formed on oak leaves the summer before and that have lain on the forest floor since autumn.

Unlike their mother's generation, however, all her children have wings, mate, and give birth to another generation of all female wasps. The generation of male and female wasps hatch from unfertilized eggs, while the generation of all female wasps hatch from fertilized eggs. The generations of gall wasps alternate, with grandmothers and granddaughters having more in common than mothers and daughters. Fathers never have sons, only grandsons. Mothers always have daughters and granddaughters, but only in alternate generations do they have sons or grandsons. No wonder biologists were puzzled by the strange ways of gall wasps until the German scientist Hermann Adler had the patience in 1875 to rear many of these wasps and to observe carefully the relationships among wasps, their galls, and their sex lives.

PARASITIC WASPS

CLASSIFICATION
Phylum Arthropoda
Class Insecta
Order Hymenoptera
Suborder Apocrita

PLACE IN FOOD WEB
Parasites

SIZE
1 mm–4 cm in length

NUMBER OF SPECIES
100,000

Parasitic Wasps

Parasitic wasps scurry about on spindly legs, waving and tapping their antennae as they track down the odors of their hosts. Unlike parasitic tapeworms and roundworms, parasitic wasps only choose other insects, spiders, mites, and a few other arthropods as hosts. All types of arthropods of the leaf litter—predators, decomposers, herbivores, and even other parasitic wasps—can be hosts for the larvae of parasitic wasps. About 15 percent of all insect species are parasitic, and half of the estimated 200,000 species of Hymenoptera (bees, wasps, ants) are parasites. Some wasps are very specific about which hosts and which host stage they choose; others are less particular and are content with trusting their eggs to any number of eligible hosts. Many parasitic wasps of the soil, like some tiny gall wasps and tiny flies of the leaf litter, have completely lost their wings. Down in the cramped spaces of the leaf litter and the tortuous passageways of the soil where mother wasps go in search of the best hosts for their eggs, wings are probably more of a hindrance than an asset.

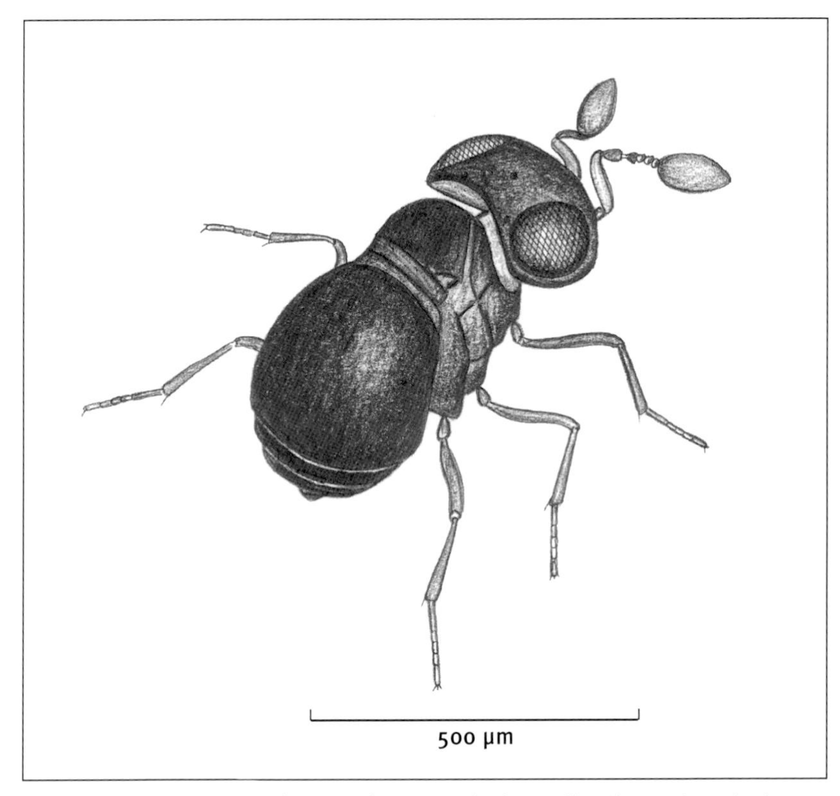

This tiny parasitic wasp chooses the eggs of other soil arthropods as its hosts.

Digger Bees and Velvet Ants

Before honey bees arrived from the Old World in the 1600s, native bees such as sweat bees and mining bees were the only bees that visited and pollinated the flowers of the New World. Most of these bees are digger bees that nest in the soil. Even though each bee digs its own burrow, it often digs it only an inch or two (25–50 millimeters) from the burrow of another bee. So many burrows may exist side by side that a community of digger bees may cover many acres, and as many as 1.5 million bees may nest on an acre (4,840 square yards; 4,050 square meters) of land. By far the largest community of digger bees ever recorded was discovered in 1963 along the River Barysh

DIGGER BEES

CLASSIFICATION
Phylum Arthropoda
Class Insecta
Order Hymenoptera
Family Andrenidae
Family Halictidae
Family Colletidae
Family Apidae

PLACE IN FOOD WEB
Diggers, Herbivores

SIZE
5 mm–1.5 cm in length

NUMBER OF SPECIES
20,000

VELVET ANTS

CLASSIFICATION
Phylum Arthropoda
Class Insecta
Order Hymenoptera
Family Mutillidae

PLACE IN FOOD WEB
Parasites of insects

SIZE
6 mm–2 cm in length

NUMBER OF SPECIES
5,000

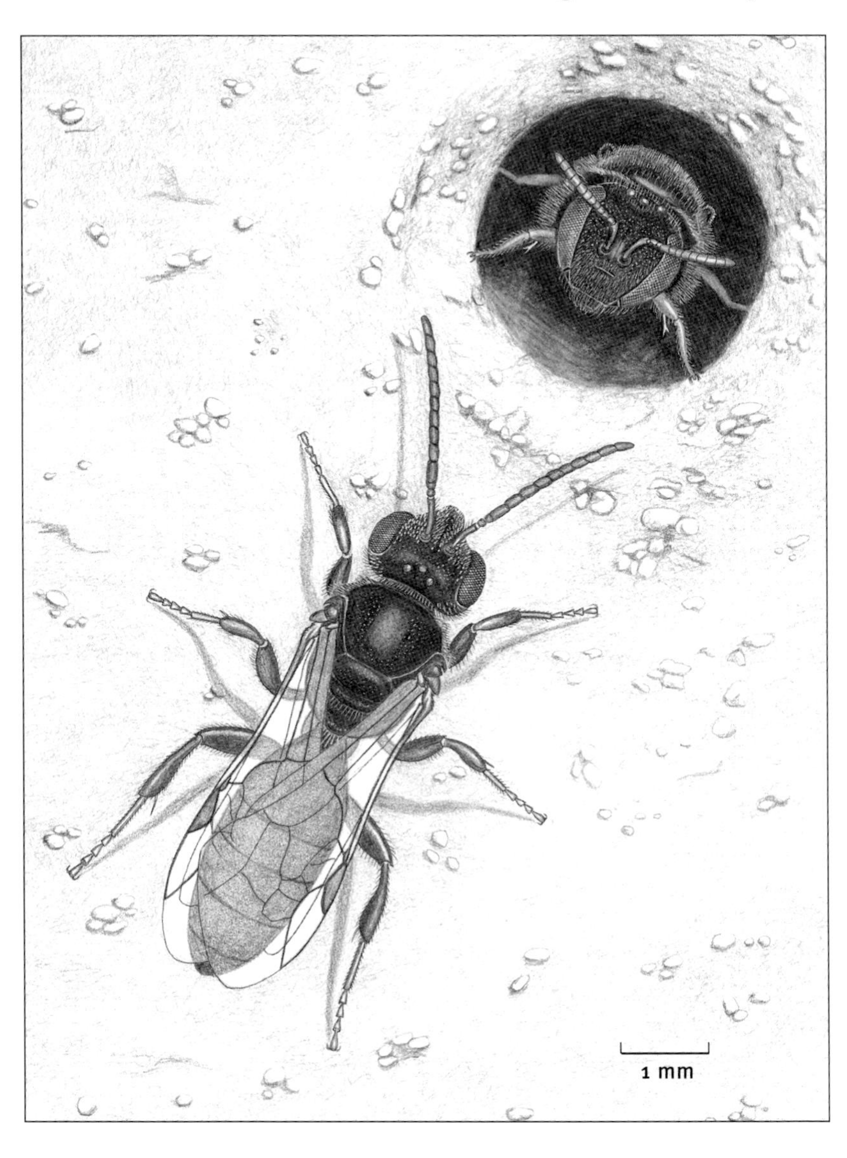

A male halictid bee (left) awaits the first appearance of a newly emerged female halictid bee from her brood nest.

that flows through Russia. There, along a four-mile (6.4-kilometer) stretch of one river bank, 12.2 million nests covered an area of about 90 acres (435,600 square yards; 364,590 square meters or 36.5 hectares). These nests of digger bees can take a number of forms, with each species of bee having its own architectural design. Some bees dig burrows only two or three inches (50–75 millimeters) deep whereas other bees may dig down two or three feet (60–90 centimeters). Anywhere from one to many chambers containing immature bees and known as brood cells can be arranged either horizontally or vertically around the main shaft of a burrow. Sometimes the brood cells are clustered like grapes at the end of the main shaft, sometimes they are spaced at wider intervals along its length. Within each of the brood cells the mother bee places a mixture of pollen and honey. Just the right amount is added to carry each bee larva through its metamorphosis.

Mining bees of the family Andrenidae leave their burrows only in the spring, exactly when the particular pollen and nectar that they supply to their brood cells is available. The life cycle of each bee is intimately coupled to the life cycle of its favorite spring flowers. After mining bees mate and lay their eggs, their larvae grow quickly in the brood cells, transforming to pupae by early summer. Here they wait through the winter for another spring and the arrival of their short-lived host flowers. For some species of mining bees, no other flowers seem to suffice.

In the spring, sweat bees of the family Halictidae begin appearing as well. All the sweat bees that wintered in the soil are females that mated the previous autumn. They begin their life aboveground by digging new brood nests and then stocking them with honey and pollen for their larvae. By midsummer bees begin emerging from the brood nests, with the males appearing first. Vast numbers of males cruise over the thousands of burrows in the community of digger bees, awaiting the emergence of the females. On a hot July day one can walk through a town of digger bees and see a cloud of males hovering a few inches above the entrances to the burrows. The males are too intent on finding an eligible mate to notice a human intruder. There is an urgency in each male's search for a mate. Unlike most females, who will safely spend the coming winter underground, the males will die within a few days.

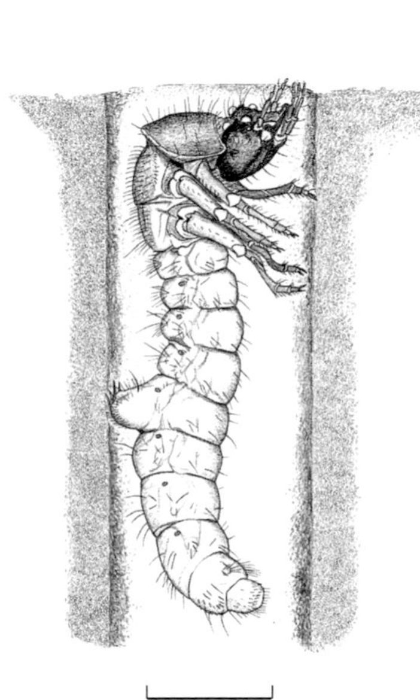

A mother velvet ant, looking for a digger bee colony in which to lay the eggs of her parasitic larvae, is about to become a meal for a tiger beetle larva.

As the male sweat bees flit overhead, females of a related species of bee may be on the ground, dashing from burrow to burrow in search of someone else's brood cells in which to lay their eggs. These females are parasitic bees that have come to rely on other bees to dig burrows and gather pollen for their larvae. The parasitic larva has strong jaws with which it can quickly dispatch the rightful resident of the brood cell. It eliminates its nest mate as soon as possible, since just enough pollen is placed in each cell to feed a single larva.

In the cities of digger bees, other insects have found a number of ways to make their livelihoods. Among those insects is a wasp called a velvet ant. Although the male velvet ant has wings but no stinger and looks like a wasp, the female has a nasty stinger but no wings and looks like an ant. Both the male and female velvet ants are colored with red, orange, yellow, and white hairs that give them a velvety appearance. The females spend most of their time moving from burrow to burrow, trying to find unprotected ones in which they can leave their eggs and raise their larvae. Unlike bees that survive as larvae on the pollen of a brood cell, velvet ants are wasps that survive as larvae on the flesh of other insects. The mother velvet ant naturally looks for brood cells with well-developed, pollen-fed bee larvae as homes for her own larvae. She paralyzes a bee larva with her stinger, lays an egg, and moves on in search of another well-fed larva.

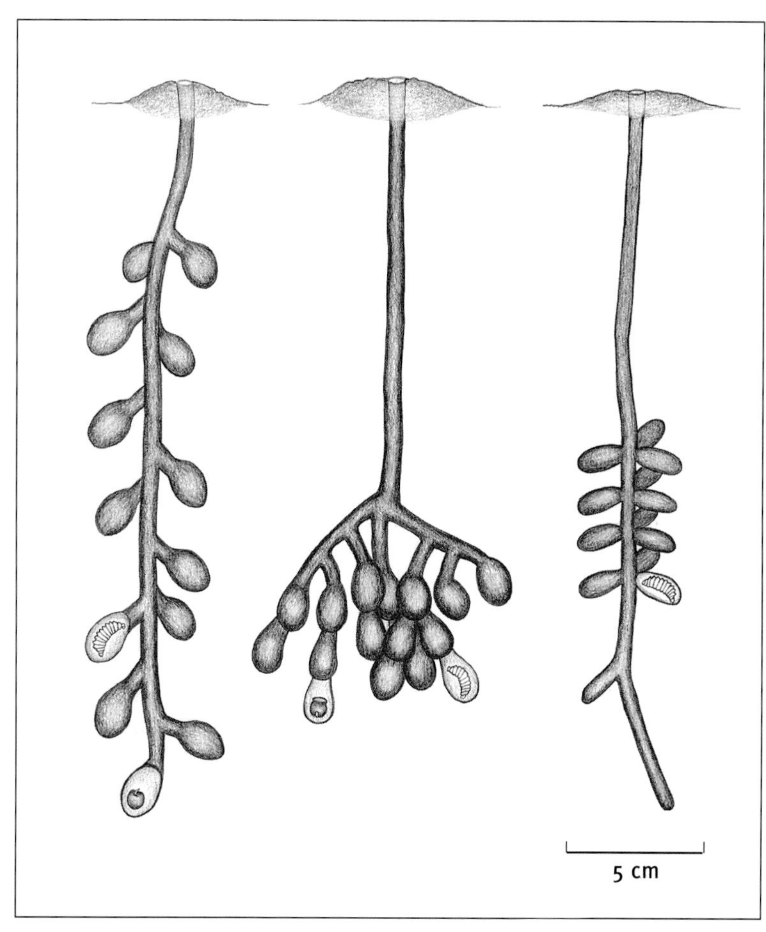

The brood nests of different digger bees have their own distinctive architecture. On the left and right are the nests of two different halictid bees, and in the center is the nest of an apid bee. Some chambers were drawn in cross section to show either bee larvae or the ball of pollen that serves as a provision for the larvae.

Generation after generation, year after year, a city of digger bees manages to survive threats from wasps and other bees. Just imagine how much soil a million of these digger bees can move in a single year on a single acre of land. If each female bee in the city digs a burrow two feet (60 centimeters) deep, or even one foot deep, mineral matter and organic matter of the soil are bound to be well circulated.

SAND WASPS AND CICADA KILLERS

CLASSIFICATION
Phylum Arthropoda
Class Insecta
Order Hymenoptera
Family Sphecidae

PLACE IN FOOD WEB
Diggers, Predators

SIZE
1–3 cm in length

NUMBER OF SPECIES
7,700

Digger Wasps

While digger bees provision the underground chambers for their larvae with pollen and nectar, digger wasps stock their burrows with all types of insects and spiders—grasshoppers, crickets, caterpillars, moths, true bugs, flies, bees, beetles, leafhoppers, treehoppers, even butterflies and trapdoor spiders.

The name digger wasp refers to a number of different wasps, each with its own hunting preference and its own distinctive features. The digger wasps known as thread-waisted wasps have skinny waists where the thorax joins the abdomen, and each of these wasps grows up on a diet of caterpillar, grasshopper, or cricket meat. Spider wasps, as their name implies, prey on spiders, including those that hide behind trap doors. They are long-legged wasps, most of which

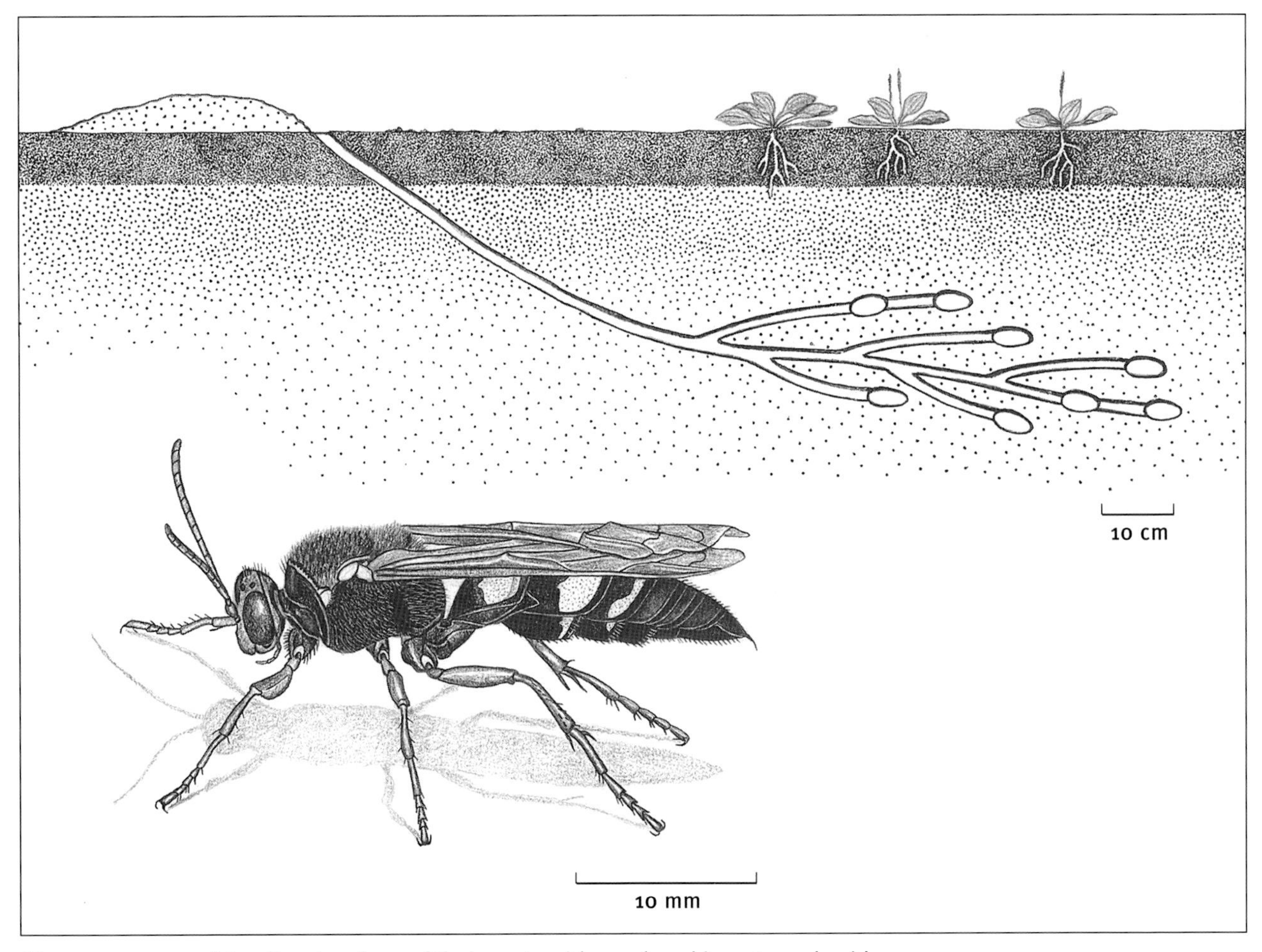

Digger wasps provision the chambers of their nests with paralyzed insects and spiders.

have dark bodies as well as dark wings. Parasitic digger wasps dig through the soil in search of beetle grubs as hosts for their larvae. Sand wasps usually have pale green markings and a fondness for just about any reasonably large flies. A single larva of a sand wasp can eat as many as 30 flies, and a mother sand wasp continues bringing flies to its growing larvae even after their growth is well along. Of all the digger wasps, the cicada killer is one of the most striking in terms of size and color. This large black, tan, and yellow wasp is large enough and strong enough to subdue a cicada that weighs from four to six times as much as it does. Once the cicada killer has paralyzed the cicada with its long sting, it somehow manages to maneuver its hefty victim into its burrow or drags the paralyzed cicada up a nearby tree, gaining just enough altitude to glide and fly to its destination.

The underground nurseries that digger wasps prepare for their larvae are simpler and less numerous than the burrows and chambers of digger bees. Each wasp burrow slopes downward to a depth that rarely exceeds a foot but that extends in length anywhere from 1 to 3 feet (30–90 centimeters). As predators or parasites on other insects and spiders, digger wasps have limited numbers of edible resources to feed their larvae. Pollen and nectar that bees use for larval food are often present in abundant supply, whereas insects that end up as provisions in the burrows of digger wasps are usually in limited supply. The land simply cannot support as many carnivores as it can vegetarians. This is true whether the carnivores are lions, tigers, wolves, or digger wasps. Rarely do digger wasp colonies exceed a few hundred burrows, and entrances to these burrows are usually more widely separated than the closely packed entrances in a densely populated colony of digger bees.

Like the males of digger bees, the males in a digger wasp colony typically emerge from their burrows a few days before the females. While awaiting the emergence of the females, the males fly back and forth over the colony. A female rarely has an opportunity to fly from her burrow before a male spots her and immediately mates with her. Males may continue hanging around the colony for weeks. They continually visit flowers for nectar during this time, but they never join in the digging, hunting, and provisioning of burrows that the industrious females so dutifully carry out.

PARASITIC DIGGER WASPS

CLASSIFICATION
Phylum Arthropoda
Class Insecta
Order Hymenoptera
Family Scoliidae
Family Tiphiidae

PLACE IN FOOD WEB
Diggers, Parasites

SIZE
1-3cm in length

NUMBER OF SPECIES
300 (Scoliidae)
1,500 (Tiphiidae)

This parasitic digger wasp burrows through the soil in search of beetle grubs on which it lays the eggs of its larvae.

ANTS

CLASSIFICATION
Phylum Arthropoda
Class Insecta
Order Hymenoptera
Family Formicidae

PLACE IN FOOD WEB
Diggers, Predators, Herbivores, Fungivores, Scavengers

SIZE
2–5 mm in length

NUMBER OF SPECIES
8,800

Ants

Mites and springtails may be the most common arthropods of the soil; but among the soil arthropods represented by the insects, ants are almost everywhere the most abundant. Only in the few places such as mountain habitats high enough to be uninhabited by ants do other animals of the soil and the leaf litter such as spiders and ground beetles actually increase in abundance and take over some roles played by ants. Anywhere from a few to several million individuals can make up an ant colony. All these ants can move substantial amounts of soil and can add substantial amounts of debris to the compost heap of plant and animal remains that surrounds their colony. An ant's reputation for carrying large and heavy objects between its sturdy jaws is legendary and well deserved.

However a person calculates the amount of earth moving that ants are responsible for, the numbers always come out large. Subsoil and the elements that have been carried down to it by rain and melting snow are constantly being moved to the soil's surface during the construction of an ant hill. The galleries of harvester ants in the deserts of the southwestern United States can extend as deep as 15 feet underground (4.6 meters). The workers of another species of desert ant move 150 to 300 pounds (68–136 kilograms) of subsoil to the surface each time they build an anthill. Ants in a Massachusetts field moved enough soil each year to cover the surface with a 0.2 inch (5 millimeter) layer, enough to weigh 30 tons per acre (27 metric tones per 4,050 square meters).

The mound-building ants of the eastern United States seem to build some of the most imposing ant hills. These insect earthworks are several feet in diameter and often two to three feet (60-90 centimeters) high. Generations of ants can occupy a mound through many summers and many winters, continually expanding their excavations and their composting. Ants range widely from their mounds along well-worn trails, carrying seeds, other insects, and pieces of plants back to their colony where much of this plant and animal matter is composted along with dead ants and ant droppings.

The seeds that are carried by harvester ants of the desert to their underground granaries total 15 million per year on an acre of land. Since the total crop of seeds on an acre of desert is about 1.5 billion, the harvester ants add about 1 percent of the seed crop to the soil in the immediate vicinity of their nest.

In the forests of Europe, wood ants keep organic and mineral matter in constant circulation around their nests. Each day during the warmer months of the year the foragers for a nest of about 1 million wood ants bring at least 100,000 insects into their nests as food for the colony.

Higher levels of nutrients derived from decomposition of organic debris accumulate in the soil found around an ant colony than in the soil beyond the ant nest. With the great variety of organic matter added to it, the compost of an ant's nest is especially rich in plant nutrients and provides a rich environment for decomposers as well as a rich nursery for young, delicate seedlings that are setting down their first roots.

In some cases the ants assure survival of not only the seedlings but also the animals that have come to depend on these seedlings for their own survival. The fruits that eventually form on lobeira seedlings happen to be the favorite fruit of a long-legged wolf that inhabits the grasslands of South America. Much of the this wolf's habitat and its favorite fruit have been lost to humans and agriculture in recent years. If it were not for the activities of some leaf-cutter ants, however, there would probably be even fewer wolves and lobeira plants than there already are. An intricate relationship has formed among the

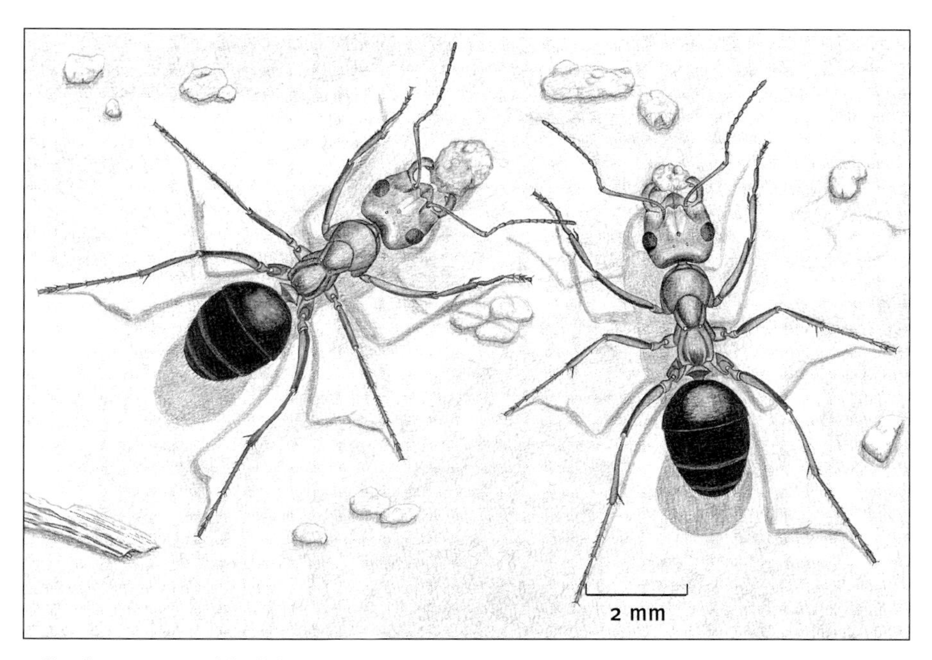

Allegheny mound-building ants are notorious warriors as well as movers of earth. Other ant species that enter the neighborhood of their large mounds are soon attacked and decapitated.

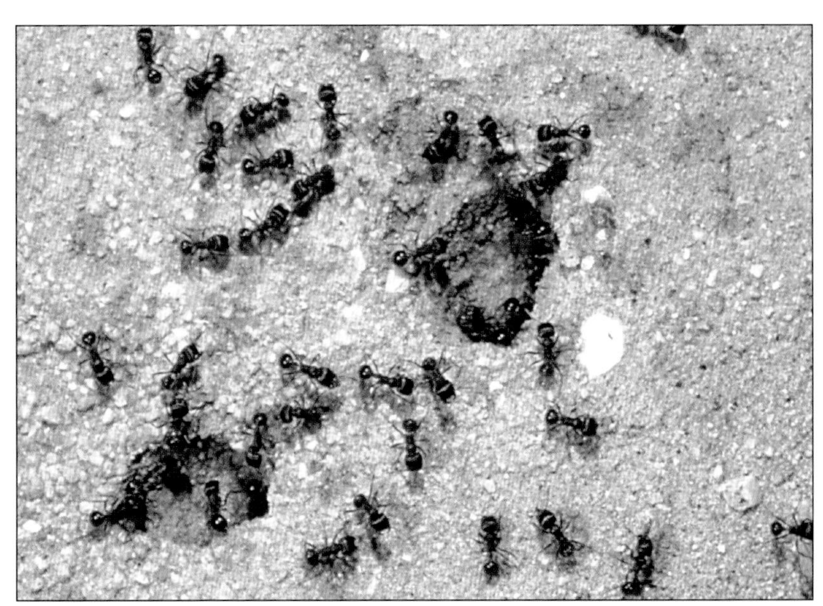

In deserts, ants are not only the most abundant arthropods of the soil, but also the most abundant animals.

ants, the wolves, and the lobeira plants of the grasslands. Lobeira seeds that are swallowed by a wolf germinate better than seeds that do not end up as part of a maned wolf's meal. The lobeira fruit and wolf droppings containing seeds of the fruit also happen to be popular with the leaf-cutter ants, with the lobeira seeds eventually ending up as debris that is added to the compost of the ant nest. Not surprisingly, more of the lobeira seeds that are dumped by the ants in their rich compost heaps germinate than those seeds that have never associated with either ants or wolves.

Other relationships have developed between ants and a variety of arthropods known as myrmecophiles (*myrmex* = ant; *philo*= love of) that take up residence in ant nests either as scavengers and nest cleaners or as purveyors of sweet honeydew for their hosts. Many beetles of the leaf litter and soil such as rove beetles, hister beetles, short-winged mold beetles, antlike stone beetles, and even tiny featherwing beetles are right at home in ant colonies.

Certain mites, bristletails, some tiny cockroaches, as well as a cricket named *Myrmecophila* often steal food from their hosts or raid their refuse piles. Some ants carefully tend aphids as well as caterpillars of certain small butterflies for the honeydew that they provide. The ant hosts are so tolerant that they accept some related caterpillars that brazenly feed on the larvae of the ants. Many myrmecophiles mimic not only the chemical and tactile communications that ants use among themselves but also mimic the appearance of ants. Arthropods that share the spacious underground chambers of ants have discovered that being the guests of ants has many fringe benefits.

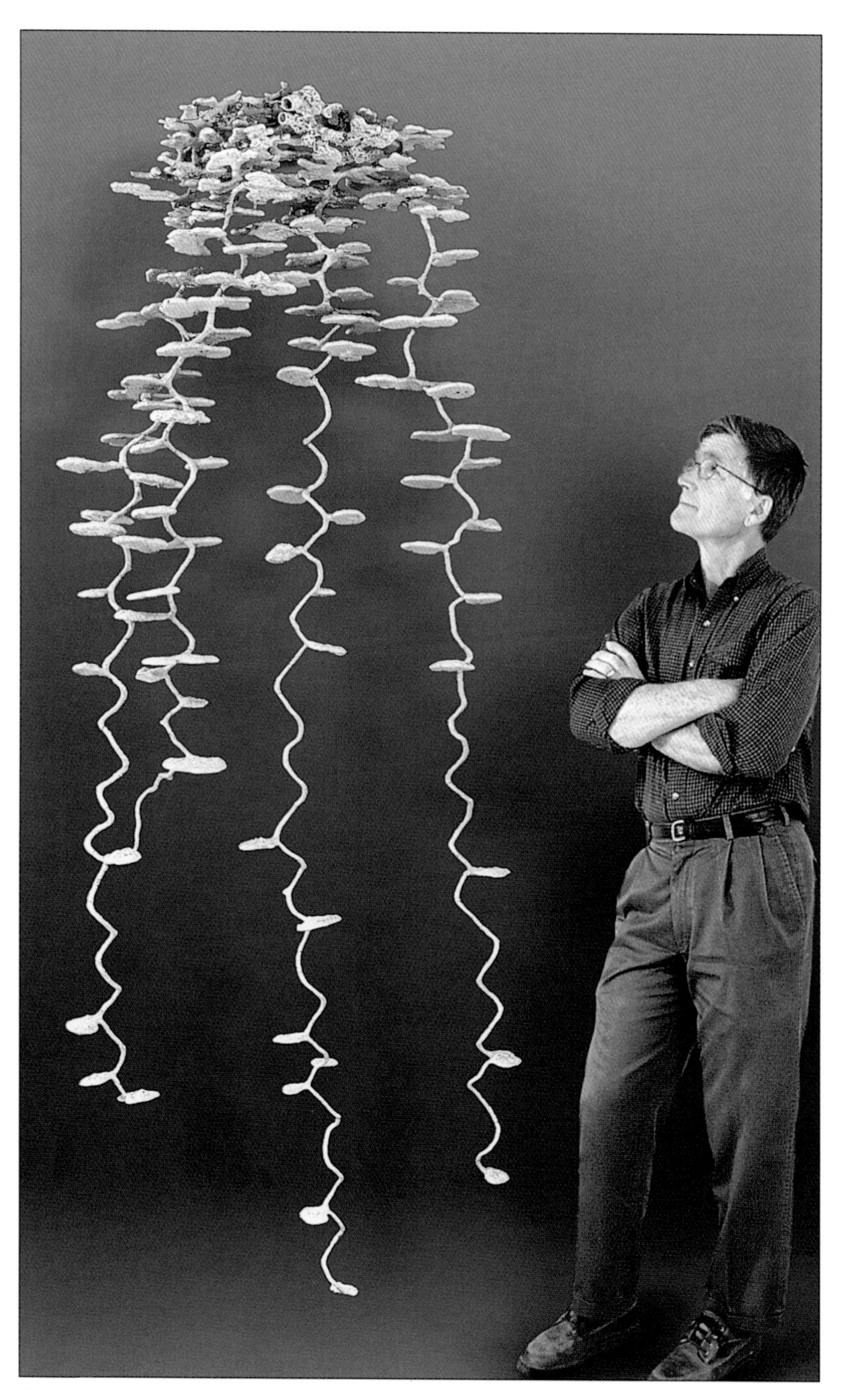

An authority on ants, Dr. Walter Tschinkel, poses with the cast of a harvester ant colony that he carefully excavated after pouring plaster down the colony's burrow. Five thousand ants dug these tunnels and chambers in only five days.

VERTEBRATES

LUNGLESS SALAMANDERS

CLASSIFICATION
Phylum Chordata
Class Amphibia
Order Caudata
Family Plethodontidae

PLACE IN FOOD WEB
Diggers, Predators

SIZE
3.8–20 cm in length

NUMBER OF SPECIES
230

LIFESPAN
3 years

MOLE SALAMANDERS

CLASSIFICATION
Phylum Chordata
Class Amphibia
Order Caudata
Family Ambystomatidae

PLACE IN FOOD WEB
Diggers, Predators

SIZE
7.5–20 cm in length

NUMBER OF SPECIES
18

LIFESPAN
4–25 years

Salamanders

Salamanders live and breathe only where soils are moist. Australia does not have a single salamander, and Africa only has three species. Europe and Asia have a few, but practically all the approximately 380 species of salamanders, representing eight families, can be found in North America. The leaf litter and moist soils of the southern Appalachians are particularly rich in salamander species. Among these lush, green mountains, salamanders hide their lovely patterns and bright colors under rocks and in the leaf litter of the forest.

The redback salamander is a common lungless salamander in the damp woods of eastern North America.

Those salamanders of the soil, known as mole salamanders start out life living in ponds and breathing with gills. Later on they come ashore, losing their gills and forming lungs. Like their namesakes, the moles, these salamanders stay in burrows most of the year. Although some species leave their burrows to breed in autumn, the rains of late winter and spring entice most species to migrate to nearby ponds where they join their fellow salamanders for an evening or two of courtship, mating, and egg laying.

The spotted salamander is one of 18 mole salamanders that live only in North America.

During their migrations, sometimes hundreds or even thousands of animals congregate in temporary ponds for this rite of spring, traversing lawns, hills, roads, or whatever may lie between their burrows and the nearest pond. People in many communities, concerned about the threats of speeding cars, have even built tunnels under roads to provide safe passage for the salamanders. Once their eggs have been deposited, the adults retire to burrows beneath the leaf litter, and every year for 10 or more years return to the same pond.

Adult lungless salamanders of the soil have neither gills like tadpoles and some other salamanders nor lungs like their relatives the frogs, toads, and mole salamanders. Instead they breathe through their thin, moist skins. When examined at close range, the oxygen-carrying blood cells can easily be seen streaming through the tiny blood vessels of their thin, translucent skins. Unlike most of their fellow amphibians, many of these lungless salamanders live strictly on land, even as larvae.

After her courtship and mating, the female goes off to a secluded spot under a log or beneath a stone where she lays only 6 to 12 eggs and invests her attention in them for the next two months. Mother salamanders can be found coiled around their few eggs, somewhat like mother centipedes and mother earwigs that huddle with their eggs, warding off animal predators and licking off any fungi that may try to engulf their defenseless embryos. These lungless salamanders are found almost exclusively in North America and make up only one family of salamanders, yet they account for 230 of the 380 species of salamanders on earth.

TRUE TOADS

CLASSIFICATION
Phylum Chordata
Class Amphibia
Order Anura
Family Bufonidae

PLACE IN FOOD WEB
Diggers, Predators

SIZE
5–9 cm in length

NUMBER OF SPECIES
300

LIFESPAN
5–10 years

SPADEFOOT TOADS

CLASSIFICATION
Phylum Chordata
Class Amphibia
Order Anura
Family Pelobatidae

PLACE IN FOOD WEB
Diggers, Predators

SIZE
4.4–6 cm in length

NUMBER OF SPECIES
69

LIFESPAN
5 years

Toads

The sight of a toad in the garden is a sight to gladden the heart of any gardener. Toads watch over the flowers and vegetables of a garden, alerted by any movements that might signal the presence of a slug, beetle, earwig, or other garden pests. With a flick of its long and sticky tongue, a toad gracefully snaps up these meals. Before gardens become populated with plants and pests, a toad's main concerns, however, are courting and mating. Hundreds, even thousands, of males sometimes congregate at seasonal pools in preparation for these momentous events. The musical trills of male toads fill the air over these shallow pools as the males inflate their vocal sacs, sit erect, and look very self-important. Soon females find the performance irresistible and succumb to the charms of the males, allowing the males to embrace them as they expel their thousands of eggs in two strings of clear jelly. Within about a week, black tadpoles hatch and begin feeding on the algae in the water. Life as a tadpole is brief because the pools in which they swim are drying in the spring sun. In a few weeks, they sprout legs, lose their tails, and begin their overland treks to promising hunting grounds. Gardens and the night lights around our homes are often favorite destinations for toads, for they also happen to be favorite attractions for the insects that toads like to eat.

As they set out for the first time on land, little toads face many new dangers. During their transformation from tadpole to toad, however, they pick up several new defenses that serve them well as new challenges arise. Among the many warts that they acquire when they become toads are a pair of particularly large warts on the neck and just behind the eyes. These are the toad's parotid glands, which secrete a milky white poison if the toad is provoked and threatened. A predator that tries a mouthful of toad is quickly disappointed with the flavor and often becomes nauseated and very ill.

Each toad has a small territory and a small burrow where it can be regularly found.

Spadefoot toads make rare appearances above ground, usually only at night and during heavy rains.

The arrangement of warts, spots, and splotches over the toad's skin blends in so well with the surrounding soil and leaf litter that toads can seem invisible at certain times and in certain places. Toads can actually make themselves invisible by burrowing into the soil, where they hide from heat, cold, or drought, and where they can rest during the day. Some toads spend almost their entire lives beneath the ground, only making brief appearances above ground to mate or to hunt on a rainy night. Practically all toads burrow to some extent, but spadefoot toads have special "spades" for digging. On the soles of their hind feet, spadefoots have horny, dark pads which expedite digging burrows that can be a few inches or several feet long. In subterranean sanctuaries of their own excavation or in a portion of some other animal's burrow that they borrow, toads can escape many of the perils of heat, cold, and predators.

The only other order of soil-dwelling amphibians besides the salamanders (order Caudata) and the toads (order Anura) is an order of totally legless creatures found only in the tropics of Asia, Africa, and Latin America. These caecilians (order Caecilia) resemble oversized earthworms and the worm lizards whose habitats they often share. Most caecilians are burrowers whose eyes are so reduced that they, instead, depend on two sensory tentacles that actually look more like pimples, one on each side of their head. Even though about 150 species have been described, we still know very little about the habits of these rarely seen amphibians.

LIZARDS

CLASSIFICATION
Phylum Chordata
Class Reptilia
Order Squamata
Suborder Lacertilia

PLACE IN FOOD WEB
Diggers, Predators

SIZE
7 mm–300 cm in length

NUMBER OF SPECIES
3,000

WORM LIZARDS

CLASSIFICATION
Phylum Chordata
Class Reptilia
Order Squamata
Suborder Amphisbaenia

PLACE IN FOOD WEB
Diggers, Predators

SIZE
18–65 cm in length

NUMBER OF SPECIES
135

Lizards

Lizards of the soil are very streamlined, having either tiny legs like certain skinks and flap-footed lizards, or no legs at all like legless lizards and worm lizards. As they glide through underground tunnels, lizards come across the abundance of termites, insect larvae, and earthworms that can inhabit soils with a variety of textures. For these lizards of the underground, legs would be an encumbrance in the narrow passageways that they travel every day.

Most skinks are swift runners, as anyone who has ever tried to catch one of these sleek little lizards can attest, but sand skinks and mole skinks have legs that are too little for running. These skinks might not move swiftly aboveground, but underground they tuck their little legs against their bodies and practically swim through dry and sandy soils.

Flap-footed lizards of Australia and New Guinea represent a family of 36 assorted species ranging from those that are burrowers and resemble eyeless worm lizards to those with well-developed eyes that have adopted the graceful locomotion of snakes. All lizards of the family Pygopodidae (*pygo* = rump; *pod* = foot) have hind legs reduced to mere scaly flaps and have tails that are at least twice as long as their bodies The assorted pygopodid species can be found in assorted habitats. Those with well-developed eyes feed aboveground on other lizards, and those that dwell underground feed on abundant soil invertebrates.

Most skinks are swift runners and some are accomplished burrowers in sandy soils.

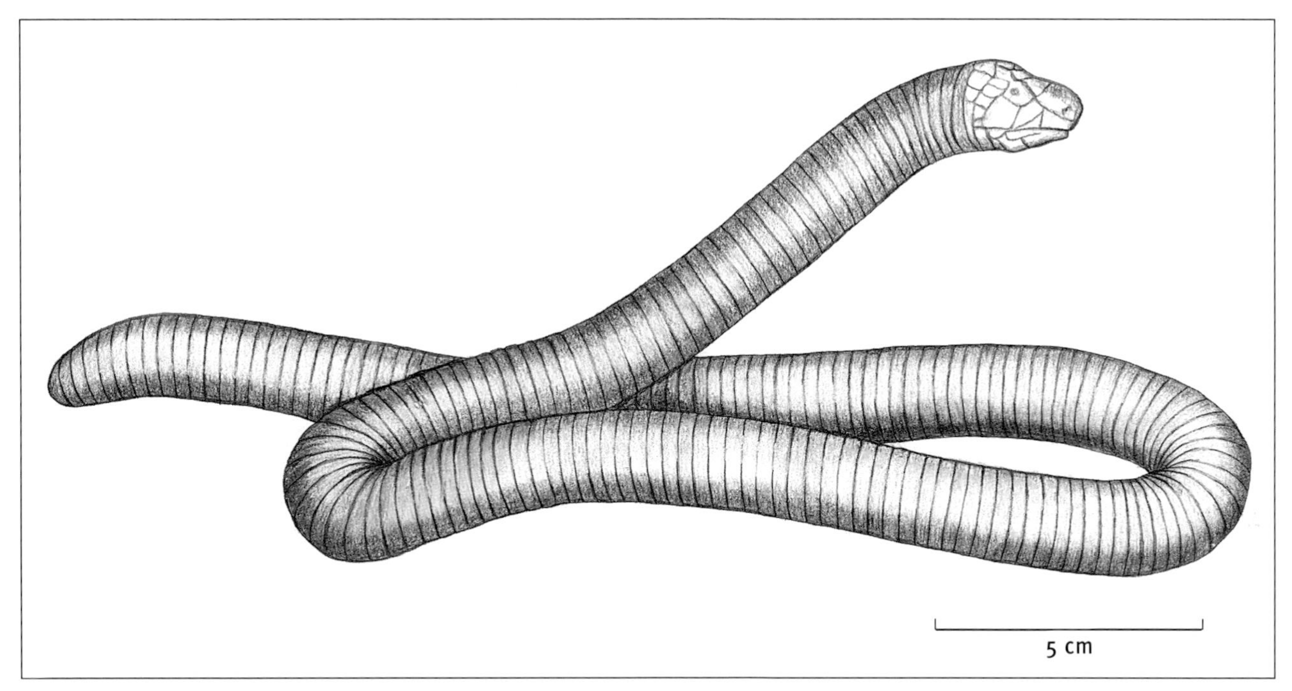

About 135 species of worm lizards are found in Latin America, Africa, and in the Mediterranean region. One species lives in Florida. They grow to about 65 cm long.

If it were not for its eyelids and ear openings, which snakes do not have, a legless lizard could also easily pass for a snake. The scientific name for its genus is *Ophisaurus* (*ophi* = snake, Greek; *saurus* = lizard), and the name for its family is Anguidae (*angui* = snake, Latin), names that convey the striking resemblance. These lizards have very long tails that readily break off but regenerate whenever they are roughed up by predators. While the rest of the lizard dashes to safety, the tail jerks and twitches long enough to distract predators that make the mistake of approaching these lizards from the rear. Snakes may look like legless lizards, but they have never mastered this trick of foiling predators by leaving their tails behind when the occasion demands a sacrifice.

Worm lizards have neither eyelids nor ear openings like other lizards and look more like large earthworms. As the translation of their suborder name Amphisbaenia (*amphi* = double; *baen* = walk) implies, worm lizards move sometimes backward, sometimes forward; and to confuse matters even more, they have heads that look like tails. Earthworms, worm lizards, and caecilians are examples of totally unrelated creatures whose very similar forms have been molded by very similar environments.

SNAKES

CLASSIFICATION
Phylum Chordata
Class Reptilia
Order Squamata
Suborder Serpentes

PLACE IN FOOD WEB
Diggers, Predators

SIZE
12–900 cm

NUMBER OF SPECIES
2,700

LIFESPAN
5–20 years

Snakes

With no legs to impede their movements in narrow underground passageways, snakes are well suited for burrowing. Not all snakes burrow, but several of them do, from large bull snakes to small garter snakes and tiny worm snakes. A snake's nose has a lot to do with its ability to burrow. Heavy nose plates apparently help snakes push and prod their way through the soil. The importance of noses in the lives of burrowing snakes can be inferred from the common names that have been given to many of them, such as hog-nosed snakes, hook-nosed snakes, long-nosed snakes, and shovel-nosed snakes. Many of these snakes, along with colorful sand snakes and poisonous coral snakes, inhabit the sands of deserts. The much damper environment of swamp mud is home to several handsome snakes with red bellies: mud snakes, swamp snakes, and rainbow snakes.

Larger snakes like those from the swamps eat rodents, frogs, toads, and crayfish, but the smaller snakes of the soil such as worm snakes, blind snakes, and sand snakes that are only about a foot (30 centimeters) long feed mainly on earthworms and perhaps a few insect larvae.

While most burrowing snakes have noteworthy noses, one exotic family of burrowing snakes from Sri Lanka and southern India called shield-tailed snakes is best known for its one-of-a-kind tail, which ends in a flat disc that the snake may use to stopper its burrow. These snakes of the family Uropeltidae

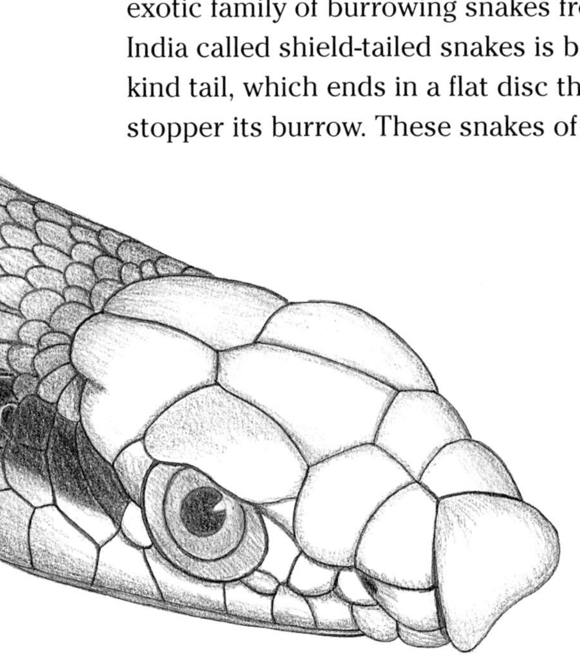

The patchnose snake is one of many snakes with noses that are used for burrowing.

Ringneck snakes are tiny, harmless snakes that twist, coil, and expose their bright bellies when they are threatened.

(*uro* = tail; *pelt* = shield) rarely grow longer than 15 inches (38 centimeters) and rarely feed on anything larger than an earthworm, but they represent another example of how exquisitely adapted to a burrowing life some snakes have become.

Anyone with a fear of snakes would probably soon change his or her opinion of these legless reptiles after finding a gentle ringneck snake. They are colorful, with orange or yellow neck rings as well as bellies that are even brighter shades of orange. They are slender and rarely grow longer than two feet (60 centimeters) in length. But even these gentle snakes can be provoked. Rather than trying to bite with their tiny jaws, they secrete a white, stinky, and very unappetizing fluid. Ringneck snakes like moist soils, where they live under logs, under stones, or among the fallen leaves. Their largest prey are probably salamanders and small toads, but they will eat the slugs, earthworms, and insects that they find there as well.

TORTOISES

CLASSIFICATION
Phylum Chordata
Class Reptilia
Order Testudines
Family Testudinidae

PLACE IN FOOD WEB
Diggers, Herbivores, Predators of slugs and earthworms

SIZE
12–140 cm in length

NUMBER OF SPECIES
39

LIFESPAN
50–60 years

BOX TURTLES

CLASSIFICATION
Phylum Chordata
Class Reptilia
Order Testudines
Family Emydidae
Genus Terrapone

PLACE IN FOOD WEB
Diggers, Herbivores, Predators of slugs and earthworms

SIZE
11.5–16 cm in length

NUMBER OF SPECIES
5

LIFESPAN
50–100 years

Turtles and Tortoises

There are several documented cases of box turtles living for more than a century. During their long lifetimes box turtles rarely venture beyond an area the size of a city block—about 250,000 square feet (27,800 square yards; 23,250 square meters). The fortunate ones whose habitats remain undisturbed during this long period of time become well acquainted with the topography, fauna, and flora of their territories. They know where the earthworms are most plentiful each spring, where slugs appear on overcast days, and where mushrooms are most likely to sprout each autumn. Like all turtles of land or water, box turtles always bury their eggs in the ground. The young turtles may dig their way to the surface after about three months or may stay in the nest until the following spring. At the approach of winter or during a heat wave, box turtles retire to favorite sanctuaries in the soil and leaf litter. Part of the box turtle's secret of longevity depends not only on its ability to tightly close its shell to intruders but also on its

At the end of each day, a box turtle settles down in the leaf litter and mosses of its home territory. It builds a simple domelike chamber in which it nestles each night.

At sunset in the Arizona desert, a tortoise leaves its burrow and sets off for an evening of cactus grazing.

tendency to spend some of the more vulnerable days of its life underground.

In drier and hotter climates, larger relatives of box turtles, the tortoises, also find it expedient to hole up in a relatively cool burrow during the hottest and driest times of the year. Desert tortoises of the southwestern United States can survive miles from any body of water. Only for brief periods after a spring or summer rain can they feast on the ephemeral plants that carpet the desert floor. During the remainder of the desert year they survive mostly on the fruits and stems of cacti. Not only can tortoises endure the desert heat, they can also devour the spines that cover the pieces of cacti. Shy gopher tortoises of the southeastern United States dig large burrows 10 to 40 feet (3 to 12 meters) long that they occupy for years, returning night after night to the quiet of their refuges. Sometimes, however, these spacious refuges become crowded with uninvited guests, from small insects to large mammals like raccoons, rabbits, and possums; from harmless burrowing owls and indigo snakes to poisonous rattlesnakes and scorpions.

BIRDS

CLASSIFICATION
Phylum Chordata
Class Aves
Order Dinornithiformes (kiwis)
Order Sphenisciformes (penguins)
Order Procellariiformes (seabirds: petrels, shearwaters)
Order Galliformes (pheasants, quails, turkeys, guinea fowl, chickens)
Order Charadriiformes (woodcocks, puffins)
Order Psittaciformes (kakapo parrots)
Order Strigiformes (burrowing owls)
Order Coraciiformes (kingfishers, motmots, bee-eaters)
Order Passeriformes (bank swallows, thrushes and thrashers, towhees and fox sparrows, some warblers)

PLACE IN FOOD WEB
Diggers; Predators of earthworms, arthropods, snails

SIZE
10–75 cm in length

NUMBER OF SPECIES
9,000

Birds

While birds of most species soar through the sky and over the trees, those of a few other species delight in literally scratching out a living from the soil. Rather than catching their food while flying or in the treetops, these birds spend their days searching through the leaf litter and soil in eager pursuit of worms and insects. Birds come down to earth and relate to soils in a variety of ways. Some survive on creatures that they find as they scratch in the leaf litter or poke in the ground. Others such as kingfishers, puffins, penguins, and other seabirds find their meals elsewhere but dig burrows for nesting. Finally there are those few flightless birds of New Zealand, the kiwi and the kakapo, that are truly at home on the ground, where they scratch, poke, and also burrow.

Large birds like pheasants, quails, grouse, turkeys, and guinea fowl vigorously comb the ground and stir up whatever insects, worms, and snails lie near the surface. A number of smaller birds such as woodcocks and robins have a fondness for earthworms. Fox sparrows and a few warblers scratch and poke around for whatever they can find in the litter. Thrashers, thrushes, and towhees also join in the scratching when they are not searching the bushes for insects and berries.

A robin listens for earthworms that are pulling fallen leaves into their burrows.

As long as the soil does not freeze and earthworms do not move too far beneath the surface, a woodcock can continue poking about for earthworms with its long bill. Not only is the woodcock's 3-inch (75 millimeter) bill disproportionately long for a bird that is only 11 inches (270 millimeters) long, but its legs are also disproportionately short. A woodcock's bill, however, is beautifully designed for locating and retrieving earthworms. It even has a hinge near the tip that allows it to open and gingerly pluck out an earthworm when the rest of the bill is buried underground. The tip of the bill is also filled with many nerves and blood vessels that endow it with fine sensitivity to odors and movements in the soil.

During its fall migration, a fox sparrow searches for insects among fallen oak leaves.

As a woodcock probes in the soil for food, it will hesitate a few seconds as though waiting to see if it detects any signs of an earthworm before withdrawing its bill and immediately moving on and poking again. Short legs and a short neck can actually be advantages to a bird that goes around poking its bill into the soil. A woodcock does not have far to stoop even when its bill has been poked in as far as it will go. Its large, dark eyes appear to be perched too far back on its head, but from their vantage point these eyes can survey a 360-degree field of vision. Thus the woodcock can keep a lookout for danger from above and from all sides while it is busily engaged in hunting earthworms. Only predators with the sharpest vision, however, have a chance of spotting this bird whose plumage blends in so perfectly with the fallen leaves among which it moves. Although most of a woodcock's attributes may seem very strange to us, they are ideal for a creature that lives among leaf litter and survives on a steady diet of earthworms.

Woodcocks are great fans of earthworms and frequent the same haunts in fields and open woods that earthworms do.

Each spring and each fall fox sparrows pass through the American forests where they tarry for five or six weeks on their way to and from the north woods of Canada and the forests of the southern United States. Often, the sound of loud rustling in the leaf litter at these times of year can be traced to a fox sparrow scratching away with sheer abandon as it kicks aside dead leaves with both feet at once. The full range of earthy colors—umber, sienna, ocher, chestnut, russet, mahogany, chocolate—can be found on the feathers of sparrows, but the richest tawny colors are found on this largest member of the sparrow family. Years ago when ornithologists frequently examined the contents of birds' stomachs, they found that in the spring and fall fox sparrows eat large numbers of millipedes and ground beetles of the leaf litter, arthropods that would turn the stomachs of most animals. Even though millipedes and most ground beetles secrete unpleasant chemicals, these chemical defenses do not seem to deter the fox sparrows.

Only a few of the over 100 wood warblers of the New World spend more time on the ground than they do in the trees. At a distance these ground warblers are easily spotted, because unlike other warblers they are deliberate walkers, not hoppers or runners. Ovenbirds and their relatives the water thrushes belong to the genus *Seiurus* (*sei* = wave; *ura* = tail). As their name implies, they are constantly bobbing their tails as they promenade across the forest floor, over logs, and under ferns. Worm-eating warblers belong to the equally distinctive genus *Helmitheros* (*helmin* = worm; *thero* = hunt for), a name that alludes to their prowess as hunters of worms. Warblers of the treetops are known for their bright plumage, but the earthy colors of the ground warblers blend in well with the browns, grays, olives, and whites of the forest floor.

Many birds nest in burrows, usually of their own making. The kakapo parrot and the kiwi are two flightless birds of New Zealand that retire to the safety of their burrows after a night spent roaming the forest floor. The long, stiff bristles surrounding their bills are touch-sensitive and help guide the birds in the dark. The wings of these birds may be weak, but they have plenty of strength

An ovenbird inspects a mossy log for hidden insects.

in the muscular legs and large bills that they use for digging. Kookaburras and kingfishers, bee-eaters, and motmots belong to an order of birds with powerful bills that they use to excavate burrows that are several feet long. Most of these colorful birds are tropical, but a few kingfishers are at home in colder parts of the world. Puffins nest on isolated islands where they dig holes in which each mated pair lays a single egg and vigilantly guards their precious investment. If danger threatens, the powerful bill and sharp claws that dug the nesting burrow can be put to use quickly and effectively. Other birds of the sea such as many penguins, petrels, and shearwaters come ashore to dig burrows and to nest underground.

Burrowing owls can dig their own burrows in the ground if the soil is not too hard and if no deserted dens of badgers, foxes, tortoises, or prairie dogs are available in the neighborhood. If an abandoned prairie dog hole meets its needs, a burrowing owl will move into town and will be readily accepted by the good-natured rodents. These owls become part of the prairie dog community, even helping the prairie dogs keep an eye out for intruders.

Bank swallows and rough-winged swallows also dig their own burrows and form large colonies along stream banks. Of all the birds he studied, the swallows were Gilbert White's favorites. In his *Natural History of Selborne,* he recorded many observations of their affairs in and around the village. He wrote:

> "Perseverance will accomplish anything, though at first one would be disinclined to believe that this weak bird, with her soft and tender bill and claws, should ever be able to bore the stubborn sand-bank without entirely disabling herself; yet with these feeble instruments have I seen a pair of them make great dispatch: and could remark how much they had scooped that day by the fresh sand which ran down the bank, and was of a different colour from that which lay loose and bleached in the sun."

For years the view prevailed that swallows overwinter in their laboriously constructed burrows, even though Gilbert White had pointed out in 1774 that the swallows use the burrows only as summer homes.

MAMMALS

CLASSIFICATION
Phylum Chordata
Class Mammalia

PLACE IN FOOD WEB
Diggers, Herbivores, Predators

NUMBER OF SPECIES
4,070

Mammals

We live in the Age of Mammals. When mammals inherited the earth from the dinosaurs, they quickly colonized all the land masses and all the seas. A few, such as the bats, took to the air, but most remained earthbound. Many adapted to life above ground in trees, some to life on the ground, and others to life beneath the surface of the earth. Mammals of very different orders and families have made themselves at home on every continent and have adapted in similar ways to similar habitats.

Burrowing mammals face some of the same challenges wherever they are found and have many of the same adaptations for digging even though they are different in many other ways. Burrowing has been fashionable among mammals. Our domesticated hamsters, gerbils, rabbits, and guinea pigs are all descended from long lines of burrowers. Spiny anteaters and duckbill platypuses, the only mammals that lay eggs, have powerful feet for digging. The spiny anteater has perfected a singular style of burrowing. Rather than digging a hole at an angle like other mammals, the spiny anteater digs a shaft straight down, soon disappearing completely from sight.

In addition to being home to the egg-laying mammals, Australia, Tasmania, and New Guinea also have the greatest diversity of marsupial (pouch-bearing) mammals on earth. Each of these marsupials has its counterpart among the mammals found in other parts of the world. To the Australians, the marsupial wombat is known as a "badger," and it is easy to see why. The wombat has short, sturdy legs and sharp claws with which it can match the badger in digging prowess. Bandicoots, with their long, pointed snouts and long foreclaws, act like skunks as they dig and poke around in the ground for insects and worms. Marsupial moles of Australia, the moles of northern Europe, North America, and Asia, as well as the Mediterranean mole rat of southeastern Europe all look and behave alike, even though they are not closely related. Many of the same adaptations for digging and burrowing are as likely to appear among the mammals of Australia and New Guinea as among the mammals of America and Europe.

Another strange group of practically toothless mammals includes anteaters and armadillos of the Americas and the

Once it decides to dig, a spiny anteater, or echidna, quickly disappears underground.

aardvarks of Africa. All of these mammals are great lovers of termites and their long, sticky tongues can sweep up hundreds of termites with each lick. These animals have only small, peglike teeth that are worthless for defense, but they have stout claws that make aardvarks and armadillos renowned diggers.

Aardvarks, anteaters, and armadillos have marsupial counterparts in Australia, known as numbats or banded anteaters, that look like squirrels with digging claws, pointed snouts, and transverse stripes across their rumps. Marsupials have more teeth than other mammals, but the numbat rarely uses its many teeth. Instead it relies on its long, sticky tongue to lick up termites and ants that it simply swallows whole.

With its large, shovel-shaped claws, the aardvark digs a burrow about 10 feet (3 meters) long in which it sleeps during the day. At other times, it uses its claws to dig into termite and ant nests. With each lick of its long, sticky tongue, the aardvark sweeps up hundreds of these insects. Aardvark is a Dutch name that translates to "earth pig."

Most of the world's burrowing rodents live in South America, and they occupy niches similar to those filled by woodchucks, gophers, and prairie dogs of North America. Viscachas from the Pampas of South America are root-eating rodents that live in community burrows appropriately called "viscacheras," their version of a prairie dog town. Familiar guinea pigs and rabbitlike agoutis are rodents without tails that spend the daylight hours in their underground burrows, coming out at nightfall to feed on leaves and fallen fruit. *Ctenomys* (*cteno* = comb; *mys* = mouse) has large comblike claws, tiny eyes, and tiny ears like the gophers of North America.

Also like gophers, they and octodontid (*octo* = eight; *odon* = tooth) rodents are great movers and mixers of soil. The octodontids have eight molar teeth on each side of the upper and lower jaws rather than the usual three molar teeth that other rats and mice have. Each of these rodents is credited with helping to transform barren ground into fertile landscapes.

Burrows can create a sense of community. Prairie dogs actually build underground cities with miles of tunnels extending from one entrance hole to another. The mountain beaver, or sewellel, on the west coast of the United States lives in underground colonies with extensive subway systems that lead to its favorite feeding stations aboveground. The rabbits of Europe, unlike the cottontails and jack rabbits of the North America, live in communal burrows known as warrens. But even a burrow occupied by only a single mammal can provide homes for many other animals in the neighborhood long after the original occupant has left.

Woodchucks and Skunks

From the entrance of an abandoned woodchuck den where it has lived since last fall, a skunk peeks out and sniffs the air. Skunks rarely get involved in large-scale digging projects; they usually rely on woodchucks to do most of the digging for them. Because of this reliance, the well-being of skunks is not surprisingly intertwined with the well-being of the woodchucks with whom they share the forests and pastures.

When a campaign to eliminate many of the woodchucks from agricultural land in New York was conducted in the first half of the 20th century, William Hamilton at Cornell University observed that the skunk population in an area declined every time that area's woodchucks were destroyed. Poison gas poured into woodchuck dens killed not only the woodchucks but also the skunks that had been sharing the dens. In the short-sighted act of eliminating many woodchucks to save a few alfalfa, corn, or soybean plants in each cultivated field, the exterminators also destroyed the skunks that happen to be

WOODCHUCKS

CLASSIFICATION
Phylum Chordata
Class Mammalia
Order Rodentia
Family Sciuridae
Genus *Marmota*

PLACE IN FOOD WEB
Diggers, Herbivores

SIZE
40–51 cm in length

NUMBER OF SPECIES
15

LIFESPAN
9 years

GESTATION
30 days

SKUNKS

CLASSIFICATION
Phylum Chordata
Class Mammalia
Order Carnivora
Family Mustelidae

PLACE IN FOOD WEB
Diggers, Predators, Herbivores

SIZE
33–46 cm in length

NUMBER OF SPECIES
13

LIFESPAN
10 years

GESTATION
42–66 days

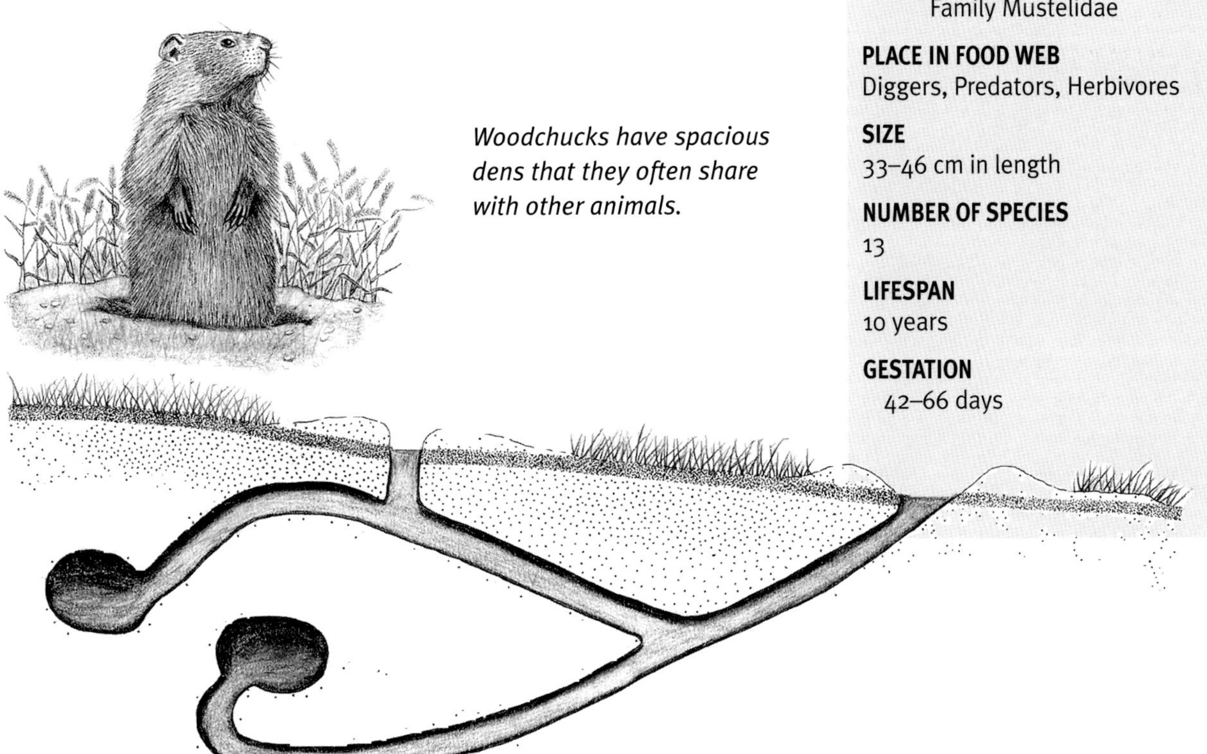

Woodchucks have spacious dens that they often share with other animals.

avid eaters of beetle grubs and mice. These insects and small rodents feed in the same fields as the skunks and woodchucks, and probably do more damage to the crops than a few woodchucks could possibly do.

On early summer mornings you may see mother skunks and their children systematically searching for crickets, digging larvae from the soil, and inspecting cow pads for beetle grubs and other insects. Pastures and meadows are often pockmarked with their neatly dug holes, about an inch (25 millimeters) wide and two or three inches (50–75 millimeters) deep. The naturalist Henry David Thoreau noted the thoroughness of his neighborhood skunks: "During the succeeding half hour, it [a skunk] did not cover a space greater than three or four rods square, but literally every foot of this area was carefully inspected. Not content with rooting into every bunch of dead leaves, it dug dozens of holes, first plunging its sharp nose into the ground and then using its fore-feet, making the dirt fly." The Canadian Entomological Service in Manitoba estimated that on one eight-acre tract, skunks destroyed 14,520 beetle grubs per acre. Skunks seem to be particularly partial to these grubs and cutworm larvae. Once they discover a patch of soil grubs, they begin digging and continue to scour the area until satisfied that they have found most of the larvae.

Skunks may not dig their own burrows, but they are constantly rooting around for insects in the soil and leaf litter.

Woodchucks are better known to many humans as groundhogs, and their mountain relatives are known as marmots.

Woodchucks are better known to many humans as groundhogs, those weather forecasters whose purported prowess in foretelling the arrival of spring is celebrated every year in the United States on February 2. In their own wildlife communities woodchucks are tolerant rodents who provide new habitats and refuges for their fellow wildlife. During the winter months while woodchucks sleep soundly in their underground chambers, other animals in addition to skunks may move in to share some of the den's extra space. Rabbits, raccoons, mice, possums, foxes, and snakes have all been known to settle down in woodchuck dens when snow falls and temperatures plummet. Abandoned woodchuck dens are often occupied as family homes by some of these same animals. Even quail, pheasants, and woodcocks may find refuge in a woodchuck den during a winter snowstorm or a prairie fire.

Clearly a woodchuck's den can be quite spacious and accommodating. While excavating a single den, a woodchuck moves about 700 pounds (318 kilograms) of subsoil along with its associated minerals to the surface, and brings air as well as organic matter to its chambers in the deeper layers of the soil. Despite their bad reputations with some farmers and gardeners, woodchucks are important and valued members in their own communities, continually improving soil conditions as well as wildlife habitat.

BADGERS

CLASSIFICATION
Phylum Chordata
Class Mammalia
Order Carnivora
Family Mustelidae
Genus *Taxidea*

PLACE IN FOOD WEB
Diggers, Predators, Herbivores

SIZE
42–81 cm in length

NUMBER OF SPECIES
9

LIFESPAN
25 years

GESTATION
4–12 months (delayed development in winter)

Badgers

Strong, muscular front legs with long claws mark badgers as powerful diggers. They dig well, and often. Constructing new burrows, remodeling old burrows, or digging for food, badgers are often so preoccupied with their digging that they are oblivious to whoever is watching as they vigorously kick loose soil from their excavations. Even their daily toilet demands some digging, for badgers seem to be as tidy as cats, usually digging a shallow hole for their droppings and promptly covering them with soil. These badger latrines are most often located around the edges of badger territory, where they serve as boundary markers for badgers living in adjoining territories.

A badger's den is its shelter by day and a nursery in the spring. Each badger designs its den according to the terrain, soil conditions, and individual preference. Many badgers remodel or reuse dens that have been vacated by other badgers or other animals. The badgers of the American grasslands have a series of many dens that they dig over an area of one to two square miles (2,500–5,000 square meters). In this familiar home territory a badger will never be too far from one of its dens. The badgers of Europe and northern Asia are less nomadic and more sociable than their North American relatives, and settle down in dens known as setts that are often occupied by generations of badgers. Some of the more ancient setts have been continually occupied for at least 200 years. Here a clan of anywhere from a few to as many as 20 badgers may live together.

The well-worn tunnels are often packed hard by years of badger traffic. The pounding of their paws on the hard soil below can sometimes be heard by listening at one of the entrances to the den. Setts vary greatly in their architecture, but a typical sett is a complex of interconnected tunnels and chambers that can be several stories deep, hundreds of yards or meters in length, and have as many as 40 entrances. Its many cozy chambers are bountifully lined with grasses and leaves that the badgers use for bedding. To dig such a series of tunnels, about 25 tons (22.6 metric ton) of soil is moved to the surface.

Hunting for daily meals demands a great deal of digging for a badger. Its favorite foods are usually hidden in the soil. The American badger is a carnivore that relishes prairie dogs, ground squirrels, and other rodents that share the prairie with it. Insects also can make up a portion of its diet. The sociable

Badgers are the most accomplished diggers in the mammal family Mustelidae that includes minks, weasels, otters, skunks, and wolverines.

European badger has more diverse tastes. Earthworms are without doubt its favorite food, but depending on the season, insects of the soil, mice, rabbits, fruits, and seeds are also consumed.

Recently researchers in Britain were puzzled to find that some badger clans covered immense territories while other clans of the same size covered much smaller territories. What they eventually discovered was that the number of badgers on a given territory was related to the earthworm population of that territory. Thus, richer soils with larger earthworm populations support larger clans of badgers.

In many cultures badgers have been associated with medicine and curative powers. To many Native Americans the badger was known as the keeper of the medicine roots. Even across the Atlantic, in Italy and Belgium, a locket of badger hair was believed to offer protection from sickness and evil spirits. Although the origins of these beliefs have been long forgotten, imagining how the beliefs originally arose is not difficult for anyone who has ever watched a badger in action. With all the digging that a badger does in its lifetime, every now and then it is bound to kick up a number of plant roots with medicinal value. The roots of prairie plants are well known for their medicinal properties, and it is probably more than just a coincidence that some of the most highly valued medicinal roots are those of plants that share their habitat with badgers. The Native Americans who were adventuresome enough to sample some of

A badger shows off its long digging claws.

the roots uncovered by badgers not only were spared the effort of digging in the hard prairie soils but were also sometimes introduced to roots with remarkable healing properties that the badger had inadvertently tossed aside during its fervent digging.

All badgers have reputations as very able diggers. In addition, each of the nine different species of badgers scattered around the world has its own noteworthy idiosyncrasies. The honey badger *Mellivora* (*melli* = honey; *vora* = to eat) of Africa and southern Asia has a fondness for honey and young bees, and has developed a collaboration with birds known as honey-guides that also are very fond of the contents of honey bees' nests and are constantly scouting for these nests. Whenever a honey-guide comes across a nest, the bird begins a series of high-pitched calls to alert a nearby honey badger about its find. The badger follows the calls of the bird to the nest and begins tearing it apart to reach the honey and young bees while the honey-guide patiently waits for its share of the feast. When honey and bees are not available, the honey badger settles for meals of small animals or the contents of ant mounds and termite mounds.

The stink badgers of Indonesia use a smelly defense similar to that of skunks and even have the same white stripe down their backs. Any attacker that ignores this white warning stripe may have the contents of the badger's stink glands sprayed in its face. The hog badger of southeast Asia has a particularly long snout for a badger and uses it to root around in the leaf litter and soil for earthworms, insects, and other badger treats. No matter where these badgers happen to live, they all have an unmistakable physique: short legs with long claws and a short, thick neck on a stout, muscular, wedge-shaped body.

Prairie Dogs

Early in this century, the artist and naturalist Ernest Thompson Seton wrote and illustrated many popular books about the animals of prairies and forests. In his books Seton portrayed animals as intimate friends, for he had gathered his knowledge of America's wildlife from his firsthand encounters in the field, having grown up on the Canadian prairies and traveled to many of America's wild places during his long, adventurous life.

Seton had known prairie dogs since his childhood on the prairies of Manitoba. Prairie dogs were still abundant during his childhood, many years after the first Europeans had settled the prairie and begun claiming land that these endearing rodents had inhabited for many generations. Seton estimated that as many as 5 billion prairie dogs lived on the prairies of North America in the days before they shared the land with humans. Some of their towns covered up to 100 acres (405,000 square meters, or 40.5 hectares). However, human settlers were not willing to share the prairie with such a large number of rodents that littered the land with their deep holes and piles of soil.

People might not enjoy the company of prairie dogs, but prairie dogs clearly enjoy each other's company: their burrows

PRAIRIE DOGS

CLASSIFICATION
Phylum Chordata
Class Mammalia
Order Rodentia
Family Sciuridae
Genus *Cynomys*

PLACE IN FOOD WEB
Diggers, Herbivores

SIZE
28–32 cm in length

NUMBER OF SPECIES
5

LIFESPAN
8–10 years

GESTATION
28–32 days

Prairie dogs spread mineral-rich subsoil around the entrance to their burrow.

are located anywhere from a few feet to 50 feet apart (15 meters). Having neighbors who can sound an alarm if an enemy like an eagle or a badger should show up in town makes life more secure on the flat and treeless prairie. Since the burrows are really the only places where prairie dogs can hide on the open prairie, these rodents devote much of their time to building and maintaining their homes for protection from threats of predators and weather. With their dexterous paws and blunt snouts, prairie dogs continually mold and pound the soil around the entrances. This mounded soil acts both as a dike to keep out water after a heavy downpour of rain and as a barricade against predators.

Being perennially curious, a prairie dog finds it hard to resist peering over the edge of its dike even when danger threatens. With its high-set eyes, a prairie dog can peer out with little more than its eyes visible above the dike. However, a threat can send the prairie dog plunging down the deep,

Prairie dogs are congenial mammals that peacefully coexist in their densely populated communities.

vertical shaft of its burrow, which may be as shallow as 3 feet (1 meter) to as deep as 16 feet (5 meters). But when curiosity once again overcomes a prairie dog's terror, it may stop at or return to a ledge or small room called the "listening post" on one side of the shaft just below the entrance. Here the prairie dog will wait and listen to decide whether it is safe to return to business as usual outdoors or whether it should remain hiding indoors where it can curl up and fall asleep in its cozy bedroom.

The vegetation that prairie dogs eat around their burrows grows in soil that has been enriched and well aerated by their digging.

After decades of displacement and persecution, only a tiny fraction of America's original population of prairie dogs survived. Their best defenses were no match for the deadly strychnine that humans used to poison them. Few people had anything good to say about these rodents that dug burrows and piled dirt and rocks on land that people could plow or use for grazing livestock.

To counter the negative reputation that prairie dogs had gained, two inquisitive soil scientists set out in 1947 to calculate the positive contribution that prairie dogs make to the enrichment of prairie soil. On a one-acre (4,840-square-yard; 4,050-square-meter) patch of shortgrass prairie in eastern Colorado, they counted 50 fresh mounds. The mounds of soil that prairie dogs pile around each of their burrows range in diameter from 2 to 18 feet (0.6–5.5 meters) and from 6 to 18 inches (15–45 centimeters) high. From the weight of soil in an average mound, the two scientists calculated that prairie dogs had piled about 22 1/2 tons (20 metric tons) of soil on the surface. This soil from as deep as 8 to 10 feet (2.5–3 meters) is rich in minerals that renew the fertility of the prairie, and the simple act of churning and loosening the soil makes it a more hospitable environment for the roots of plants.

A recent plan developed by the U. S. Forest Service that oversees America's grasslands noted that plant production is 24 percent higher in prairies inhabited by prairie dogs than in areas that are grazed by cattle. In the soils of the shortgrass prairies where there are few deep roots of trees or tall grasses to help circulate the soil's minerals, prairie dogs help bring minerals to the surface from deep in the soil every time they dig a new burrow or expand an old one. This contribution of prairie dogs to the health and fertility of prairie soils had gone practically unnoticed and unappreciated by the early settlers.

GROUND SQUIRRELS

CLASSIFICATION
Phylum Chordata
Class Mammalia
Order Rodentia
Family Sciuridae
Genus *Spermophilus*

PLACE IN THE FOOD WEB
Diggers, Herbivores, Predators of insects and gastropods

SIZE
15–27 cm in length

NUMBER OF SPECIES
36

LIFESPAN
10 years

GESTATION
28 days

CHIPMUNKS

CLASSIFICATION
Phylum Chordata
Class Mammalia
Order Rodentia
Family Sciuridae
Genus *Tamias*

PLACE IN THE FOOD WEB
Diggers, Herbivores, Predators of insects and gastropods

SIZE
10–18 cm in length

NUMBER OF SPECIES
24

LIFESPAN
10 years

GESTATION
28 days

Ground Squirrels and Chipmunks

According to early explorers of the West, ground squirrels were, in places, even more numerous than prairie dogs. Around the turn of the century, Ernest Thompson Seton estimated that as many as 5,000 Richardson's ground squirrels lived on a square mile of prairie, making their burrows 3 inches in diameter, 3 to 6 feet deep, and anywhere from 12 to 48 feet long. Their relatives on the West Coast, the equally abundant California ground squirrels, can dig tunnels extending as far as 140 feet and having as many as 20 entrances.

The burrows of the antelope ground squirrel lie only about a foot beneath the hot, dry surface of the desert soil; but within the horizontal tunnels that extend about 12 feet in length through hard-packed sand and gravel, the air is a cool retreat from the scorching temperatures above. Among the rocks and fallen trees of mountain slopes, golden-mantled ground squirrels dig a very similar system of tunnels that shelter them from the cold and snow of the western mountains.

Ground squirrels do not wander many feet or many yards from the security of their burrows. The security of having a deep, dark, and narrow burrow nearby probably gives a

Throughout the months of winter, ground squirrels hibernate in their burrows. After arising from their winter's sleep, they mate, and several weeks later, their young venture forth from the burrows for the first time.

ground squirrel the courage to be notoriously curious about the world that is centered around its home. Ground squirrels are constantly rearing up on their hind legs with backs straight, holding their front legs close to their bellies, and bracing their bodies from the rear with their long tails as they strain to see what is happening in the neighborhood of their burrows.

A chipmunk in Yellowstone National Park spends a good portion of its short summer gathering seeds and nuts to store in its underground den.

Ground squirrels can be as large as tree squirrels and as small as chipmunks; they can be found in the mountains, in the deserts, and on the prairies. Judging from the large numbers of different ground squirrels that live in these places, these mammals have adapted well to life in soils with many different textures.

Most species of ground squirrels belong to the genus *Spermophilus,* a name that translates into "lover of seeds"; and several more make up the related genera of "lovers of seeds with prominent ears" (*Otospermophilus*), "lovers of seeds and sand" (*Ammospermophilus*), and "beautiful lovers of seeds" (*Callospermophilus*). In North America these different species of ground squirrels range from Mexico to the Arctic and throughout the western half of the continent; but they are absent in the eastern parts of Canada and the United States, where forests and hills replace stretches of desert and grassland. In the rest of the world, ground squirrels are found throughout most of Africa as well as across the grasslands of central Asia and a small adjoining portion of eastern Europe.

In their cozy and spacious burrows, ground squirrels and chipmunks spend the colder months of each year in hibernation and store piles of seeds that they can eat when they awaken in spring before other seeds, green sprouts, or many insects are available as food. Because most species of ground squirrels spend so many months in hibernation, they only have time to raise one litter during the few months that they wander beyond their burrows. As though to make up for the brief time they have to court and mate, the litters that they do raise can be as large as 14 babies. During these warmer months spent above ground, they fatten up on greens and the high-protein meat of insects. In anticipation of shorter and colder days, the ground squirrels stuff their capacious cheek pouches with various seeds that they store in their underground chambers.

A ground squirrel's fondness for insects, and in particular grasshoppers, can have a significant beneficial impact on nearby crops. Much like the contributions of the much-maligned

A curious ground squirrel rushes to the entrance of its burrow, where it can survey its dominion.

prairie dogs, however, the contributions of ground squirrels to pest control, soil aeration, and soil enrichment are rarely, if ever, acknowledged by the people who share the same piece of land. In this narrow, biased view of the deeds of ground squirrels, their occasional trespassing and destruction in cultivated fields is neither overlooked nor forgiven.

Every autumn the woods of North America, northern Europe, and northern Asia are filled with the excited chips and chirps and chucks of chipmunks as they rustle through the fallen leaves, gathering acorns, mushrooms, buds, and many seeds. *Tamias,* the Greek name for chipmunk, means "storer," and the harvest from the forest floor will provision the storage bins that surround each chipmunk's cozy sleeping chamber. In many woods, the density of chipmunks can be surprisingly high, and chipmunk dens can be as numerous as two or three to an acre. The soil that a chipmunk moves as it digs its burrow is eventually carried off and scattered, leaving their whereabouts on the forest floor well hidden. The entrance where most of the soil is removed serves as a work entrance that is later plugged, while the entrance that is actually used by the chipmunk is well hidden from view and remarkably hard to find.

Moles

No one would consider a mole to be particularly handsome, with its stubby legs, squat body, and beady eyes. About the only handsome feature of a mole is its soft, velvety fur that remains spotless even in the dirtiest of the mole's tunnels. The massive digging muscles of its front legs and shoulders take up so much space at the front end of the mole's body that little space remains for a neck. As it lives out its days in dark passageways, a mole is far too busy digging and devouring earthworms and insects to be concerned about appearances. A mole has neither the eyes nor enough light in its dark galleries to appreciate the beauty of its fellow moles.

A highly developed sense of smell and sense of touch are far more useful to it than keen vision. One species, the star-nosed mole, has one of the most unforgettable noses in the animal kingdom. As its name implies, its nose looks just like a star, with 22 wriggling rays that look like tentacles radiating from the two nostrils. A nose like this can pick up not only the slightest odor but also the slightest touch. Anyone who has tried to sneak up on a mole knows how sensitive it can be to the slightest vibration of the ground. The rigid sensory whiskers, or vibrissae, that line the head, the tail, and the feet of every mole can amplify even the most insignificant tremor of the soil and send the mole dashing to the safety of a deep tunnel.

Just as squirrels and chipmunks store nuts and acorns, the mole stores little balls of earthworms. Rather than immediately eating every worm that it catches, a mole will nibble off a few segments from the end of a worm and then roll the rest into a ball that it tucks into one of the crevices or cavities lining its gallery. Even though each worm in the ball is still alive, it stays semi-paralyzed and immobilized in the mole's pantry until the mole decides to eat this particular leftover from an earlier meal. Once its tunnels are dug, a mole regularly patrols each of them. Earthworms and larvae of insects that happen to stumble into one of these many tunnels as they roam through the topsoil may soon end up in the mole's stomach or its pantry. Considering that a mole eats about half its weight each day, it must consume many generous servings of worms in its short lifetime.

MOLES

CLASSIFICATION
Phylum Chordata
Class Mammalia
Order Insectivora
Family Talpidae

PLACE IN FOOD WEB
Diggers, Predators of earthworms, arthropods, and gastropods

SIZE
11.5–16.5 cm in length

NUMBER OF SPECIES
29

LIFESPAN
3–5 years

GESTATION
30–42 days

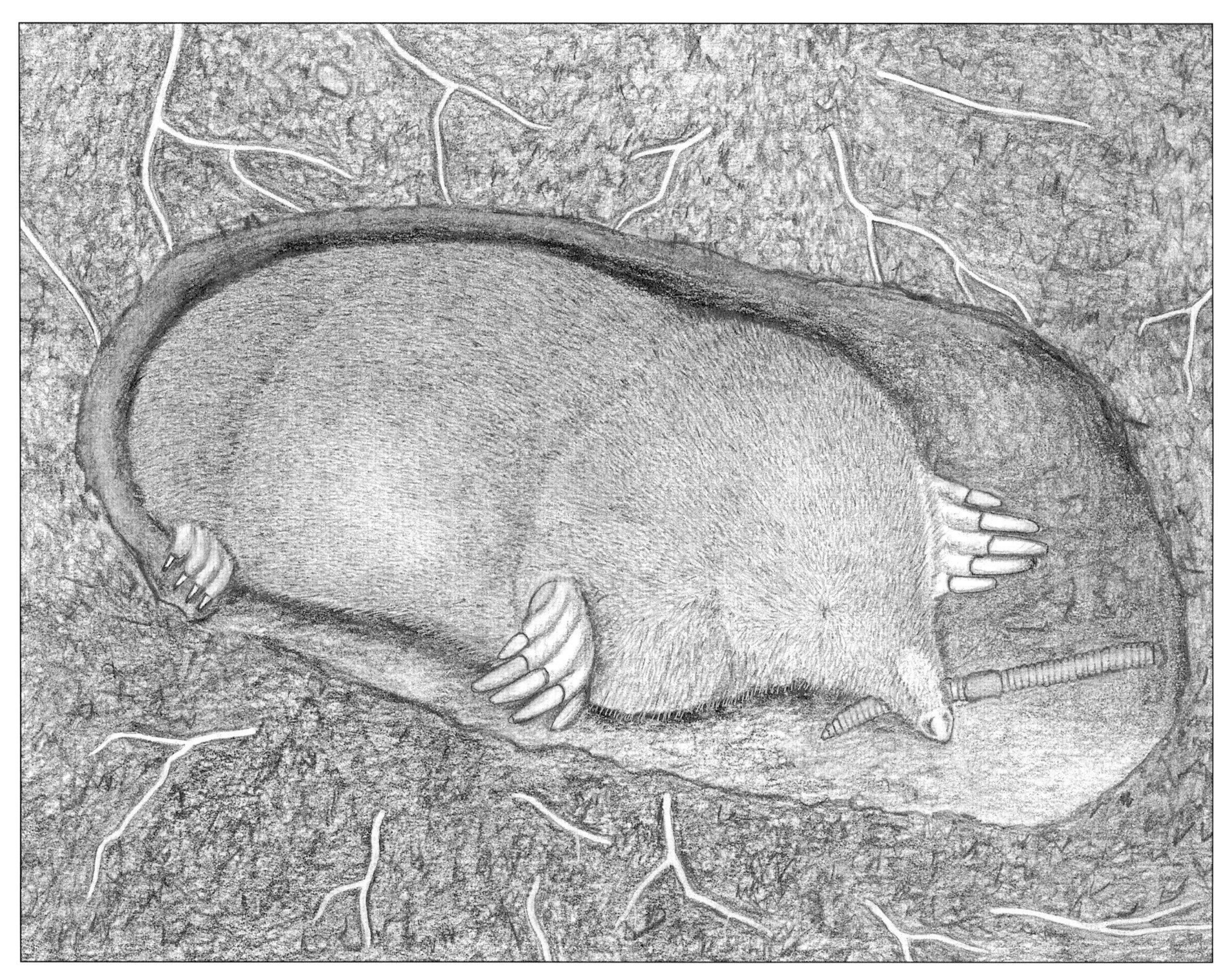

Moles do most of their foraging for earthworms and insects in shallow tunnels that lie just beneath the soil's surface; they retreat to their deep tunnels where they nest and rest during droughts and the months of winter.

Every mole excavates a series of surface tunnels for feeding and a series of deeper tunnels about 2 feet (60 centimeters) below where it can nest and avoid predators as well as heat and cold. Even in compact soil a mole can progress at the rate of 12 to 15 feet (3.5–4.5 meters) an hour. As it digs, the mole shoves the soil to its rear; when a sufficient amount of soil has built up behind it, the mole flips around and begins shoving the pile of soil through the tunnel and back toward the surface where it eventually pours forth as a molehill.

All this exertion and labor demands a lot of energy, as well as food and oxygen to generate the energy. In addition to a mole's managing to find half its weight of worms in a single day, it is also able to extract oxygen from the stale air of its stuffy, poorly ventilated tunnels. A mole's large lungs make up 20 percent of its body weight. In addition, its volume of blood and the amount of hemoglobin that carries oxygen around its body are twice that of other animals its size. The demands of its subterranean life have molded the mole into a creature beautifully adapted to its poorly lit, poorly ventilated, and usually damp home.

A mole that has been removed from its tunnels has the physique of an accomplished digger: broad front legs, a short neck, and large, muscular shoulders.

In Africa the niches occupied by moles in other parts of the world are occupied by mole rats and golden moles. Golden moles belong to a family of mammals related to the familiar moles. Their name comes from the iridescent glow of their thick fur, and they have the muscular shoulders and front legs that make true moles such excellent diggers. Also like true moles, golden moles are insectivores and feed mostly on earthworms, insects, spiders, and snails. Mole rats, however, are rodents that survive on roots and tubers. The two front teeth, or incisors, that protrude from the mouth of a mole rat like buck teeth supply its digging power. Whenever mole rats are digging with their front teeth, lip folds behind the incisors cover the mouth and keep the mole rats from swallowing dirt as they dig.

Of all the mole rats, only the naked mole rats form colonies in which they actually collaborate on their digging projects: one mole rat excavates with its teeth and passes the soil down its line of companions until it is eventually tossed out of the molehill.

The molehills that punctuate African landscapes are the handiwork of either golden moles or mole rats and represent as much as half a ton of soil moved each month by a single animal.

Mole hills on a lawn.

SHREWS

CLASSIFICATION
Phylum Chordata
Class Mammalia
Order Insectivora
Family Soricidae

PLACE IN FOOD WEB
Diggers, Predators of earthworms, arthropods, snails, and slugs

SIZE
3.5–29 cm in length

NUMBER OF SPECIES
246

LIFESPAN
12–20 months

GESTATION
13–24 days

Shrews

Shrews are like miniature moles that spend more time hunting aboveground than they spend digging belowground. The smallest living land mammal happens to be the pygmy shrew. A really large pygmy shrew may be only two inches (50 millimeters) from the tip of its nose to the base of its tail and weigh as much as an American dime. Shrews are the busybodies of the forest floor, constantly searching for food to maintain their extravagant metabolic rate. A shrew's heart beats about 160 times a minute. Its breathing rate is also around 160 times per minute, a rate 10 times that of most humans. A shrew's digestion is so rapid that food is converted to droppings in three hours. Living life at such a pace quickly takes its toll. For most shrews, old age arrives in about 18 months. By this time a shrew's teeth are usually worn to the gums, and it soon collapses from starvation.

In the fall and winter, you often can find dead shrews lying among the grasses of meadows or the litter on the forest floor. Dogs, foxes, raccoons, and other animals may sniff at dead shrews, but they leave them untouched. Even possums, which have reputations for eating just about anything, do not eat

On the forest floor, a tenrec meets a crane fly. This relative of shrews may look like a shrew, but some of the other species of tenrecs on the island of Madagascar look like otters, moles, and hedgehogs.

shrews. Perhaps to compensate for the vulnerability of being so small, shrews emit a foul odor from glands in their skin that repels other mammals; however, it does not seem to discourage carrion beetles (p.125). In the spring and summer when these beetles are about, they quickly lay claim to carcasses of shrews as nurseries for their larvae.

This shorttail shrew has found an earthworm on a forest floor in Virginia.

When shrews finally take a break from hunting insects, earthworms, and snails, they retire to their tunnels under the forest litter. Here, in a nursery chamber lined with grass or leaves, each shrew begins its life. In keeping with the frenetic pace of its outdoor activities, a shrew's home life can be equally demanding. One female shrew can have anywhere from one to 10 litters in a single year. Digging tunnels also takes energy, and most shrews prefer to dig their own and then fervently defend them if another shrew should have the audacity to trespass. Only one specie of shrews, has been observed to collaborate with its fellow shrews in constructing colonial tunnels.

Shrews are found on every continent except Australia; but there they have marsupial counterparts among a large family known as the dasyurids (*dasy* = hairy; *uri* = tail). Some dasyurids like the large Tasmanian devil do not resemble shrews at all, but about half of the dasyurid species weigh less than 3.5 ounces (100 grams), look like shrews, and act like shrews. Some of these small insect-eating dasyurids even look more like shrews than some of the hedgehogs, tenrecs, and solenodons that represent the closest relatives of shrews and moles. About 12 species of hedgehogs are scattered across Europe, Africa, and Asia, and about 30 species of tenrecs are found on the island of Madagascar. Only two species of solenodons tenuously survive in the remote forests of Cuba and Hispaniola. Like the shrews and moles, most of these other members of the Insectivora are diggers, and they all seem very fond of earthworms and other soil invertebrates. Their long, probing snouts have noses with acute senses of smell and long whiskers with fine senses of touch. Even in the disarray of leaf litter and the dark labyrinths of the soil, these snouts can track down the most elusive insects and worms.

POCKET GOPHERS

CLASSIFICATION
Phylum Chordata
Class Mammalia
Order Rodentia
Family Geomyidae

PLACE IN FOOD WEB
Diggers, Herbivores

SIZE
13–22.5 cm in length

NUMBER OF SPECIES
34

LIFESPAN
4 years

GESTATION
17–20 days

Pocket Gophers

On the vast and fertile grasslands of the world—the prairies of North America, the steppes of Asia, the savannahs of Africa—herds of grazing animals have dined and left their droppings generation after generation, enriching the soil and at the same time pressing and packing the rich soil beneath their hooves. The plants that live on this soil are particular not only about the nutrients and water that the soil contains but also about the ease with which their roots can grow and breathe in the soil. In the economy of the grasslands, it is the digging creatures that continually restore the spongy, crumbly structure to the soil that the hoofed animals just as continually compress and compact. With their incessant urge to burrow, the rodents, badgers, and insects of the grasslands are ceaselessly mixing layers of soil and recreating the rich, porous structure of soils in which plant roots grow so well.

While most burrowing animals such as prairie dogs, badgers, and woodchucks spend a good portion of their waking hours traveling aboveground, the gophers of the grasslands almost never leave their burrows. Here in their subterranean tunnels all their needs are met: protection from owls, hawks, and other predators; shelter from bad weather; and a bountiful supply of roots and tubers. When traveling to new destinations, gophers simply dig their way there. A lifetime of traveling underground can add up to a lot of digging and a phenomenal amount of earth moving. A gopher can dig 300 feet (92 meters) of tunnel in a single night. If the ground gets very hard and the going very tough, the gopher starts using its teeth as well as its claws.

Even if gopher burrows only occupy 0.1 percent of a soil's surface, each year on every acre of land 250 pounds of soil (114 kilograms on 4,050 square meters) will be moved from the subsoil to the surface where new rocks will be weathered and new minerals will be freed for the growth of plants. Gophers and ground squirrels can be so abundant in places that their new mounds may cover 15 to 20 percent of the soil's surface and involve the movement of many tons of soil in one year alone. One naturalist estimated that pocket gophers move 8,000 tons (7,256 metric tons) of soil each year in California's Yosemite National Park.

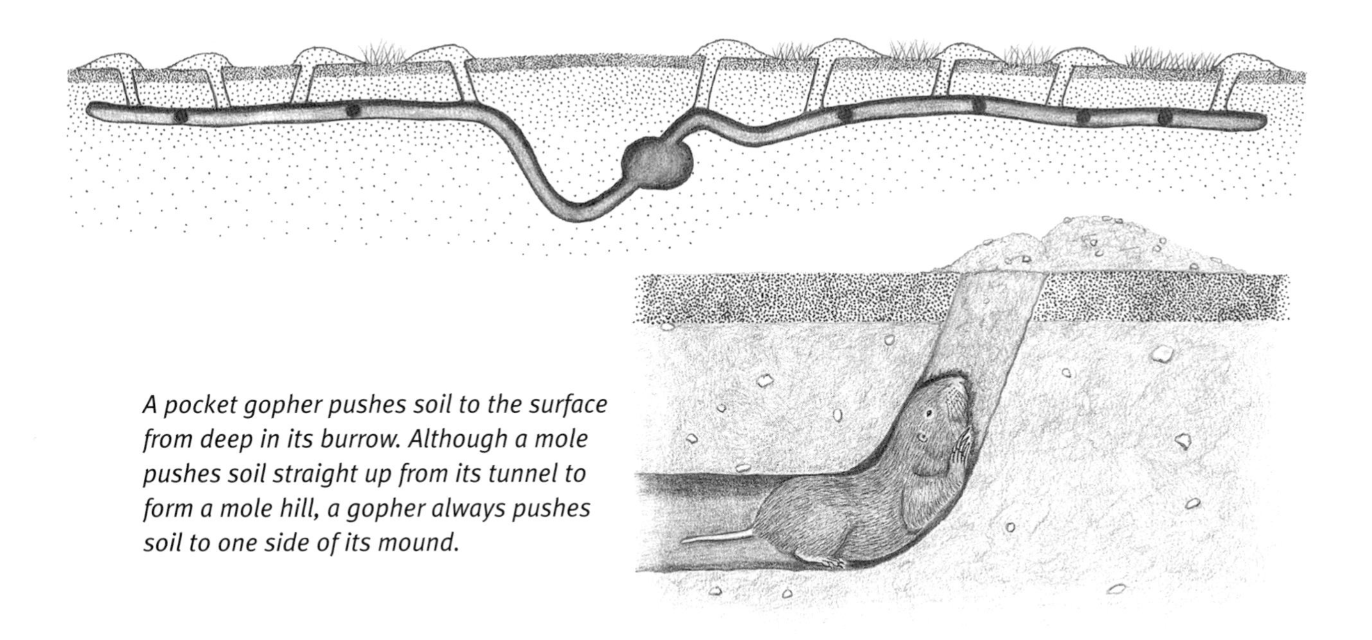

A pocket gopher pushes soil to the surface from deep in its burrow. Although a mole pushes soil straight up from its tunnel to form a mole hill, a gopher always pushes soil to one side of its mound.

According to a 1947 article, a large colony of pocket gophers on a single acre in eastern Nebraska managed to pile up 56,000 pounds or 28 tons (25,425 kilograms or 25.4 metric tons) of subsoil during a single autumn. These are impressive figures for a small mammal that is less than a foot (30 centimeters) in length from the tip of its nose to the end of its short, naked tail. For a life of constant digging in dark, narrow tunnels, gophers have just the right combination of traits: tiny ears for tight tunnels, tiny eyes for dark tunnels, and strong front legs for digging. Numerous calculations have been made to determine how much soil is moved by each kind of rodent as well as how abundant each one is, and gophers always seem to score highest on all counts.

The name "gopher" can be traced to the French word *gaufre,* meaning honeycomb. One gopher's tunnels can extend over an acre or more. The soil can be so perforated by these tunnels that a cross section of the soil inhabited by a gopher really does look like a honeycomb. The main tunnel of a pocket gopher's home is about 4 inches (10 centimeters) in diameter, between 6 and 9 inches (15-23 centimeters) belowground, and may run for 500 feet (153 meters). Many side tunnels branch off the main tunnel, some leading to the surface where excavated soil is pushed out of the opening and spread in a

In a rare appearance aboveground, a pocket gopher snacks on some stems and roots.

flat, fan-shaped mound. Other tunnels lead to toilet chambers, feeding chambers, and storage chambers. One tunnel descends several feet to the gopher's grass-lined nest chamber. An intricate network of twisting tunnels connects the many mounds of a pocket gopher's home.

In its tunnels, a gopher can find all the roots, bulbs, and underground stems that it needs to satisfy a healthy appetite for half its weight in food each day. After each meal the gopher's droppings and scraps are left to mix with the soil in the tunnels, adding organic matter and enriching soil well below its surface. Traffic in the tunnel system is two-way, with organic matter moving downward and mineral matter moving up to the soil's surface.

When the tunnels need expanding, the pocket gopher moves mineral soil from the depths of its burrow to the surface, where it is mixed with the organic remnants of plants. So much exchange of organic matter and mineral matter takes place around gopher tunnels that the surface of the ground in the vicinity of a gopher's den probably turns over at least once every two years. The contributions of gophers to overgrazed grassland are easily spotted from afar as oases of lush, green grass surrounded by stunted grass struggling to grow in hoof-trodden soil. Wherever gophers have turned and crumbled the soil, plants thrive in the hospitable environment.

Kangaroo Rats

Beneath the desert mounds that mark the homes of kangaroo rats lives a whole menagerie of desert creatures. Toads, snakes, lizards, centipedes, millipedes, ants, beetles, crickets, scorpions, and roaches are known to move in and share the spacious passageways that lie from two to three feet (50–90 centimeters) below the surface and that can occupy three or four levels as they twist and turn in this or that direction. The kangaroo rat seems to tolerate all of these tenants and provides them a cool refuge from the heat of the desert sun.

Here, in its underground chambers, the temperature almost never rises above 85°F (30°C) even though the temperature at the surface of the soil may rise to 160°F (72°C). The kangaroo rat avoids the desert heat and many desert predators by sealing itself in its burrow and resting during the daytime hours. Kangaroo rats cannot withstand much heat and soon succumb if they are exposed for only a few hours to temperatures over 100°F (38°C).

Most animals keep cool by losing heat as water evaporates from their bodies. Kangaroo rats, however, do not use this standard strategy for keeping cool. They do not pant like a dog or sweat like a horse. Instead, they stay cool and at the same time conserve precious water by avoiding the heat and concentrating their urine. They also lose very little water in their hard, dry droppings, and what little they do lose from their bodies, they manage to reuse. By eating their semidry droppings, kangaroo rats manage to extract any remaining water and nutrients that their digestive tracts failed to absorb the first time around.

Kangaroo rats are quintessential water conservationists, surviving on whatever water they produce from digestion of their diet of desert seeds and conserving even this small amount of water as they spend their days beneath their desert mounds in the relative coolness of their underground sanctuaries. In some areas of the desert as much as 30 percent of the land area is covered by the mounds of kangaroo rats. Although well-beaten trails lead from burrow to burrow, about the only time a kangaroo rat actually shares its burrow with another kangaroo rat is during the mating season. Each mound can measure 10 to 15 feet (3 to 4.5 meters) in diameter

KANGAROO RATS

CLASSIFICATION
Phylum Chordata
Class Mammalia
Order Rodentia
Family Heteromyidae
Genus *Dipodomys*

PLACE IN FOOD WEB
Diggers, Herbivores

SIZE
10–16 cm in length

NUMBER OF SPECIES
22

LIFESPAN
1 year

GESTATION
33 days

and as much as 4 feet (1.2 meters) in height. Most mounds represent the combined efforts of many generations of kangaroo rats. Each generation extends some tunnels, seals off others, adds doorways, and always seems to add a little more mineral soil to the mound. The quantities of organic matter in the form of seeds and dried grass that kangaroo rats carry

The burrows of kangaroo rats are a common sight on the landscape of American deserts. Their passageways provide a cool oasis for many desert creatures.

into their burrows commonly range from three to six bushels (105 to 210 liters) but 14 bushels (493 liters) of plant matter was found in the burrow of one particularly industrious kangaroo rat.

A number of other small mammals seem to have much in common with these handsome, big-footed rodents. Kangaroo rats share their desert habitat with closely related but even smaller pocket mice. These dainty mice with big hind feet burrow into the desert soil and survive on the seeds that desert plants are able to provide.

On the other side of the world, in the steppes and deserts of Asia and Africa, another kangaroolike rodent, the jerboa, has hind feet that are even larger than any of its American relatives. What is equally striking about the jerboa are its big ears. Some species of jerboas have ears that are half the length of their 3-inch (7.5-centimeter) bodies. The jerboa belongs to the family Dipodidae (*di* = two; *podi* = feet) and gets around fine on its two big feet, holding its small front legs above the ground. The deserts and savannahs of Asia and Africa are also home to the familiar gerbils, which could be mistaken for jerboas if their ears and hind legs were larger. In their deep burrows, insulated from heat and cold, gerbils and jerboas hoard seeds and socialize.

On the grasslands of south and east Africa live some larger big-footed, burrowing rodents, called springhares, that have been assigned a family of their own by biologists. Their family name, Pedetidae, translates to "leapers" and seems a very appropriate choice for these rodents that can leap 10 to13 feet (3 to 4 meters) with their 6-inch (15-centimeter) feet. With the ears as well as the head of a rabbit, the body of a kangaroo, and a tail slightly longer than its 14- to 17-inch (36-43-centimeter) body, the springhare looks as though it has been pieced together with parts from different animals.

PART 3

THE GIFT OF GOOD EARTH

Erosion

It is one of the ironies of nature that the same forces of wind and water that help create soils can also do a thorough job of destroying soils. Each year wind and water erosion are notorious for carrying away soil from cultivated fields in the United States that weighs not just thousands of pounds or millions of pounds, but rather about 2 billion tons (1.8 billion metric tons).

Although this figure represents a significant reduction in the rate of erosion in recent years (thanks to the introduction of new soil conservation measures), the damage from soil erosion still comes with a high price tag to society. Crop productivity losses from erosion contribute on-site costs to both the farmer and the consumer, while sedimentation, flooding, and pollution from soil erosion contribute off-site costs to the public. Expressed in terms of dollars, the on-site costs have been roughly estimated to be $27 billion and the off-site costs to be $17 million each year.

Nevertheless, erosion is a natural process that has shaped the familiar prairies, mountains, and river valleys that grace the surface of the earth. It is part of a natural cycle of wearing down and building up that has always marked the history of the earth, with the rate of soil formation keeping pace with the rate of soil erosion. Soil formation varies from place to place around the world because the rate at which a soil forms depends on several features of a place, including its climate, its soil-forming rocks, its flatness or steepness, and its plants and animals. A rough estimate of the average rate of soil formation has been given as a foot (30 centimeters) of soil developing every 10,000 years.

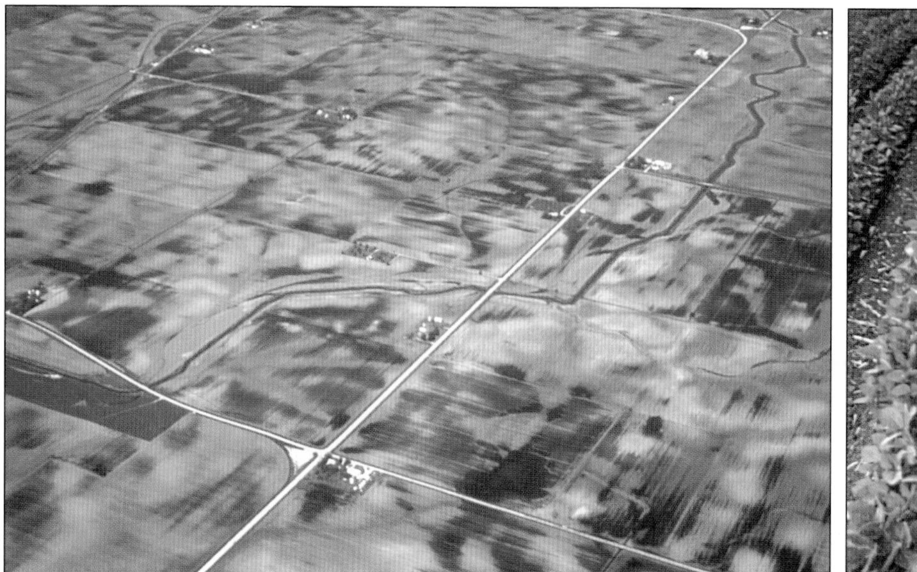

From the air (left), conventional tillage of land can be easily spotted. Most of the soil in the fields is exposed to wind and rain erosion. Equipment used to till the soil between rows of soybeans (right) compacts the soil and disturbs the habitat of soil creatures.

By leaving some soil untilled, the farms in these photographs practice conservation tillage. The farmers minimize the disruption of soil structure and soil habitats by minimizing their use of farm equipment. In combination with fence rows and windbreakers, land that is infrequently tilled attracts not only a diverse population of soil creatures but also birds and insects that help keep the populations of crop pests in check.

In many locations, the intervention of human farming has disrupted and distorted this natural cycle of soil erosion and soil formation, accelerating soil loss to such an extent that the normal processes of soil regeneration simply can not keep pace. On other land, judicious farming practices have actually built soil at rates faster than this estimated natural rate of soil formation.

Tillage is the way we mechanically work the soil to grow crops and to control weeds, using plow, disk, and harrow. By exposing soil to the elements of wind, rain, and snow, tillage dramatically modifies the environment of the soil and exposes it to erosion. Far fewer plant species now dwell on the land, often only the species that is being grown as a crop, along with the few weeds that manage to escape herbicide and harrow. Compared with native vegetation, crop plants leave behind far less organic matter; their root systems cover less territory underground and bring up fewer nutrients to the surface of the ground.

Conventional tillage of the earth, which has been practiced since the birth of agriculture, is being replaced as gentler and less disruptive methods of tilling the land are being tried and perfected. After the harvest, the crop residues that linger on the field have traditionally been plowed under, exposing the bare earth, but today many farmers choose to leave residues on the surface of the field to protect against erosion and to provide a haven for the decomposers and the makers of humus. These same farmers also leave strips of land untouched by the plow. There, trees are planted as windbreaks and fence rows are allowed to harbor a variety of plants and animals. This practice of reduced tillage, known as conservation tillage, may have the drawback of not controlling weeds as well as conventional tillage does, but it saves on fuel and equipment use, and reduces erosion by 40 to 50 percent.

At the Land Institute in Salina, Kansas, researchers are experimenting with perennial crops that would require no additional tillage after being planted. Unlike annual crops such as corn, soybeans, wheat, and rye, whose roots and shoots die back every autumn, perennial crops have root systems that survive for many years and shoots that resprout every spring. During the winter the living roots of perennial crops would hold the soil in place, and the remains of their leaves and stalks would provide both cover and nutrients for the soil. The plant debris left behind at the end of each growing season would provide a hospitable home for a large and diverse population of soil creatures. Annual autumn tillage could be abandoned, and the soil beneath the perennial crop could be spared the ravages of winter winds and spring rains.

Whenever soil blows or washes away, the nutritive elements of the soil disappear as well. What goes first is the topsoil and the humus and plant nutrients that are concentrated in topsoil. What remains after the topsoil has disappeared is the far less productive and fertile subsoil. Humus and organic matter hold water and mineral nutrients in the topsoil and provide a home for the microbes and animals that are responsible for the formation of humus and organic matter from plant and animal debris. Humus in cool and temperate climates decomposes very slowly and releases only a small percentage of its nutrients each year. As long as they are continually replenished, organic matter and humus are a storehouse for nutrients that plants can use.

Excessive Use of Fertilizers

Nutritive elements are lost from soils not only by wind and water erosion. They can be depleted from the surface soil as water from rain or snow soaks deep into the soil and carries elements out of reach of most plant roots. A soil that is spongy and rich in humus, however, will bind many of the soil nutrients and prevent them from being rapidly depleted from the topsoil. Earthworms, other deep burrowing animals, and deep roots of plants help retrieve nutrients that have been leached from the topsoil and recirculate them to the soil's surface.

Elements are also lost from the soil every time crops and animals are taken from the farm to the market. As crops grow and as livestock graze on the farm, they directly or indirectly take up elements from the soil. All plant crops obtain elements from the soil, and livestock obtain elements from these crops. Some crops and farm animals remove more of certain elements than do others. Each bushel of corn and each bushel of wheat contains about a pound (0.5 kilogram) of nitrogen, a quarter-pound (0.1 kilogram) of phosphorus, and a quarter-pound of potassium that came from the soil in which they grew. Crops of legumes such as soybeans, clover, and alfalfa certainly add nitrogen to the soil, but they also remove many pounds of calcium, phosphorus, and potassium from the soil.

A 1,000-pound (454-kilogram) cow indirectly takes about 25 pounds (11.4 kilograms) of nitrogen and about seven pounds (3 kilograms) of phosphorus from the soil where it grazes. No wonder that each time crops and livestock are taken from farm to market, the farm's soil becomes a little poorer in nutrients. As animals and plants are harvested from the land that nourished them, all the elements they took from the soil go with them. The nutrient cycles of farm soil are restored when the nutrients used by plants and animals during life are returned to the same soil after their death.

The constant demand on farmers to increase their output of crops to feed ever-increasing populations of humans and livestock, as well as the constant demand by farmers that their land be more profitable, has established a sinister pattern of accelerated loss of nutrients from the soil and accelerated consumption of synthetic fertilizers to make up for these losses. Between the years 1900 and 1950, the quantities of fertilizers that were used in England and Wales to replenish the major soil nutrients of nitrogen, phosphorus, and potassium increased several fold. Fifteen times more nitrogen, four times more phosphorus, and 36 times more potassium were added to cultivated fields in 1950 than had been added 50 years earlier. In the United States we use at least three times as much fertilizer as we used 30 years ago.

Synthetic nutrients are continually poured on agricultural fields with the mistaken belief that increasing the production of a soil also increases the fertility of a soil. Commercial fertilizers can quickly boost plant nutrition and the production of a soil. But soon the positively charged nutrients like calcium, potassium, and magnesium are leached from the topsoil and washed out of reach of plant roots, unless they are bound by negatively charged particles of humus.

Without the spongy, crumbly structure that humus gives to a fertile soil, many nutrients are simply leached from the topsoil by rain before roots have a chance to put them to use in building plant tissues. By adding too much nitrogen to the soil in the form of nitrate fertilizer, the leaching of positively charged nutrients from humus and topsoil is actually accelerated. This occurs because the negatively charged nitrates attract positively charged nutrients and drag them deeper into the earth and eventually into groundwater, streams, and lakes. In these aquatic environments, excess nutrients from the fertilizers that have passed beyond the reach of roots stimulate the growth of algae and contribute to pollution of the waters.

The nutrients that the crops and livestock of a farm take from the soil can be best replenished by adding organic matter in the form of compost, animal manure, and green manures.

If this situation were not bad enough, denitrifying bacteria put the excess nitrates to use by converting them to toxic nitrites and atmospheric pollutants of nitrogen oxides. Fertilizing fields with common mixes of nitrogen, phosphorus, and potassium may often aggravate deficiencies in other nutrients. Excess levels of these important nutrients can actually make a soil more acidic and depress the plants' uptake of other nutrients such as calcium or magnesium.

Soil without humus and with few living creatures will continue to produce only as long as fertilizer is added. The soil has no nutrient reserves of its own unless it also has humus to hold nutrients where plant roots can reach them.

How do we return something to these impoverished soils that might make a more lasting impression than pouring pound after pound of fertilizer on soil that has no place to store these nutrients? Compost, animal manures, and green manures not only contain the essential nutrients for plant growth, they also add large amounts of organic matter to the soil. This improves the structure of the soil, provides a refuge for organisms that live underground, and by acting as a storehouse for nutrients, slowly releases them at rates of about 2 to 4 percent each year.

Rye, oats, mustard, or legumes are often planted at the end of summer for use as "green manures" after the primary crops of summer such as corn and soybeans have been harvested from the land. These late-planted cover crops grow quickly, protecting the soil from the rains and winds of fall, winter, and spring. Whatever fertilizer was not taken up by the primary crop plants during the preceding summer can now be salvaged by the fast growing roots of the green manure before nutrients from the fertilizer are leached from the land and washed into the groundwater.

When cover crops are plowed under the following spring to make way for the primary crop, their remains make life more hospitable for creatures of the underground, the irreplaceable creatures that do what no human can do alone. Only these creatures can improve the structure of the soil by decomposing plant remains into humus and liberating the mineral nutrients that these plants recovered from the earth during their growing days.

Even the weeds in a garden or field serve a useful function as a form of green manure. Weeds have a knack for partitioning resources of the soil. By spreading their roots different distances both horizontally and vertically, plants can tap different mineral resources. Some weeds have a real appetite for particular minerals and gather them up from the nearby soil. Their roots bring up minerals from below ground, and whenever the weeds are hoed or pulled their remains leave a dose of minerals and organic matter on a compost pile or on the surface of the garden's soil that is within easy reach of the roots of garden vegetables.

Acid Rain

Hydrogen is probably the single most important element in the soil, not because it alone is so important for the well-being of plants but because it is so important in determining the availability and solubility of just about all the other essential elements of the soil. Soils with high concentrations of hydrogen ions—greater than one part to 100,000—are acidic soils, and soils with concentrations of hydrogen ions less than one part to 100,000,000 are alkaline soils. Soils with relatively low concentrations of hydrogen ions somewhere between these two concentrations (considered slightly acid, slightly alkaline, or neutral) are where most plants seem to grow best.

In acidic soils some elements form insoluble compounds with other elements, while in alkaline soils another group of elements forms other insoluble compounds. Since plant roots can use only soluble elements and compounds, any elements that form insoluble compounds are unavailable for their use.

While acidic soils have sufficient concentrations of available iron, zinc, nitrogen, and manganese, they are deficient in soluble phosphorus, potassium, calcium, sulfur, and magnesium. This is why plants showing iron, manganese, or zinc deficiency are often treated by adding hydrogen ions to the soil rather than by adding iron, manganese, or zinc. These elements are already there in the soil; they simply are not soluble and available for uptake by roots. In acidic soils with high concentrations of hydrogen, these elements become soluble and free to be taken up by roots. Too many hydrogen ions, however, can create real problems for roots and other inhabitants of the underground, as we are learning from recent studies of acid rain.

Rain rapidly leaches nutrients from soil that is poor in humus, but acid rain does an even more thorough and sinister job. By contributing to the acidity of soil, acid rain can have devastating effects on life underground, setting off a chain of events that soon has dire consequences for life both above and below ground. Acid rain forms when moisture in clouds combines with sulfur oxides and nitrogen oxides released mainly by automobiles, factories, and power plants.

Some of the nitrogen oxides also arise from excessive use of fertilizers. These nitrogen gases are released into the atmosphere when nitrates from fertilizers are broken down by denitrifying bacteria of the soil.

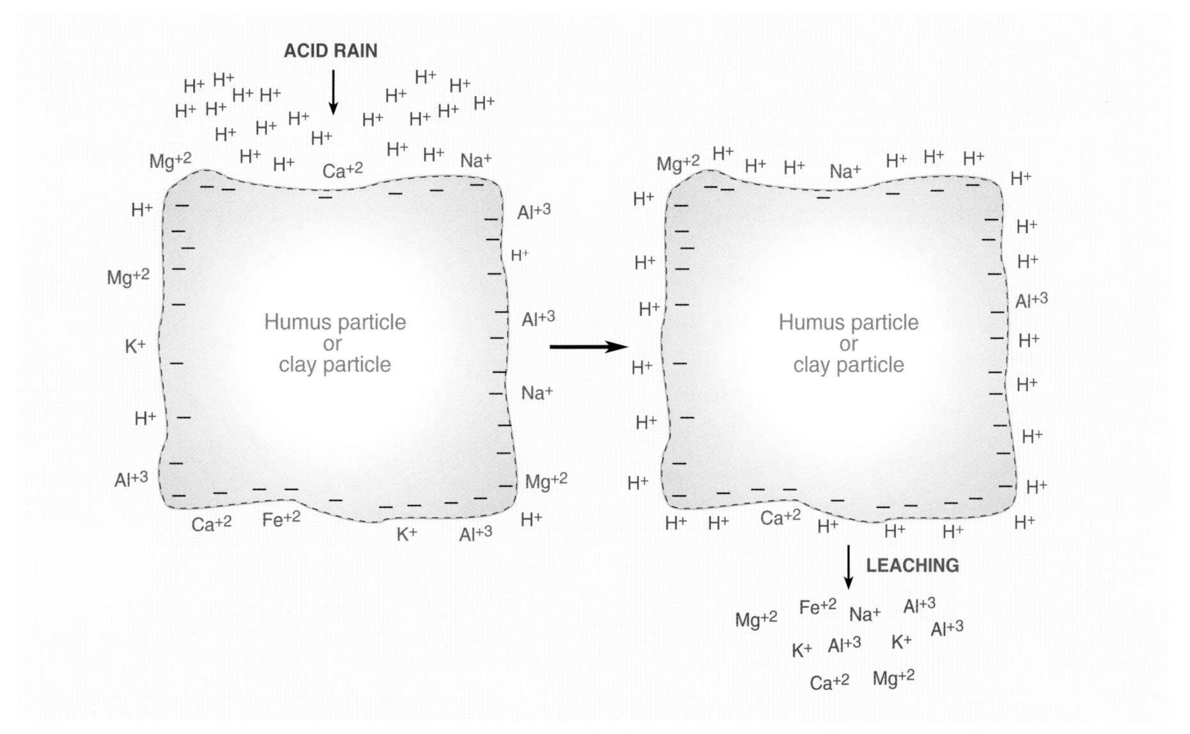

The large number of positively charged hydrogen ions (H^+) found in acid rain (arrow, top left) displaces the positively charged nutrients that are bound to surfaces of negatively charged clay and humus particle (arrow, middle). The positively charged elements (Na^+, K^+, Mg^{+2}, Fe^{+2}, Ca^{+2}, Al^{+3}) eventually are leached from the soil particles (arrow, bottom right)

Sulfur oxides react with water to form sulfuric and sulfurous acids; nitrogen oxides react with water to form both nitric acid and nitrous acid. When these acids fall to the earth, like other acids they release hydrogen cations.

Not only do the numbers of hydrogen cations often exceed the numbers of other nutrient cations but they also bind more strongly to negatively-charged particles like clay and humus. As hydrogen cations from acid rain percolate through the ground they displace other nutritient cations such as calcium, magnesium, and potassium from soil particles, pushing them beyond the reach of plant roots.

Other cations such as aluminum that are toxic to plant roots are insoluble and safely impounded in most soils—but not in acid soils. This is because anytime the hydrogen concentration of the soil becomes particularly high, toxic cations such as aluminum, or cadmium are replaced by hydrogen ions from the humus and clay particles that bind them. These toxic cations are now free, soluble, and harmful to plants and animals. Acid rain not only leaches essential elements from the ground, it also releases toxic elements that poison life in the soil.

Loss of Soil Structure

Healthy soils with humus and organic matter support an abundance of animal and plant life. These soils absorb water just as a sponge does, and the water they hold measures about six times their weight of humus and organic matter. Rain that falls and snow that melts on these soils quickly infiltrates and soaks the spongy soil rather than rushing downhill and carrying soil particles with it. The water travels throughout the ground, eventually to emerge in clear bubbling springs. Where spongy soil covers the hills above a stream, the waters flow clear and unhurried after most rains.

But land that is ill-treated and not respected has a very different fate. Agricultural land that is low in organic matter, that is overtilled, or that has been compacted by equipment or livestock has soil that has lost its vitality. Any slope to the land sends water rushing downhill to nearby streams rather than allowing the land to absorb the water among its rocks, mineral particles, and organic particles where it can be slowly released later. The more water that stays on the surface of the soil and the faster it flows, the more soil it carries along with it. Once the rich life of the soil and the humus it produces are lost, the spongy structure of a soil disappears, and the streams that drain this soil now rush by, muddy and overflowing after a summer rain or a spring thaw. The rushing streams carry nutrients from the land, diminishing its fertility after every rain and snow melt.

Great civilizations of the ancient world arose in river valleys where the fertility of the land was replenished each year by natural floods. The civilizations that arose along the Tigris and Euphrates of Mesopotamia, the Indus, the Mississippi, the Nile, and the Yangtze Rivers endured as long as their soils remained fertile.

The grandeur of ancient Egypt was based on gifts from the Nile. Each spring as the rains fell across northern Africa, humus and clay particles from the rich soils of the upper Nile were carried to Egypt in the flood waters of the river. Accompanying these negatively-charged particles was a rich supply of positively-charged nutritive elements such as potassium, calcium, and magnesium as well as trace amounts of other essential elements. The fertility of the Nile delta was replenished as these fine particles settled on the flooded fields.

This annual gift of humus from the forests of the upper Nile was taken for granted until, in modern times, high dams were built on the upper Nile that held back the flood waters and trapped the humus before it could be carried off to the delta. Now, farming in the Nile delta must be done with expensive fertilizers that are soon lost from the soil. The great river valleys, where early civilizations began with such promise, eventually met a similar fate. Once the forests along the river valleys had been cut and the spongy soil on which they had grown began to wash away, little humus remained to restore fertility to the fields in the valleys.

Plato's dialogue, *The Critias,* dating from the 4th century BC, reminds us that we do not always learn from the mistakes of our past. He describes the sad state of the once rich soil in terms that have become all too familiar:

> "What now remains of the formerly rich land is like the skeleton of a sick man, with all the fat and soft earth having wasted away and only the bare framework remaining. Formerly, many of the mountains were arable. The plains that were full of rich soil are now marshes. Hills that were once covered with forests and that produced abundant pasture now produce only food for bees. Once the land was enriched by yearly rains, which were not lost, as they are now, by flowing from the bare land into the sea. The soil was deep, it absorbed and kept the water in the loamy soil, and the water that soaked into the hills fed springs and running streams everywhere."

In his book *Man and Nature,* written over two millennia later in 1864, George Perkins Marsh echoed these words from the Greeks. "With the disappearance of the forest, all is changed. . . . The face of the earth is no longer a sponge, but a dust heap, and the floods which the waters of the sky pour over it hurry swiftly along the slopes, carrying in suspension vast quantities of earthly particles."

In 1948, the publication of *A Sand County Almanac* by Aldo Leopold helped shape a new appreciation for the gift of good earth. In stating his philosophy of land use, he wrote, "We abuse land because we regard it as a commodity belonging to us. When we see land as a community to which we belong, we may begin to use it with love and respect." Many people have taken Leopold's words to heart, fervently defending the integrity of the land and challenging its flagrant abuse.

The simple message is that healthy soil, healthy food, and healthy people are inextricably linked. Wherever good stewardship of the land is practiced—by controlling erosion and acid rain, by minimizing use of pesticides and tillage, as well as by using compost and manures in preference to commercial fertilizers—we benefit by having richer soils and more nutritious food. At the same time, these practices preserve habitat for soil creatures, our irreplaceable partners in assuring that the gift of good earth will be cherished and not squandered.

Composting

Rotten to the core. This quality just comes naturally to a compost pile and endears it to the decomposers and the company they keep. You can create a wildlife refuge for these creatures in your backyard, help solve the world's garbage problem, and provide a bountiful supply of organic nutrients for your garden by becoming a composter. All plant matter contains nutrients from the soil in which it grew. To dispose of any plant materials in a landfill, whether they are lawn clippings, fallen leaves, produce from the grocery, or even weeds is to waste a wonderful opportunity to give back to the soil some of the nutrients and organic matter that we have squandered.

By participating in nature's processes not only will you feel good about your contribution, but also the fruits, vegetables, and flowers of your garden will certainly benefit from the improved structure that compost gives to the garden's soil as well as the extra nutrients and moisture that will come their way. Your compost will be a refuge for many small and fascinating creatures that will quickly and unobtrusively move in to carry out their noble job of recycling, renewal, and restoration.

By composting we create a hospitable environment for many of the soil's decomposers so they can move in and perform the same tasks they do among the plant debris on the forest floor, in a meadow, and even in all but the most heavily sprayed and fertilized lawns and fields. Once the decomposers have arrived, the conditions in the compost pile encourage them to stick around and multiply.

Composting speeds up the natural process of decomposition that occurs constantly wherever weeds die, leaves fall, and logs rot. Composting is based on four simple and interdependent principles. By (1) interspersing green, moist matter with brown, dry matter and by (2) constructing a pile that is just the right size, a composter (3) assures that air circulates through the compost and (4) that the compost maintains a moisture content that best suits the needs of the decomposers. Even if it is not possible to adhere to all of these principles, your compost will still decompose, although it might take longer to do so. Nature always seems to compensate for imperfections and will complete the job of decomposition at its own pace.

The few steps outlined here will give you a good idea how simple, straightforward, and rewarding composting can be.

1. Begin by finding a good location for the compost pile. Choose a place away from walls and fences that can decay and stain. Avoid any spots that have poor drainage, but if you can locate the compost near a source of water and within reach of a hose, you will have the advantage of easily maintaining the optimal amount of moisture for composting.

2. Learn what sort of items the decomposers of the compost pile find acceptable. As long as the items are organic and biodegradable or inorganic and nourishing, the decomposers can extract sufficient nutrition and energy for their growth. However, avoid adding meat scraps that might attract rodents and pets to the compost pile. Also leave out rags and tires, charcoal and coal ashes, diseased plants, and pet litter; even though they are organic, they either do not degrade well or can contain toxins as well as harmful organisms. Shred or pulverize large and hard materials like corn cobs, stalks, shells, and fruit rinds before adding them to the pile. Chopping up these items will accel-

The act of composting enhances the well-being of both the soil and the composter.

erate their decay by increasing the surface area on which bacteria and fungi can work.

If we made a detailed list of items, we would soon see that the items could be grouped into general categories: (a) plant matter, whether green, dried, or processed (including shredded newspapers, coffee grounds, wood ashes, and wood chips); (b) mineral matter such as ground stone or phosphate rock; (c) dried animal matter such as feathers, bone meal, blood meal, fish meal, hoof and horn meal, egg shells, and shellfish; and, of course, (d) a variety of manures.

Each new addition to the pile contains a different mix of nutrients. Some, like seaweed, are rich in the essential trace element boron; onion and cabbage scraps are rich in sulfur; and shells of all sorts are excellent sources of calcium. The greater the variety of items placed on a compost pile, the greater the diversity of microhabitats you will provide for decomposers, and the richer and more balanced the mix of nutrients in your compost.

What is important to remember is that the decomposers require nutrients of their own to provide the energy for their survival and work. Microbes also need a certain proportion of carbon to nitrogen in order to multiply and carry out the job of decomposing the compost; usually a carbon: nitrogen (C:N) ratio somewhere between 15:1 and 30:1 is ideal.

Nitrogen is the nutrient that is almost invariably in short supply. Nitrogen added to compost in the form of manure, fertilizer, or green vegetation such as weeds and grass clippings provides the missing element for microbial growth and really speeds up the decay of the compost. Fresh, green plant matter is higher in nitrogen than dry, dead plant matter like straw, sawdust, or dry leaves and is always a good addition to the compost pile. The following C:N ratios for various materials can serve as a useful guide in choosing the best nutrition for the decomposers in your compost pile.

Garden soil	12:1–15:1
Manure	15:1–20:1
Grass clippings or weeds	20:1–25:1
Dry leaves or straw	30:1–60:1
Pine needles	60:1–100:1
Sawdust or wood chips	150:1–700:1

3. Collect a critical mass of organic materials. Use leaves, grass, weeds, or kitchen vegetable scraps for optimal composting. Decomposers thrive best on about equal portions of carbon-rich and nitrogen-rich materials. These should be added to the pile in alternating layers, each about four inches (10 centimeters) thick. Experienced composters often have a separate bin for stockpiling materials before adding them to an actively decomposing pile. Compost will heat up more quickly and break down more rapidly if materials are collected in advance and then added simultaneously.

4. Decide on what form the compost pile should take. You can simply heap compost on the ground and let gravity and the decomposers mold the shape of the pile. Books on composting, however, describe pits, bins, barrels, tumblers, boxes, steel drums, garbage cans with holes in their bottoms and sides, and even plastic bags for storing and processing compost. If space is limited, begin your composting in a trash can, large plastic bin, or a large wooden box. Add several holes to the container to make sure that air can circulate around and through the compost.

5. Decide how large the pile should be. A pile that is too small will lose a large amount of the heat generated by the microbes that are rapidly breaking down or oxidizing carbon compounds to carbon dioxide. However, a pile that is too large may become too hot or too airtight at its core. The heat may kill off many of the decomposers, and the lack of oxygen will eliminate many of the aerobic microbes that are most efficient at decomposition. High temperatures speed up the process and destroy plant pathogens as well as the seeds of any weedy plants that happened to find their way into the pile.

However, high temperatures generated inside many compost piles can reach 165°F (74°C) as bacteria, actinomycetes, and fungi reach population densities of 10 billion microbes for every gram of compost. Temperature fortunately does not affect the nutrient content of the finished compost or humus. The most important aspect of composting is giving nature the chance to decompose even if the conditions under which it must work are not particularly ideal. Once again, the decomposers can adapt to any of these forms and containers. So be imaginative and creative in designing your compost pile.

6. Add a "starter" or "activator" to speed up the arrival of decomposers in your compost. Starters are always rich in nitrogen compounds that promote the rapid growth of bacteria and fungi. In addition, many starters such as manure, well-decomposed compost, or rich soil also come with their own populations of bacteria, fungi, and some larger decomposers. Bread makers use the same strategy when they add a starter of yeast to their bread dough. In the same way that different yeasts contribute different flavors to the bread, different compost starters add different amounts of nitrogen-rich matter as well as different populations of decomposers.

7. Make sure the microbes in your compost have plenty of air. A well-aerated compost undergoes thorough decomposition to carbon dioxide, water, minerals, and humus, as opposed to the partial, smelly decomposition that occurs in compost that is unmixed and airtight. A layer of coarse material such as cornstalks or tomato stalks at the very bottom of a pile allows air to enter the pile from below. Turning the pile about a week after it has reached its highest temperature will improve the air supply and hasten the decomposition.

Contrary to popular belief, a compost heap that is properly tended does not stink. As long as the bacterial and fungal decomposers in the compost pile are getting enough oxygen, they continue adding oxygen to carbon-containing compounds until most of the carbon in these compounds has been converted to carbon dioxide. This conversion process is known as oxidation and the microbes that carry out the process are known as oxidizers or aerobes. They have a real talent for quickly breaking down dead plant and animal matter into humus, minerals, carbon dioxide, and water.

During this chemical transformation, considerable energy is given off in the form of heat. The very same basic components—carbon dioxide, water, minerals, and energy in the form of sunlight—that green plants use during photosynthesis as they form the organic compounds of leaves, wood, and fruit eventually also arise in compost piles as the result of decomposition. The pathway followed by carbon dioxide, water, minerals, and energy comes full circle as these three components pass from living plants and animals to the decomposers of the soil and then back to plants and animals again.

However, if the breakdown of compost is turned over to the bacteria and fungi that can survive in the absence of oxygen, these anaerobes (*an* = without; *aero* = air) ferment certain large organic compounds into smaller organic compounds without completely converting them to carbon dioxide.

Students prepare a worm composting box as part of a school garden project. The earthworms shred plant material added to the box and increase the surface area on which the bacterial and fungal decomposers can work.

During bread making and wine making, anaerobic microbes are the ones that convert sugars to alcohol along with some carbon dioxide. These microbes also decompose plant and animal debris to compounds of carbon such as butyric acid, lactic acid, or alcohol, as well as stinky gases like hydrogen sulfide and ammonia. Compost piles should clearly be managed to encourage aerobic decomposers rather than their anaerobic relatives.

8. Keep your compost properly moist. Water is an essential requirement for composting. As mentioned earlier, locating the compost pile near a hose or water source is a good idea. The decomposers do their best work when the compost is uniformly moist but not waterlogged. Accomplished composters say that the pile should have the water content of a squeezed sponge.

Nature keeps the generation of humus simple and there is no reason why composting should not be a simple process as well. Nature carries out the processing of organic matter at its own pace and sees to it that the populations of various bacteria, fungi, actinomycetes and larger decomposers coexist in the proper proportions. You can sit back and watch as the decomposers work their magic in the backyard compost or in the leaves underfoot.

GLOSSARY

Acid soils Soils having concentrations of hydrogen ions greater than one part in 10 million.

Actinomycetes Microscopic organisms that have attributes of both bacteria and fungi. They form branched, multicellular filaments and look like fungi, but their genes resemble bacterial genes. The rich odor of moist, freshly plowed earth arises from the hordes of actinomycetes that inhabit the soil.

Aerobes Organisms that survive and grow only in the presence of air or oxygen gas.

Algae Autotrophic organisms that use the energy of sunlight captured with chlorophyll to produce sugars from carbon dioxide and water. These simple soil organisms without stems, roots, or leaves are considered members of three different kingdoms: Plants (green and red algae); Eubacteria (blue-green algae); and Protista (algae with flagella, yellow-green algae, and diatoms).

Alkaline soils Soils having concentrations of hydrogen ions less than one part in 10 million.

Anaerobes Organisms that survive and grow in the absence of air or oxygen gas.

Anion A particle of a negatively charged element or compound.

Arachnids Arthropods that have four pairs of legs, no antennae or wings, and only two main body regions (cephalothorax and abdomen) instead of three regions (head, thorax, abdomen) as in insects.

Arthropods A large group of animals that do not have backbones but have jointed legs as well as other appendages that are jointed.

Autotrophs Creatures that obtain the energy they need for survival from either the sun or from the reactions of inorganic (mineral) components of the soil. The carbon that these creatures need to form organic compounds comes from carbon dioxide.

Casts Nutrient-rich aggregates of soil that are the droppings of earthworms.

Caterpillar The larva of a moth or butterfly.

Cation A particle of a positively charged element or compound.

Cellulose Long chains of sugar molecules found in all plant tissues. Cellulose forms fibers that support and strengthen these tissues.

Cerci A pair of sensory appendages on the 10th segment of an arthropod's abdomen that are sometimes used as pincers.

Chelicerae The jaws of spiders, mites, daddy longlegs, pseudoscorpions, and other arachnids that can take the form of fangs, pincers, or beaks.

Clay A class of inorganic soil particles that measure less than 0.00008 inch (0.002 millimeter) in diameter. These soil particles are formed by the chemical weathering of rocks such as granite.

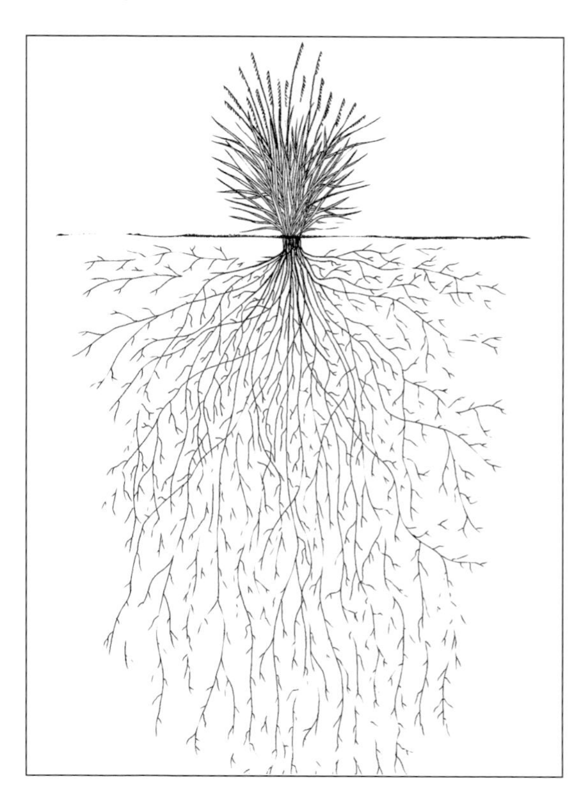

Composting The act of generating humus from organic materials that have been collected and mixed outside of the soil, where they decompose with minimal loss of nutrients.

Compounds Substances that are made up of two or more elements.

Coniferous Category of trees and shrubs that produce cones and are usually covered with evergreen leaves shaped like needles or scales.

Coprophages Organisms that feed on dung and droppings of other creatures.

Deciduous Category of plants that shed their leaves each year at a certain season.

Decomposer An organism that obtains nutrients by breaking down the remains or waste products of other organisms.

Denitrification The conversion of compounds of nitrogen and oxygen known as nitrates (NO_3^-) and nitrites (NO_2^-) to nitrogen oxide gases (NO or N_2O) or dinitrogen gas (N_2). As oxygen is released from the nitrates and nitrites of soil, nitrogen in these compounds is converted to nitrogen gases and is lost from the soil.

Detritivore An organism that feeds on dead plant and animal matter, also known as detritus.

Elements Substances that cannot be broken down to other substances with different properties.

Fossorial Adapted for digging.

Fungi Organisms that are considered unique enough from plants and animals to be placed in their own kingdom. While some fungi feed on other living creatures, most fungi are decomposers and exist as either single cells or multicellular organisms. Fungal cells form filaments called hyphae.

Fungivore An organism that feeds on fungi.

Gastropod A snail or slug.

Herbivore An organism that feeds on plants.

Heterotrophs Creatures that obtain their energy and carbon from the decomposition of organic compounds produced directly or indirectly by autotrophs.

Humus The dark organic matter that remains after most plant and animal debris has decomposed.

Hyphae Filaments of fungal cells.

Immobilization The transformation of an element (nutrient) from its inorganic form in the soil to an organic form within a plant or microbe. Once incorporated within living tissue the element is no longer readily available to other plants or microbes of the soil.

Inorganic Matter Any chemical or material that does not contain compounds having both carbon and hydrogen.

Larva An immature insect that shows little resemblance to its adult form. If the adult insect has wings, these wings first form inside the body of the larva.

Leaching Removal of nutrients by water passing through the upper layers of the soil.

Lichen A composite organism that is part alga and part fungus. The alga and fungus live together in a cooperative arrangement, often surviving in habitats where neither partner could survive alone.

Lignins Large organic molecules of plants that impart rigidity to plant tissues and are particularly resistant to the decomposition that accompanies the formation of humus. Lignin molecules hold together cellulose fibers.

Loam A soil texture in which sand, silt, and clay contribute almost equally.

Manure Any material containing organic matter as well as inorganic nutrients that enriches the soil by its addition.

Microbes Organisms that cannot easily be viewed without a microscope. These organisms include bacteria, actinomycetes, fungi, algae, and protozoa.

Minerals The inorganic particles of soil derived from rocks.

Mineralization The conversion of elements in the remains of plants and animals to their inorganic forms.

Mor A type of humus layer that is clearly separate from the underlying mineral layers of soil. This type of humus or organic layer is typical of coniferous forests.

Mull A type of humus layer that mixes with the underlying mineral layers of soil. This type of humus is characteristic of deciduous forests.

Nitrification The conversion of ammonium (NH_4^+) first to nitrite (NO_2^-) and then to nitrate (NO_3^-) by the addition of oxygen. The first step of the process is carried out by autotrophic bacteria called *Nitrosomonas* while the second step of nitrification is carried out by other autotrophic bacteria, called *Nitrobacter.*

Nitrogen fixation The microbial conversion of dinitrogen gas (N_2) of the atmosphere to nitrogen compounds that can be used by living organisms.

Nutrients Elements or compounds that nourish and promote the growth of organisms.

Nymph An immature insect that usually resembles its adult form. If the adult has wings, these wings first form on the outer surface of the nymph's body.

Organic matter Plant or animal material found in various stages of decay. Organic matter always contains combinations of the elements carbon and hydrogen.

Oxidation The loss of negative charge by a substance, often accompanied by the chemical combination of the substance with oxygen gas.

Pedipalps A pair of sensory appendages on the head of an arachnid that are the counterpart of an insect's antennae and that are sometimes used as pincers.

Podzol A type of soil that forms under coniferous forests and has a characteristic bleached horizon from which nutrients have been leached by precipitation, leaving a pale layer of sand grains.

Producers Plants, algae, and autotrophic bacteria that produce organic nutrients from simple inorganic compounds using energy from sunlight or from the reactions of inorganic compounds.

Protozoa Single-celled organisms that include amoebae with and without shells; those having flagella (*flagellum* = whip); and those having cilia (*cilium* = small hair).

Reduction The gain of negative charge by a substance, often accompanied by a loss of oxygen from the substance or the addition of hydrogen.

Rhizobia (*rhizo* = root; *bios* = life) The group of bacteria in the genus *Rhizobium* that live symbiotically in root nodules of certain plants. In the root nodules, the rhizobia obtain energy from the plants to convert dinitrogen gas in the air to compounds of nitrogen that the plants can use.

Rhizomorph An aggregation of several thousand parallel filaments (hyphae) of fungi that grows as a single unit.

Rhizosphere The region of soil immediately surrounding plant roots. Bacteria and other microbes seem to be especially abundant in this zone.

Saprophytes or Saprobes Organisms that feed on nonliving organic matter. This name is synonymous with detritivores, decomposers, and scavengers.

Silt A class of inorganic soil particles measuring between 0.00008 and 0.002 inch (0.002 and 0.05 millimeter) in diameter. Silt particles are silky to the touch and arise from the weathering of rocks.

Soil horizon A layer of soil that usually lies parallel to the surface of the ground. Each layer can have characteristic chemical and physical properties.

Soil structure The arrangement of soil particles into naturally occurring clumps called aggregates. If the clumping of soil particles is caused by tillage, the clumps are called clods.

Soil texture The relative proportion of sand, silt, and clay in a soil.

Subsoil The layer of soil (horizon) that lies below the topsoil; the layer that is not turned during cultivation.

Symbiosis An intimate, continuous, and mutually beneficial interaction between two different organisms.

Tillage The mechanical disruption of soil that modifies soil conditions for the production of crops.

Topsoil The layer of the soil that is disrupted and mixed during tillage.

Urogomphi A pair of dorsal processes that project from the posterior end of the ninth segment of a beetle larva's abdomen.

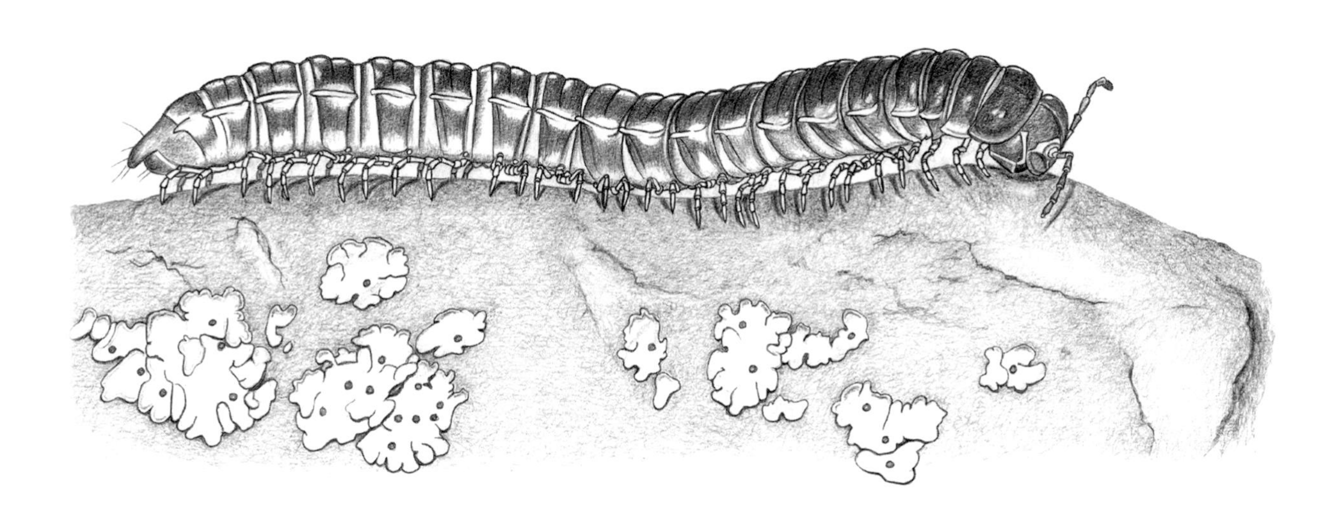

FURTHER READING

General

Bial, Raymond. *A Handful of Dirt.* New York: Walker, 2000.

Brady, N. C. and R. R. Weil. *The Nature and Properties of Soils.* Upper Saddle River, N.J.: Prentice Hall, 1996.

Dindal, Daniel L., ed. *Soil Biology Guide.* New York: Wiley, 1990.

Hillel, David J. *Out of the Earth: Civilization and the Life of the Soil.* New York: Free Press, 1991.

Logan, William B. *Dirt: The Ecstatic Skin of the Earth.* New York: Riverhead, 1995.

Wolf, David W. *Tales from the Underground: A Natural History of Subterranean Life.* Cambridge, Mass.: Perseus, 2001.

Vertebrates

Behler, John L., and F. Wayne King. *The Audubon Society Field Guide to North American Reptiles and Amphibians.* New York: Knopf, 1979.

Boitani, Luigi, and Stefania Bartoli. *Simon and Schuster's Guide to Mammals.* New York: Simon and Schuster, 1983.

Macdonald, David, ed. *The Encyclopedia of Mammals.* London: George Allen & Unwin, 1984.

Perrins, Christopher, and C. J. O. Harrison. *Birds: Their Life, Their Ways, Their World.* Pleasantville, N. Y.: Reader's Digest Association, 1979.

Tyning, Thomas F. *A Guide to Amphibians and Reptiles.* Boston: Little, Brown and Company, 1990.

Zim, Herbert S., and Donald F. Hoffmeister. *Mammals: A Guide to Familiar American Species.* New York: Golden, 1991.

Invertebrates

Aaseng, Nathan. *Invertebrates.* New York: Franklin Watts, 1993.

Borror, Donald J., and Richard E. White. *A Field Guide to the Insects of America North of Mexico.* Boston: Houghton Mifflin, 1998.

Buchsbaum, Ralph M., J. Pearse, and V. Pearse. *Animals without Backbones: An Introduction to the Invertebrates.* Chicago: University of Chicago Press, 1987.

Levi, Herbert W., and Lorna R. Levi. *Spiders and Their Kin.* Rev. ed. New York: Golden, 1990.

Fungi and Non-Flowering Plants

Arora, David. *Mushrooms Demystified: A Comprehensive Guide to the Fleshy Fungi.* 2nd ed. Berkeley: Ten Speed Press, 1997.

Hudler, George W. *Magical Mushrooms, Mischievous Molds.* Princeton, N.J.: Princeton University Press, 1998.

Lincoff, Gary H. *National Audubon Society Field Guide to North American Mushrooms.* New York: Knopf, 1981.

Shuttleworth, Floyd S., and Herbert S. Zim. *Mushrooms and Other Non-Flowering Plants.* New York: Golden, 1987.

Composting

Campbell, Stu. *Let It Rot! The Gardener's Guide to Composting.* Pownal, Vt.: Storey, 1998.

Martin, Deborah L., and Grace Gershuny, eds. *The Rodale Book of Composting.* Emmaus, Pa.: Rodale, 1992.

Nancarrow, Loren, and Janet Hogan Taylor. *The Worm Book.* Berkeley: Ten Speed Press, 1998.

WEB SITES

Insect Answers
http://entowww.tamu.edu/extension/insctans/
The Department of Entomology at Texas A&M University maintains this user-friendly site that provides images and brief descriptions of several soil-dwelling creatures.

Invertebrates of the Compost Pile
http://www.cfe.cornell.edu/compost/invertebrates.html
Cornell University Science and Engineering site containing information and images about the invertebrates active in compost piles.

Microbes and Composting
http://commtechlab.msu.edu/sites/dlc-me/zoo/zdcmain.html
Web site from Michigan State University offering information about the microbes that aid in composting.

Natural Resources Conservation Service on Composting
http://www.nrcs.usda.gov/feature/backyard/compost.html
Information and instructions for composting from the United States Department of Agriculture's Natural Resources Conservation Service site.

Soil Biology Movies
www.agron.iastate.edu/~loynachan/mov/
Soil biology site contains QuickTime™ movies on life in the soil

Soil Ecology Database
http://www.fhsu.edu/agriculture/soilsecologywebsites.htm
Fort Hays State University site offers links to articles on a wide variety of soil-dwelling organisms.

Soil Foodweb
http://www.soilfoodweb.com/articles.html
Soil Foodweb Incorporated site features many articles about soil, including those on composting, testing for life in the soil, and soil organisms.

Soil Macrofauna
www.interactive.usask.ca/skinteractive/modules/agriculture/soils/soilliv/soilliv_macfa.html
Canadian government site covering topics including soil fertility, soil management, and soil and the environment.

Soil Organisms & Living in the Soil
http://www.soils.agri.umn.edu/academics/classes/soil2125/doc/s9chap1.htm
The University Of Minnesota sponsors this kid-friendly site called.

Soil Quality Institute
http://www.statlab.iastate.edu/survey/SQI/soil_biology.htm
The United States Department of Agriculture's Soil Quality Institute provides information and images about soil biology, land management, and overall soil health.

Soil Science Education
www.statlab.iastate.edu/soils/nssc/educ/Edpage.html
Soil Science Education site of the National Soil Survey Center offers ample information, including a glossary, articles on soil formation, and a photo gallery, to help people better understand the soil.

Underground Adventure
www.fieldmuseum.org/ua
The special "Underground Adventure" exhibit at the Field Museum in Chicago highlights life in the soil.

INDEX

Acknowledgments

Over the years the text and drawings for this book grew in the fertile environment provided by a community of friends and colleagues. They are the ones who offered advice, read and critiqued sections of the manuscript, helped me find information, and also brought me creatures from the soil. The book is all the richer for their input.

Thanks to Jennifer Anderson, Catherine Birdseye, John Bouseman, Beth Chato, Gretchen Colon, Tish Cundiff, Colin Favret, Susan Gabay-Laughnan, Michelle Garland, Lowell Getz, Rosanna Giordano, Ed Hadley, Larry Hoffman, Chris Johns, Carie Nixon, Gary Olsen, Jason Pitzl, Joyce Scott, Carol Shearer, Felipe Soto, Pamela Sutherland, Betty Ujhelyi, Dave Voegtlin, Don Webb, Mark Wetzel, Jim Whitfield, Jackie Worden, Francis Young, Heather Young, and Ed Zaborski.

Molly Scott, an artist at the University of Illinois, contributed many hours of talent and patience in preparing diagrams and scanning illustrations for this book.

As editors for this book, Casper Grathwohl, Karen Fein, and Megan Schade at Oxford University Press were fine partners with whom to work. Their imagination and enthusiasm not only enriched the book but also constantly encouraged and inspired me.

As designer for this book, Valerie Sauers skillfully blended the illustrations and the text.

Most of the photographs in this book are the contribution of Michael Jeffords, Senior Professional Scientist and Education and Public Relations Liaison at the Illinois Natural History Survey. Jefford's photographs have appeared in numerous publications and speak eloquently for nature.

About the Author and Illustrator

James B. Nardi is a biologist at the University of Illinois, Urbana-Champaign. He is the author of *Once Upon a Tree: Life from Treetop to Root Tips* (Iowa State University, 1993) and *Close Encounters with Insects and Spiders* (Iowa State University, 1988).

Nardi is involved in local educational outreach programs sponsored by Urbana's Anita Purves Nature Center, Champaign County Audubon Society, and the Illinois Natural History Survey.